Edward Backhouse

Witnesses for Christ and Memorials of Church Life

From the Fourth to the Thirteenth Century

Edward Backhouse

Witnesses for Christ and Memorials of Church Life
From the Fourth to the Thirteenth Century

ISBN/EAN: 9783337005313

Printed in Europe, USA, Canada, Australia, Japan

Cover: Foto ©Lupo / pixelio.de

More available books at **www.hansebooks.com**

WITNESSES FOR CHRIST

AND

MEMORIALS OF CHURCH LIFE

From the Fourth to the Thirteenth Century.

BY

EDWARD BACKHOUSE

AND

CHARLES TYLOR.

Second Edition.
REVISED AND SOMEWHAT ABRIDGED.

LONDON:
SIMPKIN, MARSHALL, HAMILTON, KENT & CO., Limited.

1894.

JUSTINIAN AND THEODORA.

Drawn by Edward Backhouse after the Mosaics in the Church of St. Vitale, Ravenna; etched by W. B. Scott.

That very religion which the mercy of God designed to be free, with very few ceremonial sacraments, and of the plainest kind, is oppressed with slavish burdens, so that the condition of the Jews is more tolerable, who, although they knew not the time of their deliverance, are yet subjected to the yoke of the law, not to the weight of human assumptions.—AUGUSTINE.

There is but one Divine element of life which all believers share in common; but one fellowship with Christ which proceeds from faith in Him; but one new birth. All who possess this, all who are Christians in the true sense, have the same calling, the same dignity, the same heavenly blessings.—JOVINIAN.

TO THE READER.

The title "Witnesses for Christ" was originally chosen by Edward Backhouse for the entire work, of which these volumes form the second instalment. It seemed however more appropriate to designate the former volume, the second edition of which was published in 1885, *Early Church History*. In the two volumes now presented there is little attempt at a consecutive history of the Church, and the original title is therefore reverted to.

With regard to the authorship of these volumes it should be stated that the idea and inception of the whole belong to the late Edward Backhouse, who had collected much material (extending even to the seventeenth century), and whose artistic taste supplied many of the illustrations. For the remainder of the work Charles Tylor is responsible.

1887.

The work having been favourably received, it is thought well to issue a new edition in a cheaper form, so as to place it within the reach of a larger circle of readers. The whole has been revised, and a few chapters which were less closely related to the object of the writers and the title of the work, have been either entirely or partially omitted.

1894.

A cordial acknowledgment is due to several friends who have rendered aid in various ways in the preparation of this work; especially to Joseph Bevan Braithwaite and Thomas Hodgkin. Valuable assistance has also been received throughout from R. Hingston Fox.

CONTENTS.

PERIOD I.

FROM THE DEATH OF CONSTANTINE, A.D. 337, TO THE DEATH OF AUGUSTINE, A.D. 430.

	PAGE
CHAPTER I.	
The Arian Epoch	3
CHAPTER II.	
Athanasius	10
CHAPTER III.	
The Cappadocian Bishops	15
CHAPTER IV.	
Ulfilas	50
CHAPTER V.	
Martin of Tours	58
CHAPTER VI.	
Ambrose	61
CHAPTER VII.	
Chrysostom	71
CHAPTER VIII.	
Jerome	109
CHAPTER IX.	
Augustine	130
CHAPTER X.	
The Spirit of the Age:—	
I. Public Worship	158
II. Baptism and the Eucharist	161
III. Virginity	162
IV. Fasting	165
V. Almsgiving	167
VI. Saint-Worship	167
VII. Relics	172
VIII. Monachism	173
IX. The Church and the World	179
CHAPTER XI.	
Jovinian and Vigilantius	182

PERIOD II.

FROM THE DEATH OF AUGUSTINE, A.D. 430, TO THE ACCESSION OF POPE GREGORY THE GREAT, A.D. 590.

CHAPTER I.
	PAGE
The Nestorian Strife	201

CHAPTER II.
Christian Art and Mary-Worship	225

CHAPTER III.
Benedict	235

PERIOD III.

FROM THE ACCESSION OF POPE GREGORY THE GREAT, A.D. 590, TO THE END OF THE TENTH CENTURY.

CHAPTER I.
Gregory the Great	245
Note on the Papacy	255

CHAPTER II.
Christianity in Britain	257

CHAPTER III.
The Gospel in Northumbria	270

CHAPTER IV.
British Missionaries to the German Nations	294

CHAPTER V.
The Mohammedan Conquest	303

CHAPTER VI.
The Paulicians	306

CHAPTER VII.
Witnesses from the Eighth to the Tenth Century	312

PERIOD IV.

FROM THE TENTH CENTURY TO THE TERMINATION OF THE CRUSADE AGAINST THE ALBIGENSES, A.D. 1229.

                                                            PAGE

CHAPTER I.
Monastic Life in the Middle Ages—Cluny 333

CHAPTER II.
Monastic Life in the Middle Ages (*continued*)—Cîteaux 344

CHAPTER III.
Monastic Life in the Middle Ages (*concluded*)—Clairvaux, and Bernard .. 352

CHAPTER IV.
The Paulicians in Western Europe 369

CHAPTER V.
The Reformers of the Twelfth Century 378

CHAPTER VI.
The Waldenses 396

CHAPTER VII.
The Crusade against the Albigenses 407
    Conclusion 428

AUTHORITIES 432

INDEX 433

ILLUSTRATIONS.

Justinian and Theodora .. .. *Frontispiece.*	
	PAGE
Episcopal Chair of Ambrose	61
Doors of the Basilica of St. Ambrose	68
Palace of Theodoric, Ravenna	225
Fac-simile from the Durham Book .. .. *To face*	282
Monkwearmouth Church	286
Sculpture from the same	287
Ornamentation from the Durham book	287
Jarrow Church	288
Ceolfrid's Farewell	289
Bede's Chair	290
Death of Bede	292
Baptismal Vow, Old German	303
Queen Thyra's Cup and Cross	321
The Jellinge Stone, Jutland; Pagan Face	321
,, ,, Christian Face	322
,, ,, Inscription	322
Seal of Bernard of Clairvaux	341
Waldensian Candlestick	406
Fac-simile from the Troubadour's Lay	422

PERIOD I.

FROM THE DEATH OF CONSTANTINE, A.D. 337,
TO THE DEATH OF AUGUSTINE, A.D. 430.

CHAPTER I.

THE ARIAN EPOCH.

FROM the time of Constantine the history of the Church becomes the history of the world. To continue the subject in the historical form of the previous volume would lead us far beyond our limits. The purpose of the present work is rather to seek out true WITNESSES FOR CHRIST, whether amongst those upon whom the Church has bestowed the title of saint, or amongst the rejected and proscribed, whom she has branded with the name of heretic. The former, however great and good, were for the most part contented with the Christianity by which they were surrounded; and if they made any attempts at reformation, did little more than aim at the correction of abuses in discipline and manners. They left the fungus growth of superstition untouched, and in some cases even more rank than they found it. The heretics, such of them as are worthy of memorial, are those who, not always, it is true, in its completeness, discovered the truth through the mist which hid it from the eyes of the many, and who ventured loss of character, liberty, and life in order to persuade others to embrace it.

At the close of the first century we found Christianity numbering but few followers, little known and despised, yet steadily permeating the great Roman Empire, and wherever it came effecting a marvellous change in the dispositions and conduct of men. From age to age the Church grew, and asserted her reality and her power in the teeth of all manner of calumny and opposition. In spite of adverse laws and cruel edicts, she won her way, step by step, even before the days of persecution ceased, to a recognised place of influence and honour.

When Constantine declared himself her nursing-father, a new era opened before her. Suddenly her relations with the world were changed: her implacable enemy was cast under her feet; she ceased to be persecuted, and, alas! she became a persecutor. From this time we look upon the Roman Empire as no longer pagan, but Christian: the laws are Christian; the magistrates are Christian;

the Emperor is Christian. Pagan temples and sacrifices, if they do not at once disappear, are gradually replaced by Christian churches; and paganism soon begins to hide itself in the corners of the earth.[1] The wholesale admission of the people into the Church after the accession of Constantine brought with it a crowd of abuses, and powerfully accelerated that declension which, in spite of the purifying effect of persecution, had been going on for several generations.

Another point of difference between the history of the Church before and after the edicts of Milan (A.D. 313, 314) must be noticed. The historic materials, which before were scanty, now become abundant. A host of Church writers appear at once upon the scene. Homilies, orations, lectures, commentaries on Scripture, controversial treatises, confessions, epistles, histories, biographies of saints and hermits, hymns, poems, are poured forth in such volume that only a few amongst modern scholars have patience enough to master the folios in which they are preserved. This brilliant era of Christian literature lasted but little more than a century; it did not survive the irruption of the barbarian hordes. After the Goths, Vandals, Franks, and Huns had swept over the empire, trampling down civilisation, the lamps of knowledge became few and dim, and were soon all but extinguished.

It will be convenient to divide the present work into chronological epochs, the first of which will embrace the period from the death of Constantine in 337, to that of Augustine in 430. A brief outline of events between these two eras may serve as an introduction to our biographies of the Witnesses of this age.

On Constantine's death he was succeeded by his three sons, who divided his empire between them. Constantine II. received the Western provinces, Constantius the Eastern, and Constans had Illyricum, Italy, and part of Africa, for his share. Constantine, whilst invading the dominions of Constans, was killed in battle, A.D. 340. Constans was slain A.D. 350 by one of his generals, who was in turn overcome by Constantius, in 353. Constantine and Constans favoured the Catholic or orthodox party; Constantius, like his father in his later days, espoused the cause of the Arians, but with a more blind zeal and greater intolerance. The nature of the Arian error has already been set forth in *Early Church History.* Arius, whilst ascribing to our Lord divine honour, taught, contrary to the plain testimony of Scripture, that He had a beginning, and

---

[1] The name *pagan* is derived from the Latin *pagus*, a canton or country district, because it was there the old idolatry survived the longest. In like manner, *heathen* signifies one who lives on the *heath*, that is, in the open country.

is not of the same substance or essence (*homo-ousion*) as the Father. Partly from the Oriental love of speculation, partly from an honest dread of sensuous ideas and unscriptural terms, a great portion of the Eastern Church became his followers. The chief opponent of Arius was Athanasius. The whole life of this remarkable man was devoted to the defence of our Lord's proper deity, the cardinal truth which it was the object of the Council of Nicæa to settle and confirm.[1]

We have seen that at the death of Constantine the Great, Arianism was in the ascendant. That Emperor, in the part which he took in theological controversies, never lost sight of the interests of the State. It was otherwise with his son Constantius, who entered the polemical lists as if he had been himself a bishop.[2] His reign, with those of the succeeding Arian emperors, was a period of intense agitation in the Church. " Council was held against council; creed was set up against creed; anathema was hurled against anathema." " As many creeds exist as inclinations," wrote the orthodox Hilary of Poictiers in his exile, "as many doctrines as modes of life. . . . Whilst we are disputing about words, searching into novelties, catching at ambiguities, anathematising one another—scarcely one belongs to Christ. . . . We make creeds every year, nay every month; we repent when we have made them; we defend those who repent; we anathematise those whom we have defended; we condemn either other people's opinions in our own, or our own in other people; mutually devouring one another we are at length mutually consumed." " The posting service of the empire," says Ammianus Marcellinus, "was thrown into confusion by the troops of bishops galloping hither and thither to the assemblies which they called synods." And Athanasius rebukes " the restless flutter of the clergy, who journeyed the empire over to find the true faith, and provoked the ridicule and contempt of the unbelieving world." But it was not

---

[1] *Early Church History*, pt. ii. c. 11.

[2] He accepted with complacency the lofty title of "bishop of bishops." The reign of Constantius is described by Thomas Hodgkin as "one of the most peculiar of which history has preserved a record; the reign of a man deeply dyed in the blood of relatives and friends, who used the obsequious service of eunuchs instead of entrusting the affairs of the State to honest and capable ministers, whose feeble haughtiness and cowardly ambition bear no trace of the influence of Christianity upon his life, but who, nevertheless, plunged into theological discussions with an eagerness, and continued in the same with a patient endurance, such as we should scarcely find nowadays in a salaried professor of Divinity." Like his father, Constantius deferred baptism till shortly before his death.

the clergy only who took part in the strife. The points of the Arian controversy were the fashionable topics of conversation amongst all ranks, from the highest to the lowest. "Every corner and nook of the city" (Constantinople), writes Gregory of Nyssa, "is full of men who discuss incomprehensible subjects—the streets, the markets, the dealers in old clothes, the money-changers, the hucksters. Ask a man how many oboli it comes to, he will dogmatise on generated and ungenerated being. Inquire the price of bread, you are answered: 'The Father is greater than the Son, and the Son subordinate to the Father.' Ask if the bath is ready, and you are told: 'The Son of God was created from nothing.'" The war was very far, however, from being confined to words; the intolerance of the age showed itself in innumerable acts of violence, in which the Arians seem to have far outdone the Catholics. The great cities of the East especially were the frequent scenes of confusion and bloodshed.

From A.D. 341 to the death of Constantius in 361, no fewer than twelve councils, or synods, were held, at which the balance continually vibrated between orthodoxy and Arianism, but with a general inclination towards the latter. This was due to the arbitrary will of the Emperor, who at the Council of Milan propounded an Arian formula which he pretended to have received by revelation, and at the same time attempted to quench all freedom of debate by saying, "Whatever I will let that be esteemed a canon!" During the strife the Arian party split into two camps, the Semi-Arians or Homoi-ousions (a name adopted to express that the essence of the Son is *like* but not the *same* as that of the Father), and the thorough Arians, who held more distinctly than Arius himself that the Son is essentially a creature unlike the Father, not only in substance but in will. The Orthodox body were called Homo-ousions, to signify their belief that the Son is of the *same* essence as the Father, but a different person. During the storm Athanasius, Hosius of Cordova, Liberius of Rome, Hilary of Poictiers, and other eminent bishops of the Catholic party, were deposed and banished. "The whole world," exclaims Jerome, "groaned in astonishment to find itself Arian."

This state of things, however, did not last long. On the death of Constantius in 361, Christianity itself was for a time set aside by the accession of Julian, surnamed *the Apostate*, nephew to Constantine the Great. As soon as this prince ascended the throne, he declared himself in favour of the ancient idolatry, and restored it to its former place as the religion of the State. He sought to infuse new life into the dying creed by adopting the moral code of

Christianity and introducing many of its forms. The laws which he enacted against the Church were indeed mild in comparison with those which his predecessor had issued against heathenism, yet in the course of his short reign the Christians had to endure no little hardship, both from the government and the people.

One form in which Julian's enmity to the Gospel showed itself was the attempt to rebuild the Temple at Jerusalem. He seems to have supposed that he could falsify our Lord's prediction of its perpetual ruin. At his call Jews from all the provinces of the empire assembled on the holy mountain of their fathers, and entered with fanatical zeal into the great national work. The rich used spades and mattocks and baskets of silver, and ladies carried the earth and stones of the holy spot in their silken aprons. But as soon as the rubbish had been cleared away, and the old foundations laid bare, "fearful balls of flame" are said "to have burst forth from the earth, burnt the workmen, and again and again driven them from the spot."

The reign of restored paganism was short. Julian died in 363, and was succeeded by Jovian, a zealous upholder of Christianity, but who, from the critical circumstances of the times, left the pagans unmolested. At his death, after a reign of only eight months, the purple fell jointly to Valentinian I. and Valens, under whom the final division of the empire was made, Valens taking the East and Valentinian the West. Valens trod in the footsteps of Constantius, and suffered himself to become the tool of the Arian clergy. His reign was in consequence a period of deplorable desolation in the Oriental Churches. "Worthy bishops were driven from their sees; worthless men, who had their patrons among the Imperial eunuchs and chamberlains, were imposed on the Churches as priests and bishops." Many of the orthodox clergy were put to death. On the death of Valens, in 378, the Catholics recovered their power, and the Arians in their turn were driven from the Churches, never to regain their former influence.

The legal toleration of paganism continued in the first years of the Emperors Gratian and Valentinian II. in the West, and Theodosius in the East; until, in 381, Theodosius, whose character and military genius could brook no breach of uniformity, directed the whole force of his authority to its suppression; and his efforts were zealously seconded by the clergy and the Christian populace.

But Theodosius was not only a "*most Christian*," he was a "*most Catholic*" Emperor. Summoned by Gratian to deliver the East from the Goths, and baptized when dangerously ill into the Nicene faith, he set himself to combat with equal skill and success the enemies of the Catholic Church and those of the empire. To him was due the second general council (that of Constantinople, A.D. 381), by which the Nicene Creed was finally established with the addition of a clause stating in express terms the divinity of the Holy Spirit.[1] The soldier theologian thus makes known his Imperial will. The decree, directed in the first place against the Arians, was meant to reach all dissenters. "It is our will that all the nations who are subject to the rules of Our Clemency shall adhere to that religion which the divine Apostle Peter handed to the Romans, as is sufficiently shown by its existence among them to this day. . . . We believe the One Godhead of Father, Son and Holy Ghost with equal majesty in the Holy Trinity. We order those who follow this law to assume the name of Catholic[2] Christians: we pronounce all others to be mad and foolish, and we order that they shall bear the ignominious name of heretics,[3] and shall not presume to bestow on their conventicles the title of churches: and they are to be visited, first by the divine vengeance, and secondarily by the stroke of our own authority, which we have received in accordance with the will of heaven." This edict being found insufficient, another, more stringent, was issued the next year. "Let there be no place left to the heretics for celebrating the mysteries of their faith, no opportunity for exhibiting their stupid obstinacy. . . . Their crimes being made manifest, let them receive a mark of opprobrium, and be kept utterly away from even the thresholds of the churches. If they attempt any outbreak, we order that their rage shall be quelled, and they shall be cast forth outside the walls of the cities, so that the Catholic churches, the whole world over, may be restored to the orthodox prelates who hold the Nicene faith."

These measures, although not in all cases rigorously enforced, were successful. "Neither heathenism nor sectarianism," observes Robertson, "had much inward strength to withstand the pressure of the laws which required conformity to the Church." Expelled from the old Churches of the empire, Arianism found refuge amongst the barbarians, especially the Goths and Vandals, the

---

[1] The creed as adopted at the Council of Nicæa will be found in the *Early Church History*, p. 236. As enlarged by the Council of Constantinople, it is, with one exception, the same as we find in the liturgy of the Church of England. In this liturgy the word *Filioque* (*and the Son*), denoting the procession of the Holy Ghost from the Father and the Son together, has been added.

[2] Catholic, katholikos (kath holou, on the whole), *general, universal*. This term was employed by very early Christian writers in the same sense in which it is still used.

[3] Heresy, hairesis, signifies—(1) a *choosing;* (2) an opinion which any one *chooses* for himself; (3) something *different* from the *Catholic* opinions.

latter of whom, when they acquired possession of North Africa, A.D. 429, cruelly persecuted the adherents of the Nicene faith.

But with the overthrow of Arianism its disastrous consequences did not disappear. By this half-century of theological contention a severe blow had been dealt at the life of Christianity. "Whilst," observes Ullmann, "the sanctifying and beatifying doctrines of the Gospel which point to the conversion of the inner man were suffered to lie inactive, every one from the Emperor to the beggar occupied himself with incredible earnestness in the discussion of propositions, concerning which the Gospel communicates just so much as is profitable to us and necessary to salvation." "This contentious spirit," writes Gregory Nazianzen, "has torn asunder the Church; thrown cities into commotion, driven the people to take up arms, and excited princes against one another; separated the priests from the congregation, and the congregation from the priests. Everything which bears a holy name has been profaned; . . . an insolent presumption has usurped the place of law; and we are divided, not merely tribe againt tribe, as was Israel of old, but house against house, family against family, nay, almost every one is distracted within himself."

The irruption of the barbarian nations has been already slightly alluded to. It is the grand political event of this period, and it influenced in the highest degree the future of the Christian Church. Already, in the third century, the Goths had broken through the barriers of the empire and settled themselves in some of its fairest provinces. They were succeeded by other tribes—Vandals, Sueves, &c., and continual wars with alternate success were waged until, in 402, Alaric, king of the Visigoths, invaded Italy, and in 410 took Rome. For six days the Imperial city, which had stood for nearly twelve hundred years, was delivered up to the licentious fury of the barbarians. At the same time the Vandals and the Burgundians poured into Gaul, and the former, after establishing a kingdom in Spain, crossed over into Africa, A.D. 429, and made themselves masters of all the Roman dominions in that country.

In bringing this brief outline to a close, we may notice an event which happened in the reign of the Emperor Honorius. Neither the attempt of Constantine to put an end to the combats of gladiators,[1] nor the protests of Christian writers renewed from age to age, could induce the Roman people to relinquish their favourite pastime. It seemed to require some act of heroic self-devotion to

---

[1] See *Early Church History*, p. 219. Constantine's edict seems to have been only local.

break the spell by which they were bound to these shameful barbarities. The Emperor Honorius, after the victory gained by his general Stilicho over Alaric and the Goths at Polantia in the year 404, was celebrating a triumph with the usual games. An Eastern monk named Telemachus left his cell and travelled all the way to Rome in order to protest against the unchristian spectacle. He entered with the multitude into the theatre of the Coliseum. Gazing with agonized heart upon the revolting scene, and seeing no other way of making his protest known, he leaped down into the arena and attempted to separate the combatants. A cry of execration arose. The spectators, "possessed," says the historian, "by the demon who delights in the effusion of blood, and maddened at the interruption to their sport, stoned him to death." But the Emperor, struck with admiration at his self-devotion, and probably pricked in his own conscience, ordained that these sanguinary spectacles should be abolished, and that the name of Telemachus should be entered on the roll of martyrs.[1]

CHAPTER II.

Athanasius.

THE representative men whom we have selected from the ranks of the Catholic Church in this epoch were all contemporary; Augustine, the youngest of them, had nearly reached man's estate when Athanasius died. They are as follows:—

	Born	Died		Born	Died
Athanasius	296	373	Martin of Tours	316	396
Basil	329	377	Ambrose	340	397
Gregory Nazianzen	329	389	Chrysostom	347	407
Gregory Nyssen	331	395	Jerome	346	420
Ulfilas[2]	311	381	Augustine[3]	354	430

---

[1] It was, however, only the combats of men with men that were discontinued. Encounters between men and wild animals, in which human life was often sacrificed, and which took place even on the highest festivals of the Church, were as numerously and passionately attended as ever. To the disgrace of Christendom, the Roman games of the amphitheatre still exist in the bull-fights of Spain, France, and South America.

[2] Ulfilas was not in fact a Catholic; he represents the Arian party.

[3] Other leading Churchmen of this century may be named: the learned Hosius, bishop of Cordova (A.D. 256-357), counsellor of Constantine the Great,

We have, in the former volume, followed the eventful history of Athanasius until the death of Constantine.[1] His course under that Emperor's successors continued to be of the same stormy and eventful nature; at one time a fugitive and exposed to hardship, at another returning in triumph to Alexandria and wielding his crozier with increased authority and vigour.[2] Inflexible of will, he alone, amidst the waves of party strife which during this time swept over Church and State, remained consistent to the one grand purpose of his life, viz., to preserve the orthodox faith pure from the taint of heresy. For this end he braved all dangers and withstood the mandate of the Emperor himself. He was five times driven into exile. His sufferings only augmented his fame, which extended to the extreme confines of Christendom.

During his second exile (A.D. 341-346), Athanasius spent three years in Italy, a residence memorable for the introduction of the monkish life into the countries of the West. Two strange uncouth figures in cloak and girdle accompanied him to Rome. These were Ammonius and Isidore, youthful monks from the Nitrian desert.[3] The former, one of four brothers called from their unusual stature the Tall Brethren, was a learned man, and could repeat, it is said, the Old and New Testaments by heart, as well as passages from Origen and others of the Church Fathers; yet he cared nothing for the ancient monuments or magnificent works of the great city, but only to visit the martyr churches of Peter and Paul. The fastidious taste of the Roman people was at first offended by the appearance and manners of the strangers, but this feeling soon gave way to admiration and reverence, as they heard them dilate

---

and for a long period the most prominent figure in Western Christendom; Hilary, bishop of Poictiers (died 368), the great champion of the Trinitarian doctrine in the West ("a very Rhone of eloquence," as Jerome styles him); Ephrem, a deacon of Edessa, "the prophet of the Syrians" (308-373); Cyril, bishop of Jerusalem (315-386), celebrated for his catechetical discourses on the mysteries of the faith. Some of these dates, and of those in the text, are only approximate.

[1] *Early Church History*, pt. ii. c. 11, 12.

[2] His return from one of his exiles (the second) is described by Gregory Nazianzen as a most imposing spectacle. "The vast population of the great city streamed forth to meet him like another Nile; innumerable faces gazed upon him; the air resounded with shouts of joy and was made fragrant with clouds of incense. Within the city the streets were spread with carpets of the gayest colours, and myriads of lamps lighted up the night."

[3] Anthony, the first Christian hermit, was then living. Isidore afterwards became governor of the great hospice at Alexandria. He must be distinguished from the more famous Isidore of Pelusium, who lived in the succeeding century.

upon that life of bodily self-mortification and spiritual exaltation of which Rome had hitherto only heard rumours.

After the death, in 350, of the Emperor Constans, Constantius, having procured the condemnation of Athanasius at the Council of Milan (A.D. 355), proceeded by force to eject him. The bishop was presiding over an all-night vigil in St. Thomas' Church, in his city of Alexandria, when Syrianus, general of the army in Egypt, with a force of 5,000 legionaries, encompassed the building. Athanasius himself has left an account of what took place. "I sat down on my throne, and desired the deacon to read the psalm of the day [the 136th] and the people to respond, 'For his mercy endureth for ever,' and then all to return home. Presently the doors were forced and the soldiers rushed in, sounding the trumpet, discharging their arrows, clashing their arms, and brandishing their swords in the light of the church-lamps. Many of the people who had not time to escape were trampled down, others fell pierced with arrows; several of the virgins were slain, and the soldiers laid hands on others, who dreaded their touch more than death itself." Athanasius himself had a narrow escape. "Seeing the soldiers ready to seize me, the clergy and some of my people present began clamorously to urge me to withdraw. I refused to do so until everyone in the church had got away. Standing up, I called for prayer, and desired all to go out before me; and when the greater part had gone, the monks and the clergy who were about me came up the steps and dragged me down. Thus, under the Lord's guidance, I passed through unobserved, glorifying God that I had not betrayed the people."[1]

When the Emperor Julian came to the throne he restored the exiled bishops to their sees; and Athanasius returned for the third time to Alexandria (A.D. 362). But his energy in opposing paganism alarmed the new Emperor, and he had again to make his escape. His followers, full of grief, gathered round him. "Be of good heart," he said, "it is but a cloud, it will soon pass away." Finding a vessel lying near the bank of the Nile, he embarked to ascend the river to Thebes. But the Emperor had determined to take his life, and agents of the government were sent in pursuit. One of his friends contriving to outstrip the Imperial boat, brought him intelligence of the danger. His companions besought him to disembark and take refuge in the desert. He, however, directed the steersman to put the helm about, and return to Alexandria. They

---

[1] The two contemporary authorities and eye-witnesses differ slightly in the details. According to one of them, "The bishop was seized, fell into a swoon, and was almost torn to pieces. We do not know how he escaped, for they were bent upon killing him."

were met by the government boat, and hailed: "Where is Athanasius?" "He is not far off," was the answer, uttered perhaps by Athanasius himself. Suspicion was not excited, and the vessel passed on. He reached Alexandria in safety, and remained concealed until the accession of Jovian in the same year, 363, restored him to his beloved flock.

The Emperor Valens, influenced by the firmness of the Alexandrians and by fear of Valentinian, suffered Athanasius to remain for a while in his see; but in 365 he was once more compelled to fly, and it is said that he lay hid four months in his father's tomb at the gate of the city. He was finally reinstated in 366, and his long and chequered life came to a peaceful close in his own house in 373. He had occupied the see of Alexandria forty-six years. Athanasius was small of stature, somewhat stooping, and emaciated by fasting and many hardships. His countenance was handsome and expressive, and his eye piercing, so that his presence inspired even his enemies with awe.

Gibbon, who seldom bestows eulogy upon Christian heroes, loves to extol the character of the great Alexandrian divine. "The immortal name of Athanasius will never be separated from the Catholic doctrine of the Trinity, to whose defence he consecrated every moment and every faculty of his being . . . His pastoral labours were not confined to the narrow limits of Egypt. The state of the Christian world was present to his active and capacious mind; and the age, the merit, the reputation of Athanasius, enabled him to assume, in a moment of danger, the office of Ecclesiastical Dictator."

To this, must be added Hooker's panegyric. "In Athanasius there was nothing observed throughout the course of that long tragedy, other than such as very well became a wise man to do, and a righteous to suffer. So that this was the plain condition of those times: the whole world against Athanasius, and Athanasius against it; half a hundred of years spent in doubtful trial which of the two in the end would prevail—the side which had all, or else the part which had no friend but God and death, the one a defender of his innocency, the other a finisher of his troubles."

The writings of Athanasius are numerous, and have always been greatly prized by the Church.[1] His great mission, as we have seen,

---

[1] "When you meet with a saying of Athanasius," said Cosmas the monk in the sixth century, "and have not paper on which to copy it, copy it on your clothes." The creed which bears the name of Athanasius was not composed by him, nor even in his lifetime, but seems to have originated about the middle of the fifth century.

was to uphold against the Arians the proper deity of the Son of God. "When the Arians maintained that the Son of God is only distinguished from other created beings by the fact that God created Him first of all, and then all other beings by Him, Athanasius answers: 'It is a narrow-minded representation that God should require an instrument for creation; it is as though the Son of God came into existence only for our sakes. By such a representation we might be led to regard Him, not as participating immediately in the Divine Essence, but as requiring an intermediate agency for Himself. . . . If we do not stand in connection with God through his Son, as thus conceived of, we have no true communion with Him, but something stands between, and we are not his children in a proper sense. For as to our original relation to Him, we are only his creatures, and he is not in a proper sense our Father; only so far is He our Father as we are placed in communion with Him through Christ. Without this it could not be said that we are partakers of the Divine Nature.' . . . The Arians believed that they ought, according to the Scriptures, to pay divine honour to Christ: Athanasius charged them with inconsistency, seeing that, on their own showing, they thus become idolaters and worshippers of a creature. The Arians objected to the Nicene doctrine, that the idea of the Son of God cannot be distinguished from that of a created being, unless words are used representing Him with human attributes and affections. Athanasius replied that undoubtedly all expressions regarding the nature of God are symbolical, and have something of a human idea at their basis, and this we must abstract in order to come at a correct conception. This we do in the case of creation. In like manner we must abstract from the expressions Son of God, and Begotten of God, what belongs to human relations, and then there is left to us the idea of Unity of Essence."

The opinions of Athanasius on violence and persecution deserve to be written in letters of gold. "Nothing more forcibly marks the weakness of a bad cause than persecution. Satan, who has no truth to propose to men, comes with axe and sword to make way for his errors. Christ's method is widely different. He teaches the truth, and says: 'If any man *will* come after Me and be my disciple;'—when He comes to the heart He uses no violence, but says, 'Open to Me, my sister, my spouse.' If we open He comes in; if we will not open He retires; for the truth is not preached with swords and spears, not by bands of soldiers, but by counsel and persuasion. But of what use can persuasion be where the Imperial Ego dominates? Or what place is there for counsel when resistance to Imperial authority must terminate in exile or death?"

Allusion has been made to the life, by Athanasius, of Anthony the Hermit. It is the first of a long series of saintly biographies, held in the highest esteem by the Church of Rome. The work has probably been interpolated by a later hand; but, allowing for this, it is marvellous that the sagacious and powerful mind of Athanasius should have given forth such a narrative, not indeed devoid of instruction, but mixed with so much of absurdity. It is only to be accounted for by the influence of superstition, even on the strongest minds, in an age when freedom of thought was not present to counteract it. Most of the biography is taken up in relating Anthony's encounters with the devil. The demonology of the monks was derived from the Neo-Platonists; and "when the solitary had reduced his hated enemy, the body, to a skeleton, and thus weakened his understanding and inflamed his imagination, he was in a fit state to hear strange voices, and behold fearful apparitions."

CHAPTER III.

The Cappadocian Bishops.

The name of Gregory Thaumaturgus, bishop of Neo-Cæsarea in Pontus, is familiar to the readers of the *Early Church History*.[1] The fruit of his pastoral work is met with in the household of a Christian lady named Macrina, who, with her husband, concealed herself in the forests during the persecution under Galerius and Maximinus Daza. Their son Basil and his wife Emmelia had a family of ten children, and in the ordering of their household and the bringing up of their family, they diligently followed the example set them by their parents. It is related of the eldest daughter, who was named Macrina after her grandmother, that she knew the whole of the Psalms by heart, as well as many portions of the books of Solomon.

Macrina was beautiful, and, being also rich, her hand was sought by many. In accordance with the custom of the age, the choice lay with her father, who selected a young advocate of gentle birth. Before the time came for the marriage, the young man died.

---

[1] P. 192.

Macrina possessed a soul of no common order, and regarding her betrothal as a virtual union, and her affianced husband as still living, though in a far-off land, to be joined to her again at the resurrection, she refused to listen to any further proposals of marriage. At her father's death, when she was about twenty-two years of age, the care of her widowed mother and of the younger children devolved upon her, and she even undertook the management of the family estates, which lay in three different provinces. She brought up her infant brother Peter, contracted eligible marriages for her four sisters, and, not disdaining household work, she baked the bread for the family, and prepared her mother's food with her own hands.

BASIL, the first of the three subjects of this chapter, was next to Macrina in age, and was born A.D. 329. When a child, he was sent to the country house of his excellent grandmother, from whom he received the germs of Christian instruction. "She taught me," he tells us, "the words of the most blessed Gregory." These early lessons and his father's teaching prepared him to enter into competition with boys of his own age at the grammar school in Cæsarea, the chief city of Cappadocia, where he distinguished himself by his brilliant talents and exemplary conduct. From thence he was removed to Constantinople, and studied under the sophist Libanius, one of the most noteworthy defenders of expiring paganism. The tutor has recorded his admiration of the eloquence of the young Cappadocian, and of his self-restraint amid the temptations of the New Rome.

On leaving Constantinople Basil repaired to Athens to drink philosophy at that ancient fountain-head; and here also he had heathen preceptors for his guides, who still lectured under the colonnades or in the gardens where Plato, Aristotle, and Epicurus once taught.

At Athens Basil found a fellow-countryman of his own age, a native of Arianzus, a village or estate in the west of Cappadocia. This was GREGORY NAZIANZEN, the second of our Cappadocian worthies. Like Basil, he was the child of pious parents. His father Gregory, bishop of Nazianzus, had belonged at the time of his marriage to a half heathen sect called *Hypsistarians* (worshippers of the Most High), and had been won over to the Church by the persevering influence of his wife. This happened just when several bishops passed through Nazianzus to attend the council of Nicæa, and he was baptized in their presence. The credulity of the age invested his baptism with miracles and prophecies. Gregory's mother was Nonna, a woman of a masculine character, in whom religion was all powerful, but it was the religion of the age, narrow and formal. She had unlimited confidence in prayer, and had attained such mastery of her feelings that when affliction came she never uttered a lamentation till she had given thanks to God. She carried her notions of almsgiving to such an excess as often to say that she would gladly sell herself and her children to provide money for the poor. She was so exclusive that she would never shake hands with or kiss a heathen woman, or eat salt with an idolater.

Gregory, the younger was born about A.D. 330, and was dedicated, even before his birth, to the service of the Lord. Not many days after his birth his mother carried him to the church, and laid his infant hands on a volume of the Gospels. He used afterwards to compare himself to Isaac offered in sacrifice to God, and to Samuel, who was consecrated as a child by his mother Hannah. When old enough, he was, like Basil, sent to school at Neo-Cæsarea, where, probably, the friendship between them commenced; and from thence successively to Cæsarea in Palestine and to Alexandria. But his heart was set on Athens; and though the time of year was unfavourable for a voyage, he hastened to quit Alexandria and sail thither. When the ship arrived off Cyprus, a violent storm arose; the thunder, lightning, and darkness were accompanied by the creaking of the yards, the quivering of the masts, and piteous cries for help to Christ, even from some, as Gregory tells us, who had never before called upon his name. They had besides lost their store of fresh water, so that death from thirst or from shipwreck alike stared them in the face. A Phœnician vessel coming up, managed with great difficulty to supply them with water; still the storm did not abate, and for many days their fate hung in the balance. It was not the fear of death itself which tormented Gregory; but, in accordance with a frequent practice, his baptism had been deferred,[1] and death without baptism had come to be looked upon as the loss of heaven. Overwhelmed with the thought, he dedicated himself anew to God, and prayed for mercy and deliverance for himself and the ship's company. The prayer, as he tells us, was answered; all on board were saved, and so affected by their deliverance that they received "spiritual as well as temporal salvation," which doubtless means that they underwent the rite of baptism.

He arrived at Athens some time before Basil. The university, which had lost its ancient simplicity and freedom, was divided into

---

See *Early Church History*, p. 245.

rival schools, and it was the chief aim of the professors to spread their own fame and increase the number of their pupils. Fresh students were waylaid and fought for by the rival parties, and sometimes torn away from the very teacher whom they had come expressly to attend.

The acquaintance between the two compatriots speedily ripened into an ardent friendship. Dissimilar in character, they were attracted to each other by their very dissimilarity: "Gregory, the affectionate, the tender-hearted; Basil, the man of firm resolve and hard deeds." "They occupied the same chamber and ate at the same table. They studied the same books and attended the same lectures." "We knew," says Gregory, "only two streets of the city: the first and more excellent, that which led to the churches and the ministers of the altar; the other, to the schools and the teachers of the sciences. The streets which led to the theatres, games, and other places of unholy amusement, we left to others. Holiness was our chief concern; our sole aim was to be called Christians, and to be such."

Amongst the fellow-students of Basil and Gregory was Constantine's nephew, Julian, afterwards Emperor and well known by his surname of "the Apostate." The young prince attached himself to Basil, who responded to his advances. They united in the study of classic literature, and even read together in the Sacred Scriptures. Gregory, however, regarded Julian with suspicion, discerning, as he tells us, his true character in his incessant restlessness and hesitating speech, and in every feature of his countenance; and he warned his fellow-students that that young man would one day bring evil upon the empire.

Basil spent five years at Athens (A.D. 851–856). He had won a name in the university, and it was with pain he tore himself away, yet a conviction of the emptiness of the world, even under its noblest aspects, seemed to have taken possession of him, and he described Athens as "hollow blessedness." Gregory remained there a short time longer.[1]

Returning to Cæsarea, where his father resided, Basil commenced practice as a rhetorician. The success he met with and his college reputation filled him with vain and ambitious thoughts. He looked with contempt on his superiors in rank; he adopted the airs of a fine gentleman; and began to indulge in the pleasures of the city. His sister Macrina perceived his danger. Her loving heart was

---

[1] The school at Athens, which had stood 900 years, the last refuge of heathen teaching, was abolished by Justinian I., A.D. 529. Its seven remaining professors went into exile and found protection with Chosroes, king of Persia.

deeply stirred at seeing her brother choose the broad way. But she was scarcely a wise counsellor for a young man in whose pathway the world had spread its snares. It is doubtful, indeed, if a wise counsellor was at that time anywhere to be found. The mistaken idea that in order to live above the world it was necessary to flee from it had been steadily gaining force ever since Paul and Anthony retired into the Libyan desert; and, although monasticism had not yet been introduced into Asia Minor, the devout members of the Church were everywhere turning towards an ascetic life. It would have been a marvel if Macrina had escaped the general contagion. By her sisterly warnings she infused into her brother's soul the same disregard of earthly pleasures and distinctions, the same enthusiasm for self-mortification which ruled in her own breast.

The idea of a recluse life was not new to Basil. He and his friend Gregory had already, when at Athens, pledged each other one day to turn their backs upon the world. Nevertheless, Basil describes himself as awaking, under the effect of his sister's admonitions, out of a deep sleep, and in the light of Gospel truth discerning the folly of this world's wisdom to which he had begun to devote himself. Interpreting literally our Lord's words: "If thou wilt be perfect, go, sell that thou hast, and give to the poor, and thou shalt have treasure in heaven; and come, follow Me"; he at once resolved to give up his profession, and withdraw into solitude. Accordingly, about the year 357, he left Cæsarea to visit the most renowned ascetics of Egypt and Syria. "Their abstinence and endurance, their mastery over hunger and sleep, their indifference to cold and nakedness," excited in him the warmest admiration, accompanied by an ardent desire to imitate them. On his return he wrote to Gregory, reminding him of their mutual vow, and proposing they should withdraw together into the desert.

Gregory had been two years at home since his return from Athens. His parents were advancing in age, and the duty which he owed to them weighed against the allurements of a life of prayer and meditation. He reflected also that the desert would not afford the opportunity which his studious disposition craved, for a critical acquaintance with the Scriptures. But, on the other hand, he longed to devote to God every faculty he possessed, and in his hours of contemplative abstraction the examples of Elijah and John the Baptist would present themselves, as most worthy of imitation. Evidently he did not understand that it is in the New Covenant only the Christian can find his perfect Exemplar; that Christians are called "to go into the world with Christ, not out of it with Elijah and the Baptist." For a while Gregory sought to reconcile the two conflicting influences, and attempted to live a hermit life in the midst of society. His food was bread and salt, his drink water, his bed the bare ground, his clothing coarse. Incessant labour filled up the day; prayers, hymns and meditations, a great part of the night. He condemned his former life; the mirth in which he used to indulge now cost him many tears. He even gave up music, as being a gratification of the senses. But he soon found that the abstraction of mind required by this mode of life was incompatible with his domestic duties. "Many cares," he says, "fretted me by night and by day; ruling servants was a very network of evil; and I could no more look after property, with its attendant plagues of tax-collectors and law-courts, than a man can approach a house on fire without being blackened and scorched by the smoke." In this state of mind he replied to Basil's letter, by proposing that the latter should join him at Arianzus. Basil accordingly made him a visit. But the place disgusted him, for he found it cold and damp and intolerably muddy, to use his own words, "the very pit of the whole earth."

By this time Basil's family had settled on the ancestral estate in Pontus, beside the river Iris, the spot where he himself had passed his childhood. Here his sister Macrina and her mother converted their household into a religious sisterhood, to which the daughters of the noblest families in the province resorted. Basil was not slow to perceive the superiority of the brotherhood to the solitary life. "God," he writes, "has made us like the members of our body, dependent on one another's help. What discipline of humility, of pity, or of patience can there be if there be no one for whom these duties are to be practised? Whose feet wilt thou wash; to whom wilt thou be as a servant; how canst thou be last of all, if thou art alone?" Here unhappily he stopped. God, who made man to live in society, gave him also marriage, and set him in families; and has revealed Himself to us through that endeared relation of Father, which the Church of the fourth century presumptuously denied to her priests and her elect children. If, instead of placing himself at the head of a retrograde movement, and trying to give it a more practical direction, this man of commanding talents and unbending will had taken his stand on the New Testament, and withstood the popular current altogether, he might have conferred priceless benefits on his own and succeeding ages.[1]

---

[1] Basil was not actually the first to introduce monachism into Asia Minor; he was preceded by the Arian, Eustathius of Sebaste. On his return from the East, Basil joined himself to some disciples of this bishop, the counterpart of

The spot which Basil selected for his monastery was in the immediate neighbourhood of his mother's religious house, but on the opposite bank of the river. It was not a dreary wilderness, like the Egyptian deserts, but a charming retreat, such as every lover of nature might covet. "God has shown me," he wrote to his friend Gregory, "a region which exactly suits my mode of life; it is in truth what in our happy hours we often dreamed of. That which imagination pictured in the distance I now see before me. At the foot of a high mountain, covered with thick forest, spreads out a wide plain, plentifully watered, and enclosed by a belt of many kinds of trees, almost thick enough to be a fence. On two sides deep ravines serve as a protection, whilst on a third the mountain torrent, which breaks upon the wall of projecting rock, and rolls foaming into the abyss, forms an impassable barrier. From my cottage on the summit I overlook the plain and the windings of the Iris. Shall I go on to describe the fragrant smell of the meadows, the refreshing breezes from the water, or the vast numbers of song-birds and flowers? In all these another might take delight; but as for me, my mind is not at liberty to enjoy them. To me the greatest charm of this retreat is the quiet that reigns here. Remote from the tumult of the city, its silent repose is only now and then broken by a solitary hunter, who is in pursuit, not of bears or wolves, but of the deer, the roe, and the hare."[1] Even here, however, Basil could not escape from himself. In another letter he writes: "What I do in this solitude I am almost ashamed to say. I have abandoned my residence in the city, as being the source of a thousand evils, but myself I cannot leave behind. I am like voyagers unaccustomed to the sea, who, when attacked with sickness, leave the large ship because of its violent rolling, and descend into a little boat, but find no relief. Thus I, too, bearing about with me my inherent passions, have made but little spiritual progress by virtue of my solitary life."

In the *Rule* which Basil instituted for the government of his monastery, and which still regulates the cloisters of the Greek Church, industry was combined with devotion. It was a common

---

the ascetics whom he had seen in Egypt and Syria; but when he discovered they were the followers of a "heretic," he left them, concluding that they were "unsanctified hypocrites."

[1] The Iris runs through a valley some miles to the west of Neo-Cæsarea (now contracted into Niksar), with a fine mountain region between. Although the site of the monastery has not been identified, the description of the region by modern travellers answers to Basil's picture. "No description is adequate to paint the brilliancy and luxuriance of vegetation and the picturesque forms."

proverb: "A laborious monk is beset by one devil, an idle monk by a legion." By the labour of Basil's monks many a barren tract was converted into corn-fields and vineyards. His rule was severe. His monks wore coarse garments (seldom washed), a belt, and shoes of raw hide; their hair uncombed, their looks downcast.[1] One meal only a day was allowed, of bread, water, and beans without salt. "With us," wrote Basil to the Emperor Julian, "as is becoming, the cook's art has no place; our knives never touch blood; our daintiest meal is vegetables with coarse bread and half-sour wine."[2] The night, as well as the day, was divided into definite portions, and the intervals of sleep filled up with prayers and psalmody.[3] Basil himself had but one outer and one inner garment; he slept in a hair shirt, with the ground for his bed, and never made use of a bath. But Basil's rule was more than severe. Like the pattern which he found in Egypt, it was an outrage against humanity. "It is the devil's craft," he says, "to keep alive in the mind of the monk a recollection of his parents and kinsfolk, so that under colour of aiding them he may be diverted from his heavenly course." And when some (for there seem to have been a few reasonable men still remaining) pointed to Paul's words, "If any provide not for his own, and specially his own household, he hath denied the faith, and is worse than an unbeliever," Basil, with perverse ingenuity, answered, that Paul speaks here to the living, not to the dead; whereas a true monk is, as regards all secular obligations, a dead man. The solitude of the cell was looked upon as the very essence of the Christian life. With a singular ignorance of human nature he declares: "Solitude puts to sleep the vicious motions of the mind, and leisure affords a way of extirpating them altogether." Intercourse with women was especially prohibited. It was forbidden to speak with, or even to look at them, except in cases of extreme necessity. But the rule did not stop even here. "Shun the society of young men of thy own age" (such is Basil's injunction to the novice); "flee from them as from a burning flame; if thou leave thy cell, thou leavest

---

[1] Gregory's pattern of the true monk agrees with Basil's: "Vigils, fasts, prayers, tears, smitings of the breast, standing the night through, the mind going forth to God; disordered hair, feet naked in imitation of the Apostles, neglected clothing, unwandering eyes."

[2] Basil, however, was still human. "Send me some fine pot-herbs," wrote Gregory Nazianzen to a friend, who, with Basil, was about to pay him a visit, "if thou dost not wish to see Basil hungry and cross."

[3] "If any one is cross on being awaked, what punishment is he to have? At first, separation and deprivation of food; but if he continue insensible, let him be cut off as a diseased limb."—*Shorter Rule.*

thy virtue." "What sort of virtue," asks Isaac Taylor, "is that which evaporates the moment it is exposed to daylight?" Girls were not allowed to profess before their sixteenth or seventeenth year; any irregularity fallen into by those who devoted themselves after this age, was punished with inexorable severity.

Basil aimed at making the cloister a school for the priesthood. He held the strange opinion that the austerities of monastic discipline were the best training for the Christian ministry; and when he became bishop he ordained scarcely any but monks, preferring those who carried self-mortification to the greatest extreme.[1]

The alluring picture which Basil drew of his retreat brought Gregory to his side. They prayed, toiled, fasted, and sang psalms together, and studied the Scriptures and Origen. Prior to Augustine, no one of the Fathers exercised so powerful a spell over men's minds as did Origen.[2] Admired by some as the first of Christian philosophers, shunned by many as a dangerous heretic, anathematized by councils, the shibboleth of rival theologians, it was at the copious well-spring of Origen's intellect that ardent, youthful spirits slaked their thirst for knowledge. Gregory and Basil culled from his works a selection of choice passages, which they named Philocalia (Love for the Beautiful).

Possibly, however, at this time Gregory may have found Basil's cloister life somewhat severe, for on his return home he wrote his friend a bantering epistle. "With Homer let us 'sing the garniture within,' to wit, thy dwelling roofless and doorless; the hearth without fire or smoke; walls nevertheless baked enough lest the mud should trickle down on us while we suffer Tantalus' penalty—thirst in the midst of water. And that beggarly fare for which thou called me from Cappadocia! I shall never forget the broth and the bread; bread so hard that the teeth made no impression, and when they did effect an entrance were set fast as in a paste. Unless that true lady-bountiful, thy mother, had promptly come to my help, I had been dead long ago. Nor can I omit that misnamed garden, void even of pot-herbs; or the Augean heap which we

---

[1] Chrysostom herein differed altogether from Basil. "The monk," he writes, "lives in a calm, where there is little to oppose him. The skill of the pilot cannot be known till he has taken the helm in the open sea in rough weather. Too many of those who have passed from the seclusion of the cloister to the active sphere of the priest or bishop, have lost their head; and often, instead of adding to their virtue, have been deprived of the good qualities which they already possessed. Monasticism often serves as a screen to failings which active life draws out, just as the qualities of metal are tested by fire."

[2] See *Early Church History*, pt. ii., c. 4, &c.

cleared off and spread over it; or how, in levelling a rugged bank, we dragged that heavy cart full, thou the gentleman, and I the vintager, with neck and hand which still bear the marks of my toil."

Finding that Basil did not take his pleasantry altogether in good part, Gregory wrote again: " What I wrote before concerning thy Pontic abode was in jest, not in earnest; but now I write very much in earnest. Who shall give me back those psalmodies and vigils, those prayers which transported us from earth to heaven, that life which seemed to have nothing in it of material or corporeal? O that I could live again the sweet time we spent in the study of the divine oracles, and enjoy the light which, through the guidance of the Spirit, we found in them. Or let me speak of lower things, the bodily labours of the day, gathering the wood and quarrying the stone, the planting and the draining. And especially of that golden plane-tree, more honourable than that of Xerxes, under which, not a pleasure-sated king, but a weary monk did sit, planted by me, watered by Apollos (that is thy excellent self), and made by God to grow up to my honour, and as a monument of our mutual toil."

Basil's reputation for sanctity attracted to him so large a number of devotees that his retreat quickly assumed the appearance of a town. He also repeatedly made missionary journeys through Pontus, and everywhere there sprang up conventual houses of both sexes for the joint practice of industry and piety. In these institutions children were taken charge of, slaves protected, solitaries received, and (most mistaken charity!) a home made for married persons who imagined they were serving God by living apart. By his means also hospitals and other homes of beneficence were founded.

In A.D. 360 the Emperor Constantius used all his authority to obtain the signatures of the bishops to the Arian confession of faith, known as the creed of Ariminum (Rimini). Gregory's father was one of those who yielded, but afterwards, through the influence of his son and of the monks of his diocese, who were devoted to Athanasius, he made a public confession of orthodoxy. Dianius, bishop of Cæsarea, also gave way. Basil, who, like Athanasius, regarded it as the great mission of his life to uphold the Trinitarian faith, was grieved beyond measure at his bishop's weakness, and refrained from all communion with him. When, however, two years afterwards, Dianius was stricken for death, he entreated Basil to come to him and comfort his dying hours. The aged bishop expired in Basil's arms, protesting with his last breath that he had never intentionally departed from the Nicene faith, and that it was in the simplicity of his heart he had given his adherence to the Arian creed.

Shortly before the death of Dianius, Julian ascended the throne, A.D. 361. It was the desire of the new Emperor to surround himself with the associates of his early days; and he invited Basil to come at once to court. Basil was at first disposed to accept the invitation, but when he found that Julian had turned his back upon the Christian faith, and was preparing to restore paganism, he refused.[1] Julian was deeply offended, and determined to be revenged. Hearing that the citizens, so far from apostatising with himself, and building new heathen temples as he had commanded, had pulled down the only one still standing—the Temple of Fortune; he expunged Cæsarea from the catalogue of cities, and inflicted severe penalties on the clergy and the wealthy inhabitants. He even demanded of Basil a fine of a thousand pounds' weight of gold. Basil, in his reply, reminded the Emperor of the time when they two studied the Holy Scriptures together, and upbraided him with the folly of requiring so vast a sum from one who had not enough even to buy himself a meal. The Emperor was further exasperated by another occurrence. Eusebius, a distinguished layman, was chosen bishop in the place of Dianius, mainly through the exertions of Basil and Gregory. The choice, which was opposed by many of the neighbouring prelates, was offensive to Julian, who grudged the Church the possession of so able a citizen, and vowed that when he should return in triumph from his Persian campaign he would reserve the two friends, "as Polyphemus did Ulysses," for his latest victims. He did not live to return, but was slain in the expedition.

Basil had soon to repent of the part he had taken in the election of Eusebius. The new bishop, desiring to avail himself of Basil's theological knowledge and intellectual power to compensate for his own deficiencies, obliged him, against his will, to receive ordination as a priest. Shortly before, in 362, Basil's friend Gregory had also been, by his father's authority and the will of the people, driven or entrapped into the priesthood. The perversion of the Christian ministry to a sacerdotal office, and the mistaken notions derived from the old Eastern religions, regarding the mortification of the body, made Gregory shrink with extreme dread from ordination. "I felt myself unequal to this warfare, and therefore hid my face

---

[1] The student of history may recollect the two laconic epistles which passed between the Emperor and Basil. *Julian:* "I have read, I have understood, I have condemned." *Basil:* "Thou hast read, but not understood; for if thou hadst understood, thou wouldst not have condemned."

and slunk away. My body of humiliation wages an eternal war with my passions. I toss to and fro through the senses and the delights of life; I stick fast in the deep mire; the law of sin wars against the law of the spirit, and tries to efface the royal image in me. Before we have subdued with all our might the principle which drags us down, and have duly cleansed the spirit, and have much surpassed others in approach to God, I consider it unsafe to undertake the cure of souls or the mediatorship between God and man, which belong to a priest." When to his conscientious scruples was added the forced manner of his ordination, which appeared to him nothing less than an act of spiritual tyranny, it was more than he could support, and leaving his new charge he betook himself to Pontus (A.D. 362), to seek consolation from his old friend. The Nazianzen Church was offended at Gregory's flight, and on his return demanded from him a public apology. He set himself to answer in a manner worthy of the occasion. The result was one of those eloquent discourses which have made his name famous as a master of Christian oratory.[1]

To return to Basil. A rupture soon broke out between himself and the new bishop. The latter was not only his inferior in worth, but was far less popular; and when, envious of his superiority, Eusebius treated Basil with coldness, if not with insolence, the latter might easily have wrested the episcopal authority out of his hands. Basil, however, had the prudence to withdraw from the contest, and shut himself up in his monastery in Pontus. Here he remained till 365, when the arbitrary measures adopted by the Emperor Valens for the spread of Arianism, brought him back to Cæsarea. Through Gregory's mediation he became reconciled to Eusebius, and gave him his powerful support in this hour of common need. The Arians assumed a threatening aspect, but Basil compelled them to leave the city. The insurrection of Procopius at Constantinople, which just then broke out, prevented Valens for the moment from taking his revenge; and Basil had time to organise his defence. He also exerted himself to mitigate the suffering from drought and famine by which, in the year 868, Cappadocia was laid waste. He gave up the property which had recently come to him at the death of his mother, persuaded the rich merchants who had bought up the corn to open their stores, set on foot a public subscription, and himself superintended the distribution of bread to the starving multitude.

---

[1] The discourse is practically a treatise on the pastoral office, and is a storehouse whence Chrysostom, Gregory the Great, Bossuet, and other orators of various times have drawn their ideas.

In 370 Eusebius died. Basil saw that the cause of orthodoxy in the province depended upon his own elevation to the vacant see. The election of a bishop in the great cities had come, since the accession of Constantine, to be an affair of State, a matter of great political no less than ecclesiastical importance, and where parties ran high, it was often accompanied by tumults and bloodshed.[1]

In this instance the prize to be contended for was of no common value. The bishop of Cæsarea was the possessor of power reaching far beyond the limits of the city itself. He was metropolitan of Cappadocia and exarch of Pontus.[2] In the latter capacity his authority, more or less defined, extended over more than half Asia Minor, and embraced eleven provinces. Basil, beloved and popular as he was, felt, nevertheless, that his election was insecure. The people generally with the clergy and monks were on his side, but the rich chafed under his ceaseless calls to charity, the authorities dreaded the displeasure of the Arian Emperor Valens, and the neighbouring bishops were jealous of his superior reputation and abilities. Instead of leaving the matter in the hands of Him who alone has the right to appoint his shepherds, Basil began to devise measures for the accomplishment of his purpose. He sent for Gregory, but, fearing that if his friend were apprised of the real

---

[1] In the contest for the see of Rome, in A.D. 366, between Damasus and Ursicinus, a sanguinary street war was waged. Damasus, it is stated, followed by a furious mob, forced his way into the churches, and trampled down all opposers. After this, with a band of gladiators, he seized the Lateran Basilica, where he was ordained; and, having bribed the magistrates, caused his opponent to be sent into exile. The people would have hindered him from taking possession of the episcopal chair, but he cleared his way through them with blows; and then, with the ecclesiastics of his faction, joined by gladiators, charioteers, and armed rustics, besieged one of the churches where the adverse party were assembled. Setting fire to the doors, he forced his way in, slew 160 persons, men and women, and wounded many. "Notwithstanding all this," adds Roberts, "Damasus was a saint, and miracles were ascribed to him after his death!" How widely the Church had departed from the apostolic rule in the election of its officers, even where such outrages were unknown, let Chrysostom declare. "The elections are generally made on public festivals, and are disgraceful scenes of party feeling and intrigue. The clergy and the people are never of one mind. The really important qualifications for the office are seldom considered. Ambitious men spare no arts of bribery or flattery to obtain places. One candidate for a bishopric is recommended to the electors, because he is of a noble family; another, because he is wealthy and will not burden the funds of the Church; a third, because he is a deserter from the opposite party."

[2] As metropolitan he had fifty country bishops under him. The term exarch was nearly synonymous with that of patriarch.

nature of the business he might shrink from undertaking it, he stooped to employ artifice. As though he were on his death-bed, he wrote, begging him to come and receive his last commands. The wretched maxim that deceit and falsehood are permissible when religion is to be promoted, was fast taking root in the Church.[1]

As soon as he received the letter Gregory prepared to go to his friend's help, but before he set out he discovered the deception which had been put upon him. He protested against the fraud, refused to come to Cæsarea, and urged Basil to leave the city until the election was over. Such affairs, he told him, were not managed by men of piety, but by active and popular agents. But Basil was not thus to be deterred; he turned from the son to the father, the aged bishop of Nazianzus. Convinced that the cause of orthodoxy was involved in Basil's election, the old man roused himself for the occasion. Using his son as his amanuensis, he dictated two letters —one to the clergy and people of Cæsarea, calling on them to lay aside party feeling and choose Basil as bishop; the other to the electing prelates, reminding them (as Basil's state of health had been made an objection) that they were not choosing an *athlete*, but a spiritual teacher. He also wrote to a bishop of wide influence, Eusebius of Samosata, urging him to visit Cæsarea and undertake the direction of this difficult business. Eusebius found the city in a state of distraction, but his influence and tact overcame all obstacles. Even the bishops yielded, or rather pretended to do so, for when the time came for the consecration, two of them only were found willing to join in it. The rule of the Church required three.[2] But if the adverse party hoped in this way to nullify the election, they were disappointed. The aged Gregory, though scarcely able to stand, caused himself to be lifted from his bed and carried in a litter to Cæsarea. With his own hands he consecrated the newly-elected prelate, and placed him in his episcopal chair.

We now follow Basil from his cell on the Iris to his throne in the capital of Pontus. His election filled the orthodox everywhere with exultation. Athanasius, then seventy-four years old, and nearing the end of his course, congratulated Cappadocia on possessing a bishop whom every province might envy. At Constantinople the news was received with far different feelings. Valens

---

[1] In his *Rule*, Basil took a higher standard than in his own practice. He enjoined truthfulness to the exclusion of expediency even for a good end, adducing the words of Christ (John viii. 44).

[2] The fourth canon of the Council of Nicæa directs that, if possible, a bishop should be ordained by all the bishops of the province, but that in any case three, at least, should be present.

regarded it as a serious check to his designs for the triumph of Arianism. Basil was not an opponent to be despised; if he could not be made to bend, he must be got rid of.

Basil had hoped that his friend Gregory would become his coadjutor in this new office, but he was disappointed. Gregory, whose affection appears to have been somewhat cooled by Basil's trickery, expressed satisfaction at his election, but excused himself from joining with him in public life; and although after a while he yielded to his importunity and went to Cæsarea, it was only to refuse all Basil's public attentions and marks of dignity, and soon to retire again to his quiet home at Arianzus.

For some years Basil's episcopal rule was troubled by those bishops who had opposed his election. They withheld their sympathy and help, and delighted in thwarting his plans. One of them was his own uncle, who had filled a parent's place to him on his father's death, but who from some cause had left him and joined the party of opposition. Basil's younger brother Gregory, distinguished by the surname of Nyssen, interposed his offices to effect a reconciliation; but the means which he adopted were the worst that could have been devised. He, too, seems to have been imbued with the fatal error of the age, and to have supposed that a pious end justifies fraudulent means. He wrote forged letters to Basil in his uncle's name. The fraud, which was quickly discovered, only had the effect of widening the breach between the uncle and nephew. Neither would take the first step towards reconciliation; the former standing upon his prerogative of age and relationship, the latter on his rank as a metropolitan dealing with his suffragan. In the end, however, the more noble part in Basil prevailed, and he wrote his uncle a letter of affection and duty. The old man had only waited for this, and peace was restored between them.

GREGORY NYSSEN is the third in our trio of Cappadocian bishops. He was two years younger than his brother Basil, and was of a retiring disposition. He had his brother's feebleness of constitution in a still greater degree, but did not possess the same strength of mind. As a youth, the observances of religion as then practised, had but little attraction for him. Martyrs' festivals were greatly in vogue; and his mother Emmelia having come into possession of some relics of the Forty Martyrs (soldiers who were said to have suffered in Armenia under Licinius, A.D. 320), appointed a solemn festival for the translation of the same to a chapel adjoining her nunnery. High service, to which the whole country had been invited, was held in her garden throughout the night. She sent to

Cæsarea for her son Gregory to take part in the ceremonial. He obeyed the summons, but with so little goodwill that he passed the night asleep in an arbour. Whilst thus sleeping he had a dream, in which he saw himself beaten by the martyrs with their rods, and almost shut out from the garden. Terrified by this vision, and full of remorse for the dishonour he had done to God's saints, he determined to devote himself to the Church, and undertook the office of reader. Soon wearying, however, of his new vocation, he relapsed into the world and became a professor of rhetoric. He also married, and his wife is described as a "very worthy lady, full of piety and good works." His friends were deeply grieved at his defection, and Gregory Nazianzen, who had extended the friendship he had for Basil to this younger brother, adjured him in the strongest terms to retrace his steps, styling his desire of worldly distinction, a "demoniacal ambition." Nyssen was not deaf to these entreaties. After some struggles, he resolved to quit the world, abandon his virtuous wife, and betake himself to his brother Basil's monastery. Here he passed several years, studying the Scriptures, and composing a treatise on Virginity, in which he laments most poignantly what he looks upon as the fatal error, by which, as by a wall or gulf, he had for ever separated himself from that angelic state of perfection!

It was towards the close of his residence in the monastery, A.D. 371, that Gregory Nyssen so unhappily essayed to effect the reconciliation of his brother with their uncle. On the discovery of the deceit, Basil wrote him a letter of severe rebuke. He ridicules him for his simplicity, upbraids him with his unbrotherly conduct, and although, as we have seen, Basil himself had been guilty of the same thing, reproaches him with endeavouring to serve the cause of truth by deceit!

To return to Basil. In 371 the Emperor Valens divided Cappadocia into two provinces, making Tyana the capital of the new division. Anthimus, bishop of that city, choosing to consider that the ecclesiastical rule should follow the civil, claimed metropolitan jurisdiction over it in the place of Basil, and began to appropriate its revenues. To such a course Basil was not the man tamely to submit. He summoned his friend Gregory Nazianzen to his side. Gregory wrote in reply, "I will come if thou wishest: if so be that the sea wants water or Basil a counsellor, I will come. At all events, I am ready to bear ill-usage in thy company." In the scene which followed, the parties on both sides figure in a manner unbecoming to the Christian ministry. As soon as Gregory arrived, the two friends set out together for a monastery on the Taurus range, situated in the severed province, to receive the produce of an estate which, up to this time, had belonged to the see of Cæsarea. As the rents were paid in kind they took with them a train of sumpter-mules. Anthimus, hearing of the expedition, hastened, full of wrath, to intercept the convoy. Notwithstanding his advanced age, he put himself at the head of a band of armed retainers, whom he stationed at a defile near Sasima, through which the train had to pass on its return. An affray ensued; Gregory was injured, and Basil had his mule taken from him,

To strengthen himself against his rival, Basil determined to erect two new bishoprics as defensive outposts on that frontier of his diocese, and to fill them with the two Gregorys. The onerous duties of a bishop were, however, distasteful to them both, and so reluctant were they to abandon their retirement and enter upon public life, that in each case compulsion had to be used before they would suffer the ordaining hands to be laid upon them. But Basil was one of those men who, when they have a clear sight of their object, will make their way to it at any sacrifice; and when Gregory Nazianzen took to flight to avoid consecration, he even went so far as to pursue and bring him back. Gregory was deeply wounded. At his ordination he gave vent to his feelings, in these plaintive words: "Once more has the Holy Spirit been poured out upon me, and once more I enter upon my calling, sad and dejected."

The new bishoprics were Sasima and Nyssa. The latter, over which Basil placed his brother, was an obscure town, so insignificant, that Eusebius of Samosata wrote to remonstrate against a man of such talents being thus buried. Basil replied that his purpose was to make the see famous by its bishop, not the bishop by the see. The choice of Sasima for Gregory Nazianzen was still more unworthy. It was a mean village or posting-station, situate within the new province of Tyana. The revenues of the Church were meagre, and it was a spot in the highest degree distasteful to the sensitive nature of Gregory, who, in one of his poems, has left us a description of it somewhat caricatured. "On a highway of Cappadocia, at a point where three roads join, is a halting-place where is neither water nor anything green, nor any mark of civilization. It is a frightful and detestable village. Everywhere you meet nothing but noises, dust, waggons, howls, groans, chains, instruments of torture, and the executioner. The whole population consists of foreigners and travellers. Such was my church of Sasima."

Basil was universally censured for appointing Gregory to such a place. Finding him slow to enter upon his office, he sent his brother of Nyssa to quicken his resolution. Gregory Nazianzen prepared to obey, but hearing that Anthimus had appointed a rival bishop to the see, he retired from the contest. Basil reproached him for his pusillanimity. Gregory could bear no more. Loving and gentle as he was, his whole soul recoiled against these repeated insults, and he thus poured forth his wounded feelings: "Wilt thou never cease to slander me, merely because I am bold enough to recognise how I have been treated? I know now the deception thou hast practised upon me, which I can no otherwise explain, than that thy elevation to the episcopal throne has suddenly lifted thee up. . . . The most charitable accuse thee of making use of me, and then casting me aside, just as the framework of an arch, as soon as the structure is completed, is struck away and counted good for nothing. . . . I am not going to arm myself and learn the art of war, in order to fight the martial Anthimus. Fight him thyself; or if thou art in want of warriors, wait till he surrounds the pass and lays hold of thy mules. To what purpose is it that I should fight for sucking-pigs and chickens, and these not my own, as if they were men's souls and Church canons. . . . Sweep everything into thy own lap, as the rivers do the mountain torrents, to swell thy own glory; so long as thou dost not set friendship and intimacy above right and piety." From this moment the confiding friendship which had subsisted between Basil and Gregory ever since their boyhood was broken. Basil, indeed, went once again to Nazianzus to visit Gregory; but so far as appears, no more familiar letters passed between them. After Basil's death Gregory endeavoured to offer an apology for his friend's conduct, but the attempt only shows how incurable was the wound. In his funeral oration over him he says: "Admiring as I do, all he did more than I can express, I cannot praise his extraordinary and unfriendly conduct towards me, the pain of which time has not removed. To this I trace all the irregularity and confusion of my subsequent life. Unless, indeed, I may be suffered to make this excuse for him, that having views beyond this earth, he slighted friendship, only when it was his duty to prefer God, and to make more account of the things hoped for, than of the things that perish."[1]

It is doubtful whether Gregory ever entered upon the bishopric of Sasima; but at his father's urgent request he became his coadjutor in the see of Nazianzus, A.D. 372. How much every call to public service cost him may be seen by a sermon which he preached

---

[1] Church historians have been so tender of Basil's reputation that we have been obliged to consult Gregory's original epistles to complete the story.

at this time. "Between my inward longing and the Holy Spirit, I am almost torn asunder. The one urges me to fly to the solitude of the mountains, to withdraw from all sensuous things, and to retire into myself, that I may commune with God undisturbed. But the Spirit would lead me into active life to serve the common weal, to spread light, and present to God a people for his possession, a royal priesthood."

It was a year or two before this happened, namely, in 371, that Basil found himself engaged in a personal encounter with the Arian Emperor Valens. The Emperor had entered upon his theological crusade against the Catholics, and was on his march through the provinces of Asia Minor. For awhile his progress was one of uniform victory. "The Catholics had everywhere fallen before him. Bithynia had resisted, and had become the scene of horrible tragedies. The fickle Galatia had yielded without a struggle. The fate of Cappadocia depended on Basil. His house, as the Emperor drew near, was besieged by ladies of rank, high personages of state, even by bishops, who entreated him to bow before the storm and appease the Emperor by a temporary submission." But Basil had no ear for such counsels; he rejected their entreaties with disdain. The arrival of Valens was preceded by a band of Arian bishops, aiming to strike awe into their opponents by their numbers, but Basil straightway refused to hold communion with them. They were followed by officers of the Imperial household, who threatened him in violent language. One of these was Demosthenes, the *chef de cuisine*, whom the Emperor carried everywhere with him, but to whom Basil paid no attention except to bid him return to his kitchen fire. Another was Modestus, the prefect of the Pretorium :—

Modestus. What is the meaning of this, thou Basil (not deigning to style him bishop), that thou standest out against so great a prince?

Basil. What dost thou mean?

Modestus. Thou dost not worship after the Emperor's manner, although the rest of thy party have yielded.

Basil. Such is not my Heavenly Sovereign's will, nor can I worship any creature.

Modestus (amazed). For whom dost thou take me?

Basil. For a thing of nought while thy commands are such.

Modestus. Is it, then, nothing to have men of rank like us on your side?

Basil. Thou art a prefect, and illustrious, I grant; but God's Majesty is greater. It would be an honour to have thee on my side, but yet no more so than to have any member of my flock; for Christianity consists not in distinction of persons, but in faith.

The prefect was enraged at this reply, and rising from his chair, abruptly asked Basil if he did not fear his power.

Basil. Fear what?

Modestus. Any one of the many penalties a prefect can inflict.

Basil. Let me know them: confiscation, exile, tortures, death? None of these can move me.

Modestus. How so?

Basil. That man is not obnoxious to confiscation who has nothing to lose, except old tattered garments and a few books. Nor does he care for exile who is not circumscribed by place, but is everywhere at home on God's earth. Nor can torture harm a frame so frail that it would break under the first blow; and death would be gain.

Modestus. No one ever yet spoke to Modestus with such freedom.

Basil. Peradventure Modestus never before met with a true bishop. O prefect, in other things we are gentle, and more humble than all men living, but when God's honour is at stake we overlook all else. Fire and the sword, beasts of prey, irons to rend the flesh, are an indulgence rather than a terror to the Christian. Therefore threaten, insult, do thy worst, make the most of thy power. Let the Emperor be informed of my purpose.

Finding threats useless, Modestus tried promises and flattery, but with no better success. He had to report to his master that all his attempts to bring Basil to submission had been fruitless. Such rare intrepidity produced its natural effect on the feeble mind of Valens. He refused to sanction harsh measures against the bishop, and even condescended to present himself in the chief church of Cæsarea on the Feast of the Epiphany. The service had already commenced. When the Emperor, in the glowing words of Nazianzen, "heard the chanted psalms which rose like a peal of thunder, and beheld the sea of worshippers within and around the sanctuary, ranked in an order so comely as to resemble angels rather than men, and the bishop himself standing, like Samuel, erect before the people, body, eyes and soul, absorbed in God and the altar, and the priests on either side in reverential awe—the Emperor's spirit forsook him, and he swooned away." Gregory says that Valens had never before beheld such a spectacle. This can hardly have referred to the service itself, for that would surely be as imposing in the cathedral church at Constantinople. It was rather the oneness of purpose and spirit by which the assembly was animated, their love to Basil and their devotion to the Nicene faith. It must be remembered, too, that the Trinitarians were at that period the Nonconformists, and that persecution had weeded from their ranks the nominal and the lukewarm. Add to this the sight of the bishop himself as he stood before the altar—tall, spare, erect, with hollow cheeks and piercing eyes, and armed as he conceived with the majesty of heaven. When the time came for Valens to make his offering, and the ministers were hesitating whether they should receive an oblation from the hand of a heretic, Basil came forward, and himself accepted the gift.

The next day Valens again visited the church, and was admitted by the bishop within the sacred veil. The cook, Demosthenes, rudely joining in the conversation, made a grammatical mistake. Basil smiled, and quietly observed: "We have here, it seems, a Demosthenes who cannot speak Greek; he had better attend to his sauces than meddle with theology." The retort amused the Emperor, who was so well pleased with his theological opponent, that he made him a grant of land on which to erect a poor-house.

But the favourable impression thus made on Valens soon wore off. The Arian bishops recovered their influence, and an imperial order was issued for Basil to quit the city. He was to start at night, to avoid the risk of popular disturbance. The chariot was at his door, and his friends, Gregory amongst them, were bewailing his departure, when he was stopped by an imperial messenger sent in consequence of the sudden illness of the Emperor's only son. The Empress attributed their child's danger to the Divine displeasure at the treatment of Basil, and the Emperor sent to entreat Basil to come and pray over the sick child. On condition that it should be brought up in the orthodox faith, Basil consented. As he prayed, the child grew better.[1] But the Arians contrived that it should be baptized by one of their own bishops. The child (so the historians relate) grew immediately worse, and died the same night. Basil's enemies, however, were not even now in despair; they returned once more to the attack, and with the usual result. His exile was again determined on; but when Valens attempted to sign the order, the pens, it is declared, refused to write, and thrice split in his hand! This supposed miracle put an end to all further proceedings. "Valens left Cæsarea, and Basil remained master of the situation."

Thus left free to devote his energies to the internal administration

---

[1] The prefect Modestus also, who fell sick, attributed his own recovery to the prayers of Basil.

of his diocese, Basil set himself vigorously to the correction of the abuses which had grown up within it. He was an energetic promoter of morals, good order, and discipline. He had, however, no thought of bringing back the worship and government of the Church to its primitive pattern; rather were the superstitious practices of the time strengthened, and the authority of the bishops enhanced under his rule. In his own province he usurped the control of episcopal elections, and even travelled into Armenia to appoint new bishops and infuse fresh life into those who were already in office. His incessant labours were performed under the pressure of extreme bodily weakness, so that, even when considered in health, he describes himself as being "weaker than persons who are given over."

Basil's heaviest trial was yet to come. A suspicion of his orthodoxy was artfully and successfully propagated throughout the Churches. He was unjustly accused of denying the proper divinity of the Holy Spirit.[1] This brought great odium upon him. In his extremity he turned first to Athanasius, whom he designates "that great and apostolic soul who from boyhood had been an athlete in the cause of religion," and then to the Western Church. The former was unable to assist him; the Western bishops sent assurances of attachment and sympathy, but nothing more. They could not move without the bishop of Rome; and the bishop of Rome was offended, because Basil did not appeal to him as supreme. This assumption of superiority was lost on Basil; he only remarked, it was in vain to send messages to "one who sat aloft, high and haughty, and would not listen to the truth from men who stood below."

Even whilst he lay under the imputation of heterodoxy, Basil did not relax in the conflict he was always waging against Arianism. "Polytheism," he writes, "has got possession. A greater and a lesser God are worshipped. All ecclesiastical power, all Church ordinances, are in Arian hands. Arians baptize; Arians

---

[1] Fear of Sabellianism restrained Basil for some time from committing himself entirely to the Homo-ousion doctrine. His usual form of doxology was "Glory be to the Father through the Son, in the Holy Spirit." On which Hooker remarks: "Till Arianism had made it a matter of great sharpness and subtilty of wit to be a sound believing Christian, men were not curious what syllables or particles of speech they used. When St. Basil began to practise the like indifferency, and to conclude public prayers, glorifying sometime the Father *with* the Son and the Holy Ghost, sometime the Father *by* the Son, *in* the Spirit, . . . some (because the light of his candle too much drowned theirs) were glad to lay hold on so colourable a matter, and were exceedingly forward to traduce him as an author of suspicious innovation."

visit the sick; Arians administer the sacred mysteries. The pious are banished; the houses of prayer are closed; the altars forbidden; the orthodox meet for worship in the deserts, exposed to wind and rain and snow, or to the scorching sun."

Before his death, however, Basil was permitted to see the dawn of a brighter day. A new invasion of the Goths in 377 drew off Valens from the persecution of the orthodox; the next year his army was defeated with immense slaughter near Adrianople, and the Emperor himself perished. His successor, the youthful Gratian, belonged to the Catholic party, and one of his first acts was to recall the banished orthodox prelates. So that, before his death, Basil had the joy of seeing many of his friends restored to their sees.

Basil died January 1, A.D. 379, at Cæsarea. Although only fifty years old, his constitution was completely worn out. His deathbed was surrounded by the citizens, "willing if so it might be," says his friend Gregory, "to give a portion of their own lives to lengthen that of their bishop." He breathed his last with the words, "Into thy hand I commend my spirit: Thou hast redeemed me, O Lord God of Truth." His funeral was attended by immense crowds, who almost tore the bier to pieces to secure a relic of the departed saint. "The press was so great that several persons were crushed to death; almost the object of envy, because they died with Basil."

Basil was pale, and wore a beard; through life he retained his monkish dress. In speech he was deliberate, in manner reserved and sedate. His friend Gregory especially commends his trumpet eloquence, his great and various learning, his charity, his compassion, his affability. "Who," he exclaims, "more loving than he to the well-conducted? who more severe with transgressors? his smile was praise, and his silence a reproof to the uneasy conscience. If he were not full of talk, or a jester, or a boon companion, what then? This, with men of sense, is not his blame, but his praise. Yet, that he was most agreeable in social intercourse, I who knew him so well can testify. None could relate a story with more wit; none maintain the sport of words so playfully; none convey the timely hint with greater delicacy."

Basil is often called The Great, as much on account of his writings as of his character.[1] The following passage will serve as a

---

[1] He has left nearly 400 letters. Dr. Jessopp thus compares the three great letter-writers of this age, Augustine, Jerome, and Basil. "St. Augustine's can really hardly be called letters at all; they are for the most part treatises on the

specimen of his style:—" The love of God cannot be taught. We did not learn from any one else to take pleasure in the light, nor to desire life. No one taught us to love our parents or our nurses. Thus, or rather far more, the learning of the love of God comes not from without, but a certain seminal power of reason is ingrafted in us, which possesses from its own store the means of that appropriation which leads to love. Which power the school of the divine commandments takes in hand, tills with care, nourishes with skill, and, by the grace of God, brings to perfection. . . . We naturally love the beautiful (though to different persons different things may seem beautiful), and we delight to display all good to those who do us good. Now what more admirable than the Divine Beauty? What conception more attractive than the Majesty of God? What longing so vehement and irresistible as that which is engendered of God in the soul which is purged of vice, and which cries out of unfeigned desire, 'I am sick of love?' . . . Alienation and aversion from God is worse than any torments of hell. It is as the privation of light to the eye, even if no pain be present; or as the deprivation of life to a living thing. . . . Our Lord Jesus Christ, who endured a most shameful death that he might restore us to the glorious life, exacts no recompense, but is satisfied if he be only loved for what he gave. And when I think of all these things, I am in an ecstasy

---

interpretation of sacred Scripture, or on theological or philosophical questions. . . . In St. Jerome's we have some valuable notices of the religious life of the time, and we get a most curious impression of the awfully high pressure at which devout people were living at the close of the fourth century. The men and women are not men and women, but creatures who are trying to be something else and who believe themselves to be something else. Jerome himself is up in a balloon, and he seems to assume that everybody else is, or ought to be, or wishes to be, or is trying to be up in a balloon too. . . . St. Basil's letters are very much less known, but they are far more real, genuine, human, and interesting than those of Augustine and Jerome. They have a wide range of subjects, and his correspondents were people of all ranks and classes and opinions—pagan philosophers and professors, governors of provinces, ladies iu distress, rogues who had tried to take him in, and, of course, a host of bishops and clergy. . . . He can laugh and be playful—witness his letter to the governor of Cappadocia, who had cured himself of an illness by dieting himself on pickled cabbage. 'My dear sir,' says Basil, 'I am delighted at the news. I never believed in cabbage before, still less in pickled cabbage; but now I shall praise it as something superior to the lotus that Homer talks of—yea, not inferior to the very ambrosia that served as the food of the gods!' The governor answered that letter very briefly, and his answer has been preserved. 'My right rev. brother,' says the governor, 'you are right, there's nothing like pickled cabbage! Twice to cabbage kills—so the saying has it. I find, many times to cabbage cures. Come and try. Dine with me to-morrow on pickled cabbage—that and nothing more!'"

of fear lest ever, through inattention of mind or occupation with vanities, I should fall from the love of God and become a reproach to Christ. . . . The reproach which our fall will bring on Christ, and the glorying of the enemy, seem to me worse than the punishments of hell."

We must now go back a few years. It was only in condescension to his father's will that Gregory Nazianzen consented to become his coadjutor. On his father's death, however (which took place in 874), he continued to administer the see until a new bishop was elected. During these years some of his most brilliant discourses were delivered. He was sensible, however, of the worthlessness of mere words, and at last announced to his congregation that he had resolved not to preach before them again, in order that by his silence he might "check the mania for theological discussion, which was leading everybody to teach the things of the Spirit without the unction of the Spirit."

Suddenly, in 375, Gregory disappeared. He had retired to a monastery in Isauria, where he remained three years in strict seclusion. He returned home before Basil's death, but was taken so dangerously ill that he could neither visit him on his dying bed nor be present at his funeral. Like Basil, he had become prematurely old. Though only fifty years of age, his bald head bent towards his bosom, and his countenance was wasted by tears and fasting, and furrowed with wrinkles. With characteristic melancholy he writes to a friend: " Thou inquirest how I am ; I answer, very ill.' My spiritual brother [Basil] and my natural brother [Cæsarius] are both gone. Age shows itself on my head; my cares multiply; friends prove untrue; the Church is without shepherds ; good is disappearing; evil shows itself bare-faced. We are journeying in the night; there is nowhere a torch to give us light; Christ is asleep. What, then, is to be done ? Alas for me ! there is only one escape, and that is death!"

But there was work yet for Gregory to do, and that on a higher stage than before. For fifty years Arianism had been dominant in Constantinople. The adherents of the Nicene faith had dwindled down to a small number, and were without church or bishop, being obliged to conceal themselves in the remote quarters of the city. The accession of Gratian restored their courage. Looking round for a pastor, they cast their eyes on Gregory, whose praise for eloquence and sanctity was in all the Churches; and they sent him an urgent appeal to take charge of their little flock. Long he remained unwilling to quit his beloved retirement, but at length he yielded to the conviction that the time for action had arrived;

and he turned his face towards the great city. His opinion of the state of the Church there is conveyed in a few words: "It had passed through the death of infidelity: there was left but one last breath of life. What the people needed was solid teaching to deliver them from the spider-webs of subtleties in which they had been taken." Nevertheless, on some points the teaching of the Arians was more enlightened than that of the Catholics. Sir Isaac Newton remarks that before Gregory came to Constantinople, the city was free from that superstitious reverence for the martyrs with which it shortly after began to be inflamed.

Gregory began his work in a private house; but the building quickly became too small for the multitudes which flocked to it, and a church was erected in its place. To this church he gave the name of Anastasia (*Resurrection, i.e.* of the true faith). Here he delivered a fresh series of those discourses which have made his name famous. The success of his preaching raised up a host of enemies, who envied whilst they affected to despise him, even ridiculing his person and attire.[1] A fierce attack was made upon his church during the hour of service. From the Arian cathedral of St. Sophia there issued a motley crowd of monks, beggars, and women more terrible than men. The assailants made free use of stones, sticks, and firebrands. The altar was profaned, the consecrated wine was mixed with blood, the house of prayer was made a scene of outrage and unbridled licentiousness. Personally, Gregory cared little for the assault; stones, he said, were his delight; his care was only for his flock.

In the year 380 (Nov. 26) Theodosius made his entry into Constantinople. One of his first acts was to remove the Arians from the churches and restore these to the orthodox. To Demophilus, the Arian bishop, was offered the alternative of subscribing the Nicene Creed, or of resigning his office. Demophilus did not hesitate a moment. Assembling his followers in the cathedral, he said: "My brethren, it is written in the Gospel, 'If they persecute you in one city, flee ye into another.' Seeing that the Emperor excludes us from the churches, we will henceforth hold our assemblies without the city." Towards Gregory, the Emperor manifested the greatest respect. On his way to the cathedral he conversed with him for a long while, and, as though anticipating what was about to take place, concluded with these words: "This temple God delivers to thee by our hand as a reward for thy devoted labours."

When the day arrived on which the orthodox were to take pos-

---

[1] "I was," he says, "the very image of a beggar."

session of the churches, the city was violently agitated; cries of the most opposite kind filled the air, some shouting with joy, many more venting their grief and disappointment in tears and threats. The Emperor, in warlike state, and followed by an imposing train, proceeded to the Church of the Apostles, which he had caused to be strongly guarded. Gregory was at his side, breathing feebly from a recent fit of sickness, but full of confidence and thankfulness. The streets through which the procession marched were crowded with an innumerable multitude of either sex and of every age. The windows and roofs of the houses were thronged, and a tumultuous sound arose, in which grief and rage predominated, so that, as Gregory himself describes it, "the city resembled a place which had been taken by storm, and was in the hands of some barbarian conqueror." The morning was gloomy; a thick fog filled the church. The Arians began to exult in this sign of heaven's displeasure, and the orthodox were dispirited, when (so Gregory relates), at the first accents of the chants, the sun broke forth and shone upon the vestments of the priests and the swords of the soldiers, reminding him of the glory which descended upon the ancient tabernacle. At the same time a cry arose from the congregation, "Gregory shall be our bishop." Unable himself to speak from bodily weakness, he desired another priest to address the people in his name: "Silence, silence; this is the time to give thanks to God; it will be time enough hereafter to settle other matters."

The following year Theodosius convened a general council of Oriental bishops at Constantinople. The chief objects were to confirm the Nicene faith, and to appoint a bishop for the metropolis. Although the orthodox were especially invited, other parties, in the hope thereby of promoting union, were admitted; but when the Nicene confession was presented to the synod for its adoption, the Semi-Arian bishops, of whom thirty-six were present, refused to subscribe, and left the city in a body. The wish of Theodosius, that Gregory should be bishop of Constantinople, was well-known; and no opposition being made in the council, he was elected. The inaugural oration was preached by his friend Gregory Nyssen.

Nazianzen's enjoyment of his lofty position was of the very briefest duration.[1] Hardly had his consecration taken place than the bishops began to repent of their choice. His homely manners and ignorance of the world offended them, and they characterised

---

[1] He was actually bishop only a few weeks.

as lukewarmness the tolerance he showed to the now persecuted Arians. But this was not all. It was a time of bitter party spirit and great confusion. Meletius, bishop of Antioch, who presided over the council, held his bishopric only by a compromise between two contending parties. He died whilst the council was in session, and the question who should be his successor in the see of Antioch, rent asunder the Asiatic Church and the council itself. Gregory, by virtue of his office, had become president of the council. He was no party man, and his endeavour to preserve peace between the two parties was misinterpreted and resented; he was, indeed, of too gentle a nature to govern the ship in such a storm. At this crisis there arrived from Egypt and Macedonia a fresh party of bishops, who objected to Gregory's appointment to the see of Constantinople, alleging that, having been formerly consecrated to the see of Sasima, he could not now (according to the 15th canon of the Council of Nicæa) fill any other.[1] In vain did Gregory and his defenders reply that this law, if not already antiquated, had been superseded by the act of the council itself. The opposition only became fiercer, and Gregory saw that there was nothing left but to resign his episcopate. He delivered an address to the council, in which he sought to pour oil upon the troubled waters. Its only effect was to call forth a universal uproar, the younger ecclesiastics especially venting their ill-will towards him, "like screaming jackdaws or a swarm of angry wasps."[2] He wound up his speech with these words: "I now request permission to resign my bishopric, and to lead, if a more inglorious, yet a more peaceful life." Once again he appeared before the council, and exhorted them to occupy themselves with matters worthy of their high calling, and to cherish mutual harmony. "He was ready to be another Jonah to calm the angry waves. He owed but one debt, the debt of death, and that was in God's hands. He had but one anxiety, and that was for his beloved doctrine of the Trinity." From the council he went to the Emperor, who reluctantly consented to accept his resignation.

It was hard to tear himself away from his beloved flock. They entreated him not to leave them. "Who," they asked, "will nourish thy children, if thou shouldst forsake us?" He took a public farewell of the congregation, at which the council were present; and although the cathedral was filled to every corner, not a dry eye was to be seen. "Farewell"—so he wound up his cele-

---

[1] This canon forbade the translation of bishops.
[2] Elsewhere he compares them to "cranes and geese," and says it was a "disgrace to sit amongst such hucksters of the faith."

brated but floral oration—"farewell my beloved church, Anastasia, by which the true faith has been raised up. And thou, too, more majestic temple, our new possession, which hast now first received thy true greatness from the true preaching of the everlasting Word. . . . Farewell, O Holy Trinity, my sole thought, my only jewel; may this my people keep Thee, and mayest Thou preserve them. Cherish, O my children, the truth I have committed to you, and remember the persecutions I have endured for its sake. . . . The grace of our Lord Jesus Christ be with you all! Amen."

Sorrow for the loss of his church was, however, tempered by self-gratulation on his escape from the atmosphere of the court. "Never more shall I be entertained at the tables of princes, bashful and speechless, not breathing freely, feasting like a slave. No magistrate shall again punish me with a seat either near him or below him, giving the higher place to some grovelling spirit. No more shall I clasp bloodstained hands, or take hold of beard, to gain some small favour. No more, hurrying with a crowd to some birthday, burial, or marriage feast, shall I seize on all I can, something for myself, something for my attendants, with their greedy palms, and then late in the evening drag home my ailing carcase worn out with fatigue, and panting with satiety." On his way home to his native village he preached his memorial oration over the grave of Basil.

Once again in his beloved retirement, Gregory partially recovered his shattered health. There was at Arianzus a little garden with a shady walk and a fountain, which he had reserved to himself when all his other property was given to the poor. Here he soothed his irritated spirit, and half forgot the turmoil and vexations of the great city. "If any of our friends," he writes, "should inquire what Gregory is doing, say that he is enjoying in perfect quiet a philosophical life, and that he troubles himself as little about his enemies as he does about persons of whose existence he knows nothing."

From his solitude he sent forth to his friends messages of sympathy, both in their joys and in their tribulations. Although he had himself renounced marriage, and had always extravagantly extolled the virgin state, yet we find him in his declining years entering into hearty sympathy with a young friend in the prospect of marriage. "Thy beloved is now thine; the moment of your union has arrived; and I who ought to have been present, and taken part in the solemn service, am obliged to remain at a distance. Several times I have made the attempt to set out, but have always been overcome by sickness. It must be for others to invoke the genius of love (for playful mirth becomes the nuptial festival), and paint the beauty of the bride and the manliness of the bridegroom. Nevertheless, I will sing you my marriage song: 'The Lord bless you out of Zion, and grant harmony upon your union. Mayst thou see thy sons (thy sons' sons, I was ready to say) still nobler than thyself.'"

The next year, 382, he was invited in the Emperor's name to attend a synod at Constantinople. He thus replied: "To tell the truth, I am in such a temper of mind that I shun every assemblage of bishops, because I have never yet seen a good issue to any synod, have never been present at any which did not do more for the multiplication than it did for the suppression of evils. An indescribable thirst for contention and rule prevails in them; and a man who dares to lift up his voice against what is base in others, will be far more certain to bring down reproach upon himself than to succeed in removing such baseness."

The spread of the Apollinarian heresy[1] alarmed the clergy and people of Nazianzus, and they entreated Gregory to return thither and help them. Very reluctantly he yielded to their importunity, and for a short time administered the affairs of the diocese. But his bodily weakness returned, and as soon as he could induce the neighbouring prelates to consecrate a new bishop, he withdrew again from public life, and spent his last six years in seclusion. He was not idle, however, but continued to occupy himself with the various interests which surrounded him, political, ecclesiastical, and personal. In the mortification of the body, to which he had devoted himself from early life, he suffered no relaxation to overtake him in old age. But these austerities failed to bring him peace. To the burden of a weak and suffering body was often added a spiritual agony so great as to take from him all hope both for this world and the next. At other times, faith lifted him above his tribulations, and he could say: "I suffer and am content, not because I suffer, but because I am for others an example of patience. If I have no means to free myself from pain, I gain from it at least the power to bear it, and to be thankful, as well in sorrow as in joy; for I am convinced that, although it seems to us the contrary, there is in the eyes of the Sovereign Reason nothing opposed to reason in all that happens to us."

He died A.D. 889 or 390, aged about 60 years.

In Gregory's preaching, the lessons of practical religion are never lost sight of. He often sets before his hearers the danger of

---

[1] See below, Period II., Chap. I.

empty talkativeness about divine things, and disputation on theological questions, to which they were addicted. He taught that true piety consists in doing God's will, and that the knowledge of God is attainable only in proportion as the soul is purified from the defilement of sin.

In toleration of heretics Gregory was before his age. His counsel in dealing with such breathes the true Gospel spirit: "Do not rashly condemn thy brother; to condemn and despise is nothing else than to shut out from Christ the sole hope of sinners. It is the same as pulling up with the weeds the hidden fruit which is possibly of more value than thou art. Raise up thy brother gently and lovingly, not as an antagonist, not as a physician who administers medicine by force, or knows of no remedy but cauterising and cutting. Learn rather to know thyself in the spirit of humility, and to search out thy own infirmities. It is not one and the same thing to pull up or destroy a *plant* and a *man*. Thou art an image of God, and thou hast to do with an image of God; thou who judgest wilt thyself be judged. . . . In our Father's house are many mansions, and the ways which lead to them are various." Hear how he speaks to some who denied the divinity of the Holy Spirit: "Such is the love I cherish for you, such the respect I feel for your becoming attire, your abstemiousness, your holy societies, the honour you pay to virginity, your nightly psalm-singing, your love of the poor, your brotherly kindness, your hospitality, that I could even wish myself accursed from Christ if ye were but united with us." At times, however, the old bitter feeling against the Arians, so long triumphant over the Catholics, will break forth; so that if we had no other evidence than Gregory's writings, we should pronounce the whole party to be utterly base and diabolical.

Gregory's pensive spirit was especially open to the sweet influences of Nature. Thus he writes in spring: "How beautiful is everything that meets the eye. The meads send forth their fragrance; the plants bud; the young lambs frisk on the green plains. The bee now leaves her hive, spreads her wings, displays her sagacious instinct, and robs the flowers of their sweetness. All creation praises and glorifies God with inarticulate voice. Yes, it is now [in allusion to the Easter festival], the spring of the world, of the souls of men as well as of their bodies, the visible and the invisible spring, the same which we shall taste above if we are transformed and renewed here." Again, during a time of trial in his ministry at Constantinople, he tells his hearers: "As the day was declining I wandered alone by the sea-shore, for I was accustomed to disperse my cares by this kind of diversion; for the string will not bear to be always on the stretch, but must occasionally be loosened from the bow's end. Thus I wandered, my feet moving mechanically, whilst my eye swept over the expanse of waters. But it was not then as when the purple waves roll gently forward and break softly on the shore, for, to use the words of Scripture, 'the sea had arisen, by reason of a great wind that blew.' The billows, as they approached from a distance, increased in size, reared their crests, and discharged themselves on the beach with a thundering sound. But, roar as they might, the rocks stood unmoved, regardless of the waves that broke against them. As I gazed I thought a profitable lesson was to be learnt from the sight, and how I might apply it to my own state of mind, when, as has recently happened, some untoward occurrence has burst upon me."

Notwithstanding his rich Christian experience, Gregory was steeped in the superstitious spirit of the age. At Constantinople, as already remarked, he revived the practice of keeping birthday festivals, and publicly returned thanks to the martyrs for having so triumphantly assisted the true believers in their recent victory. We shall treat this subject more fully by-and-by.

The annexed passage from his *Oration on the Nativity* will convey an idea of his power to soar into the regions of abstract thought. "God ever was, and is, and will be. Or rather, He ever is; for the terms *was* and *will be* are portions of *our* fleeting duration and transient nature, but *He* always *is;* and thus He designated Himself when He appeared to Moses on the mount. For He comprehends in Himself all existence without commencement, without end, as it were a boundless and unfathomable ocean, rising above every conception both of time and nature. He is shadowed forth by the intellect alone, and that most obscurely and imperfectly, and not from the things which are inherent in Him, but from those which move around Him. Ideas collected from all parts of the creation combine to form a faint image of the Truth, which escapes before it is seized, and flies before it is understood, beaming for an instant on our mind, as the evanescent lightning glances on our sight; in order, as I suppose, that by the small portion which is comprehended it may allure us to itself (for that which is wholly incomprehensible is unhoped for and unattempted); and by what is unapprehended, may be admired; and being admired, may be loved the more; and being loved, may purify; and purifying, may render us divine."

Another passage, less abstruse, will close this notice of Gregory.

"Christ was born indeed on the earth; but in his supernal nature He had been begotten. He was born of a woman indeed, but she was a virgin. If this was natural, that was preternatural. He was without a father in his earthly geniture, and without a mother in his heavenly generation. . . . He was oppressed with hunger, yet He fed thousands in the desert; and He is the living and celestial bread. He was parched with thirst, yet He cried aloud, 'If any man thirst, let him come unto me and drink.' He was weary, yet is He the rest of those who are weary and heavy-laden. He paid tribute, obtained miraculously from a fish, whilst He ruled over those to whom He paid the tribute. . . . He wept, but He made tears to cease. Because He was a man, He asked where Lazarus was laid; but He raised Lazarus from death, because He was God. He was sold for thirty pieces of silver, yet He bought the world at an inestimable price: for He bought it with his blood. He who drinks vinegar and is fed with gall, is He who converted the water into wine, who has destroyed the bitterness of death, who is altogether sweetness, the desire of the heart. He dies, yet He gives life; and dying, He destroys death."[1]

We left Basil's brother Gregory newly installed in his bishopric of Nyssa. This, it may be remembered, was in the reign of the Arian Emperor Valens. A full share of the troubles of the time fell to Gregory's lot, aggravated, it would seem, by an inaptitude on his part in dealing with men. The Imperial cook Demosthenes, whose acquaintance we have made, was appointed vicegerent of Pontus, with the understanding that he was to do all in his power to crush the adherents of the Nicene faith. Gregory was one of those who felt the weight of his tyrannical hand, and refusing to appear before a synod which was summoned to hear charges against him, he was deposed and banished, A.D. 376. In his exile he bewailed the cruel necessity which had compelled him to leave his spiritual children, and also dwells pathetically on the home of which he had been deprived—his fireside, his table, his pantry, his bed, his bench, his sackcloth, contrasting it with the stifling hole in which he was now forced to dwell, of which the only furniture was straitness, darkness, and cold. But he took comfort in the assurance that his brethren would remember him in their prayers.

On the death of Valens in 378, as already related, Gratian recalled the exiled bishops; and to the joy of the faithful, Gregory was restored to the see of Nyssa. His return was a triumphal progress. The inhabitants of the villages through which he passed

---

[1] See a similar passage from Hippolytus in *Early Church History*, pp. 159.

poured forth to meet him, and escorted him along the road with acclamations and tears of joy. In the town the crowd was so dense as to impede his progress, and when he approached a church, a stream of flame poured into it from the multitude of lighted tapers, borne before him by the virgins who had come to welcome back their beloved bishop.

The happiness of Gregory's return was, however, short-lived. Beside the severe labour and anxiety entailed upon him by the confusion consequent on the long reign of Arianism, he had to mourn the death of his brother Basil and his sister Macrina. It was many years since Gregory had seen his sister, and when at last he was able to visit her (in Pontus), he found her "hopelessly ill of fever, with parched lips, and drenched with cold sweats. She was stretched on a couple of planks on the ground, one of them being sloped to support her head and shoulders, the wood barely covered with a piece of sackcloth. Her pallet faced the east. On her brother's approach she made an effort to rise and do him honour as a bishop; Gregory prevented her. With great self-command she restrained her groans, checked her asthmatic pantings, and, putting on a cheerful countenance, endeavoured to comfort her brother, who she saw was full of grief. When she spoke of Basil's death, Gregory broke down; but she rebuked him for sorrowing as those who have no hope," and in a rapturous spirit discoursed on the resurrection and the immortality of the soul. "Seeing he was weary, she sent him into the garden to rest in an arbour. The following day she employed her little remaining strength in consoling, animating, and instructing him. Then she prayed: "Thou, O God, has taken from me the fear of death. Thou hast granted me that the end of this life should be the beginning of true life . . . Remember me in thy kingdom; forgive whatsoever I have done amiss. Receive my soul without spot into thy hands as a burnt offering before Thee.' At last her voice failed; only her lips moved; she signed herself with the cross, gave a deep sigh, and her spirit took its flight." Round her neck was found an iron cross, and a ring containing a particle of the "True Cross." She was buried by her brother in the grave of her parents, in the chapel of the Forty Martyrs. After her death many miracles were said to have been performed at her tomb.[1]

After settling some difficulties at home, Gregory undertook, by

---

[1] Texier says that in the village Melebuhi, in Cappadocia, a few miles from Nyssa, the inhabitants, who are Greeks, still worship Saint Macrina, whose bones are supposed to lie in the neighbourhood. Possibly Gregory transported them thither; his own name is nearly forgotten.

THE EVIL OF PILGRIMAGES. 49

the desire of the Council of Antioch,[1] a long and toilsome journey to Babylon. He found the church in that city in a deplorable state. The people had "grown hardened in heresy, and brutish in their manners; lying was more natural to them than to speak the truth." His labour for their reformation seems to have met with but little success.[2]

During the half-century which had elapsed since the pretended discovery by the Empress Helena of the "True Cross," pilgrimages to Jerusalem had become frequent. On his way home Gregory visited the Holy City, the Emperor placing at his disposal one of the imperial carriages. Of this vehicle he made "both a monastery and a church," where he and his retinue kept up their daily fasting, psalmody, and hours of prayer. He visited Bethlehem, Calvary, the Mount of Olives, and the Church of the Holy Sepulchre. But although largely imbued with credulity and superstition, his faith received no confirmation from what he saw. His conscience was shocked by the gross immorality prevailing in the Holy City itself, which he describes as a sink of all iniquity. The evil was aggravated by Arian influences, to counteract which all his efforts were ineffectual. He returned home depressed and sorrowful. In letters written soon afterwards, he records his sense of the evil of pilgrimages. He points out that pious ladies travelling lonely roads with male attendants lay themselves open to suspicion; that the inns are notorious for dissolute conversation and loose manners; and that robbery and violence are not infrequent, even in the Holy Land itself, whose moral state he describes as infinitely below that of Cappadocia. He asks, moreover, whether a man will believe Christ's virgin-birth the more by seeing Bethlehem, or his resurrection by visiting his tomb, or his ascension by standing on the Mount of Olives. "Change of place," he wrote to a Cappadocian abbot, "brings God no nearer; God will come to thee if only the inn of thy soul is ready for Him."[3]

---

[1] A.D. 379.

[2] From the time of Cyrus, Babylon rapidly declined; and at the commencement of the Christian era, the greater part of the city was in ruins. It continued to exist a few centuries longer, when it sank into the condition predicted by Isaiah, ch. xiii. 19—22.

[3] The pilgrims carried back with them water from the Jordan, earth from the Redeemer's sepulchre, and chips from the True Cross. Many even visited Arabia to behold Job's dunghill! But the East was not the only quarter to which pilgrimages were made. Chrysostom lamented that want of time and health prevented him from going to Rome to kiss the chains of Peter and Paul, which "make devils tremble and angels rejoice." Jerome, however, though on his return to Bethlehem after one of his journeys, he quickened his steps that

Two years later he attended the Council of Constantinople, where, as already said, he delivered the oration on the enthronement of Gregory Nazianzen. The last mention we have of him is his presence at a synod held in the same city, A.D. 394, which was probably not long before the close of his life.

CHAPTER IV.

ULFILAS.[1]

HITHERTO we have traced the course of some of the most gifted leaders in the Christian Church within the pale of Roman civilisation. It was within the empire that Christianity was founded and established, and for a long time its organisation did not extend far beyond the frontiers. But a change was now coming over the existing civilisation. "All that is expressed by the words Christian and Teutonic is coming in; all that is expressed by the words Pagan and Roman is dying out. . . . The Teuton rent away the provinces of the empire; but, in rending them away, he accepted the faith, the tongue, and, to a great extent, the law, of the empire."[2]

Of all the Teutonic nations, the Goths were the first to embrace Christianity, and their history is the most closely interwoven with that of declining Rome. "Driven like a wedge into the eastern side of Europe by the superincumbent weight of the Huns, they pass along the whole length of it, to be similarly thrust out at the west by the Franks. During this whole course they hold a place intermediate between barbarism and civilisation. . . . They are not heathens, yet they are not acknowledged as Christians. Planted

---

he might adore the manger and cradle of his Saviour, reminds his readers that "Britain is as near heaven as Jerusalem (Et de Ierosolymis et de Britaniâ æqualiter patet aula cœlestis), and that what is worthy of praise is not to have been at Jerusalem, but to have led a godly life there." It is curious to see Britain instanced as a very *Ultima Thule*.

[1] Chronologically, this chapter should have preceded the last; but the historical order seems to be better consulted by following out the course of Arianism within the Empire, before referring to its fortunes beyond it.

[2] "This was of a truth the greatest conquest that Rome ever made; if Greece once led captive her Roman conqueror, far more thoroughly did Rome lead captive her Teutonic conqueror."—*Freeman*.

in an indefensible position by their Arian creed, they are crushed between the opposing masses of heathenism and Catholicism."[1]

The way in which Christianity was first made known to this people is related by Sozomen. "From the time of the wars under Gallus and his successors, between the Romans and the Goths, many priests were taken captive, and dwelt among those tribes. They healed the sick, purged those who were possessed, and led a holy and blameless life; and the barbarians, marvelling at their life and miracles, sought to imitate their example." So also Philostorgius: "During the reigns of Valerian and Gallienus (253-268), a great body of Goths laid waste Eastern Europe, and crossing into Asia, invaded Cappadocia and Galatia, whence they returned laden with spoil, and bringing with them many captives, amongst whom were not a few ecclesiastics. These pious men induced many of their conquerors to embrace Christianity."

These vague generalities are all that we know of the conversion of the Gothic tribes until we come to Ulfilas. With the name of this illustrious man the Gothic Church is identified; he may almost be regarded as its founder, leader, and bishop; from his hands it received not the Scriptures only, but the very alphabet by which to read them. "He is," said Constantine the Great, "the Moses of the Goths." The sources of information regarding him, though still very scanty, were augmented in 1840 by the discovery, in the library of the Louvre, of a manuscript containing a notice of him, and especially of his creed, by his friend and pupil Auxentius, Arian bishop of Dorostorus (now Silistria).

Ulfilas was born about the year 311, and appears to have been a descendant of the Cappadocian captives mentioned above. When still a youth he was sent with others of his countrymen by the ruler of the Gothic nation on an embassy to the court of Constantine, A.D. 332. From this time it is probable he resided (perhaps as a hostage) in the city of Constantinople. Here he acquired or perfected his knowledge of Greek and Latin, became a reader in the church (*lector*), commenced his translation of the Bible, and formed an acquaintance with Eusebius, the Arian or Homoi-ousion

---

[1] The campaign which Clovis undertook against the Visigoths, A.D. 507, was in fact a war of the Catholic priesthood against the Arians. Rich presents were sent to the shrine of St. Martin at Tours to purchase the saint's favour; and as the messengers crossed the threshold of the church, the precentor, as if by accident, chanted forth the verse: "Thou hast girded me with strength unto the battle; Thou hast subdued under me those that rose up against me" (Ps. xviii. 39). Assured by this token, Clovis pressed forward in full reliance on the protection of the saint.

bishop of Nicomedia.[1] Sozomen says that before he went to Constantinople he held the orthodox faith, but that the theological arguments of the Arian bishops, or their promise to forward his suit with the Emperor if he would conform to their opinions, caused him to join their party. This statement is contradicted by Ulfilas himself; his Arian creed, as preserved in the manuscript of Auxentius, commencing with the words, "I, Ulfilas, bishop and confessor, have always thus believed."

At the age of thirty, A.D. 341, Ulfilas was consecrated bishop of the Goths by Eusebius, and sent beyond the Danube to preach the Gospel to his countrymen. Here he laboured until the success of his efforts alarmed the Gothic sovereign, and gave rise to a persecution in which "many servants and handmaids of Christ yielded up their lives." At the end of seven years Ulfilas himself, with a great body of his converts, was expelled, and crossing the Danube took refuge within the empire, where he was honourably received by the Emperor Constantius. They settled in Mœsia, at the foot of the Balkan Mountains, "possessors," says Jordanes,[2] "of cattle, pastures, forest, and a modicum of wheat, but otherwise poor and unwarlike." Here Ulfilas continued to govern and instruct them, and they in return yielded to him the most confiding obedience, being firmly convinced that he could neither utter nor do anything evil.

From this time we hear no more of Ulfilas for twenty years, except that in 360 he attended a synod of Arian bishops at Constantinople, at which the creed of Ariminum was adopted, and was subscribed by Ulfilas.

In 370 the Gothic ruler Athanaric renewed the persecution in Dacia, and many Christians were put to death or driven to take refuge on Roman soil. In this instance it was not only Arians who were thus harassed, but also Catholics and Audians. These last were the followers of Audius, a zealous man of pure life, who in Syria made himself obnoxious by censuring the vices of the clergy. Being banished to Scythia,[3] he made his way into the interior of Gothia, and himself and his successors gathered congregations and founded convents for men and women. The names of some of the martyrs in this persecution have been preserved. One was Saba, respecting whom the afflicted Church, after the manner of the

---

[1] Auxentius speaks of him as preaching constantly in Greek, Latin, and Gothic.

[2] Sometimes written Jornandes.

[3] Scythia parva, now the Dobrudscha.

Church at Smyrna,[1] when it testified to the victorious faith of Polycarp, issued an encyclical letter: "The Church of God which is in Gothia to the Church of God which is in Cappadocia, and to all Christians of the Catholic Church." From this letter it appears that the Gothic magistrates insisted on the Christians eating meat which had been sacrificed to idols. Some of the heathens, touched with compassion, secretly substituted instead of the offerings meat which had not thus been polluted; but Saba, who had known the faith from a child, scorned the subterfuge, declaring that no true Christian could accept escape on such terms. The persecution cooled for a season, but broke out again in a general inquisition, from which Saba's would-be friends again sought to shield him by swearing that there were no Christians in the village. But Saba burst into the assembly, exclaiming, "Let no one swear for me, for I am a Christian." Summoned before the chief persecutor, he was, on the discovery of his poverty, contemptuously dismissed, as one who could do neither good nor harm. Some time afterwards it became known that Saba was keeping Easter with a presbyter. The king's son came into the village by night with a band of armed men, and carried off both Saba and the presbyter naked and bound. Neither torture nor promises could induce Saba to touch the polluted meat. Left for the night made fast to a log, he was released by a compassionate woman, but nevertheless refused to escape. A beam being fastened to his neck, he was thrown into the river Musæus and drowned, confessing with his last breath his faith in God, and glorifying the Saviour's name. His body was recovered and taken away by Julius Soranus, the *dux*, or Roman governor, of Scythia, himself a Christian, who, to use the words of the Church Letter, "has by permission of the presbytery sent the same to Cappadocia to your Church, a precious gift, and glorious fruit of the faith."

The bulk of the Gothic nation still remained pagan. In 375 the shock of the Huns, that "terrible 'riding folk,' who had just passed the Gate of Nations and entered Europe," shattered the empire of the Ostrogoths on the Volga. Pursuing their wild victorious march, they came upon the Visigoths in Dacia, and drove them forward as far as the waters of the Danube. The Romans from the southern shore of the great river beheld the opposite bank crowded with a countless multitude—men, women, and children, "looking behind them with terror for the approach of the dreaded foe, and stretching out their hands to the land of plenty and of safety which lay before

---

[1] See *Early Church History*, p. 47.

them. Their chief, Frithigern, sent envoys to the Emperor Valens, begging him to receive his flying people, and give them leave to settle on Roman soil. Valens, after long debate with his advisers, consented, and almost before the negotiations were complete, the impatient people, 200,000 armed men with their families, began to cross. Some attempting to swim over were drowned, others crossed on rafts and canoes; while the main body were transported in boats. The passage lasted through several days and nights."

With their change of country the Visigoths exchanged also their national religion. The Catholic historian Jordanes relates that when the envoys besought the Emperor to grant them shelter, they promised, if he would give them teachers in their own tongue, to become Christians; and that the Emperor, who was infected with the heresy of the Arians, and had suppressed all the orthodox Churches, sent them for preachers supporters of his own creed. "The Goths," continues Jordanes, "having come thither ignorant and unlearned, were thus imbued with the poison of this perverted faith; and afterwards, in their turn, sending forth preachers to carry the Gospel in the same guise to the Ostrogoths and Gepidæ, all the nations of this speech were drawn into the same sect."

Through the greed and folly of the imperial officers, the conditions of the treaty were, in the absence of the Emperor, shamefully violated, and the Goths were turned from subjects into enemies. They flew to arms and invaded Thrace, and in 378 a great battle was fought between them and the imperial forces near Adrianople, which was so disastrous to the Roman arms as to be called a second Cannæ. Valens himself was slain. He was carried wounded to a cottage, to which the barbarians, ignorant of the prize it contained, set fire, and thus destroyed at once the enemy of their nation and the champion of their faith.

On the form of Christianity which the Goths received, Mr. Scott observes: "In this dim twilight of Arianism the figure of the Christ appeared familiar to them, and comprehensible by its resemblance to their own old deities who stood between man and the absolute divine—the All-Father. It did not cost them much to exchange these demi-gods, who were only just one step removed from heroes, for one heroic figure, in whom all the powers and qualities of the rest should combine. But the All-Father remained as far removed as ever from reach and contact of human needs. Christ was not God come down from Heaven to reveal the God-head in the flesh, to deliver man from sin; He was a creature like man, exalted above man by the design and will of the Father, not by virtue of his own divine essence. . . . It was thus that the Arian Christ found responsive acceptance in the Teutonic mind. They pictured Him as a king upon earth, moving about the highways of Palestine, attended by troops of loyal followers, from among whom He had chosen the Twelve as captains. When He 'went up into a mountain,' and took his seat, his captains stood in obedient readiness before Him, and all below and around, the faithful host was waiting to hear his commands. Or if at any time the Teutonic mind took a deeper and more spiritual view of the Saviour's work, it was as the *Healer* that they loved to behold Him, moving about amongst suffering humanity, touching for the evil, restoring sight and power and hearing. Nevertheless," he continues, "Teutonic Arianism is to be carefully distinguished from Hellenic Arianism. Even if the two could be shown to occupy the same platform of belief, the moral value of the same faith was very different in and for the two parties who had approached it from different directions. For the Goth it was an upward step in faith when he confessed a belief in an historic revelation, and submitted himself to the teaching of the Gospel through which Jesus was manifested as the Son of God. For the Hellenic Christian the acceptance of an Arian creed, or of any of the Post-Nicene compromises, was a step backwards and downwards. He left the high-level of conception of the nature of God, to which, after a great struggle and, as it were, by a supreme effort, the Nicene Council had sprung; and he fell back upon a philosophical heathenism, which began by denying the God-head of Christ, and afterwards sought to bring about a compromise of faith with reason at the cost of logic, by proclaiming Christ to be God, but God in the 'second degree.'"

Ulfilas' own creed has been preserved and expanded by Auxentius. The diversity between its language and that of Nicæa is of the most subtle kind, but amounts, when pursued to its logical issue, to this. Whilst the Son is held to be the Creator and Maker of all things, King, Redeemer, Saviour, and Judge, he is yet only a "Second God," subject and obedient in all things to the Father; and the Holy Spirit is neither God nor Lord, but the minister of Christ, subject and in all things obedient to the Son.

Ulfilas' translation of the Bible marks an era in the history of the Church. It was the earliest version of the Scriptures into an unlettered tongue; it was, moreover, the first translation into one of the dialects of that great family of nations "in whose hands was the future of the world." Philostorgius tells us that Ulfilas translated all the books of both the Old and New Testaments, with the exception of Samuel and the Kings, which he omitted because of the wars that are related in them, judging that his people, who were passionately fond of war, were more in need of a bit than of a spur.[1] The translation was lost to sight for many centuries; but about the year 1500 the four Gospels[2] were discovered in the monastery of Werden in Westphalia, near Düsseldorf, arranged in the order of Matthew, John, Luke, and Mark. This is the famous *Codex Argenteus* (or Silver Book), now in the library of Upsala University. At the end of the sixteenth century it found its way to Prague, whence it was carried off by the Swedes after the siege in 1648, and presented by the victorious Königsmark to Queen Christina.

The manuscript is referred to the close of the fifth century, a hundred years after the death of Ulfilas, and is believed to have been written in Italy, probably at Ravenna. It is on purple vellum, in letters of silver, "a few words at the beginning of each section being blazoned in gold. At the bottom of each page a sort of gallery of four arches resting on Corinthian columns, suggests the influence of the architecture of Ravenna on the mind of the amanuensis, and serves the useful purpose of enclosing the numbers which under the well-known name of the *Eusebian Canons* enabled the student, before the introduction of chapters and verses, readily to compare the text of one gospel with the parallel passages in the other three."[3]

We naturally ask whether any trace of Arian doctrine is to be discovered in Ulfilas' translation. Little evidence of this kind has been detected; but in Philippians ii. 6, "Who being in the form of God thought it not robbery to be equal with God," the Greek *isa* (equal) is rendered by the Gothic *galeiko* (German *gleich*, English *like*), a word everywhere else used for the Greek *homoios* (like). "The substitution of *likeness* for *equality* in the relation of the Son to the Father is the point most characteristic of the party to which Ulfilas belonged."

Another inquiry, interesting equally to the missionary and the scholar, is, how did Ulfilas, in this first essay to clothe the Gospel

---

[1] Socrates and Sozomen say that Ulfilas invented the Gothic letters. He formed them chiefly from the Greek.

[2] Or rather portions of them, for nearly half the leaves were missing.

[3] In 1736 a Gothic manuscript came to light at Wolfenbüttel, which was found to contain large portions of the Epistle to the Romans; and in 1817 Cardinal Mai deciphered several other manuscripts, apparently of the sixth century, from the monastic library at Bobbio in Lombardy. By means of these a considerable part of Paul's Epistles and of the missing portions of the Gospels has been supplied, together with some verses from Nehemiah and Esdras, a quotation from the Psalms, and allusions to passages in Genesis and Numbers. With these exceptions, the whole of the Old Testament, together with the Acts of the Apostles, the Catholic Epistles and the Apocalypse, are still wanting.

in the language of an uncivilized tribe, render the Greek terms relating to Sin and Redemption? Mr. Scott thus answers the question: "The word for law is not command, but *Vitoth*, from *vitan*, to know, and thus signifies self-knowledge, conscience, corresponding exactly with the Apostle's description, 'a law unto themselves.' Sin is *Fra-waurhts* (compare our *froward*). As to condemnation: Amongst tribes where every stranger was a foe, the simplest and worst punishment an injured community could inflict was to drive the offender from their midst. He became a wanderer on the face of the earth, or in Teutonic phrase, a *vearges*, or wolf; and Ulfilas making use of *gavarjan* and its derivatives, pictured the sinner after judgment as the outcast and the wanderer." In his treatment of the words *hades* and *ge-enna*, Ulfilas manifested a more critical mind than the translators of our Authorised Version, who rendered both alike by the word Hell. In the Gothic it is the former only which is thus represented, namely, by "Halja (the hollow place), in accordance with the old Teutonic mythology in which Hel was known as the goddess of the place of darkness and of the newly-departed." The word *ge-enna*, the valley of Hinnom, he left untranslated, writing it *gaiainna*. "Parallel with the notion of sin as a crime, and redemption as the payment of the penalty it had entailed, was the conviction, deep-rooted in Teutonic thought and language, that Sin is a disease, and the Redeemer a healer. The Greek *sozein* (to save) is represented by the Gothic *nasjan*. Salvation was regarded as 'healing'; the Saviour was the Nasjands, the 'Healer.'"

But the importance and interest which the Gothic translation possesses for the Christian and the scholar is doubled in the case of those nations which, like ourselves, belong to the Teutonic stock. The language of Ulfilas is the eldest branch of the Teutonic tree, and in its grammar and vocabulary it is easy to trace a close affinity with the English of the present day. More than this, to the student of comparative philology these fragments of the Gothic Scriptures are invaluable, as supplying a link in the chain between the various forms of the Teutonic tongue and the ancient Sanskrit with which they are radically connected.

The translation thus made was a priceless treasure to the northern tribes for many ages. "Goths and Vandals alike carried it with them on their wanderings through Europe. Whether as a religious observance, or in the superstitious hope of reading the future on the chance-appointed page, it was consulted on the battle-fields of Gaul before the fight began. The Vandals took it into Spain and Africa, and with their leader Genseric it came round to Rome."

Besides the Bible, Ulfilas made other translations, and composed treatises in Gothic for the use of his people. In 381, the year of the great Orthodox Council, Theodosius summoned Ulfilas to Constantinople. Although the Emperor was bent on crushing the Arians, it was yet his policy to flatter the Goths, whose stalwart warriors were the support of his throne. A schism had taken place in the Arian ranks, and it is no slight tribute to Ulfilas that he appears to have been chosen as the only man who could reconcile the disputants. He was aged and infirm; and he had no sooner reached the city than he was seized with a mortal sickness. The matter on which he had been called had weighed much on his mind, but before he had begun to put his hand to it, he was, in the words of his admiring biographer, "taken up to heaven after the manner of Elijah the prophet."

Great as was the work of Ulfilas, and mighty as was his influence in his own age, that influence had little of lasting effect. The changes of events in the West were rapid, and they destroyed any abiding traces of his labours. Moreover, "the professor of an Arian or Semi-Arian creed could not become the apostle of Teutonic Christendom, and the Goth, foremost and noblest branch of the great family, was too soon cut off by the sword of the East-Roman or trampled under the horsehoofs of the Saracen."

CHAPTER V.

Martin of Tours.

The reputation of Martin of Tours for holiness and miraculous power has perhaps been greater and more universal than that of any other saint in the calendar. He is best known as having, when a soldier, divided his martial cloak with a beggar. He deserves also to be known for refusing after his conversion to serve any longer in the army. "Hitherto," he said to his general, "I have been *thy* soldier; let me now be *God's*. I am the soldier of Christ; it is not lawful for me to fight."

Martin was born about A.D. 316. In 360 he planted, near Poictiers, what is believed to have been the earliest monastery in Gaul, and in 371 he became bishop of Tours. Here the discharge of his episcopal duties did not satisfy him; he pined for his monkish way of life. Leaving the city therefore, he founded a monastery two miles eastward, at the foot of a precipitous rock on the north bank of the Loire. Some of the cells were built of logs rudely joined together, but most of the eighty brethren, whom he gathered round him, dwelt in grottoes, or cavities of the rock. The author visited the spot in the spring of 1888. The following is an extract from his diary:—" The cliff, which is of sandstone, is one-third of a mile from the river. It is about eighty feet high, and is pierced with natural grottoes, some at its base, others at some distance up the face of the rock. Devotion and art have changed the original character of these caves, and adorned the face of the cliff with chapels, steps, and oratories. In front of one of these is the burial-place of Martin's disciples and successors, whose bones, it is said, were cast out at the Revolution. The grotto shown as that in which Martin himself lived is probably authentic; it was for many centuries one of the most popular places of pilgrimage in Europe. When the age grew more luxurious a vast monastery was erected on the gently sloping ground between the grottoes and the highway which skirts the river. It was called Marmoutiers (*Majus Monasterium*), and with its garden covered many acres. All that remains of the edifice is the picturesque gateway, on the roadside, erected in the 13th century. A girls' boarding-school now occupies the place, the large garden being probably the same as in the days of the monks. It is laid out with a fine avenue of trees, and with vines, fruit, vegetables, and flowers. Some of the girls were walking up and down the avenue, others were at play in the quadrangle."

The miracles with which Martin is credited were wonderful even for that age; some of them are of the magical type familiar to us in the Arabian Nights.

His biography, by his friend Sulpicius Severus, was the most popular work of the day. As soon as it appeared in Rome there was an eager scramble for it, to the great profit of the booksellers; and at Alexandria nearly all the people had it by heart.

Martin is associated with the name of the Priscillianists, Spanish dissenters from the Orthodox Church, who seem to have partaken of both Gnostic and Manichean errors. Although not more inclined than Ambrose of Milan, or Damasus and Siricius, who successively filled the see of Rome at that time, to grant actual toleration to the followers of Priscillian, Martin's kindlier nature led him to interpose on their behalf when extreme measures were determined against them. In his ardour to spare their lives, he even did violence to his own conscience by partaking of the communion with the bishops whose hands, in his view, were stained with the blood of the heretics. Priscillian was beheaded, with six of his adherents, amongst whom was Euchrotia, the widow of a distinguished poet and orator; Instantius, a bishop, was banished to the Scilly Islands; others of the party were variously punished.

Although blindly devoted to the Church, Martin was a man of truly Christian life and blameless character. "He was," says Farrar, "full of pity and gentleness, wearing always on his countenance a sort of celestial joy; never was anything on his lips but Christ, never anything in his heart but piety, peace, and pity." He died about A.D. 397, on November 11th, named from him Martinmas Day.

Martin is credited with having had frequent interviews with Satan. One of these is thus related by Cardinal Newman: "One day, while Martin was praying in his cell, the Evil Spirit stood before him, environed in a glittering radiance, by such pretence more easily to deceive him; clad also in royal robes, crowned with a golden and jewelled diadem, with shoes covered with gold, with serene face and bright looks, so as to seem nothing so little as he was. Martin at first was dazzled at the sight; and for a long while both parties kept silence. At length the Evil One began: 'Acknowledge, O Martin, whom thou seest. I am Christ, I am now descending upon earth, and I wished first to manifest myself to thee.' Martin still kept silent, and returned no answer. The devil ventured to repeat his bold pretence: 'Martin, why hesitate believing, when thou seest I am Christ?' Then he, understanding by revelation of the Spirit, that it was the Evil One, and not God, answered: 'Jesus, the Lord, announced not that He should come in glittering clothing, and radiant with a diadem. I will not believe that Christ is come, save in that state and form in which He suffered, *save with the show of the wounds of the Cross.*' At these words the other vanished forthwith as smoke, and filled the cell with so horrible an odour as to leave indubitable proof who he was. The application of this vision," observes the cardinal, "to Martin's age, is obvious. I suppose it means in this day, that Christ comes not in pride of intellect, or reputation for ability. These are the glittering robes in which Satan is now arrayed. Many spirits are abroad; more are issuing from the pit: the credentials which they display are the precious gifts of mind, beauty, riches, depth, originality. Christian, look hard at them with Martin in silence, and then ask for the print of the nails."

CHAPTER VI.

AMBROSE.

THE other Catholic Witnesses whom we have selected, all of whom were bishops except Jerome, rose to ecclesiastical rank through the regular gradations of the priesthood, and most of them also by the

Episcopal Chair of Ambrose, of white marble, in the church of St. Ambrose, Milan. (*From a photograph*).

way of the monastic cell. It was quite otherwise with Ambrose. From the ivory chair of the Roman magistrate (*sella curulis*) he stepped at once to the marble chair (*cathedra*) of the bishop, which he filled to so much purpose as to leave it at his death superior in authority to the imperial throne. The scene of his sovereignty was Milan, the usual residence of the Western Emperors from the reign of Diocletian till the invasion of the Goths under Alaric.

The father of Ambrose was a Roman of rank, and prefect of that division of the empire to which Gaul, Spain, and Britain belonged.

His son was born about A.D. 340. After receiving a liberal education, the young man devoted himself to the profession of the law, which was the customary road to promotion in the State. He made rapid advances, and was appointed to the high dignity of "Consular" magistrate at Milan, in which post he gained the good opinion of all parties. Whilst he held this office, the Arian bishop of the city died, and the Catholics determined to elect one of their own party in his place. The Arians resisted, and a vehement strife arose; the public peace was in danger. The Consular hastened down to the church and made a speech to the people, exhorting them to peace and mutual concord. Whilst he was speaking, a cry was heard, "Ambrose for bishop." The voice was said afterwards to have been that of a child. However this may have been, the name met with an instant and enthusiastic response, the whole multitude, with one voice, shouting out, "We will have Ambrose for our bishop." Ambrose, who had not even been baptized, made all the resistance he could to this popular nomination, even resorting to very doubtful means to divert the people from their object. All was of no avail, and when he tried to escape the citizens took him into friendly custody, and sent a letter to the Emperor Valentinian I., praying for his approval of their election. As soon as the imperial confirmation was received, the bishop-elect was baptized, passed summarily through the intermediate ecclesiastical stages, and on the eighth day received episcopal consecration. This was in 374, a year after the death of Athanasius, and two years after Basil had compelled the two Gregorys to accept the same honour. Ambrose was thirty-four years of age.

On his ordination he at once divested himself of his private property, bestowing part on the poor and the Church, reserving a portion for his sister's maintenance, and placing the rest under the management of his brother Satyrus. To this voluntary poverty he joined the rigid asceticism of the times. He attended no banquets, dined only on Sundays, Saturdays, and festivals, and devoted the greater part of the night to prayer. It was one of his first cares to make up by study for his want of education in Christian doctrine. "Hurried as I was from the judicial bench to the priesthood, I began to teach what I had not myself learned, so that I had to learn and teach at the same time, because I had not had time to learn before."

In Ambrose the stern rule of the Roman magistrate[1] was united

---

[1] He was several times employed in political negotiations; his statesmanship was second only to his churchmanship.

to the zeal of the ambitious churchman; he was, as Milman expresses it, "the spiritual ancestor of the Hildebrands and the Innocents." Of such a man it was not to be expected that he would oppose the growing superstitions of the age. On the contrary, he promoted some of them to the utmost of his influence. He was never weary of extolling the merits of virginity, on which he discoursed with such eloquence that the mothers of Milan locked up their daughters lest they should come under his spell. Nevertheless, troops of virgins flocked to him for consecration, some of them even so far as from Mauritania. Still his success fell short of his desires, and he even commended those who took the veil in spite of their parents.

No less did he foster the growing veneration for relics. A splendid basilica had just been erected.[1] As a check to the Arians, the orthodox wished it dedicated with the same pomp as had been used in the case of another new church near the Roman Gate. To this Ambrose consented, on condition that some new relics should be found to consecrate it. These were discovered in the church of St. Felix and St. Nabor. Let us hear his own account of the matter. "Since," he writes to his sister, "I never conceal from thy Sanctity anything which takes place, thou must know that we have actually discovered some holy martyrs. I felt an ardent presentiment of what was to happen. Notwithstanding the diffidence of the clergy, I commanded the earth to be removed from the space before the rails. I recognised the appropriate tokens; and some persons being presented for the imposition of hands, the holy martyrs began so to bestir themselves, that before I had spoken, an urn was snatched up, and thrown down on the place of the holy sepulture. We found two men of extraordinary size,[2] such as a former age has produced; all the bones entire, and plenty of blood. There was a great concourse of people during two days. We transferred the remains to the church, which they call the Ambrosian; and while we were removing them a blind man was cured." "The miracles of old time," he adds in a sermon preached on the occasion, "are now revived; for you see many healed by the mere shadows of the saints' bodies. How many kerchiefs are displayed in triumph! How many coverlets are sought for, as having by mere contact with these most holy relics become capable of curing disease!"[3]

---
[1] On the site of the present cathedral.
[2] Afterwards identified as Gervasius and Protasius, two brothers supposed to have been martyred under Nero at Ravenna, and thence removed to Milan.
[3] The Arians derided the whole affair as a trick. An annual procession used

Under Ambrose the ceremonial of Divine service was invested with increased solemnity and magnificence. During the anxious vigils of the congregation, when his basilica was beset by the soldiers of Valentinian II., Ambrose introduced from the East the practice of antiphonal singing, in which, instead of leaving the psalmody to the choristers, the whole congregation, divided into two choirs, bore an alternate part.[1]

Profound, however, as was his veneration for the externals of religion, Ambrose knew how to disregard them when weighed against the lives and liberty of men. The Gothic invasion brought with it unutterable calamities. From Thrace and Illyricum, especially, an immense number of captives were carried off; and these the Church, as in the days of Cyprian, hastened to redeem. When the common chest of the Milanese Church had been emptied, and the rich offerings of piety exhausted, Ambrose caused the sacramental vessels to be melted down and sold, to supply money for the ransom. "The Church," he wrote, "possesses gold, not to treasure up, but to distribute for the welfare and happiness of men. It is not merely the lives of the men and the honour of the women which are endangered in captivity, but the faith of their children. The blood of redemption which has gleamed in these golden cups has sanctified them, not for the service alone, but for the ransom of man."

Ambrose had not long taken possession of his office when he was brought into sharp collision with the Imperial authority. The see of Sirmium was vacant. Disregarding the limits of his own diocese, he went thither to prevent the election of an Arian and to secure the appointment of an orthodox bishop. By this act he incurred the displeasure of Justina, the mother of the youthful emperor, Valentinian II., who was a zealous Arian, and had her residence at Sirmium. Some years afterwards she demanded the basilica in Porta Romana at Milan, which was outside the walls of the city, for the Arian worship. The answer of Ambrose was: "A bishop cannot alienate that which is dedicated to God." A second demand for the possession of a new church within the walls met with the same repulse. The Imperial officers were ordered to take possession of the church; a tumult arose, and an Arian priest was severely handled, and only rescued by the interference of

---

to take place at Milan in honour of these saints, but it was forbidden by the authorities, because the people of Piacenza threatened, if it occurred again, to produce *their* relic, the third leg of St. Protasius!

[1] Ambrose's care in this matter has been perpetuated in the name of the Ambrosian Chant, but the connection of this latter with Ambrose is uncertain.

Ambrose. Many wealthy citizens were thrown into prison, and heavy fines imposed. But the bishop was inflexible; and when the Empress commanded him to tranquillize the populace, he answered, "It is in my power to refrain from exciting their violence, but it is for God to appease it when excited." The soldiers surrounded the church. The bishop who was performing the religious rites was apprised of their arrival, but went on as if nothing was happening. The doors were burst open; the affrighted women began to fly; but when the soldiers saw the dignified and undisturbed countenance of the bishop, as of one whose soul was absorbed in his office, they fell on their knees and assured him that they came to pray, and not to fight.

In 386 an edict was passed permitting free worship to the Arians, and rendering liable to capital punishment all who should obstruct them. Under this edict the basilica of Porta Romana was again demanded, but Ambrose again refused: "God forbid that I should yield the heritage of Jesus Christ. Naboth would not part with the vineyard of his fathers to Ahab, and should I surrender the house of God—the heritage of all the faithful bishops who have been before me?" An order of banishment was served upon him, but in terms very unusual in the imperial chancery: "Depart from the city, and go whither thou pleasest." Ambrose, however, did not please to depart, but remained in the city preaching with the utmost fearlessness, and even attacking the Empress-mother in a style which cannot be defended. He took his text from the book of Job, and compared the Empress to the patriarch's wife, who bade her husband blaspheme God. He went on to liken her to Eve, to Jezebel, and to Herodias. Upon this the youthful Emperor Valentinian II. sent his private secretary, not to expel the refractory prelate, but to deprecate his tyranny. "If I am a tyrant," replied Ambrose, "why not strike me down? So far from being a tyrant, my only defence is the power to expose my life for the honour of God." He added, with sacerdotal pride, "Under the ancient law, priests *bestowed* empire, they did not condescend to assume it; kings desired the priesthood, not priests the sovereignty." When the Emperor himself was urged to confront Ambrose in the church, he replied: "His eloquence would compel you yourselves to lay me bound hand and foot before his throne."

But it was not boys[1] and dowagers only that Ambrose brought to his feet. The great Theodosius I., Emperor of the East, was in his turn compelled to give way before the commanding genius and spiritual assumption of the bishop. A synagogue of the Jews in

---

[1] Valentinian was not more than fourteen when these events took place.

Mesopotamia had been burnt by the Christians, at the instigation, it was said, of the bishop of the place. At the same time the church of the Gnostics had been destroyed and plundered by the furious zeal of some monks. Theodosius commanded that the local bishop should rebuild the synagogue at his own expense, and that the Gnostics should be indemnified and the rioters be punished by the governor. The party spirit of the Christian world was affronted, and the "pious" indignation of Ambrose aroused, by this equitable decree. He stood forward as the champion of the faith, and in a letter to the Emperor vindicated the conduct of the bishop: " I protest that I would myself have burnt the synagogue, certainly that I would have given orders for it, that no place might be found where Christ is denied." " If," he continues, " the bishop shall comply with the mandate he will be an apostate, and the Emperor will be answerable for his apostasy. What has been done is but a trifling retaliation for the acts of plunder and destruction perpetrated by the Jews and heretics against the Catholics."

No answer being returned to this letter, Ambrose had recourse to the pulpit. In a sermon delivered in the presence of the Emperor, he compared the Christian priest to the prophets of the Old Testament whose duty it was to proclaim God's message to the king himself; and he admonished Theodosius that he owed everything to God's mercy, and that therefore it was his duty to wash and kiss the feet of the Church, the body of Christ, to honour all the disciples, even the least, and to pardon their faults. As he was leaving the pulpit the Emperor stopped him, asking, " Is it I whom thou hast made the subject of thy discourse ?" " I have said that which I deemed useful for thee," was the reply. ' I own," rejoined Theodosius, " that my commands have been a little severe, but I have already relaxed them, and these monks commit many crimes." This concession did not satisfy Ambrose. " I am going," he said, " to offer for thee the sacrifice ; enable me to do so with a clear conscience." The Emperor sat down and nodded assent, but the pertinacious prelate remained standing. " Suppress the whole matter," he said, " swear it to me, and on thy sworn promise I will proceed to offer the sacrifice." The Emperor swore. Ambrose celebrated the Eucharist. " But," as he wrote the day after to his sister, " I would not have done it unless he had given me his solemn promise ; and never did I experience such sensible marks of the presence of God in prayer."

Two years later, A.D. 390, Theodosius was again compelled to humble himself before Ambrose, and this time for worthy cause.

"With all his wisdom and virtue the Emperor was liable to paroxysms of ungovernable fury." A tumult had arisen in Thessalonica about a favourite charioteer of the circus. The riot was quelled with difficulty. The imperial officers were treated with the utmost indignity, and some of them brutally murdered. When the news was brought to the Emperor, who was then at Milan, his rage was unbounded. But Ambrose was at his side, and succeeded for the time in calming his excitement, and in obtaining from him a promise that the affair should be judicially dealt with. Unhappily the bishop was called away to preside at a synod, and during his absence other counsellors, particularly Rufinus, the master of the household, obtained the Emperor's ear, and in an evil moment he sent secret orders to Thessalonica for a general massacre. A fresh exhibition of games was announced, and, in order to make the number of victims as large as possible, the whole population were invited to them in the Emperor's name. Eager to propitiate their offended sovereign, the citizens crowded into the circus. The troops were ready; instead of the games the signal for the massacre was given, and before sunset seven thousand, at the lowest computation, men, women, and children, had been "mown down like ears of corn at harvest time."

On hearing of this atrocity, Ambrose withdrew into the country and wrote to the Emperor. The letter set forth the horror which he and his brother bishops felt at this inhuman deed, in which he should consider himself an accomplice if he did not avow his detestation of its guilt, and refuse to celebrate the Eucharist in the presence of one so stained with blood. He exhorted Theodosius to penitence, and promised to offer up prayers on his behalf. When the Emperor presented himself with his royal retinue at the door of the church, to join as usual in the public worship, he was confronted by the indignant prelate in his episcopal robes: "How wilt thou dare, O Emperor, to set foot in the sanctuary, and with hands dripping with the blood of men unjustly slain, to receive the body of the all-holy Lord, or dare to raise his precious blood to lips from which words of so great wrath and destruction have proceeded. Retire, and add not a fresh crime to those with which thou art already burdened."

The Emperor returned to his palace conscience-stricken and weeping. For eight months he endured his ignominious exclusion. The festival of Christmas came, and found him utterly disconsolate. Rufinus inquired the cause of his grief. He replied, "I am lamenting my unhappy lot; the church of God is open to slaves and beggars, but is closed to me. Heaven, too, is closed; for our

Lord said, 'Whatsoever ye shall bind on earth, shall be bound in heaven.'" "I will go to Ambrose," answered Rufinus, "and compel him to release thee from this bond." "It is in vain,"

Doors of the basilica of St. Ambrose, Milan, containing (at the top of each) a small panel of cypress wood, believed to be part of the gates which Ambrose closed against the Emperor Theodosius. *From a photograph.*

replied the Emperor, "thou wilt not persuade Ambrose to violate the Divine law from any fear of Imperial power." Rufinus, however, sought an interview with the bishop, who spurned him as the chief counseller of the massacre. And when Rufinus said the Emperor was approaching: "If he comes," replied Ambrose, "I will repel him from the vestibule of the church."

The minister returned to the Emperor, and advised him to remain in his palace. But the Imperial will was now thoroughly subdued. "I will go," he answered, "and receive the chastisement I deserve." Proceeding to the consecrated precincts, he found the bishop sitting in his parlour, and humbly begged for absolution. The bishop sternly asked, "What penitence hast thou shown for thy great fault? What remedy hast thou applied to the incurable wound thou hast inflicted?" "It is *thy* duty," answered the penitent, "to prescribe the remedies; *mine* to obey." Ambrose imposed two conditions, that the law of the Emperor Gratian should be re-enacted, which required on every sentence of death or confiscation the lapse of thirty days before execution, and that Theodosius should perform public penance in the church. The conditions were accepted; the enactment was signed; and "the sovereign of the Roman Empire—the victor in so many battles, the legislator of the world—entered the sacred enclosure as an abject penitent. Laying aside every ornament that marked his rank, prostrate on the pavement, smiting his breast, tearing his hair, watering the stones with his tears, he cried aloud, 'My soul cleaveth to the dust, quicken Thou me, according to thy word.'" In this position he remained during the first portion of the Liturgy. When the offertory began, he rose, advanced within the choir to present his offering, and was about to take the seat usually accorded to the Emperor in the midst of the clergy. But Ambrose took advantage of his humiliation to put an end to this practice. A deacon stepped up to Theodosius and informed him that no layman might remain in the choir during the celebration. The submissive Emperor withdrew outside the rails.[1]

In 395 Theodosius died. Calling for Ambrose on his death-bed, he entreated him to be a father to his youthful sons Arcadius and Honorius,[2] as he had been twenty years before to Gratian and Valentinian. But only two more years were allotted to Ambrose. They were years of activity and busy work. Clouds were gathering on the northern horizon, but the high-souled churchman did not live to share the troubles which beset the sons of Theodosius. He passed away whilst Alaric was even now planning the invasion of Italy, which ended in the sack of Rome.

---

[1] When Theodosius returned to Constantinople he was invited by the bishop Nectarius to occupy his accustomed chair in the choir. "No," replied Theodosius with a sigh; "I have learned at Milan the insignificance of an Emperor in the church, and the difference between him and a bishop. But no one here tells me the truth. I know not any bishop save Ambrose who deserves the name."

[2] Arcadius was twelve, Honorius eleven years old.

The great Stilicho, who ruled the West in the name of Honorius, held Ambrose in the same esteem as Theodosius had done. When he heard that the bishop was dying, he summoned the clergy, and, with mingled entreaties and commands, persuaded them to go to his bedside, and bid him pray to be permitted to live. The dying prelate calmly replied, "I have not so lived among you as to be ashamed to live on; but I do not fear to die, for our Lord is good." As the end drew near, the question arose who should succeed him. Four deacons, standing at the farther end of the gallery in which his couch was placed, were conversing in a low tone on this subject. The dying man overheard them, and when they mentioned the name of Simplician, they were startled to hear him say three times, "Old, but good."[1] Ambrose died A.D. 397, in his fifty-eighth year. His body was laid in state in the cathedral until Easter Eve, and buried in the church which now bears his name,[2] in presence of an immense crowd, Jews and pagans joining with his flock to pay him honour.

Ambrose left a multitude of works, which, "though deficient in originality," have acquired for him a distinguished place as a teacher in the Western Church. "The West owes a vast debt to Ambrose; he, more than any other Father, checked the waves of Arianism, which, but for him, would have rolled over Italy." He is esteemed by many Protestant writers, especially by Luther. "Amongst the Fathers," says the great Reformer, "St. Augustine holds unquestionably the first place, Ambrose the second, Bernard the third. Ambrose is admirable when he treats upon that most essential article, the forgiveness of sins."

Amongst the best known of Ambrose's works are his hymns. With one of these Augustine consoled himself the day after his mother's death. "I slept," he says in his *Confessions*, "and awoke again, and as I lay alone on my bed and called to mind those verses of Thy Ambrose, I found my grief not a little assuaged."

---

[1] Simplician was elected his successor.
[2] The basilica of St. Ambrose. The present building is of Lombard style, and dates from the latter part of the ninth century. Its chief feature is the rich facing of the altar in gold and silver work, richly set with precious stones. The twelve bas-reliefs on the back represent scenes in the life of Ambrose; they appear to have been executed about 835.

CHAPTER VII.

CHRYSOSTOM.

WE return now to the East. John, who was surnamed for his eloquence Chrysostom, or the golden-mouthed,[1] was a native of Antioch and was born A.D. 345 or 347. His father was a military officer of rank; his mother Anthusa, who was left a widow at the age of twenty, refused to marry again, that she might devote herself to the education of her infant son and the care of his property. When his pagan tutor Libanius, who, we may remember, was also Basil's instructor, and who had returned to his native city of Antioch, heard that Anthusa remained unmarried, he exclaimed, "Good heavens, what women these Christians have!" And when on his death-bed, many years afterwards, Libanius was asked by his friends which of his pupils he thought most worthy to succeed him in his professorship, he replied, "John, if the Christians had not stolen him from us."

On the completion of his education Chrysostom commenced life as an advocate, a calling for which his brilliant powers of oratory especially qualified him; but the pious instructions of his mother were beginning to bear fruit, and he recoiled from the practices in use in the legal profession. His disinclination to the law and to the worldly life by which he was surrounded was strengthened by the influence of Basilius,[2] "the companion of his studies and the sharer of all his thoughts and plans." Like most of the earnest spirits in that age, Basilius had adopted the monastic life, and Chrysostom prepared to follow his example. It was, as he afterwards said, a sense of the glaring contrast between the Christianity of the Gospel and the Christianity of ordinary life which drove him to this resolution. The world seemed to him "to wage an implacable warfare against the commands of Christ, and he determined therefore to seek in seclusion that kind of life which he saw exhibited in the gospels, but nowhere else." He does not seem to have asked himself, What is to become of the community of men if the salt is taken away?

---

[1] This epithet was not in common use until the fifth century; in his lifetime he was always called John.

[2] This name and Basil are the same; the Latin form is here used to distinguish Chrysostom's friend from Basil of Cappadocia.

Up to this time he had not been baptized. Of all the eminent men whose lives we are passing under review not one can be shown to have received baptism in infancy, and of most it can be said with certainty that they were not baptized until they were of full age; yet all, except two, were the sons of Christian parents, and Augustine's mother was a Christian. Chrysostom was about twenty-three years old when he received the rite, and the public profession of his faith thus made was very helpful to his character. "From the hour of his baptism," says his biographer Palladius, "he neither swore, nor defamed any one, nor spoke falsely, nor cursed, nor even tolerated facetious jokes."

When Chrysostom's mother heard of his intention to become a monk her affectionate heart sank within her. Taking him by the hand she led him into her chamber, and making him sit beside her on the bed, burst into tears, and "with words more moving than tears" thus poured out her heart. "Not long, my child, was I permitted the enjoyment of thy father's virtues, whose premature death brought orphanhood on thee, and on me the miseries of untimely widowhood. Words cannot describe the troubled sea into which a young woman who has just left her father's roof, and is unused to the world, is suddenly plunged by this insufferable calamity; what idleness and misconduct of servants she has to put up with, against what cabals of kinsfolk she has to defend herself; what insolence of assessors and tax-gatherers she has to submit to. By none of these difficulties, however, was I prevailed upon to contract a second marriage, but endured the tempest without shrinking, being supported in the first place from above, and next by thy features, on which I gazed incessantly as on the living image of my departed husband. I have not suffered thy patrimony to diminish, but, whilst I have denied thee nothing which thy condition required, the expense has been defrayed from my own purse and my father's dowry. Do not think however that I say this to reproach thee. In return for all I have but one favour to entreat; make me not a second time a widow, awaken not again my slumbering sorrows. Wait for my death, which cannot be very long; and when thou hast laid me in the dust and mingled my bones with those of thy father, then travel whither thou wilt, even beyond the sea. Only so long as I live be contented to dwell with me, and do not rashly provoke God by afflicting thy mother."

Chrysostom could not withstand so tender an appeal. He did not, however, entirely relinquish his purpose. Like Gregory Nazianzen, prevented from entering a monastery he made a monastery of his home, and withdrew from all worldly occupations and amusements. He ate little and seldom, slept on the bare ground, and rose frequently for prayer; he rarely left the house, and lest he should fall back into the habit of evil speaking he maintained almost unbroken silence. In this recluse manner of life he was joined by several youthful companions. One of these was Theodore, afterwards bishop of Mopsuestia, famous for his advocacy of the rational as opposed to the allegorical method of scripture interpretation.

We have more than once had to deplore the low standard of truthfulness which prevailed at this period, even amongst the most devoted Christians. Chrysostom shared this failing. Several sees became vacant in Syria which it was desirable to fill without delay. A body of bishops met at Antioch for this purpose. Amongst those deemed eligible Chrysostom and Basilius were named, although they were not yet even deacons. Basilius proposed that they should act in concert, and either both accept or both refuse the office, and to this Chrysostom pretended to agree; but, terrified at the bare idea of ordination, he secretly resolved to elude the appointment and let his friend be chosen alone. When the time arrived, and Basilius was seized and carried before the bishops, Chrysostom was not to be found. To his inquiries for him Basilius received the evasive answer, "that it would be strange indeed, if, when the self-willed Chrysostom was yielding submissively to the decision of the fathers, Basilius, his superior in understanding and experience, should show any reluctance." On the faith of this, Basilius allowed the ordaining hands to be laid upon his own head. Discovering too late the trick which had been played upon him, he upbraided Chrysostom with his breach of their friendly compact. So deeply were his feelings touched that words choked his utterance. But Chrysostom, unmoved by his reproaches, answered only with a burst of laughter, and forcibly seizing his hand and kissing it, gave thanks to God for the success of the plot. He went further and defended the fraud, on the oft-asserted but rotten principle that deceit is praiseworthy when practised in a good cause. A century and a quarter before, Julius Africanus had penned this memorable maxim, "May the opinion never prevail in the Church of Christ that any false thing can be fabricated for Christ's glory."[1] Unhappily the Church has too often lost sight of this golden rule.[2]

---

[1] See *Early Church History*, p. 171.

[2] "Jerome not unfrequently violated the sanctity of truth. He defends himself by the examples of Plato, Xenophon, Aristotle, and still more by the practice of Christian controversialists, as Origen, Methodius, Eusebius, Apollinaris, who often allowed themselves to advance what they knew to be untrue,

Just at this period paganism was rigorously proscribed. An imperial decree, issued by Valentinian and Valens against such as practised magical arts, was being enforced at Rome and Antioch. The mere possession of a book of divination might lead to torture, banishment, or even death.[1] It happened that Chrysostom, walking

---

in order to strengthen their argument. This laxity concerning truth passed under the name of *oikonomia* in Greek, and *dispensatio* in Latin [both signifying management], or sometimes *officiosum mendacium* [serviceable falsehood]. It had footing chiefly in the Greek Church." These loose principles were not shared by Augustine, who stands almost alone amongst the Fathers of this age in his steadfast adherence to truth. "Every lie is a sin. Speech was given to man, not to deceive another, but to make known his thoughts; and to use it for deception, and not for its appointed end, is a sin. Nor are we to suppose that there can be a lie which is not sinful, because it is sometimes possible by telling a lie to serve another. It cannot be denied that those have reached a high standard of goodness who never lie except to save a man from injury, but it is not the deceit, but the good intention that is praiseworthy. It is quite enough that the deception should be pardoned without being made the subject of laudation, especially among the heirs of the New Covenant, to whom it is said, 'Let your communication be yea, yea, and nay, nay, for whatsoever is more than these cometh of evil.'"

[1] Of the dominion which magic exerted over the ancient world we have at this day little conception. The stringent and frequent repetition in the Old Testament of the law against enchantments, necromancy, familiar spirits, and other forms of divination, proves the prevalence of this superstition in the early ages of the world; nor was its hold less powerful on the nations, classic or barbarian, over which the Roman Empire extended. In the Acts (xix. 19) we read of the converts at Ephesus (one of the chief centres of the magical art) burning the books they were accustomed to use, to the value of nearly £2000.

It was a piece of treasonable practice which provoked the inquisition at Antioch. Many plots were in agitation against the life of the Emperor Valens, and in one of these the conspirators fixed upon Theodorus, an Imperial Secretary, to be Emperor in his stead. To confirm this choice, the magical art was invoked. According to the evidence of one of the actors given under torture, a tripod of laurel twigs was constructed in imitation of that of the famous oracle at Delphi, and, after being consecrated with mysterious incantations, was placed in the middle of a room which had been purified by Arabian incense. On the tripod was set a metal dish with the twenty-four letters of the Greek alphabet engraved round the edge. Then a priest, clothed in linen, and holding a sprig of vervain, called upon the divinity who presides over foreknowledge, and extending his hand above the tripod, let fall a ring suspended by a flaxen thread of extreme fineness. As the ring, gently set in motion by his fingers, touched and bounded off from the successive letters, the priest following the order in which the letters were touched gave forth metrical replies to the questions put by the bystanders. And when one of them inquired who should succeed the present Emperor? the ring touched successively the four letters ΘΕΟΔ (THEOD), on which some one exclaimed: "This is the decree of fate; Theodorus is to be our Emperor." On the discovery of the plot Theodorus was put to death in a barbarous manner, and with him a multitude of persons of

with a friend through the public gardens by the banks of the Orontes, fished out of the river some leaves of a book. "A playful contest for the prize ensued, but was changed into horror on finding it to be a book of magic. Their dismay was increased by seeing a soldier approach. What was to be done? To keep the leaves or to throw them away seemed equally dangerous. At last they flung them back into the water. The soldier's suspicions had not been aroused, and the two friends passed on unchallenged." "Chrysostom always gratefully looked back to this escape as a signal instance of providential deliverance."

Shortly after this occurrence (his mother probably being then deceased), Chrysostom left his home to join a monastic community on the mountains to the south of Antioch. Here he spent four years, "a hallowed and peaceful time," to which he loved to recur in after-life. He paints the daily round of the cloister in warm colours. "Before the first rays of sunlight the abbot went round, and with his foot woke up those who were still sleeping. When all had risen, and before they broke their fast, they united in a hymn of praise and in prayer. At sunrise each went to his allotted task—some to read or write, others to manual labour. Four hours during the day—the third, sixth, ninth, and at even—were appointed for prayer and psalmody. When the day's work was over, reclining on strewn grass, they partook of a common meal of bread and water, with occasionally vegetables and oil for the sick. After this they again sang a hymn, and then betook themselves to their straw couches, and slept, Chrysostom says, free from those anxieties which beset men in the world. No need was there of bolts and bars, for the monk had nothing to lose except his life, the loss of which he counted an advantage, since he could say, 'to me to live is Christ, and to die is gain.' When death entered the monastery no sound of lamentation was heard. It was not said such a one is dead, but, 'he has been perfected;' and his body was carried forth to burial with hymns of thanksgiving, and the prayers of his companions, that they, too, might soon see the end of their labours, and be permitted to behold Jesus Christ."

But being still unable to attain the object he had in view, namely, "the utter extirpation of his human instincts, he proceeded to abandon altogether the society of man, and taking up his abode in one of those solitary caves with which the mountains

---

various ranks, some of whom, it would seem, were guilty of no other crime than owning in their names the fatal syllables. The actual successor of Valens was Theodosius.

abound, he braved the intense cold of that elevated region, and limited himself to the smallest portion of food and sleep on which life could be sustained. At the end of two years his health so completely broke down that he was forced to quit his cave, and forsaking 'the life of angels' for that of men, he returned with a shattered constitution to his home in Antioch."

After teaching as a deacon for five years, Chrysostom was ordained presbyter in 386, and for ten years diligently occupied himself with the duties of his office, sometimes preaching five days in the week. Bishop Flavian opened the pulpit of the cathedral to him, and whenever it was his turn to preach, the building was sure to be thronged. In the great cities the congregations were of a very motley character; and there also the most popular preachers were to be found. An unseemly and reprehensible practice had crept in of signifying approbation by applause. It is a notable evidence of the decay of the Church that the manners of the theatre should thus have been imported into divine service. So inveterate had this habit become, that when Chrysostom rebuked his auditory for their irreverent behaviour, they applauded the very rebuke. Such, too, was the charm of his eloquence that, in these crowded audiences hanging in rapt admiration on the preacher's lips, pickpockets found a profitable occasion for plying their trade, and Chrysostom had to warn his hearers to leave their purses at home.

Here it may be well to pause a moment and inquire whether the Church has not been mistaken in offering so high a premium for pulpit oratory. The popular admiration of this gift and the prizes offered to those who excel, lead to a contempt of simple Gospel ministry when unaccompanied by learning and eloquence. When, in the still earlier period of the Church, the free exercise of prophecy and teaching in the congregation was exchanged for the ministry of one man only, grievous loss was incurred; and this loss was yet more enhanced when it came to be held of first importance that the minister should be both scholar and orator. No warranty for such a change is to be found in the New Testament, where a sound knowledge of scriptural truth, with faith and love, and the anointing of the Holy Spirit, are set forth as the only and sufficient qualifications of the Gospel herald. This departure from the original Christian institutes brought with it a train of evil consequences. Not only were those gifts stifled which the Apostle so fully recognizes as the spiritual possession of the many, but the congregation no longer came together to realise the presence of Christ in their midst, and to wait for the manifestation of his spirit. They came to see, to hear, and to be entertained. "The preachers," as Gregory Nazianzen observes, " too often seek to adorn the artless piety of our religion by introducing into the sanctuary a new sort of secular oratory, borrowed from the forum and the threatre. The multitude seek not priests, but rhetoricians ; and I must say something in their defence. We have thus brought them up, by our desire to become all things to all men,—I know not whether for the *perdition* or *salvation* of all."

Chrysostom himself whilst at Antioch suffered from this perversion of Gospel order. "Most men," he says, " listen, not for improvement, but to be pleased, and to criticise, just as though a player or musician were before them. They require eloquence more peremptorily from preachers than from professed rhetoricians. . . . The most eloquent preacher, unless his discourses come up to the measure of their expectations, is exposed to innumerable sneers and censures from his audience, none considering that a temporary depression of spirits, some anxiety, perhaps a fit of ill-humour, may dim the brightness of his intellect, and hinder the development of his thoughts ;" and, in a homily delivered some years afterwards at Constantinople, he brings out the bitterness of a more extensive experience. "Many take infinite pains to prepare a long sermon, and if they win applause, it is as though they had gained the kingdom of Heaven itself, but if silence follows their discourse the dejection which covers their spirits is worse than hell. This has turned the churches upside down ; because both *you* are impatient of those discourses which might produce compunction, and will endure only such as tickle your ears by their composition and euphony ; and *we* act a pitiful part in suffering ourselves to pander to your appetites, when we ought to be combating them. . . . When, as I discourse, I hear myself applauded, at the moment as a man (why should I not confess the truth ?) I am delighted, and indulge in the pleasurable feeling ; but when I get home, and bethink me that those who have applauded have derived no benefit from my sermon, but that the good they ought to have received was dissipated by their plaudits, I am in pain, I groan and weep, and feel as though I had spoken all in vain."

In 397 Chrysostom's connection with Antioch was suddenly dissolved. Nectarius, bishop of Constantinople, an amiable and indolent prelate, died. The appointment to the vacant place virtually rested with the eunuch Eutropius, the chief minister of the feeble Emperor Arcadius. He cast his eyes upon Chrysostom, but fearing lest the people of Antioch should refuse to part with their favourite preacher, he had recourse to a stratagem. On a false pretext, Chrysostom was induced to visit a martyr's chapel outside the city walls. Here he was apprehended by one of the Imperial officers, conveyed to the first post-station on the road to Constantinople, and being placed in a public chariot and guarded by a military escort, he was whirled along from stage to stage over the 800 miles which intervened.[1]

Whether the dignity of bishop of the Imperial city, thus thrust upon him, was welcome or otherwise, Chrysostom submitted to it with a good grace. The probability is that, although it was a wrench to be snatched from his native city in the midst of his loving labours, the extended field now opened before him for pastoral work and for the exercise of his unrivalled powers as a preacher fully reconciled him to the change. He was consecrated, A.D. 898, by Theophilus, bishop of Alexandria, who had been summoned to Constantinople for the purpose. But Theophilus who had set his mind on another candidate performed the ceremony with the utmost reluctance: he would even have entirely refused to act, if it had not been for the threats of Eutropius.

The citizens were not long in perceiving the difference between the new bishop and his predecessor. Nectarius had lived in a style of luxury and magnificence, which to Chrysostom's severe character seemed to be utterly inconsistent with the profession of a Christian bishop. He accordingly disfurnished the episcopal residence, sold the costly plate and rich carpets, and with the proceeds erected hospitals for the sick and strangers, and provided for the support of virgins and widows. He even disposed of some of the marbles and other ornaments of the churches. Instead of interchanging grand dinners with the wealthy, he ate the simplest fare in his solitary chamber. He avoided the Court and the company of the great, and even seems to have regarded social intercourse with his fellow-men as waste of time. The bishops who visited Constantinople no longer found the episcopal palace open to them, Chrysostom alleging that there were houses of the faithful in abundance where they would meet with a welcome. One, a Syrian bishop named Acacius, was so provoked by the meanness of the table and lodging which had been provided, that he exclaimed, "I'll season his pot for him."

Besides carrying into the episcopal palace the habits he had acquired in the cloister, and thus ignoring some of the duties of his exalted station, Chrysostom provoked hostility by his ecclesiastical reforms. The moral tone of the clerical order had sunk to a low

---

[1] From Antioch to Constantinople was reckoned a week's journey travelling day and night.

ebb—worldliness, avarice, flattery of the great, and yet graver faults were common. A thorough reform was needed, and Chrysostom set himself to the arduous task with unsparing severity. His measures were rendered the more unpalatable by his unbending manner and irritable temper. From the reform of the clergy he passed to that of the Court. The dissolute manners and frivolous lives of the nobles and Court ladies furnished a frequent theme for his discourses, and the fulminations he uttered from the pulpit, whilst they drew immense crowds to the cathedral and daily increased his popularity with the multitude, continually raised up new enemies against him.

Before, however, we enter on the memorable contest with vice and folly in high places, which in the end caused Chrysostom's downfall, we must introduce two episodes—his work of evangelisation amongst the Goths, and his connection with the fate of the minister Eutropius.

Many thousand Goths dwelt in Constantinople and the neighbouring provinces, and Chrysostom, zealous for the recovery of this people from the Arian doctrine, set apart one of the churches in the city for divine service in their native tongue. One Sunday, about the year 398, he himself attended. The Bible was read in the translation of Ulfilas, and a discourse delivered in Gothic by a Gothic preacher. A number of Chrysostom's own congregation seem to have been present, and he took advantage of the scene before him to deliver an eloquent discourse (interpreted into Gothic) on the transforming power of Christianity. Quoting Isaiah (lxv. 25), "the wolf and the lamb shall feed together, and the lion shall eat straw like the ox," he said: "The prophet is not speaking here of lions and lambs, but predicting that, subdued by the power of the divine doctrine, the brutal sense of rude men should be transformed into gentleness, and they should unite in the same community with the meek. And this you have witnessed to-day, the most savage race of mankind standing side by side with the lambs of the Church—one pasture, one fold for all, one table set before all." Besides his care for the Goths in and around the city, he also sent forth missionaries to those tribes which had remained on the banks of the Danube, consecrating a native to be their bishop; and he showed a like interest in the Syrian nomads. Up to the end of his life, he did not cease, in sickness and exile, to further these cherished aims.

Between Chrysostom and the minister Eutropius, by whom he had been raised to the primacy, there was nothing in common. The latter was cruel and rapacious; and he found in the new bishop, instead of a subservient tool, a man of lofty spirit who vigilantly guarded the ecclesiastical prerogative. When the victims of Eutropius' extortions fled to the churches to claim the right of asylum, they found in Chrysostom a powerful and resolute protector. In an evil hour for himself the minister had procured from the feeble Emperor a law abolishing the privilege of sanctuary. By a change of affairs at Court, Eutropius suddenly fell from his lofty station. Deprived of his rank, his property confiscated, driven from the palace, and exposed to the insults of the populace, he found himself homeless and friendless. Whither should he flee? No asylum remained but through the very door which he had done his best to close. He might still find that door open. The law which he had made was hateful to the clergy, it might be that the bishop would connive at its violation, even by the very man who had framed it. "In the guise of a suppliant, tears streaming down his cheeks, his scant grey hairs smeared with dust, he crept into the cathedral, pushed aside the curtain which divided the chancel or sanctuary from the nave, and, clinging closely to the 'holy table,' awaited the approach of the bishop or any of the clergy. The enemy was on his track. As he lay quaking with terror, he could hear on the other side of the thin partition the trampling of feet, mingled with the clattering of arms and voices raised in threatening tones by soldiers on the search. At this crisis he was found by the bishop in a state of pitiable and abject terror, his cheek blanched with a death-like pallor, his teeth chattering, his whole frame quivering, as with faltering lips he craved the asylum of the Church. . . . Chrysostom led the unhappy fugitive to the sacristy, and, having concealed him there, confronted his pursuers, asserted the inviolability of the sacred precincts, and refused to surrender the refugee. 'None shall penetrate the sanctuary save over my body; the Church is the bride of Jesus Christ, who has entrusted her honour to me, and I will never betray it!' The soldiers threatened to lay violent hands on the bishop; but he freely presented himself to them, and only desired to be conducted to the Emperor, that the whole affair might be submitted to his judgment. He was accordingly placed between two rows of spearmen, and marched like a prisoner from the cathedral to the palace." In the presence of Arcadius he maintained the same lofty tone: "What were human laws when weighed against divine?" The Emperor was unable to resist the authority with which he spoke, and promised to respect the asylum. But when the soldiers heard this, they were furious at the loss of their victim, and it was only by a passionate harangue, ending with a flood of tears, that Arcadius succeeded in restraining them from breaking into the chancel and dragging forth the suppliant.

"The next day was Sunday. The places of public amusement were deserted, and the cathedral was filled with a vast concourse of men and women. All were in a flutter of expectation to hear what the Golden Mouth would utter in defence of the Church's privilege, and in defiance of the law. The bishop took his seat in the ambo;[1] all faces were upturned; but, before the preacher uttered a word, the curtain which separated the nave from the chancel, was partially drawn aside, and disclosed the cowering form of the unhappy Eutropius clinging to one of the columns which supported the holy table. Presently the bishop burst forth: 'Vanity of vanities! Where is now the pomp of yonder man's consulship? Where his torch-light festivities? Where the applause which once greeted him? Where his banquets and garlands? They are gone, all gone; one rude blast has shattered all the leaves, and shows us the tree stripped quite bare, and shaken to its very roots. . . . Vanity of vanities; all is vanity. These words should be inscribed on our walls and on our garments, in the market-place, and by the wayside, but above all on our consciences.' Then, turning towards the pitiable figure by the holy table: 'Did I not continually warn thee that wealth is a runaway slave, a thankless servant? but thou wouldst not heed. Lo, now experience has proved to thee that it is not only fugitive and thankless, but murderous also; for this it is which causes thee now to tremble. Did I not tell thee, when thou rebuked me for speaking the truth, that I loved thee better than thy flatterers? If thou hadst endured my wounds, the kisses of thy enemies would not have wrought thee this destruction. . . . The Church which thou treated as an enemy has opened her bosom to receive thee; the theatre which thou favoured has betrayed thee, and whetted the sword against thee.'" . . . Then, turning back again to the audience, he declared that the trembling suppliant whom they beheld was "the ornament of the altar." "'What,' you will say, 'this iniquitous rapacious creature an ornament to the altar!' Hush! the sinful woman was permitted to touch the feet of Jesus Christ Himself." . . . Addressing himself especially to the rich, he said: "Such a spectacle as this, of one lately at the pinnacle of power, now crouching with fear like a hare or a frog, chained to yonder pillar, not by fetters, but by fright, is sufficient

---

[1] Or reading-desk, from which, on account of his low stature, he could be better heard than from the pulpit. The most usual practice was for the preacher to sit, the people to stand.

to subdue arrogance, and teach the truth of the Scripture precept, 'All flesh is grass, and all the glory of man as the flower of grass.'"

After remaining several days in the sanctuary, perhaps finding his asylum no longer safe, Eutropius quitted it, and escaped in disguise from the city. He was taken, tried on sundry charges of treason, and beheaded.

The beautiful Eudoxia, the haughty and intriguing wife of Arcadius, was the real sovereign of the East. For a short while Chrysostom enjoyed her favour. Soon after his arrival she was seized with "a fit of religious excitement," which found vent in the translation of some martyrs' relics to the great church of St. Thomas in Drypia, nine miles from the city. The august ceremonial took place at night; "the Empress in her royal diadem and purple, attended by nobles and ladies of distinction, walked by the side of the bishop in the rear of the chest enclosing the sacred bones," and so vast was the number of torches that Chrysostom compares the procession to a river of fire. It was dawn before they reached the church. The bishop ascended the pulpit and preached a sermon full of "extravagant laudations of Eudoxia, and of ecstatic expressions of joy" at this auspicious event.

But Eudoxia's devotion presently "burnt itself out." Chrysostom soon saw occasion to change his opinion of her, and even to censure her conduct, as well as that of the courtiers, a course of action which turned her imperial favour into implacable enmity.

Chrysostom's zeal for the maintenance of Church discipline carried him beyond the bounds of discretion. Not content with setting his own diocese in order, he quitted the capital for Asia Minor, A.D. 401, to correct some flagrant abuses in Ephesus and the neighbouring sees. He left Constantinople in charge of a bishop named Severian. The harshness with which Chrysostom exercised his usurped authority at Ephesus increased the number of his enemies; and the length of his absence from the capital gave them opportunity to conspire against him.[1]

On his return he found that through the treachery of Severian the affairs of the Church at Constantinople had fallen into confusion. Instead, however, of adopting the measures which prudence would have dictated, he was excited to a vehement display of his feelings. In his very first sermon he attacked Severian. A few days later he aimed his shafts higher, and held up to public odium the whole cabal of bishops who played the part of court flatterers, and even

---

[1] He deposed twenty bishops in the course of his visitation.

Eudoxia herself. Like Ambrose, he compared the Empress to Jezebel. "Gather together to me," he exclaimed, "those base priests that eat at Jezebel's table, that I may say to them, as Elijah of old, 'How long halt ye between two opinions?' . . . If Jezebel's table be the table of the Lord, eat at it; eat at it till you vomit." The allusion was too patent to be mistaken. From that moment his fate was sealed.

The conduct of Chrysostom on this occasion has been much praised. No one will deny that it manifested daring courage: but courage is not everything in a Christian minister. This outburst of indignation was indeed far nobler than his previous flattery, but it was not wise or defensible. To speak of the faults of others behind their back is contrary to Gospel rule, and it does not mend the matter if the defamation is public, and in the presence of thousands. Moreover, the respect and honour which are due to all men, are doubly due to kings and those in authority. When Paul administered a richly deserved rebuke to the high-priest Ananias, he apologised, because of the commandment, "Thou shalt not speak evil of the ruler of thy people." Again, the object of reproof is reclamation, but the offender is hardly likely to give heed to the reproof when it is wrapped in words of fire, and published through a trumpet. Evil, too, must have been the effect of Chrysostom's philippics on the people of Constantinople. Denunciations of rulers and public characters from his golden lips could not fail to render the Church more attractive than the theatre. What flattery is sweeter to the populace than to be told of the vices of their superiors? And when the ear is filled with such words, no room is left for the great purpose for which men come together in the church, the worship of God.

Chrysostom was not without personal friends in high station. Besides several men of influence, some eminent women were devoted to him and his cause. The most celebrated of these was the deaconess Olympias. She was early left an orphan, and came under the oversight of Gregory Nazianzen, whom she addressed as "father," and who loved to call her his "own Olympias." Her husband, the prefect of Constantinople, died about two years after their marriage, and Olympias regarded this event as an intimation that she should consecrate the rest of her days to the Lord. After she was made deaconess she seldom departed from the church night or day. She gave her time and scattered her wealth with profuse liberality, assisting the clergy of Greece, Asia, and Syria in their charitable works. Between her and Chrysostom there was a strong bond of mutual affection; "she repaid his spiritual care by many womanly attentions, especially by seeing that he was supplied with wholesome food, and did not overstrain his feeble constitution by a too rigid abstinence."

The time was not yet ripe for the enemies of Chrysostom openly to show themselves. The Empress even found it expedient to maintain for a while the semblance of friendship with the popular preacher. When, on a charge being preferred against Severian, Chrysostom, without inquiry, excommunicated that bishop and commanded him to leave the city, Eudoxia presented herself before him in the church of the Apostles, placed her infant son on his knees and conjured him to reverse the sentence. But Severian, though restored, was not reconciled, and the number of Chrysostom's enemies from the ranks of the Court ladies and the offended ecclesiastics increased daily. They were joined by the bishop Antiochus of Ptolemais, and by Acacius mentioned above, who was not at all displeased at the prospect of fulfilling his coarse threat.

Courtiers and offended bishops were not the only foes against whom Chrysostom had to contend. The Arians who had been deprived of their churches by Theodosius were determined, if possible, to recover their influence in the city. They assembled at night in the public piazzas to sing responsive hymns, and at break of day marched in procession through the midst of the city, passing out at the gates to their places of worship. To make these demonstrations more defiant they interspersed with the hymns insulting questions or expressions. Chrysostom, to counteract their influence, organised similar processions of the Orthodox, and as these were the more numerous party, and the Empress placed her purse at their disposal, they presently surpassed the others in pomp, carrying crosses of silver illuminated by wax tapers. This display provoked the Arians to attack their rivals. Blood was shed on both sides, and the Imperial eunuch who was leading the Homoousion choir was wounded. On this the Emperor forcibly put a stop to the Arian processions. The historian who relates this occurrence refers to it as the origin of such public demonstrations: "The Orthodox party," he says, "having thus commenced the practice of singing hymns in procession, did not discontinue it, but have retained it to the present day."[1]

---

[1] "Chrysostom in Constantinople sealed the victory of the Catholic party. He achieved what all the edicts of Theodosius failed to do; detached the populace of the city from their persistent and often tumultuous support of Arianism, and before the end of his brief opportunity made them devoted adherents of himself, and through himself of the Catholic Church."

The Court party only wanted a leader to open the campaign against Chrysostom. One was found in Theophilus, the bishop of Alexandria, who had so unwillingly consecrated him to the episcopal chair. He was "a man who knew better how to manage a court intrigue than how to resolve a question of divinity, and the only rule by which he shaped his opinions was interest or ambition." It suited his purposes to institute a persecution of the monks of the Nitrian desert, and particularly of the Tall Brethren spoken of in a former chapter, now far advanced in years. Many fled from the country, and the four Brethren with about fifty companions. after many hardships, arrived at length at Constantinople.

They repaired at once to Chrysostom, who received them with great respect, and shed tears of compassion when he heard the tale of their sufferings and wanderings. But he acted with caution. He lodged them in the precincts of the church of Anastasia, but refused to admit them to the Eucharist until their cause was examined and their excommunication revoked. Finding themselves still pursued by the emissaries of Theophilus, they resolved to make an appeal to the Empress. One day, as she was riding to church, a party of them presented themselves before her, in their "white sheepskins and bare arms and knees." She stopped her litter, bowed graciously to them, and implored their prayers on behalf of the Emperor, herself, and her children; and when they besought her protection, she promised that a council should be convened, and Theophilus summoned to attend.

On receiving these tidings Theophilus was furious. Epiphanius, bishop of Cyprus,[1] a restless controversialist, was foremost amongst the opponents of Origen, whom he designated the "ancestor of the Arian heresy." This man, then verging towards ninety years old, Theophilus sent to Constantinople, at once to extinguish Origenism, and to bring Chrysostom to account for sheltering the Tall Brethren. On Epiphanius' arrival, Chrysostom received him courteously, and invited him to take up his abode in the episcopal palace; but Epiphanius, rejecting his overtures, called together the bishops who were then in the city, and laying before them the decree of his own provincial council against the writings of Origen, required them to put their hands to it. Some complied; others refused. Amongst the latter was a Goth who had adopted the name of Theotimus, and had been appointed metropolitan of Lesser Scythia. He was not

---

[1] The same we met with in the *Early Church History* as protesting against oaths and pictures in churches, and also as condemning. in his work *Against Heresies*, the reformer Aërius, pp. 134, 270, 311.

only bishop; he was also physician and commercial agent to the nomadic tribes. Only half a convert to Greek habits, he still allowed his long hair to float over his episcopal robe. Educated in Greece, he had carried back with him some precious books; and when not galloping across the plains, or baptizing some barbarian, he would unroll his parchments, and drink at the flowing spring of knowledge which the earlier writers, especially Origen, had opened. The anathemas uttered against his favourite author by Epiphanius and those who sided with him, astonished and shocked him. He made no reply at the moment, but when the bishops met again, the Gothic bishop drew from the folds of his garment a roll which he began to read in a loud voice. It contained passages from Origen of unimpeachable doctrine, glowing with elevated thoughts and ardent faith. Passage succeeded passage; and when at length Theotimus paused, it was only to give vent to his pent-up indignation. "I cannot comprehend, my brethren, how any one should dare to asperse a man who has written a thousand passages as excellent as these, and to pronounce him a child of Satan and an arch-heretic. If you find in his books anything less admirable than what I have read, or even something which you cannot approve, lay it on one side; leave the bad and choose the good."

Epiphanius had not been long at Constantinople before he discovered that he had come upon a fool's errand, and growing weary of the miserable business he returned to Cyprus. He bade farewell to the bishops who accompanied him to the ship, with these words: "I leave you your city, and your Imperial palace, and all this stage-acting."

In accordance with the promise given by Eudoxia to the monks, Theophilus was summoned to Constantinople. He hailed the occasion as the wished-for opportunity of accomplishing the ruin of Chrysostom. He was attended by a strong body-guard of sailors, and took with him costly presents for the disaffected clergy and persons of rank. He did not even scruple to give out, whilst on his journey, that he was going to depose Chrysostom for grave offences. Many bishops accompanied him from Egypt and Asia, some of the latter being those whom Chrysostom had deposed. So far from conducting himself as one accused, he made his entry into Constantinople "surrounded by the pomp and dignity of a judge."

Chrysostom did not fail to offer to Theophilus the hospitality due to a brother bishop, but it was disdainfully rejected. Theophilus took up his lodging in one of the Emperor's palaces in the suburb of Pera. During the three weeks he resided there he refused all communication with Chrysostom. "His house was the resort of the disaffected clergy, and the affronted ladies and gentlemen, who were drawn thither, not only by a common hatred to Chrysostom, but also by the handsome gifts, the dainty repasts, and the winning flattery of Theophilus."

Chrysostom was directed by the Court to repair to Pera and open an inquiry into the offences of which Theophilus was accused. Either from some scruple as to his ecclesiastical jurisdiction, or from the love of peace, he declined. It was now Theophilus' turn to bring his rival to account. Not daring to institute proceedings in the city itself, he assembled a synod in the Asiatic suburb of Chalcedon, which, from the position of the mansion in which it was held, near to a celebrated tree, was called the Synod of the Oak. It was attended by only thirty-six bishops, of whom twenty-nine were Egyptians. Two deacons who had been degraded by Chrysostom for gross misconduct were suborned to prefer charges against him, and he was summoned to defend himself before the council.

The scene which took place when Chrysostom received the summons is thus described by his biographer, Palladius. We give it as translated by Mr. Stephens. "We were sitting, to the number of forty bishops, in the dining-hall of the palace, marvelling at the audacity with which one, who had been commanded to appear as a culprit at Constantinople, had arrived with a train of bishops, had altered the sentiments of nobles and magistrates, and perverted the majority even of the clergy. Whilst we were wondering, John [Chrysostom], inspired by the Spirit of God, addressed to us the following words: 'Pray for me, my brethren, and if ye love Christ, let no one for my sake desert his see, for I am now ready to be offered, and the time of my departure is at hand. I know the intrigues of Satan, that he will not endure any longer the burden of my words delivered against him.' Seized with inexpressible sorrow, some of us began to weep, and others to leave the assembly, after kissing, amid tears and sobs, his sacred head and eyes and eloquent mouth. He, however, exhorted them to return, and as they hovered near like bees humming round their hive, 'Sit down, my brethren,' he said, 'and do not weep, unnerving me by your tears, for to me to live is Christ, to die is gain. Recall the words which I have so frequently spoken to you: our present life is a journey; both its good and painful things pass away; present time is like a fair: we buy, we sell, and the assembly is dissolved. Are we better than the patriarchs, the prophets, the apostles, that this life should remain to us for ever?' Here one of the company, uttering a cry, exclaimed, 'Nay, but what we lament is our bereavement, and the widowhood of the Church; the derangement of sacred laws; the ambition of those who fear not the Lord and violently seize the highest positions; the destitution of the poor, and the loss of sound teaching.' But John replied, striking (as was his custom) the palm of his left hand with the forefinger of his right, 'Enough, my brother—no more; only, as I was saying, do not abandon your churches; for neither did the office of teaching begin with me, nor in me has it ended. Did not Moses die, and was not Joshua found to succeed him? Did not Samuel die? but was not David anointed? Jeremiah departed this life, but Baruch was left. Elijah was taken up, but Elisha prophesied in his place. Paul was beheaded, but did he not leave Timothy, Titus, Apollos, and a host of others to work after him?'"

At this point it was announced that two deputies had arrived from the Synod of the Oak. Chrysostom inquired of what rank they were, and on hearing they were bishops, begged them to be seated, and to declare the purpose of their coming. "We are," said they, "the bearers of a document which we request thou wilt command to be read." It was a citation, and as though Chrysostom had already been degraded, he was addressed only by his name. "The Holy Synod assembled at the Oak to John. We have received," so ran the paper, "an infinite number of charges against thee: present thyself therefore before us, bringing with thee the priests Serapion and Tigrius, for their presence is necessary." Chrysostom's friends were indignant at the insolence of the message, and drew up a reply addressed to Theophilus, of which three bishops and two priests were the bearers. It was in these words: "Subvert not nor rend the Church for which God became incarnate; but if, in contempt of the canons framed by 318 bishops at Nicæa, thou wilt judge a cause outside thy jurisdiction, cross over into our city, which is at least governed by law, and do not, after the example of Cain, call Abel out into the open field. For we on our side possess charges of palpable crimes against *thee*, drawn up under seventy heads; and we by the grace of God are assembled after a peaceful manner, not for the disruption of the Church, and are besides more numerous than you, for with thee there are but thirty-six, but we are forty, seven of whom are metropolitans."

Chrysostom approved of this answer, but sent also a separate letter on his own behalf, addressed not to Theophilus, but to the synod. "If you wish me to appear before you, eject from your assembly my declared enemies, Theophilus whom I could convi of having said, 'I am setting out for the capital to depose John,' Acacius, Severian, and Antiochus. If these are removed, I am ready to appear, not before you only, but before a council of all Christendom. But know that, unless this is complied with, I will still refuse to present myself, though you should summon me ten thousand times over."

The charges against Chrysostom were presented under twenty-nine heads; some of them were contemptibly frivolous, and some utterly false. "He had struck people on the face; had calumniated and even imprisoned his clergy; had illegally deposed bishops in Asia, and ordained others without sufficient inquiry; had alienated the property and sold the ornaments of the church; had held private interviews with women; had dined gluttonously by himself as a cyclops; had robed and unrobed himself on his episcopal throne; had eaten a lozenge after holy Communion; and had administered both sacraments after he himself or the recipients had broken their fast." The culminating offence was that of uttering treasonable words against the Empress (in comparing her to Jezebel), which was construed into exciting the people to rebellion. To the citation four times repeated, to appear before this packed tribunal, Chrysostom's reply was always the same. refusal to attend, and an appeal to a general council. Thus baffled, "the cabal expended their fury on his messengers; they beat one bishop, tore the clothes of another, and placed on the neck of a third the chains they had designed for Chrysostom himself; their intention having been to put him secretly on board ship and send him off to some remote part of the empire." Sentence was pronounced against him: he was "condemned as contumacious, and deposed from his bishopric. The charge of treason his judges left to be dealt with by the civil power, secretly hoping that a capital sentence would be the issue. To their mortification, however, the Imperial rescript, which confirmed the sentence of deposition, condemned the bishop only to banishment for life."

But if the disappointment of his enemies at the lenity of the sentence was great, "the wrath of the populace at the condemnation of their favourite preacher knew no bounds. As evening wore on, the news flew from mouth to mouth, and a crowd collected at the doors of his residence and of the great church, to keep watch lest he should be forcibly carried off. This voluntary guard protected him for three days and nights, during which he continually passed from one building to the other. His power over the popular mind was never greater." He had the wisdom not to abuse it. "The sermons he addressed to the vast crowds which filled the cathedral[1] inculcated patience and resignation to the Divine will." He himself determined to bow to the storm. On the third day he took advantage of the hour of the noontide meal to slip out unperceived by a side door, and quietly surrendered himself to the Imperial officers, by whom he was conducted after dark to the harbour, and put on board a vessel which conveyed him to the Bithynian coast.

"The victory of his enemies seemed complete. Theophilus entered the city in triumphal state, and wreaked his vengeance on the bishop's partisans. The people, who had crowded to the churches to pour forth their lamentations, were forcibly dislodged, not without bloodshed. Furious at the loss of their revered teacher, they thronged the approaches to the Imperial palace, clamouring for his restoration, and demanding that his case should be heard before a general council. Constantinople was almost in revolt."

The following night the city was convulsed by an earthquake. The shock was felt with peculiar violence in the Empress's bed-chamber. Eudoxia, as superstitious as she was vindictive, fell at Arcadius' feet, and entreated him to avert the wrath of Heaven by revoking the sentence against Chrysostom. The flexile Emperor complied. Messengers were despatched in pursuit of the banished prelate, bearing letters from Eudoxia, couched in terms of abject humiliation. "Let not thy holiness imagine that I was cognizant of what has been done. Wicked men have contrived this plot. I remember the baptism of my children by thy hands. God whom I serve is witness of my tears."

"The news of Chrysostom's recall caused a universal jubilee. Late in the day as it was, his friends took shipping, and a fleet of barks put forth to meet him. The Bosphorus blazed with torches and resounded with psalms of welcome. Chrysostom at first halted outside the city, claiming to be acquitted by a general council before resuming his see. The people suspected treachery, and loudly denounced the Emperor and Empress. Apprehensive of a serious outbreak, Arcadius sent a secretary to desire Chrysostom to enter the walls without delay. As a loyal subject he obeyed. On passing the gates he was borne aloft by a crowd, carried into the church, placed on his episcopal seat, and forced to deliver an extemporaneous oration. His triumph was now as complete as that of his enemies had been a few days before." The leaders of the cabal could scarcely show themselves in public; and

---

[1] The Church of St. Sophia.

after a short delay, Theophilus, on the plea that his diocese could no longer dispense with his presence, left the city by night, and sailed for Alexandria. His flight was speedily followed by the assembling of about sixty bishops friendly to Chrysostom, who annulled the proceedings of the Oak, and declared him to be still the legitimate bishop of Constantinople.

For a while the Empress yielded to the tide, and professed to be completely reconciled to Chrysostom. Strange to say, he responded to her overtures, and they vied with each other in compliments and eulogistic phrases. It is not easy to account for such weakness on the part of a man of Chrysostom's high character. The servile adulation paid to Oriental monarchs might perhaps be advanced as an excuse, if Chrysostom had not shown how easily he could break through such trammels. A more probable cause is to be found in the fatal maxim he had adopted, that the end sanctifies the means. He doubtless persuaded himself that to propitiate the Empress was essential to the interests of the Church, even at the expense of truth. But this delusive calm was presently succeeded by another storm.

Lofty as was her position, Eudoxia aspired to still higher honours. Not content with the virtual rule of the East, she panted for that half-divine homage which by ancient custom was still paid to the Emperor himself.[1] She caused her statue to be cast in silver, and set up on a lofty column of porphyry in the centre of the market-place, in front of the church of St. Sophia. Its dedication was accompanied by the boisterous revelry of the old pagan rites, which the Christian Emperors, in their short-sighted and faithless policy, had retained as a means of preserving the loyalty of the people. The sound of the music and dancing was heard in the church, and disturbed the service. "Chrysostom's holy indignation took fire; he rushed to the reading-desk, and

---

[1] "When on rare occasions, Arcadius condescended to show himself in public, he was preceded by a vast multitude of attendants glittering in gold. The streets were cleared before the Emperor's approach, who stood or reclined in a gorgeous chariot adorned with precious stones, and drawn by white mules in gilded trappings. The cushions were snow-white; the carpets of silk, embroidered with dragons in the richest colours. Gilt fans, waved by the motion of the chariot, cooled the air. The Emperor himself was laden with jewels, ears, arms, and brow; whilst his robes of imperial purple, to which colour none else might aspire, were embroidered in all their seams with precious stones. He was attended by a bodyguard carrying shields with golden bosses set round with golden eyes. Ships were employed for the express purpose of bringing gold dust to strew the pavement, that the Emperor's foot might touch nothing but gold."

thundered forth a homily, embracing in its fierce invective all who had any share in these profanities; the prefect who ordered them, the people who joined in them, and, above all, the arrogant woman whose ambition was the cause of them. 'Herodias,' he is reported to have exclaimed, 'is once more maddening; Herodias is once more dancing; once more Herodias demands the head of John on a charger.'[1] These scathing words were reported to Eudoxia. Can we wonder that all her former fury revived, and that she demanded of the Emperor signal redress for such treasonable insolence? Compromise was no longer possible; the bishop or the Empress must yield."

The hostile bishops who had returned to their dioceses now flocked again to the metropolis, ready, with the fashionable ladies and the worldly clergy of the city, to contrive new plots for Chrysostom's ruin. He had demanded a general council; let such a council be called, and let his treasonable language against the Empress be laid before it, and the result could not be doubtful. But to make matters still more secure, Theophilus put forward a canon of the Council of Antioch, A.D. 841, pronouncing the *ipso facto* deprivation of any bishop who after deposition should appeal to the secular power for restoration. The general council met towards the end of the year (408), and seems, without passing any formal sentence, to have considered this canon as decisive.

The Emperor accepted this conclusion, and accordingly, on Christmas day, refused to attend divine Service in the cathedral. But this token of imperial displeasure was lost on Chrysostom. Supported by forty-two bishops, he continued to administer his episcopate, and to preach to the people as before. Matters went on in this way until near Easter, when it was resolved that Chrysostom must be removed at all hazards. Arcadius sent him an order forbidding him to enter the church during Easter. Chrysostom's dignified reply was, "I received this church from God my Saviour, and am charged with the salvation of this flock, which I am not at liberty to abandon. Expel me if thou wilt, since the city belongs to thee, that I may have thy authority as an excuse for deserting my post."

Fearing to use force, lest he should again provoke the vengeance of Heaven, Arcadius, on the advice of Acacius and Antiochus,

---

[1] These words are now extant only as the exordium of a homily, ascribed to Chrysostom, but pronounced by some of the best critics to be spurious. That they nearly represent what was uttered is probable, both from Chrysostom's language on the former occasion, and because they could not have been laid hold of for his ruin unless they had been in the highest degree offensive.

commanded the bishop to remain a prisoner in the episcopal palace, not leaving it even for the church without permission. The Emperor could scarcely have looked for obedience to this command, least of all on Easter Eve (the great season of baptism), when three thousand catechumens were expected to present themselves. The bishop again answered that he would not desist from officiating, unless compelled by actual force. "When the time arrived, he calmly left his residence and proceeded to the cathedral. The Imperial guards, forbidden to use violence, dared not interfere. The perplexed Emperor summoned Acacius and Antiochus to his presence, and reproached them with the failure of their counsel. They replied that Chrysostom being no longer a bishop was acting illegally in administering the sacraments, and that they would take on themselves the responsibility of his ejection."

On this, the Emperor at once ordered the guards to act. The church was thronged with worshippers keeping the vigil of the Resurrection, and baptism was being administered to the long files of catechumens, male and female, whom the deacons and deaconesses had prepared for the rite by the removal of their outer garments. Suddenly the din of arms broke the solemn stillness. A body of soldiers, sword in hand, burst in, and rushed, some to the baptisteries, some up the nave to the altar. The catechumens were driven from the fonts at the point of the sword; women as well as men, half-dressed and shrieking, rushed into the streets. Many were wounded, and the baptismal water was red with blood. Others of the troop, some of whom were pagans, forced open the inner doors, and not only gazed on the sacred vessels, but handled the Eucharistic elements, and spilt the wine on their garments. The clergy in their liturgical robes were forcibly ejected from the church, and with the mingled crowd of men, women and children, chased along the dark streets. Taking refuge in the baths of Constantine, and hastily "blessing" the profane building, to serve as a baptistery, they began to collect the terrified catechumens and proceed with the ceremonial. But they were again interrupted by the soldiery, who drove them out as before; and the same scene was enacted wherever the scattered congregations endeavoured to re-unite. "The horrors of that night remained indelibly imprinted on the minds of those who witnessed them, and were spoken of long afterwards with shuddering." For the greater part of the week Constantinople wore the aspect of a city which had been taken by storm. The partisans of Chrysostom, now called "Joannites," were hunted out, thrown into prison and scourged, the sound of the scourge and the oaths of the soldiers being heard even in the churches.

For two months, however, the timid Arcadius could not summon resolution to sign the decree for Chrysostom's banishment. At length it was signed. The bishop received it with submission, and entering the cathedral, said to those who accompanied him, "Come and let us pray. At my own fate I can rejoice: I only grieve for the sorrow of my people." Then entering the baptistery, he sent for Olympias and three other of the deaconesses, to whom he said, "Come hither, my daughters, and hearken to me. I have finished my course; perchance you will see my face no more. Submit to the authority of my successor. Remember me in your prayers." Overwhelmed with grief, they threw themselves at his feet; he made a sign to one of the priests to remove them, lest their wailing should be heard outside. Being informed that the troops were in readiness to compel him to withdraw, and advised by one of his friends to take his departure in secret, he directed that his mule should be saddled, and led, according to custom, to the western gate of the cathedral. Whilst the people's attention was diverted by this feint, he passed out unobserved at a postern, and surrendered himself to some of the soldiers. Two faithful bishops accompanied him, and a vessel bore them under cover of night across to the Asiatic shore.

When the people discovered that the bishop was gone, they became violently agitated. Some rushed to the harbour, others made an attack upon the cathedral, and battered the doors, which had been locked by the soldiery. Suddenly flames burst forth from the building; all attempts to extinguish them were in vain, and this magnificent structure, the erection of Constantine the Great, was in three hours reduced to a heap of cinders.[1] The flames spread to the senate-house, which was also destroyed. Suspicion, real or affected, fell on Chrysostom and his flock; and a fresh chapter of persecution followed, worthy of pagan rule. In fact, the government of the city was at the time in the hands of a pagan prefect, who hunted down the follows of the bishop with relentless cruelty. To the pretended crime of incendiarism was added that of refusal to recognise Chrysostom's successor, Arsacius, a very old man, described by Palladius as "more dumb than a fish and more incapable than a frog," and who appears to have been appointed by the sole fiat of the Emperor. Clergy and laymen, and even

---

[1] It was again destroyed A.D. 532, and was rebuilt with yet greater skill and splendour, by Justinian, in 544. In 1453, at the capture of the city by Mohammed II., Justinian's church was converted into a mosque which still bears the name of St. Sophia.

women, were subjected to intimidation, imprisonment, insult, and torture.

Those ladies who were most distinguished for their friendship with the deposed bishop were taken before the prefect, and admonished to acknowledge Arsacius. Some from timidity complied, but others met the arbitrary command with a dauntless spirit. Amongst these was the deaconess Olympias. Being asked why she had set fire to the great church, "My manner of life," she answered, "is a sufficient refutation of such a charge. One who has expended large sums of money to restore and embellish the churches of God is not likely to burn them." "I know thy past course of life well," cried the prefect. "If thou knowest aught against it," was the intrepid reply, "descend from thy place as judge, and come forward as my accuser." Unable to fix any charge upon her, the prefect changed his tone, and advised her and the other accused ladies to save themselves further trouble by "communicating" with Arsacius. Her companions yielded, but Olympias boldly replied: "It is an injustice, that, after being publicly calumniated, I should be called upon to clear myself of charges utterly foreign to the issue. Not even on compulsion will I hold communion with those from whom it is my duty to secede." She was mulcted in a heavy fine, which she paid, and then withdrew to the other side of the Straits.

Chrysostom and his friends sent four bishops of their party to the bishop of Rome and the Western Churches to inform them of the ordeal through which the faithful in Constantinople were passing. Innocent expressed his sympathy with the sufferers; and at the request of the Italian bishops, the Emperor Honorius wrote letters to his brother Arcadius. But the sympathy and the letters were alike fruitless. The bearers were insulted and ill-treated, and compelled to return to Italy; and the four Eastern bishops were banished to distant quarters of the empire, and harried on their way with brutal insults and indignities.

Arsacius survived his elevation to the patriarchate less than a year. His successor Atticus was equally determined to stamp out the Joannites. The wealthier clergy of the party mostly made their peace by concession, the poorer sought refuge in flight, either to Rome or the monasteries; some obtained a precarious livelihood by manual labour, farming or fishing: laymen were degraded, fined, and banished. On the other hand, the delinquent bishops whom Chrysostom had expelled were restored; and ordinations were conducted with feasting, drunkenness, and bribery. "The spirit of lawlessness and selfishness which was let loose during this period of misrule, dealt a blow to morality and discipline from which the Church at Constantinople never recovered."

Landing on the Asiatic coast, Chrysostom was conveyed to Nicæa. Not until he reached that city was he informed of his destination, the mountain village of Cucusus on the borders of Cilicia and Armenia, in a lonely valley of the Taurus range. The climate was inclement; the country was exposed to perpetual inroads from the Isaurian marauders: it was the hottest season of the year (July), and the journey was long and toilsome. His heart sank within him. His guards had received instructions to push on with all speed; and although they compassionated the sufferings of their prisoner, they dared not disobey. The squalid villages, where the convoy halted, furnished no food but black bread, which had to be steeped before Chrysostom could masticate it. The water was unwholesome, exciting rather than allaying thirst. Chrysostom was seized with ague, yet he was not permitted to halt, but was hurried forward to Cæsarea in Cappadocia, some 600 miles from the capital.

"I entered Cæsarea," he writes to Olympias, "worn down and exhausted, and in the crisis of a tertian fever. There was at first no one to nurse me, no physician to be had, no alleviations necessary for my state. Soon, however, the clergy, the people, monks, and medical men flowed in upon me, proffering their services: only Pharetrius (the bishop) came not.[1] After a time the disorder abated, and I began to think of setting forward, when news was brought that the Isaurians were laying waste the country, and that the tribune had marched out to oppose them. Whilst things were in this posture, a cohort of monks, set on by Pharetrius, came to the house where I lodged, and threatened to set it on fire if I did not immediately leave the city. So furious was their behaviour that the soldiers who came to protect me were overawed, for these brutes boasted that they had on former occasions shamefully handled the city guard. The prefect sent to Pharetrius, imploring him not to expose me to the Isaurian bands, but to allow me a few days' delay. But all was of no avail; the next day the monks renewed their attack; and about noon, throwing myself into my litter, I quitted the city, all the people bewailing my departure, and devoting to perdition the man who had occasioned it.

"Hearing what had taken place, the excellent lady, Seleucia, besought me to take up my abode at her villa, some five miles

---

[1] He was secretly in league with the enemies of Chrysostom, and had many of the monks on his side; but his clergy were Joannites almost to a man.

distant, where there was a strong tower, proof against any attack which could be made upon it. At the same time she ordered her steward, if the monks should pursue me, to summon the peasants from her other villas, to contend with them hand to hand. But in the middle of the night Pharetrius came to the villa, and with vehement threats insisted upon my being ejected. The lady was unable to withstand his importunity, and the presbyter Evetheus, coming into my chamber, and supposing the alarm to be caused by the Isaurians, waked me, crying out, 'Rise, I pray thee, the barbarians are upon us!' The night was moonless and gloomy; we had no guide, nor any to help us. Expecting death at any moment, and almost sinking under my trials, I rose and ordered torches to be lighted; these, however, the presbyter extinguished, lest the barbarians, attracted by the light, should rush upon us. The way being stony, the mule which carried my litter fell, and I was thrown to the ground. Raising myself, I crawled along, Evetheus, who had leaped from his horse, holding my hands. From the roughness of the way and the darkness of the night I was unable to use my feet."

It was the end of August before Chrysostom reached Cucusus. His reception almost made him forget the sufferings of the journey. Every comfort was provided for him; friends from Constantinople and Antioch came to visit him, some even to share his exile. Far removed as he now was, he did not settle down in inaction. "The three years spent at Cucusus were the most glorious of his life." Hitherto, in the perilous position of a popular preacher, his infirmities of temper and character had marred his work. Now exiled, shorn of outward honour, and chastened by suffering, he yet laboured unremittingly as ever for the weal of his fellow-men. His letters are very numerous, and bear witness to his care, not alone for his flock in the Imperial city, but for the interests of the Churches far and near. "Never did he exert a wider and more powerful influence. His advice was sought from all quarters; no important ecclesiastical measure was undertaken without consulting him. The East was almost governed from a mountain village of Armenia."

His chief hardships were occasioned by the forays of the brigands, and the extremes of the climate. With difficulty could he endure the severity of the winter. "I am just recalled," he says, in another letter to Olympias, "from the gates of death, having passed two months in a state of suffering more grievous even than the agonies of death itself. All that I seemed to live for was to be sensible of the ills with which I was encompassed. Whether it

H

was morning or noon, it mattered not; all was all night to me. I passed whole days without rising from my bed; and although I kept a good fire, enduring the smoke, and was covered with a pile of blankets, and never ventured to the door, I suffered extreme torture; each sleepless night was like a long sea voyage. As soon, however, as spring appeared all my ailments left me."

In the winter of 405, an alarm was raised that the marauders were coming. Nearly the whole of the inhabitants fled. Chrysostom and a few faithful companions wandered hither and thither, sometimes even passing the night without shelter, until they reached a mountain-fort, sixty miles from Cucusus. Here, cut off from his friends by the snow and by the brigands, who one night had nearly captured the castle, unable to procure his usual medicines, and the place crowded like a prison, he struggled through the winter. With the return of spring the Isaurians retired, and Chrysostom went back to Cucusus. After the hill-fort "this desolate little town seemed to him a paradise. His wonderful preservation from danger, and the manner in which his feeble health, instead of sinking under the accumulated trials of his banishment, became invigorated, awoke sanguine anticipations, and in his letters written at this time he confidently foretold his return to Constantinople." But this was not to be.

"The unhappy Eudoxia had preceded the victim of her hatred to the grave to which she had destined him, but she left other not less relentless enemies behind. Stung with disappointment that the climate of Cucusus had failed to do the work they intended, they obtained a rescript from Arcadius, transferring the exile to Pityus, a frontier fortress on the eastern shore of the Euxine, where the roots of the Caucasus come down to the sea. This was the most inhospitable spot they could choose, and therefore the most certain to rid them of their victim, even if the long and toilsome journey should fail to quench the feeble spark of life."

"Two prætorian guards of ferocious temper were selected to attend him, with instructions to push forward with merciless haste, the hint being privately given that they might expect promotion if he died on the road. One of the two furtively showed some little kindness to the sufferer, but the other followed literally his instructions. The journey was to be made on foot; towns where Chrysostom might enjoy any approach to comfort, or have the refreshment of a warm bath, were to be avoided; all letters were forbidden, and the least communication with passers-by was punished with blows." So slow was the progress that in three months they had travelled no further than Comana, in Pontus.[1] Here it was evident that the bishop's strength was exhausted: "his body was almost calcined by the sun. Nevertheless his guards hurried him through the town 'as if its streets were no more than a bridge.'"

"Five or six miles beyond Comana stood a chapel erected over the tomb of a martyred bishop. Here they halted for the night. It is said that in his sleep Chrysostom saw the martyr standing by his side, and bidding him be of good cheer, for on the morrow they should be together; and that the priest in charge of the chapel saw in a vision the same martyr, bidding him 'prepare a place for our brother John.' In the morning Chrysostom earnestly begged for a brief respite, but in vain; he was hurried off, but had scarcely gone three miles when a paroxysm of fever compelled his guards to carry him back to the chapel. On reaching the place he was supported to the altar, and having asked for the white robes of baptism he put them on, distributing his own clothes to the bystanders. He then partook of the bread and wine, prayed a last prayer, uttered his accustomed doxology, 'Glory be to God for all things,' and yielded up his spirit." He died A.D. 407, in the sixtieth year of his age, and was buried by the side of the martyr in the presence of a large concourse of monks and nuns.

Thirty-one years afterwards, when Theodosius II. was Emperor, Chrysostom's body was exhumed and translated with great pomp to Constantinople. "As once in his lifetime to greet him on his return from exile, so now, but in still greater numbers, the city poured itself forth to receive all that remained of their beloved bishop. The corpse was deposited near the altar in the church of the Apostles, along with the dust of Emperors and bishops, the youthful sovereign and his sister Pulcheria assisting at the ceremony, and asking pardon of Heaven for the wrong inflicted by their parents on the sainted bishop."

---

[1] This does not appear to lie in the direct route from Cucusus to Pityus, which would surely be up the Euphrates valley. No doubt the *détour* was purposely made. Armenian tradition places the site of Comana at some ruins on the banks of the Iris, situated two hours' journey east of the large manufacturing town of Tokát. Here Henry Martyn, in 1812, a few months after completing the translation of the New Testament into Persian, closed his brief devoted life, and lies buried in the Armenian cemetery. There is a similarity in the closing scene with that of the brother who had preceded him by so many centuries. Like Chrysostom, he was on a long journey across Asia Minor; he was worn by fever, and harassed by hardships, far from friends and loved ones, and with none near him but "merciless" and alien attendants. "O, when shall time give place to eternity," is the last entry in Martyn's journal.

Chrysostom, as has been already remarked, was "small of stature: his limbs were long, and so emaciated that he compared himself to a spider. His forehead was lofty, expanding at the summit, and furrowed with wrinkles; his head bald; his eyes deep-set, but keen and piercing; his cheeks pallid and withered; his chin pointed and covered with a short beard."

Chrysostom's genius was comprehensive and his industry unwearied. In eloquence he was without a rival. "His virtues were those of the monk rather than of the Christian citizen." Himself of dauntless courage and inflexible purpose, he was unable to make allowance for the more pliable temperament of others; and he was wanting in discernment of character, and tact in the management of men. His naturally irritable temper was aggravated by feebleness of digestion, "the excessive austerities of his youth having rendered him incapable of taking food, except in very small quantities and of the plainest kind." In spite, however, of his infirmities, he was, as we have seen, greatly beloved by those who were most intimate with him.

His writings are very voluminous and highly esteemed, especially his commentaries on Scripture.[1] He was, however, no reformer. The state of the Church cried aloud for teachers of clear vision and honest heart, to bring back the golden days ere men began to teach for doctrines their own inventions and commandments. Chrysostom gave no answer to this call. Spiritually-minded as he was, we yet find him giving his countenance to the worst superstitions of the times, and even urging them forward with all the force of his eloquence. We have seen how profound was his reverence for the ascetic life. In a future chapter we shall notice his extravagant views on celibacy, fasting, and almsgiving, as well as the support he gave to the worship of saints and their relics. Let us here consider what he has to say on the priesthood and the Eucharist. Surely no man ever carried sacerdotal pretensions to a greater height, or ever set them forth in more rhapsodical language.

"Although the priesthood is discharged upon earth," so he writes in his celebrated treatise, "it is ranked among heavenly ordinances; for it was established by the Comforter Himself, who has entrusted men yet dwelling in the flesh with a ministry like that of angels. For if the institutions of the law were awful and most impressive, yet that which was made glorious had no glory at all

---

[1] The Benedictine edition of his works is contained in thirteen large folios, one-half being a translation into Latin. In the Greek Church he ranks above all other Church writers.

by reason of the glory that excelleth. . . . Although their abode and home is on earth, the priests are entrusted with the management of things in heaven, and receive an authority such as God never granted either to angels or archangels: to whom it was never said, 'Whatsoever ye shall bind on earth shall be bound in heaven, and whatsoever ye shall loose on earth shall be loosed in heaven.' For though even temporal rulers have authority to bind, their power reaches only to the body; whereas this bond penetrates the very soul, and passes up into the heavens, where God ratifies the act of his priests. . . . Out upon the madness which would despise an office so important, without which it is impossible for us to obtain either salvation or the blessings which are promised! For if, except a man be born again of water and of the Spirit he cannot enter into the kingdom of God, and if he who does not eat the flesh of the Lord and drink His blood is rejected from eternal life, and if all these blessings are dispensed only by the holy hands of the priest, how can any one without their ministry either escape the fire of hell or obtain the crowns which are laid up for us? . . . . Wherefore those who despise the priestly office commit a greater crime, and are worthy of a sorer punishment, than even the followers of Dathan."

Not less repugnant to New Testament teaching is the picture which presents itself to the preacher's fervid imagination when the priest blesses and distributes the bread and wine. "When you see the Lord sacrificed and laid upon the altar, and the priest standing and praying over the sacrifice, and all the people empurpled with his most precious blood, do you then fancy yourself still among men, or are you not instantly transported into the heavens, so as, laying aside every fleshly sentiment, to look around with naked soul and disembodied spirit on celestial objects? O the wondrous loving-kindness of God! He who sits above with the Father is at that instant holden in the hands of every one, giving Himself to those who clasp and embrace Him, as all may clearly see with the eyes of faith. . . . Then, too, there are angels standing near the priest; and all the order of the heavenly powers raise their voice in honour of the victim. I once heard a certain person relate what an aged and venerable man accustomed to revelations told him, namely, that when the sacrifice was offered he suddenly beheld a multitude of white-robed angels encompassing the altar and bowing down their heads, as soldiers do homage to their prince; and I believe it."[1]

---

[1] In the *Order of the Divine Sacrifice*, in the Liturgy of the Church of Constantinople, the "bloodless sacrifice," as the Fathers loved to call it, is made to

The communicants, however, were not always thus transported. Chrysostom has often to reprove them for occupying the very moment of the consecration with worldly business and merriment. Many also, he tells us, presented themselves only on great festivals, and then in a most disorderly manner. They hustled one another in their eagerness first to reach the table; and as soon as they had partaken of the bread and wine, hurried out of the church without waiting for the conclusion of the service. Many who came to partake of the "awful and terrific table," passed their days on the race-ground, or hastened away to the forbidden spectacles of the stage. " You leave the well of blood, the terrific cup, to go to the Devil's well, where your own soul suffers shipwreck. If souls were visible, how many could I show you floating there, like the corpses of the Egyptians in the Red Sea."

It was a common belief in that age, as now in the Romish Church, that heaven is to be purchased by good works and self-mortification. Such a doctrine is almost inseparable from the ascetic life; Chrysostom thus gives it shape. "As those who are in a foreign country, when they wish to return to their own land, take pains, a long time beforehand, to collect means sufficient for their journey, so surely ought we, who are but strangers on this earth, to lay up a store of provisions through spiritual virtue, that when our Master shall command our return into our native country, we may be prepared, and may carry part of our store with us, having sent the other in advance." In one of his letters to Olympias he invites her to count over her own perfections and to dwell with complacency on the heavenly reward which is in store for her. The sufferings of life, no less than good works, were similarly assigned in the celestial ledger to the credit of the believer. When Chrysostom was driven out of Cæsarea and dragged along the mountain path, he wrote to Olympias: "Are not these trials sufficient to blot out many sins, and to suggest to me a hope of future

---

resemble the Offering on the Cross. The bread was fashioned cross-wise, or in four limbs, and impressed with the sign of the cross on each limb. The priest taking a "holy spear," performed various touchings and piercings of the cruciform cake, elevated it, and replaced it in the charger. Then the deacon, addressing the priest, says, " Slay, Sir"; and the priest immolates the "holy cake," saying, " The Lamb of God is slain who taketh away the sin of the world." Then the deacon says, "Prick, Sir"; and the priest pierces the cake on the right side with the "holy lance": at the same moment the deacon pours wine and water into the chalice. This *Order*, however, it should be stated, although appended to the works of Chrysostom, is, at least in its actual form, of a very much later date.

glory?"[1] But when Olympias, pursuing this mistaken notion to its legitimate issue, wrote, "My only thought is how I may increase my suffering," Chrysostom seems to have become conscious of having ventured too near the precipice. He thus admonishes her: "I regard it as something highly sinful that thou professest, voluntarily and designedly, to encourage thoughts which bring sorrow with them. Thou certainly art in duty to thyself bound to contrive everything to obliterate sadness from thy mind, but thou dost what is agreeable to Satan by augmenting thy grief and trouble."[2]

We turn with pleasure from the legal and ritualistic side of Chrysostom's character to the spiritual and Christlike. He was quite alive to the vanity of mere outward observances. "We go to the church, not merely for the sake of spending a few moments there, but that we may come away with some great gain in spiritual things. If a child goes daily to school and learns nothing, is his regular attendance an excuse for him? Does it not rather aggravate his fault? . . . When you have sung together two or three psalms and gone through the ordinary prayers and return home, you suppose this is sufficient for your salvation. Have you not heard what God says: 'This people honour me with their lips, but their heart is far from me'?" "In our prayers we pay less respect to God than a servant does to his master, a soldier to his general, or even a friend to his friend. For we speak to our friends with attention, but whilst we are on our knees asking pardon for our sins and treating with God about the business of our salvation, our

---

[1] There is an obvious confusion of ideas in these words. That "our light affliction, which is for the moment, worketh for us more and more exceedingly an eternal weight of glory," is one thing; that our sins can be purged by calamities or sufferings, is another, and a wholly unscriptural doctrine.

[2] Roberts' reflections on Chrysostom's letters (all written from Cucusus) are very pertinent. "One shade of melancholy rests upon them all, but the melancholy of a mind receiving every dispensation as the work of mercy, and the discipline of grace. He bore his banishment, not indeed without occasional complaint, but in general with the cheerful fortitude of a Christian soldier. . . . Still in these letters we do not perceive, in their just and beautiful proportions, those supports under affliction which we look for in a sainted Father of the Church of Christ. There are not found in them any distinct references to the Cross of Jesus, or to the love and sympathy of that Divine Participator in human sorrows, who has offered the refreshment of his hallowed rest to the weary and heavy-laden. If we do not find in Chrysostom too high an opinion of his own deserts, we cannot but discover in his letters a tendency to claim the rewards of Heaven on a title simply based on his sufferings and persecutions."

mind is at court, or at the bar, and there is no correspondence between our thoughts and our words."

Like Gregory Nazianzen, Chrysostom deprecated the intolerance of that uncharitable age. "To anathematize," he says, "is presumptuous; it is as great a usurpation of Christ's authority as for a subject to put on the Imperial purple. The part of a Christian is 'to instruct in meekness those who oppose themselves, if God peradventure will give them repentance to the acknowledging of the truth.' But if any man refuse to accept thy counsel, do not hate him, turn not from him, but catch him in the net of sincere charity." Nevertheless, in this as in other things, he was not always consistent with himself. We shudder as we read the following to Olympias:—"If in addition to the rewards of her chastity, her fasts, her vigils, her prayers, her boundless hospitality, Olympias wishes to enjoy the sight of her adversaries, those iniquitous and blood-stained men, undergoing punishment for their crimes, that pleasure also shall be hers. Lazarus saw Dives tormented in flames. This thou too wilt experience. For if he, who neglected but one man, suffered such punishment, what penalty will be exacted of men who have overturned so many churches and surpassed the ferocity of barbarians and robbers?"

In words no less apt now than when they were spoken does Chrysostom urge upon his hearers the debt of Christian love which every man, whether called lay or clerical, owes to his fellow. "There are many who possess farms and fields, but all their anxiety is to make a bath-house to their mansion, to build entrance courts and servants' offices: *how the souls of their servants are cultivated they care not.* . . . Ought not every Christian landholder to build a church, and to make it his aim before all things else that his people should be Christian? . . . Nothing can be more chilling than the sight of a Christian who makes no effort to save others. Neither poverty, nor humble station, nor bodily infirmity, can exempt men and women from the obligation of this great duty. To hide our Christian light under pretence of weakness is as great an insult to God as if we were to say that He could not make His sun to shine. Every house should be a church, and every father of a family a shepherd over his household, responsible for the welfare of all its members, even of the slaves, whom indeed the Gospel places in their relation to God on the same level with their owners. Whilst in earlier days," he was accustomed to say, "the house was by the love of heavenly things turned into a church, now the church itself, through the earthly mind of those who attend it, is become an ordinary house."

The commentaries of Chrysostom on Scripture are, as already said, among the choicest of his works. "One of his maxims was, that sound doctrine cannot be extracted from Holy Scripture except by a careful comparison of many passages not isolated from their context. . . . He had a clear conception of the essential coherence between the Old and the New Testament. 'The very words, Old and New,' he used to say, 'are relative terms: New, implies an antecedent; Old, preparatory to it.' . . . The commandment, 'Thou shalt not kill,' attacks the fruit and consequence of sin; the precept, 'Whosoever is angry with his brother without a cause,' strikes at the root." He held that the entire Bible was written under Divine inspiration, and that no passage, no word even, is to be disregarded. "Men wrote as they were moved by the Holy Spirit; yet this was not independent of their own human understanding and personal character. The prophet retained his peculiar faculties and style; only all his powers were quickened, energized by the Spirit, to the utterance of words which, unassisted, he could not have uttered."

Chrysostom was accustomed to impress on all his hearers the duty of reading the Bible for themselves. This was a point on which the Church teachers of this age were unanimous, thus unconsciously rebuking and condemning the times which succeeded, when those who were appointed to teach the Truth took away the Book from their flock, and sealed it up as though it were a fountain of error. "Give yourselves to the reading of Holy Scripture; not merely hearing it at church, but when you return home take your Bible in hand and dive into the meaning of what is written therein.[1] . . . . Seating yourselves, as it were, beside these waters, even although you may have no one at hand to interpret them, yet will you by the diligent perusal of them acquire great benefit. . . . . Divine Providence ordained that the Scriptures should be written by publicans, fishermen, tentmakers, shepherds, goatherds, in order that the things written should be readily intelligible to all, that the artificer, the poor widow, the slave might derive advantage from them; . . . as says the prophet, 'They shall be all taught of God.'" "If," he says again, "after repeated perusal, the meaning of the text is still obscure, have recourse to some one wiser than thyself, to a teacher; God, seeing thy fervour, will Himself, even if man does not, open the meaning to thee." . . . Elsewhere he does

---

[1] It was Chrysostom's practice to give out his text beforehand, in order that the congregation might prepare themselves for the sermon by Scripture searching and reflection. Augustine likens the zealous Christian who stores up Scripture in his memory, against a time of need, to the industrious ant.

not shrink from fully setting forth the truth on this matter : "Holy Scripture does not need the aid of human wisdom for its true understanding, but only the revelation of the Spirit." The common excuse of the absorbing occupation of the present life he thus answers: "Let no one give the cold reply, 'As for me, I am fully occupied with business in court, or the interests of the State or my craft; I have a wife to care for, children to maintain, a household to manage; I am a man of the world, and it is not for me to read the Scriptures. This duty belongs to those who have betaken themselves to the mountains for that very purpose.' How! Is it not precisely because thou art surrounded with worldly cares that thou hast more need than they to read thy Bible? . . . Ignorance of Scripture is a great precipice and a deep pit. It begets heresies, leads to a corrupt life, and throws everything into confusion." "Better the light of the sun should be extinguished than that David's words should be forgotten."

Often did his admonitions remain unheeded. Commencing his lectures on the Acts of the Apostles, he asserts that many of his hearers were not aware of the existence of such a book. "We find draughts and dice, but books nowhere, except among a few. And even these lock them away in cases, all their care being for the fineness of the parchment and the beauty of the letters. For they did not buy them to be benefited, but to show their wealth and pride." "Gentlemen," he says again, "are acquainted with the characters, families, and native cities of charioteers and dancers, and can tell the breeding, training, sires and dams of the horses that run in the races; but not one probably knows the titles of Paul's Epistles."[1]

Chrysostom is clear and emphatic on the nature of Sin. "There is only one thing," he writes to the faithful Olympias, "which is really terrible; there is only one real trial, and that is Sin. Spoliation of goods is freedom; banishment is but a change of abode; death is but the discharge of nature's debt, which all must pay. These, and all other evils, when compared with Sin, are but as dust and smoke." Sin is "a terrible pit, containing fierce monsters, and full of darkness; as fire, which when once it has got a hold on the thoughts of the heart, if it is not quenched, spreads further and further; as a weight, heavier and more oppressive than lead." He combats the error of supposing that sin is more pardonable in a man of the world than in a monk. Anger, uncleanness, swearing are equally sinful in all. "Nothing," he says,

---

[1] The Scriptures at this time were not so scarce as we sometimes imagine. Copies were greatly multiplied and widely diffused. "Even Britain," says Chrysostom, "abounds with the word of Life."

"has inflicted more injury on the moral tone of society than the supposition that strictness of life is demanded of the monk only."

But on Repentance our author is not equally sound. In his nine homilies on this duty delivered at Antioch, he enumerates the several paths which lead to it. They are (1) Confession; (2) Mourning for sin; (3) Humility; (4) Almsgiving (the queen of virtues, the readiest of all ways of getting to heaven, and the best advocate there); (5) Hourly prayer; (6) Fasting (which makes angels of men). The confession here spoken of was not the auricular confession of the Romish Church, now required as a necessary condition of Communion, but was usually public, and when private, was always voluntary. On this point Chrysostom's testimony is of great value. "I do not require thee to discover thy sins to men, but to show thy wounds unto God, who will not reproach but only heal thee. . . . Is it to a man that thou confessest, to a fellow-servant, who might expose thee? Nay, it is to the Lord, thy physician, thy friend, who says, 'Confess thy sin to Me alone, and I will deliver thee.'"

The reader of the *Early Church History* may remember the beautiful passages from Tertullian, Clement of Alexandria, and Origen on the subject of Prayer.[1] Chrysostom is not unworthy to be placed beside them. "The effect of prayer on the heart is like that of the rising sun on the natural world. The wild beasts come forth by night to prowl and devour, but the sun arises, and they get them away and lay them down in their dens; so, when the soul is illuminated by prayer, the irrational and brutal passions are put to flight. Prayer is the treasure of the poor, the security of the rich; the poorest of men is rich if he can pray, and the rich man who cannot pray is miserably poor. . . . It is impossible that a man who with becoming zeal calls constantly on God, should sin; he is proof against temptation so long as the effect of his praying endures, and when it begins to fail he must pray again. And this may be done anywhere, in the market or in the shop, since prayer demands the outstretched soul rather than the extended hands. Avoid long prayers which give opportunity to Satan to distract the attention; prayers should be frequent and short; it is in this way we can best comply with Paul's direction to pray without ceasing."

Notwithstanding his legality, Chrysostom could preach salvation by Christ free and full. "What reward shall I render unto the Lord for all His benefits? Who shall express His glorious acts, or

---

[1] *Early Church History*, pp. 77, 78.

show forth all His praise? 'He abased Himself that He might exalt thee; He died to make thee immortal; He became a curse that thou mightest obtain a blessing. . . . Say not, I have sinned much; how can I be saved? *Thou* art not able, but thy Master is able so to blot out thy sins that no trace even of them shall remain. In the natural body, though the wound be healed yet the scar remains; but God does not suffer the scar even to remain, but together with release from punishment, grants righteousness also, and makes the sinner to be equal to him who has not sinned. . . . Sin is drowned in the ocean of God's mercy, just as a spark is extinguished in a flood of water."

We will pluck one more leaf from his spiritual meditations. The subject is thanksgiving. "Let us give thanks to God continually. For it is monstrous that, enjoying as we do his bounty in *deed* every day, we should not so much as in *word* acknowledge the favour; and that too, although the acknowledgment again yields all its profit to *us*, since *He* needs not anything of ours, but we stand in need of all things from Him. . . . But let us be thankful, not for our own blessings alone, but also for those of others; for in this way we shall be able both to destroy our envy, and to strengthen and purify our charity; since it will not be possible for thee to go on envying those in behalf of whom thou givest thanks to the Lord."

It is evident that two opposite influences strove together in Chrysostom, the ritual and the spiritual. Isaac Taylor, remarking on the impossibility of holding the two in equipoise, and on the vain endeavour of certain of the Fathers to do this, adduces Chrysostom as the most illustrious example of failure. "How does he toil and pant in this bootless task! Personally too much alive to the spiritual and vital reality of the Christian scheme, to be quietly willing to let it disappear; and yet far too deeply imbued with the Gnostic and the Brahminical feeling, and too intimately compromised as a public person with the Church doctrines of the times, he could never rest. . . . Few great writers offer so little repose; few present contrasts so violent; as if his cynosure had been a binary star, shedding contrary influences upon his course. And so it was in fact. Scarcely is there a homily all of a piece; hardly are there two consecutive passages that can be read without a surprise, amounting to a painful perplexity, until the secret of all this contrariety is understood; and then it becomes manifest enough that, within the writer's soul, a spiritual Christianity, which *should* have been uppermost, was ever wrestling with Church doctrines and Gnostic sentiments, which *would* be uppermost."

CHAPTER VIII.

JEROME.

EUSEBIUS HIERONYMUS was born about the year 346[1] at Stridon, near Aquileia, at the head of the Adriatic. At the age of seventeen,[2] he was sent to Rome to complete his studies: his teacher was the famous grammarian Aelius Donatus. Here Jerome used on Sundays to visit the catacombs;[3] he also began to collect a library, which he afterwards carried with him wherever he went.[4] He relates that he yielded to the temptations which the great capital so plentifully presented, and fell into sin.

At the age of five and twenty we find him at Aquileia, one of a circle of young men who devoted themselves to sacred studies and to the ascetic life. The most celebrated of these was the historian Rufinus, between whom and Jerome there sprang up so ardent a friendship that they were compared to Damon and Pythias. But Jerome was as violent in his antipathies as in his friendships; and he gave full scope to the acerbity of his nature when, on his retirement with his brother Paulinian to lead a hermit life on their paternal estate at Stridon, he fell under the displeasure of the bishop. In his correspondence with that dignitary, his language was most abusive, and it was now that he commenced the offensive practice of holding up his antagonist to ridicule by fastening upon him an opprobrious epithet, a practice which unhappily he followed through life.

There floated before Jerome's imagination an alluring vision of the East, the cradle and paradise of monasticism; and in 373 the two brothers with a few intimate friends directed their course thither. Passing through Cæsarea in Cappadocia, they made the acquaintance of Basil, who by the recent death of Athanasius had become the leading churchman of the Catholic party in the East.

At Antioch, Jerome fell sick and had a strange vision connected with his classical studies which sat uneasy on his conscience.

---

[1] Or about A.D. 340. The dates assigned greatly vary.
[2] Or fourteen.   [3] See *Early Church History*, p. 272.
[4] "The Alexandrian manuscripts," he says, "emptied my purse." When he was permitted to use the library of Pamphilus in Cæsarea, containing all the works of Origen, he thought himself richer than Crœsus.

What he saw he related long afterwards in a letter to a noble Roman lady:—" When, years ago, I had torn myself from home, and parents, sister and friends, for the kingdom of heaven's sake, I could not part with the books which with very great care and labour I had collected at Rome. And so, unhappy man that I was, I followed up my fasting by reading Cicero; or, after a night of watching, after shedding tears, which the remembrance of my past sins drew from my inmost soul, I took up Plautus. If sometimes, coming to myself, I began to read the prophets, their inartistic style repelled me. When my blinded eyes could not see the light, I thought the fault was in the sun, not in my eyes. While the old serpent thus deceived me, about the middle of Lent a fever seized me, and so reduced my strength that my life scarce cleaved to my bones. They began to prepare for my funeral. My whole body was growing cold, only a little vital warmth remained in my breast; when suddenly I was caught up in spirit, and brought before the tribunal of the Judge. So great was the glory of his presence, and such the brilliancy of the purity of those who surrounded Him, that I cast myself to the earth, and did not dare to raise my eyes. Being asked who I was, I answered that I was a Christian. 'Thou liest,' said the Judge, 'thou art a Ciceronian and no Christian, for where thy treasure is there is thy heart also!' Thereupon I was silent. He ordered me to be beaten, but I was tormented more by remorse of conscience than by the blows: I said to myself, 'Who shall give thee thanks in hell?' Then I cried, with tears, 'Have mercy upon me, O Lord, have mercy upon me!' My cry was heard above the sound of the blows. Then they who stood by, gliding to the knees of the Judge, prayed Him to have mercy on my youth, and He gave me time for repentance on penalty of more severe punishment if I should ever again read pagan books. I, who in such a strait would have promised even greater things, made oath and declared by his sacred Name, 'O Lord, if ever I henceforth possess profane books or read them, let me be treated as if I had denied thee!' After this oath they let me go, and I returned to the world. To the wonder of all who stood by, I opened my eyes, shedding such a shower of tears, that my grief would make even the incredulous believe in my vision. This was not mere sleep, or a vain dream, such as often deludes us; the tribunal before which I lay is witness, that awful sentence which I feared is witness; so may I never come into a like judgment. I protest that my shoulders were livid, that I felt the blows after I awoke, and thenceforward I studied divine things with greater ardour than ever I had studied the things of the world."

Jerome kept this vow for many years. But on his settlement at Bethlehem he resumed his classical studies; and in later life he seems to have treated the vision either as a solemn reality or an idle fancy, just as for the moment it suited him.

In Syria he met with an aged hermit named Malchus, whose romantic history intensified his desire for the ascetic life. The desert which he made choice of was that of Chalcis, some fifty miles east of Antioch. It was peopled by monks and hermits, in the midst of whom Jerome took up his abode, supporting himself by his own labour. At first he seems to have been charmed with the solitude. One of his companions having gone back to Aquileia, Jerome wrote to him in a tone of reproach: "What art thou doing in thy home, O effeminate soldier! Where are the rampart and the fosse, and the winter spent in the tented field! . . . O desert, blooming with the flowers of Christ! O wilderness, where are shaped the stones of which the city of the Great King is built! O solitude, where men converse familiarly with God!"

But a letter written after he had left the desert tells a very different tale. "I sat alone, I was filled with bitterness; my limbs were uncomely and rough with sack-cloth, and my squalid skin became as black as an Ethiop's. I spent whole days in tears and groans; and if ever the sleep which hung upon my eyelids overcame my resistance, I knocked against the ground with my bare bones which scarce clung together. I will not speak of my meat and drink, since the monks, even when sick, take nothing but cold water, and regard cooked food as a luxury. Through fear of hell I had condemned myself to such a dungeon, with scorpions and wild beasts as my companions." With all this, however, he could not escape from himself. Solitude served only to inflame his passions, and his imagination carried him back to the forbidden delights of Rome. "Though my face was pallid with fasting, yet my soul glowed with carnal desire in my cold body. My flesh had not waited for the destruction of the whole man, it was dead already, and yet the fires of the passions boiled up within me. I often imagined myself in the midst of girls dancing." At times, however, hope and peace would break through the gloom, although the false notion of penance as the necessary price at which the Divine favour is be purchased deprived him of the full and abiding assurance of faith. "Destitute of all help, I cast myself at the feet of Jesus; I bathed them with my tears, I wiped them with my hair. I tried to conquer this rebellious flesh by a week of fasting. I often passed the night and day in crying and beating my breast, and ceased not until, God making Himself heard, peace came back to me. Then I feared to return to my cell, as if it had known my thoughts, and full of anger against myself I plunged alone into the desert. Sometimes after shedding floods of tears, with my eyes lifted up to heaven, I believed myself transported into the midst of the choirs of angels, and, filled with confidence and joy, I sang, 'Because of the savour of thy perfumes, we will run after Thee.'"

During the four or five years spent by Jerome in the desert, he studied and wrote diligently. In one of the nearest monasteries was living a converted Jew, of whom he learnt Hebrew, as a means, he said, of self-mortification.[1] He also disputed on the ecclesiastical politics of the see of Antioch with the neighbouring monks and solitaries, by whom he was persecuted as a heretic. The hatred was mutual.[2]

Weary of the desert, he returned to Antioch in 379. The Church in that city was split up into three parties, each of which had its own bishop, of whom Jerome says: "I know nothing of Vitalis; I reject Meletius; I do not acknowledge Paulinus." Nevertheless, he accepted ordination as a priest at Paulinus' hands, but on the condition that he should not be required to leave his monastic life, or to perform any functions of the priestly office.

In the year 380 Jerome went to Constantinople, where, as has been related, he placed himself under the instruction of Gregory Nazianzen. He remained in the Eastern metropolis during the council of 381, and must have been a spectator of Gregory's fall; but to these events he makes no allusion. Thence he removed to Rome, which at this time he calls "The light of the world, the salt of the earth, the only place where the Gospel remains uncorrupted"(!). Here his reputation as a scholar became established. Two main objects henceforth shared his affections,—scriptural study, and the promotion of the ascetic life. The former drew him into his most celebrated work, a new translation into Latin of the Old and New Testaments from the original languages, of which we shall speak presently. Of asceticism, which was introduced into Rome nearly forty years before, by Athanasius and the Egyptian monks, Jerome was now the foremost champion.

In Rome he became the guest of Marcella, a widow of illustrious birth and great wealth, who had consecrated her ancestral palace on Mount Aventine to the service of religion. His companion, our

---

[1] He complains that its grating sound destroyed the elegance of the Latin speech.

[2] The monks took away his paper, so that he was obliged to write on an old rag. His companions said: "We had rather live with wild beasts than with such Christians as these."

old acquaintance Epiphanius, bishop of Cyprus,[1] was entertained by Paula, another Roman matron, equally noble and wealthy. These ladies were the centre of a society of religious women, which was being formed when Jerome was a student in Rome. Some of them he knew by person, all were acquainted with him through his letters, and he soon became "the soul of this patrician circle. He answered their questions of conscience; he incited them to celibate life, lavish beneficence, and enthusiastic asceticism; and flattered their spiritual vanity by extravagant praises. He was their oracle, biographer, admirer, and eulogist." But he was not a safe guide. "The letters which he wrote to these ladies," observes Maitland, "are a fearful monument of the social effects of the monastic system. Amidst elaborate and far from spiritual interpretations of Solomon's Song—amidst fulsome eulogies of the nuns and dissertations upon their peculiar relationship to the Bridegroom—the religion and the Christ of the New Testament seem missing. The Lord of life is departed, the grave-clothes alone remain to show the place where He lay."

Marcella was as intellectual as she was pious. "All the while I was in Rome," writes Jerome, "she never saw me without putting some question on history or theology; nor was she ever satisfied by authority only, without examination; and often my place was changed from teacher to learner." " Paula was descended on one side from the Scipios and the Gracchi, on the other from the half fabulous kings of Sparta and Mycenæ. Left a widow at thirty-five by the death of her Greek husband Toxotius, she carried mourning in her heart more than on her garments, and for a time her grief was so violent that her life was in danger. She had four daughters —Blesilla, Paulina, Julia-Eustochium, and Rufina. To exalted and refined sentiments, Paula joined an excessive delicacy of body and softness of habitude. Half a Greek, brought up in an opulence which had no equal in the West, she lived an Asiatic life, nearly always reclining, and when she walked she was supported, or rather carried, on the arms of her eunuchs. Nevertheless, she possessed an invincible strength of mind in resisting tyranny and wrong. Her understanding was solid and well cultivated; she spoke Greek as a family language, and knew Hebrew well enough to read and sing the Psalms of David in the original.

"Paula's daughter Eustochium, then barely sixteen years of age, was a pattern of calm, reflective will, and of firmness, even stubbornness in her resolutions; her education had fully developed the innate germ of Christian stoicism in her heart. Entrusted in

---

See *ante*, p. 85.

infancy by her mother to the care of Marcella, she had breathed a serene and peaceful atmosphere, not always to be found in her own home. She early announced her intention not to marry, but to assume the virgin's veil. It was the first example of such a resolution given by a girl of her rank, and all the world believed she would change her mind when she became of age. But when the time arrived, and Eustochium prepared to take the vow, a cry of surprise and exasperation arose; her friends exerted themselves by alternate threats and caresses to turn her from her purpose, but in vain. Her father's sister Prætextata was a zealous pagan, and with her husband saw in their niece's determination a disgrace to their name and a sacrilege against their gods. Finding all their warnings and entreaties fruitless, they tried to entrap her on the side of feminine coquetry. They invited her to their house. As soon as she entered her aunt's apartment, some women, who had been engaged for the purpose, stripped off her woollen garments, and letting down her long hair, braided it and frizzled it in the newest fashion, painted her eyes, lips, and neck, clothed her in a magnificent silk robe, and covered her with jewels. Eustochium quietly submitted to the metamorphose, listened with her habitual serenity to all the blandishments which were lavished upon her; and then, when the hour came to return to Marcella, put on again her old serge dress and went her way."

"Less difference existed between Paula and her eldest daughter Blesilla. Both were weak in body, and subject to alternate mental depression and exaltation; but the latter wasted her energy in vain agitations and pleasures. A widow after seven months of married life chequered with cares, although scarcely twenty years of age, she rejected all proposals for a second union. This resolution was not like her sister's, prompted by love for the ascetic life; she chose rather thenceforth to live for herself, for the daily round of pleasure, and the charms of the toilet; she might almost be said to have passed her life before the mirror. In this condition she was attacked by fever, but recovered when at the very point of death. She believed her cure to be miraculous, and renouncing the world, assumed the habit of a church widow. Her pagan friends were scandalized; Jerome seized the pen in her defence: 'She stank somewhat of negligence, and was buried in the grave-clothes of riches, and lay in the sepulchre of this world, but Jesus groaned in spirit, and cried, "Blesilla, come forth," and she arose and came forth, and now sits at the table with Christ.'" His letter provoked answers from Helvidius, a lawyer, and the monk Jovinian. Of his controversy with the latter we shall speak in a future chapter.

Jerome's advocacy of the ascetic life was as violent as it was blind. "I love to praise marriage, because it supplies us with virgins; of these thorns we gather roses." "Although your little nephew should hang about your neck; although your mother, with hair dishevelled and garments rent, should show you the breasts at which she nourished you; although your father should lie on the threshold; trample on your father and set out! Fly with dry eyes to the banner of the cross! The only kind of piety is to be cruel in this matter." "Peter," he has the audacity to say, "was only an apostle; but John, because he was a virgin, was apostle, evangelist, and prophet. John the single, expounds what the married could not: 'In the beginning was the Word,' etc. To him, a virgin, was committed the charge of the virgin-mother by his virgin Lord; and for the same cause was he more beloved of the Lord, and reclined on His bosom."[1]

When Eustochium took the veil, Jerome addressed a letter to her, which was in effect an elaborate eulogy of virginity. In his defence of Blesilla he had lashed the manners of the high *pagan* society; his letter to Eustochium contained "a scathing satire on the vices of the *Christians*." "How many virgins daily fall! 'Why,' say they, 'should I abstain from food which God created to be used?' And when they have flooded themselves with wine, they add sacrilege to drunkenness, and say, 'Be it far from me that I should refrain from partaking of the blood of Christ!' And when they see any one pale and sad, they call her a wretch and a Manichæan." The clergy were not spared. "All their anxiety is about their dress, whether they are well perfumed, whether their shoes of soft leather fit without a wrinkle. Their hair is curled with the tongs, their fingers glitter with rings, and they walk on tiptoe lest the wet road should soil the soles of their shoes. You would take them for bridegrooms, rather than for clerics; their whole thought and life is to know the names and houses and doings of the rich ladies."

Blesilla's health gave way, and now her disorder terminated in death. The world insisted that Jerome and her mother had killed her with austerities. Her relations gave her a pompous funeral; and a vast crowd collected to see the procession pass along the Appian Way to the family mausoleum. Paula, who followed the bier, was overcome with grief, and fainted. This incident produced a strong sensation. "See this mother," cried the spectators, "who weeps

---

[1] Although Jerome speaks of this letter as written when he was a young man, he praises Fabiola (see below) for having learnt it by heart, and acted on it.

for the daughter she has killed with fasting. Let us drive the cursed race of monks out of the city; let us stone them; let us throw them into the Tiber."

A month after these occurrences bishop Damasus died. Jerome, now become the first ecclesiastic in Rome and the acknowledged leader of the most influential circle, aspired to the vacant chair; but he was obnoxious to many of the clergy, and his temper entirely unfitted him for so responsible an office. His rival, Siricius,[1] was elected. This disappointment was aggravated by a calumnious story regarding his relations with Paula, which took such hold of the public mind that he was hooted in the streets.

Jerome now began to suspect that he had been mistaken in coming to Rome, and that his true vocation after all was the desert. He therefore determined to shake off the dust of the great city, and return to a solitary life. On the eve of his departure he wrote to one of his friends: "In haste, dear Lady Acella, whilst the vessel is spreading her sails, I write these lines between my sobs and my tears, giving thanks to God that I am found worthy of the hatred of the world. Pray for me that, leaving Babylon, I may arrive at Jerusalem; that, escaping the dominion of Nebuchadnezzar, Ezra may lead me back to my country. Fool that I was, to wish to sing the Lord's songs in a strange land, to abandon Mount Sinai, and ask help from Egypt!" Paula resolved to be Jerome's companion. With Eustochium and a band of maidens taken from all classes, she set sail for Antioch, A.D. 385. At Cyprus they made a stay of ten days, receiving from Epiphanius the same hospitality which Paula had shown Jerome in Rome. Jerome, with his brother and a friend, travelling by another route, reached Antioch before them. On the ladies' arrival the two parties formed a caravan, the ladies riding on asses, with their luggage on pack-mules. They arrived in Jerusalem early in 386.

Paula was profoundly affected as she approached the scene of the Saviour's passion. "The whole city," says Jerome, "was witness of her tears and groans. In the church of the Sepulchre she threw herself on the stone with which the tomb was supposed to have been closed, and embraced it so vehemently that we could scarcely disengage her. But when she entered the sepulchral chamber, when her knees felt the ground which the limbs of the Saviour had touched, and her hands pressed the stone couch on which His divine body had lain, she fainted away. Regaining consciousness, she covered those lifeless relics with kisses, clinging to them with her

---

[1] As fierce an advocate of celibacy as Jerome himself.

lips, as one parched with thirst at a long sought spring, as though she purposed to dissolve the rock by her tears and kisses." Such a demonstration on the part of this noble Roman lady may seem strange to us, and the outcome of a morbid excitement, but we shall do well to consider whether our love to the same Saviour equals hers.

The pilgrims made the round of the Holy Places, from Mamre and the Dead Sea southward, to Nazareth and the Lake of Galilee in the north; after which they went down into Egypt. "At the monasteries of Nitria they were received with great honour. They heard the strange tales of the monks, assisted at all their services, ate their hard fare, lay in their hard cubicles, and were indeed almost persuaded to take up their abode in the Egyptian desert. But the superior attractions of Palestine prevailed, and returning thither the whole company settled at Bethlehem in the autumn of the same year. There Jerome spent the remaining thirty-four years of his life, pursuing unremittingly the two great objects to which he had devoted himself."

The first work of the pilgrims was to build a monastery, and three convents over which Jerome and Paula presided. They erected a church also, in which the inmates of all the houses met, and a hospice or house of entertainment for the pilgrims, who came from all parts of the world to visit the holy places. "Now," cried Paula, "if Joseph and Mary should again come to Bethlehem, they would have a place to lodge in." Jerome took possession of a cave or grotto next to that "of the Nativity,"[1] where he surrounded himself with his books, papers, amanuenses and other appliances of study: he called it his paradise. "I find myself," he wrote to Augustine, "well hidden in this hole, to weep for my sins whilst

---

[1] Jerome's grotto is still a principal object of curiosity at Bethlehem. The genuineness of the cave which now bears his name is a question which depends on that of "The Grotto of the Nativity," both being rock-hewn and situated underneath the present church of St. Mary. That the stable where our Saviour was born was a *grotto* was an article of early belief, and it was in this belief that Jerome took up his abode there. That he did live in one or other of the several rock-hewn chambers here existing (and which have since undergone much alteration) may be considered as certain, but whether in that which is now called the Chapel of St. Jerome, is much less so. The earliest mention of this chapel is in 1449. It is entirely hewn out of the rock except on the north side, where a window looks towards the cloisters of the church. There is a painting in the chapel representing Jerome with a Bible in his hand. The Emperor Constantine, in 330, erected a basilica over the Grotto of the Nativity, and it is pretty generally agreed that the present church is substantially identical with that basilica.

waiting for the Day of Judgment." As soon as he was settled he opened a free school for the inhabitants of Bethlehem, to whom he taught Greek and Latin. Thus carried back to the books he had so passionately loved in his youth, he forgot his dream, and eagerly drank again at the forbidden fountain. Virgil, the lyric and comic poets, Cicero, Plato, Homer, became again his daily delight, and he never wearied of expounding them to his pupils.

In figure and visage Jerome was spare, his naturally pale complexion embrowned by the Eastern sky: he wore his hair short and straight. His inner and outer garment were those of the hermit, of a dark brown colour, the same he had worn even in Rome; and if we may judge by his directions to others, they were not over cleanly.[1] He fasted till sunset, when he supped on vegetables and bread; he allowed himself flesh and wine only in sickness.

No inconsiderable part of Jerome's time was taken up with the care and discipline of the monastery, and with the crowds of monks and pilgrims who flocked to the hospice. Yet Scriptural studies were his main pursuit, and his diligence in these is almost incredible. Sulpicius Severus, who visited Bethelehem, says: "The presbyter Jerome who rules the Church there is so well versed in Latin, Greek, and even Hebrew learning, that no man can stand before him. He devotes himself wholly to books and study, resting neither night nor day. I stayed with him six months, and when I departed, his household accompanied me along the road, and I returned with a light heart to Alexandria." Jerome wrote, or rather dictated, with great rapidity. The translation of the three books of Solomon was the work of three days, when he had just recovered from a severe illness; and he rendered the book of Tobit from the Chaldee in a single day. When confined to his couch with sickness he would take down from his shelves one volume after another, and dictate to an amanuensis.[2]

Of the manner of life at Bethlehem we have a picture from the

---

[1] "Cleanliness of body," so he wrote to some of his lady friends, "is the filth of the soul. A mean sombre garment is the index of a mind at peace." "No one of the Roman matrons," he says elsewhere, "was ever able to command my homage, except she mourned and fasted and appeared in squalid clothing." Sometimes, however, he expresses himself more reasonably: "Shun equally sordid and showy garments. Foppery and filth are alike to be avoided; the one as redolent of voluptuousness, the other of vain-glory." "Thy clothes," he tells Eustochium, "should not be exactly clean, yet not filthy." Chrysostom commended the squalid attire of his beloved Olympias.

[2] Jerome's reputation was spread throughout the Christian world. One day six strangers presented themselves at his cell; they were sent by a pious and wealthy Spaniard, who desired to possess copies of all his works.

hands of Paula and Eustochium, coloured by their own fervid feelings and imagination. It is in a letter to Marcella at Rome. "It would take too long to recount who of the bishops, the martyrs, the doctors of the Church, have visited Jerusalem, esteeming themselves imperfect in religion and knowledge until they had received the finishing touch, and adored Christ in those places where first the Gospel shone forth from the cross. . . . We do not say this because we deny that the 'kingdom of God is within us,' and that there are holy men in other quarters; but they who are foremost in all the world are gathered together here. . . . The Gaul, and even the Briton, severed from the rest of the world, whosoever among them has made any progress in religion, hastens hither, eager to see for himself the places mentioned in the Holy Scriptures; not to speak of the Armenians and Persians, the people of Arabia and Ethiopia, Egypt teeming with monks, Pontus, Cappadocia and Mesopotamia. . . . There are almost as many choirs of choristers as there are different nations. There are no distinctions amongst them; the only strife is who can be most humble. . . . In what words," they continue, " can we place before thee the cave of the Saviour and the manger in which He uttered his first cry? Here one does not see the broad porticoes, the gilded ceilings, the palace halls which wealth erects, that man's worthless little body may walk about more sumptuously. See, in this little hole of earth the maker of the Heavens was born; here He was wrapped in swaddling clothes; here visited by the shepherds; here pointed out by the star; here adored by the Magi. . . . In this little city of Christ all is rustic. The silence is only broken by psalms. Wherever one turns, the ploughman holding the plough sings alleluias; the toiling reaper cheers his labour with psalms; the vine-dresser, pruning the vine with his hook, sings something of David. These are the ballads of this country; these the love-songs; this the shepherd's pipe; these its rustic sports." Jerome added a postscript to their letter: " Here bread and herbs, the produce of our own hands, with milk, afford us plain but wholesome food. Living thus, sleep does not overtake us in prayer, satiety does not interfere with study. In summer the trees afford us shade; in autumn the air is cool, and the fallen leaves afford us a quiet resting place; in spring the fields are clothed with flowers, and we sing our psalms the sweeter amid the singing of the birds; and when the winter's cold and snow come we have no lack of wood, and I watch, or sleep warm enough."

The repose of the community at Bethlehem was, in the year 395, rudely interrupted by a threatened invasion of the Huns, who had overrun Syria, laid siege to Antioch, and were directing their course towards Palestine. The monasteries were broken up. Jerome and Paula hurried down to the sea of Joppa, where they erected a temporary camp for the protection of the sisterhood, and hired ships to carry them to a place of safety. At this juncture, news was brought that the Huns had changed their course, and instead of crossing Lebanon had turned to the north and west.

About this time Fabiola, one of the group of noble ladies who remained in Rome, was on a visit at the convent. She had come to consult Jerome on a case of conscience. Ill-treated by her husband, she had sought relief in divorce, and to escape the temptations of her unprotected state she had married again. Could she, without performing penance, be in communion with the Church, her first husband being still alive? She returned to Rome without having conferred with Jerome; but the case being made known to him by a priest of her company, he sent his judgment in writing. In regard to the plea that she married a second time from necessity, he says: "We all favour our own vices, and what we have done of our own will we attribute to the necessity of nature." On the question of her second marriage while her husband was living, he quotes the Apostle's sentence: "'The woman is bound by the law to her husband so long as he liveth, but if, while her husband liveth, she is married to another man, she shall be called an adulteress.' Therefore, if this sister wishes to receive Christ's body and not to be called an adulteress, let her do penance." Fabiola accepted the conditions, and "Rome beheld a daughter of the ancient and illustrious house of the Fabii kneeling amongst the penitents on the steps of the Lateran church in mourning habit, with dishevelled hair, and sprinkled with ashes."

During his residence at Bethlehem, Jerome was involved in several long and bitter controversies. The earliest of these was his contest with his old friend Rufinus respecting the doctrines of Origen. Like Basil and Gregory, Jerome and Rufinus had early been captivated by the philosophy of that profound thinker. But as time went on the former became convinced that some of Origen's dogmas could not be defended, and that his own reputation for orthodoxy was in danger. So that when the question again agitated the Churches of Palestine, A.D. 395, Jerome hastened to repudiate the charge of being one of Origen's disciples. This produced an acrimonious correspondence between himself and Rufinus, and although after a while they professed to be reconciled, and took each other's hands over the Saviour's tomb in the church of the Resurrection, yet on Rufinus' removal to Rome in 397, the quarrel broke out afresh. For several years an exchange of controversial, or more properly speaking, abusive tracts took place between the two angry disputants. Augustine was deeply pained to witness such strife between men of advanced age, of reputation for learning and piety, and who had once been familiar friends and fellow-students of Scripture. "I am pierced through," he writes to Jerome, "by darts of keenest sorrow when I think how between Rufinus and thee, to whom God has granted to feast together on the honey of the Holy Scriptures, the blight of such exceeding bitterness has fallen. This, too, at a time when you were living together in that very land which the feet of our Lord trod when He said, '*Peace* I leave with you, my peace I give unto you.' If I could anywhere meet you both together (which, alas! I cannot hope to do), so strong is my agitation, grief and fear, that I think I would cast myself at your feet, and there weeping till I could weep no more, would, with all the eloquence of love, appeal first to each of you for his own sake, then to both for each other's sake, and for the sake especially of the weak, for whom Christ died, imploring you not to scatter abroad these hard words against each other, which if at any time you were reconciled you could not recall, and which you could not then venture to read, lest strife should be kindled anew." Sad to say, this pathetic pleading was ineffectual; even Rufinus' death did not disarm Jerome.[1]

With Augustine himself, somewhat his junior in age, Jerome had a curious correspondence, which only escaped embitterment owing to the patience displayed by the former. Jerome, in his commentary on the Epistle to the Galatians, had put forward the monstrous hypothesis that the dispute between the apostles Peter and Paul, there described, was merely feigned. Peter, he asserted, only pretended to separate himself from the Gentiles the more forcibly to bring out the incongruity of a Christian continuing to keep the Mosaic law. This appeared to Augustine as imputing to the apostle an acted lie, and he accordingly wrote to Jerome, A.D. 394,[2] showing what evil consequences must ensue if it could possibly be supposed that any teaching of the apostles was illusory. He asks, with a sly hit at Jerome's extravagant notions on celibacy, if we are to consider that the passages in which Paul eulogises marriage are fictitious. Unfortunately the presbyter to whom Augustine com-

---

[1] "The scorpion," wrote Jerome, "is buried under the soil of Sicily, with Enceladus and Porphyrion; the many-headed hydra has ceased to hiss against us." Of Jerome's controversies with Jovinian and Vigilantius, we shall speak when we come to the history of those reformers.   [2] Or 395.

mitted his letter, together with some of his own writings for Jerome's perusal, died before he had set out on his errand, but not before he had shown the letter to several persons, and copies had been taken. A second letter, which Augustine wrote three years later, when he discovered that the first had never been received, also miscarried: the messenger to whom it was committed never started, alleging that he was afraid of the sea. But of this letter, too, copies were taken, and a deacon, who had met with one on an island of the Adriatic, bound up with other writings of Augustine, either brought a copy, or described its contents to Jerome. Soon afterwards, some pilgrims returning from the Holy Land, informed Augustine that it was the talk of the monasteries of Bethlehem how he had attacked Jerome in a letter which he had not sent to him. Augustine hastened to exculpate himself, and to point out that what he had written was never intended for publication. He also begged Jerome to use an equal freedom in criticism, and concluded with the earnest desire that he could have personal intercourse with his correspondent. "In Jerome's reply, friendship struggles with suspicion and resentment." He professes to know little of Augustine's works, concerning which, nevertheless, he might have something to say in the way of criticism, and insinuates that Augustine was seeking to increase his own reputation at his expense. Augustine's rejoinder opens with language of profound respect, and after explaining how his first letter had miscarried, he enters again on questions of Biblical interpretation. He commends Jerome's version of the New Testament, but, with the mistaken reverence of the times for the Septuagint, entreats him not to continue the translation he had begun of the Old Testament from the original Hebrew. Jerome again complains that he had not received Augustine's original letter. "Send me," he says, "your letter signed by yourself, or else cease from attacking me, and let me beg you, if you write to me again, to take care that I am the first whom your letter reaches." Augustine now (some ten years after his first letter was written) sent to Jerome authentic copies of both his letters, at the same time begging that the matter might not, through the mishaps which had occurred, grow into a feud like that between Jerome and Rufinus. On the receipt of this packet Jerome returned an immediate and full reply. He touched on all the points raised, appealing, on the question of Peter's conduct at Antioch, to Origen and other Eastern expositors of Scripture to bear him out.[1] It would seem, however, that Jerome was at last

---

[1] The Eastern Churches continued to maintain Jerome's interpretation of Peter's conduct; the Western followed Augustine.

convinced, for Augustine, writing at a later date, cites a passage from him, in which he admits that no bishops are immaculate, since Paul found something to blame even in Peter. The correspondence was carried on some time longer with increasing goodwill on both sides.[1]

In 403 Paula died, at the age of 56. Her health had been undermined by years of excessive austerities. "She was," says Jerome, "always mourning and fasting; and had become almost blind with weeping." As she was departing she murmured in Hebrew some verses in Psalms xxvi. and lxxxiv., commencing, "O Lord, I have loved the beautiful order of thy house and the place of the habitation of thy glory." Then applying her finger to her mouth, she made the sign of the cross upon her lips. "There were present at her death the bishops of Jerusalem and other cities, and an innumerable company of priests and deacons, virgins and monks. There was no doleful cry, but a universal chant of the Psalms. Her body was carried to the tomb by the hands of bishops, and laid in the midst of the church of the Nativity. The cities of Palestine came to her funeral; the widows and the poor, after the example of Dorcas, showing the clothes that she had given them. . . . During the whole week the Psalms were sung in order in Hebrew, Greek, Latin and Syriac." . . . "If," writes Jerome, "all my being should become tongue and voice, I should still be unable worthily to declare her virtues. Noble by birth, she was yet more noble by her sanctity; once powerful by her wealth, she became still more powerful by her poverty in Christ; the descendant of the Gracchi and the Scipios, she preferred Bethlehem to Rome, and a mud roof to the gilded ceiling of a palace. Never," he adds, "from the death of her husband to the day of her own going to sleep, did she eat with any man however holy, not even if he were a bishop. She never entered the bath unless she was sick; even in a dangerous fever

---

[1] In this correspondence, as in all the letters of the time which have come down to us, we are struck with the adulatory titles made use of. We have seen the commencement of this weakness in Cyprian's days. — See *Early Church History*, p. 177, note. As the honour paid to the bishops became more profound, the style of address became more fulsome. Augustine salutes Jerome as "My lord most beloved and longed for," "My venerable lord Jerome"; and addresses him and others as "Your charity, your holiness." Jerome in reply styles Augustine "My lord truly holy and most blessed father (*papa*)," and calls him "Your excellency," "Your grace." At the Council of Ephesus, A.D. 431, Cyril is styled "Most saintly, most sacred, most devoted to God, our father and bishop." The bishops were saluted with bowing the head, kissing the hand, and even kissing the feet.

she used no soft bed, but rested on the hard ground with a scanty covering of hair-cloth, if indeed that is to be called rest, which joined days and nights together by almost ceaseless prayers. . . . Farewell," he exclaims, "O Paula, and help by thy prayers the old age of him who bears thee a religious reverence. Thy faith and works have joined thee to Christ, and being now present with Him thou wilt more easily obtain what thou desirest. I have raised to thee a monument more durable than brass, which time shall never destroy. But," he adds, "we do not weep that we have lost her; we thank God that we once possessed her. What do I say? We possess her still, for the elect who ascend to God still remain in the family of those who love them."

"The picture of Paula's death," writes Joseph Bevan Braithwaite, "gains nothing in our eyes from the ascetic colouring spread over it. Yet we may be instructed as we trace in her self-denying faith, her care for the poor, her patience in tribulation, her childlike trust in God, the genuine marks of the followers of Jesus. We would especially notice her love for the Scriptures. She had stored them in her memory. The facts of the Bible were to her the foundation of truth; and she still sought after an insight into the spiritual meaning for the edification of her soul. Much as we must deplore the evils of monasticism, we cannot mark the conduct of these devoted women in laying aside the wealth and honours of earth for what they believed to be the service of Christ, without, in some measure at least, entering into the feelings of Jerome as he watched by the couch of the dying Paula, and listened to the descendant of so many illustrious heathens testifying of her longing to depart and to be with Christ; and breathing forth her spirit in language more ancient than the earliest triumphs of Rome, but which is for ever new in the experience of the children of God: 'How amiable are thy tabernacles, O Lord of Hosts! my soul longeth, yea, even fainteth for the courts of the Lord.'"

It was now that the nations of the north of Europe—Goths, Vandals, Sueves, and Alans—having broken down the military barriers of the Empire, poured their hordes over her fairest provinces. In 405 the Isaurians laid waste the north of Palestine; the monasteries of Bethlehem were beset with fugitives, and Jerome and his friends were brought into great straits for the means of living. But another and a sorer calamity was at hand. Already the Goths were ravaging the northern provinces of Italy; and in 410 Rome was taken by Alaric. Many of the inhabitants were massacred; a far greater number were suddenly reduced to the miserable condition of captives and exiles. The city was given up to pillage; the booty was immense. "The acquisition of riches served only to stimulate the avarice of the rapacious barbarians, who proceeded by threats, by blows, and by torture, to force from their prisoners the confession of hidden treasure. The noble Marcella, the venerable head of the religious sisterhood in the city, was verging upon extreme old age. The blood-stained Gothic soldiers who rushed into her house expecting large spoils from so stately a palace, eagerly demanded that she should surrender the treasures which they were persuaded she had buried. She showed her mean and threadbare garments, and told them how it came to pass that she, a Roman matron, was destitute of wealth. The words 'voluntary poverty' fell on unbelieving ears. They beat her with clubs; they scourged her; she bore the strokes with unflinching courage, but fell at their feet and implored them not to separate her from the youthful Principia, her adopted daughter, dreading the effect of these horrors on the maiden, if called to bear them alone. At length their hard hearts softened towards her. They accepted her statement as to her poverty, and escorted her and Principia to the basilica of St. Paul.[1] Arrived there she broke forth into a song of thanksgiving, 'that God had at least kept her friend for her unharmed, that she had not been made poor by the ruin of the city, but that it had found her poor already, that she would not feel the hunger of the body, even though the daily bread might fail, because she was filled with all the fulness of Christ.' But the shock of the cruelties she had endured was too great for her aged frame, and after a few days she expired, the hands of her adopted daughter closing her eyes, and her kisses accompanying the last sigh."

Many of the fugitives took refuge in Africa and Syria, and some even found their way to Bethlehem. "Jerome describes himself as struck dumb with amazement at the capture of the city that had conquered the world; and as the intelligence followed in quick succession, of the desolation of the provinces, and of the ruin which foreshadowed the breaking up of the Empire in the West, he often sought relief in the words of his own translation of Psalm cxx. 5, 'Woe is me that my pilgrimage is lengthened out!'" . . . . "It was," he says again, "as though the end of the world was come. Who would have believed that obscure Bethlehem would see begging at its gates nobles lately laden with wealth? The daughters of the queenly city wander from shore to shore; her ladies have become servants; her most illustrious personages ask bread at our gate,

---

[1] Alaric had given orders that the right of asylum in the churches should be respected, especially in the two great basilicas of St. Peter and St. Paul.

and when we cannot give bread to them all, we give them at least our tears. In vain I try to snatch myself from the sight of such sufferings by resuming my unfinished work; I am incapable of study; I feel that this is the time for translating the precepts of Scripture, not into *words*, but *deeds*, and not for saying holy things, but doing them."[1]

We have spoken of the Vulgate, the celebrated translation of the Bible into Latin from the original languages. It arose out of Jerome's connection with the Roman bishop Damasus. Whilst he resided in Rome, a council was held in the city, to which he was appointed secretary, and when it was dissolved the bishop retained his services for himself in the same capacity. During their intercourse on matters of Scripture interpretation, Damasus urged Jerome to undertake a thorough revision of the Latin Gospels. Jerome recognised the need of such a work. "Mistakes," he says, "have been introduced by false transcription, by clumsy corrections, and by careless interpolations, so that there are almost as many forms of text as copies." This revision was accomplished whilst he was in Rome; and after he removed to Bethlehem, at the urgent request of Paula and Eustochium, he extended his labours to the Old Testament.[2] He had, as has been said, already commenced the study of Hebrew;[3] and now he engaged as his teachers, at much difficulty and expense, three Rabbis, one of whom was from Lydda, and another from Tiberias.[4] Great preparation was needed for the work. He consulted Biblical students; he searched every library in Palestine and Egypt, especially those of Alexandria and Cæsarea; he made use of the Hexapla of Origen; by the help of linguists he

---

[1] "The fall of Rome," says Thierry, "turned men's brains as with a vertigo and delirium. There was no longer any government, pity, or justice, and for many men no longer a God. 'The world crumbles away, and our head knows not how to bow down,' cried Jerome in terror. 'That which is born must perish; that which has grown must wither. There is no created work which rust or age does not consume:—but Rome! Who could have believed that, raised by her victories above the universe, she would one day fall, and become for her people at once a mother and a tomb?'"

[2] Eustochium, as well as Paula, understood Hebrew. They used to go to Jerome's cave at certain hours to read the Hebrew Bible with him; and from the conversations which arose on these occasions many a passage in his version of the Vulgate was settled.

[3] Jerome's knowledge of Hebrew was much greater than that of Origen, Epiphanius, or Ephrem, the only other Fathers who understood it at all.

[4] It is said of the Jew of Lydda that his thirst for gold was equal to his love of knowledge. To read Daniel and Tobit, Jerome was obliged to change his instructor for one who understood Chaldee: the Rabbi rendered the text into Hebrew, which Jerome dictated in Latin for his scribes to write down.

made himself acquainted with the Ethiopic and Syriac versions; and he availed himself of the traditional knowledge of his Jewish instructors on orthography, vowel sounds and interpretations, as well as on Biblical topography. On the last point he was not satisfied with information at second-hand, but made a tour of Palestine, identifying, as well as he was able, the sites of the cities and villages, mountains, and sacred spots of the Old and New Testaments. This was not all. He exercised his sound and penetrating judgment in replacing passages which had been omitted, and rejecting such as had been interpolated. Nor were learning and genius alone necessary for the accomplishment of this vast undertaking; it required a rare intrepidity to call in question the authority of the Septuagint, and to restore to its proper place the original Hebrew. It must also be borne in mind that the task was undertaken and completed by one man on his own individual responsibility. "No scholar, for fifteen hundred years," remarks Westcott, "was so fitted to accomplish it." In the words of Milman: "Whatever it may owe to the older and fragmentary versions of the sacred writings, Jerome's Bible is a wonderful work, still more as achieved by one man, and that a Western Christian, even with all the advantage of study and of residence in the East. It almost created a new language. The inflexible Latin became pliant and expansive, naturalizing foreign Eastern imagery, Eastern modes of expression and of thought and Eastern religious notions, most uncongenial to its own genius and character; and yet retaining much of its own peculiar strength, solidity and majesty. If the Northern, the Teutonic languages, coalesce with greater facility with the Orientalism of the Scriptures, it is the triumph of Jerome to have brought the more dissonant Latin into harmony with the Eastern tongues. The Vulgate, even more perhaps than the Papal power, was the foundation of Latin Christianity."

Like all innovations, however good, the labours of Jerome were received at first with an outcry of alarm. He was accused of disturbing the repose of the Church, and shaking the foundations of the faith. But although the Vulgate was an appeal from tradition to truth, it came itself in course of time to represent that very idolatry of tradition which it had sought to overthrow. Barely tolerated during the life-time of its author, its intrinsic merit made way for it, until by the seventh century it had entirely superseded the older versions. Its daily and hourly use in all the churches and monasteries of Europe, coupled with ignorance of the original languages on the part of the clergy, raised its authority, in time, to the place of an article of faith; so that the Council of

Trent, in 1546, declared: "The Vulgate edition shall be held for authentic in public lectures, disputations, sermons and expositions, and none shall dare to refuse it."[1]

A long period of sickness preceded Jerome's death. By the help of a cord fixed to the ceiling of his cell, he used to raise himself from his couch whilst he recited his *Hours*.[2] He was attended in his last illness by the younger Paula (grandchild of his friend Paula), and another of the nuns. He died 419 or 420 A.D., at the age of seventy-four.

All critics agree in extolling Jerome's learning and the soundness of his theology. "What Jerome was ignorant of," said Augustine, "no mortal has ever known." The words of Erasmus are: "The divine Jerome is among the Latins so incontestably the first of theologians that we have scarcely another worthy the name. What a pitch of Roman eloquence in him! How great a skill in languages! What a depth of acquaintance with the history of all antiquity! How retentive a memory! How happy a union of all qualities! How absolute a knowledge of mystic science! Above all things, how ardent a spirit, and how admirable an inspiration!" "His commentaries on Scripture," says Roberts, "are among the best which the Fathers have bequeathed to us. His *Letter to Demetrias* is valuable for the clear and sound exposition it contains of Divine Grace as the gift of gratuitous mercy."

Although his notions were at least as superstitious, and his prejudices more violent than those of his contemporaries, yet his powerful intellect often grasps the truth with singular firmness, and holds it up to view unsullied and luminous. The traditions of the Church had become by this time of equal authority with Holy Scripture. "Of the dogmas which are preserved in the Church," writes Basil, "there are some which we have from Scripture, and others from the tradition of the Apostles, and both have the same force. What written precept have we, for instance, for signing believers with the cross? or for turning to the east in our prayers? The words of invocation, when the bread of the Eucharist and cup of Blessing are consecrated, which of the saints has left to us in writing? We bless both the water of baptism, and the oil of unction, and the person who is baptized—out of what Scripture? Is it not on the authority of the silent mystical tradition?" However inconsistent he may have been in practice, Jerome disposes in

---

[1] On the invention of printing, the Vulgate was the first book of any considerable size which was issued from the press.

[2] The prayers and psalms repeated at stated times were thus named.

a few words of all such pretensions. "Do not suffer yourselves to be seduced by pretended apostolical traditions. Hypocritical priests require men to worship their traditions and statutes as other nations worship idols; but to us God has given the law and the testimony of the Scriptures. . . . I place the Apostles apart from all other writers; they always speak the truth; others err like men. We ought not, like the scholars of Pythagoras, to regard the prejudicated opinion of the teacher, but the weight and reason of the thing taught."

But the case is far otherwise when we come to consider Jerome's spirit and temper, and his influence on his own and succeeding ages. There is too much ground for the protest of Isaac Taylor against the "vile legendary trash" of which Jerome's *Life of the Hermit Paul* largely consists. "It is not," he adds, "without an emotion profoundly painful, that one turns from the turbid, frothy, and infectious stream of Jerome's ascetic writings, to the pellucid waters of Plato, Xenophon, and Cicero, reason darkened indeed, but struggling toward the light, and exempt from virulence, from hypocrisy and from absurdity. Such a contrast powerfully impresses the mind with a sense of the infinite mischief that has been done to mankind by men, who, when Christianity, with its simple grandeur and its divine purity, was fairly lodged in their hands and committed to their care, could do nothing but madly heap upon it, and often for selfish purposes, every grossness and folly which might turn aside its influence, and expose it to contempt. It may be a Christian-like and kindly office to palliate the errors, and to cloak the follies, and to give a reason for the false notions, of the Nicene divines; but when, on the other side, one thinks of the long centuries of woe, ignorance, and persecution, and religious debauchery, which took their character directly from the perversity of these doctors, it is hard to repress emotions of the liveliest indignation."

We will conclude with the masterly analysis of Jerome's character in the *Dictionary of Christian Biography.* " He was vain and unable to bear rivals; extremely sensitive as to the estimation in which he was held by his contemporaries, and especially by the bishops; passionate and resentful, but at times becoming suddenly placable; scornful and violent in controversy; kind to the weak and the poor; respectful in his dealings with women; entirely without avarice; extraordinarily diligent in work, and nobly tenacious of the main objects to which he devoted his life. . . . His writings contain the whole spirit of the Church of the Middle Ages, its monasticism, its contrast of sacred things with profane, its credulity and superstition, its subjection to hierarchical authority, its dread of heresy, its passion for pilgrimages. To the society which was thus in a great measure formed by him, his Bible was the greatest boon which could have been given. But he founded no school, and had no inspiring power; there was no courage or width of view in his spiritual legacy which could break through the fatal circle of bondage to received authority which was closing round mankind."

CHAPTER IX.

AUGUSTINE.

OF Augustine, "the tenderest, most devout, and in all respects most noble-minded of the Christian Fathers," more is known than of any other, chiefly because he has left an autobiography, the well-known *Confessions*, written when he was about forty-three years old. The son of a pagan citizen of Thagaste, in Numidia, he was born A.D. 354. His mother, Monnica, "the pattern of mothers," was a Christian, and to her patience and faithfulness her husband mainly owed his conversion, and her son his character and greatness.

Augustine was sent first to an elementary school in his native town, "where," as he tells us, "*one and one are two, two and two are four*, was a hateful singsong" to him, and when he did not learn, he was beaten. He calls this discipline "a great and grievous ill," and in his distress he used earnestly to pray to God that he might not be so punished. "We boys," he says, "wanted not memory or capacity, but we delighted only in play, and for this we were punished by those who were doing the same things themselves. But the idleness of our elders is called business, whilst boys who do the like are punished by those same elders."

In due time he was promoted to a higher school in the neighbouring large town of Madaura, where the majority of the inhabitants were pagans, and the statues of the gods still stood uninjured in the forum. Here Virgil delighted him,—"the wooden horse full of armed men, and the burning of Troy, and the spectral image of Creusa;" but although Homer contained the same "sweetly vain fiction," the difficulty of mastering Greek embittered all the romance of the Iliad. To make the youthful scholar comprehend the Greek poet, harsh threats and blows were freely used.

It is worthy of notice that when Augustine in after years looked back upon his school days with a ripened judgment, and from a Christian standpoint, he condemned the classic method of instruction, that "torrent of hell" as he calls it, by which learning was poured into the boyish mind through the obscene fables of heathenism. He also brings out into strong relief the scrupulous care with which the scholars were trained in the niceties of grammar, whilst moral truth and practice were neglected ; so that, as he expresses it, "it was accounted a greater offence for a scholar to drop the aspirate and say '*ominem*, instead of *hominem* (man), than if, in opposition to the divine commandments, he, a human being, should hate a human being."

At the age of sixteen he returned home to his parents, and the next year was sent to college at Carthage to complete his education. During this period, notwithstanding his mother's loving counsel and entreaties, he fell into dissolute habits. "My mother's admonitions to chastity appeared to me but womanish counsels which I should blush to obey." . . . . "Blindly" (he says again) "I rushed on headlong; when I heard my equals pluming themselves on their disgraceful deeds, I made myself out worse than I was that I might not be dispraised. . . . A cauldron of unholy loves bubbled up around me; and yet foul and dishonourable as I was, I craved, through an excess of vanity, to be thought elegant and urbane." He and his companions, *habitués* of the theatre and the circus, prided themselves on their gallantry, and practised shameful tricks and rough jokes in the public streets. But in the midst of all this dissipation he found time for study, and his natural genius asserted itself so strongly that he became head scholar in the school of rhetoric.

In the course of his studies he lighted upon the "Hortensius" of Cicero, a dialogue in praise of philosophy, of which fragments only remain. "This book," he writes, "changed my affections, and turned my prayers to Thee, O Lord.[1] Suddenly all my vain hopes became worthless, and with an incredible warmth of heart, I yearned for the possession of immortal philosophy, and began to arise that I might return to Thee. . . . One thing alone checked my ardour, that the name of Christ was not in the book. For this name had my tender heart piously drunk in, even with my mother's milk, and whatever was without that name, though never so erudite, polished and truthful, could not take complete hold of me." But he was not yet humble enough to receive the spiritual teaching of

---

[1] His *Confessions* are throughout addressed to God.

the Scriptures. "They were such as the lowly can understand; but they appeared to me unworthy to be compared with the dignity of Cicero; my full-blown pride shunned their simple style, nor could the sharpness of my wit penetrate their inner meaning."

In this condition of mind he met with the Manichæans,[1] whose rationalistic system entangled him like "bird-lime," and for a long time held him a willing prisoner. Years afterwards, when he had escaped, and had come into the reality of the Gospel, he saw how deceitful had been the illusion which had been put upon him. "O truth, truth, how did the marrow of my soul pant after thee! They sounded out thy name to me, but it was but a voice. As fictitious dishes served up to one in hunger, so instead of Thee they served up to me thy sun and moon, thy beauteous works, but not Thyself; and glowing phantasies and empty fictions; and I fed upon them, but was not nourished but famished. For I hungered and thirsted, not so much after thy works, but after Thee Thyself, the Truth, with whom is no variableness, neither shadow of turning; and far from Thee was I wandering, cut off even from the husks of the swine whom with husks I was feeding."

Augustine returned from Carthage an avowed Manichæan, and not content with holding these opinions himself, he used all his skill as a trained disputant to win converts to the same error. His pious mother (his father was then dead) "wept for him more than mothers weep the bodily death of their children." She did more than grieve. Shrinking from, and detesting the blasphemies of his heresy, she began to doubt whether it was right in her to allow her son to live with her and to eat at the same table. From this perplexity she was delivered by a dream. She saw herself standing on a wooden rule,[2] bowed down with grief, when a shining youth advanced towards her, and with a smile inquired the cause of her sorrow. She answered that she was lamenting her son's perdition; he bade her be comforted, and told her to behold and see that where she was, there was her son also. She looked, and saw Augustine standing near her on the same rule. On her relating to him the vision he pretended that it signified she should not despair of being some day what he was. "No," she replied promptly and decidedly, "it was not told me, where he is, thou shalt be, but where thou art, he shall be." He confesses that his mother's answer, showing that she was not deceived by his sophistry, moved him more than the dream itself.

---

[1] See a brief notice of their rise and doctrines in *Early Church History*, p. 226.
[2] *Regula;* symbolical of the rule of faith.

About the same period his mother in her distress applied to a bishop, reported to be well skilled in refuting errors and teaching sound doctrine, entreating him that he would have some talk with her son. He refused, alleging that Augustine was as yet unteachable, being puffed up with the novelty of the heresy he had embraced, and with having already silenced many by his arguments. "Leave him alone for a time," he said, "only pray for him; he will of himself, by reading, discover his error; for I myself, when a youth, was by a misguided mother betrayed to the Manichæans, and not only read but wrote out almost all their books; and yet I came to see, without argument or proof from any one, how that sect was to be shunned." But Monnica could not be satisfied; she besought the good bishop still more earnestly and with many tears, that he would see and discourse with her son. A little displeased at her importunity he exclaimed, "Go thy way and God bless thee, for it is not possible that the son of these tears should perish." She went away comforted, accepting his answer as a voice from heaven.

Augustine now commenced to teach rhetoric at Carthage. His pupils were mostly studying for the law. "In those years I made sale of the art of victorious loquacity. Yet I preferred to have honest scholars, as they are esteemed, to whom I without artifice taught artifices, not to be practised against the life of the guiltless, although sometimes for the life of the guilty." Many heathen notions and practices still lingered, and amongst them that of soothsaying. "When I would compete for a theatrical prize," Augustine continues, "a soothsayer demanded how much I would give him to make me win. He was to sacrifice certain living creatures, and so induce the devils to favour me. I answered him: 'Although the garland I was to win should be made of imperishable gold, I would not suffer a fly to be destroyed to secure it.' But I said this not out of pure love for Thee, O God of my heart, for I knew not then how to love Thee, but because I detested and abominated such foul mysteries, although I myself was sacrificing to devils by the superstition in which I was enthralled." Accordingly he did not hesitate to consult another kind of impostors, the astrologers, or "mathematicians," who observed the stars, but offered no sacrifices and invoked no spirit in their divinations.

At twenty, Augustine had mastered nearly all the science of the age. Whilst others were scarcely able to understand Aristotle with the aid of skilful tutors, he read him unassisted. "Whatever was written on rhetoric, logic, geometry, music, or arithmetic, I understood without an instructor, because of the quickness of intelligence and acuteness of observing which Thou, O my God, gave me."

By degrees Augustine discovered that the professors of Manichæism could not solve the questions which sprang up in his astute mind, and that what Manes had taught regarding the universe was contradicted by science. His confidence was further shaken by the most renowned bishop of the sect, who discerned Augustine's genius, requesting to become his pupil. All this time, during which he was wandering in the labyrinth of a false religion, Augustine was in bondage also to the indulgence of his unsubdued appetites.

Amongst the pupils in his school of rhetoric was Alypius, a youth of great promise, but "the vortex of Carthaginian customs had inveigled him into the madness of the games." Although not yet himself converted, Augustine perceived clearly the folly of such a manner of life. "One day," he writes, "when I was sitting in my accustomed place, with my scholars before me, Alypius came in, saluted me, and fixed his attention on the subject I was handling. Whilst I was explaining there occurred to me a simile borrowed from the circus, as likely to make what I wished to convey pleasanter and plainer, imbued at the same time with a biting gibe at those who were enthralled by that madness. I had no thought at the moment of curing Alypius of that plague. But he applied my words to himself, and thought I spoke them only for his sake. And what any other would have made a ground of offence against me, this worthy young man took as a reason for being offended at himself, and for loving me more fervently." But although Augustine's sharp reproof brought Alypius for the time to his senses, he was not in reality "cured of his plague." In Rome, not long afterwards, he was one day met by a knot of acquaintances and fellow-students returning from dinner, who with friendly violence drew him towards the amphitheatre, he all the while resisting. "You may," he protested, "drag my body thither and seat me there, but you cannot force me to lend my mind or my eyes to the spectacle." Nevertheless they carried him in with them and took their places. Soon the customary excitement seized the vast crowd. For a while Alypius kept his eyes firmly closed, but on the fall of one of the combatants, there arose so mighty a cry, that, overcome by curiosity, his resolution gave way, and he looked on the scene before him. Instantly the sight of the blood brought back all the old craving; he fixed his gaze until he was intoxicated with the sanguinary pastime, and joined in the universal shout. "From all this, didst Thou," adds Augustine, "with a most powerful and a most merciful hand pluck him, and teach him not to trust in himself but in Thee."

The schools of rhetoric at Carthage were very disorderly, and although that of Augustine enjoyed a high reputation, he longed for a more quiet chair, where discipline still held something of her ancient sway. He resolved to go to Rome. This resolution was a great grief to Monnica. Unable to part with him, she went down to the harbour, determined either to prevent his voyage, or to bear him company. To free himself from her, he pretended that he had a friend whom he desired to see off, and who was waiting for a favourable wind. "By the help of this device, I hardly persuaded her to remain that night in a place close to our ship, where there was an oratory in memory of the blessed Cyprian." During the night, whilst she was weeping and praying that he might not be permitted to leave her, the wind rose, filled the sails, and bore Augustine out of sight of land. His reflections in after-years on the events of this sad night are full of tenderness and wisdom. "I lied to my mother, and such a mother, and got away. Thou, O God, mysteriously counselling and hearing the real purpose of her desire, granted not what she then asked, that Thou mightest make me what she was ever asking." When the next morning she came to the shore and found the ship was gone, "she was wild with grief."

Augustine came to Rome in 383. He had been there only six months when the city of Milan applied to Symmachus, the pagan prefect, an upright and eloquent man, for a teacher of rhetoric. Augustine, through some Manichæan friends, made application for the appointment; and Symmachus, having satisfied himself of his fitness, sent him to Milan at the public expense. Alypius would not leave him. "He clave to me," writes Augustine, "by a most strong tie, and went with me to Milan, both that he might not leave me, and that he might practise something of the law he had studied, more to please his parents than himself. At Rome," he continues, "he had thrice sat as assessor with much uncorruptness, wondered at by others, he wondering that they should prefer gold to honesty."

The great attraction for Augustine at Milan was Ambrose. "To Milan I came, and to Ambrose the bishop,[1] thy devout servant, known to the whole world as among the best of men, whose eloquent discourse did at that time strenuously dispense unto thy people the flour of thy wheat, the gladness of thy oil, and the sober intoxication of thy wine. To him was I unknowingly led by Thee, that by him

---

[1] He had then occupied the see nine years.

I might knowingly be led to Thee. He received me as a father, and I began to love him, not at first indeed as a teacher of the Truth, which I utterly despaired of finding in thy Church, but as a man friendly to myself. I studiously hearkened to him preaching to the people, but not with the intent I ought to have done, for of the matter I was careless and scornful, but testing his eloquence whether it came up to its fame. Yet all the time, little by little, I was unconsciously drawing nearer to him. For although I took no pains to learn *what* he spoke, but only to hear *how* he spoke, yet along with the words which I prized there entered into my mind also the things about which I was indifferent; for I could not separate them: so that whilst I opened my heart to admit how *skilfully* he spoke, by degrees there entered also the conviction how *truly* he spoke. In the end I resolved to become a catechumen in the Catholic Church."

Augustine found but little opportunity of private intercourse with the bishop. "It would seem that Ambrose, after the fashion of hot countries, sat habitually in a corner of the cloister or verandah which surrounded the open court of the house, so that those who wished to speak to him could watch for an opportunity of finding him disengaged." "When," writes Augustine, "he was not occupied with the crowds of busy people to whose infirmities he devoted himself, he was either refreshing his body with necessary sustenance, or his mind with reading. Often when we had come and seen him thus intent, and had sat long silent, we were fain to depart, inferring that he was unwilling to lose the little time he thus secured for replenishing his mind."

Monnica could not long remain absent from her beloved and erring son, but followed him to Milan. The vessel in which she sailed was in danger of shipwreck, and the sailors themselves were alarmed, but Monnica, so Augustine relates, was comforted by a heavenly vision and able to predict a safe termination to their voyage.

Shortly before her arrival Augustine and Alypius were joined by another young man, Nebridius, "who left Carthage and his fine paternal estate, his house and his mother, and came to Milan for no other reason but that with me he might live in a most ardent search after truth and wisdom. "So," he continues, "were there three indigent persons sighing out their wants one to another, and waiting upon Thee that Thou mightest give them their meat in due season." These three, with a few others of like mind, formed the project of separating themselves wholly from the turmoil of the world. Each was to throw his possessions into the common stock;

and the cares of the household were to be committed to two of them as stewards, that the rest might devote themselves undisturbed to the pursuit of wisdom. But an important element had been left out in their calculation. "We began to ask whether the wives whom some of us possessed already, and others hoped to have, would give their consent, and all our plans which had been so skilfully framed broke to pieces, and were utterly wrecked and cast aside. So we fell again to sighs and groans, and our steps again followed the broad and beaten tracks of the world."

Augustine found himself still under the shackles of his old sins. He had brought with him to Milan his son Adeodatus, and the youth's mother. Monnica was very solicitous that he should break off the unlawful connexion, and contract an honourable marriage. A maiden was even chosen for him and his consent obtained; but the time of reformation was not yet come; he fell back again into his former mode of life.

He had now cast off the doctrines of the Manichæans, and had allied himself with the Neo-Platonists, with whom, however, he did not long remain. "Being," he says, "warned to return to myself, I entered into my inward parts, Thou leading me on; and with the eye of my soul I saw above my mind the unchangeable light. Not this common light which all flesh may look upon, nor a greater one of the same kind, though much more resplendent, but very different from these. Neither was it above my mind as oil is above water, nor as heaven is above earth, but it was above me because it made me, and I was below it because I was made by it. He who knows the truth knows that light, and he who knows that light knows eternity. Love knows it. O eternal truth, and true love and beloved eternity! . . . I found not the way to enjoy Thee, until I embraced that Mediator between God and man, the Man Christ Jesus, who is over all God blessed for ever, and who called to me saying, 'I am the way, the truth, and the life!'"

There was at Milan a good man named Simplician,[1] one who had been spiritually helpful to Ambrose, and who is described by him "as having traversed the whole world to acquire divine knowledge, and given his entire life to holy reading, night and day." "Thou God!" exclaims Augustine, "didst put into my mind, and it seemed good in my eyes, to go to this man. I went therefore and unfolded to him the tortuous course of my errors." Simplician related to him the history of Victorinus, who after worshipping idols all his life, became in his old age a child of Christ, and made a public

---

[1] He succeeded Ambrose as bishop of Milan.—See *ante*, p. 70.

confession of his name. As Augustine listened—"I burned," he says, "to imitate Victorinus, and when I heard that in the time of the Emperor Julian a law was made forbidding Christians to teach grammar and rhetoric, and that this man chose rather to relinquish the school of words than to give up thy Word, he appeared to me not more courageous than happy in having thus discovered an opportunity of serving Thee only;—which thing I also sighed for in my bonds; bonds not imposed by another, but by my own iron will. The enemy being master of my will had made a chain of it, and bound me with it. Out of a perverse will came lust; and lust indulged became custom; and custom unresisted became necessity. And that new will which had begun to rise in me, freely to serve Thee and to wish to enjoy Thee, O God, the only sure delight, was not as yet able to overcome my former wilfulness made strong by long indulgence. Thus did my two wills—one old, the other new; one carnal, the other spiritual—strive within me, and by their discord undid my soul."

Another hand of help was extended to him by his fellow-countryman Pontitianus. This man, coming to the house where Augustine and Alypius dwelt, saw on the table a copy of Paul's Epistles; and in the conversation to which the volume gave rise he related to them the anecdote of the two gentlemen, who were turned from the pursuit of worldly honour to embrace the ascetic life by reading Athanasius' *Life of St. Anthony*.[1] The narrative sank deep into Augustine's soul. "Thou, O Lord, whilst he was speaking didst turn me towards myself, taking me from behind my back where I had placed myself, and setting me before my face that I might see how foul I was, how crooked and defiled, bespotted and ulcerous. I beheld and loathed myself, and whither to flee from myself I found not. And whenever I sought to turn away my gaze from myself, Thou again didst set me over against myself, and thrustedst me before my own eyes that I might find out my own iniquity and hate it. . . . Pontitianus," continues Augustine, "having finished his story and the business he came for, went his way, and I withdrew into myself. With what scourges of rebuke did I not lash my soul to make her follow me, struggling to go after Thee! Yet she drew back, she refused. All her arguments were spent and confuted; there remained only a mute shrinking; she dreaded, as if it were death itself, the plugging of that flow of habit whereby she was wasting to death. I grasped Alypius, and exclaimed, ' What ails us? What is it? The unlearned start up and take Heaven by

---

[1] See *Early Church History*, p. 300, note.

force, while we with our learning, but wanting heart, behold! where we wallow in flesh and blood.' Some such words I uttered, and in my excitement flung myself from him, while he gazed after me in silent amazement."

" There was," he goes on to relate, " a little garden belonging to our lodging, of which we had the use. Thither the tempest within my breast hurried me, where no one might check the fiery struggle in which I was engaged with myself, until it came to the issue which Thou knewest, though I did not." Alypius followed, "for his presence did not destroy my privacy, and how could he desert me so troubled? We sat down as far from the house as we could."

The fever which consumed Augustine's soul communicated itself to his body; he tore his hair; he smote his forehead; with close-knit fingers he clasped his knee. The two natures, the two wills within him, the good drawing this way, the evil that way, were locked together in a death-struggle for the mastery. " The very toys of toys and vanities of vanities, my old mistresses, held me in their thrall; they shook my fleshly garment and whispered softly, Dost thou part with us? From this moment shall we no more be with thee for ever? What they said I did not so much as half hear, for they did not openly show themselves and contradict me, but muttering as it were behind my back, furtively plucked me as I was departing, to make me look back upon them. For on that other side toward which I had set my face and whither I still trembled to go, the chaste dignity of continence shone upon me full of cheerfulness, honestly alluring me to come and doubt nothing, and extending her holy hands, full of a multiplicity of good examples, to receive and embrace me."

At length he could could contain himself no longer; the storm which raged within him found vent in a torrent of tears. Feeling entire solitude to be the fittest place for weeping, he stole away from Alypius, and flung himself under a fig-tree, where his heart found relief in words. " 'Thou, O Lord, how long? How long, Lord, wilt Thou be angry for ever? O remember not against us former iniquities. How long, how long? To-morrow, to-morrow? Why not now? Why not this hour an end to my uncleanness?' Thus I said, and wept in the most bitter contrition of my heart, and behold I heard the voice, as of a boy or girl, I know not which, coming from a neighbouring house, chanting and oft repeating, *Tolle, lege; tolle lege*'; ' Take up and read, take up and read.' Instantly my countenance altered; I began to think most intently whether children were wont in any kind of play to sing such words;

and I could not remember ever to have heard the like. So checking my tears I rose up, interpreting it to be no other than a command to me from Heaven, to open the book and read the first chapter I should light upon. . . . Eagerly, therefore, I returned to the place where Alypius was sitting, for there I had laid the volume of the Apostles. I seized, I opened, and in silence read that paragraph on which my eyes first fell: 'Not in rioting and drunkenness, not in chambering and wantonness, not in strife and envying; but put ye on the Lord Jesus Christ, and make no provision for the flesh to fulfil the lusts thereof.' No further would I read, nor needed I, for instantly as the sentence ended, by a serene light as it were infused into my heart, all the darkness of doubt vanished away. Then putting my finger, or some other mark, in the place, I closed the book, and with a tranquil countenance made known to Alypius what had passed. He asked to see what I had been reading. I showed him; he looked further and read, 'Him that is weak in the faith, receive ye,' which he applied to himself and was strengthened. Thence we go in to my mother. We tell her; she rejoices; we relate how it all took place; she leaps for joy, and triumphs and blesses Thee, who art able to do exceeding abundantly above all that we can ask or think, for she saw that Thou hadst given her for me more than she was wont to ask in her pitiful and most sorrowful groanings. For Thou didst so convert me to Thyself, that I sought neither a wife nor any other of this world's hopes, standing on that rule of faith where Thou hadst showed me to her in a vision so many years before."

It was only in accordance with the spirit of the age that Augustine, having now given himself to the Lord, should take the vow of perpetual celibacy and withdraw altogether from secular concerns. Throwing up his professorship, he retired to a country house at Cassiacum,[1] which was placed at his disposal by one of his Milanese friends. There he passed the seven months which intervened till his baptism. He was accompanied by his mother and his son, then not quite fifteen, Alypius and Nebridius, and six other chosen friends. To this select company the time spent at Cassiacum was the realization of the happy life of which some of them had already dreamed. They rose early, sometimes passed the morning in reading, dined frugally together, and in the afternoon assembled under a spreading tree in the meadow, for pleasant and profitable conversation. When it rained they removed to a hall of the baths which were attached to the villa. "Of these *réunions* Augustine was the life and soul; it was a little school of Christian philosophy

---

[1] Now Cassago de Brianza, twenty miles from Milan.

of which he was the professor. Some had their tablets always ready, and with the stylus noted down rapidly what was said. When the discussion was prolonged into the twilight, a servant brought a lamp that the writers might not lose any of the master's words." These conversations were the germ of several of Augustine's philosophical treatises.

After his baptism, which was performed (A.D. 387) by Ambrose himself, his son and Alypius being baptized at the same time, Augustine and Monnica proceeded to Rome, intending to return to Africa. But the sweet prospect of again living together in their native country was not to be realized: Monnica's earthly race was nearly run. At Ostia she was taken with fever, which carried her off in nine days. Augustine bewailed her loss with the most poignant sorrow.

Augustine tarried nearly a year in Rome before returning to Africa. In 388 he took up his dwelling in his native town, Thagaste. Distributing half of his patrimony to the poor, he retired with a few chosen friends, of whom Alypius was one, to his own house, and entered upon a life of fasting, prayer, meditation, and study. Like Basil and Jerome, he exerted himself for the establishment of monastic houses, but it was chiefly the lower classes and liberated slaves whom he persuaded to take the vows.

At the end of three years, having occasion to go to Hippo, he was present in the church when the bishop Valerius was discoursing on the necessity of appointing an additional priest for the Catholic service. He was recognized and laid hold of, and notwithstanding his resistance, presented to the bishop, who ordained him on the spot. When he removed to Hippo[1] he took with him his brotherhood, and settled his monastery in the gardens adjoining the church. In a few years Valerius, finding his strength decline, associated Augustine with him in his episcopal duties, and at his death in 396 Augustine became bishop. He thus meditates on his new position. "Nothing is better than the study of Divine wisdom without distraction; but to preach, to refute, to reprove, to edify, to take care for each individual soul, is a heavy burden and toil. Who would not shun it? But the Gospel makes me afraid when I think of the slothful servant who buried his Lord's talent." The episcopal residence now became both a cloister and a school of theology. Many who were there trained for the priesthood rose to offices of rank and influence.[2]

---

[1] The modern seaport town of Bona, in the east of Algeria, is built out of the ruins of the ancient Hippo, the site of which lay a mile to the south.

[2] Combining the clerical life with the monastic, Augustine became unwit-

Augustine required his clergy to live with him as a religious community in celibacy and poverty. There was, however, no display of asceticism. He himself wore the black dress of the Eastern cœnobites, but retained his linen and shoes. "I applaud your courage," he said to those who went barefoot; "do you bear with my weakness." The table service was of wood, earthenware and marble, and the spoons of silver. Hospitality was freely maintained. The diet of the brotherhood was mostly vegetable; but flesh and wine were provided for the visitors, of whom there was a continual succession. On the dining-table was carved a Latin distich:—

"He who slanders the absent is forbidden to sit at this board."

If any one infringed this rule, Augustine used to tell him that either the verses must be effaced, or he must leave the table. Another reprehensible custom in conversation was the frequent taking of the name of God to witness the truth of what was said. The penalty which the bishop imposed on his guests for this offence was to go without wine at dinner.

Augustine was a powerful and very diligent preacher; often preaching five days in succession, sometimes twice a day. The fire which burnt in his own soul kindled a corresponding flame in the souls of his hearers. Like all true Christian preachers, he depended for success on the help of the Holy Spirit. "The Christian orator," he says, "will succeed more by prayer than by gifts of oratory. Before he attempts to speak he will pray for himself and his hearers. And when the time is come, before he opens his mouth, he must lift up his thirsty soul to God to drink in what he is about to pour forth, and to be himself filled with what he is about to dispense. For who knows what it is expedient at any given moment for us to say, or to be heard saying, except God who knows the hearts of all? And who can enable us to say what we ought, and in the way we ought, but He in whose hand are both ourselves and our words? He therefore who would both know and teach, should learn all that is to be taught, and acquire a faculty of speech, suitable to his office; but when the hour for speech arrives let him give heed to our Lord's words, 'Take no thought how or what ye should speak, for it shall be given you in that same hour what ye shall speak; for it is not ye that speak but the Spirit of your Father that speaketh in you.' If the Holy Spirit speaks thus in those who for Christ's sake are delivered to the persecutors, why

---

tingly to himself the founder of the Augustinian order, which 1100 years afterwards gave Luther to the world.

not also in those who deliver Christ's message to those who are willing to learn?"

At the same time he has a word of reproof for such as from sloth or a fanatical spirit despised the helps which God has provided. "If any one says we need not direct men how or what they should teach, since it is the Holy Spirit that makes them teachers, he might as well say we need not pray, since our Lord says, 'Your Father knoweth what things ye have need of before ye ask Him'; or that the apostle Paul should not have given directions to Timothy and Titus as to how or what they should teach to others. These three apostolic epistles ought to be constantly before the eyes of every one who has attained to the position of a teacher in the Church."[1]

Augustine's practice agreed with his precepts. "One day he had prepared an eloquent discourse, designed to produce a strong impression on cultivated minds. Suddenly in the midst of his preaching he broke the thread of his argument, and turned abruptly to a more simple and popular subject. On his return home he related how he had yielded to an impulse of the Holy Spirit which had driven him to set aside the original plan of his sermon. Hardly had he spoken, when a man knocking at the door, entered, bathed in tears. He had been arrested by the diverted portion of the discourse, and now confessed himself to be won over to the Gospel."

It was early in Augustine's episcopal life that he came into conflict with the Donatists.[2] This sect, confined to the North African province, had increased rather than diminished under the successors of Constantine, and its adherents were here as numerous as the Catholics. Hippo was a very hotbed of the schism. With the same faith, the same worship, and nearly the same discipline, there

---

[1] With all this wisdom, Augustine, like most of the Fathers, indulged in a symbolism often fanciful and sometimes absurd. See for example his comment on the healing of the impotent man at the Pool of Bethesda. "The pool is the Jewish people shut in by the five books of Moses as by five porches. The law only brought forth the sick, it could not heal them. Christ, by his teaching and mighty acts, troubles sinners, troubles the water, and arouses it to his own death. To descend into the troubled waters means to believe in the Lord's death. That only one was healed signifies unity; those who came afterwards were not healed, because he who is outside unity cannot be healed. Christ found in the impotent man's age the number of infirmity. The number forty is consecrated by a kind of perfection. Why should we wonder that he was weak and sick whose years fell short of forty by two? Finding the man thus lacking, Christ gave him two precepts, ordered him to do two things, 'Take up thy bed—and walk.' Thus filling up that which was lacking of the perfect number."

[2] For an account of the rise of the Donatists, see *Early Church History*, Part ii. c. 10.

were two rival communities, each claiming to be the true Church. This was a condition of things which Augustine could not endure to behold. He not only yearned to bring all men to what he looked upon as the peculiar privileges of the Catholic Church; he sincerely believed that outside her pale there is no salvation.[1] He confounded the authority of Christ with that of the visible Church, and claimed for the latter the same absolute obedience as for Christ Himself. From the moment therefore when he became bishop of Hippo, no object lay nearer to his heart, than to bring back the Donatists into the Catholic communion. His confidence in his own theological principles induced him to believe that if the bishops of that party could only be brought calmly to investigate the questions at issue, they would acknowledge their error. In 397 a public disputation took place between himself and an aged Donatist bishop, named Fortunius, which however led to no practical result. In 408 another effort was made. At a Council held at Carthage the Donatists were invited to choose delegates prepared to discuss the contested points with delegates of the Catholic party. The invitation would seem to have been prompted by the spirit of charity, but the terms in which it was couched were not conciliatory; it was the language of men who believed themselves the sole possessors of the truth, addressed to men in error, and whose errors moreover it was their business to correct. The Donatists naturally rejected the overture.

It happened several years afterwards (410) that some Donatist bishops who had been summoned before the higher civil authorities, let fall the assertion that they would be well able to prove the truth of their cause if they were but allowed a patient hearing. The Catholic bishops, or Augustine on their behalf, seized eagerly upon the words; and the next year the Emperor Honorius gave orders for a conference to be held at Carthage between the two parties. The Pro-consul of Africa, Flavius Marcellinus, a man of ability, and friendly with Augustine, was appointed to preside. The terms on which the Donatists were invited to meet their opponents had the sound of extreme liberality. The Catholics declared themselves ready to surrender their bishoprics to the Donatists if these should be able to prove their case. But there is little merit in the profession of great sacrifices when there is not the remotest chance of

---

[1] "Why," he asks, "should any hesitate to throw themselves into the arms of that Church, which has always maintained herself by the succession of bishops in apostolic sees, by the faith of the people, the decisions of councils, and the authority of miracles? It is either a matchless impiety or a foolish arrogancy not to acknowledge her doctrine as a rule of faith."

these being called for. More feasible was another proposal, that if the Donatists should lose their cause, and should be willing to return to the Catholic Church, their bishops should be recognized as such; or, if preferred, the bishops of both parties should resign, and Donatists and Catholics unitedly choose new officers. "Be brothers with us in the Lord's inheritance," pleaded Augustine; "let us not for the sake of preserving our own dignities hinder the peace of Christ." He endeavoured at the same time to inspire his Catholic brethren with the charity that animated his own breast: "The eyes of the Donatists are inflamed, they must be treated tenderly. Let no one defend his faith by disputation, lest the spark let fall should kindle a great fire. If you should hear reviling language, endure it; be as though you had not heard it; be silent. 'Shall I be silent,' you may ask, 'when charges are brought against my bishop?' Yes, be silent, not that you are to allow the charges, but to bear them."

Accordingly there met at Carthage (A.D. 411) 286 bishops of the Catholic, and 279 of the Donatist party.[1] The latter, who stood in awe of the superior logic of Augustine, came to the conference reluctantly and full of distrust: this was manifest from the first. As the numbers were so great, Marcillinus directed that seven disputants from each side should be chosen. To this the Donatists objected; and the greater part of the first day was spent in debate on this point, and on other questions of a formal nature. At length they yielded, and nominated their representatives, of whom Petilian was the chief spokesman. Augustine of course was the leader on the Catholic side; and amongst his colleagues was Alypius.

When the deputies met again on the second day, the Donatists refused to be seated, saying: "The divine law forbids us to sit with the wicked." No notice was taken of this most offensive remark; but the Catholics declining out of courtesy to sit whilst their opponents were standing, Marcellinus also ordered his own chair to be removed. Two subjects chiefly occupied the conference. The first related to an historical question of a hundred years before, viz., the traditorship of Felix[2] and the validity of Cæcilian's con-

---

[1] One hundred and twenty Catholic bishops are said to have been absent, and sixty-four sees were vacant. Many of the Donatist bishops also were absent. It must be borne in mind that many of the villages of this province, as well as the towns, were then presided over by bishops.

[2] See *Early Church History*, pp. 222, 224. The *traditores*, or betrayers, were those who in the Diocletian persecution gave up to the magistrates their copies of the New Testament to be publicly burnt.

secration: into this we need not here enter. The other resolved itself into the great theological problem: What is the Church?

That which had been the apple of discord between Cyprian and Novatian,[1] the definition of the Church, was now keeping the Catholics and Donatists asunder. Both parties confounded the visible with the invisible Church, the cup with that which it contains. The Catholics maintained that, apart from the communion with the one visible Catholic Church, derived from the Apostles through the succession of bishops, there can be no communication of the Holy Spirit, and no salvation. Augustine thus confounded what Christianity had effected through the Church, with the Church itself as an outward institution. He did not see that the mighty effects brought about by the Gospel had been due to its inherent divine power; nay, that it might have produced far purer and mightier effects, had it not been in so many ways disturbed and checked in its operation by the imperfect vehicle of its transmission. In his exclusion of dissenters from the benefit of the Gospel, Augustine does not come behind Cyprian: "No one," he says, "attains to salvation, and eternal life, who has not Christ for his Head. But no one can have Christ for Head, who does not belong to his body, which is the Church. The entire Christ is the Head and the Body; the Head is the only-begotten Son of God, and the body is the Church. He who agrees not with Scripture in the doctrine concerning the Head, although he may stand in external communion with the Church, belongs not to the Church; and he who holds fast to all that Scripture teaches respecting the Head, and yet cleaves not to the unity of the Church, belongs not to the Church." Whenever the Donatists appealed to miracles, answers to prayer, visions, and the holy lives of their bishops, as evidences that the true Church was with them, Augustine met them by a reference to such passages of Scripture, as Matt. xxiv. 24: "There shall arise false Christs, and false prophets, and shall show great signs and wonders." "Let them not try to prove the genuineness of their Church by the councils of their bishops, or by deceitful miraculous signs, seeing that our Lord has put us on our guard against such proofs, but let them confine themselves to the Law and the Prophets, and the word of the only Shepherd."

The Donatists, like the Novatians, held that every Church which tolerates unworthy members within it, is itself polluted by communion with them, and thus ceases to be a true Christian Church; and by a natural but mistaken egotism, they took it for granted that they were themselves the true Church, and that the rest of

---

[1] See *Early Church History*, pp. 183—185.

Christendom was apostate and corrupt. Petilian argued that religious acts are operative only in a pure Church; that none but a blameless priest can administer the "sacraments." Augustine replied: "Often the conscience of man is unknown to me, but I am certain of the mercy of Christ."

Petilian: Whoever receives the faith through an unbeliever receives not faith but guilt.

Augustine: But Christ is faithful, from whom I receive faith and not guilt.

Petilian: The character of a thing depends on its origin and root; a genuine new birth can come only from good seed.

Augustine: My origin is Christ; my root is Christ; my head is Christ. He alone makes me free from 'guilt, who died for our sins and rose again for our justification; for I believe not in the minister by whom I am baptized, but in Him who justifies the sinner, so that my faith is counted to me for righteousness.

It was a foregone conclusion that Marcellinus should give sentence against the Donatists. They were adjudged to have lost their cause and to be guilty of heterodoxy. It was determined that the sect should be utterly blotted out; that all who would not conform should be deprived of both place and name, so that the whole province might be brought back into the Catholic unity. To this object, unhappily, Augustine lent the weight of his eloquence, learning, and character. The pro-consul forbade the Donatists thenceforth to assemble for worship, and ordered them to give up their church-buildings to the Catholics; at the same time admonishing the bishops to return to the one true Church. Appeal to the Emperor proved useless. Honorius, in 412, issued a decree enacting severe penalties against the sect. The malcontents were to be heavily fined in proportion to their rank, and if obstinate were to forfeit all their property. Slaves and peasants were to be scourged into conformity, and their Catholic masters who should neglect to act on this order were to be punished as Donatists. Bishops and clergy were to be banished, and the church property confiscated.

Very many yielded, whole communities even, as at Cirta, returning bodily to the Catholic Church. A greater number, however, nobly preferred to suffer the loss of liberty and property rather than do violence to their consciences. Three hundred bishops and thousands of the inferior clergy were torn from their churches and banished to the islands. Some even, in the madness of despair, committed suicide. "The persecution," says Julius Lloyd, "was as unrelenting as that by which Louis XIV. coerced the Huguenots. Some yielded through fear of the Imperial Edict, others through the extraordinary ability and fascinating influence of Augustine. Not Francis de Sales, Bossuet and Fénélon together, exercised over the Protestants of France a greater influence than Augustine alone, in winning to his side all who were accessible to eloquence or argument."[1]

The measures adopted were only too successful. The remnant of the Donatist Church, on the irruption of the Vandals, sided with the conquerors against the Empire, and were taken under their protection, but this Church never regained its influence. The Donatists lingered, however, till the pontificate of Gregory the Great at the end of the sixth century, but after his adverse edicts they disappear from history.

During this long controversy Augustine vacillated between gentle and forcible methods of overcoming the Donatists. At one time we find him appealing to the example of Elijah, who slew with his own hand the prophets of Baal; at another protesting against the penal measures by which it was proposed to coerce the schismatics: "You must go forward," he said, "simply with the word of truth; you must seek to overcome by argument, else all the effect will be that instead of open and avowed heretics you will have hypocritical Catholic Christians."

In a letter assigned to the year 408, Augustine defends with sophistical arguments the principle of coercion. "If any one saw his enemy running headlong to destroy himself, when he had become delirious through a dangerous fever, would he not in that case be much more truly rendering evil for evil if he permitted him to run on thus than if he took measures to have him seized and bound? ... Who can love us more than God? And yet God quickens us by salutary fear, and the sharp medicine of tribulation; afflicts with famine even the patriarchs, disquiets a rebellious people by severe chastisements, and refuses though thrice besought to take away from the Apostle the thorn in the flesh. . . . Whatever the true Mother does, even when something severe and bitter is felt by her children at her hands, she is not rendering evil for evil, but is applying the benefit of discipline to counteract the evil of sin, not with the hatred which seeks to harm, but with the love which seeks to heal."

At the Conference this question was necessarily uppermost in the

---

[1] A section of the Donatists, the Circumcelliones, burned the churches, maltreated the Catholic clergy, committed many other outrages, and laid wait for Augustine himself. The moderate Donatists looked on in horror, but were powerless to check these excesses. See *Early Church History*, p. 225.

minds of the Donatist leaders over whose heads the sword of the magistrate hung suspended by a hair. "Did the Apostles," asked Petilian, "ever persecute any one, or did Christ ever deliver any one over to the secular power? In dying for men he has given Christians the example to die, but not to kill." Another Donatist bishop, Gaudentius, pleaded: "The Saviour of souls sent fishermen, not soldiers, to preach his faith. What must that man think of God who defends Him with outward violence?" To these unanswerable arguments Augustine had nothing to reply but the same kind of sophism; "It is no doubt better to be led to God by instruction than by fear of punishment or affliction; but although the former is better, the other is not to be neglected. Bad servants must be reclaimed by the rod of temporal suffering." No atrocities, alas, will be wanting when for the sake of the supposed good, either of the whole or of individuals, the question, What is right? comes to be thus subordinated to the question, What is expedient? With a strange perversity of interpretation, Augustine adduced as a Scriptural warrant for the most flagrant acts of oppression, our Saviour's command in the parable of the Supper, "*compel* them to come in." His sanction of persecution became from this time forward a precedent of great authority in the Church. In it is to be found the germ of that whole system of spiritual despotism and intolerance which culminated in the Inquisition.

Whilst persecution was raging against the Donatists, Augustine embarked in the Pelagian controversy. Hitherto the doctrinal differences which agitated the Church had come from the East; this arose in the West.[1]

---

[1] The *germ* of the Pelagian doctrine had however for some time existed in the Eastern Church. Marius Mercator asserts that it had its birth in the Antiochian School, chiefly with Theodore of Mopsuestia (A.D. 392), and was carried to Rome by Rufinus, who, not daring himself to publish it, taught it to Pelagius. But it is to be noted that the cardinal doctrine of Pelagianism, man's natural goodness, is put by Athanasius, half a century earlier, into the mouth of Anthony. In his sermon to the monks the anchorite is made to say: "Virtue needs only the consent of the will, since it is within us, and originates in the mind, for the soul was created beautiful and upright. If it turn from its original nature, this is called vice. The thing therefore is not difficult; for if we remain as we were originally created, we are in a state of virtue. Now if this had to be obtained from without, there would be real difficulty; but since it is within us, let us guard the soul as a precious deposit which the Lord has committed to our keeping, in order that He may acknowledge his work to be as He made it.... In this we have the Lord for our fellow-worker." Upon which Ruffner observes: "The origin of this doctrine was not the Bible, nor even apostolical tradition, but the Platonism of the Fathers from the time of Justin Martyr. Plato taught the entire moral ability of man to purify his soul from sin."

About the end of the fourth century Pelagius,[1] a British monk, a man of learning and reputation, took up his abode in Rome, where he became the disciple of Rufinus. Amongst his acquaintances was Cælestius,[2] a native of Ireland, who had forsaken the profession of an advocate for the ascetic life. The two friends began to put forth views in direct antagonism to those of Augustine, who had for some time taught that man is by nature wholly evil, and in himself impotent to embrace and pursue good. They remained, however, unmolested until the sack of the city in 410, when Cælestius fled to Carthage. Here his doctrines excited alarm, and were condemned by a Council held in 412. Augustine brought his powerful intellect to bear upon the infant heresy, refuting it both by preaching and writing.

Pelagius, meantime, had gone to Palestine, where (415) he was charged with heresy before bishop John of Jerusalem, and a synod of his clergy. Orosius, a young Spanish ecclesiastic, who had been living with Jerome, stood forth as his accuser. When Orosius supported his charge by a reference to Augustine, Pelagius contemptuously asked, "What is Augustine to me?" Orosius answered, that a man who presumed thus to speak of the bishop to whom the North African Church owed her restoration, deserved to be excommunicated. John, who also made little account of the authority of Augustine, exclaimed, "I will be Augustine," and undertook himself the defence of Pelagius.[3] The synod, on the ground of jurisdiction, referred the question to the bishop of Rome. In the same year, before a synod at Diospolis, the ancient Lydda, Pelagius was tried and pronounced innocent. It was easy for a doctrinal heresy to take root in the East.

Cælestius, who had returned to Rome, seized this occasion to appeal against the sentence of the Carthaginian synod. A council was called by Zosimus, the Roman bishop; and on Cælestius disavowing all dogmas which the Roman See had condemned, he was exculpated, Zosimus sending a letter of reproof to the Africans for listening too readily to charges against good men. But Augustine and the African prelates were not to be thus trifled with. They assembled again in synod at Carthage (A.D. 418), asserted their independence of Rome, and passed nine canons, which came to be regarded as the bulwark of the Church against Pelagianism. The Emperor Honorius now interposed, declared the Pelagians to be

[1] This name is the Greek form for Morgan—i.e., *sea-born*.
[2] Jerome describes Cælestius as *Scotorum pultibus prægravatus*, "heavy with Scotch porridge." The term Scot at that time signified a native of Ireland.
[3] John spoke only Greek, Orosius only Latin, but Pelagius both languages.

heretics, and subjected them to disabilities and penalties. Upon this Zosimus, pressed by the Court and by the anti-Pelagian party, re-opened the matter, and summoned Cælestius before a fresh council. But Cælestius quitted Rome; and Zosimus excommunicated him and Pelagius as heretics, at the same time requiring all bishops to subscribe the African canons. Pelagius and his adherents were banished.[1]

The Pelagian doctrine may be thus stated. Adam was created mortal and would have died, even if he had not sinned; and men come now into the world in the same state in which Adam was created. Adam's sin brought injury to his descendants, not by transmission, but by the influence of example. As man is able to discern good from evil, so he has power to will and to work what is good; as by our own free will we run into sin, so by the same free will are we able to repent and reform, and raise ourselves to the highest degree of virtue and piety. Pelagius, indeed, spoke of grace, but by it he understood that knowledge of his will which God has given—the law and the Gospel, the example of the Saviour's life. He denied that the help of the Holy Spirit is necessary to man's salvation. He professed to follow Scripture, but when Scripture crossed his opinions he forsook that safe guide, and gave himself up to the beguiling direction of his own reason.

Augustine's teaching was the very opposite of all this. He held that death, temporal and eternal, with all the diseases of the body, are the consequences and penalty of sin. He denied, sometimes absolutely, sometimes in a modified sense, the freedom of the will, and taught that without grace man can do only evil. Original sin, derived from Adam's transgression, he held to be a cardinal doctrine of the Gospel, and that God exacts the penalty due to his broken law, even from the heathen and from infants of the tenderest age if unbaptized. In intimate connection with this doctrine he maintained the existence of an eternal decree, separating antecedently to any difference of merit one portion of the human race from another—ordaining one to everlasting life, abandoning the other to everlasting misery. This he allowed to be a perplexing mystery, and repugnant to our natural ideas of God's justice, but he defended it on the ground of his inscrutable and sovereign will. Predestination, moreover, implied irresistible grace and final perseverance.

Augustine did not all at once arrive at these conclusions; and even when he had matured his system he shrank from its legitimate

---

[1] Cælestius went to Constantinople, where he was kindly received by Nestorius.

consequences. His charity was better than his logic. We find him reproving some who asserted that God has predestinated the wicked, not only to suffer eternal punishment, but also to commit sin, their sinful actions being determined by an inevitable necessity. And in a letter (A.D. 426) he writes, "We have been visited by two young men who report that your monastery has been agitated by dissension. Some, they told us, entertained such exalted views of grace as wholly to deny free-will, and even maintained that in the day of judgment God will not render to every one according to his works. Most of you, however, hold a different opinion, maintaining that man's free-will is assisted by God's grace, and by it disposed to what is right; and that when the Lord shall come to render to every one according to his works, He will judge those works only to be good which he has prepared for us to walk in; and this I pronounce to be the right opinion. . . . If there be no grace of God, how does He save the world; if there be no free-will, how is He to judge the world?"

Augustine erred through supposing that divine truth can be fully grasped by human reason, and was obliged to explain away a host of clear and positive statements of Scripture, which controverted his positions.[1] "His was the error," observes Canon Mozley, "of those who follow without due consideration the strong first impression which the human mind entertains, that there must be some definite truth to be arrived at on the question, and who therefore imagine that they cannot be doing other than good service if they only add to what is defective, enough to make it complete, or take away from what is ambiguous, enough to make it decisive. . . If revelation as a whole does not speak explicitly, revelation did not intend to do so; and to impose a definite truth upon it when it designedly stops short of one, is as real an error of interpretation as to deny a truth which it expresses."

Dr. Schaff refers the two systems to the characters of their authors. "Pelagius was an upright monk, who, without inward conflicts, won for himself in the way of tranquil development a legal piety which knew neither the depths of sin nor the heights of grace. Augustine passed through sharp convulsions and bitter conflicts, till he was overtaken by the unmerited grace of God. He had a soaring intellect and a glowing heart, and only found peace after he had long been tossed by the waves of passion; he tasted

---

[1] For instance, he distorts the plain words in 1 Tim. ii. 4, "Who willeth that all men should be saved," into "all manner of men," rich and poor, learned and unlearned, and he makes the sense to be, that all who are saved, are saved only by the will of God.

all the misery of sin, and then all the glory of redemption. . . . The Pelagian controversy turns upon the mighty antithesis of sin and grace. . . . It comes at last to the question whether redemption is chiefly a work of God or of man; whether man needs to be born anew, or merely improved. The soul of the Pelagian system is human freedom; the soul of the Augustinian is divine grace. The one system proceeds from the liberty of choice to legalistic piety; the other from the bondage of sin to the evangelical liberty of the children of God. The one loves to admire the dignity and strength of man; the other loses itself in adoration of the glory and omnipotence of God. The one flatters natural pride, the other is a gospel for penitent publicans and sinners. Pelagianism begins with self-exaltation, and ends with the sense of self-deception and impotency. Augustinianism casts man first into the dust of humiliation and despair, in order to lift him on the wings of grace to supernatural strength, and lead him . . . up to the heaven of the knowledge of God."

For his clear setting forth of the doctrine of divine grace, apart from the presumptuous theory of predestination, the Church owes to Augustine a debt of lasting gratitude. In his enunciation of this evangelical truth he stood opposed to the traditional principle of salvation by good works, which was taught by almost every writer of the time. And although it was left for the Reformed Church fully to endorse his apostolic teaching on this point, yet in every century, thoughtful and humble disciples accepted it for themselves, and were edified by his Christlike spirit. But the Catholic Church, through her doctors and councils, continued to uphold the efficacious merit of good works, on which the Council of Trent, in 1546, set its seal, ruling that "If any one shall say that justifying faith is none other than a trust in the divine mercy forgiving our sins for Christ's sake, or that it is that trust alone by which we are justified, let him be accursed."

Hitherto the North African province had escaped the scourge of the Northern hordes which had laid Europe waste. Its turn was now come. Genseric, King of the Vandals, the most terrible of all the barbarian leaders, crossed from Spain in 429, and ravaged the country with all the atrocities in which uncivilized races indulge when let loose upon a wealthy and luxurious population. The miseries the Catholics had inflicted on the Donatists were now multiplied upon themselves.

After overrunning nearly the whole province, the invading army laid siege to Hippo. During several months the city was successfully defended by the Roman general Count Boniface. Augustine was old and infirm. "The devastation of his country," says his biographer Possidonius, "embittered his days. He saw the towns ruined, the country houses destroyed, the inhabitants slain or fugitives, the churches destitute of priests, the virgins and monks dispersed. Some had succumbed to torments, others had perished by the sword, others again were taken captive and served hard and brutal masters."

Several bishops, with the remnant of their flocks, took refuge in Hippo, and found shelter in Augustine's house. "The misfortunes," writes Possidonius, "of which we were witnesses were the topic of our daily conversation. We pondered the terrible judgments which the Divine justice was accomplishing before our eyes, and we said: 'Thou art just and good, and thy judgments are true.' We mingled our griefs, our groans and our tears, and offered them to the Father of all mercies and God of all comfort, beseeching Him to deliver us from the evils we endured and those we feared." "What I ask of God," said Augustine one day at table, "is, that He would be pleased to deliver this city from the enemies who besiege it; or if He has otherwise ordained, that He will give his servants strength to endure the evils He shall permit to befall them; or at least that He will withdraw me from this world and call me to Himself." This last prayer was soon granted.

In the third month of the siege, Augustine was attacked with fever. A man brought to him his sick son, and entreated him to lay his hands upon him. The dying bishop asked why, if he had the power to heal the sick, he should not exercise it first upon himself? The father replied that he had had a dream, in which he heard a voice say: "Go seek the bishop Augustine, ask him to lay hands on thy son, and he shall be healed." Upon this, Augustine did as the man requested, and (so Possidonius relates) the youth immediately recovered.

It was a maxim with Augustine that even the most experienced Christian ought not to die without a season of penitential retirement. Accordingly, as he felt death approaching, he begged his friends to leave him entirely to himself, and not to enter his chamber, except with his physician or the attendants. He caused the penitential psalms to be written out large, and hung before him upon the wall; and in this manner, in solitude and prayer, he passed the last six days of his life. He died on the 28th of August, 480, aged seventy-six years.

With Augustine departed the glory of the North African Church. "Rising with Tertullian towards the end of the second century, it ran a fervid course like its own ardent sun, and set almost as precipitately in the early part of the fifth." The name of Christian still survived, but little more was left than the dregs of Christianity, to withstand, two centuries later, the fury of the Mohammedan invasion.[1]

Since the apostles, no man has occupied a more important place in the Church than Augustine, or has exercised more lasting influence on mankind. "He was," says Schaff, "a philosophical and theological genius of the first order, towering like a pyramid above his age, and looking down commandingly upon succeeding centuries. He had a mind uncommonly fertile and deep, bold and soaring, and with it, what is better, a heart full of Christian love and humility. He stands of right by the side of the greatest philosophers of antiquity and of modern times. . . . With royal munificence he scattered ideas in passing which have set in mighty motion other lands and later times."

Want of courage, no less than an undue reverence for tradition, hindered Augustine from standing forth as a Church Reformer. He confesses that Christianity, which God made free, appointing few sacraments and easy to be observed, had in his time become more burdened with ceremonies than the Jewish Church itself; and he professes himself ready to abolish those customs which are neither contained in Scripture, nor enjoined by councils, nor confirmed by universal practice. But here he stops. The more flagrant abuses of the age were left untouched. "I dare not," he says, "condemn more freely many things, because I must take care not to offend the piety of some and the pugnacity of others."

It is with no desire to dwell with harshness on the defects in Augustine's character, but because his surpassing gifts must not blind us to his deficiencies, that we add Isaac Taylor's words. "Everyone must allow this eminent man to have been a fervent and heavenly-minded Christian. That grace which prevails over nature, rendering whoever receives it a new creature in Christ Jesus, shone in him conspicuously; and his devotional writings come home to the heart of every spiritually-minded reader. . . . No moment in the history of the Church can be named more fearfully critical than when the bishop of Hippo stood before Christendom in the prime and vigour of his religious course. The fate of Europe was trembling on the point between an abyss of ignorance and anarchy, and a possible renovation. . . . There was

---

[1] At the period of the Vandal conquest the North African provinces numbered no fewer than 500 Catholic bishops; in A.D. 457, less than eighteen years afterwards, only three remained. There appears to have been no bishop of Hippo after Augustine.

a downward rush toward all those follies and abuses which rendered Christianity an object of contempt to the Saracen conquerors of the next century. Yet was there at the same time a rising movement towards reform; more than two or three raised a remonstrant voice against the frauds and illusions of the age. . . . Who better than Augustine might have led this early reformation? . . . O, that it had been whispered to him at that dark moment, to think, and speak, and act as a true father of the Church! . . . Fruitless regrets! Augustine, the last hope of his times, joined hands with the besotted bigots around him, who would listen to no reproofs. Superstition and spiritual despotism, illusion, knavery, and abject formalism, received a new warrant from the high seat of influence which he occupied."[1]

Augustine was a most voluminous writer. His *Confessions* have been freely used in the foregoing narrative. The treatise *On the Trinity* is associated with a well-known legendary anecdote. As he was walking to and fro on the sea-shore of Hippo, he saw what appeared to be a little boy busily employed in digging a hole in the sand and then filling it with water, which he fetched in a cockle-shell from the sea. Augustine paused and spoke to him: "What art thou doing, my child?" "I am trying to empty the sea into this hole which I have dug." "My child, it is impossible to get the great sea into that little hole." "Not more impossible, Augustine," replied the angel (for such he was), "than for thy finite mind to comprehend the mystery of the Trinity."

His most famous work is entitled *The City of God*. "The later opponents of Christianity among the heathen charged the misfortunes and the decline of the Roman Empire on the overthrow of idolatry. Augustine answered the charge in his immortal work *The City of God* (that is, the Church of Christ), upon which he laboured twelve years, from 413 to 426, amidst the storms of the great migration, and towards the close of his life. He was not wanting in appreciation of the old Roman virtues, and he attributes to these the former greatness of the empire, and to the decline of them he imputes her growing weakness. But he rose at the same time far above the superficial view which estimates persons and things by the scale of earthly profit and loss, and of temporary success. *The City of God* is the most powerful, comprehensive, profound, and fertile production in refutation of heathenism and

---

[1] Augustine not only endorsed Ambrose's discovery of the buried martyrs under the altar at Milan (see *ante*, p. 63), but himself presents us with a tissue of miraculous cures wrought by the bones of the martyr Stephen, quite as incredible.

vindication of Christianity, which the ancient Church has bequeathed to us, and forms a worthy close to her literary contest with Græco-Roman paganism. It is a grand funeral discourse upon the departing universal empire of heathenism, and a lofty salutation to the approaching universal order of Christianity. While even Jerome deplored in the destruction of the city the downfall of the empire, as the omen of the approaching doom of the world, the African Father saw in it only a passing revolution preparing the way for new conquests of Christianity. Standing at that remarkable turning-point of history, he considers the origin, progress and end of the perishable kingdom of this world, and the imperishable kingdom of God, from the fall of man to the final judgment, where at last they fully and for ever separate into hell and heaven."

We conclude our notice of Augustine with the passage in which he gives "a local habitation" to the faculty of Memory,

"I come to the fields and spacious palaces of my MEMORY, where are the treasures of countless images brought into it from all manner of things by the senses. There is stored up, also, whatsoever we think, either by enlarging or diminishing, or any other way varying those things which the senses apprehended: yea, and whatever else has been committed to it which forgetfulness has not yet swallowed up and buried. When I enter this store-house, I require what I will to be brought forth, and some things come instantly; others must be longer sought for, and are fetched, as it were, out of some inner receptacle; others, again, rush out in troops, and whilst something else is desired and enquired for, start forth, as who should say, 'Is it perchance we?' These I drive away with the hand of my heart from before the face of my remembrance, until what I wish discovers itself and comes to view out of its secret place. Other things present themselves without effort, and in continuous order as they are called for, those in front giving place to those that follow, and as they make way returning to their hiding-place ready to come forth again when I will. All which takes place when I repeat a thing from memory. All these things, each of which entered by its own avenue, are severally and under general heads there laid up, being received into that great store-house of the memory, in her numberless secret and inexpressible windings, to be forthcoming at need. Yet it is not the things themselves that enter in, but only the images of the things, which how they are formed who can tell? Even when I dwell in darkness and silence, in my memory I can produce colours if I will, and discern betwixt black and white; sounds also are there lying dormant, and laid up as it were apart. For these, too, I call, and forthwith they appear; and though my tongue be still and my throat mute, yet can I sing as much as I will. The same with the other things piled up by the other senses; so that I discern the scent of lilies from violets, though smelling nothing. In that vast court of my memory there are present also with me heaven, earth, sea, and whatever I can think upon in them. There also meet I with myself and recall myself, and when, where, and what I have done, and under what feelings. Out of the same store do I myself with the past combine fresh and fresh likenesses of things which I have experienced or have believed, and thence again infer future actions, events and hopes, on all which I reflect as if present. Excessive great is this power of memory, O my God, a large and boundless chamber; who has ever sounded the depths of it? Men go abroad to admire the height of the mountains, the mighty billows of the sea, the broad flow of the rivers, the compass of the ocean, and the courses of the stars, and yet they omit to wonder at themselves."

CHAPTER X.

The Spirit of the Age.

Public Worship.—"Three centuries and more," says Cardinal Newman, "were necessary for the infant Church to attain her mature and perfect form and due stature. Athanasius, Basil, and Ambrose are the fully instructed doctors of her doctrine, morals and discipline." Strange interpretation of Church History! The presumptuous forbidding to marry, the plagiarism of Brahminical self-torture, the invocation of the martyrs and adoration of their bones and ashes, the fond belief in lying wonders, the exaltation of priestly rule to the prejudice of the civil power instead of the unworldly kingdom of Jesus, are these the tokens of fully instructed teaching in doctrine, morals and discipline?

The preceding biographies have presented in some fulness the state of the Church in the fourth and fifth centuries. It will only be necessary here to add a few additional touches.

To begin with the order of public worship, as it was conducted in Constantinople and other great cities. "A stranger on entering the spacious open court in front of the church, which was flanked on either side by cloisters, beheld the fountain where the worshippers were expected to wash their hands before entering the divine presence. Lingering in these cloisters, and pressing around the faithful to solicit their prayers, he would observe men, pale, dejected, and clad in sack-cloth. These were the first class of penitents, men of notorious guilt, whom only a long period of humiliating probation could admit even within hearing of the service. As he advanced to the church door, he had to pass the scrutiny of the doorkeepers, who guarded admission, and distributed the several classes of worshippers to their proper seats. Nearest to the door were placed the catechumens and the less guilty penitents of the second order. Amongst these also Jews and heathens were admitted, that they might profit by the religious instruction. He would see the walls of the church lined with marbles; the roof often ceiled with mosaic, and supported by lofty columns with gilded capitals; the doors inlaid with ivory or silver, the distant altar glittering with precious stones. In the midst of the nave stood the pulpit or reading desk, around which were arranged the choristers. When the chanting was ended, one of the inferior clergy ascended the pulpit, and read the portion of Scripture for the day. He was succeeded by the preacher, a presbyter, or a bishop, selected for his learning and eloquence, whose discourse was frequently interrupted by the plaudits of the auditory. Around the pulpit, also, was the last order of penitents, who prostrated themselves in humble reverence during the prayers and the benediction of the bishop. Here the steps of the uninitiated stranger must pause. He might only behold at respectful distance the striking scene : first of the baptized worshippers in their ranks, the women in galleries above; beyond, in still further secluded sanctity, on an elevated semi-circle, the bishop in the midst of his attendant clergy. Even the gorgeous throne of the Emperor was below this platform. Before it stood the altar, spread with a cloth of fine linen, and in some churches overhung with a richly-wrought canopy. In the East, embroidered curtains or light doors altogether hid it from view. Such was the ceremonial as it was addressed to the multitude. But as soon as the liturgy commenced, the catechumens were dismissed, and the church doors were closed.[1] To add to the impressiveness, night was sometimes chosen for the Christian, as it had formerly been for the pagan mysteries."

How unlike all this to the simplicity of the primitive worship! If,

---

[1] The dismissal of the uninitiate was called *Missa Catechumenorum*, that of the baptized at the end of the service came in later ages to be known as *Missa Fidelium*. By degrees the word *Missa* was retained only for the latter, and was applied, not to the act of dismissal, but to the service itself; and thus in its slightly altered form of *Mass* it came to signify the consecration and oblation of the *Host* (*hostia*, victim or sacrifice).

however, the stranger had happened upon the birthday of some popular Saint, he would have beheld a still greater contrast. "As soon as he passed the door his senses would be greeted by the perfume of flowers,[1] and the noon-day glare of lamps and tapers. He would see the floor covered with a prostrate crowd of pilgrims, imprinting their devout kisses on the walls and pavement, and directing their prayers to the relics of the saint, which were usually concealed behind a linen or silken veil." Suspended on the walls or on the pillars of the church he would see the votive offerings of the faithful, the model in gold, silver or wood, of an eye, a hand, a foot, the picture of a shipwreck, the memento of some special blessing. How early this imitation of a pagan usage was first practised, cannot be said with certainty, but it was already in vogue, both in the East and West, at the period we are now reviewing.[2]

The truth is that the public worship of the Christians had approached perilously near to that of the ancient Greeks and Romans. Thus there were in both rituals splendid robes, mitres, tiaras, croziers (identical with the *lituus*, or crook of the augur), processions, lustrations, images, gold and silver vessels, and, in the course of the fifth century, incense. The heathens supposed that their country would be more prosperous in proportion as the temples of the gods and heroes were multiplied, and this notion descended to the Christians. New churches were continually being dedicated to Christ and the saints, in order to render heavenly assistance

---

[1] The use of flowers, whether for strewing the graves of the dead, or adorning the churches, dates from the latter part of the fourth century. The former of these two customs (they would not have dreamed of the latter) was repudiated by the Early Christians as a heathen observance. One of the earliest passages in which it is alluded to is in Ambrose: "I will not sprinkle his tomb with flowers, but with the sweet scent of Christ's spirit; let others scatter baskets of lilies; our lily is Christ." Jerome says: "Some husbands strew over the tombs of their wives, violets, roses, lilies, and purple flowers." The practice was soon extended to the churches, first to those of the martyrs, which in their origin were only enlarged sepulchres, and then to the basilicas. Jerome commends Nepotianus for decorating both kinds of buildings with flowers, foliage, and vine leaves.

[2] The classical student is familiar with this custom. Many offerings, arms, legs, and other parts of the body, in metal, stone, or clay, which were formerly hung up in the temples, are still preserved in museums and cabinets. Persons saved from shipwreck used to hang up their clothes in the temple of Neptune, with a picture representing their danger and escape. Soldiers discharged from service suspended their arms to Mars; gladiators, their swords to Hercules; and poets, the fillets of their hair to Apollo. The temple of Æsculapius, however, in which were hung up tablets recording the cures wrought by that god, seems to have been the chief model for the Christian shrine.

more powerful and certain. As was to be expected, the idea of sanctity which had become attached to places of worship lost nothing of its force; as we have more than once seen in preceding chapters, the churches, like the persons of the priests, were surrounded with an ever increasing halo of solemn mystery.

BAPTISM AND THE EUCHARIST.—We drew attention in the former volume to the explicit declarations of John the Baptist, our Lord Himself, and Peter, that whereas John's baptism was with water, Christ's disciples should be baptized with the Holy Ghost; and we at the same time pointed out, how early this grand distinction began to be lost sight of. Even the more thoughtful so identified the spiritual change with the external rite, as to be unable to conceive of the one without the other; whilst in the belief of the multitude, who lost sight altogether of the former, immersion in water removed, as by a magical and instantaneous process, all the defilement of sin, and made men fit for Heaven.

The writers of the previous century, Tertullian, Hippolytus and others, insist so unmistakably on this almost talismanic power as to leave little to be added by those who followed them. Chrysostom clothes the same idea in his own fervid language. "Although a man should be foul with every human vice, the blackest that can be named, yet when he descends into the baptismal pool, he comes up from the divine waters purer than the beams of noon. . . . The baptized put on a royal garment, a purple dipped in the blood of the Lord." Basil urged baptism in his most declamatory style. "Beware lest procrastinating and providing no oil, thou should come upon the fatal day. Who in that hour shall administer the rite? It is night; no helper is at hand; death is near. . . . 'Alas, I neglected to cast off the burden of my sins when it would have been so easy! Miserable wretch! I washed not my sins away in the sweet waters of baptism; and lo, I perish! Even now I might have been sitting in the choir of angels, might have shared the delights of heaven.'" Gregory of Nyssa states that when alarmed by earthquakes, pestilences, or other public calamities, such multitudes rushed to be baptized, that the clergy were oppressed by the labour of receiving them. It was the same superstitious view which induced Constantine the Great to defer his baptism to the latest hour of life.[1]

Each successive age contributed its share towards the conversion of the morsel of bread which the priest had blessed, into an object of adoration and supernatural efficacy, as it is this day regarded in

---

[1] See *Early Church History*, p. 245.

the Romish Church. It is true that the best writers of this period see beyond the external, and dwell upon that inward and heavenly communion with Christ, of which the outward observance, if now of any further service, is only a sign and a memorial. Thus Athanasius, commenting on John vi. 62, declares that the partaking of the flesh and blood of Christ is not there to be understood in a literal sense. "Christ," he says, "mentions on this occasion his ascension to heaven for the very purpose of turning away men's minds from sensuous notions, and leading them to the idea of a spiritual nourishment, inasmuch as He communicates Himself to each after a spiritual manner." And Jerome: "If the bread which came down from heaven is the Lord's body, and the wine which He gave to his disciples his blood, let us go up with the Lord into that great and high room, and receive at his hand the cup which is the New Covenant. He invites us to the feast, and is Himself our meat; He eats with us, and we eat Him. . . . Jesus Christ has given his blood to redeem us, and this may be taken either for his spiritual and divine flesh, whereof He saith Himself, 'My flesh is meat indeed, and my blood is drink indeed;' or for his flesh which was crucified, and his blood which in his passion was spilt with the soldier's lance." So Augustine: "The flesh without the spirit profits nothing. The inward act of feeding is to be distinguished from the outward. The former is a privilege only of believers; the unbelieving and the unworthy receive nothing but the *sacrament* of the body and blood of Christ."

But the Fathers of the fourth century do not always write thus soberly. Take an example from Ambrose's funeral oration over his brother Satyrus. The vessel in which Satyrus was returning to Italy ran upon the rocks. Unbaptized and uninitiated in the "mysteries," the young man sought amongst those on board for a morsel of the consecrated bread, which when he had found he wrapped in a sacrificial kerchief and tied about his neck. Thus armed, he fearlessly leapt into the sea, believing himself to be so well protected as to need no other help.

VIRGINITY.—Foremost amongst the elements of which the ascetic life was composed is the vow of perpetual celibacy. How the unmarried state came in the fourth century to occupy the place that martyrdom had held during the times of persecution, and how, by its introduction as a rule of devout Christian life, one of the most awful and emphatic predictions of the New Testament was accomplished, has already been shown in the *Early Church History*.[1]

---

[1] Pt. ii. c. xvii. "God, when he would form a happy and holy world, said, 'It is not good for man to be alone.' Satan, inspiring the apostacy to make

From the time of the Council of Nicæa, the virgin state is the favourite theme with all the great Church writers; and is presented by them sometimes in the very language of the Oriental theosophy. The great object was the mortification of the flesh; and in this exercise, observes Ruffner, Virginity was the most difficult to attain, requiring the aid of all other mortifications. "So to thin the blood, attenuate the flesh, enfeeble the nerves, dry up the marrow, and exhaust the constitution, as to destroy the natural appetite," in this it was considered lay the secret of overcoming "both the demon without and the demon within." Even Origen, so early as the third century, says: "When we abstain from flesh, we do it to chasten the body and reduce it to servitude, in order that we may extinguish our carnal affections, and so put to death our corporeal actions." This kind of teaching was carried much further by the writers of the next century.

To begin with Athanasius. "The Son of God has, besides his other gifts, granted us to have on earth an image of the sanctity of angels, namely, Virginity. The maidens who possess this virtue, and whom the Church Catholic is wont to call the brides of Christ, are admired even by the Gentiles as being the temple of the Word. Nowhere, except among us Christians, is this holy profession perfected; so that we may appeal to this very fact as a convincing proof that with us the true religion is to be found." "A great virtue truly is virginity," exclaims Basil, "which, to say all in a word, renders man like to the incorruptible God. For the soul, holding to the idea of the true good, and soaring up to it as on the wing of this incorruptness, and perceiving that by this alone the incorruptible God can be worthily worshipped, brings up the virginity of the body as an obsequious handmaid to assist her in the worship of beauty like her own."

The two Gregorys teem with the same kind of dreamy philosophy. Nazianzen thus addresses a virgin: "Thou hast chosen the angelic life, and hast ranged thyself with those who are unyoked [the angels]; be not thou borne downward to the flesh; be not thou borne downward to matter." Nyssen writes: "In order that we may, with a clear eye, gaze upon the light of the intellectual universe, we must disengage ourselves from every mundane affection"; "that," in the words of Chrysostom, "the soul disengaged from its trammels and all earthly thoughts may wing its way to its home and its native soil." Chrysostom indeed falls into

---

the world and even the Church unholy and unhappy, said, 'It is good for man to be alone; nay, it is *better* for him to be alone.'"

a rhapsody when he contemplates the lustre of virginity. "The virgin when she goes abroad should strike all with amazement, as if an angel had just come down from heaven. All who look upon her should be thrown into stupor at the sight of her sanctity. When she sits at church it is in the profoundest silence, her eye catches nothing of the objects around her, she sees neither women nor men, but her Spouse only. Not only does she hide herself from the eyes of men, she avoids the society of secular women also. Who is it that shall dare approach her? Where is the man that shall venture to touch this flaming spirit? All stand aloof, willing or unwilling, all are fixed in amazement as if there were before their eyes a mass of incandescent and sparkling gold."

Between these soaring imaginations, however, and the actual life of multitudes of those who assumed the vows of celibacy, a great gulf intervened. In the same treatise from which these words are taken Chrysostom thus discloses the reverse side of the picture. "Alas, my soul! our virginity has fallen into contempt. The veil that parted it off from matrimony is rent by shameless hands; the holy of holies is trodden under foot, and its grave and tremendous sanctities have become profane, and are thrown open to all; and that which once was had in reverence, as so much more excellent than wedlock, is sunk far below it. Nor is it the enemy that has effected all this, but the virgins themselves!"

That the monastic vow was very imperfectly kept, both by men and women, is notorious. Denouncing the practice of the unmarried clergy, who, under the name of spiritual sisters, kept young women, often "consecrated virgins," as housekeepers, Chrysostom exclaims: "What a spectacle it is to enter the cell of a *solitary* brother, and see the apartment hung about with female gear. But it is a greater riddle still to visit the dwelling of a *rich* monk; for you find the *solitary* surrounded with a bevy of lasses, just, one might say, like the leader of a company of singing and dancing girls. What can be more disgraceful! Forbidden by the apostolic precept to meddle at all with temporal matters, he spends his time, not only in mundane, but even in effeminate trifles. He is sent to the silversmith's to inquire if my lady's mirror is finished, if her vase is ready, if her scent-cruet has been returned; for matters have come to such a pass that the virgins use more toilet luxuries than those who have not taken the vow. From the silversmith's he must run to the perfumer's to inquire about her aromatics; from the perfumer's to the linendraper's; and thence to the upholsterer's. For the good man is so complaisant that he will perform any errand, however trivial. Add to all these cares the jarrings and scoldings which beset a house full of pampered women! Paul says: 'Be ye not the servants of *men;*' how then shall we be the slaves of women!"

Of the 150 extant epistles of Jerome, the greater part have Virginity for their subject, and abound in exhortations, cautions, and rebukes, to these "holy pets of the Church." "Some priests," he says, in a letter to Eustochium, "walk forth in the most public manner, and by sly winks draw after them crowds of young men. They dress in thin purple robes, and tie their hair loose that it may fall over their shoulders, over which a mantle is thrown. They wear short sleeves and thin slippers, and go mincing as they walk. And this is all their virginity." The monks were no better. "Some you may see with their loins girt, clad in dingy cloaks, with long beards, who yet can never break away from the company of women; but live under the same roof, sit at the same tables, are waited upon by young girls, and want nothing proper to the married state except—wives!"

The upholders of celibacy relied upon the example of the Virgin Mary; the dogma of her perpetual virginity was essential to their position: so early a writer as Clement of Alexandria alludes to it. The unsophisticated reader of the New Testament is left in no doubt that Mary had children after the birth of our Lord. The language of Matt. i. 25, and Luke ii. 7, with the mention of the brothers of our Lord,[1] is too plain and conclusive to be touched by any authority of Church Father, Council, or Pope. "To have admitted," remarks Isaac Taylor, "the plain sense of the intelligible phrase employed by the inspired evangelist would have been tantamount to a betrayal of the whole scheme of religious celibacy. Only let it have been granted that the virtue of the 'mother of God' was nothing better than real virtue, and that her piety was a principle of the heart, and that her purity was the purity of the affections; and only allow that she was a 'holy woman,' and an exemplary wife and mother, such as the Apostles speak of and commend; only to have done this, would have marred the entire scheme of theology and morals, as fancied and fashioned by the ancient Church. The perpetual inviolateness of the blessed virgin was well felt to be the keystone of the building."

FASTING.—This observance had been gradually removed from the place which it occupies in the New Testament and in the earliest class of Church writers, into a different sphere. New motives and

---

[1] Matt. xii. 46; John vii. 5. In this case, as in others, the plainest meaning of words and fullest testimony of Scripture were set at nought by the Church to attain her object.

a new object gave to it a totally new character. The Church at Antioch fasted as they ministered to the Lord, and again when they separated Saul and Barnabas for the work of the Gospel; and Paul shows us how the combat in the spiritual arena is to be waged: "I buffet my body and bring it into bondage, lest by any means after that I have preached to others I myself should be rejected."[1] The widely different place which this observance occupied in the fourth century, and the scrupulous and painful manner in which it was practised,[2] has been repeatedly presented in the foregoing biographies. "What," asks Athanasius, "does Christ require of thee, but a pure heart and a body unsoiled and brought down with fasting?" "Wouldst thou learn," writes Chrysostom, "what an ornament fasting is to men, what a guard and preservative? Look well to the monastic tribe, blessed and admirable! Men though they are, fasting makes angels of them. God, when He made man, instantly committed him into the hands of Fasting as to a loving mother entrusted with his safety.[3] If, then, fasting were indispensable even in Paradise, how much more so out of Paradise?"

These maxims of Chrysostom's made, however, but a faint impression on the volatile people of Constantinople. "If," he says, in one of his sermons, "I ask why hast thou been to the bath to-day? thou wilt reply, to cleanse my body in preparation for the Fast. And if I ask why didst thou get drunk yesterday? again thou wilt reply, because I am to fast to-day." "We see," he says again, "nothing but people making merry, and saying to one another, 'Victory is ours; Mid-Lent is over.' . . . I know some who, in the middle of Lent, dread already the fast of the next year." The mass of the population indeed alternated between ceremonial observances and sensual excess. The Church fasts, which were observed with superstitious strictness, were succeeded by disgraceful outbreaks of debauchery. Basil gives on one occasion as a reason for protracting his sermon, that although it was in the midst of the fast, many of the congregation, as soon as the service was over, would fly to the gaming-table.

The Fasts were sometimes observed with such scrupulosity that the Church had to interfere. Timothy, bishop of Alexandria, was called upon to decide the question, gravely propounded, whether a

---

[1] Acts xii. 2, 3; 1 Cor. ix. 27.

[2] The Christian anchorites performed miracles of fasting, but they scarcely come up to those of the Hindoo saints. In one of the Brahminical fasts the devotee is neither to eat nor drink for twelve days and nights. In another he drinks only warm water.

[3] Does this refer to Genesis ii. 16, 17?

man who fasted in order to communicate, and who had by chance swallowed a drop of water, ought to refrain. He replied that he ought so much the more to communicate, because it was an artifice of the devil to hinder him.[1]

ALMSGIVING.—When the fatal maxim was admitted that salvation is to be purchased by good works, the blessed grace of " considering the poor" soon lost its original savour, and was degraded into a matter of barter between the soul and heaven. Chrysostom asks, "What! hast thou not understood, from the instance of the ten virgins in the Gospel, how that those who, although proficients in virginity, yet possessed not Almsgiving, were excluded from the mystical banquet? Virginity is the fire of the lamps, and almsgiving is the oil. As the flame unless supplied with a stream of oil disappears, so virginity unless it is united with Almsgiving is extinguished. Now who are the vendors of this oil? The poor who sit for alms about the doors of the church. And for how much is it to be bought? For what thou wilt, for so much as thou hast. Hast thou a penny? Buy Heaven; not indeed as if Heaven were cheap, but the Master is indulgent. Hast thou not even a penny? Give a cup of cold water. Heaven is in the market, and we heed it not! Give a crust, and take back paradise. Alms are the redemption of the soul. As vases of water are set at the church gates for washing the hands, so are beggars sitting there that thou mayst wash the hands of thy soul."

SAINT-WORSHIP.—The inducement which the martyrs' festivals offered to the heathen to join themselves to the Church, and the evil consequences which ensued from this compromise with idolatry, are fully stated in our former volume.[2] To the nominal convert, the substitution of the saint for the idol would make but little difference. The old classic mythology may be said to have been replaced by a new Christian Pantheon.[3]

---

[1] One of the charges brought against Chrysostom by the *Synod of the Oak* was "that he had eaten a lozenge after Holy Communion."—See *ante*, p. 89.

[2] *Early Church History*, p. 280.

[3] The deification of the martyrs naturally excited the mockery of the heathen. "Instead of many gods," writes the Emperor Julian, "the Christians worship many wretched men." Eunapius the Sardian, one of the last of the pagan authors, exclaims: "These are the gods the earth now brings forth—the intercessors with the gods, men called martyrs, before whose bones and skulls, pickled and salted, the monks kneel and prostrate themselves, besmearing themselves with filth and dust." In like manner the Manichæan Faustus reproves the Catholic Christians: "Ye have changed the idols into martyrs whom ye worship with the like prayers, and ye appease the shades of the dead with wine and flesh."

Dr. Middleton, commenting on the idolatry of modern Rome, invites his readers to enter the temples, and see the altars which were built originally by the old Romans to the honour of their pagan deities. "We shall hardly see any other alteration than the shrine of some old hero filled by the meaner statue of some modern saint; nay, they have not always given themselves the trouble of making even this change, but have been content sometimes to take up with the old image, just as they found it, after baptizing it only, as it were, or consecrating it anew, by the imposition of a Christian name. This their antiquaries do not scruple to put strangers in mind of, in showing their churches; and it was, I think, in that of St. Agnes, where they showed me an antique statue of a young Bacchus, which, with a new name, and some little change of drapery, stands now worshipped as a female saint. The noblest heathen temple," he continues, "now remaining in the world, is the Pantheon, which, as the inscription over the portico informs us, having been impiously dedicated of old by Agrippa to Jove and all the gods, was piously re-consecrated by Pope Boniface IV.[1] to the blessed Virgin and all the saints. With this single alteration it serves as exactly for the Popish as it did for the pagan worship for which it was built. For as in the old temple every one might find the god of his country, and address himself to that deity whose religion he was most devoted to, so it is now; every one chooses the patron whom he likes best; and one may see here different services going on at the same time at different altars, with distinct congregations around them, just as the inclinations of the people lead them to the worship of this or that particular saint."

We have seen how profound in the time of Cyprian was the veneration for the victorious confessors.[2] This feeling gathered rather than lost strength after the Diocletian persecution, and working on the natural tendency of mankind to deify its benefactors and heroes, ended in a universal worship of the saints. Possibly, also, the controversies respecting the Trinity and the nature of Christ may have tended indirectly towards the same result. Although his human nature was in theory as clearly asserted as his divine, yet it was not dwelt upon in the same emphatic manner, and people began to seek out, or eagerly to turn towards, other beings who were supposed to be in closer sympathy with man. These they found in the martyrs. The spirits of the martyrs were believed to hover about their tombs, or even, as Jerome pretended, to be

---

[1] A.D. 608—615.
[2] *Early Church History*, p. 165.

ubiquitous, and prayers were addressed to them as intercessors with God.

Another preparation for saint-worship may perhaps be found in the semi-divine honours which were paid to the Roman Emperors, and which produced a thraldom of the mind extremely favourable to superstitious notions.

Prayers, thanksgivings, vows, and offerings were everywhere made to the saints. And as in the older mythology there were tutelary gods, to whom the guardianship of special nations and cities, trades and conditions of life, were assigned, so now every country and place, every order and profession of men came to have its patron saint.[1]

The Fathers of the age were leaders in the very fore-front of this superstition. A few specimens out of many, taken from their writings, will suffice. Basil, in an oration delivered on the "birthday" of one of the martyrs, thus appeals to the bystanders: "As many of you as in this place have been assisted by him in prayer, as many as he has brought back into the right way, as many as he has restored to health, or who have had their dead children recalled to life, be ye mindful of the martyr." Again, on the festival of the Forty Martyrs: "Behold a fountain of blessing, a refuge prepared for the Christian! A church of martyrs! Often hast thou laboured to find one who might intercede for thee. Lo! here are forty, emitting one voice of prayer. The wretch bowed down with anguish flees to them. O, indissoluble band! Guardians of mankind!"

---

[1] Thus James became the patron of Spain; George the Martyr, about whose identity and even existence there has been a voluminous controversy, the guardian saint of England. John was the patron of theologians; Luke of painters; Anthony was venerated as a protector against pestilence; Apollonia against toothache. To Phocas, a gardener at Sinope (through some strange freak of the genius of superstition), was especially entrusted the care of mariners, the ancient office of Castor and Pollux. At the daily meals on shipboard, it was customary to assign him a ration, as to an invisible guest, the proceeds of the sale of such ration being distributed among the poor as a thank-offering for a prosperous voyage. Calendars of the saints were commenced in the fourth century; and as the number of martyrs exceeded that of the days of the year, many festivals often fell on the same day. The *Lives of the Saints* (Acta Sanctorum) are contained in sixty-three folio volumes. This colossal work, which was commenced (or rather sketched) by Rosweyd, before the close of the sixteenth century, was continued by the Bollandists in the seventeenth and eighteenth, and is still in progress. When Rosweyd's prospectus, which contemplated only seventeen volumes, was shown to Cardinal Bellarmine, he asked, "What is the man's age?" "Perhaps forty," was the answer. "Does he," asked the Cardinal, "expect to live 200 years?"

Gregory Nazianzen thus invokes Athanasius, in the oration delivered after his death: "Look down propitiously upon us, and govern this people, who are perfect adorers of the perfect Trinity. If peace should come, preserve me and feed my flock with me; but if war, take me home and place me beside thyself and those who are like thee."

Gregory Nyssen does not come behind either his friend or his brother. Thus he speaks of the martyr Theodorus. "Last year he quieted the savage tempest, and put a stop to the horrid war of the fierce Syrians. If any one is permitted to carry away the dust with which his tomb is covered, it is to be laid up as a thing of great price. O Theodorus, we want many blessings; intercede for thy country, with the common King. If there be need of more intercession and deprecation, call together the choir of thy brethren the martyrs. Exhort Peter, excite Paul and John the beloved disciple, that they may be solicitous for the Churches which they have founded, that the worship of idols may not lift up its head against us, that heresies may not spring up like thorns in the vineyard; but that by the power of thy prayer, and of the prayers of thy companions, the commonwealth of Christians may become a field of corn."

After reading such rhapsodies we may well exclaim with Bishop Hooper, "What intolerable blasphemy of God, and ethnical idolatry is this!" And these things were not done in a corner. On the occasion of Gregory's oration, the birthday of Theodorus, the people streamed to the shrine in such multitudes, that he could compare it to nothing but an ant-hill.

As was to be expected, the fervid imagination of Chrysostom carries him even beyond his brethren. "Let us in this fire of love fall down before the relics of the saints! Great boldness had they when living, but much more now that they are dead; for now they bear the *stigmata*[1] of Christ, and when they show these, they can obtain all things of the King. O wonderful pyre! What a treasure does it hold! That dust and those ashes, more precious than gold or jewels, more fragrant than any perfume." Some relics of the "Egyptian Martyrs" were transported from Alexandria to Constantinople: the city poured itself out to welcome the landing of the inestimable treasure, and to accompany it to the sacred shrine where it was to be deposited in gold and marble. The voice of the preacher is lifted up: "Now is our city more securely defended

---

[1] Marks of the wounds in the body of Jesus; hence, generally, marks of martyrdom.

than by ramparts of adamant; now is it walled about with lofty rocks on this side and on that. For these ashes of the saints repel not merely the assaults of visible enemies, or exclude merely sensible evils, but even the machinations of invisible demons, confounding all the stratagems of the devil; and this they do with as much ease as a strong man sweeps down a child's playthings." Nevertheless Chrysostom, when the evangelical mind was uppermost in him, could say: "A great man can be reached only through porters and parasites, but God is invoked without the intervention of any one, without money, without cost of any kind."[1]

As time goes on, the shades of error deepen. Sulpicius Severus, in his eulogy of Martin of Tours, after lamenting the heavy burden of his own sins, exclaims: "There is a hope, however, left, our sole and last hope, that what we cannot obtain of ourselves we may at least merit by Martin's intercession." And Prudentius thus addresses St. Agnes:—

"O blessed virgin! O new glory!
Noble inhabitant of the celestial height!
Incline thy face with double diadem
To behold our vile impurities;
To whom it has been given by the Universal Parent
To render pure even the vault of heaven itself.
I shall be cleansed by the brightness
Of thy countenance, easy of propitiation,
If thou wilt fill my heart.
All is pure which thou pious one deems worthy to look upon,
Or to touch with thy bounteous feet."[2]

Augustine, more enlightened, laboured to explain away or to excuse the worship paid to the saints; but his disclaimer is contradicted by facts, and his pleas are unwarranted by Scripture. "We do venerate the memory of the martyrs, and this is done both to excite us to imitate them, and to obtain a share in their merits and the assistance of their prayers. But it is not to any martyr that we build altars, but to the God of the martyrs. No oné ever says, We bring an offering to thee, O Peter, O Paul, or O Cyprian! Our emotions are intensified by the associations of the place, and love is excited both towards those who are our examples, and towards Him by whose help we may follow such examples. We regard the martyrs with the same affection that we feel towards holy men of God in this life; only there is more devotion in our sentiment

---

[1] Dr. Pusey observes: "Through volumes of St. Augustine and St. Chrysostom there is no mention of any *reliance* except on Christ alone."

[2] Sulpicius died about A.D. 420; Prudentius flourished about 405.

towards them, because we know that their conflict is over, and we can speak with greater confidence in praise of those who are already victors in heaven than of those who are still combating here. That which is properly divine worship, which the Greeks call *latria*, and for which there is no word in Latin, we give only to God. To this worship belongs the offering of sacrifices, as we see in the word *idolatry*, which means the rendering of this worship to idols. Accordingly we never offer sacrifice to a martyr, or to a holy soul, or to an angel. Any one falling into this error is instructed either in the way of correction or of caution."

RELICS.—It is not easy for us in this Protestant age and country to comprehend the high value set upon relics, especially from the time when the Empress Helena made the "discovery of the true Cross." No church was complete without the possession of these treasures; no altar was looked upon as truly sanctified, except a bone of one of the Apostles, or the ashes of some distinguished martyr, or a splinter of the Cross itself, was enshrined within it.[1] The passion for relics finds a place in all the great writers. Ambrose is seeking the remains of a predecessor who was banished to Cappadocia; Basil is able to send him the coveted treasure, affirming with great emphasis the genuineness of the article. The devout sons of the West made pious journeys eastward in quest of the much coveted relics, and not unfrequently the cunning Greeks, who received their genuine coin, sent them home laden with spurious merchandise. Later, as Pope Gregory the Great tells us, Greek monks came to Rome to dig up common bones near St. Paul's church for sale in the East as holy relics. Imperial legislation and the decrees of councils were equally powerless to check this profitable traffic. "Let no one," so runs a law of Theodosius in 386, "remove a buried body; let no one carry away or sell a martyr." Individuals, no less than churches, coveted the possession of these jewels. We may remember how, so early as the year 311, the lady Lucilla kept by her the bone of a martyr to kiss before she partook of the Bread and Wine.[2] This mania soon became universal. Scarcely any one ventured to go about unprovided with such a talisman. Chrysostom speaks of particles of the True Cross being set in gold and suspended about the necks both of men and women.

The epoch we are now reviewing was the very age of wonders and legends. Speaking of Butler's *Lives of the Saints*, which he

---

[1] The second Council of Nicæa (A.D. 787) decreed that the presence of relics was indispensable to an altar.—Canon 7.

[2] *Early Church History*, p. 222.

terms "the fairy-land of unbounded credulity," Isaac Taylor says: "Let any one open the volume at hazard and, without looking at the dates, select a few [narratives] which appear the most ridiculously absurd or on any account peculiarly offensive, and I will venture to predict that they will turn out to be Nicene and not Popish stories. In fact, they will be found to be translations from Athanasius, Basil, Palladius, Jerome, or some of their contemporaries. On the contrary, any lives that may appear to be less objectionable, and in a sense edifying, will be those of modern Romanist saints."

MONACHISM.—We come now to the peculiar feature of the age: the Monastic Life. In the former volume we touched upon the origin of the anchorite's cell and its gradual development into the monastery.[1] The period we are now reviewing saw the new institution spread from Egypt and Syria over all the provinces of the Empire, absorbing into itself the best life of the Church. It will be worth while to examine more closely the features of this singular phenomenon.

Monachism did not spring out of the gospel. Its essential idea has not only nothing in common with New Testament doctrine; it is repugnant to its whole spirit and object. We must go back for the origin of asceticism to an antiquity greater than even Greek philosophy can show, and to countries beyond the Ganges. The elder form of Hindoo superstition,—Brahminism,—was Pantheistic. It proposed to man, as the highest good, absorption into the universal God; and the means by which this felicity was to be obtained were seclusion from society, mental abstraction, and the mortification of the body even to suicide. The great Brahminical code, the Laws of Menu, written a thousand years before the Christian era, lays down the following rules for the man who would attain perfection: "Let him retire from the world, and gain the favour of the gods by fasting, subduing the lusts of the flesh and mortifying the senses. Let him crawl backwards and forwards on his belly; or let him stand all the day on his toes. At sunrise, noon, and sunset let him go to the water and bathe.[2] In the heat of summer let him kindle five fires about him; when it rains let him bare himself to the storm; in winter let him wrap himself in a wet garment. So let him rise by degrees in the strength of his penances." What have we here but the very type and pattern of the fourth-century asceticism?

---

[1] See *Early Church History*, Pt. ii. c. xvii.
[2] This observance puts to shame the Christian devotees.

In the sixth century B.C., or earlier, the Buddhist reformation took place, by which Nihilism was substituted for Pantheism, and the world not so much despised as bewailed for its emptiness. Less fanatical than the original creed, it yet united self-mortification with contemplation and prayer. The monastery now took the place of the cave or cell, and convents both for men and women were spread over Eastern Asia. The two governing principles of Hindoo philosophy, whether Buddhist or Brahminical, are, first, that matter is essentially evil; and secondly, that happiness consists in exemption from all the affections and influences which spring from matter, in other words, in profound, imperturbable repose, the soul being occupied only with the ceaseless contemplation of the Divine Essence from which it is derived.

"Considering the misery that originates in affection, let the man wander alone like a rhinoceros. So long as the love of man toward woman is not destroyed, so long is his mind in bondage. He who has no desire for this world or the next, and who after leaving human attachment has overcome divine attachment,—he is indeed to be called a Brahman. As a man might with loathing shake off a corpse bound upon his shoulders, so let me, leaving this perishable body, this collection of many foul vapours (as men deposit filth upon a dung-heap), depart, regretting nothing, wanting nothing. The 'Four Resources' of a religious life are (1) morsels of food received in alms; (2) for clothing, rags taken from a dust-heap; (3), for shelter, to dwell at the root of a tree; (4) for medicine, the four kinds of filth—dung, urine, ashes and clay."

Both these doctrines found their way into the Christian Church. With the most famous of the Anchorites, who were held up as the great objects of imitation, the body, instead of being cherished as God's creation, was contemned as "a machine for producing sin, a loathsome prison of the spirit."[1] "All earthly things which can

---

[1] Dorotheus, an Egyptian monk, never gave way to sleep of his own will. It sometimes happened that, utterly overcome with lassitude, he would fall down on his mat. Then he would be sorely grieved, and say in an undertone, "You could as easily persuade angels to sleep as men of the true watchful spirit." He was once asked, "Why do you kill your body in this way?" He answered, "Because my body kills me." Another, an aged man named Benjamin, being afflicted with dropsy, requested those who came to visit him to pray for his soul. "I care little," he said, "for my body; for when it was well it did me no good, and now that it is sick it can do me no harm."

Eusebius, a Syrian monk, employed another to read to him from the Gospels. His attention being drawn off by some men ploughing in the neighbouring field, it was necessary to read the passage a second time. To punish himself for his inattention, he fastened an iron girdle round his loins, riveted a heavy collar to

afford pleasure to the senses were shunned as a snare. Cities are evil, human society is evil, green fields, shady woods, refreshing streams, balmy breezes, gay and fragrant flowers, the music of speech and the music of nature, all that is sweet to human sense, is poison to the soul. Impressed with this false and miserable estimate of his Maker's works, the Christian seeker after perfection, like the Brahminical, fled into the desert, where amid arid sands and naked rocks, noisome beasts and reptiles, and the fiery sun overhead, he spent his days in punishing his body, fighting with demons, praying to God and dreaming of heaven. It was imagined, moreover, that the more of earthly good the soul renounces and sacrifices for the sake of heaven, the more of heaven's felicity will God bestow upon it."

The Buddhist monasteries, thus originating many centuries before the Christian, have continued to flourish down to this day. They bear a strong resemblance to those of the Romish church. Their vows of celibacy, poverty and obedience, their common meals, readings and religious exercises, correspond so closely with those of the Latin convent, that the Romish missionaries to the East in the seventeenth century were utterly bewildered, and could only suppose that Satan had devised a counterfeit of the true devotion on purpose to plague them. Thus, Borri, one of their number, says: "There are so many priests and monks in that country (Cochin China) that it looks as if the devil had sought to represent among the heathen the beauty and variety of our orders. Some are clad in white, some in black, some in blue and other colours. Some profess poverty, living on alms; others occupy themselves in works of mercy. The priests wear chaplets and strings of beads round their necks, and make so many processions in prayer to their false gods that they outdo the Christians."

The preceding biographies furnish ample evidence that the monastic profession numbered within its ranks some on whom the choicest gifts of the head and of the heart had been conferred. Doubtless, under the rough cloak and girdle were to be found thousands of sincere and even intelligent Christians, who, although in the darkness of the times they had mistaken the way, yet had their citizenship in heaven.[1] But for the most part the monks

---

his neck, and by a chain drew the two together, so that his head was bent down and he could not look up. This he called foiling Satan by a stratagem. He also made a vow never to tread any path but the narrow one which led from the monastery to the church.

[1] The number of persons of both sexes who during this period devoted themselves to the monastic life was prodigious. Palladius speaks of 3000, 5000,

were a fanatical, illiterate race. Many were unable to read; the ignorance which would have been despised in the "secular" clergy, was in them admired as a token of sanctity. They were in consequence easily aroused; their partisanship was violent; they denounced every deviation from their own narrow creed and notions as the work of the devil. Beginning, moreover, with seclusion and separation from the world, they came to play the busiest part in all its transactions. "Strange contradiction of the human mind!" writes Montesquieu; "the ministers of religion amongst the ancient Romans, not being excluded from the duties of civil society, burdened themselves but little with its affairs. And when the Christian religion was first established, the ecclesiastics who were more separated from worldly affairs mingled in them with moderation. But in the fall of the Empire, the monks, bound by a more exclusive profession to flee and even to fear business, embraced every occasion of meddling with it. They ceased not to make confusion everywhere, and to stir up that world which they had left. No state matter, no peace, no war, no truce, no negotiation, no marriage was managed without the help of the monks; the councils of the prince were full of them, and the national assemblies almost entirely composed of them."

Commencing with vows of poverty, the monks soon began to acquire property and even wealth. Jerome says: "Some, when they have renounced the world, increase rather than diminish their estates, and amongst crowds of guests and swarms of servants, claim the title of solitaries. Some clericals possess a degree of wealth under the poor Christ, which they did not possess under that rich knave the devil." So John Cassianus: "We, living in common under an abbot, carry about our private keys, and wear on our fingers the rings with which we seal up our stores. Not boxes and baskets, not even chests and store-rooms suffice to hold the things we have collected, or which we received when we left the world."

Much has been said, not by Roman Catholic writers only, in praise of Monachism, and we cannot doubt that God has made use of this institution to subserve his beneficent designs. By means of the monasteries, at some epochs, the wilderness has been reclaimed, the arts of industry have been taught to rude nations, learning has

---

or even 10,000 monks as being associated under the rule of a single anchoret or abbot; and 10,000 nuns are mentioned as belonging to the religious houses of one city. Nearly 100,000 of all classes were to be found at one time in Egypt.

been preserved, a sanctuary provided from rapine and bloodshed, and a fountain opened from which spiritual life and knowledge flowed around. But all this does not prove that the institution was Christian or right; it only shows that which we see continually, that God overrules man's devious methods for the purposes of his own love and goodness. The Israelites did evil when they clamoured for a king, yet the monarchy was made use of in perfecting the divine scheme of man's redemption. It was no real extenuation of the cruel sin of Joseph's brethren, in selling him into Egypt, that he said to them, long afterwards, "Be not grieved that ye sold me hither, for it was not you who sent me but God."

Milman has portrayed in eloquent language the evil and the good of the monastic life. "It is impossible," he says, "to survey Monachism in its general influence, from the earliest period of its interworking into Christianity, without being astonished and perplexed with its diametrically opposite effects. Here, it is the undoubted parent of the blindest ignorance and the most ferocious bigotry, sometimes of the most debasing licentiousness; there, the guardian of learning, the author of civilization, the propagator of humble and peaceful religion. To the dominant spirit of Monachism may be ascribed some part at least of the gross superstition and moral inefficiency of the church in the Byzantine Empire; to the same spirit much of the salutary authority of Western Christianity, its constant aggressions on barbarism, and its connection with the Latin literature. . . . Nothing can be conceived more apparently opposed to the designs of the God of nature, and to the mild and beneficent spirit of Christianity; nothing more hostile to the dignity, the interests, the happiness, and the intellectual and moral perfection of man, than the monk afflicting himself with unnecessary pain, and thrilling his soul with causeless fears; confined to a dull routine of religious duties, jealously watching, and proscribing every emotion of pleasure as a sin against the benevolent Deity; dreading knowledge, as an impious departure from the becoming humility of man. On the other hand, what generous or lofty mind can refuse to acknowledge the grandeur of that superiority to all the cares and passions of mortality; the felicity of that state which is removed far above the fears or the necessities of life; that sole passion of admiration and love of the Deity, which no doubt was attained by some of the purer and more imaginative enthusiasts of the cell or the cloister? Who, still more, will dare to depreciate that heroism of Christian benevolence, which underwent this self-denial of the lawful enjoyments and domestic charities of which it had neither extinguished the desire, nor subdued the regret—not from the slavish fear of displeasing the Deity, or the selfish ambition of personal perfection—but from the genuine desire of advancing the temporal and eternal improvement of mankind; of imparting the moral amelioration and spiritual hopes of Christianity to the wretched and the barbarous; of being the messengers of Christian faith, and the ministers of Christian charity to the heathen, whether in creed or in character?"

We cannot wholly subscribe to these latter sentiments. It is true that the only genuine heroism in the world is the heroism of Christian self-denial for the sake of our fellow-men; and it is shameful when those who spend their lives in self-indulgence, forgetful of God and man, affect to despise a simplicity of life, a scorn of ease or a prodigality of unselfish labour, which they can neither imitate nor appreciate. But it can hardly be too much emphasized that the praise which our author is disposed to accord is due to the *motives* only of those who embraced the ascetic life. We would acknowledge in many the excellence of their motive, but we deplore the error of their method. It cannot be said that the cloister is necessary to any of the objects set forth, least of all to the work of the Christian missionary.

Isaac Taylor takes a different view. He wrote at a time when, as now, a deluge of semi-popery threatened to submerge our country. "Christianity was just about to work its proper effect upon the Roman world, when the ascetic fanaticism came in; first to poison the domestic system at the core by its hypocritical prudery, and its consequent separation of the sexes; and, secondly, to turn off the fertilising current of the most powerful sentiments from the field of common life, and to throw them all into the waste-pipe which emptied itself upon the wilderness. The mighty waters of Christian moral influence, which should have renovated the Roman world and have saved the barbarism of a thousand years, were by the ascetic institute shed over the horrid sands of Egypt and Arabia—there to be lost for ever. . . . Southern Europe was left for another cycle of centuries, and monkish fanaticism, with its celibacy and its fastings, has continued now these fifteen hundred years to be the grim antithesis of a widespread dissoluteness of manners."

Enough has been said regarding monkish austerities, but there is one type of self-mortification as yet unmentioned, which confirms in a striking manner the comparison already made between the Indian fakir and the Christian devotee. We mean the Pillar saints.

The first and most celebrated of these was Simeon Stylites, born about A.D. 390. The account of him which has been handed down is as follows. When a youth he entered a monastery near Antioch, where his austerities were so excessive that the abbot begged him to depart, lest the emulation he caused should be dangerous to the weaker brethren. He accordingly withdrew to a place about forty miles from the city, where he lived for ten years in a sort of narrow pen. Afterwards he built a pillar and took up his dwelling on the top of it, which was only about a yard in diameter. He removed successively from one pillar to another, always increasing the height, until at last it reached to sixty feet. In this manner of life he spent thirty-seven years. Day and night he professed to be continually in prayer, spreading forth his hands and bending so low that his forehead touched his feet. At three o'clock in the afternoon he addressed the admiring crowd below, heard and answered their questions, sent messages and wrote letters, for he corresponded with bishops and even Emperors. He took only one scanty meal a week and fasted altogether throughout Lent; he wore a long sheepskin robe and a cap of the same; his neck was loaded with an iron chain.

Simeon is said to have converted thousands of Arabs, Armenians, Persians, and heretics; but the conversion seems to have consisted in their being immersed in water and paying divine honour to the saint and his pillar, rather than in any change of spirit or manner of life. At Simeon's death his cowl descended to another monk named Daniel, whose mastery over his body, miracles, and sanctity rivalled those of his predecessor. The two saints found many imitators in the East, but this absurd fashion never got a footing in Europe.[1]

THE CHURCH AND THE WORLD.—The Fathers of the fourth and fifth centuries were not blind to the moral condition into which the Church had sunk in their day. "The Church," writes Chrysostom, "is like a woman fallen from her ancient prosperity, who possesses various signs of her former wealth, and displays the little chests and caskets in which her treasure was preserved, but who has lost the treasure itself." Basil likens her to "a ship driven about by the fiercest storms, whilst the crew are quarrelling amongst themselves;" and "to an old garment which tears wherever you touch it, and which it is impossible to restore to its primitive strength and soundness."

---

[1] Simeon's pillar was gradually built round with chapels and monasteries, and the figure of the saint as a protecting genius was set up at the doors of the shops in Rome. A German fanatic built himself a similar pillar near Trèves, and essayed to live upon it, after the manner of Simeon, but the neighbouring bishops pulled it down.

By this time, indeed, the distinction between Pagan and Christian had become nominal rather than real. The vile manners of the heathen were still maintained by those who called themselves Christians. Children were by needy parents exposed to perish, boys were sold as slaves for their fathers' debts. Christian parents betook themselves to magicians when their children were sick, and expected a cure to be wrought by hanging a talisman about their necks. The conversation of the market-places was filthy.

The theatre was frequented alike by Christians and heathens, and was, as in the days of Tertullian,[1] the very hotbed of vice. Chrysostom calls it "the seat of pestilence, the gymnasium of incontinence; and a school of luxury, Satan being its author and architect;" and after many unheeded warnings declares he will no longer admit play-goers to the Lord's Supper. By the force of custom, sights were tolerated there which would have been endured nowhere else. Even the celebration of the Eucharist and other rites of the Church were profanely represented.[2]

The circus evoked the indignation of Chrysostom even more than the theatre. "The indomitable passion for the chariot-races, and the silly eagerness displayed about them by the inhabitants of Rome, Constantinople, and Antioch, are among the most remarkable symptoms of the depraved state of society under the later Empire. The whole populace was divided into factions, distinguished by the different colours adopted by the charioteers, of which green and blue were the chief favourites. The animosity, the sanguinary tumults, the superstitions, folly, violence of every kind, which were mixed up with these popular amusements well deserved the unsparing severity with which they were lashed by the great preacher. 'You applaud my words, and then hurry off to the circus, and sitting side by side with Jew or Pagan, clap your hands with frenzied eagerness at the efforts of the charioteers. You plead business, poverty, want of health, lameness as excuses for absence from church, but these hindrances never prevent your attendance at the hippodrome.'"

Salvian, a presbyter of Marseilles, and a writer of uncommon elegance, has left us a forcible description of the corrupt state of the Church in the fifth century. The biting language in which he declaims is the very counterpart of that in which Cyprian speaks

---

[1] See *Early Church History*, p. 115.

[2] "We Christians," complains Gregory Nazianzen, "are brought upon the stage, and made subjects for vulgar laughter in company with the most profligate of men. Nay, there is hardly any gratification so popular as a Christian exposed to mockery and insult in a comedy."

of the heathen world.[1] "What," he asks, "what but fraud and perjury is the course of life of the merchants? What but iniquity that of those attached to halls and courts? What but false accusation that of officials? What but rapine that of all the military? You will say, surely the nobility are free from crime. Not so; for who is there, whether among the noble or among the rich (and it is one of the miseries of these times that none is accounted so noble as he who has amassed the greatest wealth), who is there that shudders at crime? I am wrong. Many shudder at crimes; they are shocked at the vices of others, whilst they themselves practise the same. They execrate openly what they perpetrate secretly. . . . A very few excepted, what else is almost every assembly of Christians but a sink of vices? You will more easily find the man who is guilty of all crimes than him who is guilty of none. But it is the laity only, you will say, who sin at this rate, surely not the clergy. Alas! under colour of religion, men who after a course of profligacy inscribed themselves with a saintly title, have changed their profession only, not their life. They have put off the garment only, not the mind of their former condition. These men well know that what I am saying is true, their own consciences bear witness to every word. . . . The entire mass of the priests is so sunk into this depravity that it has come to be regarded as a species of sanctity for one to be a little less vicious than the rest. Inasmuch as scarcely any corner is not blotted with the stain of mortal sin, what room have we to flatter ourselves with our name? . . . It will, to many, sound insufferable if I should affirm that we are inferior to the barbarians, who are either heretics (Arians) or pagans. But what if it be so? As to life and conduct, I grieve to say we are worse. . . . Ye Romans and Christians and Catholics, ye defraud your brethren, grind the faces of the poor, fritter away your lives over the impure and heathenish spectacles of the amphitheatre, wallow in licentiousness and inebriety. The barbarians, however fierce towards us, are just and fair in their dealings with one another; the impurities of the theatre are unknown amongst them; many of their tribes are free from the taint of drunkenness; and amongst all, except the Alans and the Huns, chastity is the rule."

Whatever truth there may be in Salvian's verdict regarding the priesthood, there must have been very many, in all parts of the empire, who still adorned the profession of the Christian minister. In support of this opinion we may adduce the unequivocal testimony of an outsider, the heathen historian Ammianus Marcellinus. He

---

[1] See *Early Church History*, pp. 6-8.

has been relating the sanguinary contest between Damasus and Ursicinus for the possession of the Roman See,[1] and thus concludes: "I do not deny, when I consider the pomp and display of the episcopal office in this city, that they who covet such rank are justified in striving with all their might to attain the object of their desires. For when they have gained it, they come into a state of perfect ease and luxury; the offerings of matrons are showered upon them; they ride in chariots, dress with splendour, and feast with even more than royal extravagance. They might be equally happy if, instead, they were to live like some of the provincial bishops, whom rigid abstinence, simplicity of dress, and an humble demeanour commend to the Eternal Deity and his true worshippers as pure and sober-minded men."

CHAPTER XI.

JOVINIAN AND VIGILANTIUS.

FROM the galaxy of illustrious names on which we have been gazing, we turn to that small cluster of obscure men who strove to call back the Church to Apostolic simplicity and truth. The need of reform had become more and more pressing, but the great leaders and teachers of the age had failed to perform their duty; nevertheless the truth was not left wholly without witnesses.

The name of Aërius was introduced into our former work[2] earlier than in the exact order of time. He flourished about the middle of the fourth century, and may be regarded as the first Protestant after the Council of Nicæa. His teaching on many points anticipated in a remarkable degree that of the most enlightened Protestants of the Reformation.

JOVINIAN. Little is known of the personal history of this monk. As in the case of Aërius, his own writings have perished, his opinions having come down to us only through his opponents, Jerome and Augustine. He received his education in an Italian convent,[3] but his bold and free spirit refused to be shackled by the dead forms which surrounded him, and about A.D. 388 he began to enunciate sounder and more spiritual principles. Especially he

---

[1] See *ante*, p. 27, note.
[2] See *Early Church History*, p. 310.
[3] Cave says he lived some years in Ambrose's monastery at Milan.

denied the superior merit of celibacy;[1] and as just then the popular feeling, consequent on the death of Blesilla,[2] was running against Jerome and Monachism, he made many converts, not only of the laity, but also of monks and nuns; and many of both sexes were induced to marry.

A friend of Jerome's, Pammachius, the husband of Paula's daughter, was one of the first to take alarm at the new heresy. He brought Jovinian's book to the notice of Siricius, the Roman bishop, a blind upholder of celibacy.[3] A synod was convened, A.D. 390, and Jovinian and eight of his adherents were summarily condemned and excommunicated. Jovinian betook himself to Milan, but if he expected to meet with indulgence either from the Emperor Theodosius or the bishop Ambrose, he was grievously disappointed. Siricius had been beforehand with him, and had sent three presbyters with a letter of warning addressed to the Milanese Church; and Ambrose hastened to show himself in complete accord with the Roman synod. In conjunction with eight other bishops, he endorsed the sentence of excommunication, and in a letter to Siricius stated that the Emperor also execrated the impiety of the Jovinianists, and that all at Milan who had seen the heretics shunned them like a pestilence. He stigmatizes Jovinian's opinion that there was no difference of merit between the married and the unmarried as "a savage howling of ferocious wolves scaring the flock." The matter did not end here. For, long after, in 412, we find the Emperor Honorius issuing the following edict: "Some bishops having complained that Jovinian assembles sacrilegious meetings without the walls of the most holy city, We ordain that the said Jovinian be seized and whipped, together with his abettors and followers, and that he be immediately banished to the Island of Boa."[4]

---

[1] He controverted the perpetual virginity of Mary, a point which was then becoming an article of faith in the Church.

[2] See *ante*, p. 115.

[3] See *ante*, p. 116, note. Siricius decreed by letter that if any bishop, priest, or deacon should marry, he should not look for pardon, "because it is necessary to cut off with the knife those sores which cannot be cured by other remedies." This was the first *Decretal*, the first of the *Letters* of the Bishop of Rome which became a rule to the Western Church, and thus laid the foundation of the vast system of ecclesiastical law.

[4] Boa was a rock near the Illyrian coast. Some historians have thought that the Edict of Honorius was not directed against our monk, but against another heretic of the same name. For this opinion two reasons are assigned, the one that Jovinian, as appears by Jerome, died so early as 406; the other that no such complaint as that on which the edict is founded was brought against him

Whilst the merit of the ascetic life was being re-echoed from side to side, and charity was estimated and sins graduated by the outward act, Jovinian stood forth and proclaimed the true doctrine of faith. "There is but one Divine element of life which all believers share in common; but one fellowship with Christ which proceeds from faith in Him; but one new birth. All who possess this, all who are Christians in the true sense, have the same calling, the same dignity, the same heavenly blessings. . . . The labourers of the first, the third, the sixth, the ninth, and the eleventh hour received each alike one penny; and that you may wonder the more, the payment begins with those who had laboured the shortest time in the vineyard. . . . Virgins, widows and married women who have been once baptized into Christ, if their works are right, have equal merit. . . . It amounts to the same thing, whether a man abstain from food, or partake of it with thanksgiving." But when he goes on to say that there are no half-ripe members in the Church, no progression in the spiritual life, we cannot follow him; nor when he declares that he who is once baptized cannot be overcome by temptation, and that if any are so overcome it is a proof that they have never received the true baptism. In opposition to the division of sins into mortal and venial (the former only being held to exclude from eternal life), Jovinian took his stand on high and solid ground. He maintained that the Gospel requires and confers a new holy disposition, to which every sin of every kind stands directly opposed, so that all sin, whatever outward appearance it may have, proceeds from the same corrupt fountain, and manifests the same ungodly life.[1]

The publication of Jovinian's book excited, as has been said, considerable attention in Rome. It also aroused the wrath of Jerome in his cell at Bethlehem, and without delay he set to work to extinguish the heretic. "The tone of his reply is that of a man suddenly arrested in his triumphant career by some utterly unexpected opposition; his resentment at being thus crossed is mingled with a kind of wonder that men should exist who could entertain such strange and daring tenets. The length, it might be said the prolixity, to which he draws out his answer, seems rather the outpouring of his wrath and his learning, than as if he con-

---

at the synod. The latter objection is of little weight; with regard to the former, Tillemont suggests that the date of the edict may be erroneous. Moreover, it is not probable there were two Jovinians; if there were, we have one reformer the more, or at least one more instance of a willingness to suffer for conscience' sake.

[1] Jovinian also opposed the excessive veneration for the act of martyrdom.

sidered it necessary to refute such obvious errors." He calls Jovinian's protest against the supposed merit of asceticism, "the hissings of the old serpent, by which the dragon expelled man from Paradise."[1] So violent was his language that on his reply being sent to Rome, Pammachius and others of his friends attempted to suppress it; but Jerome told them the book had been too much circulated to be recalled. Augustine, who was also opposed to Jovinian, was alarmed at the extravagant terms in which Jerome had extolled celibacy, and deprecated marriage; and to counteract the effect of his tract, wrote a treatise for the purpose of restoring marriage to its true position; although, as was to be expected, he ascribes a still higher degree of the Christian life to the unmarried state, when it is chosen from the right motives. "In this tract," observes Neander, "Augustine distinguishes himself, not only by his greater moderation, but also by a more correct judgment of the ascetic life in its connection with the whole Christian temper. Like Jovinian, he opposed the tendency to set a value upon the outward conduct, upon the mere *opus operatum*, without regard to its relation to the disposition of the heart. By giving prominence to the latter, Augustine approached Jovinian, and he would have come still nearer to him, had he not been on so many sides fettered by the Church spirit of the times."

The names of two other witnesses of Jovinian's age and country, if not actually his disciples, have also come down to us, Sarmatio and Barbatianus, both of them monks in Ambrose's cloister at Milan. They disputed the benefit of asceticism and the peculiar merit of the unmarried life. Not being suffered to utter their opinions in the cloister, they renounced their vows,[2] and removed to Vercelli, where they hoped to be able to teach their doctrines unmolested. But Ambrose put the Church in that city on its guard against the heretics. Of the further history of these men we have no account.

Thus persecuted by the bishops, written down by the greatest doctors of the age, outlawed by synods, detested by the whole body of the clergy, Jovinian and his adherents were soon forgotten. But though the mouths of the witnesses were closed, the truths they pro-

---

[1] We take no notice of the charge of gluttony brought by Jerome against Jovinian. It is probable it had no other ground than that on which the Pharisees rested their accusation against our Lord: "The Son of Man is come eating and drinking; and ye say: Behold, a gluttonous man, and a winebibber, a friend of publicans and sinners."

[2] The monastic vow was not then irrevocable; it was first so made by Benedict of Nursia, A.D. 529.

claimed were not so easily destroyed. They presently sprang up again in a new quarter.

VIGILANTIUS was born about A.D. 364, at Calagorris, a *mansio* or posting-station, forty-five miles south-west of Toulouse. His father, a descendant of the robbers whom Pompey drove out of Spain,[1] was the innkeeper of the place, and made his fortune by supplying post-horses and refreshment to travellers.[2] Vigilantius assisted him, and it was probably his business to wait on the travellers, drive the cars and act as guide across the Pyrenean mountains.

The ecclesiastical writer Sulpicius Severus, with whom we have already met in the life of Martin of Tours, resided at a villa between Toulouse and Narbonne, and possessed estates on both sides of the Pyrenees. His way from one to the other lay through Calagorris, and the young man attracting his notice, he took him into his service. Here Vigilantius would meet with the best society of which Gaul could boast, and would hear the news of the Christian world retailed, and theological questions discussed. Sulpicius, besides his charity towards the sick and poor, and his care for the maintenance of public and family worship, was occupied in preparing an abridgment of the Holy Scriptures. But in this reasonable and exemplary manner of life he seems to have been disturbed by bishop Martin of Tours, who persuaded him that his benevolent and pious actions were of no value without the practice of austerities. Sulpicius hearkened only too credulously. To what an extent he carried his self-humiliation we see by a letter from his friend Paulinus of Nola. "Thy domestics tell me thou art poor in the midst of wealth, and art living in a state of self-imposed bondage, treating thy servants as thy companions, and thy brethren as thy masters. In fact, that thou art a perfect servant of God, the enemy of riches, the living copy of the holy Martin, an entirely obedient follower of the Gospel."

In 394 Vigilantius and a companion were sent by Sulpicius to Nola to visit Paulinus. The reader of our former volume is already acquainted with this enthusiast, who so greatly delighted in his noon-day illuminations;[3] but in view of the protest which Vigilan-

---

[1] These robbers belonged to the Spanish village of Calagorris, and when they arrived in Gaul they gave the same name to their new settlement.

[2] The posting system was under the direction of the State, and officials or government messengers were carried along at the rate of upwards of eight miles an hour in four-wheeled carriages or light two-wheeled cars, drawn by horses or mules.

[3] See *Early Church History*, p. 272.

tius was soon to raise against the superstitions of the age it may be well to acquaint ourselves more closely with what must have come under his notice at Nola. The fame of Paulinus was in all the churches. He held a correspondence with Augustine, by whom he was addressed in a style of warm friendship, reverence, and even flattery; and his influence was so great that he was able to set at nought the displeasure of the Roman bishop Siricius.[1]

Paulinus had fitted up his villa, which stood close to the tomb of his patron saint Felix,[2] as a monastery and a house of reception for strangers. Ample pleasure grounds which had been adorned with fountains, statues and flowerbeds, were transformed into an orchard and a cabbage garden. During Vigilantius' visit, his host began to rebuild the church. The pavement and walls were laid in marble, and on the ceiling of the dome there were wrought in mosaic emblematical representations of the Trinity and the evangelists.[3] Under the cupola stood the high altar, enshrining ashes of the Apostles, relics of martyrs, and a splinter of the "true Cross." The lofty nave was flanked by aisles, and beyond these were four chapels for private devotion and the burial-places of the faithful. From the church you passed by three latticed arcades to the mausoleum of St. Felix, and from this again in the same manner to his oratory. The building when completed, surmounted as it was by three cupolas and encompassed with walls, had almost the appearance of a little town.[4]

When all was finished, processions were formed, the relics of the saint were displayed, clouds of incense rose, and lights were burned before the tomb, whilst votive offerings were presented by the multitude, who cried aloud, "Hear us, holy Felix! blessed Felix!" A festival which took place in honour of the saint whilst Vigilantius

---

[1] Paulinus was meant for better things. "Rigorous abstinence, periodical fastings, night watchings, coarse vestments, the accumulation of bones and rags of saints, and especially the hourly prostrations at the shrine of St. Felix, absorbed all the capacities of a mind once distinguished by the graces and refinements of the scholar, the poet and the rhetorician."

[2] A legendary confessor in the Decian persecution, whose life was said to have been miraculously preserved.

[3] This is the first mention in the West of allegorical figures or historical pictures in churches. In the East they are spoken of by Gregory Nyssen a generation earlier.

[4] In imitation of Paulinus, Sulpicius in Gaul built two basilicas, with a baptistery between them, on the walls of which were painted likenesses of Martin and of Paulinus himself. Paulinus is popularly said to have been the inventor of church bells. It is clear that some sonorous instrument (signum) was first employed about this time to call Christians to worship.

was at Nola is described in almost the very words of Prudentius' rhapsody over the pilgrimage to the shrine of Hippolytus in the Roman catacombs.[1] Paulinus himself was somewhat shocked with the prodigal consumption of wine on this occasion, although he is at first inclined to regard the excess with indulgence. "Would they could offer up their vows of joy with more sobriety, and not be quaffing cups of wine within the sacred precincts! Yet I think some allowance may be made for those who indulge a little in these festivals, since rude minds are liable to error, and simple piety is scarcely conscious of the faults it commits." But the sight of an inebriate provokes his wrath: "Thou hast now reason to dread Felix; thou art insulting him by thy drunkenness; wretched creature, thou art making him the witness and the avenger of thy revels. I have thought it right," he continues, "to have the walls of the sanctuary decorated with paintings, that in the sacred history, and the pious examples held up to their view, the rustics may forget their wine and become sober."

The rule of the monastery was severe. Paulinus tells us of one of the brotherhood who, after he had been some time at Nola, was much altered; his body grew lean and his face pale; and adds, "He rarely drinks at table, and in such small quantities as is scarcely sufficient to wet his lips, but he does not now complain of an empty stomach or a dry throat." The cloister cooks leaving, one after another, Sulpicius sent to Paulinus "brother Victor," who proved a rare treasure to his new master. "His dishes," says Paulinus, "are of a kind to destroy the fancies and delicacies of a senator. He thoroughly understands how to dress beans, to make vinegar from beetroot, and to prepare coarse broth for hungry monks. More than this, he seasons his meagre porridge with such salt of grace and such sweetness of charity, that the want of material condiments is not felt."[2]

---

[1] *Early Church History*, p. 277.

[2] The monks of the West fell short of the Oriental standard in the discipline of the body as well as in the power of abstraction. In one of Sulpicius' dialogues, himself and Gallus (a disciple of Martin of Tours), being present, Postumian, the pilgrim, relates how the ship he sailed in was almost driven on the quicksands (Syrtes), and how, just escaping, he and his companions went ashore to explore the desert country of the African coast. They saw before them a hut shaped like the keel of a ship, and an aged hermit clad in sheepskins and turning a hand-mill. Finding they were Christians, the old man received them lovingly, and invited them to join in prayer. "'Laying some skins on the ground for us to recline upon, he set before us a plentiful dinner, half a barley loaf and a handful of a sweet herb. There were four of us and he the fifth. We made a hearty meal.' At this word Sulpicius smiled and said to Gallus, 'How

Cleanliness and becoming attire were as little regarded at Nola as the delicacies of the table. "Give me," exclaims Paulinus, "the society of those who wear hair-cloth shirts, and whose loins are girdled with a rope. I cannot do with those insolent persons who pride themselves on their well-dressed hair: give me those who for the sake of holy deformity, wear it short and badly cut, such as live in honourable neglect of the niceties of life, who despise personal beauty, and purposely disfigure themselves, that their hearts may be clean."

We must not, however, pass over a redeeming element in the monastic life at Nola, which so long as it remained served as a bulwark against corruption and decay. This was the study of Holy Scripture, a pursuit to which Paulinus devoted himself as ardently as Sulpicius. The difficulties which the Biblical student of that time had to surmount, were such as in our day can scarcely be imagined. Books were all in manuscript and took up much room. It was a rare thing to possess the whole Bible in one volume. Origen, Eusebius, and Jerome had introduced into the Scriptures certain divisions, but these fell very short of the chapters and verses which we now possess; and headings of chapters, marginal notes, indexes and concordances were unknown. Paulinus was considered so good a textuarian, that Augustine consulted him, and submitted some of his writings to his correction. The study of the Holy Scriptures by the side of the semi-heathen rites practised at Nola, although it failed to open the eyes of a Sulpicius or a Paulinus, may have been to the more free and inquiring mind of Vigilantius, as a lamp shining in darkness.

On the death of his father in 395, Vigilantius returned for a short time to Calagorris, whence he again set out on a journey to Palestine and Egypt. Revisiting Nola on the way, he was furnished by Paulinus with a letter of introduction to Jerome at Bethlehem. The great recluse received him courteously, and took him to the sacred places, "crossing himself at every step." As Vigilantius

---

wouldst thou like to dine on a handful of herbs and half a loaf for five men?' Gallus blushed and answered: 'Thou art at thy old tricks, Sulpicius, letting slip no opportunity of taxing us Gauls with voracity; but it is cruel to expect us to live like angels, though for myself I can believe that the angels eat too. As to that half of a barley loaf, I should think it a poor mouthful for myself alone, but that meagre Cyrenian might be well content with it; for hunger belongs to him either by necessity or by nature. Nor do I wonder that half-starved and weather-beaten mariners should think it a good dinner; but for our part, we are far from the sea, in a plentiful country; and what is more, as I have often told thee, we are Gauls.'"

appears to have made his visit only three years after Jerome had crushed Jovinian, it is not very unlikely that the opinions of that reformer formed a topic of conversation between them. Another topic was furnished by the Origen controversy, which was then going on, and which seems to have occasioned some interruption to their friendly intercourse. From Bethlehem Vigilantius proceeded to Jerusalem, where he appears to have spent some time with Jerome's opponent, Rufinus, and when on his way home he repeated his visit to Jerome, the suspicious nature and ill-humour of the latter burst forth, and Vigilantius quitted Bethlehem abruptly. On his way back to Gaul he tarried a while in Alexandria, whence, proceeding to the shores of Italy, he made his way home by the Cottian Alps.[1] Wherever he went he seems to have spoken freely of Jerome and his opinions, and to have found many sympathisers.

The recollection of their quarrel rankled in Jerome's mind, and when he heard of the manner in which his late visitor had occupied himself on his journey he vented his spleen in a stinging epistle (A.D. 398). "It would have been just had I given thee no satisfaction by letter, since thou hast given no credence to thy own ears. But since Christ has given us in Himself an example of perfect humility by kissing his betrayer, I intimate to thee in thy absence the same things which I told thee when present. . . . Thou hast left Egypt and all the provinces where so many defend thy opinions with effrontery; and hast selected me as an object of persecution, me who reprehend all doctrines contrary to the Church and publicly condemn them. So Origen is a heretic! What is that to me, who do not deny that in many points he is a heretic? If I did not daily anathematize his errors, I should be a partaker of them. . . . I as a Christian, speaking to thee as a Christian, beseech thee brother not to aim at being wise above thy knowledge. From thy childhood thou hast learned another trade, thou hast been used to another kind of training. It is not for the same man to examine both gold coins and the Scriptures, both to sip wines and to understand the Apostles and Prophets. . . . Call to mind I pray thee the time when I descanted on the true resurrection of the body, how thou leaped aside, clapped thy hands and stamped thy feet, proclaiming that I was orthodox. But when thou got out to sea, the offensive odour of the bilge-water struck into thy brain, and thou remembered that I was a heretic. I gave credence to the

---

[1] Some have connected this journey over the Cottian Alps with the early Protestantism which manifested itself in the valleys of Dauphiné and Piedmont, but without, as it seems, sufficient ground.

letters of the holy presbyter Paulinus, not imagining that his judgment of thee could be erroneous; and although I noticed that thy conversation was unpolished, I set it down to rusticity and simplicity rather than to folly. . . . Thy name must have been given thee by *antiphrasis*, for thy whole mind slumbers as in a lethargy. Thy tongue ought to be cut out and torn to shreds."

Several years may have elapsed before Vigilantius put forth the treatise which has made his name honourable, and which drew down upon him a still more severe infliction of Jerome's wrath. As soon as it was published, information of the writer's audacity in attacking the ruling follies of the age was sent to Jerome by Riparius, a priest of the diocese of Toulouse. It drew forth (A.D. 404) a characteristic reply.

"Thou sayest," writes Jerome, "that Vigilantius (he should rather be called Dormitantius) is again opening his foul mouth, and is casting forth the most villainous filth against the relics of the holy martyrs, styling us who receive them 'cinder-gatherers and idolaters,' because we venerate the bones of dead men. . . . I am surprised that the holy bishop[1] in whose diocese he is said to be a presbyter, should wink at such madness, and should not with his apostolic rod of iron, dash in pieces the worthless vessel, and deliver him for the destruction of the flesh that the spirit may be saved. . . . If the relics of the martyrs are not to be honoured, how is it that we read 'Precious in the sight of the Lord is the death of his saints'? If their bones pollute those who touch them, how was it that Elisha when dead raised to life the dead man? Were all the camps of the Israelitish host unclean because they carried the bodies of Joseph and the patriarchs in the wilderness? And did they carry unclean ashes into the Holy Land? . . . This tongue should be cut off by the surgeons, or rather this mad head should be cured, that he who knows not how to speak may learn sometimes to keep silence. I once saw this marvel and wished to bind the madman with Scripture testimonies; but he went off, he departed, he escaped, he burst away, and has railed against us between the billows of the Adriatic and the Cottian Alps. . . . I could have wished to say more did not the brevity of a letter impose on me the obligation to silence, and hadst thou thought it expedient to send me his doggerel books that I might know what I ought to answer. At present I am beating the air, and give proof rather of my own orthodoxy than of his heterodoxy which is manifest to all men. But if thou wishest that I should write a longer book against him,

---

[1] Exuperius, bishop of Toulouse.

send me his dirges and drivellings, that he may hear John the Baptist announcing, 'Now also the axe is laid unto the root of the tree ; therefore every tree which bringeth not forth good fruit is hewn down and cast into the fire.'"

In accordance with this letter, Riparius, and another priest, Desiderius, sent a copy of Vigilantius' tract to Jerome, and with it a formal charge against the reformer. They represented that the whole neighbourhood was in commotion, and that their own people were infected by the blasphemous doctrines of the heretic. The infuriated monk immediately set to work, and in one night forged the engine which was to " crush the serpent." This was in the year 406.[1]

Vigilantius' treatise is known only through Jerome's answer. It is plain, however, that in his protest against the abuses of the times, Vigilantius takes a wider range than his predecessor Jovinian had done. We have seen that he denied the tombs of the martyrs to be the proper objects of veneration. He calls their relics a heap of ashes and wretched bones, and asks of what use it is to honour and adore and even kiss dust folded up in a linen cloth ? He derides the prodigies said to be wrought in the churches of the martyrs, and condemns the vigils performed in them, asserting, as Tertullian and Lactantius had done before him,[2] that the practice of burning tapers by daylight came from the heathen. "How," he asks, " could men think of honouring by the light of miserable wax candles, those martyrs on whom the Lamb in the midst of God's throne is shedding all the brightness of his majesty ?"

In his answer Jerome does not deny that these practices were borrowed from the pagans, but asserts that the same homage, which is to be detested when offered to idols, is to be approved when offered to martyrs. He maintains, further, that Christians are far from intending to pay to creatures the honour which is due to the Creator alone ; that their devotion sees in what Vigilantius describes as "wretched bones," something of much greater worth ; that they venerate in the tomb nothing which is dead, but through it look up to the saints alive with God, who is in truth not the God of the dead but of the living. In defending the vigils, he could not deny that they often served both as a pretext and an occasion for gross immoralities. To the objection advanced against the lighted tapers, he could only answer that, even though the laity or

---

[1] Jerome tells us that he wrote his answer "in a single night," because the brother who was to take the letter could not tarry longer.

[2] See *Early Church History*, p. 271.

pious women might be mistaken in supposing the martyrs to be so honoured, yet we are bound to respect such pious feelings, though they may err in the mode of expression. But the conclusive argument on which he relies is, universal authority. "Was the Emperor Constantius," he asks, "guilty of sacrilege, who transported the holy relics of Andrew, Luke and Timothy to Constantinople, before which the devils (such devils as inhabit Vigilantius) roar, and are confounded? Or the Emperor Arcadius, who translated the bones of the blessed Samuel from Judæa into Thrace? Are all the bishops not only sacrilegious but infatuated, who carried this worthless trash and these loose cinders in silk and gold; and all the people gathered together from Palestine even to Chalcedon, who met them, and received them as if it were the living prophet? Is the bishop of Rome sacrilegious, who offers sacrifice on the altar under which are the venerable bones (the vile dust would Vigilantius say?) of Peter and Paul; and not the bishop of one city alone, but the bishops of all the cities of the world, who enter the church of the dead in which this most worthless dust and ashes are deposited?"

Vigilantius also denied the efficacy of prayers addressed to departed saints. "According to the Holy Scriptures," he says, "only the living pray for one another; the martyrs moreover cannot be everywhere present, to hear men's prayers and to succour them. The souls of the Apostles and martyrs have settled themselves either in Abraham's bosom, or in a place of refreshment, or under the altar of God; and they cannot escape and present themselves where they please. Do they so love their ashes as to hover always round them, lest if any suppliant should happen to draw near they might not hear him?" These opinions may be fanciful, but Jerome's reply is no better founded. "If the Apostles and martyrs in this earthly life, before they had yet come safely out of the conflict, were able to pray for others, how much more can they do so, now that they have obtained the victory! and seeing it is asserted of them that they follow the Lamb whithersoever He goes, and the Lamb is everywhere present, we must believe that the faithful are in spirit everywhere with Christ."

Vigilantius spoke lightly of fasting and mortification, and the various austerities of the monks, and even of the hermit life itself. "Should all retire from the world and live in deserts, who would remain to uphold the public worship of God? Who would exhort sinners to virtue? This would not be to fight, but to fly." Especially he denied the merit of virginity, and that celibacy is incumbent on the clergy. It is evident that his teaching had made some converts among the higher clergy, for Jerome declaims against some bishops, who (evidently because they feared the pernicious consequences of a constrained celibacy) would ordain no others as deacons, but those who were married.

Another point on which Vigilantius sought to bring men back to Scripture and common sense, was that of the right stewardship of earthly possessions. He showed that those who managed their own property themselves, and distributed their incomes prudently amongst the poor, did better than those who gave away the whole at once; and that it was a more Christian act for a man to provide for the poor of his own neighbourhood, than to send his money to Jerusalem for the support of the monks in that city who lived on charity. On these as on some other points, Jerome has nothing to oppose but flimsy sophistry. What he lacks in reason, however, he makes up in abuse. "Many monsters have been born into the world, centaurs and satyrs, owls and bitterns, Cerberus, the chimera and the many-headed hydra, and the three-formed Geryon. Gaul alone has had no monsters, but has always abounded in brave and eloquent men. Suddenly Vigilantius has arisen, who, in his unclean spirit, fights against the spirit of Christ."

From this time we almost lose sight of the reformer. According to some, the bishop Exuperius, who refused in the first instance to take part against Vigilantius, and was even said to favour him, was eventually induced by the invectives of Jerome, and the influence of Innocent I. of Rome, to have him banished from Aquitaine. One historian records that he served a church in Barcelona, and this may well agree with the statement just related. It is thought that he may have perished about the year 409, in that great hurricane of the Northern barbarians, which after desolating Gaul, broke over the Spanish peninsula, and converted it into a desert.

The Catholic worthies whose lives we have endeavoured to portray are the men to whom the Romanists of the present day, and many who bear the name of Protestant, look up, as to the Fathers of the Church; and the century in which they flourished is regarded as its golden age. No constellation of luminaries so bright and so numerous is to be met with again until we come to the Reformation. At the same time how far all these celebrated churchmen were, as individuals, true Witnesses for Christ, is a question on which there may well be a difference of opinion. Few of the readers of this volume are likely to follow Cardinal Newman in the reasons he gives for honouring Jerome: "I do not scruple to say, that were he not a saint, there are words and ideas in his writings from which I should shrink; but as he *is* a saint, I shrink with greater reason from putting myself in opposition, even in minor matters and points of detail, to one who has the infallibility of the Church pledged to his saintly perfection. I cannot, indeed, force myself to approve or like these particulars on my private judgment or feeling; but I can receive things on faith against both the one and the other. And I readily and heartily do take on faith these characteristics, words, or acts of this great Doctor of the Universal Church; and I think it is not less acceptable to God or to him to give him my religious homage than my human praise."[1] To argue in this manner is to impose on one's self a slavery worse than that of Egypt. Many of our readers will agree with Newman in his private opinion regarding Jerome, and some will perhaps go further, disposed, like Isaac Taylor, to challenge the claim of that extraordinary man to any place at all amongst the true Witnesses for Christ.

It is clear that these renowned Fathers of the Church have not earned our gratitude in some essential matters. They found the episcopal authority already inordinately great; they left it absolute. They found the system of celibacy and monkery and the worship of saints and relics a young and sturdy plant; they left it a mighty tree overshadowing the whole land. They found the Church half resolved to employ force in compelling men's consciences; they left her fully embarked on this fatal course. Down to their time, schismatics (not to say heretics) were regarded with some measure of charity, and treated with some show of consideration; but after the time of Augustine all this has vanished; it is, "Recant, or die; return to the bosom of Holy Mother Church, or perish like a malefactor." Such from this time forward was the only alternative. At the same time the dogma of one Catholic Church, beyond the pale of which there is no salvation, became fixed and universal.

In passing judgment however upon the Church teachers and rulers of this age we must bear in mind that men are to be weighed in the balance of their own times, and not in that of any other. The degree of light which prevailed in their day must always be taken into account. The fourth and fifth centuries formed an age not only of rank superstition, but of profound moral corruption. The social and political sores went on festering until they became intolerable, and had to be cut out by the swords of the barbarians.

In estimating, on the other hand, the motives and characters of the Reformers, Aërius, Jovinian, Vigilantius, two important considerations present themselves. They are men almost unknown to history. Scorned and proscribed by nearly the whole Church, no

---

[1] These views are sufficiently refuted by Jerome's own words, quoted above. See p. 129.

friendly biographer has traced their course or drawn their portrait; or if this was done, envy and bigotry have effectually effaced the record. And as the story of their life has perished, so it is with their writings; these have either been designedly destroyed or have become buried in oblivion. Not a fragment of all that proceeded from the pens of these three Witnesses has come down to us, except in the quotations made from their books by those who undertook to refute them.[1] No man, it is needless to say, would ever consent to be judged on the evidence of extracts from his writings made by an adversary. The meaning of quoted words may be greatly modified, or even neutralised, by the unquoted context. Other writings of the same author, or other chapters not referred to, may set his object or his motive in a totally different light, and in the place of distrust, awaken sympathy and admiration. Lastly, the extracts themselves may be garbled. And if all this is true as a general rule, it is emphatically so when the antagonist is a Jerome. Hence we draw our estimate of the character of these reformers from slender materials. We know not how far they possessed that true spirit of love and faith which is able to disarm or to rise above the persecution of man. We do know that they saw clearly some things in respect of which the eyes of the leading churchmen of the age were blinded.

If the warning voice raised by these just men had been heeded, and the Church had happily retraced her steps out of the labyrinth of error into which she had wandered, with what affection would their names have been embalmed! Their writings would have been preserved with as much care as those of Athanasius or Chrysostom, and we might have constructed biographies of them as worthy of our attention and even as full of incident as those of the champions of orthodoxy. But if their known actions are fairly weighed and duly considered, they will be found to deserve the title of Christian heroes. The whole Christian world was rapidly sinking into an easy and fatal slumber. They lifted up their voices to utter the warning cry. They were almost alone; they could hope for no inspiring echo from any other quarter. The courage of Chrysostom has been much extolled when he ventured from the fastness of his pulpit to attack the Empress Eudoxia; and of Basil and Ambrose, when they confronted Valens and his minister and the Emperor Theodosius, with a spirit as haughty as their own; but the breach into which Jovinian and Vigilantius threw them-

---

[1] The monks were the only librarians of the Middle Ages, and they admitted none but orthodox books. Thus the works of such writers as Vigilantius and Jovinian, even if not purposely destroyed, would soon disappear.

selves was one of far greater danger and for a far nobler prize. If any men ever played a part which should entitle them to the gratitude of posterity, surely it was these. And carefully must we note that, although their opponents, in order to weaken their influence, seek in every way to blacken their memory, yet no tangible accusation is made against them, either as to the honesty of their motives or the moral character of their life.[1]

---

[1] The opinion of the candid historian, Du Pin, lends support to the above. "It is a misfortune that Jovinian's and Vigilantius' books are lost; and there is reason to believe from those other disputes wherein St. Jerome was engaged, that if we knew what they said for themselves, instead of thinking them heretics, we should esteem them illustrious defenders of the Christian religion against that superstition, which an immoderate zeal for a monastical life did at that time introduce into the Church. . . . Since obstinacy is necessary to make a man a heretic, it would be rashness to call Jovinian a heretic, of whom we know nothing but what we have from his enemies."

PERIOD II.

FROM THE DEATH OF AUGUSTINE, A.D. 430, TO THE ACCESSION OF POPE GREGORY THE GREAT, A.D. 590.

CHAPTER I.

THE NESTORIAN STRIFE.

THAT long conflict of tongues and pens, and not unfrequently of swords also, which commenced with the Nestorian Controversy, has special claims on our attention. Not only does its record form a faithful mirror of the age, fraught with instructive lessons, but the contest itself powerfully hastened, if it did not actually produce, that vital decay of the Eastern Churches which rendered them an easy prey to the hosts of Islam.

The Arian controversy turned on the question of our Lord's proper deity; the Nestorian on that of the two natures in Him, the human and the divine. The problems on which the Eastern Church of the fifth and sixth centuries wasted her energy may be regarded as insoluble; and it is not always easy even to follow the subtle arguments of the disputants. But the narrative is curious; and if the reader has any faith still remaining in the purity of the ancient Church, or in the efficacy of Church councils, it will be severely tried before he has followed the story to its end.

Two schools of thought stand opposed to each other, the Alexandrian, and the Antiochian or Syrian. At Alexandria, where the enemy to be combated was the Arian denial of Christ's eternal Godhead, his divinity was insisted upon at the expense of his humanity, so that it was customary to say, "God was born, suffered, and redeemed us with his blood;" and the favourite appellation of the Virgin Mary (whose worship was just coming into vogue) was that of *Theo-tokos* (bearer or mother of God).[1] At the head of this school was Cyril, bishop of Alexandria, who seems to have regarded the Incarnation almost as a new entity, which is in every relation God and man in one. The Antiochian school, on the contrary, having to contend against the heresy of Apollinaris,[2] who taught that in Christ the human body was united with an animal soul only (the place of the rational soul being supplied by the Divine Logos[3]),

---

[1] The phrase is used by Athanasius.

[2] Bishop of Laodicea, died 392; see *ante*, p. 44.

[3] Christ was thus made a middle being, between God and man. Apollinaris regarded the orthodox view of a union of full humanity with full divinity in one person—of two wholes in one whole—as an absurdity.

took an opposite direction. This school, distinguished for sound learning and sobriety of interpretation, but with a tendency towards rationalism, was founded by Diodorus of Tarsus[1] and Theodore of Mopsuestia.[2] In its scheme the divine and human nature were held so rigidly apart as to make Christ, though not professedly, yet virtually, a double person. The effect was to weaken the cardinal truths of his sufferings, death and resurrection, and thus impair the reality of his work of redemption. To this school belonged Nestorius, who however held its doctrine in a more modified form than his friend and teacher Theodore. In the course of the struggle a third standard was raised by the monk Eutyches of Constantinople, who, whilst he aimed at supporting Cyril and the Alexandrian party, created a fresh schism by going still further, and teaching that there is only one nature in Christ, the divine.

If it is difficult at the beginning of the contest accurately to mark out the relative position and front of the combatants, it is still more so to follow the hostile banners through the shifting scenes of this fiercely contested field. "Never was there a case," observes Milman, "in which the contending parties approximated so closely. Both appealed to the Nicene Creed; both admitted the pre-existence, the impassibility of the Eternal Word; but the fatal duty which the Christians in that age, and unhappily in subsequent ages, have imposed upon themselves, of considering the detection of heresy the first of religious obligations, mingled as it now was with human passions and interests, made the breach irreparable." "The real differences between the combatants on either side," remarks Roberts, "in the maintenance of the dogmas of Eutyches and Nestorius, were often undiscernible amidst the dust and smoke of the combat; and the sharpest feeling of hostility in either party arose out of their mistakes of each other's meaning."

Nestorius succeeded to the episcopal chair of Constantinople, A.D. 428.[3] He began his rule as an ardent Catholic. On the fifth day after his ordination he endeavoured to deprive the Arians of their church: they burned it down in despair. "Give me," he cried in his inaugural discourse before the Emperor Theodosius II., "the earth purged of heretics, and in exchange I will give thee heaven. Help me to destroy the heretics, and I will help thee to conquer the Persians." All the while however he held private

---

[1] Died A.D. 394.

[2] He was bishop from 393—428; see *ante*, p. 73.

[3] He is described as "simple in dress, grave in demeanour, pale and meagre with ascetic observances, and of surpassing eloquence."

opinions which he refrained from openly avowing. The challenge came from his presbyter Anastasius, who said in public: "Let no man style Mary *Mother of God* (*Theotokos*), for Mary was human, and it is impossible that God should be born of humanity." This was followed up by a bishop of Mœsia who was visiting Constantinople, and who in one of his sermons cried out: "Let him be accursed who calls Mary *Mother of God.*"

Upon this a violent agitation arose in the city, not only amongst the clergy, but amongst all classes of the people. It was as if the denial of the name *Theotokos* had robbed mankind of the hope of salvation. The general feeling found its utterance through Eusebius, afterwards bishop of Dorylæum in Phrygia, and also through Proclus, who had been an unsuccessful candidate for the see of Constantinople. One day when Nestorius was preaching, the former stood up in full church, and in contradiction of the bishop, asserted that the "Eternal Word begotten before the ages had submitted to be born a second time." And Proclus, in a sermon, accused Nestorius and his party of believing only in a deified man, and of detracting from the honour of Mary. Nestorius was not slow to retort: he compared his adversaries to the pagans who gave mothers to their gods. Nevertheless, he declared that if any of the simple-minded were disposed to call the Virgin Mary *Theotokos*, he would not quarrel with them, provided they did not convert her into a goddess; but he proposed instead the safer and more Scriptural term *Christo-tokos* (the mother of Christ), inasmuch as the name Christ belongs to the whole person, uniting the divine and the human natures.[1]

. This did not satisfy his opponents. A large party of the clergy and monks refused to recognize him any longer as their bishop, or even to hold Church fellowship with him; and a placard was affixed to the walls of the principal church, probably by Eusebius, exhibiting a parallel between his tenets and those of the heretical Paul of Samosata, whose name was still a by-word in the Church. Once also when Nestorius was about to preach, a monk placed himself in the way, refusing to let him enter because it was forbidden to a heretic to teach in the churches. His enemies even threatened to throw him into the sea. In retaliation Nestorius made free use of deposition, whipping, banishment, and other forcible means against such as were amenable to his jurisdiction.

Cyril was watching events from Alexandria. His first act in

---

[1] As Nestorius justly points out, the Scriptures nowhere teach that God, but everywhere that Jesus Christ, the son of God, was born of Mary.

opposition to Nestorius was to publish a homily, for the Easter festival, on the union of deity and humanity in Christ, and afterwards to address to the Egyptian monks a long admonitory letter on the same subject. In both these documents he vindicated the title *Theotokos*, and sounded an alarm against the disturbers of orthodoxy. An unfriendly correspondence ensued between himself and Nestorius. But the latter, notwithstanding the arrogant speech with which he commenced his rule, and the intolerant and violent acts of which he had been guilty, seems to have been a sincere man, desirous of doing what he believed to be right. When therefore a good presbyter named Lampon proffered his friendly offices between the two disputants, Nestorius readily accepted his mediation, and sent Cyril a short conciliatory letter which closed the correspondence. "Lampon's gentleness," he wrote, "has conquered me. Nothing is more powerful than Christian gentleness. When I see such a spirit in any one I am seized with fear; it is as though God dwelt in him."

But Cyril was too envious of the Byzantine see, and too full of ill-will against his rival, to lay aside his hostility. He intrigued with the clergy at Constantinople; and when Nestorius proposed that the matters in dispute should be referred to a general council, he wrote to Celestine bishop of Rome, sending him a garbled report of the doctrines taught by Nestorius, and craftily leaving it to his decision whether the offender ought not to be deprived of the fellowship of the Church. Nestorius likewise sent Celestine an account of the controversy, but in this letter, instead of conceding to the bishop of Rome any jurisdiction over the Churches, he addressed him, as Chrysostom had done, simply as an equal. Celestine, as was to be expected, espoused the cause of Cyril. He pronounced Nestorius guilty of heresy, and directed that unless he should within ten days present a written recantation of his errors, and testify his agreement with the Roman and Alexandrian Churches on the birth of Christ, he should be degraded and excommunicated. At the same time in a letter to Cyril, full of extravagant praises, he gave to that bishop "by the sovereign authority of the Apostolic See," power to carry the sentence into execution. The copy of the decree which he sent to Nestorius was accompanied by vehement reproaches.

Thus armed, Cyril called upon Nestorius to recant, and at the same time sent him a creed or body of doctrine set forth in twelve formulas of Anathema, which he required him to subscribe. This step had the effect of converting the personal dispute between himself and Nestorius into a rupture with the Antiochian Church.

The Syrian bishops, many of them men of learning and piety, were indignant at Cyril's conduct; and their leader John, the patriarch of Antioch, selected Theodoret[1] to draw up an answer to the Anathemas. In his answer, however, Theodoret unhappily showed himself more eager to confute Cyril than to discover and set forth Scriptural truth. He did not consider, controversialists seldom consider, that victory at the expense of truth is not victory, but defeat.

Meanwhile the messengers of Celestine and Cyril presented their demands to Nestorius. Conscious of right, and of his independent dignity, the bishop treated their message with disdain. At the Imperial Court also, Cyril's conduct produced an unfavourable impression; and Theodosius II. acceded to Nestorius' request and summoned a general council.

The council met at Ephesus in the year 431.[2] With his copy of the summons Cyril received an imperial reprimand for his meddlesome and intriguing conduct. The better to secure calm deliberation and order, the Emperor sent down to Ephesus the Count Candidian, one of his wisest ministers, as his representative. The count ordered all strangers, monks and laymen to quit the city, and forbade the bishops to absent themselves from the synod during its session, and especially to visit the court. Cyril and Nestorius arrived at Ephesus at the appointed time. The former brought with him sixty Egyptian bishops, blindly devoted to his will. He had also a powerful colleague in Memnon, bishop of Ephesus itself, who had forty prelates under him. Nestorius deemed it necessary to obtain from Candidian a guard of soldiers for his protection.

The arrival of John of Antioch and the Syrian bishops, who made the journey by land, was delayed by violent rains and other causes, so that sixteen days after the appointed time they were still five or six days' journey from the city. John informed Cyril of this in a respectful letter which he sent to excuse their delay. But it chimed in so completely with Cyril's purpose to proceed in the absence of the friends of Nestorius, that he refused to wait longer. On the 22nd of June, therefore, notwithstanding the protest of Candidian and of Nestorius and forty-one other bishops, he opened

---

[1] Bishop of Cyrus on the Euphrates and a fellow-student of Chrysostom; well known also as the author of one of that series of Church histories (commencing with Eusebius) which covered the first six centuries of the Christian era, and from which we have had frequent occasion to quote.

[2] It is known as the Third General Council, Nicæa, A.D. 325, being the First and Constantinople, 381, the Second.

the synod, having allowed his party to place him in the chair. The council was held in the church of St. Mary, where, as tradition affirmed, the Virgin, the *Theotokos*, had been interred. About 200 bishops were present. Nestorius kept aloof, declaring that he would appear only when all were assembled.

Under these circumstances an orderly investigation was not to be thought of; the issue had indeed been determined beforehand. In a single day, the assembly sitting from morning till night, Nestorius was cited, arraigned, condemned, deposed, and deprived of his orders. At the conclusion of the farce, the assembly raised a tumultuous shout, "Anathema, Anathema to him who does not anathematize Nestorius!" and, as the narrative has it, "after many tears," proceeded to pass sentence against him in the following terms: "The Lord Jesus Christ, blasphemed by Nestorius, has ordained by this most holy synod, that he should be deprived of his episcopal rank, and of all sacerdotal fellowship." This sentence was signed by 198 bishops;[1] after which Rheginus of Constantia in Cyprus preached a discourse in which Nestorius was branded as "worse than Cain, as one under whom the earth ought to open and swallow him up, and fire to rain down on him from heaven that the simple might witness his end." The preacher thus concluded: "Let us worship and adore the God, Logos, who has condescended to walk among us in the flesh, without separating Himself from the essence of the Father."[2] In the message to Nestorius which accompanied the sentence he was called "a new Judas." The Ephesians were violently orthodox, and when the sentence was proclaimed by heralds, it caused tumultuous rejoicing in the city. The people, who had waited from morning till evening, broke out into shouts of triumph, and escorted Cyril and the bishops in state to their houses with torches and censers.[3] We need not stay to characterize this council as it deserves, because it was succeeded some years later by one far more violent and infamous.

---

[1] Some of the subscriptions are found in this form: "I —— have subscribed by the hand of ——, because I cannot write." It was the same with the signatures at the Council of Chalcedon, eighteen years afterwards.

[2] "As if," remarks Neander, "this worship of the incarnate God did not exist among the party of Nestorius, because they expressed themselves in other language! Thus," he adds, "a new slavery to forms of expression in religion was again to be substituted in place of the worship of God in spirit and in truth!"

[3] These events and the place suggest a parallel with Acts xix. 34, 35; as if, almost, the *Theotokos* had taken the place of the *Dio-petes*, Diana of the Ephesians.

The council sent to the Emperor a party statement of what had been done, full of perversions of the truth regarding Nestorius; and prayed for an order that the writings of that heretic might be burned wherever they were found. Nestorius and ten of his friends sent up a counter-memorial, complaining of the arbitrary and illegal proceedings of Cyril and Memnon, demanding protection, and praying the Emperor to summon a new and impartial assembly. Candidian also drew up his report, in which he gave it as his judgment that the decrees of the synod could have no legal validity.

In the midst of these transactions, John of Antioch and the Syrian bishops, thirty in number, arrived at Ephesus, and in conjunction with the other prelates friendly to Nestorius, proceeded very imprudently to constitute themselves a new council.[1] With still greater imprudence they passed sentence of deposition upon Cyril and Memnon, and excommunicated all who had taken part in the proceedings against Nestorius. Now also came upon the scene the deputies of the Roman bishop, who had been detained by contrary winds, and who, according to their instructions, approved of all that Cyril had done. Thus fortified, the Cyrillian council proceeded to summon before it John of Antioch and his associates, and when they refused to appear passed sentence of suspension against them. The Emperor, on receiving Candidian's report, sent a letter to the synod, censuring the conduct of its members, and declaring that he could not approve of any judgment upon the doctrines in dispute, which did not proceed from the whole united council. Unable to offer any reasonable bar to this equitable decree, Cyril called in the aid of fanaticism.

There was at Constantinople an archimandrite,[2] held in great verneration, named Dalmatius. For forty-eight years he had lived in seclusion. The Emperor himself had sought his help, but could never prevail upon him, even in times of public calamity, to leave his cell. Dalmatius had from the first regarded Nestorius as a teacher of error, and was wont to say to those who visited him: "Take heed to yourselves, my brethren, an evil beast is come into this city who may do you an injury." To this man Cyril sent an account of the judgment passed upon Nestorius, and of the affliction which, as he pretended, the faithful were suffering at his hands. The arrival of the letter set the whole body of zealous monks in commotion. Dalmatius imagined himself summoned by a voice

---

[1] They are henceforth spoken of as the Oriental Party.

[2] Archimandrite, "ruler over the fold," signifies an abbot or superior of monasteries.

from heaven to come forth at last from his seclusion in order to save the Church from ruin. The abbots and monks issued from their cloisters, and chanting psalms, with torches in their hands, marched in procession with Dalmatius at their head to the palace of the Emperor. Vast multitudes followed and stood before the gate, chanting in their choirs, whilst the abbots were admitted to an audience. In the presence of a full court Dalmatius addressed the Emperor in a bold and confident tone, and handing him the letter of the synod, asked, to whom he would give ear, to six thousand bishops, or to one godless man? The weak-minded Emperor promised that the Cyrillian party should be allowed to send deputies to Constantinople. When Dalmatius announced to the multitudes outside that a favourable answer had been received, the vast procession, singing the 150th Psalm, marched forward to one of the churches, where Dalmatius read the letter of the synod and gave an account of his audience. As soon as he had finished, a universal shout was raised, "Anathema to Nestorius!"

Acting on the permission thus granted, Cyril sent three bishops to Constantinople. The effect of their influence was soon apparent. Some who had hitherto numbered themselves amongst the friends of Nestorius were won over to the opposite side. To one of these the persecuted bishop wrote a touching letter, not reproaching him for his defection, but vindicating his own orthodoxy, and declaring how thankful he would be to return to the tranquillity of his old cloister life. The Oriental bishops on their part were not idle. They still had friends at court, one of whom, the count Irenæus, a colleague of Candidian, laboured to counteract the influence of the Cyrillian bishops. His success, however was only partial; the Emperor's understanding was convinced, but he was a tool of court parties, which in turn were directed by outside influences. All he could do was to order that the three deposed bishops, Nestorius, Cyril, and Memnon, should remain deposed, and that the rest of the council should lay aside their mutual contention, and prepare to return to their own sees in peace and concord.[1]

The Imperial message was entrusted to the count John, one of the secretaries of state, who invited the bishops on both sides to meet him at his own apartment in Ephesus. But instead of

---

[1] The extreme heat of the summer, and confinement within the walls of Ephesus, affected the health of many of the bishops, as well as of their attendants; several died, while many who had not made provision for so long an absence from their homes, were reduced to distress for the means of subsistence.

listening to what he had to say, the two parties, as soon as they met, fell into vehement disputes, which lasted the greater part of the day and went on even to blows. Unable to bring them to reason, the count caused Cyril and Nestorius to be forcibly removed; after which he laboured in every way to restore harmony. John of Antioch and his friends were prepared to make concessions; but the Cyrillians, to whom the person of their leader was of much more importance than that of Nestorius was to his party, were not so compliant, and when the count proposed that a common confession of faith should be drawn up, they would have nothing to do with it. One point on which the Emperor had expressly insisted was that the Oriental bishops should declare themselves in favour of the *Theotokos*. In accordance with this, the more moderate amongst them drew up a confession, in which, whilst the two natures in Christ were distinguished with precision, a sense was admitted in which the term *Theotokos* might be used. This concession, however, was distasteful to the more zealous of the party, who wholly rejected the term.

Count John seeing that all his pains to restore peace were ineffectual, advised the Emperor to send for deputies from both sides, and to enter himself into a personal investigation of the whole matter. To this the Emperor agreed; and eight bishops from each party went up to Constantinople. Soon after their departure from Ephesus, Nestorius was informed that the Emperor, in court phrase, "had given him permission" to return to his cloister. Weary of strife and care, he gladly obeyed, and retired to his cell outside the gates of Antioch. At the same time Cyril and Memnon were by an Imperial decree restored to their episcopal dignity.

When the deputies of the two parties arrived at Chalcedon, they were directed not to cross the Bosphorus into Constantinople, for fear of exciting an insurrection of the monks. This prohibition, in the case of the Cyrillians, was presently withdrawn; whilst the Oriental delegates, still detained on the Asiatic side, were set upon by the ferocious monks of the suburb, and some of them wounded. By this time the mind of the Emperor had become entirely closed against Nestorius, and when the restoration of that bishop to his see was urged by some members of the privy council, he cried, "Let no one speak to me of Nestorius; I have had enough of him already." The Oriental deputies, after five pretended audiences, seeing that their longer talliance would be to no purpose, obtained leave to return to their homes; as did also the rest of the bishops who had remained at Ephesus.

Notwithstanding all that had taken place, there was little disposition at the Imperial Court to support Cyril in his antagonism to the Orientals. His dogmatic stiffness was regarded as the cause of the continued divisions in the Church. To further his case he had recourse to the arts of cajolery and bribery, and spent so much money on chamberlains and court ladies, that the Churches of Alexandria were burdened with debt.

But if Cyril was regarded with suspicion, the hatred against Nestorius grew more and more intense. Even John of Antioch now wavered, and at length drew off from his old friend and ally. Cyril, on his part, finding his intrigues produce but little fruit, began to see that a timely concession might win over the moderate Orientals to the condemnation of Nestorius. An iniquitous compact was accordingly entered into between the two parties. Cyril subscribed a confession of faith, essentially identical with that which the moderate Orientals had sent up to Constantinople. John of Antioch consented to condemn Nestorius, and to recognize Maximian as bishop of Constantinople in his place. This compromise, made in the year 432, met with the usual fate of such hollow and artificial reconciliations. Concealing the inward schism which still continued to exist, it merely served to call forth new divisions. Cyril was accused by the zealots of his party of betraying his own cause, whilst in his "confession" the Ultra-Orientals saw the hated spectre of Apollinarianism rise again into view.[1]

But whilst there were divisions in the Oriental camp with regard to the scheme of doctrine now put forth by Cyril, there was little disposition to follow John's example in condemning Nestorius. With Theodoret at their head, the Syrian bishops declared that they would consent "neither with hand, tongue, nor heart," to the unjust and wicked sentence which had been passed upon him; and they not only continued to regard Cyril as excluded from the

---

[1] One of the Oriental bishops, Andreas of Samosata, relates a singular dream. He found himself in an assembly of bishops, where he was told that the heretic Apollinaris was in reality still living. Andreas in astonishment asked several times whether this really was so, and Alexander assured him it was. All at once they entered a house where Apollinaris, in extreme old age, lay upon a bed. As they were about to take their seats by the bedside the old man rose and distributed the elements of the Supper. The bishop John of Antioch sitting on the bed received the bread and wine from his hand. But Andreas with indignation said within himself, "What accommodation to circumstances is this! it is a sin against the Holy Ghost; it is trifling with the incarnation of our Lord." With these words he awoke, and gave earnest expression to the wish that the dream might not prove true, that Apollinaris, who had re-appeared, so to speak, in Cyril, might not bring them all over to his own doctrine.

Church, but they excommuicated all who accepted the compromise. Encroaching conduct on the part of John still further estranged them from him, and the schism which thus arose in the diocese of Antioch, spread into other parts of the East, until there was formed an association of bishops who were opposed to the three patriarchs of Constantinople, Alexandria, and Antioch.

Nestorius was still dear to many at Constantinople, and on the death of Maximian, in 433, vast multitudes assembled and demanded his restoration, threatening in case of refusal to set fire to the cathedral. This demonstration however was of no avail. Proclus, who had been, as we have seen, one of the first to oppose Nestorius, was elected patriarch, and leagued himself with Cyril and John, in supporting the unnatural compact of the previous year. The two latter, determined to overcome the resistance of the Oriental Church, employed threats and bribery, and even obtained an Imperial edict for the expulsion of such bishops as refused to accept the articles of agreement. Men who for a long period of years had given their lives wholly to their spiritual office, were now threatened with a forcible separation from the communities by whom they were beloved and respected, because the arbitrary will of a few individuals found it possible through the Court to rule over the Church.

Most of the bishops, including even Theodoret, bent before the storm. A few remained faithful, and were driven from their sees by military force. Amongst these are especially to be named Meletius of Mopsuestia and Alexander, the venerable bishop of Hierapolis, who set the noble example of preferring the answer of a good conscience above worldly advantage and imperial favour. Alexander boldly declared that even if the dead were to rise and testify in favour of the Egyptian doctrines, he must yet be true to his own conscience, and reject them. When he was torn from his own flock, a universal lamentation arose through the city; the churches were closed, and it was necessary to open them by force. Meletius, when reproached with the presumption of standing out alone against the united judgment of the whole Christian world, replied that God has given to men the dominion over their own will; whence it has often happened, as the Old and New Testaments show, that a few, inspired by faith in God, have defended the truth against the multitude. "Pardon me, I pray you," he said, "if I find myself unable to deceive my own conscience. As soon as I see the order for my removal signed by the Emperor's own hand, I shall leave the church, still praising God as before. I am ready by his grace not only to give up my church, but to die a thousand deaths rather than sin against my conscience." He was banished to Armenia. Neither of these faithful Witnesses had saved enough money to defray the expenses of his journey.

Thus forsaken by almost all his friends, and every day more hated at the Imperial Court, the very name of Nestorius became a byword and a reproach, and continued to be such for many successive ages. His enemies grudged him the tranquillity he enjoyed in his cloister before the gates of Antioch; and the Roman bishop Celestine, so early as 432, called upon the Emperor to remove from society the man who had been condemned by the judgment of the whole Church, and who still persisted in his "blasphemous errors." He was, however, left unmolested until 435, when Cyril and John, in the prosecution of their unholy alliance, procured his banishment. The place of his exile was one of the oases of Egypt, probably the Great Oasis. After remaining there a while he was carried off by some Libyan barbarians, who however had compassion upon him, set him at liberty, and warned him to seek a safer place of abode. He went to the town of Panapolis in the Thebais; but here the prefect, more barbarous than the barbarians, caused the aged bishop, now enfeebled by hardship, to be hurried by his soldiers pitilessly from place to place. Of the manner in which he ended his days, no certain account has come down to us. During his exile he enjoyed sufficient composure of mind to write a history of the controversy in which he had been engaged. In this production, which he styled *Tragedy*, and of which only some few extracts have survived, he forcibly exposes the intrigues of Cyril, but speaks with more forbearance of those who had been the dupes of that bishop.

The followers of Nestorius were numerous. Driven beyond the bounds of the Empire, their teachers sought a refuge in the school of Edessa, from whence their doctrines spread into Persia,[1] India, and Tartary, and even into the heart of northern China. They had churches also in Syria, Arabia, and Cyprus. At the present day they are found in the mountains of Kurdistan and the plain of Oroomiah on the confines of Persia and Armenia. Although ignorant, they are in many ways more simple and spiritual than the other Oriental Churches. They reject the use of images, the worship of Mary as the mother of God, and the doctrine of purgatory. They do not practise auricular confession; and their priests mainly support themselves by labour. Both bishops and presbyters are permitted to marry. Their worship is more simple than that

---

[1] Syriac became the ritual language of the Persian Church.

of the Greek Church, and they are more accessible to the message of the Gospel. They have been styled the Protestants of Asia.

The banishment of Nestorius brought no relief to his followers. The same year a new Imperial edict appeared, ordaining that the Nestorians should for the future be called *Simonians*,[1] that all who should copy, preserve, or read the writings of Nestorius should be severely punished, and that all bishops who defended him should be deposed. All meetings of Nestorians for divine worship were forbidden. A military tribune was sent into the Antiochian diocese to enforce this law. But Theodoret and some others refused to stoop to any further concession.

In the midst of these conflicts death carried off Cyril from the scene of his restless strife, A.D. 444. But the spirit of Cyril survived in his successor.[2] This was Dioscorus, a man of like ambition, of an irascible and boisterous temper, and a loose manner of life, who stuck at no means, however infamous, to attain his object. He inherited the aims as well as some of the traits of his predecessor, and laboured with equal zeal to make the doctrine of the one nature in Christ dominant, and to exalt the Alexandrian see above that of Constantinople. The Oriental Churches, led now by Theodoret, were the principal object of his attack; he had as allies within those Churches a party of monks and clergy, the abbot Barsumas at their head, who had acted as spies to Cyril and creators of disturbance.

At Constantinople there continued to be an influential body of abbots and monks, who, deficient in intellectual culture, and unable to apprehend any system but that which appealed to their feelings, naturally gravitated towards the Alexandrian doctrine, which in fact they carried to an extreme. "We hold fast to the Scriptures," so they were accustomed to say, "and these declare that the Word became flesh. In becoming flesh He assuredly underwent no change. He is the same; and this is the inexpressible wonder. God was born; God suffered; God has a body. The *how* is what no reason can explain. It is not for us to know more than Scripture reveals. All beyond is dangerous to faith."[3]

---

[1] From Simon Magus; a common epithet of detestation for inveterate heretics:—"even," says the Edict, "as the Arians were styled Porphyrians by a law of Constantine of blessed memory."

[2] In regard to Cyril, it is due to say that some historians take a much more favourable view of his character and aims.

[3] They spoke of the Saviour's humanity as "absorbed in his Godhead, like a drop of honey in the ocean."

The leader of this party was the abbot Eutyches,[1] and from him the new stage of the protracted contest has been called the Eutychian Controversy. This man had lived from youth to old age shut up in his cloister, which he had never quitted but once, namely, at the time of the Cyrillian Council at Ephesus, when he had come abroad in public to raise his voice against Nestorius. It was the writings of Theodoret which now again drew him out to oppose the "pernicious doctrines" of those who, as he expressed it, divided the one and only Christ into two Sons of God. At the same time Theodoret in a fresh treatise challenged both Dioscorus and Eutyches, skilfully attacking the whole type of doctrine which they set forth, and making an able defence of the Antiochian theology. Dioscorus, instead of defending himself with the pen, accused Theodoret before the new patriarch of Antioch, Domnus—who had succeeded to that see on the death of his uncle John—of preaching two Sons of God. Theodoret saw the danger, and expressed his readiness to condemn such as refused to call Mary *Theotokos*. But this concession came too late. Dioscorus sent a memorial to the Emperor, accusing the whole Oriental Church of Nestorianism; and Theodoret received orders to keep quiet and not to leave his own diocese.

At this juncture the scene suddenly shifted. Flavian, who in

---

[1] "As Nestorius, teaching rightly that God and man are distinct natures, did thereupon misinfer that in Christ those natures can by no conjunction make one person; so Eutyches, of sound belief as teaching their true personal conjunction, became unsound by denying the difference which still continueth between the one and the other natures."—Hooker. The same judicious writer thus sums up the four points which express the whole nature of Christ, with the corresponding heresies regarding them, and the councils at which they were condemned. "There are but four things which concur to make complete the whole state of our Lord Jesus Christ: his deity, his manhood, the conjunction of both, and the distinction of one from the other being joined into one. Four principal heresies there are, which have in these things withstood the truth: Arians, by bending themselves against the deity of Christ; Apollinarians, by maiming and misinterpreting that which belongeth to his human nature; Nestorians, by rending Christ asunder, and dividing Him into two persons; the followers of Eutyches, by confounding in his person those natures which they should distinguish. Against these there have been four most famous councils: the Council of Nicæa, to define against Arians; against Apollinarians, the Council of Constantinople; the Council of Ephesus, against Nestorians; against Eutychians, the Chalcedon Council. In four words, alēthōs, teleōs, adiairetōs, asugchutōs, *truly, perfectly, indivisibly, distinctly;* the first applied to his being God, the second to his being man, the third to his being of both One, and the fourth to his still continuing in that one Both; we may fully, by way of abridgment, comprise whatsoever antiquity hath at large handled either in declaration of Christian belief, or in refutation of the foresaid heresies."

446 succeeded Proclus as bishop of Constantinople, assembled two years later a local or *home* synod, as it was termed. In this assembly, Eutyches, whose crude theology was as hateful to many as that of his opponent Nestorius had been, was formally arraigned and excommunicated as a heretic. This rash act, committed in the face of the Emperor's displeasure, and in spite of the popularity and influence of the accused, was acquiesced in unwillingly by Flavian, who was carried away by the tide he could not stem. Eutyches and his party cried aloud for a general council.

The "Second Council of Ephesus" was accordingly summoned in 449. It was never designed to be a free assembly of the Church; it was merely an instrument in the hands of Dioscorus, Eutyches and the Emperor, for the overthrow of Flavian, and, as Theodosius expressed it, "the extirpation of the devilish root of the Nestorian heresy." Dioscorus was nominated president. Flavian was to have no vote. In order to counterbalance the still dreaded influence of Theodoret and the Oriental bishops, a seat was given to the abbot Barsumas, as the representative of the orthodox archimandrites, who, in many places of the East, were in antagonism to their bishops. Lastly two counts of the Empire were included that they might employ the secular power in support of the dominant party. The Egyptian bishops who accompanied Dioscorus were men of a violent and fanatical spirit, and Barsumas was attended by a "thousand rabid monks and a troop of brawny hospital waiters," whose fierce shouts showed they were ready for strife and outrage. But the cause of injustice derived its greatest strength from the cowardice or covetousness of many of the bishops, who loved honour and office more than the truth. They professed Christ with the lips, but in act and spirit they denied Him. When a formal complaint was about to be brought against a bishop, accused of unchastity and other offences, Dioscorus dismissed the whole matter. "If," said he, "you have a complaint against his orthodoxy, we shall receive it, but we have not come here to pass judgment on unchastity." They were, in fact, "for acting," remarks Theodoret, "as if Christ had give us a rule of *faith* merely, and not a rule of *practice*."

The proceedings were violent and disorderly from the beginning; Dioscorus turned out all reporters but those of his own party. He opened the synod by declaring that the Council of Nicæa and the Council of Ephesus had established one and the same creed, which was unalterable. "Accursed then," he exclaimed, "be he who would unsettle again what was there determined!" In response to which the assembly shouted out: "On this depends the salvation of the world! God save the bishop Dioscorus, the great guardian of the faith!"

"Eutyches laid before the council a written confession of faith, which having been read and approved, Flavian called upon Eusebius of Dorylæum to read and make good the charges he had preferred against Eutyches at the *home* synod. This was not allowed, and the acts of the synod were merely read over. No disturbance arose until the part taken by Eusebius in urging Eutyches to acknowledge two natures in Christ after the incarnation, came under review, and then all was confusion and uproar." The Egyptian bishops and the whole throng of monks who accompanied Barsumas, exclaimed : "Divide asunder the man who speaks of two natures! He who speaks of two natures is a *Nestorius*." Eusebius attempted to explain, but was interrupted by cries of, "Burn Eusebius! let him be burned alive! As he has cut Christ asunder, so let *him* be cut asunder!" The president put the question: "Is the doctrine that there are two natures after the incarnation to be tolerated?" The answer was returned: "Anathema on him who so says!" "I have your voices," replied Dioscorus, "I must have your hands! He who cannot cry, let him lift up his hands!" All hands were raised, with the shout: "Expel, burn, tear, cut asunder, massacre—all who hold two natures!"

Dioscorus then demanded the condemnation of Eusebius and Flavian. The bishops now perceived that they had gone too far, and a number of them gathered round, imploring him on their knees not to proceed further. Disregarding their entreaties he exclaimed: "Call in the counts!" The pro-consul of Asia entered, attended by soldiers and monks, with swords, clubs and chains. The bishops in terror attempted to hide themselves in corners of the church, or under the benches; they were dragged out, and with threats and blows compelled to sign a blank paper on which the condemnation of Flavian was to be written. It is said that Dioscorus and Barsumas struck the aged Flavian on the face, kicked him, and stamped on him, Barsumas shouting, "Strike him, strike him dead!" He was taken out of the council hall; and being dragged by the soldiers to Hypepe, a village at a short distance from the city, expired three days after. Eusebius and Theodoret were deposed and the former imprisoned. The Roman legates offered a fruitless resistance to these barbarous and tyrannical acts.[1]

---

[1] Neander remarks that the bishops, in palliation afterwards of their own conduct, had strong inducements to exaggerate the violence used on this occasion, and that many contradictions may be detected in their testimony. "Still,'

To this infamous assembly Leo of Rome, doubtless not uninfluenced by the treatment his own representatives had received, gave the expressive name of the *Robber Synod* (*Latrocinium*). "Terrible was the day on which it opened," writes the abbé Martin; "the true faith received in the East a shock from which it has never since completely recovered. The Church witnessed the separation from herself of nations which have never returned to her, and perhaps never will." It seems to us hardly credible that such a scene could ever be tolerated either by Church or Emperor. We see the literal fulfilment of Paul's prediction to the elders of this very city: "Grievous wolves shall enter in among you, not sparing the flock." What were such synods but herds of wolves in disguise, holding high council as though they were the true shepherds? To what purpose is it that the Holy Ghost says: "The Lord's servant must not strive, but be gentle towards all; correcting in meekness them that oppose themselves"?

So corrupt were the times that the very bishops who had taken part in the *home* synod of Constantinople under Flavian, hastened to give their adhesion to the decrees of the Robber Council. But this concession could not save the party. Many of the most worthy bishops of the East were deposed. By these measures Dioscorus succeeded at last in silencing, if he could not extinguish, the Oriental Church.

The sagacious churchman who then filled the Roman chair, and of whom it has been said that he "possessed every virtue compatible with an unbounded ambition,"[1] had been no unconcerned spectator of the Nestorian Controversy. He considered himself to be of right, as Peter's successor, the chief shepherd of the entire Church, and the hope of establishing universal dominion, no less than his own sound theological convictions, compelled him to interfere. His strong clear intellect perceived the importance of the question at issue, and two months before the Robber Council met,

---

he adds, "it is clear that force was resorted to in various ways; that the bishops were kept confined for a whole day in the church; that they were menaced by soldiers and monks till they had subscribed; and that blank papers were laid before them for their signature, which could afterwards be filled up with whatever the leaders chose."

[1] Milman says of Leo: "He was a Roman in sentiment as in birth. All that survived of Rome, of her unbounded ambition, her inflexible perseverance, her dignity in defeat, her haughtiness of language, her belief in her own eternity and in her indefeasible title to universal dominion, her respect for traditionary and written law and for unchangeable custom, might seem concentrated in him." Leo, it may be added, seems to have been almost free from the *superstition* of his age.

he had embodied his views in a letter or *Tome*, addressed to the Patriarch Flavian. This document, or one of similar import, was presented to the council, but Dioscorus always contrived to put off the reading of it. In this celebrated letter, the entireness and yet the distinctness of the two natures united in the Saviour, are defined with singular ability, and copiously illustrated. Leo demonstrates that the fundamental truth of Christianity is sacrificed quite as much by a curtailment of Christ's humanity as of his divinity. "The faith," so he wrote, in words which have become famous, "by which the Catholic Church lives and progresses is, that neither his humanity exists without his true divinity, nor his divinity without his true humanity. A denial of his veritable human nature is a denial also of his corporeal passion; and the danger is equal of believing that our Lord Jesus Christ is either God alone without being man, or man only without being God. In the one nature He suffered death, but in the other He could not die."

After the Robber Council events concurred to favour Leo's interference. In 450 Theodosius died, and his sister Pulcheria, who had been the patroness of Flavian, united herself in marriage with Marcian, a soldier of fortune on whom she conferred the Imperial diadem. A complete change now came over the court religion. The exiled bishops were recalled; and many trimmed their sails anew to suit the change in the wind. Anatolius, the new bishop of Constantinople, was recognized by Leo only on the condition of subscribing his Letter and condemning Eutyches, as well as Nestorius.

Both Leo and the Emperor were favourable to calling a new general council, as the best means of repairing the mischief done by the Robber Synod; but whilst Leo urged that the place of meeting should be in Italy, the Emperor decided on Nicæa. The assembly came together in 451.[1] Owing to the disturbances created by fanatical monks and others, the Emperor was induced to transfer it to Chalcedon.

The council met in the church of Euphemia the martyr. Evagrius the historian, who was conversant with the capital and its vicinity, describes the spot with the pen of an eye-witness: "You go up to the church by a gentle ascent, and from this commanding position, survey the plain beneath, verdant with herbage, corn, and every kind of tree. The eye takes in also a range of woody moun-

---

[1] The number of bishops is variously reckoned at from 520 to 630. All were from the East except Leo's envoys and two African bishops.

tains, and rests on the sea where the dark blue waters play with a gentle ripple on the beach, or the surging waves in their recoil sweep back the shells and seaweed. Right opposite rises Constantinople in the charm of its vastness. Here the council was under the Emperor's own eye, and he deputed nineteen officers of state to attend it as his representatives. The Roman delegates and Anatolius sat as presidents of the clergy.

Although the assembly was so numerous, and so august in its constitution, the irritation and mutual hatred of the two parties was apparent from the very outset. When Theodoret appeared in the midst as the accuser of his former judges, whilst he was welcomed by the Orientals with enthusiasm, the bishops of the Egyptian party raised a malignant cry: "Cast forth the Jew, the enemy of God, the blasphemer of Christ!" Notwithstanding, however, this burst of fanaticism, fear, court favour, and the change in religious fashion soon showed their effects. The Palestinian bishops left the seats which they had at first occupied near the Egyptians, and removed to the opposite side where the Orientals and the Roman delegates were seated. Others followed their example, until at last Dioscorus was left with only thirteen Egyptian bishops to support him. But the sense of shame was not entirely wanting. When the question arose of deposing those bishops who had taken the lead in the late council, the assembly resounded with the cry: "We have all sinned, we all ask forgiveness." Many with an ill grace excused their past conduct on the ground of Imperial authority and constraint. Even the commissioners declared such an excuse in matters of faith to be inadmissible, and Dioscorus stigmatized it as a confession of guilt. The Alexandrian bishop was as courageous as he was overbearing. He made an able and spirited defence,[1] and had even the audacity to excommunicate Leo. The sentence of the synod, which was signed by about 300 bishops, condemned him to degradation from his episcopal and priestly rank: it was confirmed by the Emperor, who added to it that of exile. Dioscorus ended his days at Gangra in Paphlagonia, A.D. 454.

Leo's letter to Flavian, already noticed, was read at the Council of Chalcedon. When the Roman delegates proposed that it should be adopted as an authoritative creed, some murmurs were at first heard; but when it was threatened to hold a council at Rome, the

---

[1] Dioscorus acknowledged Christ to be "*of* two natures," but declined to use the form "*in* two natures," thus refusing to own that the difference of natures subsisted after the incarnation. The distinction between "*in*" and "*of*" became a Shibboleth in the Church.

objectors gave way, and shouts of approval burst from all sides:
"This is the belief of the Fathers, of the Apostles! Thus do we
all believe! Accursed be he who denies that Peter has spoken by
the mouth of Leo!"[1]

We subjoin the symbol or creed adopted by the council, which
was succeeded by the usual presumptuous anathema against all
who should presume to teach otherwise: "Following the holy
Fathers, we unanimously teach one and the same Son, our Lord
Jesus Christ, complete as to his Godhead, and complete as to his
manhood; truly God, and truly man, of a reasonable soul and
human flesh subsisting; consubstantial with the Father as to his
Godhead, and consubstantial also with us as to his manhood; like
unto us in all things, yet without sin: as to his Godhead begotten
of the Father before all worlds, but as to his manhood, in these
last days born for us men and for our salvation of the Virgin Mary,
the mother of God (*Theotokos*); one and the same Christ, Son,
Lord, Only-begotten, to be acknowledged in (or of)[2] two natures,
without confusion, without conversion, without severance, and
without division; the distinction of the natures being in nowise
taken away by their union, but the property of each nature being
maintained, and both concurring in one person and substance
(*hypostasis*). We confess not a Son divided and sundered into
two persons, but one and the same Son, and Only-begotten, God
the Word, our Lord Jesus Christ; even as the prophets had before
proclaimed concerning Him, and He himself hath taught us, and
the symbol of the fathers hath handed down to us."

Although the Egyptian party had submitted, their hatred towards
the Orientals was in no degree appeased. In the eighth session of
the council the case of Theodoret came up for consideration, and he
was set upon vociferously, and urged to anathematize Nestorius, his
doctrines, and his friends. The theological opinions of Theodoret
appear to have undergone a change,[3] and he had come to the
council prepared to make large concessions. "Truly," he said, "it
is not for the sake of my bishopric that I have come here, but to

---

[1] A legend grew up respecting this letter. It was said that when the Pope
had written it, he laid it on the Apostle Peter's altar, praying that if there were
anything erroneous in it, it might be corrected. At the end of three days he
found the letter marked with sundry erasures and emendations, which he
accepted as the work of the apostle.

[2] The reading is uncertain.

[3] In one of his latest works, his *Account of Heresies*, he speaks of Nestorius
as "an instrument of Satan," and as having under the pretext of orthodoxy
denied both the divinity and the incarnation of the Only-begotten Son.

prove myself an orthodox man, to show you that I condemn Nestorius and Eutyches and every one who speaks of two Sons of God." This was not enough for his implacable adversaries, who interrupted him with repeated cries: "Say, Anathema to Nestorius and to all who think with him." He attempted to justify himself: "I cannot utter that anathema, but I believe "——. Here he was again interrupted: "He is a heretic, a Nestorian, cast out the Nestorian!" Wearied with the strife, and overborne by clamour, he at length gave way, and repeated the formula: "Anathema to Nestorius, and to every one who refuses to call Mary the mother of God, and who divides in two the Only-begotten Son." Upon this he was considered to have given sufficient proof of his orthodoxy, and at the instance of the Imperial commissioners he was restored to his Church by acclamation. It is uncertain whether Theodoret returned to his see, or spent the remainder of his days in his monastery, devoting himself to literary labour. He died A.D. 458.[1]

Theodoret's is a sad history. He was possessed of a broad, unselfish, and independent spirit, but the times in which he lived were too hard and stormy for his faith. With Nestorius and John of Antioch, he was brought up in a Syrian monastery, where he is said to have been placed at the age of seven, and to have sat at the feet of Theodore of Mopsuestia and Chrysostom. In 423 he was pressed into the episcopal office, and sent to govern the Church of Cyrus on the Euphrates, with its 800 villages. Here he set himself with extraordinary success to the conversion of heretics, and was distinguished for his skill in refuting the arguments of Jews and pagans. In one of his letters he enters, like Paul, into a forced commendation of himself: "I have never prosecuted, or been prosecuted at law ; and I can say the same of all the pious clergy in my diocese. Neither I nor my servants ever received a gift, not so much as a loaf or an egg. Long ago I gave my patrimony to the poor; and now I possess neither house, land, nor money, not even a sepulchre in which to lay my bones. Out of my episcopal revenues I have erected porticoes, built bridges, and repaired the public baths. I found the city without water, and have constructed an aqueduct by which it is plentifully supplied." When Theodoret was deposed by the Robber Synod, he wrote : "The hardships we undergo for the

---

[1] Whilst theological storms were thus agitating the Church, the world without was convulsed by a tempest of a different kind. Attila the Hun, "the scourge of God," was devastating the countries both of the East and the West. From 445 to 450, he ravaged the Empire from the Euxine to the Adriatic, after which he continued his march into Gaul, where, in 451, at Châlons, he was defeated by Aëtius and Theodoric, King of the Goths. He died in 453.

sake of the divine doctrines are welcome. It cannot be otherwise if we truly believe in the promise that ' the sufferings of this present time are not worthy to be compared with the glory which shall be revealed to us-ward.' But why should I speak of *future* blessings? Even though no reward were bestowed on the combatants, yet the Truth itself alone is enough to move its friends to encounter with all joy every danger in its behalf." Although an intense admirer of the ascetic life, and swallowing the miracles of the desert with as great an avidity as Athanasius or Jerome, he had yet a profound reverence for truth and reason. "Blind faith," he writes, "is the source of all the evils and errors of the Church. Of all heresies the most dangerous is that which in our days lifts its head so high, and with equal absurdity and injustice, exacts that man should abandon his own intelligence and receive his religion without examination, thus preventing him from ever arriving at a living and constant faith."

The acts of the Council of Chalcedon were ill-adapted to secure the object it had in view, namely, the union of the two parties. The defects and contradictions which were brought to light; the substitution of one formula of belief for another; the mischievous influence of the Court : all this was fatal to the authority of its decisions.

The prominence given in the council to the doctrine of "one nature" marks indeed only a fresh epoch in the dreary theological war, which now enters upon its third and last stage, under the name of the Monophysite Controversy. This word Monophysite (*One Nature*) became a war cry with the wild and untutored monks of Egypt and Palestine, who showed little mercy to such as differed from them. We do not propose to pursue further the history of the dispute. Were we to do so we should see adventurous monks climbing to the highest places by the ladder of fanaticism; provinces wasted with fire and sword; one Emperor vowing to make the Monophysite doctrine universal in the East; the next eagerly espousing the opposite cause; a third in danger of losing his crown because he favoured a proposed addition to a Church hymn.[1] But of reason or piety, of love to God or charity to man, of the true

---

[1] Out of the Monophysite heresy was evolved the *Monothelite* (*of one will*) in which the metaphysical point was drawn out to such a degree of fineness as to be invisible. Mosheim observes: "They admitted two wills in Christ [the divine and the human], both active and operative, and yet maintained that, in a certain sense, there is in Him but one will and one operation of will." This phase of theology arose during the reign of the Emperor Heraclius (A.D. 610—641), and divided the Eastern Church for fifty years. It was condemned by the Council of Constantinople (A.D. 680), called the Sixth Œcumenical Council.

witnessing for Christ, we should find next to nothing. Never was the Apostle's injunction to Timothy, and through him to all these bishops,—whether Alexandrian, Antiochian, Nestorian, Eutychian, or Monophysite—more needed or less regarded : " Charging them in the sight of the Lord, that they strive not about words, to no profit, to the subverting of them that hear."[1]

A few straggling rays of light, indicative, let us hope, of many more now lost in oblivion, illumined this long age of darkness. One is the character of Timotheus Salophaciolus, patriarch of Alexandria in the year 460, and again in 477. This man, by his gentleness and moderation, secured on two occasions to that distracted city an interval of tranquillity in the midst of perpetual disturbance. Himself a Duophysite (defender of the *two natures*), he protected instead of persecuting the Monophysite party, and although admonished by the Emperor Basiliscus to use greater severity towards the heretics, he was not to be turned aside from his course of rectitude. In consequence he was esteemed by all parties, the Monophysites calling to him in the streets: "Although we have no Church fellowship with thee yet we love thee."

Another gleam of brightness is found in the resistance of a North African bishop to the arbitrary will of Justinian. In 544 that Emperor published the edict of *The Three Chapters*, in which the writings of Theodore of Mopsuestia and Theodoret, the survivor of whom had been dead a century, were condemned.[2] The edict was sent through the whole Empire to receive the signatures of the bishops. Justinian's great general, Belisarius, had just recovered North Africa from the Vandals, and the Church in that desolated province had begun again to show signs of life. The bishop Facundus of Hermiana possessed a temper rare in those days. Having first thoroughly investigated the doctrinal questions in dispute, and come to a decision upon them, he abode by the result with unshaken constancy. He wrote a treatise eminently characterised by freedom of spirit and disregard of the fear of man, as well as by a candid and searching criticism. In this tract he protested against the unwarrantable dogmatism which had wrought so much mischief in the Greek Church. "Whilst," he says, "in other arts no one presumes to pass judgment on what he has never learned, in

---

[1] The external Church during this period was maintained on a magnificent scale. The cathedral of Constantinople, under the Emperor Justinian, was served by 60 presbyters, 100 deacons, 40 deaconesses, 90 sub-deacons, 110 lectors, 25 precentors, and 100 janitors—a total of 525 officers.

[2] The writings of the former were so effectually destroyed that only some titles and fragments have come down to us.

matters of theology those who have learned the least are most arrogant and peremptory in their judgments. When the civil power oversteps its office, it may indeed ruin men by betraying them to deny the truth with their lips, but it can never effect the object it has in view, for it cannot instil into their minds other convictions than they possess; it can act only on what is external; it cannot reach the soul." Of the bishops who excused their compliance by the constraint of secular power, he spoke with scorn. "As if we have been ordained bishops for no other purpose than to be enriched by the gifts of princes, and to sit among the high dignitaries of the State. And as if, when by the cares of government and the arts of the wicked, the prince has admitted anything which tends to injure the Church or disturb its peace, it were not our duty to set before him the truth for his own good, and if necessary to resist him with our Christian authority, and patiently endure his displeasure."[1]

The controversy held on its withering course throughout the fifth and the greater part of the sixth century, branching out into further dispute on the doctrines of Origen, and the edict of *The Three Chapters*. After the year 565, when death delivered the Church from that great legislator and self-deluded theologian Justinian, the Monophysites, like the Nestorians, became a separate sect outside the limits of the Church general; and thus they have continued to the present day. Their descendants are yet found in Syria, Armenia, Assyria, Egypt and Abyssinia. "They have," says Schaff, "long since fallen into stagnation, ignorance and superstition, and are to Christendom as a praying corpse to a living man." "Isolated fragments," he styles them, "of ancient Church history, curious petrifactions from the Christological battle-fields of the fifth and sixth centuries."

But if the long controversy, of which Monophysitism was the concluding act, was barren of good, it was abundantly fruitful of evil. Schism, hatred, bloodshed, the bitterest intolerance, the substitution of words for actions, of formal orthodoxy for practical piety, broke down what yet remained of vigour and life in the once flourishing Churches of the East, and left them, in the succeeding century, an easy prey to the Mohammedan conquerors. When the challenge came they surrendered their liberty, often their faith, with an alacrity which else would have been incredible; and even where they resisted, it was with the warrior's sword, not with the spirit of ancient martyrdom.

[1] To these instances may be added the enlightened testimony borne by John the Almsgiver, patriarch of Constantinople, in which he shows clearly that Slavery is abhorrent to the Gospel.

CHAPTER II.

CHRISTIAN ART AND MARY-WORSHIP.

WHILST the Church was thus torn by internal contest on questions of doctrine, Art within the Church was steadily developing in conformity with the growing elaboration of her ritual and the splendour of her priesthood. There was one Italian city which signalised itself beyond all others by the beauty and variety of the works which were there executed during this period. This was Ravenna,

Theodoric's Palace, Ravenna.

which, from the fifth to the eighth century, was virtually the capital of Italy. One reign during this long period of violence and revolution, stands forth illustrious. It is that of Theodoric the Goth. His beneficent and prosperous rule gave time to the distracted country to breathe again after her long years of agony. During his reign, 491-526, so great was the security attained in Italy that even wayfarers were safe. Ennodius calls him a "pattern of a perfect king for moderation, temperance, chastity, and sacerdotal modesty."

"The serene impartiality of Theodoric's government in religious affairs," says a modern writer, "extorts the praise of the most zealous Catholic. Himself an Arian, he attempted nothing against the Catholic faith. 'We cannot,' he used to say, 'impose a religion by command, because no one can be compelled to believe against his will.' He devoted himself to maintaining the peace, securing the welfare, promoting the civilization, and lightening the financial burdens of his people."

The churches of Ravenna and the mosaics with which they are embellished form a collection of early Christian Art which stands alone amongst the monuments of Europe. "It is well," says Freeman, "that there should be one spot from which the monuments of heathen Rome and mediæval Christendom are alike absent, and where every relic breathes of the strange and almost forgotten time which comes between the two." The art and the artists came alike from the East, and their work has been described as "more Byzantine than Constantinople itself;" and although it belongs to successive dominations so dissimilar as those of the declining Empire, the great Ostrogoth, and the Exarchate, yet the same design and the same workmanship extend unbroken through a period of 250 years.

The church of S. Vitale contains the celebrated mosaics of Justinian and Theodora, "still almost as fresh as when they were first executed." The two sovereigns, with other principal figures, form the frontispiece to this volume; it was composed by Edward Backhouse from two distinct and larger groups.

In these rich remains of Christian art from the fifth to the seventh century, nothing is more conspicuous than the advance which had taken place in superstitious ideas since the era of the catacombs. That era came to an end about the time when the Ravenna mosaics were commenced. In the monuments on the walls of the catacombs there is a marked absence of that idolatry into which the Church afterwards fell. There were, originally, no apostles in their ecclesiastical character, no saints, no madonnas, no angels, no nimbus or auriole.[1] In Ravenna we find all these, some of them, it may be, here introduced for the first time. The earliest figures of angels are to be seen in the church of S. Agata; of apostles, in that of S. Giovanni in Fonte. The nimbus was a decoration of heathen origin, and was placed around the heads of gods and emperors. It would seem that previous to the sixth century it was applied to no Christian figure as such.

---

[1] The *aureole* is the nimbus for the whole body, usually oval.

Where it is seen round the head of our Lord in the earlier mosaics, it is thought to have been added by later hands.

But the most notable departure from the earlier simplicity is in the Madonna. In the mosaics of Ravenna we have an outcome of the orthodox zeal kindled by the Nestorian Controversy; we see the Virgin-mother with her Child, seated on her throne, the object of universal worship, and giving forth blessings as though she were God Himself. Henceforth the Virgin and Child becomes the leading subject of art, presented with every kind of variation, and employing the highest genius of each successive age. These bewitching representations are not without danger for the unwary mind; and in the present age especially, when indifference, that deadly enemy of spiritual religion, has borrowed the name of charity, and the wholesome dread of Rome which acted as a restraint on our forefathers no longer exists, the seductive beauty of Italian art opens a wide door to error. That there is a real power in this fascination, such as may overcome true fidelity to Christ and to his first and great commandment, no one will deny. Mrs. Jameson writes of those "who refuse to give to this subject the honour due to a religious representation, yet regard it with a tender half-unwilling homage; and when the glorified type of what is purest, loftiest, holiest in womanhood, stands before us, arrayed in all the majesty and beauty that accomplished art inspired by faith and love could lend her, and bearing her Divine Son, rather enthroned than sustained on her maternal bosom, 'we look, and the heart is in heaven!' and it is difficult, very difficult, to refrain from *Ora pro Nobis*."[1]

It is a wide-spread but mistaken belief that Christian worship is assisted by art. This belief is one of the results of looking to man for what can only come from God. The first century, during which the Church was a stranger to art, was the most glorious era of her history, and no epoch of Latin Christianity has been further removed from the faith and holy life of the primitive age, than that in which Raphael and Michael-Angelo exhausted their skill in adorning her temples. "In the teachings of the Saviour," writes Samuel Tuke, "there was much to show that 'Grace hath use of Nature': the dressing of the lily and the provision for the sparrows supply beautiful lessons on the universal providence of the Creator, and the trust which his superior creature Man might repose in Him.

---

[1] That these grand efforts of the pencil are necessarily or even generally "inspired by faith and love," is a mere assumption, not borne out by fact. Some of the chief worshippers in the temple of the fine arts have been men of loose morals and doubtful faith.

No idea, however, appears to have entered the minds of the early disciples that they were to set lilies and sparrows before them artificially to stimulate their trust and confidence. . . . History abundantly shows that as that living faith which is the life-blood of true religion declined, so did men seek by dead forms, pageantries, and other varieties of human art to stir up something which was *like* the living power that had been more or less lost. This practice of *imitation* will be found running through all the history of the Church's depravation. Art raised up feelings in men's minds which were the *imitations* of those holy aspirations that came from God and breathe towards Him. The Gospel in its simplicity had been preached to the poor, and had wrought its miracles; it had by the accompanying power of divine grace awakened dead souls, opened blind eyes, and the ear deaf to the sweetness of truth was made to hear and understand the words of eternal life. The changes were inward, but the effects were seen outwardly, and here was the door opened for human art to be exercised, and like the Egyptian sorcerers of old, it did somewhat '*likewise by its enchantments.*' We cannot, I believe, have too much impressed upon our minds, that all the ingenious arts by which it has been attempted to quicken dormant souls to the sense of heavenly things, are but so many counterfeits of truth and seals upon error, by which men are prevented from seeking after and finding the true wisdom and riches. . . . The use of sensible imagery in religious teaching, and some imitations of the heathen mysteries, may be clearly traced in the second century, and still more largely in the third. In the fourth century the rites and institutions by which the Greeks, Romans, and other nations had formerly testified their religious veneration for fictitious deities, were adopted with some slight alterations by Christian bishops and employed in the service of the true God. Thus art came to be restored in great measure to the place which she had formerly held in connection with religion; and her sway and influence increased during the period which elapsed between what is called the conversion of Constantine, and the downfall of the Roman Empire." So was it in the era of the Renaissance: "It was just when superstition and profligacy were at their height in that which called itself the Church of Christ, and when wealth had again arisen to encourage them, that the fine arts also again made their appearance to hide by their adulterate decorations the filthiness which was within. Licentious and profligate popes patronized those extraordinary efforts of the pencil by which the events of sacred story were transferred pictorially to the walls of the great Temple of Rome or of the Vatican. There was no incongruity between the grossest sensuality and impiety, and the love and admiration of the beautiful in nature as presented by the fine arts; and though in the complicated operations of moral causes, it is not permitted us absolutely and certainly to analyse their several portions of influence, and though I am far from tracing the condition of the Church primarily to a love of the artificial, yet I think it bears the character of an important agent in the progress of deterioration, and that at least, by glozing over or hiding the real deformities and deadness of the Church, it tended greatly to obstruct the work of reformation."

" The revival of the ancient world in the classical studies," to quote another Christian moralist, " pursued as it was in Italy with such passionate ardour, revived also the spirit of the ancient heathenism, harboured it in Rome itself and upon the very throne of the Roman bishop, and threatened the world with a new heathenism, unless the Reformation had averted this danger. . . Assuredly the arts and sciences flourished in Italy, in the Medicean era as they had never done before, as they have never done since, and adorned life with an unwonted refinement of manners and education. But the foundation of true morality was wanting. Classical studies resulted in a hitherto unheard of licentiousness in life and motive. . . . The most distinguished advocates of classical learning reproach each other with sins which cannot be spoken of. Poggio wrote Jests (Facetiæ) which can scarcely be equalled for vulgarity and immorality, and which yet went through twenty editions in thirty years. The heathen spirit, under the form of refinement and scientific interest, ruled at the Medicean court. The Platonic Academy at Florence put the Platonic philosophy in the place of Christianity; and Savonarola strove with ardent zeal against heathen immorality and heathen belief as defended by the highest prelates. . . Macchiavelli says: ' We Italians are pre-eminently irreligious and wicked, because the Church, in the persons of its advocates, sets the worst example.' "

The worship of the Virgin, as already said, was almost unknown before the Nestorian Controversy: the first Council of Ephesus denotes the era of its birth.[1]

The worship of the saints in general was familiar to men's minds for some time before the Virgin Mary became the especial object of adoration. The craving for human mediators between man and God, fostered by heathen influences and a one-sided theology, found its most complete satisfaction in the person of the

---

[1] See *ante*, p. 205.

Virgin. "Directly," remarks Milman, "that Christian devotion expanded itself beyond its legitimate objects, . . . the Virgin-mother of the Saviour appeared to possess peculiar claims to veneration. . . . The higher importance assigned to the female sex by Christianity, than by any other form of at least Oriental religion, powerfully tended to the general adoption of the worship of the Virgin. Women willingly deified this perfect representative of their own sex, while the sex was elevated in general sentiment by the influence ascribed to their all-powerful patroness. The ideal of this sacred being was the blending of maternal tenderness with perfect purity—the two attributes of the female character which man, by his nature, seems to hold in the highest admiration and love."

Let us trace the steps by which Mary-worship was developed. The first germ is to be found in the parallel which, in the second century, was drawn between the Virgin and Eve. The earliest writer who refers to this is Justin Martyr. "Eve, a virgin, conceived the word of the serpent, and brought forth disobedience and death; but the virgin Mary received faith and joy, when the angel Gabriel announced the good tidings to her, and replied, 'Be it unto me according to thy word.' And from her was born He by whom God destroyed the serpent." Half a century later, this simple thought had developed in such a manner as already to trench on the Saviour's work of redemption. "If," says Irenæus, "the virgin Eve disobeyed God, the virgin Mary was persuaded to be obedient to God, that she might become the advocate of the virgin Eve. Thus, as the human race fell into bondage unto death through a virgin, so is it rescued through a virgin." Again: "As Eve being disobedient, became the cause of death both to herself and to the whole human race, so Mary being obedient became the cause of salvation both to herself and to all mankind. . . . The knot of Eve's disobedience was loosed through the obedience of Mary." These Fathers are, however, entirely unconscious of the perfections which a later age discerned in Mary; they speak of her just as they do of the other holy women of the New Testament, as simply human, liable to err, obnoxious to reproof.

We have already spoken of Mary's "perpetual virginity."[1] The first champion of this doctrine, Epiphanius, is the first also in the orthodox Church to broach the utterly baseless idea, of her "Assumption." "For myself, I am uncertain whether Mary died and was buried, or not." But so little was the Church of that day pre-

---

[1] See *Early Church History*, p. 282, and *ante*, p. 165.

pared for the actual worship of the Virgin, that the same writer strongly reprehends the practice of certain women who came from Thrace into Arabia, and who were accustomed, on a fine day, once in the year, to spread a linen cloth on a car (or throne) and perhaps in imitation of the worship of Ceres offer on it to the Virgin a cake. "The whole thing," he says, "is foolish and strange, and is a device and deceit of the Devil. Let Mary be in honour. Let the Lord be worshipped. Let no one worship Mary."

By the end of the fourth century Mary's perpetual virginity had become an article of faith. Jerome (in 383) anathematizes Helvidius and Jovinian for maintaining that she bore children to Joseph after the birth of Jesus; and a few years later, Bonosus, bishop of Sardica, was for the same offence deposed, and his church closed against him. A further step is attributed to Augustine, viz., the doctrine that Mary was free from actual, although not from original sin.

We first meet with prayer to the Virgin towards the end of this century. Gregory Nazianzen (A.D. 389) tells of a woman who in a time of danger prayed to Mary for protection; but neither Athanasius, Basil, Chrysostom, nor Augustine supplies any example of such an invocation.

It was, as already said, the Nestorian Controversy that gave the signal for the worship of Mary, raising her at once to the highest rank in the new Christian Pantheon. From the time when Nestorius was condemned by the Council at Ephesus, the title of *Theotokos* (Mother of God), which had hitherto been used only by the Alexandrian School, became general. The Eutychians vied with the Catholics in the honour they paid to the Virgin; and the Monophysite bishop of Antioch, Petrus Gnapheus, was the first to introduce her name into the prayers of his church (circa 470).[1] Churches and altars were everywhere dedicated to the "Holy Mother of God, the perpetual Virgin," and the picture of the Madonna and Child became the symbol of the orthodox faith. Every one who wished to prove his abhorrence of the arch-heretic Nestorius exhibited on the walls of his house, or on his garments or furniture, the image of the maternal Virgin holding in her arms the Divine infant.

The Apocryphal Gospels, which about this time began to find general acceptance, powerfully aided the development of Mary-worship. In these fabulous histories of our Lord and his Apostles, which had their origin amongst the Gnostics, and were for a long

---

[1] This practice appears not to have obtained in the Latin Church till the time of Pope Gregory the Great.

time rejected by the Church, are contained marvellous stories concerning Mary—the germs of those dogmas which in course of time became articles of faith. Soon the language addressed to her grew well nigh blasphemous. The opponents of Nestorius, Proclus who succeeded him at Constantinople, and Cyril bishop of Alexandria, could scarcely find words emphatic enough to express her transcendent glory. She is, " The spiritual Paradise of the second Adam, the living Bush of nature, the Sceptre of orthodoxy, the imperishable Temple." Through her "heaven rejoices and the angels and archangels are glad, the devil is disarmed and banished, fallen man is restored to heaven, and every believing soul is saved."

We add here an outline of the history of Mariolatry down to our own time.

In the sixth century we find the Emperor Justinian imploring the Virgin's intercession with God at the dedication of the church of St. Sophia, and in general for the success of his administration. His general Narses was unwilling to join battle until he had received some token of her protection; and the Emperor Heraclius (A.D. 610) had images of the Virgin on his masts when he sailed to Constantinople to overthrow Phocas. The Old Testament types and phophecies were now found to apply to the Virgin equally with the Saviour. Germanus, patriarch of Constantinople in the eighth century, finds in her, "the second tabernacle, the altar, the Holy of Holies, the Cherubim of glory, the burning bush, the temple gate entered by the Lord God which man might never open, the root of Jesse, the garden enclosed, the city of God, the Queen and the Bride." He thus addresses her. " O Mistress, Mother of God, grant to all who celebrate this thy festival, thy help, shelter, and patronage, ever saving them through thy intercessions from all dangers, diseases, and calamities, and from the future threatening of thy Son, and establish them in the palace of delight."

It remained for the learned and pious schoolman Bonaventura (in the thirteenth century), by a new device to intensify and popularize this anti-scriptural worship. In the *Virgin's Psalter*, ascribed to his pen, the Psalms are applied to Mary instead of to God.[1] It is a religious parody, and whilst as such it is abhorrent to our feelings, a few examples are necessary to show how far the Church of Rome has lost herself in the paths of idolatry.

---

[1] This book, whether from the hand of Bonaventura himself or of a contemporary, is always printed in his name, and is at the present day a most popular work in France and Italy, editions being continually issued with the papal sanction.

PSALM XV.

Remember, O Lady, and speak favourably for us, and avert from us the anger of thy Son.

PSALM XXVI.

O Lady, I have loved the beauty of thy countenance, and I have venerated thy holy majesty.

Confess her name because it is holy, and because her marvellous works are recounted throughout all ages.

PSALM CXIX.

Lead me in the path of thy mercies, thou most beautiful of women, for I have desired thee.

How have I loved thy law, O Lady; thy meditation is always present to me.

Thy word is a lamp unto my feet, and an ineffable light unto my ways.

In the *Canticles* and *Hymns*, printed with the *Psalter*, we find:—

I will confess thee, Lady, because thou hast hid these things from the wise, and hast revealed them unto babes.

Thy glory has covered the heavens, and the earth is full of thy mercy.

As the child cannot live without its nurse, so cannot salvation be obtained without our Lady.

At thy name let every knee bow, in heaven, on earth, and in hell.

Other similar works of devotion might be quoted. In a modern volume in English issued under the highest authority we read:—

Modern heretics cannot endure that we should salute and call Mary our Hope. They say that God alone is our Hope, and that He curses those who put their trust in creatures. This is what the heretics say; but, in spite of it, the Holy Church obliges all ecclesiastics and religious each day to invoke and call Mary by the sweet name of our Hope—the Hope of all.

O Immaculate Virgin, prevent thy beloved Son, who is irritated by our sins, from abandoning us to the power of the devil. . . . Through thee we have been reconciled to God. Thou art the salvation of the whole world.

We often obtain more promptly what we ask by calling on the name of Mary, than by invoking that of Jesus.

Jesus himself said, Were it not for the prayers of my Mother, there would be no hope of mercy.

Mary so loved the world as to give her only-begotten Son.[1]

---

[1] The *Glories of Mary*, translated from the Italian of St. Alphonsus Maria de Liguori. He founded the Order of the Redemptionists in 1732, and died in 1782. The *Imprimatur* runs thus: "We hereby approve of this translation of the *Glories of Mary*, and cordially recommend it to the faithful.—Nicholas Card. Wiseman, Archbishop of Westminster, A.D. 1852." "We heartily commend this translation of the *Glories of Mary* to all the disciples of her Divine Son.—✠ Henry E. Archbishop of Westminster [Cardinal Manning], Aug. 11, 1868." Unhappily the Anglican Church, in this as in so many other articles, is doing her best to overtake Rome. Since the publication of our first edition, we have met with the following Hymn to the Virgin, in a volume of Guild Hymns in use in one of our large towns:—

What is this but the "mouth speaking blasphemies"? (Rev. xiii. 5.)

The *Ave-Maria* takes its name from Gabriel's salutation, "Hail Mary," and consists of Luke i. 28 and 42, with this addition, made in the beginning of the sixteenth century, "Holy Mary, Mother of God, pray for us sinners, both now and in the hour of death. Amen." It is placed in the Romish Missal on a level with the Lord's Prayer and the Apostles' Creed, and with them forms the basis of the Rosary.[1]

The earliest festivals in honour of the Virgin, the Annunciation and the Purification, cannot be traced back further than the sixth century. The latter was also called Candlemas, from the multitude of candles which were then lighted, as was formerly done in the heathen festival of the Lupercalia, in the same month of February.[2] The feast of the Assumption, founded on the Gnostic legend of her translation to Heaven, became at Rome, in the ninth century, one of the chief festivals. Several others were added in later times.

Our sketch would be imperfect without a brief notice of the debated doctrine of the Immaculate Conception. This innovation having been propounded about A.D. 1140, by some canons of Lyons, drew down upon them the rebuke of the great Bernard: "On the same principle you would be obliged to hold that the conception of her ancestors in an ascending line was also a holy one; since she could not otherwise have descended from them after a worthy manner, and there would be festivals without number. . . . We ought

---

"Mother of Mercy! day by day,
My love of thee grows more and more;
Thy gifts are strewn upon my way,
Like sands upon the great sea-shore.

Get me the grace to love thee more;
Jesus will give it if thou plead:
And Mother! when life's cares are o'er,
O, I shall love thee then indeed!"

[1] The origin of the Rosary is thus stated by Gieseler: "Ever since virtue was supposed to attach to frequent repetitions of forms of prayer, people naturally were in want of means for facilitating and securing the enumeration of them. Thus an Egyptian monk, Paulus, used to count his prayers by the help of stones; Godiva, an English countess (about A.D. 1040), by a lace. In the thirteenth century a medallion with sacred symbols on it, set round with knobs for counting, was in use. . . . The Rosary is first heard of among the Dominicans as early as 1270, under the technical name of the Paternoster."

[2] When Ceres searched with candles for her daughter Proserpine, carried by Pluto into the regions below.

not to attribute to Mary that which belongs to Him only who being Himself free from sin can make others holy. Except Him, all who are descended from Adam must say of themselves that which one of them says in the name of all, ' In sin did my mother conceive me.'"[1] And a century afterwards the doctrine was attacked by the celebrated Dominican, Thomas Aquinas, so vigorously, that he was thought to have utterly overthrown and chased it into oblivion. But his great successor and opponent in the philosophy of the Schoolmen, the Franciscan Duns Scotus, took the fugitive dogma under his protection, and made of it the battle-cry of the Franciscan order. Round this symbol the two puissant armies waged long and deadly war. When the Franciscans appealed to the revelations made to St. Birgitta (Bridget) in favour of the Immaculate Conception, the Dominicans opposed to them the visions of a sister of their own order, the celebrated Catharine of Siena. But as usual credulity was stronger than reason. Christendom in general, and the University of Paris in particular, declared itself (A.D. 1389) in favour of the Immaculate Conception. Several Dominican doctors were forced to recant, and all candidates for academical degrees were obliged to subscribe to the new doctrine.[2] Since then it has become more and more deeply rooted in the Roman Catholic mind. In 1746 Pope Sixtus IV. appointed an annual festival in honour of it; and in 1854, in the most solemn manner, it was adopted as an article of faith by a general council held at Rome.

CHAPTER III.

BENEDICT.

THE life of a good man, under whose laws a vast number of the inhabitants of Western Europe have lived for thirteen centuries, must needs be worthy of our notice. Benedict, and Pope Gregory the Great, who wrote his biography, are the principal Churchmen of the sixth century.[3] Yet the actual materials of Benedict's history

---

[1] Bernard however held that, "like the Baptist and Jeremiah" (!), Mary was, before her birth, cleansed from original sin.

[2] In 1509 four Dominicans were burnt at Berne for getting up fraudulent appearances of saints in order to discredit it.

[3] Gregory was three years old at the death of Benedict. A halo of legend encircled Benedict's head even during his life, and his miracles probably, as in the case of Martin of Tours, gathered little by the lapse of time.

are comparatively scanty, and every incident of his life is wrapped in a thick haze of miraculous interposition.

Jovinian and Benedict were both monks, but their experience of the cloister, and their convictions as to the means by which the Church was to be renovated, led them in wholly opposite directions. The one saw that without a return to first principles and New Testament teaching, the plague which was wasting the Church could never be stayed; the other believed that the monastic life upon which the Church had entered was her true course, and that what was needed was only to give to it its proper direction and consistency.

A century had elapsed since Jerome, Martin of Tours, and John Cassianus made Europe familiar with the monastic institution. The monastery at Marseilles, founded by Cassianus in the early part of the fifth century, was a centre of Christian influence, and amid the disorders caused by the marauding incursions of the northern tribes, proved a great blessing to the people. From this convent and its branches had gone forth many pious and laborious bishops. But by the end of this distracted century, the spirit of monasticism had declined and its discipline grown lax, and the monks are described as roaming over the country, corrupting both manners and religion.

Benedict was born at Nursia in Central Italy,[1] A.D. 480. At the age of twelve he was, according to a custom which prevailed, sent to Rome to be instructed in the liberal arts; but his pure young spirit shrank from the corruption which he saw everywhere around him. He longed for solitude, and at the end of two years fled from Rome, accompanied for the first twenty-four miles by the nurse whom his parents had sent with him, and who from affection was unwilling to leave him. But Benedict still pursuing his object, escaped from her, and proceeding further, stopped at a small village not far from the town of Subiaco.[2] The rustic inhabitants, pleased with his modesty and sweetness of disposition, allowed him to take up his abode in a cell near their church. Here he fell in with a monk named Romanus, who took him to a cavern not far from his own cloister; and in this rude shelter the delicately-nurtured boy found a home. His scanty food was secretly supplied by Romanus from his own small pittance. The cave lay at the foot of the cliff on which the monastery stood; as there was no path down the rock, the bread was lowered by a rope, a small bell being attached

---

[1] In Umbria, midway between Rome and Ancona.
[2] Fifty miles east of Rome.

to give warning. So entirely was Benedict cut off from the world that he ceased to mark even the fasts and festivals of the Church. At the end of three years his hiding-place was discovered by some shepherds, who at first mistook him for a wild beast, but when they drew near, were melted into kindness by his gentle eloquence. Henceforth the story of his life is a renewal of the experiences of Paul and Anthony in the desert of the Thebaïs. There are the same heroic conflicts with the natural passions,[1] the same deadly battles with the evil one under various disguises, the same prodigality of miracles wrought often for the most trivial purposes.

Benedict's fame spread through the country, and the place of abbot in a neighbouring convent falling vacant, the office was conferred on him. His strength of will was equal to the sweetness of his temper, and he warned the monks beforehand of the discipline which he should think it his duty to enforce. This he did with so much severity, that in a short time their love was turned to hatred, and they attempted to poison him. He mildly reproved them, prayed that they might be forgiven, and withdrew again to his grotto. This was no longer a solitude. The fame of his miracles and sanctity drew multitudes to him even from a distance. The breaking up of society, consequent on the repeated irruptions of the northern nations, and the rapid changes in government, possessions, and creed, drove men to seek shelter from the storms of the world in that recluse life which promised security from earthly vicissitudes. Men of consideration at Rome placed their sons with Benedict that he might educate them for the ascetic life; even Goths of the lower ranks came to him, and these he employed in the labour of the field and the garden. In a short time there sprang up in that romantic region, on the peaks of the hills, and under the oaks and chestnuts which clothed the ravines, twelve monasteries, each containing twelve monks under a superior.

But Benedict could not remain at Subiaco. To rid himself of an envious priest, who plotted against his life and assailed the continency of his monks, he withdrew with a few followers to Monte Casino, fifty miles to the south-east, where they took up their abode in the ruins of an ancient castle. On this mountain stood a temple of Apollo in the midst of its sacred grove, and the peasants still brought their offerings to the pagan altar. By his eloquent preaching Benedict diverted the people from their idolatry, taught them the faith of the Gospel, and persuaded them to demolish the

---

[1] Effectually to mortify his sensual appetite, he one day stripped off his only vestment of skins, and rolled himself in a clump of thorns and briars which was near his grotto.

stately edifice, with its altar, statue and grove. He erected in its place a chapel, dedicated to St. Martin of Tours, and a monastery, the germ of that "great model republic which gave its laws to almost the whole of Western Monasticism." Here about the year 529[1] he framed his celebrated *Rule*, "an enduring monument of his own spirit, and of the new shaping which, through his instrumentality, was given to the cœnobitic life of the West."

In the Benedictine scheme the abbot is the representative of Christ; to him therefore all are to yield obedience, ready, cheerful and implicit. Candidates are admitted for a year on probation, at the end of which time they take upon themselves the irrevocable vow. From the beginning poverty, chastity and obedience had been indispensable to the profession of a monk; Benedict made the last still more absolute, and added what was known as the *Vow of steadfastness*. Henceforth the door of the monastery opened only inwards. Formerly, if the monk forsook his cell and married he was liable to penance, but his marriage was not annulled; now, such marriages were declared, *ipso facto*, void, and the offender was compelled to return. The vow, written out, was laid upon the altar, those who could not write signing it with their mark. The property of the novice, if not already given to the poor, was added to the common stock of the brotherhood. The beds of the monks were often searched, and punishment followed the appropriation of any valuables. No letters or presents, even from the nearest kindred, were to be received without leave of the abbot, who might transfer any gift to another than the one for whom it was intended. The abbot in his turn, although absolute, was admonished by the Rule, to temper the severity of discipline with the spirit of love; he should show mercy and gentleness to the brethren while he hated their faults; his own fallibility should ever be present with him, and he should remember that "the bruised reed is not to be broken."

"The three occupations enjoined by Benedict's system were the worship of God, reading, and manual labour. The adventitious advantages of the monastery were not contemplated by the founder; the object was not to make the wilderness blossom with fertility, to extend the arts of civilized life into barbarous regions; it was solely to employ in engrossing occupation that portion of time which could not be devoted to worship and [meditation]." And in regard to learning and study, in which of later times the Benedictines

---

[1] The same year in which the ancient classic schools of Athens were closed by order of Justinian. The two events mark a dividing line between ancient and mediæval history.

have so highly distinguished themselves, this was an innovation quite foreign to the ideas of the founder himself, whom his biographer describes as "learnedly ignorant, and wisely unlearned." Its introduction was perhaps chiefly due to the influence of Cassiodorus, a contemporary of Benedict, who in 538 laid aside the high office which he held in the State, and retired from the world in order to found a monastery at Vivarium in Calabria.[1]

The monastic day was equally divided between religious exercises and labour. Seven times[2] in the twenty-four hours prayers were chanted by the brotherhood, commencing at dawn with *matins*, before which *vigils* had been sung already. The psalms were distributed among these services in such a manner that they should all be chanted every week. Much time was spent in learning them by rote and in reading the Scriptures, Cassianus's *Conferences*, the Lives of the Saints, and other "edifying books." At meals there was reading aloud and no conversation was permitted. During harvest the monks did not return to the house, but knelt and performed their religious service in the fields. Manual labour was varied by the teaching of children, sent to reside in the cloister or in daily attendance from the neighbouring village. As time went on this occupation became of more and more importance, and gave its literary shape to the Benedictine societies.

In regard to abstinence the Rule was less severe than amongst the Eastern monks. It was not however from choice that Benedict admitted a relaxation of the ancient severity; he did so unwillingly, and only in condescension to what was then supposed to be the gradually decreasing vigour of the human frame! The monks were cooks and servitors by turn. At the end of the week, the one who went off duty and he who took his place were to wash the feet of the rest. Two sorts of grain or vegetables were served for dinner, with fruit or salad, and sometimes fish or eggs, with a small measure of wine. A pound of bread a day was allowed to each. Indulgence was shown to the aged and sick. From Easter to Pentecost there was no fast; from Pentecost till the end of September there were fasts on two days of the week; the rest of the year to Easter was a perpetual fast, with only one (evening) meal a day. In Lent a still more rigorous abstinence was enjoined, not from food only, but from sleep and speech. It was strictly forbidden to

---

[1] Cassiodorus caused his monks to transcribe even the ancient classics, by which means some at least escaped destruction.

[2] This number is taken from Psalm cxix. 164. They were (besides vigils), matins (*morning*), prime (*early*), tierce, sexte, nones (*third, sixth, ninth* hour), vespers (*even-tide*), and compline (*completion* of the day).

partake of food without the walls; if a brother was obliged to be absent the whole day, the Rule required him to fast until his return. To take away occasions of absence, every monastery contained within its enclosure a mill, a well, a bakehouse, and all other needful appliances. When a monk was sent out on necessary business he was forbidden on his return to dissipate the minds of the brethren by relating his adventures. The occupation of every monk was determined by the abbot, and if any one prided himself on his skill in any art or handicraft the Rule required him to abandon it! The laws of commercial economy being then but little understood, the monasteries, to escape the reproach of covetousness, were accustomed to sell their productions under the market price.

The clothing consisted of a coarse tunic or robe with long sleeves, which served as a shirt; at first white, afterwards changed to black. For the offices of the choir, the monks put on a large mantle with a cowl, also black, and a scapulary, consisting of two pieces of cloth joined round the neck with a hood, and hanging, one part in front, the other behind.[1] Unlike the Oriental monks, they wore shoes and stockings; their girdle was narrow and of leather. Each had two suits which he himself kept in repair. They slept in their clothes, shoes and girdle, in dormitories of ten or twenty, in separate beds, the young and old intermixed, with a deacon to each chamber. The penalty for light faults was the smaller excommunication, *i. e.*, eating alone after the others had done. For graver faults, separation from the table, from prayers and from the community, personal chastisement, and last of all expulsion.

Silence, humility, obedience, these were the cardinal virtues of the cloister life. "Everything," remarks Milman, "was concentrated on self. It was a man isolated from his kind who was to rise to a lonely perfection; all the social, all patriotic virtues were excluded." Humility was confounded with slavish fear, and a false importance was attached to the outward demeanour. Benedict took no account of the Lord's plain injunction: "Thou when thou fasteth anoint thy head and wash thy face, that thou be not seen of men to fast." Like Basil and Gregory, he thought it necessary that the temper of the mind should be exhibited in the postures of the body.[2] The head was to be constantly bowed down;

---

[1] "This was nothing else than the hooded frock of the ploughman and shepherd, borrowed from that of the slave in pagan times, such as Columella has described."

[2] See *ante*, p. 22.

the eyes directed to the earth; the thoughts to be hourly occupied in self-accusation for sin; and the brethren were to cultivate the state of mind proper to those who might at any moment appear before the Divine Judgment-seat. Benedict persuaded himself that this was the discipline which made men free. "When," he says, "the monk has passed through all these stages of humility, he will attain to that love of God, which being perfect casts out fear, and will begin to practise naturally and from custom all those rules which he before observed through fear."[1]

Not long before his death Benedict was visited by the great Totila, at the head of his victorious Ostrogoths. To test his prophetic spirit the king dressed one of his captains in his own royal robes and purple boots, gave him a numerous escort, and sent him up to the monastery to present himself as the king. The moment Benedict perceived the captain, "My son," he cried, "put off the dress thou hast on, it is not thine." Totila himself afterwards ascended the hill, and fell prostrate at the abbot's feet. Benedict raised him up, solemnly rebuked him for the cruelties he had committed, and (so it is said) foretold his conquest of Rome, his passage over to Sicily and Greece, his reign of nine years, and his death during the tenth. The greater humanity which distinguished Totila's conduct of the war from this time is attributed to his interview with the saint.

Benedict's twin sister, Scholastica, was as devout as himself, and equally powerful in attracting and ruling her own sex. She also is reported to have wrought miracles. Her convent was not far from his: they met however once only in each year. When she lay on her death-bed, about the year 543, he came to visit her, expecting it might be for the last time. With the sisterly affection which her artificial manner of life had not been able to quench, she entreated him to rest for the night under her roof. He had never passed a night out of his own monastery, and he refused, even at her solicitation, to break his rule. Scholastica bowed her head in prayer. Suddenly the serene sky was overcast, lightnings flashed and thunders pealed above them, and the rain fell in torrents. "The Lord have mercy upon thee, my sister," said Benedict, "what hast thou done?" "I prayed to thee," she replied, "and

---

[1] "The Catholic Church has recognized three other rules besides that of St. Benedict, viz.: 1. That of St. Basil, which is still retained by the Oriental monks. 2. That of St. Augustine, which is adopted by the regular canons, the order of the preaching brothers or Dominicans, and several military orders. 3. The rule of St. Francis of Assisi and his Mendicant order in the thirteenth century."

thou wouldst not hearken to me, but the Lord has heard my prayer. Go now if thou canst." They passed the night together in spiritual conversation. "Three days afterwards Benedict, from the window of his cell, saw his sister soar up to heaven in the form of a dove." He survived her only forty days. A violent fever seized him. He ordered her tomb to be opened, and caused himself on the sixth day to be carried into the chapel, where, supported by his monks, he received the *viaticum*. Then standing beside the open grave, at the foot of the altar, with his arms extended, he breathed out his spirit in prayer.

It was an era of convulsion in the political world. The fall of the Gothic monarchy and the reconquest of Italy by the generals of Justinian were succeeded by the invasion of the Lombards, under their king Alboin, in 568. Arian in name, but still half-pagan in their nature, they crossed the Alps, and poured themselves down upon the plains of Italy. So sweeping was the devastation they wrought that the end of the world was thought to have come. They were especially furious against the monasteries; and in 580 they attacked the sanctuary of Monte Casino by night, pillaged and burnt it. The monks all escaped, bearing with them, as their entire fortune, the *Rule* written by their founder, with the day's measure of wine and pound of bread which he had prescribed. Benedict is said to have foreseen the event in prophetic vision. A nobleman with whom he lived on familiar terms found him one day weeping bitterly. After watching him for a long time, and perceiving that his tears did not cease, and that they did not proceed from the ordinary fervour of his prayers but from profound melancholy, the nobleman asked the cause. Benedict answered: "This house which I have built and all that I have prepared for my brethren has been delivered up to the pagans by the sentence of Almighty God; scarcely have I been able to obtain that their lives shall be spared."

But ere he died, Benedict was comforted, so we are told, by another vision. He saw his Rule go forth over all Europe, and monasteries of his order rise up in every part of the Western world. And thus, indeed, it came to pass. Except during the temporary prevalence of Columbanus' Rule in France, that of Benedict was paramount in Europe until the thirteenth century, when the Dominicans and Franciscans partially eclipsed it; it formed the model for all other monastic orders, and was the prolific nursery of missionaries, authors, bishops and popes.

PERIOD III.

FROM THE ACCESSION OF POPE GREGORY THE GREAT, A.D. 590,
TO THE END OF THE TENTH CENTURY.

CHAPTER I.

GREGORY THE GREAT.

THE pontificate of Gregory marks an epoch in the history of the Church. In him the papacy came to maturity. Leo the Great possessed superior genius and ambition; but in his days there was still a power higher than the Church, viz., the Empire. By the time of Gregory a great change had taken place. The Western Empire fell in 476, and although in the next century Belisarius and Narses had recovered Italy for the Byzantine Emperors, it was but an ephemeral flicker of the expiring flame. The political horizon had fallen to a dead level,—the only figure which rises above it is the Roman pontiff.

With Gregory we stand on the threshold of the Middle Ages. The classic world of antiquity has disappeared. The language of Rome has almost ceased to be vernacular, and is soon only to be met with in the courts of law, the Church and the cloister. Scarcely is there to be found a single man of genius or learning either in the East or in the West. The Eastern Church, sunk down under its own corruptions and the weight of Byzantine despotism, is soon to become an easy prey to the Moslem conquerors. The Church of the West is compared by Gregory himself to "an old and shattered ship, admitting the waters on all sides, her timbers rotten and shaken by daily storms and premonitions of wreck."

In the person of Gregory the bishop of Rome first became in act and influence, if not in avowed authority, a temporal sovereign. "His acts," writes Milman, "were not the ambitious encroachments of ecclesiastical usurpation, but were forced upon him by the purest motives, if not by absolute necessity. The virtual sovereignty fell to him as abdicated by the neglect or powerlessness of its rightful owners; he must assume it, or leave the city and the people to anarchy."

Gregory was high-born[1] and wealthy, and had for some years filled the office of Roman prætor; but the monastic life of Monte Casino captivated him, and on his father's death he abandoned his high office and professed himself a Benedictine monk. He sold his

---

[1] He was born about A.D. 540.

patrimony, and the wealthy patrician who had been used to traverse the city in silk and jewels, now, habited like a beggar, was to be seen waiting on the beggars in the hospital of the monastery, which he had built at the gate of his paternal mansion. He practised the austerities of the order with the utmost rigour, eating nothing but pulse which his mother sent him ready soaked in a silver porringer. This porringer, which was the only relic of his former splendour, did not long remain in his hands, for one day a shipwrecked sailor coming to beg of him as he was writing in his cell, Gregory finding no money in his purse, gave him the bowl. Constant fasts and vigils reduced him to such a state of debility that he was scarcely able to stand.

Gregory founded six monasteries in Sicily beside that in which he lived at Rome. The fame of his abstinence and charity took, as was usual in that age, the form of miracle, and his monastery was the perpetual scene of preternatural wonders. It was whilst he was still in the convent that the well-known incident took place which led to the conversion of our Saxon ancestors; it will be related in the next chapter. At first it was Gregory's purpose himself to carry the Gospel into our remote and at that time barbarous island. He extorted the unwilling consent of the Pope (Pelagius II.) to leave his monastery for this purpose, and had actually set forth and travelled three days' journey, when he was overtaken by messengers sent to recall him. "All Rome had risen in pious mutiny and compelled the Pope to revoke his permission."

Soon after his return Italy became a scene of misery and desolation. The Lombards were wasting the peninsula; the feeble exarch of Ravenna confessed he had no power to withstand them; the Tiber at Rome overflowed and swept away the granaries of corn, and a pestilence ensued to which the pope Pelagius fell an early victim, A.D. 590. A successor had to be found; with one voice the clergy, the senate and the people summoned Gregory to the vacant chair. The prospect of the honour was a burden to him; he wrote to the Eastern Emperor, Maurice, entreating him to withhold the Imperial consent; but his letter was intercepted, a general petition for his promotion was substituted, and an Imperial rescript was received, confirming his election.

"Monasticism ascended the papal throne in the person of Gregory. In austerity, in devotion, in imaginative superstition, he was a monk to the end of his days." Nevertheless he possessed an extraordinary capacity for business, and devoted himself to his manifold duties "with the hurried restlessness of the most ambitious statesman. Nothing seems too great, nothing too insignificant for his earnest personal solicitude; from the most minute point in the ritual, or regulations about the papal farms in Sicily, he passes to the conversion of Britain, the extirpation of simony amongst the clergy of Gaul, negotiations with the armed conquerors of Italy, or the revolutions of the Eastern Empire." But in the midst of all he panted for the retirement and quiet of his monastic life. "When I lived in the cloister my soul could almost always keep in a disposition for prayer. But since I have undertaken the pastoral office, my distracted soul can hardly ever collect itself. . . . What sort of watchman am I, who stand not on the height of a mountain, but in the valley of weakness? But the Creator and Redeemer of men is able to impart to me, unworthy as I am, vigour of life and power of tongue, if from love to Him I do not spare myself."

The Roman Liturgy, with the service of the Mass, was settled by Gregory almost in the same form in which it has remained to the present day. He arranged the order of processions and the vestments of the priests and deacons. His attention to church music is perpetuated in the Gregorian Chant; he not only instituted a singing school, but himself taught the choristers, and the whip with which he admonished his inattentive scholars was preserved as a relic for centuries.[1]

Gregory's pontificate lasted thirteen years. He died A.D. 604, at the early age of 54. In his latter years he suffered much in body. "For nearly two years," he writes to the patriarch of Alexandria, "I have been imprisoned in my bed by such pangs of gout, that I can scarcely rise on great holidays to celebrate solemn mass. And the intensity of the pain compels me immediately to lie down again, that I may be able to endure my torture by giving free course to my groans."

Gregory's character exhibits in a striking light the contradictions of his age and of his office. He was charitable yet severe, humble yet ambitious, a lover of truth and yet could stoop to gross flattery, a proficient in the science of his day and a diligent expositor of Scripture, and yet immersed in the credulity and superstition which commonly belongs to ignorance.

On the great question of Slavery, Gregory was an example to the

---

[1] John the Deacon gives a humorous account of the attempts of the Germans (or Gauls), two or three centuries afterwards, to perform the Gregorian Chant: "Their thundering Alpine voices issuing from throats rasped with wine, vainly strive to give back the sweet modulation of the chant, instead of which a din like that of waggons rumbling over the stones disturbs and exasperates the hearers."

Western Church, constituting himself the protector of what was perhaps still the most numerous class of the population. Unhappily, however, he was unable to put a stop to the slave-trade which was in the hands of the Jews. On the manumission of two slaves he had a deed drawn up with these golden words in the preamble: "It is a good and salutary thing when men whom nature created free, and whom the law of nations has enslaved, are presented again with the liberty in which they were born." The Western Churches, it may be remarked, were far behind their Oriental brethren on this point. The Eastern monks refused to keep slaves, not only because they themselves performed the most menial work, but because they would not thus degrade the image of God. The good abbot Isidore of Pelusium,[1] interceding with a nobleman on behalf of one of his slaves, wrote that "he could hardly believe that a friend of Christ, who had experienced the grace which makes all men free, could still own slaves." John surnamed the Alms-Giver, patriarch of Alexandria from 606 to 616, thus reproved some who treated their slaves with cruelty: "God has not given us servants that we should beat them, but that they may serve us; perhaps not even for this purpose, but rather that they may receive sustenance out of our abundance. Tell me what price can purchase him who was created after the image of God? Hast thou who art his master a single member more to thy body, or hast thou a different soul from him? Is he not in all things thy equal? Pray, what is the gold which is paid for the right to make a slave of him, for whose sake heaven, earth and sea, and all that is therein were created; to whom angels minister; on whose account Christ washed the disciples' feet; for whose sake Christ was crucified?"

Devoted as Gregory was to ritualism, he yet, like Ambrose, caused the consecrated vessels of the altar to be sold for the redemption of captives taken in war. To say that Gregory considered the poor would not be to say much of a Roman bishop; his almsgiving was on the most princely scale. The first day in every month he distributed corn, wine, cheese, vegetables, bacon, meat, fish and oil; and every day before he sat down to his own meal, a portion was separated and sent out to the hungry at his door. Being told that a beggar had died of want in the city, he imposed on himself a hard penance as a punishment for the neglect of his stewardship. A bishop newly appointed refusing to relieve some poor aged persons who were on a journey, Gregory sent him a message. "It seems

---

[1] He died A.D. 431.

strange to me that one who has clothes, silver, and a cellar, should have nothing to give to the poor. Tell him that reading and prayer will not now be enough, that he cannot be suffered to sit alone in a corner; he must help the necessitous, he must regard the wants of others as his own, otherwise his title of bishop will be only an empty name."[1]

With all his benevolence, Gregory's government of his monastery was severe in the extreme. Many who embraced the monastic life became weary of its monotony and sought to return to the world; for such he had no pity. Nor was he more indulgent to the faults of those who remained under his charge. He forgot Benedict's injunction not to break the bruised reed. A monk named Justus, formerly a physician, attended him skilfully and with affectionate care during a long illness. Justus on his death-bed confessed to his brother that he possessed three pieces of gold. This was in direct violation of the rule of the house. The money was found concealed amongst some drugs, and Gregory resolved to make the offender sensible of the enormity of his trespass, and to awe the brotherhood by the terror of his example. He suffered no one to approach the dying man's couch, sending him only the message that he died detested by all the community. And when the miserable man had breathed his last, his body, together with the three pieces of gold, was cast out upon the dung-hill, the whole convent shouting: "Thy money perish with thee!" At the end of thirty days Gregory began to relent, and permitted mass to be offered for the tormented soul. This was repeated daily for thirty days more, when the spirit of Justus is said to have appeared to his abbot and assured him of his release from misery.

The extravagant pretensions of the see of Rome, which had been handed down from bishop to bishop for successive generations, lost nothing in Gregory's hands. The thorn in his flesh during his later days, was the attempt of the patriarch John of Constantinople to set up a rival claim for his own see, by assuming the title of Universal Bishop. In resisting this claim Gregory tries to persuade himself that he is opposing John in the common interests of the Church. "Is this the time chosen by an arbitrary prelate to invade the undoubted rights of St. Peter by a haughty and pompous title? Am I defending my own cause? Is this any special injury to the

---

[1] A great volume recording the name, age and dwelling of the objects of Gregory's bounty was long preserved in the Lateran. Economically speaking, the harm of such indiscriminate charity, in pauperising its objects, probably far outweighed the good that was effected. The papal bounty too may have been a measure of policy, the continuance of the Imperial largess which the Roman citizens were accustomed to expect.

bishop of Rome? It is the cause of God, the cause of the whole Church. Let all Christian hearts reject the blasphemous name. Whoever calls himself universal bishop is Anti-Christ." How Gregory or his successors have reconciled these words with their own assumptions, it is not easy to see. To us they seem to be the language of self-deception. The papacy never yields and never forgets, and it is fair to conclude that Gregory's indignant protest was directed not so much against the title as against the usurpation of it by his rival.[1]

The darkest stain on the memory of this distinguished man is found in connection with this rivalry. The Emperor Maurice, who seems always to have thwarted even the best of Gregory's measures, countenanced the claims of the patriarch of Constantinople, and was besides himself reputed a heretic. His end was tragical. Phocas, a soldier of fortune, "an odious and sanguinary tyrant," having risen in rebellion against him, caused Maurice to be dragged from the sanctuary to which he had fled, and with his five sons to be butchered before his face. The news of the death of the Emperor filled Gregory with exultation, and he launched out into a panegyric on the base usurper: "Glory to God in the highest! who has chosen thee and placed thee on the Imperial throne to banish by thy merciful dispositions all our afflictions and sorrows. Let the whole people return thanks for so happy a change."

The new Christian idolatry which had grown up during the fourth and fifth centuries had by this time become universal, entering into the daily life of all Christendom. Every man was surrounded by a world of invisible beings—angels, whose visits were rare, demons who were continually on the watch to seduce the unwary, and glorified saints who had become the protectors of mankind in the place of God and Christ. The literature of the age (and Gregory's pages are no exception) teems with this invisible world. In his *Dialogues*, for example, a woman who eats a lettuce without making the sign of the cross, swallows with it a devil and becomes possessed. The relics of the martyrs, those priceless jewels of the Church, had now attained a self-defensive power; profane hands touching them were withered, and such as endeavoured to remove them were struck dead. "One of the golden [?] nails of the chains of St. Peter tempted the avarice of a Lombard (probably an Arian); he took out his knife to sever it; the awestruck knife sprang up and cut his sacrilegious throat. The Lom-

---

[1] Cardinal Bellarmine endeavours to escape the difficulty by assuming that the term *episcopus universalis* is used in two very different senses.

bard King and his attendants were witnesses of the miracle, and stood in terror, not daring to lift the fearful nail from the ground. A Catholic was fortunately found, by whom the nail permitted itself to be touched; this peerless gift, so avouched, Gregory presented to a distinguished civil officer." When the Empress Constantina, the consort of Maurice, applied to Gregory for the head of the apostle Paul or at least some portion of his body, to place in a church she was building, Gregory replied: "I neither can nor dare grant that favour, for the bodies of the holy apostles, Peter and Paul, are so resplendent with miracles and terrific prodigies in their own churches, that no one can approach them without great awe, even for the purpose of adoring them. . . . I wished to make some alteration in the church near the most holy body of St. Paul, and it was necessary to dig deep in the neighbourhood of his tomb. The superior came to some bones not at all connected with his sepulchre, which he removed, but he paid dearly for his rashness. He was visited by a fearful apparition and died suddenly. . . . But that thy pious longing may not be wholly disappointed, I will hasten to send thee some filings of those chains which St. Paul wore on his neck and hands, if indeed I shall succeed in getting them off. For since the devout are continually begging permission to take away something from these chains, a priest stands by with a file; and sometimes it happens that the dust falls off easily and instantly; while at other times the file is long drawn over them, and yet nothing is scraped off."[1]

In spite however of superstition and prejudice, Gregory's opinions were often sound and enlightened. These are his words on the Christian ministry:—" The world is full of priests, yet there are but few real labourers for God's harvest, since although we have undertaken the priestly calling, we do not fulfil its duties. He who is unable to occupy the congregation with a connected discourse may instruct individuals and edify them by private conversation. Let us ask ourselves, who have been converted by our tongue? We have received our talents to trade with; what profit have we brought to

---

[1] Peter's chains, as well as those of Paul, were preserved at Rome. They were originally two, the Neronian with which he was bound by order of the Emperor Nero, and the Herodian by which he was attached to the soldiers in the prison at Jerusalem. The latter was discovered by the Empress Eudoxia, wife of Theodosius II., whilst on a pilgrimage, and sent by her as a precious relic to Rome, where the moment it touched the former it became miraculously welded to it, and thus formed one holy and inseparable chain! In memory of this miracle the feast of the Chains of Peter was instituted, and is still kept on the 1st of August. See *ante*, p. 49, note.

Him who said 'occupy till I come?' Behold, He is already come; He is looking for the profit from our traffic. What gain of souls can we show?" He does not restrict this responsibility to the priesthood. "The priest's lips should teach knowledge, for he is a messenger of the Lord; but all may attain the same high dignity if they will. Whosoever calls his neighbour from wicked ways to a right course of life, he too, certainly is a messenger of the Lord. Hast thou no bread to give to the needy? Thou hast a tongue; thou hast something of more value than bread. For it is a greater thing to refresh by the nourishment of the word a soul destined to everlasting life, than to satisfy the mortal body with earthly bread. To the poorest, even the little that he has received will be reckoned as a talent."

The Church of Rome venerates the name of Gregory as amongst the wisest of her doctors; it would have saved her from infinite loss if she had attended to his counsel on the study of Scripture. It was his constant habit to enforce upon both lay and clergy the great duty of reading the Bible. One of the Emperor's physicians excusing himself from this practice by the distractions of the times, Gregory wrote to him: "What else are the Holy Scriptures but a letter from the Almighty to his creatures? If thou wert staying at a distance from the court, and received a letter from thy earthly sovereign, thou wouldst not rest, thou couldst not sleep, till thou knew its contents. The King of Heaven, the Lord of men and angels, has sent thee his letter, giving thee directions how to attain eternal life, and yet thou art neglecting to read it. Bestir thyself, and reflect daily on thy Creator's words. Learn to know the heart of God from the words of God, so that thou mayest yearn with ardent longing after the Eternal." To a bishop who made a like excuse, namely, that his duties left him no leisure for reading,[1] Gregory quoted Rom. xv. 4, and continued: "If the Holy Scriptures were written for our comfort we ought the more to read them in proportion as we feel oppressed by the burden of our distractions." And when the bishop, referring to Matt. x. 19, "But when they deliver you up, be not anxious how or what ye shall speak, for it shall be given you in that hour, what ye shall speak," argued that the teachers of the Church had no need to study the Divine word, but might rely simply on the immediate revelation of the Holy Spirit, Gregory answered: "The outward word would have been given us to no purpose if, being filled with the Spirit, we had no need of it."

---

[1] The functions of the bishops, as of the pope, were in those unsettled times various and burdensome, including many secular duties.

Elsewhere, with an experience which will find a ready response in Christian hearts of all times, he says: "Often we believe our conduct to be meritorious, but when we compare it with the Divine word we see at how great a distance we are from perfection."

Again Gregory warns his hearers against expecting special revelations when in possession of the broad Gospel truth. A woman in a time of mental anguish wrote to him that she would give him no rest until he received a special revelation that her sins were forgiven. Gregory answered her, that he was unworthy of a special revelation, and referred her to the fountain of the Redeemer's mercy, set open for all, adding, "I know thou hast a fervid love to God, and I trust the word spoken by the lip of truth of another has also been spoken of thee: 'Her sins, which are many, are forgiven, for she loved much.'"

Like true Christian men in all ages, Gregory utterly disclaimed the false notion, that by the mere profession of sound doctrine, or by a zeal for religion, without holiness, a man can please God. To a certain bishop who boasted of the number of heretics he had converted, Gregory wrote: "I thank God that by thy instrumentality heretics have been reclaimed to the Church; but thou must take care that those who are already in the Church, so live as not to rank amongst her enemies. For if they do not love what is godly, but serve earthly lusts, thou wilt be bringing up strange children in the bosom of the Church itself."

Very wisely does he write concerning miracles, leading the minds of his hearers from the visible to the invisible, from outward signs to the purpose and end of all miracles, the work of God in the heart of man. "When Paul came to Malta and saw the island full of unbelievers, he healed the father of Publius by his prayers; yet when Timothy was ill, he bade him drink no longer water, but use a little wine for his stomach's sake, and his often infirmities. How is it, O Paul, that thou miraculously restorest the sick unbeliever to health, and yet to thy fellow-labourer prescribest only natural remedies like a physician? Is it not because outward miracles have for their object, that souls should be conducted to the inward miracle? . . . In order for faith to grow, it must be nourished by miracle; as when we plant shrubs we pour water on them, till we see that they have taken firm root in the ground. The Church works now in a spiritual manner what it then effected through the Apostles in a bodily manner. When believers who have renounced the language of their former worldly life, cause holy truths to issue from their lips, what do they but 'speak with new tongues?'

When they hear pernicious counsel, but are not carried away to commit evil deeds, do they not 'drink deadly poison, but it does not hurt them?' When they see their neighbours weak in righteousness and give them help, and strengthen them by their own example, what do they but 'lay their hand upon the sick so that they recover?' Strive after these miracles of love and piety, which are all the more sure as they are more hidden."

That Gregory had a sense of the danger of resting too much on miracles, we may see by his letter to the monk Augustine in Britain. "But my beloved brother, there is something which along with thy great joy gives reason for much fear. Thou mayest rejoice that the souls of Englishmen have been led by outward miracles to inward grace, but thou ought to fear lest the miraculous works which have been performed should puff up thy own weak mind. . . . Examine thyself strictly, learn correctly what thou thyself art, as well as how the grace of God has shown itself amongst this people, for whose conversion thou hast received the power of working miracles. Consider this power, not as conferred on thyself, but on those for whose salvation it has been given thee."

We conclude with a few more gems from the casket of Gregory's experience.

Some men ostentatiously confess their faults, but when they are reproved for them, defend themselves, and protest their innocence. This kind of mock confession proves that they are not really humble, but seek only the merit of being reckoned so.

The greater progress saints make in the divine life, the more sensible are they of their own unworthiness; for in proportion as they draw near to the light their deformity is made manifest, and the better they become acquainted with holiness the more completely do they know and understand what sin is.

He who dispenses of his earthly substance to his destitute neighbour, but does not guard his own life from sin, is like a man who should offer the meaner gift to God, and keep the more valuable for the Evil One.

It is not enough that we renounce our property, we must come out of ourselves. We must renounce ourselves in that which we have made ourselves through sin, and keep ourselves in that which we have become through grace.

True prayer consists not in the words of the lips, but in the feelings of the heart; for our desires, not our words, fall as a sound of power on the secret ear of God. If we pray with our lips, but do not desire with our hearts, our calling upon God is only a silence; but if we desire with the fulness of our hearts, our very silence is a calling upon God.

Unlike the Oriental divines, Gregory would suffer no sacrifice of truth on any pretence. "It is not allowable," he says, "to make use of falsehood even to save life."

NOTE ON THE PAPACY.

The papal supremacy attained its full proportions, although not its full exercise of tyrannical power, in Gregory I. In our former work we traced its germ and the earlier stages of its development.[1]

Siricius, bishop of Rome, A.D. 384—398, was the first to issue a Letter (or Decretal) having the force of a law to the Catholic Church. In 417, the Council of Carthage sent to Innocent I. its canons respecting the Pelagian controversy for its sanction. Innocent signified his satisfaction, and gave them to understand that, according to the sacred institutions of the Fathers, whatever was done even in the remotest provinces could not be complete until it had come to the knowledge of the Apostolic Chair. But the spirit of independence was not yet quite extinct. Notwithstanding the dictum of Innocent, the African Church resolved that no appeal against its jurisdiction should lie beyond the sea; and when his successor Zosimus put forth some canons of the Council of Sardica as canons of the great Council of Nicæa, Augustine's friend Alypius exposed the mistake, and at the death of Zosimus the Council of Carthage addressed the new pope, Boniface, in words of bold and honest admonition: "Now that thou art seated on the throne of the Church of Rome, we hope we shall no more have to endure a worldly pride unworthy of the Church of Jesus Christ."

But this was the last stroke for the independence of the Church. Leo I. might have paraphrased the words of Louis XIV., "*L'Eglise*, c'est moi." "He who disputes the primacy of the Apostle Peter will find himself powerless to lessen that dignity; but puffed up by the spirit of his own pride will plunge himself into hell." This assumption on the part of Leo was endorsed by the youthful Emperor Valentinian III. By a decree of the year 445 he ordained: "The primacy of the Apostolic Seat being established by the merit of the Apostle Peter, the dignity of the City of Rome and the sanction of a holy synod, no pretended power shall arrogate to itself anything against the authority of that seat. For peace can be universally preserved only when the whole Church acknowledges its ruler."

At the same time the personal holiness of the pope was declared, and he was exempted from the judgment of his fellow-men. Accordingly in 501, when Pope Symmachus was "accused of many horrible crimes," the bishops refused to sit in judgment upon him, because "the merit and primacy of St. Peter and the decrees of the holy councils had conferred a supreme power on the see of Rome, and it was a thing unheard of that the bishop of Rome should submit to be judged by his inferiors." Ennodius, bishop of Pavia, went further and declared that the pope had no need of reformation, because he who was promoted to this dignity was of necessity holy, and God would not suffer him to be corrupted.

How succeeding popes not only maintained this assumed prerogative of holiness and of supremacy in the Church, but even waged wars, disposed of thrones, and set their feet on the necks of kings, is well known to all readers of history, and it will to some extent appear in the following pages.[2]

---

[1] *Early Church History*, p. 259.

[2] Gregory II. in the eighth century (A.D. 727) boasted to the Greek Emperor, "All the kings of the West reverence the pope as God upon earth"; and Boniface VIII. (from 1294 to 1303) declared it to be essential to the salvation of every human being to be subject to the Roman pontiff. The title of pope (*papa*,

This brief notice of the growth of papacy would be incomplete without a reference to the *Forged Decretals* of Isidore. These documents, which made their appearance in the ninth century, consisted partly of about one hundred letters purporting to be written by earlier bishops of Rome from the time of the Apostles, or by their correspondents, partly of the acts of certain unknown councils. For many centuries, even down to the Reformation, they were accepted as genuine notwithstanding gross anachronisms.[1] In these Decretals the privileges of the clergy, and especially of the bishops, are magnified, and the pope appears as the supreme head, law-giver, and judge of the Church, the universal bishop. There was, it is true, little or nothing new in the hierarchical pretensions here set forth; "the main outline of the papacy had been marked out four centuries earlier by Leo the Great; but the consolidation of the scattered fragments into one body, the representation of the later papal claims as having come down by unbroken tradition from the Apostolic times, could not but produce a vast effect" in rendering the papal authority paramount in Europe.

Principal Fairbairn has these pertinent remarks on the origin and growth of the Romish Church system: "The old Religion had its priesthood, the new had its clergy, and so these two were made parallel. Once they had been made parallel, it was necessary to do the same for the worships; and once they were assimilated, the New Testament ceased to fulfil the Old, the Old reigned in the New. And this is what Cyprian shows us; he represents the victory of the older Religion, the rejuvenescence of Judaism, the entrance of the hieratic idea into the Kingdom of Christ, changing it into a kingdom of priests. . . . . The clergy became the Church, the Church the Religion, and the Religion a transformed Roman empire, with the pope for emperor, bishops for procurators, and the priesthood for the magistrates and legionaries that levied the taxes, enforced the laws, upheld the unity, and maintained the peace of the civilized world. Papal infallibility is but imperial supremacy transfigured and spiritualized. The Catholic Church could not have been without Christianity, but still less could it have been without Roman imperialism. It owes its life to the one, but its distinctive organization to the other. . . . . If the Church had passed the first five centuries of its existence under an Oriental despotism or amid free Greek cities, its structure had been altogether different. It seemed to vanquish the Empire, but the Empire by assimilating survived in it; the name was the name of Christ, but the form was the form of Cæsar."

---

father) was not exclusively applied to the bishop of Rome till about the year 521. The phrase Apostolic See seems to have been first used by Zosimus (417—419). The title of cardinal arose later. Gregory the Great frequently speaks of the "cardinal-presbyters and deacons" of a church. Those of the parish churches in Rome, twenty-five or twenty-eight, came to be held in special honour; and in 1059 Pope Nicholas II. formed these with seven "cardinal bishops" into a college for electing future popes.

[1] Persons are made to correspond with one another who lived centuries apart; Scripture is quoted in the words of Jerome's Vulgate some two hundred years before Jerome was born; complaint is made of the encroachment by laymen on Church property in language belonging to the period of Charles the Great.

CHAPTER II.

CHRISTIANITY IN BRITAIN.

THE early history of the British Church is very obscure. The facts relating to it, which are known with any degree of certainty, may be enumerated in a few lines. By the end of the second century the Gospel had spread through the southern parts of the island and had begun to penetrate " beyond the Roman pale"; but the legend of St. Alban, who is reputed to have suffered martyrdom in the Diocletian persecution, rests upon scanty evidence.[1] In the reign of Constantine, three British bishops attended the Council of Arles, A.D. 314. Bishops from Britain are again met with at the Council of Sardica (347), and at that of Rimini (359), where a large number were present and subscribed the Semi-Arian Creed. At the end of the same century we read of Ninyas, a Welsh missionary, preaching to the Picts in Galloway. He is said to have been educated at Rome, and on his way homeward to have visited Martin of Tours, who ordained him to his missionary work, and whose name he gave to the church of his new bishopric in Galloway.[2] About the same time Paula and Eustochium speak of pilgrims from Britain who came to visit the holy places at Bethlehem.

In the year 409 the Romans abandoned the island ; and between this date and the landing of the Jutes (449), the Pelagian heresy was introduced into Britain, as Bede relates, by a bishop named Agricola, and the British Churches, unable by themselves to refute the subtle arguments of the preacher, sought the aid of the bishops of Gaul. Germanus of Auxerre and Lupus of Troyes were accordingly sent to them, and overthrew the heretical teachers in a disputation at St. Albans A.D. 429. Germanus returned hither eighteen years afterwards to complete the spiritual victory.

From the time of the Saxon invasion we hear little more of the British Churches. In Gaul, Italy and other countries of the Em-

---

[1] See *Early Church History*, pp. 113, 307. The famous Glastonbury legend of Joseph of Arimathea and the Sacred Thorn is not older than the eleventh century.

[2] There still survives, says Dean Stanley, on a lonely hill the contemporary grave-stone of some who would seem to have been the companions of Ninyas. Being built of stone, the church was called the White House, and is identified by tradition with Whithorn in Wigtonshire.

S

pire, the conquerors adopted the religion as well as the language and manners of the conquered, but in England the case was widely different. The conquest of this country by the Saxons, which it took a century or two of hard fighting to accomplish, ended in the complete subversion both of Roman civilization and of Christianity, and in the substitution alike of the political life and the idolatry of the Germans. Bede's harrowing picture of the Saxon ravages may perhaps have gained something in colouring by the lapse of three centuries. "They plundered the cities and country, marking their course by flames from one sea to the other, and spreading themselves over almost every part of the island. Public and private buildings were alike destroyed; the priests were murdered at the altars; the bishops and their people were indiscriminately put to the sword, until there was none to bury them. Some of the wretched remnant were seized on the mountains and butchered in heaps. Others, spent with hunger, surrendered themselves and submitted to perpetual slavery for the sake of food. Some sorrowfully made for regions beyond the sea; others remained behind to lead in perpetual trembling and anxiety a hard and precarious life among the forests and mountains." Those whom Bede describes as fleeing "beyond the sea" found refuge in Armorica;[1] those who became serfs to the conquerors gradually forgot their Christianity; while such as maintained their independence in the unconquered fastnesses of Cornwall, Wales, or Cumberland, although they preserved their religion, lost their Roman civilization and the use of the Latin tongue. Thus Britain was withdrawn from the Roman world, and until the mission of Augustine was regarded as a land of mystery and fable.

One episode, however, pregnant of future blessing to Europe, belongs to the annals of the British Church previous to the Saxon conquest. The ray of historical light which reveals to us Ninyas preaching to the southern Picts, at the end of the fourth and beginning of the fifth centuries, falls also on the village of Bonaven, now Kilpatrick, in Dumbartonshire. Here was born near the year 372, Patrick, called in his native tongue Succath. His father was a deacon, and appears also to have held some office in connection with the northern Roman Wall. He gave his son a good education. But the youth lived on light-hearted from day to day, without personal interest in religion, until in his seventeenth year the course of his life was rudely interrupted.

Some pirates of the wild tribes of the Scots, who then inhabited

---

[1] Brittany and part of Normandy.

the north of Ireland, landed upon the coast and carried him and a multitude of others away as captives. Patrick was sold to a chieftain who made him keeper of his flocks and herds. Affliction led him to seek God, of whom in the days of youthful ease and liberty he had been unmindful. Abandoned on earth, he found consolation and happiness from above; and as he wandered about with his cattle he enjoyed heavenly communion in prayer and quiet meditation. Let us hear his own words written at a later period of his life: "I was about sixteen years old and knew nothing of the true God, until, in captivity, He opened my unbelieving heart, so that, though late, I thought of my sins and turned to Him with my whole soul. And He who preserved me before I could distinguish between good and evil, and watched over me as a Father, looked down on my lowly condition and had compassion on my youth and ignorance. Before He humbled me I was like a stone sunk in the mire, but when He who had power came, He raised me in his mercy and set me on a very high place. For which cause I must testify aloud in order to make some return for such inestimable blessings both in time and eternity. The fear and love of God," he continues, "was kindled in me; faith grew, so that I prayed often, one day offering a hundred prayers, and at night almost as many, and when I passed the night in the woods or on the mountains, I rose up to pray before daybreak in the snow, ice and rain. Yet I felt no suffering, nor was there any sluggishness in me, such as I now find, for then the Spirit glowed within me."

After spending six years in the service of this chief, Patrick believed he heard a voice in his sleep which promised him a speedy return to his native land, and not many nights afterwards announced to him that a vessel was ready to take him. In dependence on this call he set out, and at the end of some days met with a ship on the point of sailing. At first the captain would not receive the poor unknown youth. Patrick fell on his knees and began to pray, and ere he had finished the captain relenting, sent one of the sailors to call him. Through many sufferings and deliverances he at length reached his home. Ten years afterwards he was a second time taken prisoner by Scottish pirates, and was now carried to Gaul, whence the charity of Christian merchants again restored him to his native land, to the great joy of his parents.

But Patrick could not rest at home; he felt an irresistible call to carry the message of salvation to the people amongst whom he had passed his youth, and been born again to the heavenly life. As Paul was directed by the Lord to go over to Macedonia, so Patrick deemed he received a heavenly summons to preach the Gospel to the people of Ireland. A man from that country appeared to him in a dream, giving him a letter superscribed, "The words of the Irish"; and as Patrick read it, he seemed to hear the simultaneous voices of many, crying: "We beseech thee, child of God, come and again walk among us!" His feelings would not allow him to read further, and he awoke. Another night he heard a voice from Heaven, the last words of which were intelligible,— "He who gave his life for thee, He speaks in thee." He awoke full of joy. A third time he dreamed, and it was as though there was something within him and yet above him, praying with deep sighs. When he awoke he called to mind the Apostle's words: "The Spirit also helpeth our infirmity, for we know not how to pray as we ought, but the Spirit Himself maketh intercession for us with groanings which cannot be uttered."

His parents and friends strove to keep him from his purpose. "Many opposed my going, and said behind my back, 'Why does he rush into danger among the heathen who do not know the Lord?' Gifts were offered to me with tears if I would remain at home; but I did not yield; God overcame in me and withstood them all. How," he exclaims, "should so great and blessed a favour be bestowed upon me, to know and love God, and to leave my parents and native land, and go to the people of Ireland to publish the Gospel, and to suffer insults and persecution even to bonds! Moreover, if I am found worthy I am also ready to give up my life with joy for his name's sake." Before commencing his missionary work Patrick went again to Gaul, the better to prepare himself by intercourse with pious priests and monks.

His knowledge of the Irish language enabled him to preach with great readiness to the people. By the sound of a kettle-drum he collected large assemblies in the open air, to whom he declared the sufferings of the Saviour for sinful humanity; and the word of the Cross reached the witness for God in the hearts of many. He met indeed with much opposition, for the Druid priests and national bards whose influence was great, stirred up the people against him. But he conquered by steadfastness and faith, by glowing zeal, and by the attractive power of love. His influence over men's minds is seen in the following instance. Coming in the course of his journeys to the house of a man of rank, his message was received and the whole family were baptized. But one of the sons, not contented merely to profess the Gospel, clave to the Gospel messenger, and in spite of all the efforts of his friends, forsook all to accompany Patrick in his toils and dangers. On account of the youth's gentle disposition, he received the name of Benignus, and his sweet voice was used to influence the people by the singing of hymns. At Patrick's death Benignus became one of his successors in the pastoral office. Many of the national bards were converted by his means, and lips which had been accustomed to chant Druidical couplets, now sang the folly of idolatry and the praises of God and Christ.

Patrick sought especially the conversion of the chiefs. These when they allowed themselves to be stirred up by the priests against the new religion, could do much harm; but when they embraced the Gospel, their example formed a counterpoise to the reverence felt for the Druids. Young men of the lower rank who seemed fitted for the ministry were by him educated as teachers. He also received and protected slaves who fled to him from the harsh treatment of their owners.

Patrick was watchful against spiritual pride. After speaking in one of his letters of the miracles which God had enabled him to perform, he adds: "But let no one on account of such things suppose that I place myself on an equality with the Apostles, or the perfected saints, for I am a poor, sinful, despicable man. Be astonished, ye who fear God, both small and great, and ye eloquent talkers who know nothing of the Lord, understand and examine who it is who has called a simple person like me to serve with fear and trembling, yet faithfully and blamelessly, the people to whom the love of Christ has led me." He avoided even the semblance of seeking his own glory or profit. When many brought gifts out of gratitude to him as their spiritual father, and pious women offered him their ornaments, he refused them all, whilst he himself gave presents to the heathen chiefs (one of whom had plundered and imprisoned him), in order to secure peace for his flock, and to ransom Christians from captivity.

After labouring thirty years he thus addressed his converts: "I call God to witness that I seek not honour from you. May He never suffer me to lose the Church which he has won in this remote corner of the earth. I pray that He will count me worthy to persevere in a faithful testimony until the time of my departure, and that I may be permitted to shed my blood for his name, with my converts who are in prison, even though my body should obtain no burial, or be torn in pieces by wild beasts. For beyond a doubt we shall rise again with the glory of the Redeemer Jesus Christ, for we shall reign by Him, and through Him, and with Him. The visible sun rises daily for our benefit according to God's command, but its splendour will not endure for ever; all the unhappy beings who worship it will suffer punishment. But we worship Christ, the true Sun who will never set; and he likewise who does his will shall never set, but shall live for ever."

Patrick often desired to re-visit his native country, but could never find opportunity to leave his work. "I am bound," he says, "by the Holy Spirit, who will not hold me guiltless if I leave the work I have begun, and I am in fear also lest it should fall to the ground."

The Catholic legend of Patrick's journey to Rome, A.D. 432, where he was ordained by Pope Sixtus III. as missionary to Ireland, is unsupported by historical evidence. Like Ulfilas with the Goths, Patrick is said to have taught the Irish the use of letters. After his death his disciples carried on his labours in the spirit of their master. The Scriptures were studied, books were collected, and the monasteries became schools of missionaries, so that the country acquired the title of "The Island of the Saints."[1] In the succeeding century the grateful church sent back to Scotland the Gospel which she had received from thence. The leader in this work was an abbot of royal race named Columba, or as he was called while still a child, from his diligent attendance at public worship, Columkille (the dove of the Church). He crossed over to North Britain in a wicker boat with a small band of monks about the year 563, and established himself in the little island of Iona, called after him I-colm-kill, now included within Argyleshire. In the course of his missionary journeys he passed over the Grampians to preach to the northern Picts; and he died in 596, the very year in which the monk Augustine set out from Rome for the conversion of England. The monastery which Columba founded at Iona, and over which he presided thirty years, attained a wide reputation and became the centre of religious life to the whole land of the Picts. There Biblical and other studies, according to the standard of those early days, were carried on. Its abbots had the control and guidance of the bordering tribes and churches, and even exercised authority over bishops.

Whilst the Gospel was thus taking root in Ireland, and extending its beneficent influence to Scotland, the original British Church, which survived in the fastnesses of Wales and Cornwall, would seem, if we may trust the invectives of Gildas,[2] to have fallen into

---

[1] It is possible, however, that this appellation, in Greek hiera nēsos (*holy island*), is only a corruption of the native name Eri, or Erin.

[2] Gildas, a British or Irish Church writer, probably of the sixth century, but whose history is very obscure, writes thus in his epistle addressed to the Britons: "Britain hath clerks, but many of them are deceitful raveners;

a worldly condition. Nevertheless the Welsh clergy in the sixth century, in the events to be presently related, showed signs of religious life still existing amongst them.

Such was the state of Christianity in these islands when Pope Gregory the Great undertook the conversion of the Anglo-Saxons. The British and the Irish Church had alike sprung up independent of Rome, and the latter had prospered and had embarked on the aggressive work of the Gospel with little help, and with no control, from the Roman clergy. But neither the Welsh Britons, nor the missionaries of Ireland and Iona, had made, so far as we know, any attempt to teach the religion of Jesus to the rugged, warlike, freedom-loving Saxons. This triumph was reserved for Rome.

The incident which led to it is well known. Gregory the Great, before he became pope, saw in the forum at Rome some handsome boys, fair-skinned and with beautiful hair, exposed for sale. He inquired whence they came. "From the island of Britain." "Are they Christians?" "They are still pagans." "Alas!" he exclaimed, fetching a sigh from the bottom of his heart, "that the prince of darkness should possess such bright faces, that such grace of countenance should be devoid of inward grace! Of what nation are they?" "Angles." "Right," said he, "for they have the faces of angels, and ought to be co-heirs with the angels in heaven. What is the name of their province?" "The people of that province are called Deiri." "Right," he said again, still punning on the answers he received, "they must be rescued *de irâ* (*from the wrath to come*), and won to the mercy of Christ. What is the name of their king?" "Ælla." "Alleluia! Praise unto God the Creator must be sung."[1]

From that moment Gregory resolved upon the conversion of Britain. Unable, as we have seen,[2] to enter upon the work in person, he sent forth as soon after his accession to the papal chair as the distracted state of Italy would permit, Augustine, provost of

---

shepherds who are rather wolves prepared for the slaughter of souls. Instructing the laity, they are withal examples of the most depraved vices and manners. Despising Christ's commandments, they fulfil their own lusts."

[1] "It may well be doubted," remarks Philip Smith, "whether this scene belongs to the real history or to the legends of Gregory's life. (1) The elaborate play on words suggest a suspicion that the story is rather *ben trovato* than *vero*. (2) Bede does not relate it in its place as part of the history of the mission, but brings it in after as an episode. (3) The very words in which he introduces and dismisses the story seem to mark it as derived from those legendary histories of Gregory which were popular in England, rather than from the authentic records copied for Bede at Canterbury and Rome."

[2] See *ante*, p. 246.

his monastery in Rome, accompanied by forty monks. On their journey through Gaul, as they communed together, they became alarmed at the danger of the enterprise. The Saxon people were idolaters, a fierce and barbarous nation, and their language strange; it would be folly to proceed, the only safe course was to return home. Accordingly they sent Augustine back to Rome humbly to entreat the pope to release them from so perilous a service. But Gregory was not to be turned aside from his purpose by their fears. He wrote to them: "Gregory, the servant of the servants of God, to the servants of our Lord. It had been better not to begin the good work than to think of desisting from that which has been begun. Let not the toil of the journey nor the tongues of evil men deter you; but with all possible earnestness and zeal perform that which by God's direction you have undertaken, being assured that great labour is followed by a greater glory of eternal reward."

Thus admonished they pursued their way, and landed at Ebbesfleet on the Isle of Thanet, A.D. 597. The Gospel was not altogether unknown in Kent. King Ethelbert's wife Bertha, daughter of the Frankish king Charibert, was a Christian, and had brought with her a bishop who held divine service in an old British church outside the walls of Canterbury. The king, on receiving a message from Augustine, went down to the shore to meet him, and setting his throne in the open air for fear of magical arts, ordered the missionaries to be brought into his presence. They advanced in solemn procession, Augustine, "the dark-haired swarthy man, higher than any of the rest from his shoulders and upwards," at their head, preceded by a silver cross and the figure of our Lord painted on a board. As they drew near, they chanted their litanies for the salvation of the king and his people. When he had heard their message, Ethelbert said: "Your words and offers are fair, but as they are new to me and as yet unproved, I cannot forsake at once the faith of my nation which I have so long followed." Nevertheless he permitted them to reside in his chief city of Canterbury, entertained them hospitably, and allowed them to preach and make converts. The austere life of the monks, their fastings, vigils, prayers and preaching, the courageous trust in God which they exhibited, and perhaps above all their miracles, made a powerful impression on the rude people. By direction of the pope, Augustine went to Arles to be ordained archbishop of the English nation, and on his return to Canterbury he found the work had made such rapid progress that at the first Christmas festival the king himself and ten thousand converts were baptized. The ceremony took place in the channel which divides the Isle of Sheppey from the mainland.

Wishing to show Augustine the greatest possible honour, Ethelbert gave up to him his own palace in Canterbury, with the Roman-British church in the neighbourhood for his cathedral, adding such lands and possessions as were deemed necessary to support the newly-founded see. Thus Roman Christianity became at once the established State religion in the dominions of the king of Kent. This example was followed in time by all the other kingdoms. "Everywhere the bishop's throne was set up side by side with the king's, the king*dom* of the one became the bishop*ric*[1] of the other; the bishops sat in the Council of the Wise Men [Wittenagemote] as equal with the Ealdermen [the rank next to the king]; the clergy ranked with the thanes; the laws of the Church were laws of the State"; the union of Church and State was complete. Outside the walls of Canterbury, Augustine erected a Benedictine abbey, afterwards called by his name, which became the parent seat of learning in England.

The form of Christianity thus brought to our forefathers was ritualistic and corrupt, yet was it a gift of incalculable value. The coin had been debased by no small mixture of alloy, but the gold was still there, and it still bore the Saviour's image. The lamp of truth burnt with a flickering light, yet it was infinitely better than the heathen darkness which it made manifest.[2]

At first it was Gregory's purpose to have the idol temples of the Saxons destroyed, but afterwards, when a fresh band of missionaries under abbot Mellitus was sent to reinforce Augustine, Gregory directed that the idols only should be removed, and that those temples which were substantially built should be suffered to remain. Sprinkled with holy water, and sanctified by altars and relics, they were to be converted into churches. Like Gregory Thaumaturgus,[3] the pope even thought it expedient to humour the ignorant people in their ancient pagan practices. "Because," so he wrote to Mellitus, "they have been used to slay many oxen in sacrifice to devils, let the same solemnities be continued with a new direction, so that on the day of the dedication, or the nativities of the holy martyrs, they may build huts of the boughs of trees round the transmuted temples, keep a religious feast and slay and eat their

---

[1] The Saxon word *rice* or *ric* signifies jurisdiction: it forms part of the name Surrey, south-*rice* or south-*rige*.

[2] "The Saxons were the fiercest of the Teutonic race. On the rude manners of the barbarian tribes had been engrafted the sanguinary and brutalizing habits of the pirate. Their religion was as cruel as their manners; they are said to have sacrificed a tenth of their principal captives on the altars of their gods."

[3] See *Early Church History*, p. 281.

cattle to the praise of God, returning thanks to the Giver of all things. In this way, whilst some of their old gratifications are outwardly permitted them, they may the more readily attain unto inward joy. For it is impossible to efface everything at once from their obdurate minds; he who would ascend to the highest place must rise by degrees."[1]

At the same time the pope wrote to Ethelbert: "Bishop Gregory, to the most glorious lord and my most excellent son Ethelbert, King of the English. . . . Guard carefully the grace which thou hast received from God, and hasten to promote the Christian faith among thy people. Increase thy zeal for their conversion; edify them by great purity of life; exhort, terrify, soothe, correct, that thou mayst find thy Rewarder in heaven. For so Constantine, our most pious Emperor, recovering the Roman commonwealth from the perverse worship of idols, subjected the same with himself to our Almighty God and Lord Jesus Christ, and thus transcended in fame former princes. . . . Willingly hear, devoutly perform, and studiously retain in memory whatsoever you shall be advised by our most reverend brother bishop Augustine, who is instructed in the monastic rule, filled with the knowledge of Holy Scripture, and by the help of God endued with good works; for if you give ear to him in what he speaks for God, God will the sooner hear him praying for you. . . . I have sent some small presents which will not seem inconsiderable when accompanied by the blessing of the holy Apostle Peter."

Essex quickly followed Kent in receiving the Gospel, and London, then within its bounds, was made an episcopal see, Mellitus being appointed the first bishop. During Augustine's lifetime Christianity made no further progress in Saxon England.

"The British Church secluded in the fastnesses of Wales could not but hear of the arrival of the Romish missionaries, and of their success in the conversion of the Saxons. Augustine and his followers could not but inquire with deep interest concerning their Christian brethren in the remote parts of the island." But when they found that the practices of the British Churches differed in some particulars from those of Rome, sympathy was changed into coldness and suspicion. His narrow monastic education, if not his natural character, had unfitted Augustine to deal with an independent Church. One of his letters to Gregory asking his advice on some dubious points of discipline is still extant. Both his

---

[1] Roberts suggests that the custom of bringing deer at a certain season into St. Paul's Church, London, and laying them on the altar, was a relic of this indulgence; it was abolished at the Reformation.

questions and the pope's replies exhibit in a strong light the weakness and even the childishness of the monastic system. Nevertheless the pope shows a moderation and good sense which Augustine would have done well to imitate. "Thou knowest, brother, the custom of the Roman Church in which thou wert bred. But I direct that if thou hast found anything either in the Roman, Gallican, or any other Church, which may be more acceptable to Almighty God, thou shalt carefully choose the same, and teach it to the Church of the English, which as yet is new in the faith. 'For things are not to be loved for the sake of places, but places for the sake of good things.'" Unhappily Augustine acted in an entirely opposite spirit. He believed the Roman discipline to be perfect, and regarded every deviation from it as heretical; and he aspired to nothing less than the subjection of the whole island to the "Apostolic" see.[1]

Having received their Christianity before the settlement of the Roman ritual and hierarchy, the Britons pursued a different practice on several points. Their mode of baptism was different; their observance of Easter was otherwise regulated; they differed in their monastic rules, and in the form of tonsure of the priests; and (much more important) marriage was allowed to their clergy. Of these divergences, the time of keeping Easter seems, strange to say, to have taken the leading place in the minds of the Italian monks.[2] The Britons were not indeed, as the Eastern Churches had been, Quarto-decimanians; they did not, following the Jewish mode of reckoning, keep our Lord's Crucifixion and Resurrection according to the day of the month, regardless of the day of the week.[3] But a new and more accurate method of computing Easter had not long been introduced, and had not yet reached Britain.[4]

---

[1] Gregory and Augustine had already anticipated the spiritual conquest of Britain, and had planned a second metropolitan see at York, which, like Canterbury, was to be the centre of twelve bishoprics.

[2] As to the tonsure, the Roman clergy shaved the crown of the head, leaving a circle of hair, in imitation of the crown of thorns. They called this St. Peter's tonsure, pretending that the apostle was so shorn in memory of our Lord's passion. The British priests shaved the fore-part of the head as far as the ears, in the form of a crescent, which was called by their adversaries the tonsure of Simon Magus. There was a third fashion, the Greek tonsure, which was referred to the Apostle Paul as its author, and consisted in shaving, or rather closely clipping, the whole head.

[3] See *Early Church History*, p. 237.

[4] The new cycle was improved and settled by Dionysius Exiguus, a Scythian monk, who flourished in the latter part of the fifth century. It is to him also that we owe the practice of dating events from the birth of our Saviour, thus looking upon this event as the grand "turning-point" of history.

Rome herself had been late in accepting the new calendar, having until within three-quarters of a century observed the same rule as that still followed by the British Churches.[1] Everything must needs, however, be sacrificed to the idol of uniformity and of Roman supremacy.

Augustine sent a message to the British clergy, demanding that they should lay aside their own practices, and observe in all respects the Roman discipline. Dinooth, abbot of their great monastery at Bangor,[2] unable to comprehend such an assumption of authority, answered: "We are all ready to listen to the Church of God, to the pope of Rome and to every pious Christian, and to show perfect love to each, according to his station, upholding him by word and deed. We know not that any other obedience can be required of us towards him whom you call 'the Father of Fathers.'"

At King Ethelbert's suggestion the Britons were invited to a conference with Augustine and his clergy. They met, A.D. 601 or 602, on the banks of the Severn in Gloucestershire, the confines of the kingdom of Wessex. The conference was held under an oak, afterwards known as Augustine's oak.[3] It was not to be expected that the parties should come to an agreement. On the one side were unreasonable demands urged with inflexible rigour and haughtiness; on the other there was the consciousness of right, supported by an ancient spirit of independence. "When," says Bede, "after a long disputation, the Britons manifested no compliance with the entreaties and rebukes of Augustine and his companions, but preferred their own traditions to the consensus of all the Churches in the world, the holy father Augustine, to put an end to this tedious contention, said: 'Let us pray to God for a heavenly sign to direct us which tradition to follow. Let some infirm person be produced, and let us see by whose prayers he shall be made whole.'" The British unwillingly consented; a blind man, an Anglo-Saxon, was brought, and presented to the Welsh clergy, who prayed over him in vain. Augustine then knelt and

---

[1] Several times towards the end of the fifth century Easter was kept in different weeks by the Greek and Roman Churches.

[2] Bangor signifies *the sacred circle.* There were no fewer than sixteen places so named in Wales, besides the famous monastery on the Lough, near Belfast. Dinooth's is supposed to be Bangor-Iscoed, now Bangor, on the Dee, five miles east of Ruabon.

[3] Not improbably near the present Aust Passage, anciently Aust Clive (Southern Cliffs). This was the lowest ferry on the Severn, and is several times mentioned in the Civil Wars as the landing-place of troops coming from Chepstow. In 1375 the prebend of Aust was given by King Edward III. to Wicliffe.

prayed, and immediately the blind man was restored to sight.[1] Still the Britons did not yield; they declared they could do nothing without the consent of a larger number of their clergy. Their seven bishops accordingly came together, with learned men from the monastery of Bangor.[2] But before they ventured to renew the conference, they consulted a hermit whom they held in great veneration. The good man said they might follow Augustine if he were a man of God. "But how," they asked, "are we to know whether he is such?" "If," replied the hermit, "he is meek and lowly of heart, he bears the yoke of Christ and offers it to you; but if he is stern and proud, he is not of God, and we may disregard his words." "But how," they asked again, "shall we discern this?" "Let the Romans," said the hermit, "arrive first at the place of meeting, and if on your approach the man shall rise from his seat to receive you, hear him submissively, for he is the servant of Christ; but if he despises you and remains seated, do you also despise him." Augustine, as they drew near, kept his seat; upon which the Britons charged him with pride, and contradicted all he said. "If," answered Augustine, "you will comply with me in three points—keep Easter duly, administer baptism according to the practice of the holy Roman Apostolic Church, and join us in preaching the word of the Lord to the English,—we will tolerate all your other divergences from our customs." They replied that they would consent to none of those things nor receive him as their archbishop. The stern tones of the Roman monk close the interview. "As you will not have peace with brethren, you shall have war from foes; and as you will not preach unto the English the way of life, you shall suffer at their hands the vengeance of death."

"All which," adds Bede, his gentle heart steeled by religious bigotry, "all which through the Divine judgment fell out as Augustine had predicted. The warlike king of the Angles, Ethelfrid, having raised a mighty army, made a vast slaughter of that per-

---

[1] Dr. Hook is of opinion that no such transaction as the above ever occurred. "That Bede related faithfully the tradition of the Church of Canterbury no one doubts; but the event recorded took place some time between the years 600 and 605. Bede finished his history in 731. . . . If we read his narrative attentively, the account of the miracle looks like an interpolation. He does indeed say that the Britons confessed that it was the true way of righteousness which Augustine taught; but the statement is contradicted by the fact that he does not name a single Briton who became a convert to Augustine's opinion. . . . I treat the whole statement as a mere 'Canterbury tale.'"

[2] The bishoprics were Menevia or St. David's, Llandaff, Llanbadarn, Bangor, and St. Asaph; with perhaps Gloucester; the seventh spoken of by Bede is unknown.

fidious nation at the city of Caerleon.[1] Being about to give battle, he observed standing apart in a place of safety, a great company of priests and monks, who having fasted three days were come to offer prayers to God for their people. 'Although they are unarmed,' he said, ' yet if they cry to their God against us, it is the same as if they fought against us; let them be first attacked.' Twelve hundred are said to have fallen, only fifty saving themselves by flight. Thus," concludes Bede's narrative, " was fulfilled the prediction of the holy bishop Augustine that these perfidious men should feel the vengeance of temporal death, because they had despised the offer of eternal salvation."

The relation between the Roman and the British Churches is thus summed up by our quaint historian Fuller. "Augustine found here a plain religion (simplicity is the badge of antiquity) practised by the Britons; living some of them in the contempt, and many more in the ignorance of worldly vanities. He brought in a religion, spun with a coarser thread, though guarded with a finer trimming, made luscious to the senses with pleasing ceremonies, so that many who could not judge of the goodness, were courted with the gaudiness, thereof. We are indebted to God for his goodness in moving Gregory; Gregory's carefulness in sending Augustine; Augustine's forwardness in preaching here; but above all, let us bless God's exceeding great favour, that that doctrine which Augustine planted here but impure, and his successors made worse with watering, is since, by the happy Reformation, cleared and refined to the purity of the Scriptures."

CHAPTER III.

THE GOSPEL IN NORTHUMBRIA.

STEP by step Christianity won its way throughout the Heptarchy. It early found an entrance into the great northern kingdom, whose capital was York.

Paulinus, one of Augustine's followers, was consecrated the first bishop of York.[2] He had accompanied into the north Ethelburga,

---

[1] Caerleon, in Monmouthshire, the chief city of Wales, the Britannia Secunda of the Romans. But according to Moberly it was Chester.

[2] He is described by Bede as "tall in stature, a little stooping, with black hair, thin face, slender aquiline nose, and at once venerable and awful in

the Christian daughter of Ethelbert King of Kent, on her marriage with Edwin King of Northumbria, A.D. 625. Edwin, although still a pagan, was well disposed towards Christianity. Being about to undertake a war against Quichelm King of the West Saxons, he promised Paulinus, that if by his prayers he would procure him victory, he would renounce his idols and confess Christ. Edwin was victorious, but, before making profession of the Gospel, he desired to confer with his chief men and councillors, so that if they also were of the same mind, "all might together be cleansed in the fountain of life." Paulinus consented, and a general council was convened A.D. 627, probably at the royal villa on the Derwent. When they were assembled, the king inquired of every one in particular what they thought of the new doctrine. The chief priest Coifi was the first to answer. " O king, consider what this is which is now preached to us, for the religion we have hitherto professed has, so far as I can see, no virtue in it. For none of thy people has applied himself more diligently to the worship of our gods than I, and yet there are many who receive greater favours from thee, and are more prosperous in their undertakings. If the gods were good for anything they would favour me who have been more careful to serve them. If therefore on examination thou findest these new doctrines better, let us receive them without delay." As soon as he had spoken a thane stepped forward and said: "The present life of man, O king, compared with that part of our existence which is unknown to us, is like the flight of a sparrow through the hall where, round a blazing fire, with thy nobles and servants, thou sittest at supper in the winter time, whilst storms of rain and snow rage without. The sparrow flying in at one door and out at the other is happy only during the short space when he is within the hall; as he came from winter, so he vanishes into winter again. It is the same with the short span of man's life; of what went before, or what is to come after, we are utterly ignorant. If therefore this new doctrine can tell us something more certain, it deserves to be received." He was followed by many other elders and royal councillors; after which, at Coifi's request, Paulinus expounded the Christian doctrine: whereupon the chief priest cried out: "I have long been sensible that there was nothing in that which we worship, because the more diligently I sought after truth, the less I found it; but now I confess that in this preaching truth itself shines forth, which is able to confer on us life, salvation and eternal happi-

---

aspect." This description was derived by Bede through the abbot Deda, from an aged man who had himself been baptized by Paulinus in the Trent.

ness. I advise, O king, that we instantly abandon and set fire to our unprofitable temples and altars." When the king inquired of him who should be the first to profane the ancient sanctuaries, he answered: "I; for who should more properly than myself destroy those things which through ignorance I worshipped?" Then taking arms and mounting a stallion (neither of which was lawful for a priest), he rode to the spot where the chief temple stood. The people thought him mad, but without heeding them, as soon as he drew near, he cast his spear against it and defiled it, and at his bidding his attendants burnt it with all its precincts.[1]

The king was baptized, and Christianity became the religion of Northumbria. The blessings of peace followed quickly in its train. "In those times," says one of our old chroniclers, "was so great a peace that a woman might go from one town to another unharmed. King Edwin," he adds, "caused brass or iron cups to be fastened beside the clear wells for the refreshment of wayfarers, and so good justice did he keep, that no man dared take them away." But at Edwin's death two usurpers who were pagans shared his kingdom between them, and the Northumbrians relapsed into idolatry. The eclipse however did not last long. The two kings dying, Oswald, the rightful heir, ascended the throne, and restored the Christian faith. He had been an exile amongst the Scots, where he had learnt to esteem the Gospel as the first of blessings. As soon therefore as he was seated on the throne, he sent, not to Rome or to Canterbury, but to Iona for a missionary to teach the people anew. It is said that a monk of austere manners was at first chosen for this service, but, unable to condescend to the weaknesses and wants of a rude people, he effected nothing, and returned home declaring that the Northumbrians were too barbarous to be instructed. There was present when the missionary gave in his report, a monk named Aidan, severely ascetic in his personal habits, but full of charity and gentleness towards others. This man ascribed the missionary's want of success to his own fault, and

---

[1] This spot, called by Bede Godmunddingaham, that is, *Protecting home of the gods*, is identified with Goodmanham, near Market Weighton, upwards of twenty miles E.S.E. of York. If this be so, and if the conference was held, as it is said, on the Derwent, the high-priest must have had a ride of some twelve to fifteen miles. The village church, which stands on the crown of a gentle hill at the southern edge of the Wolds, is supposed to occupy the site of the old shrine. In the lower part of the tower are the remains of a Norman doorway, and within a porch on the south side there is a semi-circular arch; the rest of the church is of various periods, none earlier than the fifteenth century. Within are two stone fonts, the smaller of which is ancient, although there can be no foundation for the tradition that Coifi was baptized in it.

suggested that he ought, like Paul, to have fed his untutored hearers first with milk, until by degrees they should have acquired strength to receive more perfect counsel. All present exclaimed that Aidan himself was the fittest man for the work; and he was accordingly consecrated a bishop and sent into Northumbria, A.D. 635.

The king gave him, as his episcopal seat, the island of Lindisfarne, afterwards called Holy Island, which was visible, at a distance of about six miles, from his own castle of Bamborough. Between Aidan and the king a warm friendship grew up. One Easter Day when they were sitting at table together, with a silver dish full of dainties before them, and were just ready to bless the bread, the king's almoner came suddenly in to tell him that a multitude of needy persons from all parts were sitting in the street expecting alms of him. The king immediately ordered the viands to be carried to the poor, and the silver dish to be cut in pieces and divided among them. Aidan, deeply impressed with the action, took the king's right hand in his, and said, "May this hand never perish." And so it was, according to the good old chronicler, who is ever ready to credit the miraculous; when the king was slain in battle, his right arm, which had been severed from his body, remained entire and uncorrupted, and was preserved down to Bede's time in a silver case in St. Peter's church, Bamborough.

The first church on Lindisfarne was built after the manner of the Scots, of split oak, thatched with coarse grass. Here Aidan preached to the chiefs and the royal household, the king himself acting as interpreter. But as soon as he had mastered the English language Aidan travelled through Northumbria, preaching and conversing with the people.[1] "He taught," says Bede, "no otherwise than he lived; he neither sought nor loved anything of this world. He journeyed on foot, never using a horse except when compelled by some urgent necessity. All who bore him company, whether shaven monks or laymen, unlike the slothfulness of our times, occupied themselves in reading the Scriptures or learning psalms. If it happened, which was but seldom, that he was invited to eat with the king, he went with one or two of the clergy, and having taken a small repast, made haste to be gone in order to read or pray. Whatever gifts he received from the rich he distributed amongst the poor, or expended in redeeming captives, many of whom he

---

[1] The county of Durham, except some cultivated patches near its hamlets and vils, was then in a state of nature, large tracts of land being covered with forests of magnificent oak, the haunt of beasts of the chase.

educated as priests." "The religious habit," continues Bede, "was then held in great veneration; so that wheresoever any clerk or monk came he was joyfully received by all as God's servant; and such as chanced to meet him upon the way ran and bowed to him, and rejoiced to be signed by his hands or blessed with his lips. On the Lord's days the people flocked eagerly to the churches or monasteries, not to feed their bodies, but to hear the word of the grace of God. Priests, and clergy too, were so free from the plague of avarice, that no one received lands or possessions for building a monastery, unless it were enforced by the ruler of the country." Aidan was alive to the value of education. He himself taught twelve Saxon youths, and as new monasteries were founded they became schools under the care of the monks who had followed him from Scotland.

As with Augustine and the Britons, the differences between the Roman and Scoto-Irish discipline came early into view, especially the time of observing Easter.[1] Bishop Aidan and the king observed the Scottish rule; but the queen had been brought up in the Roman practice, so that whilst her husband was joyfully celebrating Easter, she was still observing a rigorous fast. During Aidan's lifetime this difference was not suffered to disturb the peace of the church. Bede generously remarks : "Although bishop Aidan could not keep Easter contrary to the custom of those who had sent him forth, yet he took every pains to promote piety, faith and charity after the manner of all holy men."

But after Aidan's death the diversity of practice soon led to dissension. Aidan was succeeded in the bishopric by Finan, 652, and he again by Colman, 661, both like Aidan monks from Iona. King Oswald's successor, Oswy, followed the practices of the Scottish Church; his queen Eanfled, a Kentish princess, was, like her predecessor, devoted to the Roman ritual. Foremost amongst the Saxons educated at Lindisfarne was Wilfrid, a youth of great energy and intelligence. Wishing to compare the customs of the Northumbrian Church with those which claimed to be Catholic, he was sent by Queen Eanfled to Gaul and Rome, and came back full of zeal for the Roman usages. On his return the king's son Alfrid made him abbot of the monastery of Ripon, displacing the Scottish monks for whom he had founded that cloister.

---

[1] The intolerance seems not to have been all on one side. Augustine's successor in the see of Canterbury, Laurentius, complains that the Scottish bishop Dagan, coming into England, refused to eat with him and his fellow bishops, and even to break bread in the same house with them.

The dispute concerning Easter came to its height in 664, when King Oswy called a synod at Whitby to bring it to a settlement. On the part of the Scots appeared bishop Colman and a Northumbrian bishop named Cedd, who had preached the Gospel amongst the East Saxons with great diligence, self-denial and success. They were supported by the saintly Hilda, in whose abbey the conference was held, in the presence of the king, the queen, and Prince Alfrid. On the other side were Agilbert bishop of the West Saxons, a native of Gaul, and Wilfrid, who from Agilbert's ignorance of English was the spokesman of the party. Bishop Colman argued for the Scottish practice from the authority of the apostle John, and the custom of the churches founded by him.[1] Wilfrid took his stand upon the custom of Rome and "of the Church of Christ in every land, except only these Scots and their accomplices in obstinacy, the Picts and Britons, who from these two remote islands of the ocean foolishly fight against the whole world." He ensconced himself in the authority of Peter, and asked "if even the holy Columba was to be preferred to the apostle on whom Christ had built his Church, and given him the keys of the kingdom of heaven." On hearing this the king exclaimed, "Is it true, Colman, that these words were spoken to Peter by our Lord?" Colman answered, "It is true, O king." "Can *you* show any such power given to your Columba?" "We cannot," replied Colman. "Do you both agree that these words were principally directed to Peter, and that the keys of heaven were given to him by our Lord?" They both answered, "We do." Upon this the king declared, "I say that Peter is the doorkeeper, and I will not contradict him, but obey him in all things, lest when I come to the gates of heaven there should be none to open them, he who holds the keys being my adversary." Bishop Cedd submitted; but Colman, says Bede, perceiving that his doctrine was rejected and his sect despised, renounced his charge and went back into Scotland, accompanied by all who would not accept the Roman Easter and the Roman tonsure. From this hour the English Church was wholly subject to Rome.

Wilfrid was in course of time appointed archbishop of York, and went to France to be consecrated by the Gallic bishops. On his

---

[1] We have seen that the Scots were not Quarto-decimanians (see *ante*, p. 267). "Colman," says Bede, "celebrated Easter, not like the Jews, on the fourteenth of the month, whatsoever the day of the week might be, but on the Lord's day, from the fourteenth to the twentieth." It may be that Colman cited the apostle John in a traditionary way, without clearly understanding the point at issue.

return the vessel was stranded on the coast of Sussex. This, the last kingdom in the Heptarchy to be Christianized, was still almost wholly pagan. The savage inhabitants, who were merciless wreckers, rushed down to plunder the ship. At their head was a priest who, like "another Balaam," stood on a rising ground uttering spells and curses. Wilfrid on board the vessel, "like Moses and Aaron when Joshua fought with Amalek," withstood him by fervent prayer; whilst the crew made a stout resistance. A stone from a sling struck the pagan priest on the forehead, and put an end to his enchantments and his life. His fall only exasperated the barbarians. Thrice they renewed their attack upon the little band, and thrice they were beaten off. As they were preparing for a fourth assault, the returning tide floated the ship, which sailed along the coast and arrived safely at Sandwich, whence they returned to Northumbria.

After occupying the see of York with renown for several years, Wilfrid became involved in disputes with the king, was degraded from his dignity, and subjected to hardship and exile. In his adversity he remembered the rude people of Sussex, and how greatly they stood in need of Christian teaching. The king and queen of the South Saxons had both been baptized, and there was a small monastery of five or six Irish monks at Bosham, near Chichester, who "served the Lord in poverty and humility, but to whom none of the natives gave heed;" with these exceptions Wilfrid found the kingdom almost entirely heathen. The arts of life were hardly better understood than the precepts of the Gospel. Although the sea and the rivers abounded in fish, the people had no skill to take any but eels. Wilfrid made his men collect the eel-nets and cast them into the sea; they caught three hundred fishes of divers kinds, one-third of which they gave to the poor, another to the owners of the nets, and kept one-third for themselves. Wilfrid's preaching was very successful; nobles, priests and people flocked to him to be baptized; and the king granted him as the seat of his bishopric the peninsula of Selsey,[1] with all its lands, chattels, and inhabitants. Here he established a monastery and school, and finding in his new domain two hundred and fifty men and women slaves, "all these, as by baptizing them he saved them from the servitude of the devil, so by giving them freedom he

---

[1] When Lanfranc removed the episcopal sees from the villages, Selsey was transferred to Chichester. In the south aisle of the choir of this cathedral some Saxon bas-reliefs brought from thence are still to be seen.

loosed them from the yoke of human bondage." By this act he set a noble example.[1]

We have spoken of Hilda. Whitby Abbey contained houses for men as well as women, all under the direction of this "Northumbrian Deborah."[2] One of the monks was Cædmon, the first English poet, of whom Bede has left a brief but charming notice. "There was," he writes, "a certain brother who, with much sweetness and humility, made pious verses in his native language. Before he entered the monastery he had lived many years without learning the art of versifying, so that at entertainments when for the sake of mirth all the guests sang in turn, as soon as he saw the instrument come towards him he rose from the table and went home. Once on a time, having left the feast and gone to the stable, where it was his business that night to attend to the horses, when he had finished his work he composed himself to sleep. In his sleep One appeared to him and said, 'Cædmon, sing some song to me.' He answered, 'I cannot sing; I left the entertainment and retired to this place because I could not sing.' He who talked with him replied, 'Thou shalt however sing.' 'What shall I sing?' asked Cædmon. 'Sing the Creation,' was the answer. Upon which he sang—

Nu we sceolan herian	Now must we praise
heofon-rices weard.	the Guardian of heaven's kingdom,
metodes mihte	the Creator's might,
and his mod-ge-thonc.	and his mind's thought;
wera wuldor-fæder.	glorious Father of men!
swa he wundra gehwæs	as of every wonder He,
ece dryhten	Lord eternal,
oord onstealde.	formed the beginning.
he ærest gescéop	He first framed
eorthan bearnum	for the children of earth
heofon to hrófe	the heaven as a roof,
halig scyppend.	holy Creator!
tha middangeard	Then mid earth
moncynnes weard	the Guardian of mankind,
ece dryhten	the eternal Lord,
æfter teode	afterwards produced;

---

[1] The redemption of slaves was long a principal duty of the religious houses. In Doomsday no slave is registered in York, and few in the neighbouring counties. At the Council of Celchyth (in Mercia), A.D. 816, bishops were directed by their wills to free all bondsmen of English descent, whom the Church had acquired during their administration.

[2] Several such double monasteries existed in Saxon England; they seem to have prospered for a time, but were soon discontinued.

firum foldan   the earth for men,
frea ælmihtig.[1]   the Lord almighty.

When he awoke he remembered what he had sung in his dream; and much more to the same effect came into his mind. He went to the town-reeve of Whitby to acquaint him with the gift he had received, and by him was conducted to the abbess, to whom in the presence of many learned men he told his dream and repeated his verses. It was seen by all that the Lord had bestowed upon him heavenly grace; and the abbess urged him to lay aside his secular habit and enter upon the monastic life, directing that he should be thoroughly instructed in the Bible. "Retaining in his memory all he learnt, and as it were chewing the cud, he turned the sacred history into most harmonious verse. He sang the creation of the world, the origin of man, the departure of the children of Israel out of Egypt and their entrance into the land of promise; the incarnation, passion and resurrection of our Lord, and his ascension into heaven, the descent of the Holy Ghost, and the preaching of the Apostles, the terror of the judgment to come, the pains of hell and the delights of heaven."

When the time of his decease drew near, Cædmon, being taken sick, desired his attendant to prepare a room for him in a hospital which was nigh at hand. As his master was still able to walk and converse, the attendant wondered at the order, but did as he was bid. The poet talked cheerfully and playfully with the other inmates of the hospital until past midnight, when he asked if they had the Eucharist. His companions answered, "What need of the Eucharist? thou art not going to die." "Nevertheless," he answered, "bring me the Eucharist." Having taken it into his hand, he asked whether they were all of unruffled mind towards him, free from all controversy and rancour. They answered they were all in perfect charity, and inquired whether he was in the same mind towards them? He replied, "My children, I am in charity with all the servants of God." Having strengthened himself with the heavenly viaticum,[2] he inquired if the time was near when the brethren were to be awakened to sing the Nocturns. They replied, "It is not far off." He answered, "It is well; let us wait for that hour;" and "signing himself with the sign of the holy cross, he laid his head on the pillow, and falling asleep, so in silence ended his life."

---

[1] Thorpe, *Cædmon's Metrical Bible*. Bede gives the verses in Latin; King Alfred's version of Bede's history gives Cædmon's original words as above.

[2] Death-bed communion; literally, provision for a journey.

Of Cædmon's poem (if indeed it be his), only one ancient copy, and that anonymous, is extant, written apparently in the tenth century. It was given by Archbishop Ussher to the learned Junius, who printed it and afterwards bequeathed it to the Bodleian library. Milton probably saw it before he composed his *Paradise Lost*. The poem contains some fine passages.[1]

"Cædmon's poetry," remarks Milman, "was the people's Bible. . . . He chose by the natural test of his own kindred sympathies, all which would most powerfully work on the imagination, or strike to the heart of a rude yet poetic race."

In the same year that Aidan died, so Bede relates, a youthful shepherd in the hill country of Lauderdale, now in the county of Berwick, but then forming part of Northumbria, was watching his flock by night, when a company of angels appeared to him, singing hymns of triumph, and bearing up to heaven a newly-departed soul. He awoke his fellow-shepherds, who only laughed at his tale; but when he learned that bishop Aidan had passed away at that very time, he left them, and rode down to Melrose,[2] where

---

[1] Satan's fall is thus described:—

Then was the Mighty angry;
The highest Ruler of heaven
Hurled him from the lofty seat.
* * * * *
He must seek the gulf
Of hard hell-torment,
For that he had warr'd with heaven's
　Ruler.
* * * * * *
The fiend with all his comrades
Fell then from heaven above,
Through as long as three nights and
　days.
* * * * * *
* * * * * *
Satan harangued,
Sorrowing spoke,
He who hell thenceforth
Should rule.
He was erst God's angel,
Fair in heaven,
Until him his mind urged,
And his pride
Most of all,

That he would not
The Lord of Hosts'
Word revere.
Boiled within him
His thought about his heart
Hot was without him
His dire punishment.
Then spake he the words:
"This narrow place is most unlike
That other that we ere knew,
High in heaven's kingdom.
* * * * * *
O! had I power of my hands!
Then with this host I——
But around me lie
Iron bonds;
Presseth this cord of chain:
I am powerless!
* * * * * *
Here is a vast fire
Above and underneath;
Never did I see
A loathlier landscape;
The flame abateth not."

[2] This was not the identical Melrose with which Scott has made us familiar, and which was a later foundation a short distance higher up the Tweed.

some Scottish monks from Lindisfarne had reared a monastic house. Here he applied for admission into the brotherhood, and was readily received. A few years afterwards Cuthbert, for this was the name of the shepherd youth, made one of that colony of Scottish monks, which Prince Alfrid first planted at Ripon, and then sent back to their own country to make way for Wilfrid and his Anglo-Romans.[1] On his return to Melrose Cuthbert devoted himself to missionary work, of which there was urgent need, for the people around were addicted to magic and sunk in ignorance.[2]

In 664 he was promoted to be prior of Lindisfarne, where he set an example of devotion and self-denial. As time went on, the spirit of asceticism grew upon him, and he forsook the island, retiring to a solitary place on the mainland, and thence to one of the little islands of Farne, lying to the southward. This islet "consists of a few acres of ground, partially covered with grass, and hemmed around with an abrupt border of basaltic rock." Here the more completely to exclude what little was left of the outer world, he raised a wall of turf and stone which he could not see over; and within this enclosure built an oratory and a hut of driftwood thatched with straw. His cell had but one window, and this after a while he closed, never opening it, except to give his blessing when his brethren from Lindisfarne, or strangers, came to seek it. At the place of anchorage he set up another cabin to shelter his visitors. On this island he passed nine years. In 684, with great difficulty and only by the personal entreaty of King Egfrid, who crossed over to Farne for that purpose, he was induced to abandon his hermitage, and to accept the bishopric of Lindisfarne.

For two years Cuthbert faithfully discharged the episcopal duties, and then resigned his see to retire again to his beloved cell, that he might die there in peace. Early in 686 he was seized with his death-sickness. Herefrid prior of Lindisfarne visited him, and after receiving directions for his burial, went home, purposing shortly to return; but a storm arising, five days elapsed before he could venture to recross. On the sixth day Herefrid, with a party

---

[1] See above, p. 274.

[2] He feared not to travel in the most inaccessible districts, on rugged mountains and by toilsome paths, where the people alike from their poverty and ignorance were quite neglected by others, and he often remained away two or three weeks, or a month even, from the monastery, dwelling among the mountaineers, and teaching them both by word and by the example of his deeds.

of his monks, found Cuthbert sitting in the little guest-chamber at the landing-place. For five days and nights he had not tasted anything nor moved from the spot. The monks carried him into his oratory, where he uttered his last request, that should they ever be compelled to desert their home, his remains should accompany them wherever they went.[1] When he died, which was at midnight, Herefrid lighted a couple of torches and waved them in the air as a signal to Lindisfarne. Cuthbert is said to have wrought many miracles, the fame of which after his death spread far and wide, and laid the foundation of the extraordinary influence and wealth of the see of Durham.

Lindisfarne was for many years a centre of learning and of ecclesiastical power. Before the conversion of York into a metropolitan see under Wilfrid, its bishop wielded jurisdiction from the Firth of Clyde to the Humber.[2] In how great a degree art and learning had taken up their abode in this remote corner of Christendom is seen in the celebrated *Durham Book*, an illuminated copy of the Gospels in the Vulgate version of Jerome written at this period.[3] This, one of the most beautiful manuscripts in Europe, is a memorial of the pious care of the monks of Lindisfarne. One abbot after another took his part in the labour of love. Eadfrith,[4] who followed Cuthbert in the bishopric and abbacy, and whose chief mission was to spread the glory of his predecessor, began to transcribe the work probably during Cuthbert's lifetime, and laid it reverently on its completion upon the shrine of the saint; Ethilwald,[5] who succeeded Eadfrith, gave the covers; Billfrith, the anchorite, wrought the ornaments and jewelled work upon the

---

[1] This charge was faithfully kept; but the incursions of the Danes made its fulfilment a very arduous matter. For many years the body was carried about to various places in Northumbria and Cumbria, and once was even taken on board a ship to be conveyed to Ireland. At last it found a resting-place on the summit of the hill at Durham, then covered with wood. Here a church was commenced, the parent of the present stately cathedral.

[2] The original rude church was replaced by a cathedral of stone. This was pulled down in 1093, when the see was transferred to Durham, and the Priory Church, whose picturesque ruins still adorn the island, was erected out of its materials. No trace now exists of the original monastic buildings. The name Holy Island, in memory of the martyrs in the Danish massacre, was given in 1093. Some remains of Cuthbert's cell are, it is said, still to be seen on Farne Island.

[3] It is the earliest specimen extant of Saxon calligraphy and decoration.

[4] Bishop from A.D. 698 to 721.

[5] Bishop from A.D. 724 to 740.

outside. Thus far it would seem was the work completed in the early part of the eighth century, and it was not until the middle of the tenth that Aldred the priest, still animated as the previous labourers had been by devotion to the memory of Cuthbert, added, in a small current hand, the interlinear Saxon version. The book was justly esteemed a priceless treasure by the island monks. They bore it with them when fleeing from the ravages of the Northmen. Once in the ninth century the monks were essaying to cross the channel to Ireland when the precious volume fell into the sea. Great was their joy to discover it three days after, stranded on the coast at Whithorn, bearing only the stains of sea-water, which are still visible. The book remained at Lindisfarne until the dissolution of the monasteries, and has since found its way to the British Museum, where it is now preserved. The volume is a square folio, written on vellum in double columns in the half-uncial character. It contains whole-page pictures of the four Evangelists, and four pages also of rich lace-work ornament of a Runic character round the figure of a cross. These illuminations with the capital letters are all richly and delicately coloured. The accompanying chromograph represents rather more than half the right-hand column of folio 88.

Matthew v. 3—8.

[3] Eadge tha bithon thærfendo vel-from of-gaste
Beati pauperes sp*iri*tu

forthon hiora is
quoniam ipsorum est

ric heofna
regnum caelorum

Eadge bithon tha thærfende thæt is un-spoedge menn vel unsynnige forthon hia agan godes r[ic]

T
M xxvi [5]
x

Eadge bithon tha milde forthon
Beati mites quoniam

tha agnegath
ipsi posidebunt

eortho
terram

Forthon tha milde gbyes hli'giendr[a] eortho

T
M xxvii [4]
u
Lu xlviii

Eadge bithon tha the gemænas
Beati qui lugunt

forthon tha
quoniam ipsi

gefroefred bithon
consolabuntur

nu
nunc

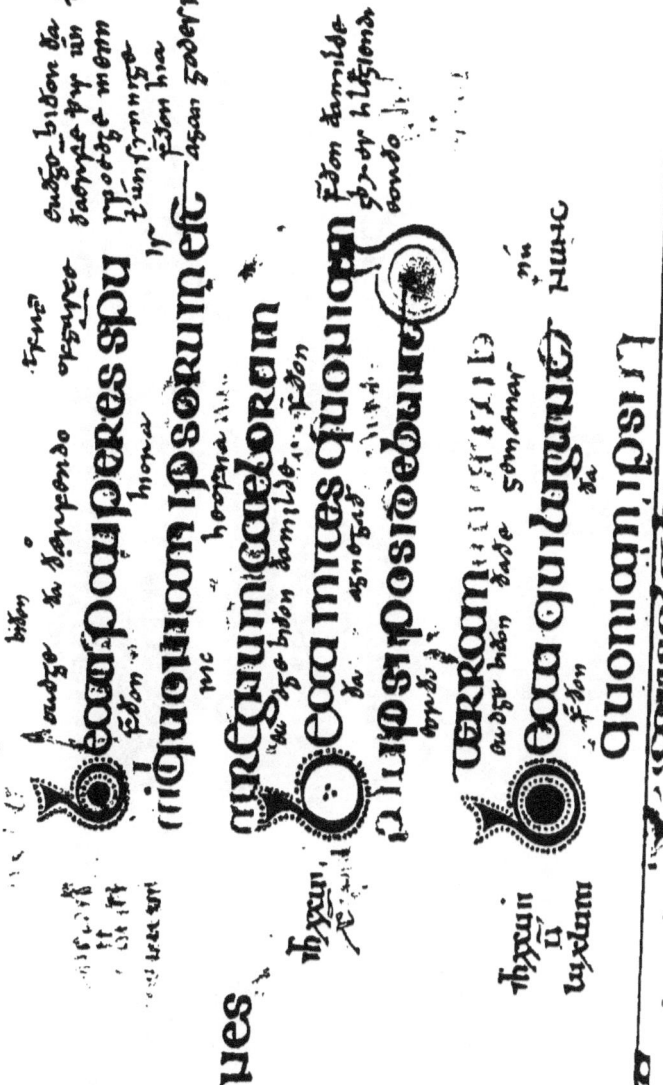

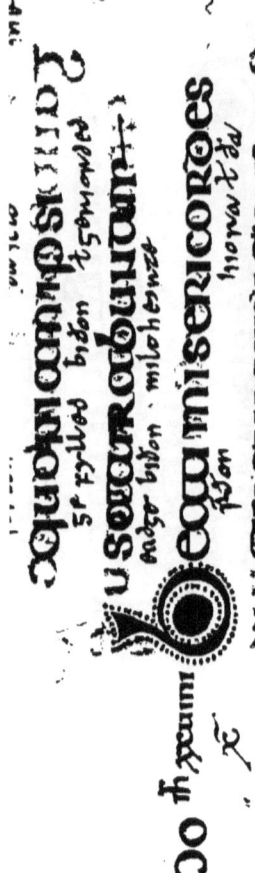

Facsimile of part of a page from the Durham Book (Lindisfarne Gospels).

T   Eadge bithon tha the hyncgrath   Eadge bithon
M xxviii [6] Beati qui esuriunt   tha the thyrstas
 u   & hyncgras
Lu xlvii & thyrstas sothfæstnisse   æfter sothfæst
    et sitiunt iustitiam   nisse forthon tha
                  gefylled bithon
     forthon tha ilco   in ece lif
    quoniam ipsi

    gefylled bithon *vel* geriorded
    saturabuntur

T   Eadge bithon milt-heorte
M xxviiii [7] Beati misericordes
 x

     forthon hiora *vel* tha
    quoniam ipsi

    milt-heortnise
    misericordiam

    him gefylges
    consequentur

    Eadge bithon claene of hearte Eadge bithon tha
       vel from   claene hearte
 [8] Beati mundo corde   bute esuice
                  & eghwoelcum
    forthon tha god   facne forthon
    quoniam ipsi d*eu*m   hia geseas
                  god in ecnise

    Blessed are the poor of spirit Blessed are the
 [3] Blessed *are* the poor in spirit destitute that is
                  poor men
    for theirs is   [or] innocent
    for theirs is   for they
                  own God's
    (the) kingdom of heaven   kingdom
    the kingdom of heaven

    Blessed are the mild (meek) for For the mild
 [5] Blessed *are* the meek for shall inhabit (the)
                  higher earth
    they shall own
    they shall inherit

    (the) earth
    the earth

    Blessed are those that mourn
 [4] Blessed *are* they that mourn

    for they
    for they

    shall be comforted
    shall be comforted

	Blessed are those that hunger	Blessed (are)
[6]	Blessed *are* they that hunger	those that thirst
		and hunger
	and thirst for truth	after truth
	and thirst after righteousness	for they
		shall be filled
	for the same	in eternal life
	for they	

shall be filled *or* refreshed
shall be   filled

      Blessed are (the) merciful
[7] Blessed *are* the merciful

for their *or* the
for   they

mercy
mercy

follows them
shall obtain

	Blessed are (the) clean of heart	Blessed are the
[8]	Blessed *are* the pure in heart	clean-hearted
		without deceit
	for they God	and wickedness
	for they God	every for
		they shall see
		God in eternity

NOTES.

The interlinear translation and marginal gloss are in the Dano-Saxon dialect, which differs in many particulars from the Anglo-Saxon.

It will be noticed that verses 4 and 5 are not in the same order as in our New Testament, but are interchanged. This is their order in the Vulgate, which has been followed by Wicliffe. Tyndale and our modern translators follow the Greek order. In verse 4 the transcriber has made a mistake, *lugunt* for *lugent*. The fragments of words on the left in the Chromo belong to the other column of the page.

The letters opposite verses [5] [4] [6] [7] are the *Eusebian Canons*. The M with the T above it stands for Matthew; the x signifies the tenth canon or table, the u (v) the fifth.

At the end of John's Gospel is the following note:—

✠ Eadfrith biscob lindis-fearnensis æcclesiae he this boc aurat aet fruma gode. & sancte cuthberhte & allum thaem halgum gimaenlice tha the in eolonde sint. & Ethiluald lindis-fearneolondinga biscob hit uta githryde & gibelde sua he uel cuthae. & billfrith se oncrae he gismiothade tha gihrino thathe utan on sint & hit gihrinade mith golde & mith gimmum aeo mith suulfre ofergylded faconleas feh : & Aldred presbyter indignus & miserrimus mith godes fultummæ & sancti cuthberhtes hit ofergloesade on englisc. & hine gihamadi mith thaem thriim daelum. Matheus dael gode & sancti cuthberhti. Marcus dael thæm biscobe. & lucas dael thaem hiorode & œhtu ora seulfres mith co inlade : & sancti iohannis dael for hine seolfne & feouer ora seulfres mith gode & sancti -cuthberhti thæte he hœbbe ondfong therh godes milsae on heofnum. seel & sibb

on eortho forth-geong & githyngo uisdom & snyttro therh sancti cuthberhtes
earnunga: ✠ Eadfrith. oethiluald. billfrith. aldred. hoc evangelarium deo &
cuthberhto construxerunt vel ornauerunt.

✠ Eadfrith, bishop of the Lindisfarne Church, (was) he (who) at the first
wrote this book in honour of God and St. Cuthbert, and all the saints in common
that are in the island. And Ethilwald, bishop of the people of the Lindisfarne
island, made it firm on the outside, and covered it as well as he could. And
Billfrith the anchorite, he wrought in smiths' work the ornaments that are on
the outside, and adorned it with gold, and also with gems, overlaid with silver,
unalloyed metal. And Aldred,[1] an unworthy and most miserable priest, with
the help of God and St. Cuthhert, glossed it above in English, and made himself familiar with the three parts: Matthew's part for God and St. Cuthbert;.
Mark's part for the bishop; and Luke's part for the brotherhood, and eight
oras[2] of silver for his admission; and St. John's part for himself, and four oras-
of silver (deposited) with God and St. Cuthbert; to the end that he may,
through God's mercy, gain admittance into heaven, and on earth happiness and
peace, promotion and dignity, wisdom and prudence, through St. Cuthbert's
merits. ✠ Eadfrith, Œthilwald, Billfrith, (and) Aldred made and adorned
this gospel book for God and St. Cuthbert.[3]

The saintly Cuthbert was yet living when, in 674, Benedict Biscop, a noble Saxon, obtained from King Egfrid seventy hides of
land on the north bank of the river Wear, and founded the abbey
of Monkwearmouth. "Its church," as Bede informs us, " was a
magnificent stone building in the Roman style, and was constructed
by workmen brought over from France. When it was nearly
finished, Biscop sent again to France for artificers skilled in making
glass, and those foreigners not only fashioned the windows, but
taught the natives the mystery of their art, by which lamps, cups,
and an endless variety of useful and ornamental articles are formed
with wonderful beauty and facility." Biscop's zeal prompted him
to make several journeys to Rome, whence he brought back the art
of Church music, many valuable books, and a copious supply of
relics and pictures of Christ, the Virgin, the Twelve Apostles, &c.,.
with which he adorned the roof and walls of his church.[4]

Biscop's fabric has not wholly perished. The church still stands

---

Supposed by some writers to be the same with Aldred the provost,. whose
name appears in the Durham Ritual about A.D. 970; but this is uncertain. It
is considered, however, that the Dano-Saxon *gloss* belongs to the period just
mentioned, namely, the latter half of the tenth century.

[2] The ora had two values, but was commonly reckoned at sixteen pence.

[3] In the foregoing description and elucidation of the *Durham Book*, we are
specially indebted to Joseph Cohen of Woolwich for kind and valuable assistance.

[4] The plate and vestments for the service of the church also came from
abroad.

in a third-rate street of the busy town of Sunderland, a memorial of England's religious zeal in the vigour of her childhood. The west porch and west wall are the very same that Benedict's skilful workmen from France raised under his eye, and on which Bede, in his

Monkwearmouth Church.

youthful wonder, gazed with so much delight. In proof of this the plan of the church and its style of ornamentation agree exactly with those of other "Saxon" churches of the seventh and eighth centuries. There is also a close and curious resemblance between the fragments of sculpture remaining on the Monkwearmouth stones and the illuminations in the Lindisfarne Gospels. Considering, remarks G. F. Browne, how very few there must have been who carried the art of "Irish ornamentation" to perfection, the hand which in so felicitous a manner handled the chisel at Monkwearmouth was not improbably the same which, more than twenty years afterwards, drew the exquisite designs of the Lindisfarne Book. One of the fragments of the artist's work is a corner of a sculptured stone of yellowish tint built into the wall of the vestry,

THE IRISH ORNAMENTATION. 287

and which may perhaps be a portion of the memorial slab laid over the body of Benedict himself, hard by the altar of his church.[1] It is presented in the following woodcut, together with a pattern from one of the four great pages of interlacements in the manuscript.

Fragment of Sculpture from Monkwearmouth Church.

Corner of a Page of Ornamentation, *Durham Book*.

[1] Mr. Browne has kindly permitted us to copy his drawing of the sculpture.

In 682 Biscop founded the sister monastery of Jarrow on the Tyne, whither he transferred seventeen monks of the Wearmouth Convent under the direction of a learned priest named Ceolfrid.[1] Ceolfrid was a pattern of discipline, a collector of books, and a great lover of Rome. After a while he was appointed by Biscop, abbot of Wearmouth as well as of Jarrow. He died A.D. 716 at Langres, in France, on his way toward Rome, where he intended to end his days. Bede has left a description of Ceolfrid's farewell to his flock. The scene is the monastery of Monkwearmouth. "Early in the morning of the 4th of June, after mass had been sung in the church of the blessed Virgin mother of God, and also

Jarrow Church.

in the apostle Peter's, and all present had received the Holy Communion, the abbot girded himself for his pilgrimage. The brethren crowded into the church, where Ceolfrid, after kindling the incense and praying before the altar, stood upon the steps, and, with the flaming censer in his hand, gave the salutation of peace. From the

---

[1] The church was dedicated A.D. 684. The present building, with a few remnants of the ancient priory, now converted into cottages, stands at the north end of the smoky and unsightly hive of industry which still bears the honoured name of Jarrow. It occupies a breezy though gentle eminence on the south shore of the Tyne, overlooking its broad and shallow waters. The church has been modernised, but in this case, as in that of Monkwearmouth, the base of the square tower is supposed to be the actual work of Biscop.

church they proceeded, mingling their sobs with the Litany, into the oratory of St. Lawrence. Here Ceolfrid uttered his last farewell, and exhorted them to preserve love to one another, and to correct offenders according to the Gospel. He forgave all who had ever incurred his displeasure, and craved the same forgiveness for

Ceolfrid's Farewell.   Designed for Edward Backhouse by W. B. Scott.

himself, if on his part he had treated any too rigorously; and begged to be remembered in their prayers. They come to the river ; they exchange again, amid their tears, the kiss of peace, and all bow the knee whilst he prays aloud. He enters the boat, his companions entering also, the deacons carrying a golden cross and lighted tapers. He crosses the stream, does reverence to the cross, and mounting his horse; disappears."

Both Benedict Biscop and Ceolfrid had a part in the education of "Venerable Bede," the glory of the Anglo-Saxon Church. This remarkable man was born about the year 673, and at the age of seven, whilst the church was in building, was brought to Biscop at Monkwearmouth to be instructed in the rudiments of learning, and initiated in the discipline of the cloister. When only nineteen, being under the canonical age, he was made deacon, at thirty was ordained priest, and afterwards became abbot of the monastery of Jarrow, numbering at that time 600 monks and scholars. Here he

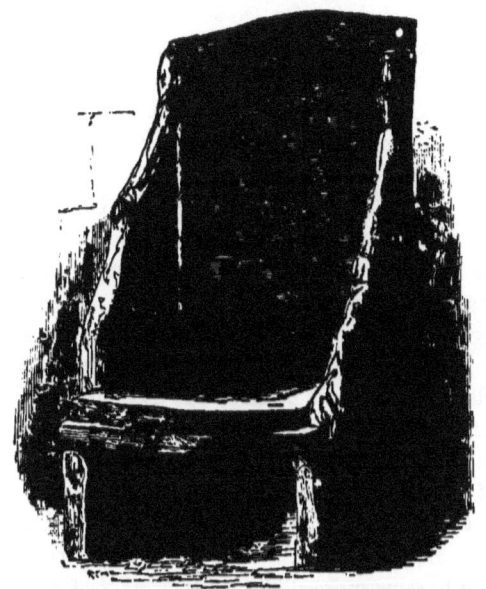

Reputed Chair of Bede, Jarrow.

spent his life, giving daily instruction in the Scriptures and all the other learning of the age; not a few of his disciples catching the enthusiasm of his gentle, humble spirit. Bede's life seems to have flowed on, "like a calm river, within the pleasant banks of study, teaching, and devotional exercises."[1] He tells us he never wandered far from his own cloister, and we have no account of any journey extending beyond York. His death happened in 735, in his sixty-third year.

---

[1] "I have ever held it sweet either to learn, to teach, or to write." He says also that he took part in the domestic work of the monastery, "the winnowing and threshing of corn, giving milk to the lambs and calves, and the work of the garden, kitchen, and bakehouse."

His disciple Cuthbert, afterwards abbot of Jarrow, has left a touching description of Bede's last days in a letter to a fellow-pupil. "I have read with much satisfaction in thy letters that masses and holy prayers are diligently celebrated by you for our father and master Bede, beloved of God, on which account it is the more pleasing to me to gratify thy desire, and to relate how he departed this world. Although much troubled with shortness of breath, he was cheerful and joyful, till the day of our Lord's Ascension, reading lessons to us and singing psalms, and giving thanks to God night and day with expanded hands. He sang the sentence of St. Paul, 'It is dreadful to fall into the hands of the living God,' and also the song in our English tongue [to the effect], 'No man is so wise as to dispense with the examination of his account before his departure.'[1] He sang also antiphons according to our custom: 'O Glorious King, Lord of Powers, who triumphing this day, didst ascend above the heavens; do not forsake us orphans; but send down upon us the Father's promised Spirit of Truth.' When he came to that word 'do not forsake us,' he burst into tears and wept much, and an hour afterwards he repeated what he had begun. We hearing it, wept with him; by turns we read, and by turns we wept, nay, we always read with tears. He often repeated, 'God scourges every son whom he receives,' and the saying of St. Ambrose: 'I have not so lived among you as to be ashamed to live on; but I do not fear to die because our Lord is good.'[2] He had two works in hand during those days—the translation of the Gospel of St. John into our own tongue, and a selection from the Book of Notes of Bishop Isidore—which he laboured to finish, saying, 'I would not leave my children anything erroneous, or have them toil fruitlessly after my death.' On the Tuesday before Ascension his breathing became more difficult, and his feet began to swell; but he passed the day pleasantly, dictating and saying, 'Go on quickly, I know not how long I shall abide, or whether my Maker will soon take me away.' Again on Wednesday, he desired we would write with speed, and when we had finished we made the customary procession with the relics of the saints till the third hour. Then one of us who was with him said, 'Most dear master, there is still one chapter of the Gospel untranslated, is it troublesome to thee to be asked any more questions?' He answered, 'It is no trouble, take thy pen and write fast.' But at the ninth hour he said to me, 'Run and bring hither the priests of the monastery.' When they came, 'The rich,' he said, 'can make presents of silver

---

[1] See *ante*, p. 154.　　[2] See *ante*, p. 70.

and gold; I have none of these, but with love and joy I present my brethren with what God has given me.' Thus saying he distributed amongst them a few peppercorns and grains of frankincense, with some church cloths, and charged them diligently to say masses and prayers for him. 'It is time,' he said, 'I returned to Him who formed me out of nothing. I have lived long, my merciful judge·

Death of Bede.   Designed for Edward Backhouse by W. B. Scott.

well foresaw my life for me; the time of my dissolution draws near; I desire to be dissolved, and to be with Christ.' Much more he spoke, and passed the day joyfully till the evening, when the lad said, 'Dear master, there is yet one sentence to write.' He answered, 'Write quickly.' Presently afterwards the youth said again, 'Now it is finished.' He replied, 'Thou hast said the truth, it is ended. Hold my head in thy hands; it is a great satisfaction to me to sit opposite to the holy place where I have been wont to pray, that I may call upon my Father, singing, 'Glory be to the Father, and to the Son, and to the Holy Ghost.' With these words he breathed his last, and we doubt not his soul was borne by angels unto heavenly joys."

Bede wrote many books, the most renowned of which is his *Ecclesiastical History of Britain*.[1] In his attainments he was abreast of all the learning and science of the age. Under Benedict Biscop and Ceolfrid he enjoyed exceptional advantages. "Nowhere else could he acquire at once the Irish, the Roman, the Gallician, and the Canterbury learning."[2] Bede understood Greek, and had some knowledge of Hebrew, was well acquainted with the Latin poets, and familiar with the works of the Fathers.[3] There was at that time no spot on this side the Alps more luminous than Jarrow : in Ireland and France, the light of knowledge was fast waning. The culture of Jarrow passed over to the school of York, which was fostered, though not founded by Bede ; and Alcuin, the most illustrious pupil of that school, carried the lamp of learning across the sea to the court of Charles the Great, before the ravages of the Danes plunged England again into barbarism.[4]

Bede's Homilies on the Gospels contain many bright spiritual thoughts. Take the following example (John ii. 1-11). "'And when they wanted wine, the mother of Jesus said to him, They want wine. Jesus said to her, Woman, what have I to do with thee? Mine hour is not yet come.' In nowise did He who commands us to honour father and mother intend to dishonour his mother; still less did He mean to deny that she was his mother, from whom He had condescended to be born. But in that He was about to perform a miracle, He signified that He had not received from his temporal mother that divine nature which He was proceeding to exhibit, but that He had enjoyed it eternally from the Father. 'What, O woman, is there in common between my Deity, which

---

[1] It was translated from the Latin into Anglo-Saxon by King Alfred.

[2] Theodore, seventh archbishop of Canterbury, 668-690, was a Greek, a native of Paul's city of Tarsus. He was accompanied to England by the abbot Adrian. They brought with them a valuable library, and are regarded as the founders of English scholarship. The larger monasteries were converted into schools of learning, Canterbury being the chief. "Many of their disciples," says Bede, "are still living, who are as well versed in Greek and Latin as in their native tongue."

[3] Copies of the Vulgate New Testament and of Cassiodorus on the Psalms in Bede's own handwriting are in the Chapter Library at Durham.

[4] It is said on King Alfred's accession, A.D. 872, not a single priest was to be found south of the Thames who understood the daily Latin service which he muttered.

I have always held indissolubly with the Father, and the human nature which I have received from thee? The hour is not yet come when by dying I may show the prevailing nature of the humanity which I have received from thee: I must previously exhibit the power of the Eternal Deity in great signs.'"

After the death of Bede, we hear nothing of the two monasteries of Monkwearmouth and Jarrow until the fatal year 870, when, with Lindisfarne and the other religious houses on the coast, they were utterly destroyed by the Danes, and monks, priests and people put to the sword.

Two hundred years afterwards they were restored by Aldwin, a Mercian monk, but in 1083 were deprived of their independent existence, and became cells of Durham Cathedral.

CHAPTER IV.

British Missionaries to the German Nations.

WE must retrace our steps to give some account of the work of the Irish and English missionaries on the continent of Europe. These messengers were amongst the most faithful Witnesses for Christ from the sixth to the ninth century. In those days Ireland was perhaps the first of the nations in knowledge and gospel charity, and the Irish Church, so far from being the most docile and devoted of Rome's servants, stood forth almost alone to resist her arbitrary will.

The leader of this band, who commenced his missionary travels seven years before the arrival of Augustine in England, was Columbanus.[1] He was born about 543 A.D. in the province of Leinster, and educated in the monastery of Bangor, on Belfast Lough, founded and governed by the abbot Comgall. At the age of thirty he conceived the idea of preaching the gospel to the pagan nations of Germany, some knowledge of whom had come into Ireland through France. The seed of Christianity had been early planted in those parts of Germany which were subject to the Roman Empire, but when these countries were overrun by barbarous pagan tribes, the precious plant was trodden down and almost eradicated.

---

[1] Not to be confounded with Columba of Iona spoken of in the last chapter, who was born forty years before.

Columbanus felt within him, as his biographer expresses it, "that fire which our Saviour said He came to kindle on the earth." The abbot gave him twelve young men as his companions. Arriving in Gaul they found the need of Christian teaching in some parts of that country so urgent, that, being invited to remain, they settled in a forest of the Vosges mountains in the country of the Burgundians. Columbanus purposely chose a spot which had first to be reclaimed by the severe labour of his monks, in order that they might acquire greater power of self-denial and of control over the sensuous nature, and might also show the untutored people how to till the soil. At first they had nothing to live upon but herbs and the bark of trees; but Columbanus had great faith in prayer, and the answers he received were so remarkable that he came to be regarded as one highly favoured by God. One of the brothers fell ill; no suitable food for him was to be had. At the end of three days, spent by Columbanus and his monks in prayer, a man presented himself at the door of the convent leading horses laden with sacks of provisions. He told them he had come in obedience to a sudden impulse to assist those who from love to Christ were enduring such privations in the wilderness. At another time a stranger priest, to whom Columbanus showed his granary, expressed his surprise that so small a store should suffice for the wants of so many; upon which Columbanus replied: "Let men but rightly serve their Creator, and they are secure from starvation, as it is written in the thirty-seventh psalm, 'I have never seen the righteous forsaken, nor his seed begging bread.' It is easy for that God to replenish the barrel with meal, who with five loaves of bread satisfied the five thousand."

Columbanus found monachism in France in a state of decay, and the rule of Benedict almost forgotten. By his exhortations and example the enthusiasm for the monastic life revived, and was spread throughout France : the three great houses of Anegray, Luxeuil, and Fontaines were founded by him. He gave to his monks a new and stringent rule, borrowed from the rigid discipline of the Irish and Scottish monasteries. All self-will was to be mortified; all the motions of the body and even the tone of the voice were regulated, chastisement following upon every transgression.[1] Perpetual silence

---

[1] Six strokes were the penalty for calling anything one's own, omitting to say Amen after the abbot's blessing, or to make the sign of the cross on one's spoon or candle, talking at meals, or failing to repress a cough at the beginning of a psalm. Ten strokes were the punishment for striking the table with a knife, or for spilling beer upon it. For heavier offences the number rose as high as two hundred, but in no case were more than twenty-five to be inflicted at once. An-

was imposed, except on urgent occasions. Meat and wine, with which Benedict had indulged the weak and ailing, were forbidden to all. One meal only was allowed, namely, in the evening. "These excessive severities," says Montalembert, "discouraged no one. Columbanus up to the last day of his life saw an army of disciples collect around him, in sanctuaries more numerous and illustrious than those of Benedict. . . . The genius of Columbanus hovers over the whole of the seventh century, of all the centuries the most fertile in the number and fervour of its monastic establishments. "But," he is obliged to add, "before the century was completed the rule of the great Irishman was everywhere replaced by the spirit and laws of his immortal predecessor." It was, in fact, impossible that so inhuman a discipline should in the end supplant Benedict's wiser rule, or should long survive the life of its founder.

Columbanus, however, was not altogether devoid of tenderness, and his command over men was unbounded. Once he was summoned from the solitude to which he had retired, by the tidings that nearly all his monks in the monastery of Luxeuil were sick. He hastened thither and commanded them to rise up and go to work in the barn at threshing out corn. At the sound of his voice many of them, forgetting their malady, rose up and went to work. Very soon, however, he bade them desist, and telling them that they must allow a little refreshment to their bodies exhausted by disease, he placed food before them; they ate and became well. Like good men in all ages, Columbanus found retirement for reading and meditation necessary to his spiritual life, and he might be seen from time to time wending his way into the dense forest for this purpose, bearing on his shoulder a copy of the Holy Scriptures. Although he insisted on the punctilious observance of outward practices, and imposed on his monks many devotional exercises

---

selm, archbishop of Canterbury in the reign of William Rufus, rebuked this discipline of the stick still practised in his time. An abbot complained to him that the youths under his care were incorrigible, notwithstanding all the stripes he administered. "You are always beating your boys," replied Anselm; "what sort of men will they grow up?" "Stupid and brutish," answered the abbot "What else can you expect," said Anselm, "when you educate men into brutes?" "Is that our fault," answered the abbot; "we try to compel them in all manner of ways to be better, and yet we effect nothing." "You compel them!" exclaimed Anselm. "If you were to plant a tree in your garden, and pen it in on all sides so that it could not spread out its branches in any direction, and should afterwards transplant it, what kind of a tree would it become? A useless stock with crooked, tangled branches. And whose fault would it be but yours who caged it in this unnatural fashion?"

which could not fail to become mechanical, yet he was careful to remind them that everything depends on the temper of the heart.

In his intercourse with popes and bishops Columbanus maintained the independent spirit of the Scoto-Irish Church. He wrote to Popes Gregory the Great and Boniface IV. on the vexed question of the time for keeping Easter, exhorting the former to reconsider the Paschal Cycle by which this festival was determined, without blindly following any former pope. "A living dog," he said, "may be better than a dead lion." He adduced the memorable example of the bishops Polycarp and Anicetus in the second century, who each maintained his own practice on this very question, and yet remained in mutual charity and unity.[1] He set the Church of Jerusalem above that of Rome; and he admonished Pope Boniface IV. that in proportion as the dignity of the Roman bishops was great, so ought their care to be great, lest by perversity they should lose it: "He only," he told him, "is the true key-bearer of the kingdom of Heaven, who by true knowledge opens the door for the worthy, and shuts it upon the unworthy, and he who acts otherwise can neither open nor shut."

Columbanus' boldness in rebuking sin brought upon him the ill-will of the Frankish king Thierry II. and his wicked grandmother Brunehaut, and in 610 he was banished from the kingdom, and ordered to be taken back to Ireland. But the veneration he had inspired and the loftiness with which he vindicated his spiritual office were such that it was some time before any one would venture to execute the order, and the attempt when it was at length made was defeated by a storm.

Instead of returning home he and his companions proceeded to Switzerland. His chief disciple was Gallus,[2] a well-educated young man, inflamed with zeal against the pagan idolatry. At Tugium (the modern Zug) he set fire to the temples of the Alemanni (or Suevi), and threw their idols into the lake. The people rose against him; the monks were compelled to fly, and Columbanus, forgetful of his Master's spirit, devoted the whole race of the barbarians to perdition. Coming to the Lake of Constance they were met by a Christian priest, who directed them to the remains of a Roman castle called Pregentia,[3] where they took up their abode. Here they rebuilt a ruined church, and supported themselves by fishing and horticulture. In common with the whole region of the

---

[1] See *Early Church History*, p. 97.

[2] In Erse, Callech.

[3] Bregetium, Bregenz, at the eastern end of the lake.

Alps the country had become re-paganised, and the chief objects of worship were three statues in gilded brass. At a festival in honour of these idols the people assembled in unusual numbers, partly out of curiosity to see the strangers. Gallus preached to them in their own language, and then broke their idols in pieces and threw them into the lake.

At the end of three years Columbanus left Pregentia, and crossing the Alps into Italy founded, near the city of Pavia, the celebrated monastery of Bobbio, A.D. 613.[1] Gallus having fallen sick was left behind. On his recovery he made his way into the forest on the south shore of the lake, where he erected an oratory with huts for his companions, and began to instruct the rude inhabitants of the country. This was the beginning of the monastery of St. Gall, the most illustrious in Switzerland both for learning and afterwards for wealth and political influence. Gallus died about A.D. 630.

The next missionary from our islands of whom we shall speak, emanated not from the Irish but from the Saxon or Anglo-Roman Church. This was Winfrid, better known in history as Boniface, a name given to him by the pope. He was a man of extraordinary energy, and his labours in the mission-field attained great success. He had no sympathy with the independence of the British Churches, but on the contrary constituted himself the ally and instrument of the papal see in extending the Roman discipline over a large portion of Central Europe, and in quenching every spark of independent practice and thought.

Boniface was born at Crediton in Devonshire in the year 680, and trained in a convent at or near Exeter. "The passion for foreign travel, which seemed innate in the monks of the British islands, combined with the nobler desire of devoting his life to the conversion of pagan nations, constrained him to leave his native land." From 715 to 722 he laboured mostly in Friesland, but in the latter year, seeing in a dream the prospect of an abundant harvest amongst the tribes in the interior of Germany, he directed his course to Hesse and Thuringia.

During one of his journeys he arrived at a nunnery in the district of Trèves, on the banks of the Moselle. After service the abbess and her guests repaired to the common hall, and as was customary a portion of Scripture was read during meal-time. The reader was Gregory, a lad of fifteen, a nephew of the abbess, and

---

[1] "An outpost of the Catholic faith in the midst of the Arian Lombards." Afterwards famous for its library, and especially for its numerous palimpsests (books written over more ancient works from scarcity of parchment). Columbanus died here, A.D. 615.

but lately returned from school. Boniface was pleased with the way in which the boy read his Latin Vulgate, and asked whether he understood what he had read? The boy, mistaking his question, read the words a second time. "Nay, my son," said the missionary, "that is not what I meant. I know thou canst read well enough, but canst thou translate the passage into thy own mother-tongue?" The lad confessed he was unable to do so, upon which Boniface himself translated it into German, and then made it the ground of a brief exhortation to the company. His words fell on the listening ear of the young Gregory like the spark which kindles a flame, and the boy was seized with an unconquerable desire to accompany the preacher in his mission, declaring that if he was not provided with a horse he would go on foot. He is known amongst the band of mediæval missionaries as Gregory of Utrecht.

The next year Boniface was summoned to Rome by Pope Gregory II., who consecrated him bishop over all the Churches he should found in Germany, giving him permission to travel whithersoever he would. On this occasion he took a solemn oath of implicit obedience to the Apostolic see. Kneeling at the tomb of the Apostle Peter, he uttered the words: "I promise thee, the chief of the apostles, and thy representative Pope Gregory and his successors, that with God's help I will abide in the unity of the Catholic faith; and if ever I find that the conduct of the presiding officers of churches contravenes the ancient decrees and ordinances of the Fathers, I will have no fellowship with such men, but will obstruct them all I can, and if unable to stop them, will report their conduct faithfully to the pope." By this transaction, observes Neander, the question was settled whether the German Church should be incorporated into the system of the Roman hierarchy, or whether there should proceed from it a reaction of freer Christian development.[1] This last would have taken place if the more free-minded British and Irish missionaries who were scattered among the German populations had acquired the preponderance. At Rome the danger which threatened from this quarter was well understood, and the commission which Boniface received was not only to convert the pagans, but quite as much to bring back to orthodoxy and obedience those whom "unauthorized" teachers had led astray.

Although Boniface had thus bound himself hand and foot to Rome, there can be no doubt whatever as to his zeal in labouring to turn the rude tribes from the darkness of paganism to the light

---

[1] Such a reaction did occur, but eight centuries had first to pass away.

of the Gospel. By the year 739 he had baptized nearly a hundred thousand of the inhabitants of Thuringia and the neighbouring districts. These wholesale conversions, in effecting which he was powerfully seconded by the authority of Charles Martel, were no doubt many of them merely nominal; but the suppression of idolatry, the abandonment of savage heathen customs and the substitution of Christian worship and instruction, must have effected a great revolution in the minds and habits of the people.

Boniface maintained frequent intercourse with England. The monasteries he founded were peopled with monks and nuns from this country, who introduced various arts, and took with them books for the instruction of the youth. From Daniel bishop of Winchester, Boniface received wise counsel for his missionary work; and Eadburga, abbess of Minster in the Isle of Thanet, supplied him with clothes and books, amongst which was a copy of Peter's Epistles, written in gold letters, to excite the admiration of the ignorant people who came to hear him. His eyes being weak, he asked his former teacher, the abbot Wimbert, to have a copy of the Prophets engrossed for him in plain large characters and without abbreviations.

Boniface's oath to oppose such as were not in harmony with the Romish tradition, did not remain a dead letter. He had several encounters with Church teachers of this description. One of these was Clement, an Irish missionary, of whom nothing is known save that he was married, that he defended from Scripture the marriage of bishops, and that he denied the writings of Jerome, Augustine, and Gregory the Great, and the canons of councils, to be binding on Christians. Another was Virgilius, also a native of Ireland, who was preaching the Gospel in Bavaria. An ignorant priest having, in the case of a baptism, pronounced the Latin formula incorrectly, Boniface declared the baptism to be invalid. Virgilius protested, and appealed to the pope, who decided in his favour. His heresy indeed seems to have been scientific rather than theological, for when he afterwards presented himself as a candidate for one of the bishoprics founded by Boniface, the latter refused to accept him because he held the "unscriptural opinion that the earth is a globe, and that consequently there are other men living under our feet." This time the pope agreed with Boniface, and directed that Virgilius should be deposed from his priestly office. Virgilius seems, however, to have succeeded in exculpating himself at Rome, for he afterwards became bishop of Salzburg and was enrolled amongst the "saints."

That the anti-Romish opinions promulgated by the Irish missionaries in France and Germany were widely diffused is evident from a letter written to Boniface by Pope Zacharias (A.D. 741-752). "Thou hast found men wandering about, more numerous than the Catholic priests, and not ordained by Catholic bishops. False vagabonds are they, adulterers, murderers, effeminate, sacrilegious hypocrites, tonsured slaves who have fled from their masters. They meet with their abettors in conventicles, and exercise their ministry in strange places, such as the cellars of country-houses where their stupid folly may be concealed from the bishops." The pope's imputation of immoral conduct must be taken for what it is worth; the fact is established, on the best authority, that there existed in the eighth century in the heart of Europe, numerous teachers and congregations of Christians who were independent of the See of Rome, and protested against its errors.

But the malpractices and superstitions of Rome were sometimes too glaring for the honest English heart of Boniface. He fearlessly rebuked Pope Zacharias for allowing money to be demanded as the price of an archbishop's pall. In a letter to the same pope he complains of the bad example set at Rome to simple pilgrims from Germany; of the heathenish practices allowed there on the first of January; and of the public sale of amulets, which the women bought to hang round their arms. "When," he says, "the people return and report that such things are done under the very eyes of thy Holiness, my Christian instructions are not a little hindered of their effect."

As his age increased, the sphere of Boniface's authority and influence widened. He was appointed archbishop of Mentz, and it was by his hand that Pepin the Little was anointed king. But his indefatigable labours were now drawing to their close. Committing his administrative work to younger men, he set out in the beginning of the year 755 on a mission to Friesland, the scene of his early ministry, under the firm persuasion that he should never return. In the book-chest which he took with him wherever he went, he carried his shroud, desiring that after his death his body might be conveyed to the great monastery of Fulda, in Hesse, which he had founded. With a small retinue of clergy, monks and servants, some fifty in all, he embarked in a boat on the Rhine, and descended towards the Zuyder Zee. The little band traversed the country, founded churches, and baptized thousands of converts. It was the fourth of June; they had planted their tents on the banks of a small stream near Dokkum, in the north of Friesland. During the day a large number of new converts had been in attendance, and were to return on the morrow to receive the rite of confirmation.

Early the next morning Boniface heard at a distance the sound of an approaching multitude, and full of joy came from his tent to meet them. But he soon found out his mistake. The clash of weapons announced other than a friendly purpose. In fact the pagan priests, maddened by the success of Boniface and his coadjutors, had devoted the very day appointed for public admission into the Church, to vengeance on behalf of their gods. They seem also to have been lured by the gold and silver vessels which they supposed Boniface to carry about with him. On their approach the younger Christians drew swords to defend their bishop, but he checked the ineffectual resistance. Taking the relics in his hands, and exhorting his attendants not to fear those who were able only to kill the body, but to confide in their Lord who would soon bestow upon them the reward of everlasting glory, he calmly awaited the issue. He had not long to wait. Laying his head upon a volume of the gospels, he received the fatal blow: most of his followers perished with him. He was in his seventy-fifth year. According to his desire his body was carried up the Rhine, and buried in the monastery of Fulda.[1]

Boniface was followed by Willehad, a Northumbrian, who preached in Friesland and North Germany, commencing in the district where his predecessor was slain. With him the stream of missionaries from Ireland and England to the continent seems to have come to an end.

In receiving the German converts into the Church, the formula made use of was very simple. It is to be observed that this baptismal vow, written down by the priest and responded to by the catechumen, takes us back to the infancy of the German language. German literature may be said to have commenced with the foundation of the Church by Boniface. The art of writing cannot, outside the Roman pale, be traced back much if at all earlier than the eighth century, and for a long time the clergy were its only possessors. The earliest known transcript of the vow is preserved in the cathedral of Merseburg in the Prussian province of Saxony, and was written in the eighth century. The following is a fac-simile of it:—

---

[1] Boniface is distinguished from other missionaries of his age, in that not a single miracle is recorded of him. A modern historian says of him: "No missionary has been more eminent in labours since the Apostle Paul."

Interrogatio Sacerdotis.
Forsahhistu unholdun? Ih fursahu.
Gilaubistu in Got Fater Almahtigan? Ih gilaubu.
Gilaubistu in Christ Gotes Sun Nerienton? Ih gilaubu.
Gilaubistu in Heiligangeist? Ih gilaub.

The priest asks.
Dost thou forsake the devil? I forsake.
Dost thou believe in God the Father Almighty? I believe.
Dost thou believe in Christ the Son of God, the Saviour? I believe.
Dost thou believe in the Holy Spirit? I believe.

CHAPTER V.

THE MOHAMMEDAN CONQUEST.

THE subversion of the Eastern Church by Mohammed and his successors should afford, one would suppose, ample material for the Church historian to record. On the contrary, this chapter in history is one of the briefest and most barren. Within a short space of years Syria, Phœnicia, Mesopotamia, and Egypt abjured the cross and prostrated themselves before the crescent. In her early days, when the Church was poor, despised, and few in number, she successfully resisted the whole weight and power of the Roman Empire; now that she had become wealthy and dominant, she had not inward strength to withstand the first onset of a false religion. Some resistance, it is true, was offered to the invaders, but it was with the sword, not with the Spirit; the annals of those years are barren of acts of faith. Where were the prophets boldly proclaiming the divine judgments,—the apologists,—the scholarly athletes wrestling with error,—the confessors,—the martyrs? The Eastern Churches were like costly garments in some tropical country, into which the white ants have found their way; to the eye they are beautiful and perfect as when they were fashioned, but at the first rude touch they crumble to dust.

It may be argued that the two cases were different. Roman paganism sought wholly to stamp out Christianity; Mohammedanism, which, it must be confessed, shot some rays of truth into the dark places of the earth, respected and even reverenced the religion of Christ. This reverence however was in profession rather than in reality. The ancient Church would never have consented, no Church in which the Spirit of Christ dwelt could have consented, to the treacherous compact by which the Eastern Christians in the seventh century purchased immunity from the Moslems.

There is no need to dwell upon the causes which produced this deplorable collapse; they have given their distinctive features to the foregoing pages, as well as to the volume to which the present work is a sequel.[1] "What Mohammed and his caliphs found," writes Isaac Taylor, "in all directions whither their scimitars cut a path for them, was a superstition so abject, an idolatry so gross and shameless, Church doctrines so arrogant, Church practices so dissolute and so puerile, that the strong-minded Arabians felt themselves inspirited anew as God's messengers to reprove the errors of the world, and authorized as God's avengers to punish apostate Christendom. The son of the bond-woman was let loose from his deserts, to 'mock' and to chastise the son of the free-woman."[2] The eloquent apologist for Monachism thus describes the part played by monks and clergy in the cowardly surrender of the fortress at the first summons of the enemy. "After an age of unparalleled virtue and truthfulness, after having presented to the monastic life of all ages, not only immortal models, but also a kind of ideal almost unattainable,—the monastic order allowed itself to be overcome, through all the Byzantine Empire, by that enfeeblement and sterility of which Oriental Christianity has been the victim. . . . The monks of the East sank gradually into nothingness. Intoxicated by the double influence of courtierism and theological discord, they yielded to all the deleterious impulses of that

---

[1] Another cause is to be found in the cruel persecution of the Paulicians. See below, Chap. VI.

[2] Of the seventh century Mosheim writes: "In this barbarous age religion lay expiring under a motley and enormous heap of superstitious inventions, and had neither the courage nor the force to raise her head or display her natural charms to a darkened and deluded world."

declining society, of whose decay despotism was at once the result and the chastisement. . . . They could neither renovate the society which surrounded them, nor take possession of the pagan nations which snatched away every day some new fragment of the empire. They knew no better how to preserve the Church from the evil influences of the Byzantine spirit. Even the deposit of ancient knowledge escaped from their debilitated hands. They have saved nothing, regenerated nothing, elevated nothing. They ended, like all the clergy of the East, by becoming slaves of Islamism and accomplices of schism."

Mohammed was born about A.D. 570; and his flight from Mecca to Medina, which forms the era of the Moslems under the name of the Hegira, took place in 622. Before his death in 632, he had subdued all Arabia and had commenced the reduction of Syria. His successors prosecuted the conquests thus begun. In 637 Jerusalem was taken; two years later the subjugation of Syria was completed, and that of Egypt in 641. Persia followed and North Africa; and in 711 the victorious Arabs, known in Europe under the name of the Moors whom they had conquered, crossed over into Spain, and subjugated that country in about two years. Thence they overran France as far as the Loire, when the great victory of Charles Martel in 732 effectually checked their progress in Western Europe.

Mohammed was not ignorant of the Bible, and he borrowed from it both in theology and morality.[1] But the truth of which he thus possessed himself was inextricably mixed with errors and absurdities; and the Koran, notwithstanding the respect with which its author speaks of Christ, contains no trace of the doctrine of Redemption.[2] He proclaimed it as his mission to carry through the earth the knowledge of the one God and of himself as his prophet, and he waged relentless war against idolatry, "Believe or die," was the sole alternative offered to the pagan. Towards the Jews

---

[1] "His acquaintance, however, both with the Old and New Testament was small, fragmentary and inaccurate, not derived from the Scriptures themselves, but from Talmudic legends and apocryphal gospels, and, as we may confidently affirm, not drawn at first hand even from these."

[2] Some missionaries in 1831 visited in the prison at Cape Town a Hottentot under sentence of death. He was a Mohammedan convert, and was attended by the Moslem teacher. The missionaries requested him the next time the priest came, to ask if the Mohammedan religion afforded any means of relieving the conscience from the burden of sin? At their next interview they inquired what answer the teacher had given. "He confessed," said the Hottentot, "that no provision exists for such a need; on which I told him that I renounced a religion which afforded no ray of hope for the anguish of a wounded conscience."

and Christians, "the people of the Book," as he styled them, he assumed a different attitude; they were not required to embrace the faith of Islam, but were suffered, under certain conditions including the payment of tribute, to worship in their own way. Nevertheless the oppression to which they were subjected, and the bribes which were held out to converts, drew multitudes over to the new religion. Whole populations of Christians at once embraced the faith of the conquerors; and the sacred land of Israel and the birth-place and original home of Christianity have ever since been trampled under foot by the followers of the false Prophet.

CHAPTER VI.

THE PAULICIANS.[1]

FROM the time when Jerome so successfully quenched the sparks of light struck by Jovinian and Vigilantius, we meet with no attempt to reform the Church for more than two hundred years. Her slumber, which grew ever more profound, was not disturbed until the seventh century, when a religious awakening took place in the East.

The birthplace of the Paulician movement was Armenia, and the root from which it sprang is thought to have been the remnant of the Marcionites, that sect of Gnostics which may be described as the most spiritual, as it was the most enduring.[2] As in the case of Vigilantius and Jovinian, no information has come down to us respecting this sect except from adverse sources.

The origin of the Church is traced to the following circumstance. In the middle of the seventh century there resided at the village of Mananalis, not far from Samosata, a man named Constantine, who gave hospitable entertainment to a certain deacon returning from captivity, probably among the Saracens. The grateful deacon presented his host with a manuscript containing the Gospels and Paul's Epistles, neither of which, as it would appear, he had ever seen before. Constantine applied himself earnestly to the study of these sacred books, especially of the Epistles, which made a deep impression upon him, and gave an entirely new direction to his

---

[1] So named, it is supposed, from the Apostle Paul, whose writings they especially valued.

[2] See *Early Church History*, p. 57.

thoughts and to his life. Unhappily his mind was preoccupied with the Oriental dualistic ideas familiar in the Gnostic systems, which represented the creation of the world as the work of a spirit atenmity with the perfect God; and when he read in the New Testament of the opposition of darkness to light, flesh to spirit, and the world to God, he seems to have mixed this pure Christian teaching with the alloy which he had derived from the Marcionites. None the less however did Constantine believe himself called to stand forth as an apostolical reformer. He laboured with great assiduity in his work of reformation twenty-seven years, and made many converts, both from the Church and from the followers of the Persian sage Zoroaster. The progress of the new society naturally provoked persecution; Constantine was stoned, and a large number of his disciples were burned alive. During the next generation the sect was rent by schism, and at the same time the advancing sword of the Saracen conquerors obliged many to leave their native country and to seek a new home in Asia Minor. Here they were in danger of extinction, when a new leader arose and led them back to the path of service and suffering.

This was a young man named Sergius, a native of a village in Galatia, who had been brought up in the Catholic Church. He was one day addressed by a Paulician woman in the following manner: "I hear, sir, that thou excellest in science and erudition, and art a man of high moral character; tell me then, why dost thou not read the sacred Gospels?" "Because," answered Sergius, "it is not lawful for us of the laity to read those books, but only for the priests." The woman replied, "It is not as thou supposest, for there is no respect of persons with God. He willeth all men to come to the knowledge of the truth. But your priests corrupt the word of God, and would conceal the mysteries which are contained in the Gospels, and this is the reason why detached portions only of Scripture are read in the churches." She then asked him of whom it was that our Lord spoke (Matt. vii. 22, 23), who had prophesied in his name and wrought miracles, but whom He would nevertheless refuse to own; or who were the sons of the kingdom of whom our Lord says that they should be thrust out of it (Matt. viii. 12). "They are those," said she, "whom you call saints, of whom you say that they work miraculous cures, and expel evil spirits, those whom you honour, whilst you neglect to honour the living God." These words sank deep into the heart of Sergius. Like his predecessor Constantine, he commenced at once to study Paul's Epistles; and was not slow to perceive the wide difference which existed between the teaching of the Apostle and the effete forms of the State religion. At the same time, like Constantine, he seems to have suffered his theology to be marred by the Gnostic Dualism.

For thirty-four years[1] Sergius preached and taught with indefatigable zeal, traversing every province of Asia Minor. "I have," he said, "run from east to west and from north to south, till my knees were weary, preaching the Gospel of Christ." Like the Apostle he supported himself by his own hands, following the trade of a carpenter. His strict morality and gentle manners extorted commendation even from his enemies, although they pretended to regard these virtues as so many marks of hypocrisy. In his teaching it was his custom to present first the practical requirements of Christianity, and afterwards, when he had gained the ear of his audience, to inveigh against the dominant Church. Many of the laity were attracted by his preaching, and even monks, nuns and priests became his willing auditors. An involuntary testimony to his character, as well as to the extent of his influence, is borne by the Catholic historian. He styles him, "the most mighty champion of the devil, a fierce wolf in a sheepskin who has changed many from sheep into wolves; a deceitful pretender to virtue, who, under this disguise, has beguiled many, and who has trodden under foot the Son of God [the mass] and counted the blood of the covenant an unholy thing." Sergius indeed, if his words have been faithfully reported, became intoxicated with his own success. In one of his letters to his flock are these words: "I am the porter and the Good Shepherd, and the leader of the body of Christ, and the light of the house of God. I am with you always, even unto the end of the world; for though I may be absent in the body, yet I am with you in the Spirit."

At first the missionary labours of Sergius fell within a favourable period. There was in the Greek Church at this time a small handful of ecclesiastics who considered it unchristian to coerce heretics with the sword, declaring that priests, whose duty it is to lead men to repentance, ought not to be partakers in the shedding of blood. Influenced by these enlightened men, or impatient of the domination of the bishops, the Emperor Nicephorus[2] refused to be the tool of the hierarchy in the persecution of dissenters. So long as he lived therefore the Paulicians enjoyed tranquillity. But when Michael I.[3] succeeded to the throne the conditions were changed. At the instance of the Patriarch of Constantinople it was determined to compel all heretics to return to the Catholic Church.

---

[1] A.D. 801—835.   [2] A.D. 802—811.   [3] A.D. 811—813.

The milder of the clergy remonstrated. Theodore, abbot of the monastery of Studium in Constantinople,[1] although a zealous defender of the Church-faith, and even a fanatical supporter of image-worship, honourably distinguished himself on this occasion. Writing to the bishop of Ephesus, who had declared that to put Manichæans to death was "a glorious work," he asks: "How sayest thou? Our Lord commanded that the tares and the wheat should grow together until the harvest; how then canst thou call the rooting up of the tares a 'glorious work?'" He quotes Chrysostom on the same Scripture passage: "This the Lord spoke, foreseeing that wars would be waged and blood shed and slaughter perpetrated. We are not to kill heretics, else would war rage for ever in the earth. And if ye begin to use the sword and slay heretics, many saints also will inevitably be destroyed with them." "Which thing," adds Theodore, "has already happened in our time. Neither ought we to pray *against* the teachers of error but *for* them, as our Lord prayed on the Cross for those who knew not what they did."

But a few individual voices availed nothing against the dominant spirit. Iconoclasts and image-worshippers alike concurred in persecuting the heretical sects. Leo the Armenian,[2] successor to Michael, although hostile to image-worship, sent a bishop and an abbot to coerce the Paulicians into conformity. In the discharge of their commission these inquisitors acted at Cynoschora with such severity that the inhabitants rose up and slew them. To escape the Imperial vengeance, the insurgents fled to that part of Armenia which had received the faith of Islam, where they were received with open arms. They soon fell into a lawless manner of life, and joined the Saracens in their incursions into the Imperial provinces. Against these excesses Sergius set his face, but his remonstrances were unheeded. After governing the community in their new location for several years, whilst he was one day at work in the mountain alone, felling timber for his trade, he was attacked by a Catholic zealot who wrested his axe from his hand and cleft him in twain, A.D. 835.

For a few years the Paulicians enjoyed some repose; but on the re-establishment of image-worship under the regency of Theodora in 842, the work of extermination was resumed. All endeavours to win them back to the Church, either by arguments or threats, being unsuccessful, the sword was once more unsheathed against

---

[1] And thence called *Studites*.
[2] A.D. 813—820.

them. The slaughter was terrible in the extreme, rivalling that of the Albigenses and Waldenses at a later period. It is said that no fewer than 100,000 persons were put to death.

Meanwhile, in the eighth century, a numerous body of this people had been transported into Thrace and Bulgaria by the Emperor Constantine Copronymus; whither also, about the year 970, another and still larger migration from Armenia took place by direction of the Emperor John Zimisces. They were chosen on account of their valour to guard the Balkan frontier of the Greek Empire, and were planted near Philippopolis.

The Paulicians were by no means free from errors. If we may trust the evidence which has come down to us, they rejected the Old Testament, with the Epistles of Peter and some other portions of the New. Many may be ready to doubt the claim of such heterodox professors to be true Witnesses for Christ, and justly indeed in the later stages of their history, when they became a military power. But with all their errors and faults, they wrought a good work in the midst of a corrupt Church, leading a godly life, and on many most important doctrines pointing men back to the first principles of the Gospel. Thus they maintained that the multiplication of external rites had imperilled the true life of religion. They contended against dependence on the magical effect of the Sacraments, the use of which indeed they entirely discarded. It was, they declared, by no means Christ's intention to institute water-baptism as a perpetual ordinance; by baptism He meant the cleansing work of the Holy Spirit. So too, they held that eating the flesh and drinking the blood of Christ consists in coming into vital union with Him through his word. They despised the wood of the cross, then an object of universal adoration, and protested against the worship of the Virgin Mary. Although their doctrines fostered the practice of strict morality no trace is to be found of the ascetic spirit; on the contrary, they treated the Church fasts with contempt. Learning from the New Testament that all believers are one in Christ, they rejected the distinction of clergy and laity, and protested against the assumption of the Jewish priesthood by the Christian minister. They had amongst them rulers and Church officers, but these were not distinguished by dress or badge, any more than by a supposed peculiar holiness.

Out of the Paulicians and a kindred sect called the Euchites, arose the Bogomiles,[1] in whom, as in the former, a clearer insight into spiritual truth than that of the Church around them was

---

[1] Slavonic: *Bog*, God; *z'milui*, have mercy.

marred by visionary fancies, even so far as to deny that Christ had a real body. The sect was widely spread through the Greek Empire. A venerated monk, Constantine Chrysomalos, who by his writings contributed to the diffusion of their doctrines, was condemned at a synod held at Constantinople in 1140. He taught that "all singing and prayer, all participation in the outward rites of the Church, and study of the Scriptures, is vain unless accompanied by that inward change by which man is delivered from the power of evil." Contemporary with him was Niphon, also a monk, who by his pious and strict life won universal reverence. He was ignorant of classical learning, but familiar with the Holy Scriptures, and he maintained correspondence with many bishops, especially in Cappadocia. This man was condemned by the Patriarch Michael to perpetual confinement in a monastery; but Michael's successor Cosmas, a man of singular piety and benevolence, restored him to liberty and made him his table companion. As Cosmas refused to abandon Niphon after the latter had been condemned by a synod, sentence of deposition was passed upon himself, upon which he retorted that it was "the Church which was corrupt, and that he himself was like Lot in the midst of Sodom."

The Bogomile doctrines spread from Thrace and Bulgaria to the Sclavonian country of Bosnia, which thus in the twelfth century became the seat of a numerous Protestant Church. The pope, who at this very time was attempting to extinguish in Western Europe the light which two centuries before had been kindled by the Paulician missionaries, extended his powerful arm towards the East to bring back the Bosnians to the Catholic faith. He succeeded for a while in recovering the Ban or sovereign, who was also the head of the sect, but a few years afterwards, 1199, that prince fell again into heresy, and his dominions became the asylum for the persecuted Albigenses, 1207—1218.[1] As soon however as the work of extirpation in Languedoc and Provence, begun by Pope Innocent III., was completed, his successors again endeavoured to strangle the reformed religion in the Bosnian mountains. The brother of the King of Hungary was the De Montfort of this new crusade, and in 1238 invaded Bosnia with a large army. Similar inroads were repeated for more than two centuries; the country was laid waste, cities were sacked, heretics burned, butchered, and cast into dungeons. But the faith of the Bogomiles was exceedingly tenacious of life; and in the fifteenth century we find them still as numerous as ever, and making common cause with the followers of John

---

[1] See below, Part iv. chap. 7.

Huss. In 1459 the Ban Stephen, a Catholic, made a last attempt to root out his dissenting subjects, and it is said drove away 40,000 of them into the Herzegovina. The expulsion however of this large number did little to diminish the strength of the party at home, and in 1468, the Turkish conquest of the Balkan cut short all such arbitrary proceedings, and once for all delivered the oppressed people from their Christian tyrants. They refused to strike a blow for their sovereign, and even hastened to surrender to the infidels their towns and fortresses.[1]

CHAPTER VII.

WITNESSES FROM THE EIGHTH TO THE TENTH CENTURY.

IT is a matter for devout thanksgiving to the Divine Head of the Church that during the darkest period of its history a succession of true Witnesses was always found, by whom either the life of Christianity was preserved or the much needed work of reformation attempted.

One of the most illustrious of these was our countryman ALCUIN.[2] He was born of a noble Northumbrian family, in the same year in which Venerable Bede finished his course, A.D. 735, and was brought up from infancy in the school at York. His master was Ethelbert, afterwards archbishop of York. The course of instruction embraced a fair knowledge of the Latin poets and of the Greek Fathers, with as much Hebrew as could be learnt from the study of Jerome. The library contained books in all these three languages, and included the works of Aristotle and Cicero. Alcuin succeeded Ethelbert as head of the school, which reached its highest reputation under his direction, many youths from distant places resorting thither.

Charles the Great (Charlemagne) was then the chief patron of learning in Europe. The ignorance this monarch perceived in the

---

[1] The intelligent traveller from whom we have derived this information discovered, in the mountain gorges, many singular sepulchres. They bore upon them various devices, but very seldom the figure of the cross; the Bosnians of the present day call them the tombs of the Bogomiles.

[2] See *ante*, p. 293, where we have already spoken of Alcuin's part in carrying the learning of Jarrow and York to the Continent of Europe.

abbots and bishops caused him to issue a circular letter, exhorting them to the diligent pursuit of literary studies that they might better understand the mysteries of holy writ. For the promotion of the same object he founded his celebrated Palatine School.[1]

Alcuin several times visited France and Italy, and was on two occasions presented to Charles, who in 781 urged him to join his court and assist him in his educational work. Accordingly he removed to France about 782, and was endowed by Charles with the revenues of two monasteries. Here, besides directing the Palatine School and organising others on the same model, he employed himself in writing and revising books for educational and ecclesiastical purposes, and in correcting the Vulgate translation of the Bible, which, through the negligence and ignorance of transcribers, had become in many places unintelligible. On the occasion of Charles's coronation as Emperor at Rome, A.D. 800, Alcuin sent him a copy of this great work.

Charles himself did not disdain to become Alcuin's pupil, and calls him his "most beloved teacher in Christ." He frequently sought his help in difficult passages of Scripture, and when absent kept up a familiar correspondence with him, in which Alcuin was accustomed to express his opinions with great freedom. The King's studies embraced the chief sciences of the age. "He spent," says Eginhardt, "much time with Alcuin, the most learned man of the day, in acquiring rhetoric and logic, and especially astronomy. He learned from him the art of computation, and with profound thought and skill calculated the courses of the planets."[2] The other savants of the court often joined the King and Alcuin in their studies: the royal daughters were also admitted.

In 790 Alcuin returned to Northumbria, but after two years we find him again on the Continent, where in the disputations which arose with certain heretics, he appeared on the orthodox side. The abbacy of St. Martin at Tours becoming vacant in 796, Charles sent him thither to restore its decayed discipline, and to institute a

---

[1] *Schola Palatina*, school of the palace. Aix-la-Chapelle, and Ingelheim near Bingen, were the Emperor's chief residences. The school probably followed the court.

[2] The king delighted in the works of Augustine, especially his *City of God*. For want of early practice, he himself could never succeed in learning to write; although he kept his tablets and writing-book under the pillows of his couch, it was all to no purpose, those rigid fingers so long accustomed to grasp the sword could not bend themselves to the pen. D. Ceillier, however, thinks that Eginhardt in this passage meant only that Charles tried in vain to imitate the beautiful characters of the manuscripts in his library.

school. He died there A.D. 804, and was buried within the church of St. Martin.

Alcuin was deeply impressed with the importance of the preaching of the Gospel and of Bible-study; and was accustomed to press upon the bishops the necessity for the latter as a preparation for the former. " Without the holy Scriptures," he wrote to the clergy of Canterbury, " it is impossible to come to the right knowledge of God; and if the blind lead the blind, both fall into the ditch." But he was far from restricting the study of the word to ecclesiastics, and desired that the Emperor should have diligent searchers of Scripture among his ministers of state. He was opposed to the taking of human life even by the authority of the magistrate. His name is associated with the stand made by the Gallic clergy in this age against image-worship. After the Iconoclastic strife in the East had raged for three-quarters of a century, the Second Council of Nicæa, A.D. 787, by its ninth canon solemnly established the worship of images. But in 794, when a great number of bishops[1] from all parts of Charles's dominions assembled in council at Frankfort, this canon was rejected by a large majority. This bold step is thought to have been due in no little degree to the influence of Alcuin, supported by his Imperial master. To the English scholar some writers attribute also the famous edicts issued by authority of the Emperor, and known as the *Capitularies* and the *Caroline Books*, in which, although images and pictures in churches were still retained as ornaments, and to keep alive the memory of pious men and pious deeds, all kinds of adoration, even reverence for them, is condemned.[2]

---

[1] Said to have numbered about 300.

[2] The opposition of the Gallic clergy to image-worship dates from an earlier period than that of Charles the Great. In the seventh century Serenus, bishop of Marseilles, observing that the worship of images was spreading amongst the rude Franks of his diocese, caused the statues and pictures of the saints to be cast out of the churches. Pope Gregory the Great, whilst professing to commend his motives, censured the rashness with which he had acted, advancing the very unsafe plea that images are especially useful for newly-converted people. Nothing can be weaker than the language of the pope's rebuke. "Where," he asks, "is the bishop who ever did the like? If nothing else could hinder thee, oughtest thou not to have refrained from the very singularity of the the act? Ought thou not to have been afraid of making people believe that thou thought thyself the only wise person in the world?" When the Iconoclastic Emperor Leo the Isaurian was endeavouring by main force to purge the Eastern churches of their pictures, Pope Gregory II. wrote to him: " Only try thy experiment here. Go into the schools where the children are learning to read and write, and tell them thou art the opponent of images; they would instantly throw their tablets at thy head, and thus the ignorant will teach thee perforce what thou wilt not learn from the wise."

CLAUDE OF TURIN.—But the most strenuous of the Frankish opponents of image-worship flourished under Charles's successor. This was Claude bishop of Turin, who may justly be styled the Protestant of his age. He forms a connecting link between Jovinian and Vigilantius in the fourth and fifth centuries and those evangelical Churches which sprang up in France and Italy in the eleventh and twelfth.

Claude was a native of Spain, and like Alcuin joined that band of learned men from various countries which adorned the court of Charlemagne. He was appointed by the Emperor's son Louis, surnamed the Pious, who was then keeping his court in Auvergne, to be his domestic chaplain. Claude was a diligent student of the New Testament, and like Leo the Isaurian in the East, was probably anxious to vindicate Christianity from the reproach of idolatry cast on it by the Mohammedans. Louis himself despised image-worship, and when he came to the throne he sent Claude to fill the episcopal chair of Turin (circa 822) for the express purpose of giving a check to the idolism to which the Italians had abandoned themselves.

With too eager haste Claude began to declaim against the prevailing superstition, and to order all the statues and pictures of the saints, the crosses and votive offerings, to be flung out of the churches. The prejudices of the people were violently shocked, and their discontent manifested itself in popular tumults. "I found," he writes, "the churches full of the lumber of consecrated gifts, and because I alone began pulling down what all adored, I was calumniated by all. Unless the Lord had helped me I had been swallowed up alive." He owed his safety to the fear of the Frankish arms; which fear also seems to have restrained the pope, Paschal I., from taking overt action against him. Of this pope he said: "He only is apostolic who is the keeper of the Apostle's doctrine, not he who boasts of being seated in the Apostle's chair and yet does not keep the Apostle's charge; for the Lord says: 'The Scribes and Pharisees sit in Moses' seat.'"

Claude had a friend, Theodemir, an abbot, who used to ply him with theological questions, and was thus the occasion of his writing several of his treatises. All the while, however, Theodemir seems to have been playing a double part, his real object being to convict Claude of heresy. On the publication of the bishop's commentary on the 1st Epistle to the Corinthians, he brought charges of unsound doctrine against him, before an assemblage of bishops and nobles. Hearing of this ungenerous proceeding Claude wrote to him: "May the Lord who is the witness of my life, and who gave me this work to do, forgive thee." Theodemir was unable to substantiate the charges, and changing his mode of attack assailed the bishop with his pen. In his reply, Claude declared that he held firmly to the unity of the Church, but that he would always with God's help fight against superstition and error. "If those who say they have cast off idolatry, worship the images of the saints, then they have not forsaken their idols but only changed their names. If men are to be worshipped, it would be much better to worship the living than the dead. If the works of God's hands, the stars of heaven for example, ought not to be worshipped, much less ought the work of men's hands. Whoever seeks from any creature in heaven or on earth the salvation which he should seek from God alone, is an idolater." He sternly rebuked the adoration of the Cross. "What these men do is quite a different thing from what God has commanded. God has commanded us to *bear* the Cross, not to *adore* it; they are for *adoring* it because they are unwilling to *bear* it." With equal boldness he contended against pilgrimages: "Foolish men, undervaluing spiritual instruction, go to Rome to attain everlasting life. One gets no nearer to St. Peter by finding oneself on the spot where his body was buried, for the soul is the real man." Claude's free opinions gave great offence in high quarters, and the Emperor was persuaded to commission Jonas bishop of Orleans to write a refutation of his errors. But this was not published until after Claude's death.[1]

It is not only as a destroyer of images and a caster-out of crosses that the name of Claude of Turin is inscribed upon the Church's record. He had largely imbibed the spirit of Paul's Epistles, to the study of which he especially gave himself, as well as to the writings of Augustine; and in all his Scripture Commentaries, he makes practical Christianity his great aim. With him "heavenly grace is the source of true sanctification; the state of the heart, the test of moral worth; love to God apart from all reference to reward,

---

[1] The Gallic clergy of that day were equally in unison with Claude on the question of pilgrimages, as they were on that of images. The Second Council of Châlons, in 813, declared: A pilgrimage to Rome or to St. Martin of Tours is accounted a panacea. By it careless ecclesiastics imagine themselves cleansed from sin, and qualified to perform their office; laymen suppose they may sin with impunity; nobles, that they may practise extortion on their dependents; whilst beggars find in it a crutch for their mendicancy. Men are so foolish as to suppose that their sins are purged by the mere sight of a holy place, unmindful of the words of St. Jerome, that it is no merit to have seen Jerusalem, but to have lived a godly life there. See *ante*, p. 50, note.

the essence of the Christian temper; worship of God in the spirit, the characteristic of true piety."[1]

The truth which Claude preached, commended as it was by his exemplary life, attracted many followers, so that Theodemir complains of him as having founded a new sect which had spread from Italy through France even into Spain.[2] We do not, it is true, meet with any society which bore his name, nor even with the traces of any association for the purpose of maintaining his doctrines, but whenever in succeeding ages God's messengers declared the simple Gospel truth in the countries where Claude's influence had been exerted, there was a remarkable readiness to receive it; and it is well known that the Waldensian Church, which came into note in the twelfth century, claimed Claude of Turin for its spiritual ancestor.

Another enlightened *Witness*, contemporary with Claude, was AGOBARD, archbishop of Lyons from about 810 to 840 A.D. He wrote a tract against image-worship, in which he says: "If Hezekiah broke the brazen serpent, made by God's express command, because the mistaken multitude began to worship it (for which act his piety was highly commended), much more now ought the images of the saints, which were never set up by God's command but are absolutely human inventions, to be broken and ground to powder."[3] Many bishops of Aquitaine and Narbonne supported Agobard, but the light which thus shone over Southern France was only transient. Under Charles the Great's successors civil and religious order declined, and men's consciences were for a time held in fetters even stronger than before by an ignorant and worldly clergy.

ANSCHAR, styled the Apostle of the North, was born near Amiens in 801. From the works of Christian love of this remarkable man, and the revelations with which he was favoured, we see how the Spirit of Christ condescended to dwell with his children, even in the darkest days of the Church. Influenced by a pious mother, until his fifth year, Anschar seems to have received religious impressions in his opening mind when a very young child. During his school-days evil communications dimmed these early revelations. They were not effaced however, and he was recalled to thoughtful-

---

[1] Claude's teaching reminds us of Vigilantius, and it is worthy of note that Jonas accuses Claude of maintaining the heresy of that early reformer.

[2] Jonas states that Germany was also infected.

[3] Strange to say, Agobard's name is to be found in the Romish Hagiography (lives of the saints), whilst his *Treatise on Pictures* is placed in the *Index Expurgatorius* (catalogue of writings prohibited by the Church)!

ness by a night vision. He imagined himself to be standing in a slippery place, thick with mire, from which he was unable to extricate himself. Not far off, on a safe and pleasant path, he beheld a graceful woman handsomely attired, accompanied by several others in white garments, one of whom was his own mother. He would gladly have gone over to them, but the slippery ground held his feet. As they drew nearer he heard the richly-adorned lady, who appeared to be the Virgin Mary, say to him, "My son, wilt thou come to thy mother?" And when he answered that he would fain do so if he could, she replied: "If thou wishest to join us, thou must eschew vanity and diligently pursue a serious life." From this time a change came over him; instead of play he gave himself to reading and meditation.

In the convent of Corbie near Amiens, whither he was sent when still a youth, he had another vision in which the glory of Heaven was revealed to him. He was transported to the assembly of the blessed, and their united hymn of praise filled his soul with inexpressible delight. All had their faces turned towards the east, where was a splendour of surpassing brilliancy and giving forth the most beautiful colours. "The splendour was so illimitable," says Anschar, "that I could see neither beginning nor end; and although I looked round on all sides I could perceive only the superficial appearance, I could not see that which dwelt within the centre of this light. Yet I believe He was there whom the angels desire to look upon; for from thence proceeded a flood of glory which shed its effulgence over the whole assembly. He was in all, and all were in Him. He satisfied all their wants, and was their guiding soul; He hovered over them, and was their support from beneath." Peter and John, who appeared as Anschar's guides, led him right in face of this boundless light, whence a voice came forth full of unutterable sweetness: "Go hence, and return to Me with a crown of martyrdom." At these words the adoring host became silent, and with bowed and reverent faces worshipped. "When I heard the words," continues Anschar, "I was sad because I was obliged to go back to the world, but was comforted with the promise that I should return from it hereafter."

Two years afterwards he had a third vision. He had been engaged in prayer in a small chapel to which he was wont to retire, and when he rose, there entered at the door a person of noble countenance clad in Jewish garb, whose eyes shone like the light. He perceived that it was the Lord Jesus Christ, and fell at his feet. As he lay prostrate he heard a voice bidding him stand up; and when in trembling awe he stood before the Lord, and was not able to look upon His countenance for the brightness of the light which beamed from His eyes, he heard the same voice, full of tenderness, saying to him: "Confess thy sins that thou mayest be justified." Anschar answered: "Lord, why need I tell them to Thee? Thou knowest all, nothing is hid from Thee." The Lord replied: "I indeed know all things, but yet it is my will that men should confess their sins to Me that they may receive forgiveness." Upon this he knelt and made confession, and the Lord said: "Fear not, I am He who blotteth out thy trangressions." With these words the Saviour vanished, and Anschar went his way full of joy and confidence. At another time, on receiving again the same assurance of forgiveness, he inquired, "Lord, what wouldst Thou have me to do?" The answer came: "Go preach the Word of God to the tribes of the heathen."

At the head of the seminary of Corbie was the learned Paschasius Radbert, and Anschar, his most industrious pupil, was promoted to be his assistant. In 822 a colony of monks from this abbey settled on a fertile spot in the valley of the Weser, and gave the name of their parent cloister (in German) *Corvey* to the new house, which became one of the chief monasteries beyond the Rhine. Anschar was one of the colonists. The Jutland king Harald, who had just been baptized at Ingelheim, being about to return home, the Emperor Louis the Pious proposed he should be accompanied by a gospel preacher. Wala the abbot of Corvey recommended Anschar for this mission, and when the Emperor asked the young man if he was willing for God's glory to accompany King Harald, he replied that he was not only willing but eager to go. Many tried to dishearten him by representing the savage character of the Northmen and the evil nature of their idolatry, but he adhered steadfastly to his purpose, and retiring alone to a vineyard prepared himself by reading the Scriptures and prayer for the great undertaking.

For upwards of forty years Anschar laboured incessantly in Denmark, Sweden and the north of Germany, enduring disappointment, distress, hardship and persecution, through which nothing but an unshaken trust in God could have supported him. Once when an army of Northmen sacked and burned the town where he was, together with his church and monastery, leaving him barely time to save the church vessels, he exclaimed, as he surveyed the desolate scene: "The Lord gave, and the Lord hath taken away, blessed be the name of the Lord." His love of meditation and prayer led him to construct a cell, which he called his "place of quiet and penitence," and to which, with a few companions who were like-minded, he from time to time withdrew. But he never suffered this to interfere with his apostolic duties, only resorting to his retreat to renew his spiritual life after long and arduous toil. He was in the habit of disciplining himself by severe mortifications, but conscious how easily self-exaltation is engendered by such outward austerities, he prayed to God for grace to save him from this danger. Too humble to aspire after miraculous gifts, he nevertheless could not prevent the coming of sick persons from distant parts, who hoped to be restored by his prayers. When however such a hope was expressed he would say: "Could I deem myself worthy to ask miracles of the Lord, I would beseech Him to grant me this one miracle, that He would make of me a holy man."

Being attacked with his mortal sickness Anschar's only regret was that the hope inspired by his early dream, that he should die a martyr's death, was not to be fulfilled. He often said his bodily pains were less than his sins deserved, repeating the words of Job, "Have we received good from the hand of the Lord, and shall we not receive evil?" Travail of spirit for the souls of those who were about him, and especially for the conversion of the Danes and Swedes, occupied him to the end. Having received the bread and wine, he prayed that God would forgive all who had done him wrong, frequently also repeating the words, "Have mercy upon me, O God, according to Thy loving-kindness: be merciful to me, a sinner; into Thy hands I commend my spirit"; and so, with his eyes uplifted, he died, as he had wished, on the anniversary of the Purification of the Virgin, A.D. 865.

After Anschar's death it was still only by slow degrees and with frequent repulses that Christianity made its way in Denmark. Gorm the Old, who died about the year 935, clung to his ancestral heathenism and persecuted the Christian missionaries, whilst his wife Thyra, a beautiful and virtuous lady, had become a Christian, and with her husband's permission maintained her own chapel and priests. Their son, Harald II., surnamed Blaatand (Bluetooth), professed the faith of his mother, and removed his court from Ledra, the ancient seat of the worship of Odin, to Roskilde in Zealand, where he erected a cathedral. He continued however to make the old palace at Jellinge, near Veile in Jutland, his usual place of residence.

Here he buried Gorm and Thyra, and piled over their tombs two huge circular barrows, which still remain. Gorm's mound is about 40 ft. high and 670 ft. round at the base.[1] Thyra's is rather

---

[1] It is not an exact circle, the two diameters being about 204 and 224 feet respectively.

smaller, and covers a rude wooden chamber 22 ft. long, 8 ft. broad, and 5 ft. high. As there is no chamber under the large barrow, it is probable that both bodies were buried beneath the smaller. Both mounds have been opened. Thyra's chamber contained, amongst

Thyra's Cross and Cup.

other relics, a silver cup lined with gold, about 2 inches high; a small bronze cross thinly coated with gold; two figures of birds in copper; a small piece of fine red silk; and an end of wax candle. In the other mound very little was discovered.

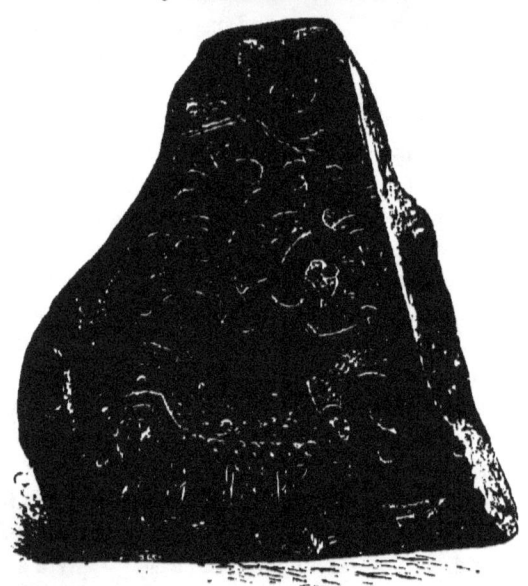

Between the graves stands a church, not so old as the mounds, but yet very ancient; and near the church are two blocks of reddish granite.[1] The larger of these is three-sided, about 7 ft. 6 in. in height and 20 ft. round at the base. On one side is carved the dragon, the pagan emblem of Scandinavia; on another a figure of Christ, with the arms extended, as on the Cross; and on the third side, which is the largest, is an inscription in Runic characters, continued also in the lower part of the other two.

---

[1] Both the blocks have been removed from their original site.

ᚼᛅᛦ·ᛏᚿᛦ ᛏᚼᛦᚿᛁᚼᚱ

ᛏᚿᛦ·ᛏᛁᛦ·   'ᛦᚱᛁᛋᛏᚿᛋ

In Roman characters it reads thus:—

> Haraltr kunukr bad gaurva
> kubl dausi aft Gurm fadur sin
> auk aft Thourvi mudur sina sa
> Haraltr jas sor van Tanmaurk
>
> ala auk Nurviak
>
> auk T (. n ....) kristno.

King Harald had these memorials made of Gorm his father and Thyra his mother; the same Harald who won for himself all Denmark and Norway, and (made the Danish people?) Christians.

The smaller stone is 6 ft. 3 in. in height; it bears a short but significant inscription.

> Gurmur Kunugr gardi kubl dusi aft Thurvi kunu sina Tanmarkar but.
>
> King Gorm made this memorial of Thyra his wife, Denmark's ornament.[1]

The place of these monuments is now far from the highways of men, and full of repose. "From the blue fiord, on whose shore the little town of Veile spreads itself, we ascended," says a recent traveller, "some 200 or 300 ft. through picturesque woods to a table-land; passing broad fields of corn ready for the sickle, and quaint farm-houses and barns, the very image of the toys we played with in our childhood. There are few hedges, and between the corn patches are long ribands of grass, where the cattle feed tethered to stakes, and tended by a boy. On a ridge to the right, before entering the hamlet of Jellinge, were seen five large barrows.

---

[1] Or *Saviour*, or *trust;* the word is doubtful. The above woodcuts are taken from a model of the stone presented to the writer by Walter Morris, with the help of the lithographs in Professor Kornerup's valuable and elaborate work, *Kongehphiene i Jellinge*, Copenhagen, 1875, for a copy of which we are indebted to the kindness of the author. The particulars in the text are also derived from this work. The similarity between the Irish school of ornament and the figures on the Runic monuments is very noticeable: compare the above woodcuts with the fragment of sculpture from Monkwearmouth church and the square of lace-work ornament from the *Durham Book*, *ante*, p. 278.

Here in this corner of the earth now so tranquil, in the rude palace long since decayed, the old sea-kings a thousand years ago hung up their weapons, glutted themselves with flesh and cups of mead, roared out their idol-songs to Odin, and recounted their deeds of plunder and merciless slaughter, with which, from century to century, they made the shores of England, Normandy, France and Sicily to groan and tremble."[1]

NILUS.—We turn again to the South of Europe. Nilus was a monk of Greek origin, and a native of Rossana in Calabria (South Italy), where he was born in 910.[2] He did not stand forth as a reformer; he did not see that the dense growth of superstition which encumbered the Church must be cut down and cleared away before the good seed could have room to take root and grow. Nevertheless his eye being single, his soul was full of light; and if those who saw his course of life and heard his words of evangelical wisdom had been willing to follow him, the light of gospel truth might have broken forth in Southern Italy even in that dark age.

Although the founder of several monasteries, he did not place his dependence on monastic austerities or spiritual marvels. In consonance with the superstitious temper of the age, the thought would often occur to him, whilst engaged in prayer or in singing, "Look towards the altar; perhaps thou wilt see an angel, or a flame of fire, or the Holy One Himself, for such sights many others have seen." But being inwardly admonished that thoughts like these grow out of spiritual pride, he would resolutely shut his eyes and give himself up the more to penitential exercise, wrestling with his soul till the sweat trickled from his forehead. Once when he was occupied with writing, reading and singing in St. Peter's at Rome, he was beset with these temptations. Throwing himself before the altar he prayed, "Lord, thou knowest that I am weak; have compassion on me and relieve me of this conflict." Thus lying he fell asleep, and saw a vision. He beheld Christ hanging on the cross, separated from him only by a thin white curtain. He cried out, "Lord have mercy upon me, and bless thy servant." The Saviour from the cross extended his right hand three times over him. He awoke, and the temptation was gone. The disciple who gives this account adds: "What much fasting and watching could not effect, was effected by thus humbling himself before the Lord, and by a knowledge of his own weakness."

---

[1] Private diary of a journey in Denmark, July, 1882.

[2] He is called Nilus *the Younger* to distinguish him from the venerable monk of the same name who resided on Mount Sinai in the fifth century.

Like Anschar, he was of a humble spirit. Being asked by a father to heal his son, a demoniac, he excused himself, saying he had never prayed for the gifts of healing the sick or casting out demons; what he had asked was that God would grant him the forgiveness of his sins and deliverance from wicked thoughts. He endeavoured however to comfort the father, by representing to him that the involuntary possession in the case of his son by one evil spirit, was a far lighter affliction than the readiness to serve them all which is manifested in a wicked life.

Some nobles and ecclesiastics came one day to prove Nilus with hard questions. When he saw them he said within himself: "They are come to entangle me in empty talk. Lord Jesus, free us from the devices of Satan, and grant that we may think and speak and do what is well pleasing to Thee." When he had so prayed he opened at hazard the book he had in his hand, a biography of a pious monk, and made a mark in the place ; and as soon as his visitors had saluted him and sat down, he gave the book to one, who was a privy-councillor, to read where he had marked. The privy-councillor read: "Scarcely one in ten thousand attains to salvation." All exclaimed with one voice: "God forbid! whoever says that is a heretic. If it be so, we have all been baptized in vain ; in vain we adore the Cross; in vain we partake of the Eucharist; in vain we call ourselves Christians." Whereupon Nilus quietly remarked: "Suppose I should prove to you that Basil, Chrysostom, Theodore Studites, the Apostle Paul, and the Gospel, all declare the same thing, what would *you* say, you who by your own wicked lives gainsay the words of holy men ? I tell you that by all these observances you gain nothing in the sight of God. Unless you become truly virtuous not one of you can be saved." At this all sighed and exclaimed, " Woe to us, miserable sinners ! " Nicolas, an officer of the Imperial guard, who trusted in his almsgiving, now spoke: "Yet Christ said, ' He who gives to a poor man but a cup of cold water shall not lose his reward.'" To which Nilus replied : " That was spoken to the poor, that none might offer as an excuse his having no wood wherewith to prepare warm water. But what wilt *thou* do who robs the poor even of the cup of cold water ? " Next a nobleman, a man of immoral life, referred to the example of Solomon, "a wonderful man and greatly commended in the Bible ; was *he* not saved ? " " What concern of ours is it," replied Nilus, " whether Solomon was saved or lost ? Not to him but to us it is said ' every one that looketh on a woman to lust after her hath committed adultery with her already in his heart.' But of Solomon we do not read as we do of Manasseh, that after having sinned he repented." Here one of the priests impertinently struck in with the question, "What was the forbidden fruit in Paradise?" "A crab apple," answered Nilus. And when all laughed, he added: " Such a question deserved such an answer."

The Imperial chamberlain, coming in state to a neighbouring castle, was offended that Nilus did not present himself before him with the other abbots. But when he heard of Nilus' independent character, he was still more desirous to see him. As soon as he entered the room the chamberlain was struck with awe at his presence, and sent for a copy of the Gospels, in order that if any matter of importance should pass between them, it might be ratified by oath. But Nilus reproved him, reminding him of what Christ said of swearing in His sermon on the mount. "Why," he asked, "dost thou furnish an occasion to mistrust thy words; and why dost thou begin our conference by transgressing the word of the Lord? He who is ready on slight occasions to take an oath, will also be ready to utter a falsehood."

Nilus' countryman John, archbishop of Placenza, a man of a restless worldly spirit, became entangled in an alliance with the Roman usurper Crescentius, who after expelling Gregory V. set up John as pope in his place.[1] Nilus wrote to him, prophetically warning him of the consequences of his ambition, and calling upon him to renounce the honours he had so unworthily gained, and to retire from the world. His words found no entrance; but within a year the doom which Nilus had foreseen fell upon the unhappy man. Gregory was restored to his chair by the arms of the German Emperor Otho III., and a cruel revenge was wreaked on the archbishop. His eyes were put out, and his tongue and his nose cut off, and in this deplorable condition he was thrown into a dungeon. Nilus was in his monastery at Gaeta when he received the tidings of John's fall and the barbarity practised upon him. Although now upwards of eighty years of age, sick and infirm (it being besides Lent, when he gave himself to penitential devotions), he forgot all in his sympathy with the sufferer, and quitting his cell travelled immediately to Rome. Presenting himself before the Emperor, he asked to be put into the same dungeon with the archbishop, that they might do penance together for their sins. The Emperor promised to comply; but presently, instead of this, the archbishop was exposed to new and more public ignominy. Upon this Nilus boldly told both pope and Emperor that their offence was

---

[1] His name is commonly omitted in the tables of the popes; when introduced he is called John XVI.

not so much against the wretched man as against God; and that as they had broken their word and shown no mercy, so they themselves could expect no mercy from God. The youthful Emperor was touched, and invited Nilus to ask any favour he pleased. "I have nothing to ask of thee," was the Christian reply, "but that thou wilt not trifle with the salvation of thy own soul. Emperor though thou art, thou must die like other men, and appear before the judgment-seat of God, to render an account of all thy deeds, good and bad." The Emperor burst into tears, and taking the crown from his head, begged the man of God to give him his blessing.

In order to do Nilus honour, the monks of the venerable abbey of Monte Casino, the mother of all the Benedictine houses, invited him to celebrate mass in their church in the Greek tongue. At first he refused, saying: "How shall we (Greeks), who are everywhere humbled on account of our sins, sing the Lord's song in a strange land?" Afterwards however he consented, and sang a hymn composed by himself in praise of St. Benedict. When the hymn was ended, the conversation turned on the diversity between the Greek and Latin Churches as to fasting on the Jewish Sabbath.[1] Nilus gave his opinion in the words of Paul: "'Let not him that eateth, set at nought him that eateth not; and let not him that eateth not, judge him that eateth, for God hath received him.' Whether *we eat*, or *ye fast*, let all be done to the glory of God." He then adduced the older Church teachers, who favoured the Greek custom; but added: "We will not however contend about this; if the Jews did but honour Christ crucified as their Lord, I should take no offence, even though they fasted on Sunday. . . . Everything depends on the state of mind in which a thing is done. *We* do right not to fast on the Sabbath, in opposition to the Manichæans, who reject the Old Testament; and *ye*, from your point of view, are bound to fast on that day, in order to purify your souls for the celebration of the day following, consecrated to our Lord's resurrection."

Nilus being near his end, the governor of Gaeta proposed that when he died, his body should be brought into the city for burial, so that his sacred bones might serve as a protection to the town. His humility was shocked at the prospect of receiving such veneration; and he determined that the people of Gaeta should not know where he was buried. Accordingly he mounted his horse and took his way towards Rome, saying to his monks as he bade them farewell: "Sorrow not: I go to prepare a place and a monastery, where

---

[1] See *Early Church History*, p. 95.

all my brethren and scattered children will meet me again." On arriving at Tusculum,[1] he rode into the small convent of St. Agatha, saying: "Here is my final resting-place." His friends in Rome invited him to continue his journey to the city, that he might perform his devotions at the tombs of Peter and Paul; but he answered: "He who has faith as a grain of mustard-seed may even in this spot honour the memory of the Apostles." He begged the monks that when he died they would not delay his burial, and that they would not lay his body in a church nor erect any monument over him; but if they wished to distinguish his grave, they should raise over it a seat for wayfaring men, such as he had always been, to rest themselves upon. For two days before he died he lay with no other sign of life than a murmur of his lips, and a slight motion of his hands making the sign of the cross. One of the monks putting his ear to his mouth, heard the words: "Then shall I not be ashamed when I have respect to all thy commandments." He fell asleep, without a struggle, A.D. 1005.

The hymn which follows is by Joseph Studites who, in the ninth century, lived many years at the court of Constantinople. It approaches more nearly to modern hymns of Christian experience than perhaps any other which has come down to us.

THE RETURN HOME.

Safe home, safe home in port!
Rent cordage, shattered deck,
Torn sails, provisions short,
And only not a wreck;
But oh! the joy upon the shore
To tell our voyage perils o'er!

The prize, the prize secure!
The athlete nearly fell;
Bare all he could endure,
And bare not always well:
But he may smile at troubles gone
Who sets the victor-garland on!

No more the foe can harm:
No more of leaguered camp,
And cry of night-alarm,
And need of ready lamp:
And yet how nearly he had failed,—
How nearly had that foe prevailed!

---

[1] Near the modern Frascati, ten miles S.E. of Rome.

THE RETURN HOME.

The lamb is in the fold
In perfect safety penned:
The lion once had hold
And thought to make an end:
But One came by with wounded side,
And for the sheep the Shepherd died.

The exile is at Home!
O nights and days of tears,
O longings not to roam,
O sins and doubts and fears,—
What matter now (whate'er men say)
The King has wiped those tears away!

O happy, happy Bride!
Thy widowed hours are past;
The Bridegroom at thy side;
Thou all his own at last!
The sorrows of thy former cup
In full fruition swallowed up

PERIOD IV.

FROM THE TENTH CENTURY TO THE TERMINATION OF THE CRUSADE AGAINST THE ALBIGENSES, A.D. 1229.

CHAPTER I.

Monastic Life in the Middle Ages.—Cluny.

> "My rule
> Is left a profitless stain upon the leaves;
> The walls, for abbey reared, turned into dens;
> The cowls, to sacks choked up with musty meal.
> . . . . . . Mortal flesh
> Is grown so dainty, good beginnings last not
> From the oak's birth unto the acorn's setting."
> —Benedict, *in Dante.*

In the foregoing pages, the reader cannot fail to have remarked how the lofty, though mistaken, object of Benedict was, as time went on, more and more lost sight of, and the separation from the world at which he aimed swallowed up in the vortex of civil and political life. In name and dress, in the unnatural and corrupting abnegation of marriage, and in the daily round of ceremonies often unprofitable, not to say idolatrous, the monk lived apart; but in all beside, not only in the petty affairs of his own township, but also in the government, in diplomacy, and even in the wars of principalities and empires, he was foremost both as adviser and actor. Instead of the cloister excluding the world, the world had taken possession of the cloister. "Most monks," remarks Mosheim, "did not even know that the rule they had bound themselves to follow was called the rule of St. Benedict." The time for reformation was fully come; but, unhappily, the reformation took place on the old unnatural lines. "Catholic efforts of revival all took, with more or less rigidity, the monastic form, and their successive failure is due to the inherent weakness of monasticism. It sets before men an unnatural and impossible ideal. It substitutes for the social and domestic virtues upon which the world rests, an ascetic and self-regarding type of holiness. It is the attempt

'to wind ourselves too high for sinful men beneath the sky,'

and so is peculiarly exposed to reaction, laxity, corruption. The story of all monastic orders, truly told, is one of perpetual striving after a holiness which hungers and thirsts after self-denial, and finds no self-maceration too hard; then of slow falling-away into formality, idleness, self-indulgence, open vice : and a period once more of enthusiastic reform, and repentant return to the old ideal."

Early in the tenth century a successful attempt to restore the monastic discipline was made at Cluny, in Burgundy. This monastery was founded in 908 by the abbot Berno, to whom William the Pious, Duke of Aquitaine, gave the village of Cluny with the neighbouring lands. Upon Odo, the second abbot, the mantle of Benedict may be said to have fallen. He not only revived the strict rule of the latter, but added fresh observances and regulations, and through his influence the old austerity of the monastic life reasserted its sway throughout Europe. Odo had been a schoolmaster and precentor of the cathedral at Tours, and came of a good stock. He says of his father: "He seemed to be a different sort of person from men of the present day; for he had by heart the histories of the ancients and the *Novellæ*[1] of Justinian. At his table there was always the reading of the Gospel." Odo himself, when he became a monk, possessed a library of a hundred volumes.

In the eleventh and twelfth centuries successive popes rivalled each other in showering privileges upon Cluny. Calixtus II., having nothing further to bestow, took his own ring from his finger and placed it on that of the abbot, declaring that for the future the abbot of Cluny should be *ex officio* a Roman cardinal, and that the Cluniacs should have the priviledge of continuing to celebrate mass, if ever the kingdom should be placed under an Interdict. The monastery besides coined money like a sovereign State, and Louis VI. styled it "the noblest member of his kingdom."

In 1122 Peter of Montvoissier was chosen abbot. "When I was raised to the office," he wrote, "I found a large monastery, religious and famous, but with a very insufficient revenue; 300 monks or more, and provision for only one hundred, crowds of guests, and always an infinite number of poor."[2] Peter was a man of a wise and charitable spirit.[3] To a recluse he wrote: "Thy outward separation from the world will avail thee nothing without the only firm bulwark against besetting sins within the soul—the Saviour. By union with Him and by following Him in his sufferings, thou wilt be safe against the attacks of all thy enemies." And to a prior: "Of what avail is all the fasting in the world to him who has no love? Abstain if thou wilt from flesh and from fish; torture thy body, give no sleep to thy eyes; spend the night in vigils and

---

[1] This was the title of the latest portion of the great body of law compiled in the reign of Justinian.

[2] Seventeen thousand poor were annually relieved at the gates.

[3] Like Chrysostom and Augustine, and many other great men in the Church, he had enjoyed the inestimable blessing of a pious mother.

the day in toil; still willing or unwilling thou must hear the Apostle: 'And if I give my body to be burned but have not charity it profiteth me nothing.'" Monk though he was, he had no sympathy with that immolation of the natural affections which was required by the rules of Basil and of Benedict. "The good man," he says, writing to a monk, "ought not to fly from his kinsmen and friends for fear of contamination; he should seek to win them by wholesome admonitions. Instead of being afraid of their earthly affections, he should communicate to them his own heavenly love. It is," he adds, "in the recesses of the heart alone that the true despiser of the world finds the true solitude, where no stranger enters, where without audible utterance is heard the gentle voice of the Master discoursing with us." To one of a kindred mind with himself he says: "When I would search with thee into the mysteries of Scripture, thou wast always ready to join me with the greatest delight. When I would converse with thee on worldly science (always under the guidance of divine grace), I found in thee a ready mind and an acute discernment. O, how often, with the doors shut, and Him alone for our witness who is never absent when discourse turns upon Himself, have we held solemn converse, on the hardness of man's heart, the entanglements of sin, the manifold snares of wicked spirits, the economy of salvation by the incarnation and sufferings of the Son of God, the dreadful day of the last judgment." His charity became almost proverbial. He declined to express an opinion regarding a deceased heretic, lest he should bring a false accusation against a dead man.

Hence it is not to be wondered at that Peter, whilst he laboured for the restoration of good manners and a holy life, made no effort to restore the severe rule of Benedict. This was reserved for the founders of two new religious houses which were just then coming into note, Cîteaux and Clairvaux. Between the great Bernard, who rendered both these monasteries illustrious, and whose history is presently to be related, and Peter, there existed indeed a close and life-long friendship; but it was scarcely possible that the indulgence of relaxed discipline on the one side, and the determination to return to primitive austerity on the other, should not sooner or later bring them into collision.

An occasion of difference between the convents of Cluny and Clairvaux had arisen before Peter became abbot. Bernard, who quitted Cîteaux for Clairvaux in 1115, took with him a young kinsman, noble and wealthy, named Robert, for whom he had a paternal affection. The young man however soon grew restless under the severe and unrelenting discipline to which he was subjected, and availed himself of the first opportunity to leave. His parents in his childhood had promised him to Cluny, and the abbot Pontius was unwilling to lose so valuable a possession. Hearing probably that Robert sighed for deliverance, he sent his prior to bring him away. In spite of his own vow and of Bernard's remonstrances the youth left Clairvaux, and accompanied the prior to Cluny. The matter was considered so important as to be referred to the pope, who affirmed the claim of the elder monastery. In the hope of moving him to a voluntary return, Bernard wrote Robert a letter of four folio pages, full of alternate wrath and tenderness. He now reproves the youth as a prodigal, gone away to indulge in riotous living, and now chides himself for the harsh enforcement of austerities, too severe for a lad brought up in the softness of secular life. The prior who had enticed Robert away comes in for a large share of Bernard's wrath. Bernard's entreaties were in vain so long as Pontius ruled; but when Peter succeeded to the abbacy he gratified his friend by sending back the young kinsman, who expiated his six years of truant indulgence by more than sixty of submission to the Cistercian rule.

At length the dissension between the two abbeys, which for some years had been smouldering, burst forth into a flame. The Cluniacs spoke of the Cistercians as upstart Pharisees, whilst these denounced the former as apostates. In 1125 Bernard, urged by the abbot of St. Thierry, seized the pen, and in a long and eloquent letter which he called his *Apology*, enumerated the abuses which had crept into the monastic life.[1] They dispense (he says) with the year's noviciate, and receive back renegades as often as they choose to come. They have discontinued the regular fasts, retaining only a shadow of them, and this more from shame towards man than from the fear of God. They have come to despise manual labour; neither the authority of Scripture nor their vow being able to withdraw from their bosom the hands become delicate through idleness. The pious practices of pouring water on the hands of the guests, washing their feet and the like, have disappeared. They possess parish churches, receive first-fruits and tithes, and claim for their own, towns, villages, peasants, tolls and taxes. And when such unlawful revenues are challenged they defend them at law, so that monks are seen conducting causes, and thus in heart turning back to Egypt and Sodom.

Bernard then proceeds to the personal life of the brethren, upon

---

[1] He does not confine his censure to Cluny, but extends it to the rich and luxurious monasteries in general.

which theme his words are vehement. "I am astonished to see among monks such intemperance in eating, in drinking, in clothes, in bed-covering, in horse-trappings, in buildings. . . . At meals no man asks his neighbour for the heavenly bread; there is no conversation concerning the Scriptures, none concerning the salvation of souls; but small talk, laughter, and idle words fill the air. And while the ear is tickled with gossip and news, the palate is stimulated by dainties; dish after dish is set on table, and to make up for the small privation of meat a double supply of fish is provided. Who can say, to speak of nothing else, in how many forms eggs are cooked? The dishes are even made to charm the eye as well as the taste; and although the stomach complains that it is full, curiosity is still excited. As for wine, directly we become monks we seem to be afflicted with weak stomachs, and set ourselves in a praiseworthy manner to follow the weighty advice of the apostle and take a little wine; but for some unexplained reason the qualification of *a little* is disregarded. You may see a cup half full carried three or four times backwards and forwards, in order that out of several wines smelled and sipped the most potent may be selected. Have we not heard that in some monasteries on great festivals the wines are mixed with honey and powdered with spices? Is this too for our stomach's sake and our often infirmities? . . . I have heard that strong hearty young men are accustomed to place themselves in the infirmary for the purpose of regaling on those viands which the rule allows only to the utterly debilitated. In order to distinguish these invalid monks they carry a stick in their hands, a most necessary token!"

Next as to clothing and style of living. "This habit of ours, formerly a sign of humility, is by the monks of our day turned into an occasion of pride. The knight's cloak and the monk's cowl are cut from the same piece of cloth. When you want to buy a cowl, you rush through the towns, visit the markets and fairs, dive into the merchants' houses, turn over their goods, undo their bundles, feel the cloth with your fingers, hold it to your eyes or to the sun, and if anything coarse or faded appears you reject it. . . . What kind of humility is it in an abbot to take his progress with a retinue of hairy men? I have seen one with sixty horses in his train. You would think them to be not fathers of monasteries but lords of castles, not shepherds of souls but princes of provinces. Then there is the baggage,—table-cloths, cups and basins, candlesticks, ornaments of the beds. My lord abbot cannot go more than four leagues from home without taking all his furniture with him, as if he were bound for the wars or had to traverse a desert. Is it quite impossible to wash one's hands in and drink from the same vessel? Will your candle burn nowhere but in that golden or silver candlestick of yours? Is sleep impossible except upon a variegated mattress or under a foreign coverlet? Could not the same servant harness the mule, wait at dinner, and make the bed? If such a multitude of men and horses is necessary, why not carry with us our provisions, and thus relieve from an intolerable imposition those who entertain us?"

Bernard has something to say of the grand and decorated churches of which that of Cluny was one of the most magnificent.[1] On this subject he manifests a degree of enlightenment beyond his age, regarding art much in the same aspect as that presented in a previous chapter, namely, as a hindrance to true worship.[2] He censures the vast height of the roof, the inordinate length and superfluous width of the building, costly polishing and strange designs which, by attracting the eyes of the worshipper, hinder the soul's devotion; these things, he says, remind him of the old Jewish ritual. "By the sight of such costly vanities men are prompted to make gifts to the church rather than to pray there. The beautiful picture of some saint is exhibited—the brighter the colours, the greater the sanctity—and men run to kiss it. The chandeliers hanging from the roof, and the tall trees of brass in the place of candlesticks, fashioned with wonderful skill, are all studied with precious stones, glittering almost as bright as the lights themselves. What do you suppose is the object of all this? The repentance of the contrite, or the admiration of the beholders? O vanity of vanities! The church's walls are resplendent, but the poor are not there. The curious find wherewith to amuse themselves, but the wretched find no consolation in their misery. . . . Again, in the cloisters, what is the meaning of those ridiculous monsters, of that deformed beauty, that beautiful deformity, before the very eyes of the brethren as they read? What are unclean monkeys there for, or ferocious lions, or monstrous centaurs, or soldiers or huntsmen? Such an endless variety of forms appears everywhere, that it is more pleasant to read in the stone-work than in books, to spend the day in admiring these oddities than in meditating on the Divine law. For God's sake, if we are not ashamed of these absurdities, why at least do we not grieve at the cost of them?"

---

[1] This church, which at the time of Bernard's *Apology* had been thirty-five years in building, was finished in 1130. It was the wonder of Christendom. It was 580 feet long and 120 wide, was supported by sixty-eight massive columns, and lighted by 800 windows.

[2] *Ante*, p. 227.

To all these charges Peter makes but a feeble defence. His case is perhaps strongest on the possession of the lands and villages which had been lavishly conferred by former lords upon the abbey. Land in the hands of the monks was generally better administered than by lay owners. Secular masters too often imposed hard service upon their serfs and treated them as mere chattels, whilst the rule of the monks was light and considerate; they regarded the peasants, not as slaves, but as brothers, and maintained them when they fell into sickness and indigence. On the question of labour Peter makes a very lame defence. "How," he piteously asks, "are a languid set of men, barely kept alive on their vegetable diet, to bear labour in the field, exposed to heat, rain and cold, which peasants and ploughmen find it hard to endure ? This is not only impossible, but it would be indecent. Does it not appear most indecent that monks, who are to abide in the cloister and devote themselves intensely to silence, prayer, reading and meditation, should put aside these things for vulgar rustic labour."

But Peter and Bernard knew one another's worth ; their souls were made for mutual sympathy; and after this temporary ruffle their correspondence was continued in the most brotherly spirit. Their epistles abound in playful and affectionate sallies, and are a fine specimen of mediæval letter-writing. We must find space for a few sentences. Peter writes to Bernard :—"I am thankful to be so excellently well placed, being as thou art pleased to write, an actual inmate of thyself, so that if I should become cold I shall undoubtedly soon grow warm again, thus cherished by thy heart of charity. . . . The messenger coming to Cluny, and not finding me, neither brought on nor forwarded thy letter, but left it there. At length I got it from the sub-prior, to whom it had been entrusted. Immediately my soul was drawn out, so drawn out that I did what I never remember to have done, except in reverence to the Holy Scriptures ; as soon as I had read thy letter, I kissed it. And that I might excite a greater love for thee, I read it over again to those around me."

Bernard to Peter :—"I wish I could send thee my mind just as I send thee this letter. Thou wouldst, I am sure, read most clearly what the finger of God has written on my heart, has impressed on my marrow, of love to thee. . . . I say this because my Nicholas[1] (aye, and thine too), being vastly moved in spirit himself, has moved me, affirming that he saw a letter from me addressed to thee, which contained some unkind expressions. Believe one who

---

[1] His secretary.

loves thee, that there neither rose in my heart nor issued from my lips anything which could offend the ears of thy blessedness. The fault is owing to the multitude of business; so that my scribes do not well remember what I tell them. They sharpen their style too much, and it is out of my power to look over what I have ordered to be written." Again: "I saw thy letter, and flew to shut myself up with that Nicholas whom thy soul loveth. I read over and over again the sweetness that flowed from it. I grieved that I was not able to answer according to my feelings, because the evil of the day called me away. For a vast multitude, out of almost every nation under heaven, had assembled. It was my place to answer every one; because for my sins I was born into the world that I might be confounded with many and multifarious anxieties."

Both Bernard and Peter reposed confidence in this secretary, Nicholas, who was a very active servant, wrote pious letters, and was "brimful of sacred and philosophical learning." He belonged originally to Cluny and it was Peter's desire to have him again. "When thy holiness was at Cluny," so writes Peter, "thou asked, 'What dost thou want with Nicholas?' I answered, 'It is no great matter.' But I confess to thee, dearest friend, they were the words of wounded feeling rather than of truth. I had one thing in my heart and another on my tongue. What my mind tacitly suggested was, 'Why repeat thy wishes so often; as thou hast been denied thy request twice before, thou mayest perhaps now be denied a third time.' Let my confession avail me—for what? That thou shouldst send Nicholas, and not only now, but whenever I shall ask for him."

The truth is, however, that Nicholas was unworthy the confidence of either. Writing some time afterwards to pope Eugenius III., Bernard says: "We have been in peril from false brethren, and many forged letters under counterfeits of our seals have gone forth. Thus compelled, I have laid aside that seal, and use the new one which thou seest, containing both a figure of me and my name." And later: "That Nicholas has gone forth from us, because he was not of us; and he has gone out, too, leaving very dirty footmarks behind. I had seen through the man a long time, but I waited in the expectation that either God would convert him, or that like Judas he would betray himself; and this has happened. Besides books and specie in gold and silver, there were found upon him three seals—his own, the prior's, and one of mine, and that not the old but the new one, which I had been forced by his tricks and rogueries to alter. Who can say to how many persons he has written just what he pleased, in my name, without my knowledge?"

We give one more short paragraph from Peter's correspondence, being part of a letter written to his own notary, who was devoting

Bernard's Seal; size of the original. The Seal is of brass, and represents Bernard in his monkish dress, with shaven hair and chin, seated on a folding chair, the arms of which terminate in a serpent's head. In one hand he holds a crozier; in the other, what has been taken for a book or a church-door. The incription is: ✠ SIGILLUM: BERNARDI: ABBATIS: CLAREVALL. The absence of the letter S (*Sancti*) before BERNARDI is a strong proof of genuineness; Bernard was canonized a few years after his death.

himself to the study of the classics. Ever since the time of Tertullian and Clement of Alexandria, the use of classic literature had been a subject of contention in the Church. Peter ranged himself on the prohibitory side; but although his sentence and counsel cannot be endorsed, the Christ-like spirit which inspired his pen is a worthy example for every student. "Truth, looking from heaven, and compassionating the misery of mortals, and taking the likeness of sinful flesh, cries: 'Come unto Me all ye that labour and are heavy-laden, and I will give you rest.' . . . See now, without the study of Plato, or the subtleties of Aristotle, the place and the way of happiness are discovered. Let man quit the teacher's chair, for the God-man sits down to teach, and says: 'Blessed are the poor in spirit, for theirs is the kingdom of heaven.' Why dost thou seek through thousands of words and multiplied labours what thou mayest obtain in plain language and with little labour? Why dost thou recite with the comedians, lament with the tragedians, deceive with the poets, and be deceived with the philosophers?"

After the death of Peter the Venerable, Cluny lost its lustre. It continued to be learned, wealthy and powerful, but its spiritual lamp was dimmed. The Cluniacs excelled in the arts of calligraphy and illumination, and from the twelfth century, owing to their labours and those of the Cistercian and Carthusian communities, there was a vast increase in the number of books. Cluny itself possessed a rich library of Greek and Latin authors.

In 1245, when Pope Innocent IV. was a fugitive in France, and the prelates and abbots rallied round him, the prior of Cluny presented him with eighty palfreys splendidly caparisoned, besides a large sum of money, and a palfrey each for the twelve cardinals; and in return he was appointed by the pope his master of the horse.

From this time we hear but little of Cluny until the Revolution. At the suppression of the monasteries, the monks were driven out and the destruction of the buildings was decreed by the Republic. The mayor of Cluny, anxious to save so magnificent a monument, went himself to Paris and petitioned that it might be converted into a hospital for invalid soldiers. But the inhabitants of the Commune, eager to make money of the materials and the site, presented a remonstrance, alleging that the vicinity of the military veterans would corrupt the morals of the town. The remonstrance prevailed. The church was first demolished; the south bell-tower and a chapel enclosing a tomb, supposed to be that of Peter the Venerable, alone being left: the bells were melted into cannon for the Republican armies. The abbey walls offered so formidable a resistance that a detachment of troops was called in to assist in the work of destruction. "When this was accomplished, when the last offending buttress had been battered down, the people made a pile of the paintings, statues of wood, and carved work, and setting fire to them in the public square, celebrated their triumph by dancing round with yells and shouting. Some years afterwards, on his way to assume the iron crown of Lombardy, Napoleon passed through the department. At a town where he stopped to change horses, he was met by a deputation from the commune with a request that he would honour them by taking Cluny in his route. 'Begone!' was the stern reply. 'You are a race of Vandals; you have suffered your grand and beautiful church to be sold and destroyed; I shall not visit Cluny.'"

What remains of the abbey, besides the church itself, has been converted into an *Ecole normale professionnelle*. The library has been taken to Paris, but a few relics are still preserved on the spot, *e. g.*, the long crook with which the monks used to set apart the abbot's tenth sheaf in the fields; a massive chest and escritoire, and some weighty coffers of oak, which were the abbot's "portmanteaux" when he travelled. The town of Cluny grew up round the great ecclesiastical edifice. Its streets are narrow and winding, and at the present time ill-kept. They abound in quaint houses, some dating from the twelfth century.

Amongst the numerous apartments and offices of a monastery, the library and scriptorium held an important place. The formation of a library at that day was a great undertaking. Books were few, for parchment was dear, and writing was a rare art, the more so as the language in which it was practised was almost exclusively Latin. There was but little trade in books, at least north of the Alps. They were to be purchased chiefly at certain Italian monasteries, in which manuscripts were multiplied for sale. It was usual for neighbouring convents to lend one another their manuscripts to be copied: sometimes these were sent long distances for this purpose. Peter, abbot of Cluny, writing to the prior of Chartreuse, tells him that he had sent him the lives of Gregory Nazianzen and Chrysostom, with Ambrose's treatise *Against Symmachus*. He had not sent Hilary *On the Psalms*, because there was in his copy the same defect as in the prior's. Prosper *Against Cassianus* he did not possess, but had sent into Aquitaine for it. He begs the prior to let him have the greater volume of Augustine, containing his correspondence with Jerome, because a great part of his own copy, whilst lying at one of the cells, had been eaten by a bear! Sometimes books were lent on the condition that a copy should be returned with the volume.

The scriptorium, at first a small cell, gradually grew, in the larger monasteries, to be a spacious chamber, where many writers were employed who daily sat down to their work in a very business-like manner. The abbot of St. Martin's at Tournay used to exult in "the number of writers the Lord had given him." In his scriptorium (not one of the largest) "a dozen young monks were to be seen, seated in perfect silence, at writing tables furnished with every appliance. Here were transcribed all Jerome's commentaries on the prophets, all the works of Pope Gregory the Great, and whatever the abbot could lays his hands upon, of Augustine, Ambrose, Isidore, Bede and Anselm." Nor was the work of the transcriber always confined to men. Diemudis, a nun of Wessobrunn in Bavaria, was very skilful in the art. Besides office books for the Church service, she engrossed "in a most beautiful character" copies of the Gospels and Epistles, an entire Bible in two volumes, and another in three, with portions of the works of many of the Fathers.

The work of the transcriber was laborious. Some have left furtive side-notes by which we may see what was passing in their minds. One prays his patron saint to deliver him from his toil; another longs to be off from his ink that he may console himself with a cup of wine; a third gives thanks that the day is drawing to a close. More devout is the prayer in a very early French Visigothic manuscript (eighth century): "Vouchsafe, O Lord, to bless this scriptorium of thy servants, and all who labour therein; that whatsoever sacred writings shall be here written or read, may be received with understanding, and bear good fruit." Very often we meet also with a solemn imprecation, sometimes in verse, on the head of any miscreant who should abstract the volume. The cloister rule of silence gave rise to a language of signs. In the library the sign for a book was to move the hand as if turning over the leaves, to which was added a particular sign for the Missal, Gospels, Epistles, Psalms, the Rule, and so on. When the monk wanted a heathen author he was to scratch his ear like a dog.

Every great house had its peculiar style of writing, so that in many cases the parentage of a given manuscript is easy to be determined. The several houses vied with one another in the beauty of their calligraphy and the splendour of their capital letters, which gleamed with gold, silver, and vermilion. These illuminated copies were show-books, to be brought out on high festival days.

CHAPTER II.

Monastic Life in the Middle Ages (*continued*).— Cîteaux.

From Cluny we must travel some leagues in a north-easterly direction, still in Burgundy, to note the foundation of a rival house, which was to eclipse that renowned convent, if not in privileges and wealth, yet in its influence on the religious life of Christendom. This was Cîteaux (in Latin, Cistercium), twelve miles south of Dijon, then a wilderness covered with woods and briars.

Two brothers of the noble house of Molesme (a castle south-east of Troyes) were riding through a forest on their way to a tournament. Suddenly each was seized with the temptation to murder the other, and thus secure the whole of their paternal inheritance. They both wrestled with the dark phantom, and mastered it. Some years afterwards they passed together again along the same dreary road, and the recollection of their former temptation came back to them. They shuddered at the fearful power of the enemy, hastened to confess themselves to a hermit, and then disclosed to each other what had been their secret thoughts. With one accord they resolved to abandon a world which bred such dreadful suggestions, and devote themselves to God. Accordingly they gathered around them in the forest of Colan, near the family estate, a small community which grew into a monastery, one of the brothers, Robert, being made the first abbot. It was affiliated to Cluny.

The course of the new monastery did not run smooth. Robert was a zealous disciplinarian; the major part of the monks were lax and ungovernable. The more earnest members of the community, weary of seeing the rules of the order perpetually disregarded, asked permission of the abbot to withdraw to some other place where they might serve God without distraction. Robert not only gave them permission, but declared that he would himself accompany them. Having obtained the sanction of the papal legate, he himself with his prior, and with Stephen Harding an Englishman, and eighteen other monks, left Molesme (A.D. 1098) to seek, as Milman expresses it, "a more complete solitude, a more obstinate wilderness to tame, more sense-subduing poverty, more intense mortification." Such a spot they found at Cîteaux.

It was not the object of this little band to found a new order of monks, but rather, as had been the case at Cluny, to recall the monastic life to the original spirit and strict rule of Benedict.[1] Fuller quaintly puts the case: "As mercers, when their old stuffes begin to tire in sale, refresh them with new names to make them more vendible; so, when the Benedictines waxed stale in the world, the same order was set forth in a new edition, corrected and amended under the names, first of Cluniacs:—these were Benedictines sifted through a finer search, with some additionals invented and imposed upon them by Odo, abbot of Cluny; secondly Cistercians, so called from one Robert, living in Cistercium in Burgundy aforesaid; he the second time refined the drossy Benedictines."[2]

---

[1] It was perhaps in order to signify more plainly his intention, that they changed the colour of their garments from black to white.

[2] Cîteaux was not the only attempt at reformation in this period on the part of those who aimed only at the correction of abuses, unconscious that the foundations themselves were out of course. A pious and learned ecclesiastic named Bruno, shocked at the profanation of holy things which he daily witnessed in the archbishopric of Cologne, sought refuge in a life of the strictest asceticism. With twelve companions, about the year 1084, he settled himself down in the wild valley of Chartreux (Carthusium) not far from Grenoble, founding the abbey since known as *La Grande Chartreuse*, where they spent their day in silence, devotional exercises, study, and manual labour. They employed their leisure hours in transcribing manuscripts. The Carthusians enjoyed the rare merit of long maintaining unaltered their strict mode of living and contemplative habits, even when their order had become famous and their monasteries richly endowed.

"These monks of Citeaux," says Morison, describing their habits in the early days, "though very wonderful, do not tempt one to join. They actually keep the whole of St. Benedict's rule literally, not conventionally and with large allowances, as is usual [even] in the strictest houses. They eat but one meal a day, and have risen twelve hours from their hard couches, and sung psalms, and worked in the fields, before they get even that. They never taste meat, fish, grease or eggs, and even milk only rarely. Their dress consists of three garments, and those of the coarsest wool. Their church shows no attempt towards picturesque beauty, but in all things aims at the austerest simplicity."[1]

For a while it seemed as though the experiment would prove a failure. The little community, unrecruited from without, was thinned by death; a season of scarcity bringing with it an epidemic sickness. But just at the moment when affairs were at their worst, new elements of life were infused. Robert being by command of the pope obliged to return to his former charge at Molesme, Alberic his prior was elected abbot in his room, and on Alberic's death in 1109, Stephen succeeded to the vacant seat. Stephen Harding was a native of Sherborne in Dorsetshire,[2] and was instructed in the priory at that place in reading, writing, music, and the services of the Church. Under the tyrannical rule of William the Conqueror he fled to Scotland, and thence removed to Paris, where he applied himself to the study of Holy Scripture and Biblical learning. After visiting Rome to view the tombs of the martyrs he joined Robert at Molesme, and thence accompanied him to Cîteaux. Stephen was a man of piety,[3] extensive learning, and large administrative capacity. He conceived the project of retaining in intimate connection with Cîteaux all the religious houses which should spring from it. A general chapter of the heads of these

---

[1] "The crosses were of iron or painted wood; the lamps, candlesticks, censers, of brass or iron, and the chalices of silver gilt."

[2] Sherborne had long been an ecclesiastical centre, having been made an episcopal town in A.D. 705, when Aldhelm, abbot of Malmesbury, was appointed to the see (since become that of Salisbury). Aldhelm was a member of the royal family of Wessex, and a man of activity, who did much to spread monastic Christianity in the west of England. He is the first Englishman whose writings have come down to us; they are however of little interest.

[3] It is related of him that when entering the church for even-song he was observed to press his finger forcibly upon the latch of the door, as if he would leave the impression of a seal. Being asked the meaning of the action, he replied: "The thoughts which occupy me during the day in the management of the monastery, I leave here, and bid them remain until I call for them to-morrow morning after praise."

houses was to be held yearly, for the transaction of the common affairs and for the weal of the whole order; and the abbot of Citeaux was himself to visit at least once a year all the affiliated houses. The document in which this scheme was embodied was called the *Charter of Charity*. Of Stephen's erudition we have convincing proof in the corrected edition of the Latin Vulgate, which with the help of some learned Jews, he made from Hebrew manuscripts.[1]

But it was not altogether or even mainly to the Charter of Charity, that Citeaux was indebted for its rescue from decay or oblivion.

Some fifteen miles north, two miles beyond Dijon, stood the castle of Fontaines, whose ruins are still to be traced. It crowned a hill-summit, and commanded a fair prospect of the city, and beyond it of the fruitful plain of the Saône in which Citeaux lay, bounded by the mountains of the Côte d'Or. Here dwelt the wealthy baron Tesselin, vassal and friend of the Duke of Burgundy. He was a true knight, the very mirror of chivalry, as gentle as he was brave. Being at one time drawn into a quarrel, it was agreed to settle the matter by single combat. Tesselin was the stronger of the two, and victory would have been easy, but his soul was disquieted. The fear of the divine judgments weighed upon him; and he resolved to be reconciled to his adversary. And so when the time came and the two champions appeared at the place of meeting, instead of drawing his sword Tesselin frankly gave up the point in dispute. His wife Alith was a pious and charitable lady. She sought out the poor, relieved their sick, and "cleansed their cups and vessels with her own hands." In her latter years she rivalled the devotions and austerities of the nuns, setting before her, alas! that mistaken pattern "of self-sacrifice and holiness which alone was attractive and beautiful in that age." So great was her reputation that when she died, the abbot of St. Benignus in Dijon (now the cathedral) came to Fontaines and begged her body as a most precious treasure. He and his monks bore it away on their shoulders, and were met by a large concourse of people with crosses and tapers, who accompanied them to the church where they buried her.[2] To Tesselin and Alith was born, in 1091, a son, the Bernard of whom we have just spoken.

---

[1] The work, written on vellum in six folio volumes, is still preserved in the city library of Dijon. Its date is 1110. It is carefully and clearly engrossed.

[2] Alith's chair, or what is traditionally believed to be such, is still to be seen in the Ducal Palace (now the Hôtel de Ville) at Dijon. It is of inlaid oak, roomy and comfortable. In the same hall is also to be seen Bernard's wooden

The boy was sent in due time to the church-school of Châtillon, where he distinguished himself by his progress, and was remarked as being not only studious but fond of retirement and "marvellously cogitative." His mother had destined him for the Church, but after her death the young nobles, his companions, sought to win him to their company by pleasures and adventures. Finding these inducements too weak to tempt so ardent and soaring a spirit, they set before him a more insidious bait. The nations of Europe were at this time arousing themselves from the slumber of the tenth century, and an extraordinary enthusiasm for literature and philosophy was springing up, especially in France; the young men who had previously aspired to honour only by the weapons of war, now sought it by those of dialectics. It was at this very period that Abelard, having overcome his rival William of Champeaux, was lecturing in Paris to a vast concourse of students. For some time Bernard was dazzled by the allurements of this new path to glory. But the impression made upon him by his mother's teaching and example survived long after her death, and could not be effaced even by this temptation. Her image was constantly before him; he pondered over the discourses she had held with him, and the plans she had formed for him; and his ardent imagination led him to believe that she appeared visibly and rebuked him for his indecision. Journeying alone to visit two of his brothers in the camp of the Duke of Burgundy, who was then laying siege to the Castle of Grancy, he thought he again beheld her and heard her speaking to him in the same accents of reproof. Retiring into a church by the roadside, "he lifted his hands towards heaven, and with a torrent of tears poured forth his heart like water in the presence of his Lord."

This was the turning-point. When he arose from his knees, he solemnly vowed that he would become a monk. Not satisfied with this, he at once sought to induce his kindred to follow him into the cloister. In this endeavour he displayed "that commanding personal ascendancy, that overpowering influence of spirit, which hardly met with a defeat during his whole life." His uncle, the opulent Count of Touillon, of high renown in arms, was the first to join him. Bartholomew and Andrew, his two younger brothers, made but small resistance to his earnest appeal. The eldest, Guido, who had wife and children, was harder to win, but at length he too yielded. Gerard, the second in age, a brave and prudent knight,

---

cup which he used at Citeaux, now bound with brass, and the crozier of Robert, the first abbot, curiously carved and ornamented.

despised this sudden resolution of the rest as an impulse of levity, and withstood all Bernard's solicitations. "I know, my brother," rejoined Bernard, "that it is suffering alone which will bring thee to reflection." Then placing his hand on Gerard's side: "It shall come to pass, and quickly too, that a lance shall pierce thee here, and make a way to thy heart for the counsel of salvation which thou now despisest." A few days afterwards, when engaged in fighting, Gerard was surrounded and carried off captive with a spear in his side. "I turn monk," he exclaimed, "monk of Cîteaux!"[1]

Many of the new votaries being married, Bernard caused a nunnery to be erected at Jouilli near Dijon for their wives, Guido's consort being appointed the first abbess. He then led his followers, about thirty in number, to Châtillon, where during six months in rigorous seclusion they prepared themselves for the monastic life. At the end of that time, Bernard and his brothers returned to Fontaines to take a final leave of their paternal home. Nivard, the youngest son, was playing with some other children in the street,[2] and Guido addressing him said, "See, my brother, the whole of our paternal inheritance will now devolve on thee." To which the boy answered: "What, do you take heaven for yourselves, and leave me only the earth? This is no fair division." He afterwards joined the fraternity; and the old baron, full of grief at the loss of his sons, retired to Clairvaux soon after the establishment of that abbey, and himself took the vows.

It did not accord with Bernard's self-denying purpose to make choice of any of the richer and more illustrious abbeys; he selected the poor and struggling convent of Cîteaux. This house, then of fifteen years' foundation, was, as has been said, reduced to a very low condition. On a memorable day, not only in the history of Cîteaux, but in that of the world, Bernard, then twenty-two years of age, presented himself with thirty companions at the gate of the monastery. This was in the year 1118. Many of the little company were of noble rank, and all were animated in a greater or less degree with the enthusiastic spirit of their leader.

Although the rule of the convent was excessively severe it was insufficient to satisfy Bernard's craving after spiritual life. In him the spirit of the ancient Egyptian monks may be said to have re-

---

[1] The story of Guido's submission is fearful. Bernard pursued his work of proselytism so pitilessly that mothers hid their sons, and wives their husbands, at his approach.

[2] An ancient narrow street still runs down from the crest of the hill where the castle stood.

visited the earth. He dwelt alone, save when on his knees with the rest in the choir. He passed whole days "in ecstatic contemplation, so that seeing he saw not, and hearing he heard not. Time given to sleep he regarded as lost." Of the scanty food which he took, rather to avert death than to sustain life, his unconscious taste lost all perception, whether it was nauseous or wholesome. Extreme weakness of stomach followed these severities, yet "his dauntless spirit never yielded." So long as he was able he joined the other monks in their hard manual labour; and when obliged to give up such work, he turned to lighter but more menial offices, that he might supply by humility his deficiency in toil.

"The visits of his friends who were still in the world were a source of great disquiet to him. Their conversation brought back thoughts and feelings which he had determined to leave for ever. After their departure, on one occasion, he went to attend the office of *Nones*, and as usual lifted his mind to prayer; but immediately found that God's grace and favour were not vouchsafed as before. That idle talk was evidently the cause. The next time they came he was prepared. Stopping his ears with little wads of flax, and burying his head deep in his cowl, although exposed for an hour to their conversation, he heard nothing, and even spoke nothing except a few words to edification."

When at work in the fields, Bernard was accustomed "to look through nature up to nature's God." "Any knowledge of divine things that I may possess," he wrote in after years, "or any facility in explaining Holy Scripture, has been obtained through mediation and prayer in the fields, with none but the beeches and oaks for my teachers." "Believe me," he wrote to a celebrated teacher of the speculative philosophy, "thou wilt find more in woods than in books, and trees and stones shall teach thee that which thou canst not learn from man."[1] Especially were the sufferings of our Lord the theme of his meditation. He compared this exercise to the bundle of myrrh which the Spouse in the Canticles gathers with pious care to plant in her bosom. "From the very beginning of my conversion, my brethren," so he expresses himself in one of his sermons, "feeling my own great deficiency, I took this nosegay, composed of all the sufferings and pains of my Saviour, of the privations He submitted to in his childhood, the labours He endured in his preaching, the fatigue He underwent in his journeyings, his

---

[1] "This our life, exempt from public haunt,
Finds tongues in trees, books in the running brooks,
Sermons in stones, and good in everything."
Had Shakspeare read Bernard?

watchings in prayer, his temptations in fasting, his tears of compassion, the snares laid for his words, his perils among false brethren, the outrages, spitting, smiting, mockery, insults, nails. In these contemplations I find relief from sadness, moderation in success, and safety on the highway of life. My most sublime philosophy is to know Jesus Christ and Him crucified."

Bernard's reputation soon drew so many votaries to Citeaux, that the convent became too small to receive them. The very year in which he was admitted a colony was settled at La Ferté, on the river Grône; the next year another was planted at Pontigny; and in 1115 Bernard himself was selected by Stephen to go forth and found a new monastery in such place as he might choose. Twelve monks, representing the twelve Apostles, were chosen to accompany him, of whom four were his brothers, one his uncle and another a kinsman. After divine service in the church, Stephen placed a cross in Bernard's hands, who at the head of his little band solemnly walked forth from Citeaux. "When," says the Cistercian Chronicle, "Bernard and his twelve monks silently took their departure, although nothing was to be heard but the voices of those who were singing the hymns, you might have seen tears in the eyes of all present."

Notwithstanding Bernard's departure the fame of Citeaux daily increased, and candidates for the white cowl flocked thither in overwhelming numbers. Within fifty years of its foundation it could reckon as belonging to it five hundred affiliated abbeys or nunneries; by the commencement of the next century these had increased to eighteen hundred; and at one time, it is stated, there were no fewer than ten thousand.[1]

Much good doubtless was effected by the planting of so many religious houses, glowing with the ardour of their first love. But this good was not unmixed. The charity of their *Charter* did not extend to those who differed from them. When the Church began to take systematic action for the suppression of heresy, it was

---

[1] Most of the great English abbeys, Tintern, Rievaulx, Fountains, Furness, Netley, were Cistercian. The first of the order in this country was Waverley in Surrey, founded 1128. "The order," says a Roman Catholic writer, "took to itself all the quiet nooks, valleys, and pleasant streams of Old England, and gladdened the soul of the labourer by its constant bells. Its agricultural character was peculiarly suited to the country." "The Cistercians," says Mrs. Green, "founded their houses amongst the desolate moorlands of Yorkshire, in solitary places which had known no inhabitants since the Conqueror's ravages, or amongst the swamps of Lincolnshire. One hundred and fifteen monasteries were built during the nineteen years of Stephen's reign, more than had been founded in the whole previous century; 113 were added during Henry's reign."

Cistercian monks whom the pope chose to confute and brow-beat the reformers, and to incite their fellow-citizens against them; it was Cistercian monks who everywhere traversed the land preaching with furious zeal the crusade against the Albigenses; and an abbot of Citeaux itself was the inspiring genius and leader of the detestable enterprise.[1]

After a time, as might be expected, abuses crept into the Cistercian monasteries, and discipline began to hang down her hands. A fruitful source of mischief was that the patron of a monastery, on the death of the abbot, sometimes conferred the revenues on some kinsman or favourite *in commendam*, as it was called. These abbots *in commendam* were often not monks at all; some never visited the abbeys whose revenues they enjoyed; others "quietly established themselves in the house with wife and children; and the tramp of soldiers, the neighing of horses and baying of hounds, made the cloister more like a knight's castle than a place dedicated to God's service."

Some remains of the ancient monastery of Citeaux still exist, and form part of a large reformatory for boys which covers the original site.

CHAPTER III.

Monastic Life in the Middle Ages (concluded).
Clairvaux, and Bernard.

We left Bernard and his twelve disciples filing out from the walls of Citeaux. They took a northerly direction, and after a journey of about ninety miles arrived at La Ferté on the river Aube, in Champagne, between Troyes and Chaumont. Four miles beyond this little town lies a shallow valley encircled by thickly-wooded hills. It was once a haunt of robbers, and was called from the abundance of the plant which grew there, the Valley of Wormwood; but after Bernard settled at the spot its name was changed to the Bright Valley (Claravallis, Clairvaux). The little company arrived in June, and began at once to provide for shelter and sustenance. "The rude fabric which they raised was long preserved by pious veneration. It consisted of a building covered by a single roof,

---

[1] See below, chap. 7.

under which chapel, dormitory and refectory were all included. The bare earth served for floor; the windows were scarcely wider than a man's hand. Immediately above the refectory was the sleeping apartment, a loft reached by a ladder. The beds were boxes or bins of planks, a small space hewn out with an axe allowing room for the sleeper to get in or out. The inside was strewn with chaff or dried leaves. At the summit of the ladder was the abbot's cell, a framework of boards was his bed, with two logs of wood for his pillows." The toil of building left the brethren but little time to provide themselves with food. They had taken possession of the wilderness too late in the year to sow the ground, and the neighbouring farmers, who at first ministered to their wants, soon became familiar with their sanctity and their necessities, and ceased to regard either. Their food was bread made of barley and millet, with beech-leaves cooked in brine, and when these failed there was nothing left but nuts and roots. Their clothes too were wearing out.

The hearts of the brethren, stout as they were, began to quail: "they would not remain in this valley of bitterness, they would return to Citeaux." It was all Bernard could do to prevent them. He had recourse to prayer. As he prayed, he thought he heard a voice from heaven: "Arise, Bernard, thy prayers are heard." On which the monks said, "What didst thou ask of the Lord?" "Wait, and ye shall see, ye of little faith," was the reply; and presently there came a stranger, who gave the abbot ten livres. Another time their supply of salt failing, Bernard said to one of the brethren, "Guibert, saddle the ass, go to the fair and buy us salt." Guibert answered, "Where is the money?" "Take faith," replied Bernard, "for as to money, I know not when we shall have any; but He who is above holds my purse in his hands." The monk smiled and rejoined, "It seems to me, father, that if I go empty-handed, I shall return empty-handed." "Nevertheless go," replied the abbot, "and go in faith. I tell thee our Treasurer will be with thee, and will supply all thou needest." Guibert received his abbot's benediction and went, though still more than doubtful of the issue. On the way he met a priest who inquired his business. Guibert told his errand, and made known the indigent state of his convent; the compassionate priest, taking him to his own house, gave him half a bushel of salt and fifty shillings. On Guibert's return with his panniers filled, Bernard said to him, "I tell thee, my son, no one thing is so necessary to a Christian as faith; keep hold of faith, and it will be well with thee all the days of thy life."

After this crisis was over, brighter days opened on Clairvaux.

Indeed, as Morison observes, the way to fame for a new monastery seems to have been " first of all to get nearly extinguished by cold and hunger." Stephen Harding had appointed Bernard abbot of the new foundation. The appointment was incomplete without episcopal ordination. Bernard received this at the hands of William of Champeaux, mentioned above. Through his emaciated frame and features, and homely, not to say ragged apparel, the bishop discerned the lofty intellect and unquenchable spirit which dwelt in so frail a tabernacle, and became his admirer and steadfast friend.

The labours and anxieties through which he had passed, added to his own excessive austerities, brought Bernard to the brink of the grave. William, hearing of his dangerous condition, came to visit him, hoping to induce him to spare himself and take rest. But Bernard would hear of no relaxation, either of his duties or austerities; whereupon William set off for Citeaux. He found the chapter assembled, and asked permission to direct and manage Bernard for one year. The leave was granted, and Bernard, obedient to the commands of his superiors, resigned himself into William's hands. The latter caused a small cottage to be built outside the monastery walls, where Bernard was to dwell, relieved from the monastic regimen, and from the daily care of the abbey. How far this prescription so affectionately intended was successful, may be learnt from his friend and biographer, the abbot of St. Thierry, who, accompanied by another abbot, visited him in his hut. "It was about this time (1116), that my visits to Clairvaux began. I found the saint enjoying a state of perfect tranquillity, and living to God as though he already tasted the delights of Paradise. When I entered the chamber and beheld the lodging and the guest, a feeling of veneration came over me as if I had been approaching the altar of God. He welcomed us with gracious kindness, and when we inquired how he fared, and how he liked his new mode of life, 'Excellent well,' he replied, with his usual benevolent smile, 'I who have hitherto ruled over rational men, am now by the just judgment of God obliged to submit myself to an irrational being.' This he spoke concerning a conceited quack to whose care he had been entrusted, and who undertook to cure him. When we sat down to table, I expected to find his diet suited to the state of so precious an invalid, but he was served on the contrary, by the doctor's orders, with lumps of rancid butter and other viands so revolting, that a healthy man pinched by hunger would hardly have touched them. We were indignant, and could scarce restrain ourselves from breaking the rule of silence, and reproaching the empiric as a sacrilegious homicide. But he to whom all this was done took it all with indifference, and approved of everything. His sense of taste seemed dead; water, he said, was the only thing pleasant to him, cooling the fever of his throat and mouth. I tarried with him a few days. I thought I saw all around me a new heaven and a new earth, crossed by the old pathways of our fathers, the Egyptian monks, and the recent footsteps of some men of our own time. The golden age seemed to have returned in Clairvaux."

The whole convent was animated by Bernard's spirit and example. Men of illustrious descent who had played a distinguished part on the theatre of the world, now toiled in the sweat of their brow, and practised the extreme of self-denial. His biographer thus describes the scene which presented itself on entering the valley. "It was a dreary spot, enclosed by gloomy woods and rugged hills, and as the traveller came down the slope he saw the valley full of men industriously occupied, but in profound silence, only interrupted by the sound of the implements and hymns of praise. So solemn was the stillness that strangers forbore to speak on any but sacred subjects, until they had passed beyond its precincts."

At the expiration of the year, Bernard hastened to throw off the surveillance of the empiric, and to resume his abbatial duties. But his health had been too far undermined to bear the convent rule, and he was compelled again to retire into a separate dwelling. It is instructive to find that in after-years he lamented the youthful enthusiasm which had led him thus to waste his strength.[1]

Some remarkable anecdotes are told of Bernard's faith and of his power over men. During one of his visits to Paris, A.D. 1125, he was requested to lecture in the schools. He did so, dilating on "the true philosophy,"—contempt for the world, and voluntary poverty assumed for Christ's sake. To his surprise and grief his discourse made no impression; not one of his hearers was converted. Returning to the house of the archdeacon with whom he lodged, he fell immediately to prayer; as his soul waxed more and more fervent, he was overcome with a torrent of tears, and his sobs and

---

[1] He thus warns beginners against the excesses of asceticism. "It is your self-will which teaches you not to spare nature, nor listen to reason. I fear lest beginning in the Spirit you will end in the flesh. Do you not know that a messenger of Satan often clothes himself as an angel of light? God is Wisdom, and requires a love which unites itself with wisdom. The cunning enemy has no surer means of banishing love from the heart than by seducing men to walk imprudently, and not according to reason."

groans were heard outside the room. The archdeacon inquired what could be the cause of such grief? A monk who knew Bernard well replied: "That wonderful man, inflamed by the fire of charity and entirely absorbed in God, cares for nothing in this world, save only to recall the wandering to the ways of truth, and to gain their souls to Christ; and because he has been sowing the word of life in the schools and has gathered no fruit in the conversion of the clerics, he thinks God is angry with him. Hence this storm of groans and tears; I confidently anticipate that a full harvest tomorrow will compensate for to-day's sterility." The next morning Bernard preached again and with a very different result; for as soon as his sermon was over, several of his hearers expressed their desire to become monks. Taking these with him he set out for Clairvaux, and passed the night at St. Denis. The next day however, instead of continuing his journey homewards, he said, "We must return to Paris, there are still some there who belong to us." As they re-entered the city they saw three ecclesiastics coming towards them, at the sight of whom Bernard exclaimed: "God has helped us; behold those for whom we returned!" When the clerics came near, they addressed him: "O most blessed father, hast thou come back to us who desired thee so much? We were minded to follow, but hardly hoped to overtake thee." "I knew it, beloved," he replied; "we will now, by God's grace, go on together." They accompanied him to Clairvaux, and continued under its rule the remainder of their lives.

A wider scene now opens before us. In 1130, on the death of Pope Honorius II., two rival factions contended for the possession of the papal chair. One chose the Cardinal of St. Angelo, who took the name of Innocent II.; the other, the Cardinal of St. Mary Trastevere, who was styled Anacletus II. The latter, with the assistance of Robert the Norman, Duke of Sicily, made himself paramount in Rome, and compelled his opponent to take refuge in France. Bernard passionately espoused the cause of the exiled pope, and it was mainly through his means that the trans-Alpine kingdoms, France, Germany and England, recognised Innocent as the lawful successor of Peter. In the course of the long journeys he undertook with this object, he had an interview with our king Henry I.:—"the wisest soldier-statesman of his age, face to face with the greatest monk of Christendom." They met at Chartres. "Henry was undecided as to which pope would suit him best. His own clergy had a leaning towards Anacletus; that might be a reason for him to choose Innocent." "Art thou afraid," asked Bernard, "of incurring sin by acknowledging Innocent? Bethink thee how to answer to God for thy other sins; that one leave to me, I will account for it." Henry joined the party of Innocent.

Innocent paid a visit to Clairvaux. "He was met by a tattered flock of Christ's poor, preceded by a cross. They came on in solemn silence, every eye fixed on the ground; no prying curiosity watching and following the movements of the brilliant cavalcade. The pope and bishops were moved to tears at the sight of so much austerity and self-restraint. The plain unornamented church, the bare walls of the monastery, offered nothing to the Romans either to admire or wish for. The hard fare of the monks appeared more wonderful still. If by chance a fish was to be had, it was placed before the pope alone."

When the tide turned in Innocent's favour and he ventured into Italy, Bernard accompanied him. As they drew near to Milan, "the whole population came out to meet the saint, as far as the seventh milestone. Nobles and common people, on horse, on foot, all proceeded to welcome, with an incredible reverence, the man of God; they kissed his feet and sought to pluck even the hairs from his garment." Equal rejoicing manifested itself on the way as he returned to Clairvaux. "Wherever he passed the shepherds came from their hills and the rustics from their fields, if it might be only to behold him afar off and implore his blessing; and when they had seen him they went back to their huts, rejoicing with one another that they had seen the saint of God."

At the end of twenty years from its foundation, the monastery had outgrown its walls, not the original barn of wood only, but the stone buildings by which that structure had been replaced. The prior with a few others of the brethren came to Bernard in his cottage to consult him. "The saint was in the heavens," says his biographer, "and they obliged him to come down and listen to their sublunary business." At first he appeared unwilling to make any change. "Our present stone buildings," he said, "have been erected at great cost and labour. If we sacrifice all this, worldly people may call us fickle, or may say that too much riches have made us mad. In truth, however, we have not the money; he who intends to build a tower must first sit down and count the cost, otherwise it will be said of him, 'This man began to build and was not able to finish.'" They answered that God who sent them so many brethren would doubtless provide the means of erecting buildings for them. Bernard was delighted with their faith, and gave his consent. Help poured in abundantly, "bishops, nobles, merchants, without being pressed, gave liberally; labourers were hired, and the monks themselves fell vigorously to work," so that the new edifice was soon completed.

We come now to an incident which exhibits in the darkest colours the spiritual arrogance of the Romish Church. In the part he played on this occasion, Bernard showed himself not inferior to Ambrose or even to Hildebrand.[1] William Count of Aquitaine had espoused the part of Pope Anacletus, and had thrust out from their sees the bishops of Poictiers and Limoges, who favoured the cause of Innocent, replacing them by creatures of his own. For this offence he was excommunicated by Innocent; and the papal legate, Geoffrey, bishop of Chartres, was sent into Aquitaine to procure the reinstatement of the deposed bishops. Unable to contend against William, he entreated Bernard to lend him his powerful assistance. They met the count at Parthenay.[2] Bernard and Geoffrey employed all their arguments and influence to induce him to restore the bishops, and even threatened him with the fate of Dathan and Abiram. The count heard them patiently, and replied that he was ready to acknowledge Innocent and Anacletus, but as to the expelled bishops, nothing in the world should induce him to receive them again; they had offended him beyond forgiveness. Finding the count intractable, Bernard and Geoffrey, with those who might lawfully do so, entered the church, William as an excommunicated person remaining outside, standing by the door. Going up to the altar, Bernard performed the "overwhelming miracle" of the Mass, and then with the Host in his hand, and in a transport of religious fury, came forth to the count. Not now with words of entreaty, but with flashing eyes and in a voice of thunder he thus addressed him. "We have entreated thee, and thou hast spurned us. The united band of God's servants have implored thee, and them too thou hast spurned. Behold the Virgin's Son, the Head and Lord of that Church which thou persecutest, thy Judge is here into whose hands thy soul must fall. Wilt thou spurn Him also, wilt thou despise Him as thou hast done his servants?" A silence as of death fell upon the terrified spectators, who, bowing their heads in prayer, waited in expectation of an immediate judgment from heaven. The count, when he saw the awful countenance of Bernard, in whose hands he verily believed his Judge and Lord to be at that moment holden, became stiffened in every limb, and fell

---

[1] For the former, see *ante*, pp. 66-69. Hildebrand (Pope Gregory VII.), sixty years before the period at which we are now arrived, had compelled the Emperor Henry IV. of Germany to stand as a penitent for three days outside the gates of Canossa, thinly clad and fasting, with the ground deep in snow.

[2] Not far from Poictiers.

insensible to the ground. Raised up by his attendant knights, he could neither speak nor see, and again fell with his face on the grass, foaming at the mouth. Bernard came close, and pushing him with his foot, told him to stand up and hear the judgment of God. "Here," he said, "is the bishop of Poictiers; go and be reconciled to him. Restore him to his see, whence thou hast expelled him." The poor man heard, although he neither dared nor was able to speak, and went at once to the bishop, gave him the kiss of peace, and reinstated him in his office. Soon the count was in friendly converse with Bernard, who admonished him for the future to avoid such impious doings, lest he should in the end weary out the Divine patience.

The history of Bernard's life introduces us to an ecclesiastical descendant of the good Patrick, and shows us into how abject a condition the once flourishing and evangelizing Church of Ireland had fallen.

Malachy was consecrated bishop of Connaught at the age of thirty years. He soon discovered that he had been appointed, "not to rule over men, but over beasts, so insolent were they in their manners, so deadly in their rites,[1] so unbelieving in religion, so rebellious against discipline, so filthy in their lives. They were Christians in name, but pagans in reality. They would not pay tithes nor first-fruits, nor enter the bonds of wedlock, nor make confession, nor perform penance." In these untoward circumstances Malachy did what he could. "He passed whole nights sleepless, his hands lifted to God in prayer; he rebuked the rebels publicly and privately, and when they would not come to church, ran after them through the streets, and searched the city[2] for such as he might win to Christ."

Celsus, the primate, by his will appointed Malachy his successor; but the Irish had the vicious custom of regarding the episcopal office as an heirloom, which ought not to be suffered to go out of the family; and Maurice, and after him Nigellus, of the "wicked seed" which had occupied the see of Armagh for two hundred years, succeeded for a while in keeping Malachy out of his office. In the end Nigellus yielded, and Malachy, to consolidate his authority, made a journey to Rome to solicit the pallium (archbishop's cloak).[3] In

---

[1] Does this point to any remains of Druidical sacrifices?
[2] Probably Tuam.
[3] This vestment was bestowed by the pope upon archbishops, at first as a token of augmented dignity and indicative of vicarial authority, but by the eighth century it had come to be conferred on all bishops as a badge of subordination to the "Apostolic See."

crossing France he halted at Clairvaux. Bernard gave him a cordial reception. He wondered to see so holy and active a servant of Christ from so barbarous a nation. "I was refreshed," he says, "by his look and word, and rejoiced as much as in all riches." At Rome Pope Innocent II. condoled with him on the length of his journey, and appointed him his legate in Ireland; but when he asked for the pallium, told him that if he would summon a general council of the bishops, clergy and chief men of the country, who should send a deputation to Rome, it should be granted. Then taking the mitre from his own head he placed it on Malachy's, giving him also the stole and maniple which he himself wore. Malachy spent a month in the city, making a round of the holy places for prayer.

Nine years afterwards he repeated his journey to solicit the pallium, and on the way again visited Clairvaux. He had been only a few days in the abbey when he was seized with fever. The monks were emulous in their efforts to relieve and restore him; but he foresaw that his days were numbered. On the former occasion he had entreated the pope for permission to live and die at Clairvaux, but his request had been refused. "Now," he said to the monks, "I shall not be baulked of my desire; He who has led me to the place which I sought will not deny me the end I have wished for. This poor body will find its resting-place here, and as concerns my soul, the Lord will provide, who saves those who place their hope in Him." When he was to receive extreme unction, he would not allow the brethren to go up to the cell where he lay, but came down to them, and having taken the *viaticum* returned to his bed. None could believe he was dying. "His countenance," says Bernard, "was not pale, nor his forehead wrinkled, nor his eyes sunken, nor his flesh wasted. Such grace was in his body, such glory in his countenance, as even the hand of death could not efface. With psalms and hymns," he continues, "we followed our friend on his homeward journey. He died in his fifty-fourth year, at the place and time he had chosen and foretold."

We have referred to the scholastic theology which arose about the end of the eleventh century. From the time of a controversy on the Lord's Supper between Lanfranc, archbishop of Canterbury, and Berengar of Tours, the relish for the treatment of theology by the method of logic, as opposed to tradition, spread through Europe with astonishing rapidity. Lanfranc's disciple Anselm, archbishop of Canterbury in 1109, is regarded as the first of the *Schoolmen*. Paris was the chief seat of the new philosophy; and next to it, after the year 1200, was Oxford. The most distinguished teacher at the beginning of the twelfth century was Bernard's friend, William of Champeaux, who taught in the cathedral-school at Paris with great reputation, until the superior genius of his famous pupil, Peter Abelard, threw him into the shade.[1]

Abelard pursued the theological speculations to which Origen in the third century had pointed the way, and with even a more daring spirit. His lectures awakened in the youthful students an enthusiastic admiration both for himself and his philosophy. The bishops and higher clergy took alarm, and a council was summoned at Soissons by the papal legate, before which Abelard was cited as a heretic, A.D. 1121. He was condemned without even being allowed to explain or defend his opinions. "The council," he says, "without discussion or examination, compelled me to burn my book" (his *Treatise on the Divine Trinity and Unity*) "with my own hands. And so it was burnt amid general silence." When he rose to expound his belief in his own words, his judges said there was no necessity for anything beyond the recital of the Athanasian Creed, "a thing which any boy could do." Thus saying, they placed before him a copy of the creed, as though it had been something altogether new to him. It was notorious that Abelard could not consistently subscribe the creed, that all he had written was in contravention of it, yet he wanted the moral courage to stand by his principles. Origen would have taught him otherwise, because in Origen the lofty flight of the intellect was controlled and regulated by a large measure of the love of Christ, and by the humility of a child of God.[2] "I read the creed," says Abelard, "as well as I could amidst sobs, sighs and tears; and then, like a convicted criminal, was delivered over to the abbot of St. Medard, to be kept in close custody in his monastery." Nevertheless this arbitrary condemnation by the synod of Soissons only increased his fame.

Bernard occupied in theology a position the very opposite to that of Abelard. Holding that the mysterious doctrines of revelation are beyond the reach of intellectual analysis, he condemned every departure from the received teaching of Scripture upon divine things. Abelard had asked: "Why may not God, by an act of his will

---

[1] See *ante*, p. 348.

[2] The honour paid to intellectual superiority blinds men to the infinitely greater worth of moral integrity. It is common, for example, to style Galileo a martyr of science, and to condone his abjuration before Pope Urban VIII. of the cosmical truth that the earth moves round the sun. But he would have left a far nobler name, and been a far greater benefactor to mankind, if he had stood faithful to his own conscience, and set an example of fidelity to truth.

alone, forgive men their sins, and deliver them from the power of Satan? What need is there in order to this, of the sufferings of Christ? Christ before his passion forgave many their sins. . . . . How can God become reconciled to man through the death of his Son, when this death could not happen without involving the sin of so many who crucified Him, which sin was certainly far greater than Adam's, the partaking of a forbidden apple? If God was so angry on account of that first sin, how can He be appeased in the case of so many far greater sins? How unjust and cruel that God should require the blood of an innocent person as the price of pardoning so many guilty!" Accordingly he looked upon the incarnation and passion of the Son of God as simply a manifestation of divine love, and inferred that the "amazing grace shown us by God, who gave his own Son to become man and suffer for us, must enkindle in us such love in return, as to make us ready to endure all suffering for his sake." In like manner he defined redemption to be, "that supreme love which is enkindled in us by Christ's passion, a love which not only delivers us from the bondage of sin, but acquires for us the true freedom of God's children." To which Bernard justly replied: "Did Christ then merely *teach* righteousness; did He not also *bestow* it? Did He *exhibit* love only; did He not also *infuse* it? . . . Who denies that other ways of redemption, justification, and deliverance were possible to the Almighty? But this can make nothing against the way and method which He has chosen. We cannot fathom the holy will of God, but we can feel the effect of the work, we can be sensible of its benefit. Why did He accomplish that by the blood of Christ which He might have accomplished by a word? Ask Himself. It is vouchsafed to me to know that the fact is so, but not why it is so. Shall the creature say to the Creator, 'Why hast Thou formed me thus?' . . . It was not the death of Christ, *in itself*, but his will in freely offering Himself, that was acceptable to God; and because this precious death, procuring the downfall of sin, could only be brought about by sin, God had not therefore pleasure in the sin, but used it for good. God did not require the death of his Son, but accepted it when offered; He did not thirst for blood, but for man's salvation."

Abelard would test revelation by reason; he defines faith to be merely "an opinion concerning that which does not yet appear." Bernard replies: "He professes to explain all things by reason, even those which lie beyond the limits of reason; he thus fights both against faith and reason, for what is more contrary to reason than through reason to seek to soar above reason? And what is more contrary to faith than to refuse our belief to that which we cannot attain by reason? . . . Far be it from us to leave aught belonging either to our faith or our hope in an *empty opinion*, so as to be removed from the sure and steadfast foundation of truth;—truth confirmed by God through prophecies and miracles, established and sanctified by the Offspring of the Virgin, the blood of the Redeemer, the glory of the Resurrection. With which outward certainty we connect the inward: ' The Spirit Himself beareth witness with our spirit that we are children of God.' . . . I behold three several objects in the work of redemption—the example of humility,. God emptying Himself; the measure of love extending even to death, death on the cross; the mystery of redemption, whereby death itself is annihilated. . . . It is one thing to follow Jesus, it is another to cleave to Him through love,—it is another still to feed upon his flesh and blood. To follow Him is a wholesome resolve; to cling to and embrace Him is a noble joy; to feed upon Him is a holy life, for He is that bread of life which cometh down from heaven, and giveth life to the world, and what is resolve or joy without life?"

Between two such champions, both zealous and both confident, it was scarcely possible that a personal encounter should long be deferred. Bernard drew up an appeal to the pope, cardinals, princes and bishops to repress the arch-heretic, whom he designated as Arius, Nestorius, Pelagius all in one, and scattered it broadcast over Europe. Abelard to protect himself persuaded the archbishop of Sens, whom Bernard had offended, and who was about to preside over a numerous synod (A.D. 1140), to summon Bernard to attend, and at the same time gave out that he was going to meet the great abbot of Clairvaux in logical combat. At first Bernard hesitated: "When all fly before his face, he selects me, the least of all, for his antagonist." But when he found that Abelard's disciples asserted that he did not dare to meet their master, he accepted the challenge. " I declined," he says, " partly because I was but a youth and he a man of war from his youth, partly because I hold it unmeet to submit matters of faith which are grounded on the sure and steadfast truth to the subtleties of human argumentation. . . . . Finally I yielded, not without great reluctance and many tears, to the counsel of my friends, and came to the appointed place at the appointed time, unprepared except with those words of Scripture: ' Take no thought how or what ye shall speak: for it shall be given you in that hour what ye shall speak'; and, ' The Lord is my helper; I will not fear; what shall man do unto me?'"

The original object of the meeting at Sens was an exhibition of relics, and as the occasion was intended to be a very solemn one, the king, Louis VII., was present with a multitude of bishops, abbots and nobles. Abelard came with a troop of disciples: Bernard with two or three of his monks. The synod was held in the church of St. Stephen. The question of Abelard's heresies came up on the second day. Abelard entered, and walked up through the midst of the assembly, which was for the most part inimical to him. As he passed one of his fellow-schoolmen he whispered the proverb, "When thy neighbour's house is burning, thine too is in danger." Bernard stood in a pulpit, with Abelard's book before him, from which he caused to be read aloud the passages he had marked for reproof, condemnation or explanation. But the reading had hardly begun, when to the amazement of all Abelard rose, refused to hear more or to answer any questions, and saying he appealed to Rome abruptly left the assembly. The synod however continued its sitting, and did not suffer his heretical opinions to go uncondemned. They were read and re-read, and, say the bishops in their letter to the pope, "proved to be not only false, but plainly heretical, both by most evident reasons, and also by testimonies from Augustine and others of the Fathers, brought forward by the abbot of Clairvaux."

Abelard proceeded towards Rome with the intention of personally pressing his appeal. Passing through Burgundy, he put up at Cluny. Peter the Venerable received him with a guileless charity. Abelard's heresies were as hateful to him as to any one, but with him charity was above everything. He wrote to the pope:— "Master Peter (Abelard), as he lately came from France,[1] came to Cluny. He told me that, being oppressed by the attacks of certain persons who had branded him with the name of heretic, which he detested, he had appealed to Rome and was going thither for protection. I exhorted him to seek Bernard, in company with the abbot of Cîteaux, and to remove and expunge from his books whatsoever he had written offensive to Catholic ears. They went together to Clairvaux, and on their return Peter told us how he met Bernard, and that the old animosities between them were removed. Urged by me, he has chosen for himself a dwelling-place in Cluny, where I beseech thee to permit him to end his days, which perchance will not be many." Abelard did not in fact long survive. On his death in 1142 the abbot of Cluny wrote to Abelard's friend, Heloise: "A long letter would be insufficient to unfold the humility

---

[1] Burgundy was not at this time part of France, but was ruled by its own sovereign duke.

and devotion of Master Peter's behaviour. He was sparing in his food and dress, and all that related to his body; he read continually; he prayed often; he was always silent, unless the conversation of the monks, or a public discourse in the convent, drew him out of himself. Having become more infirm, I sent him to Châlons, because of the softness of the climate. There, so far as his malady would permit, he suffered not a moment to pass in which he did not either pray, read, write or dictate; and so the divine visitor found him, not like many, slumbering, but on the watch."

Two years before he died, Bernard wrote a long letter to one of his disciples of the same name with himself upon his elevation to the papal chair under the title of Eugenius III. It was in effect a diatribe on the corruptions of Rome, and is a monument of his honesty and fearlessness. In reading it we are reminded of the language of Cyprian when he took a survey of heathendom, and of Salvian when he probed the festering sores of that degenerate Christianity which had taken the place of heathendom.[1] Rome in fact had never changed, but pagan or Christian had always shown herself ambitious, mercenary, carnal. "The grasping, the simoniacal, the sacrilegious, the adulterous, the incestuous and all such like monsters of humanity," writes Bernard, "flock to Rome, in order either to obtain or to keep ecclesiastical honours at the hands of the pope. . . . Whom," he asks of Eugenius, "canst thou mention in that vast city, who received thee as pope without the intervention of a reward or the hope of one? For the future thou wilt have no plan from which they will consider thou hast a right to exclude them, no secret into which they will not thrust themselves; and if thy porter were to cause only a little delay to any one of them at thy doorway, I should not like to be in that porter's place. . . . They are cunning to do evil, but how to do good they know not. They are hateful to heaven and earth, on both of which they have laid violent hands; impious they are towards God, seditious and envious among themselves, cruel towards strangers; loving no man, they are loved of none. They cannot endure subjection, yet are incapable of ruling; faithless to their superiors, intolerable to their inferiors. They are shameless in asking favours, truculent in refusing them, importunate to receive, restless till they do receive, ungrateful when they have received. They are great promisers, but scanty performers; most subtle flatterers and most biting detractors; natural dissemblers and malicious traitors. Among such

---

[1] See *Early Church History*, p. 6, and *ante*, p. 180.

men, thou, their pastor, movest about in gold and gorgeous apparel. . . . We nowhere read that Peter went about adorned with precious stones and decked with gold and silks; nor mounted on a milk-white horse and surrounded with guards, nor attended by swarms of servants: herein thou art a follower, not of the apostle Peter, but of the Emperor Constantine.[1] . . . What do the sheep get of all this? If I might speak out, it is demons, rather than sheep, which graze in these pastures. . . . Is it not unbecoming in thee to have no law but thy own will, and because there is no tribunal before which thou canst be called, to exert thy power and despise reason? Art thou greater than thy Lord who said, 'I came not to do mine own will'?"[2]

But the end was drawing nigh. Bernard could no longer take solid food; even liquids gave him pain; and sleep forsook his couch. A little while before his death he dictated these words: "Pray to the Saviour, who willeth not the death of a sinner, that He do not delay my departure, and yet that He will be pleased to keep guard over it. By your prayers sustain him who has no merits of his own, that the enemy of our salvation may find no place open to his attacks." He died in 1153, at the age of sixty-three years.

From Augustine to Luther the Church records no name so illustrious as that of Bernard. What has been already related of him portrays the leading features of his character. One word more as to his humility. Strangely transported as he sometimes was with sacerdotal pride, it was nevertheless one of his chief cares to cultivate a humble spirit. "He often told us," writes his secretary, "that when he was in the midst of honours and flattering attentions he seemed to lose his personality; he imagined himself as absent, and all that was going on before him as a dream. But when he conversed with the simple-minded of his monks he rejoiced to find himself again, and to be as it were in his own person.

---

[1] In respect of this pomp he adds, "I counsel thee to submit to it from regard to the customs of the times, but not to seek it as a thing becoming or due to thee."

[2] A contemporary of Bernard uses language if possible even stronger: "Turn to the citizens of Babylon (Rome) and observe what manner of people they be, and in what ways they walk. Come hither to the top of the mountain that thou mayest behold all the habitations of the damned city. Look on her princes and judges, cardinals and archbishops, the very seat of the Beast. Every day they are intent on doing evil, insatiably occupied with works of iniquity. They offer things sacred for sale; they purchase iniquity, and labour with all their might that that may not descend alone to hell."

He often declared that he never spoke in any company, however humble, without a feeling of awe coming over him ; he would have preferred to be silent had he not been moved by the pricks of conscience, the fear of God, and brotherly love." This testimony is confirmed by all his friends and disciples. Luther calls him "a man so godly, holy, and chaste, that he is to be commended and preferred before all the Fathers. Being grievously sick," he adds, " and having no hope of recovery, he put not his trust in his life of singleness, wherein he had lived most chastely, nor in his good works and deeds of charity, whereof he had done many ; but removing them far out of his sight, and receiving the benefit of Christ by faith, he said, 'I have lived wickedly ; but Thou Lord Jesus dost possess the kingdom of heaven by double right : first, because Thou art the Son of God ; secondly, because Thou hast purchased it by thy death and passion. The first Thou keepest for thyself as thy birthright ; the second Thou givest to me, not by the right of my works, but by the right of thy grace.'"

In person Bernard was rather above the middle height and exceedingly spare, his whole body, to use the words of the monkish chronicler, " being most delicate and without flesh." He was of a clear and sanguine complexion, with a beard slightly inclining to red. His countenance was serene and heavenly, and an expression of " angelical purity and dove-like simplicity " beamed in his eyes, which are scarcely ever spoken of by his contemporaries without the addition of the epithet *columbinus*.[1]

Before Bernard had been many years dead, the abbey was rebuilt in a magnificent style, and the abbots and monks, forgetful of his prayers and tears and the example of his dedicated life, turned aside into that course of wealth and ease which he had so strenuously censured in Cluny. Instead of a plain house arose a palace, of which the dormitories, refectory, chapter-house and library were finished in the most richly decorated style, and adorned with statues of Bernard and his fellow-monks. In process of time the abbot was raised to the rank of a bishop, having under his rule in France eighteen abbeys, twenty-eight nunneries, and forty-one abbeys commendatory, besides forty in foreign countries. His annual income was 90,000 francs, besides 1072 quarters of wheat and 700 hogsheads of wine, and the tolls of forges and forests, with

---

[1] The well-known hymn, "Jerusalem the Golden," was not written by Bernard of Clairvaux, but by a contemporoary of the same name, a monk of Cluny under Peter the Venerable. This Bernard was born of English parents at Morlaix in Brittany.

other perquisites. By way of recreation from the fatigues of office he possessed a superb country-house half a league from the monastery, with a chapel carved and gilded and a choice gallery of pictures.

The Reformation period brought no material change to the monastic orders in Catholic countries, but by the beginning of the seventeenth century these had become so corrupt that a general reform was resolved on by the pope. To this the abbot and monks of Clairvaux offered a stout resistance, and enlisted on their side the all-powerful Richelieu; and when disgusted by their irregularities he gave them over to the papal commissioners, as a last expedient they persuaded their Cistercian brethren to join them in electing Richelieu himself general of the order. Richelieu accepted the dignity, still insisting on reform, but before his measures were ripe he died, A.D. 1642. No reform was effected; the old abuses continued and new enormities were perpetrated, until the abbey fell to pieces by the weight of its own corruption. When, in 1798, the Revolution like a whirlwind overthrew everything that bore the name of religion, there were but forty-five monks left to be expelled from the once saintly, powerful and populous convent of Clairvaux.

The abbey was confiscated,[1] and some time afterwards converted into a *Dépôt de Mendicité*. Some years ago it was re-constructed as a prison or House of Industry for the reformation of criminals. From 1400 to 2000 convicts are usually here confined. The prison itself is surrounded by an inner wall, beyond which is another nearly three miles in extent, enclosing the buildings of the administration, with barracks, orchards, gardens and corn-fields. The prisoners are employed in manufactures of various kinds, the products of their labour being sold to the trade at a low price. On the nearest hill is a colossal statue of Bernard, stretching out his hands over the valley. From his feet you look down into the nearer courts of the prison; and when you are weary of meditating on the busy hive of malefactors, pursuing their silent and compulsory tasks, whom however you do not see, you may in imagination substitute for the prison the abbey such as it was in the time of the great monk. Then too the valley was full of labourers, but they were drawn from the noble and the free; their labour was equally arduous, but it was the labour of Christian love; there

---

[1] The books and manuscripts were taken to Troyes, and are now in the city library. Amongst the latter is Bernard's Bible, engrossed about the time of his birth, with marginal notes probably by his own hand.

reigned over them a stillness as profound, but it was the stillness of religious devotion. Bernard and his monks missed, as we believe, the plain and simple pathway of Christian service, yet we must never forget that the ground and aim of their life was God's commands, Christ's love, and man's salvation.

CHAPTER IV.

The Paulicians in Western Europe.

"I WILL put my law in their inward parts, and in their heart will I write it; and I will be their God, and they shall be my people. And they shall teach no more every man his neighbour, and every man his brother, saying, Know the Lord: for they shall all know me, from the least of them unto the greatest of them, saith the Lord: for I will forgive their iniquity, and their sin will I remember no more." Thus Jeremiah in prophetic vision portrays the character of the New Covenant. The fulfilment of this prophecy is the theme of the writer of the Epistle to the Hebrews, who repeats it word for word, introducing it by declaring that Christ, who has obtained a more excellent ministry than Aaron, is the mediator of this new and better covenant. In these words the relation of the Christian Church to God is plainly set forth. The Old Covenant required a human priest as mediator, in the New the believer is brought near to God through Christ, the only possible mediator. In the Old Covenant, first Moses, and afterwards the priests, received heavenly gifts and dispensed them to the people, and the people in their turn brought offerings to the priests to be presented to God through their mediation. But in the New Covenant, the Gospel of the free grace of God, the heavenly gifts are poured down direct into the hearts of the believers, and their sins forgiven, without the intervention of any priest or mediator but Christ alone. It was the rejection of this grand truth that led the Church into a labyrinth of error. Instead of proclaiming the liberty of the New Covenant, she reimposed on men's consciences the old Levitical yoke, laden with burdens more numerous and heavier than before. The preaching of the Gospel is a holy obligation, the instruction of the ignorant is a blessed work, the shepherding and ruling of the Church, "not for filthy lucre, or as lording it over the charge," is an honourable office; but to create anew an order of men to whom the gifts and offices of the Spirit are limited, and to place the rest of mankind at a distance from God, with no access to the sanctuary but through that order, is virtually to deny the New Covenant, and to make the word of God of no effect.

The attempts at reformation described in these pages were so many acts of returning faith in the fulfilment of Jeremiah's prophecy. The reformers had a sight of that goodly inheritance which the Saviour had purchased for them, and they strove according to their means to take possession of it both for themselves and for all mankind. Some of them were but partially enlightened, and their mistakes were lamentable; yet inasmuch as by their means the lamp of truth was kept alive, they have a strong claim on our gratitude; and it may be asserted that in respect of Christian doctrine, as well as of purpose and manner of life, they are far better entitled to a place in Church history, than are those who sought to smother their testimony.

Our notice of the monasteries has brought us to the twelfth century; we have now to go back about 200 years in order to mark the dawn of evangelical truth in Western Europe.

The tenth century is often spoken of as the midnight-hour of the Church's history. The Romish historians do not attempt to conceal the deplorable condition into which she had then fallen. "Behold," says Cardinal Baronius, that devoted champion of the papacy, "the 900th year of the Redeemer, the commencement of a new century, which by reason of its ruggedness and barrenness of good has been called the Iron Age, by the deformity of its exuberant evil, the Leaden Age, and by its poverty of writers, the Dark Age. The holy Roman Church which had been without spot or wrinkle, with what filth was it her fate then to be bespattered! . . . How foul was her face, when abandoned women bore rule, at whose will sees were changed, bishops presented, and false pontiffs, their lovers, intruded into Peter's chair! . . . Then was Christ evidently in a deep sleep in the ship, and the ship itself covered with the waves."

But even the darkness of the tenth century was illumined here and there, as we have seen in the monk Nilus, by streaks of golden light. Scarcely also had it closed than a new era began to dawn, —an era during which the Church will, we may trustfully believe, never entirely relapse into the former darkness, but by however slow degrees, and amid whatever dense clouds and fearful storms, will pursue an upward course towards the goal of final glory. To trace the commencement of this new epoch is the object of the present chapter.

Transplanted into Thrace by Constantine Copronymus in the eighth century, and again by John Zimisces in the tenth,[1] the Paulicians gradually made their way into Western Europe. "Taking their course from Dalmatia, they spread into Italy, where they found a soil ready prepared to receive their tenets; for ancient Manicheism had struck its roots so deep that the united efforts of emperors and popes had not been able to tear them up." Men's minds were everywhere ready to hear the gospel message. A craving for Scriptural knowledge and more soul-satisfying food than the effete Church was able to supply had arisen in the countries of the West; and many of the clergy even were ready to welcome any protest against ecclesiastical corruption.

Some of the sects which now made their appearance sprang up independently of Oriental influence. "The Cathari" (the most general name given to the reformers) "were," observes Neander, "by no means all like-minded or of a common origin." Many derived no more from the Paulicians than their first impulse and their acquaintance with the Bible. Once aroused to a living religion, their faith and practice developed itself in its own peculiar manner. Others needed no such impulsion; "in them the devotional study of the Bible produced a practical mysticism." All however in addition to the peculiar Gnostic tenets which were so deep-rooted,[2] aimed at the restoration of the Church to its spiritual and apostolic simplicity. They disclaimed those dogmas which had been added to the primitive Christian faith, such as purgatory, and the intercession of saints, together with the whole hierarchical system. "The sacraments," said some of them, "can in nowise be efficaciously administered by the degenerate priests of the dominant Church, because the question is not one of externals, but of the inward intention, in which these men are wanting. The true baptism is that of the Holy Ghost, whereby men are inwardly purified, the baptism by water being merely symbolical; infant baptism is useless, because infants are incapable either of faith, of purpose of amendment, or of the reception of the Holy Spirit. The true signification of the Lord's Supper is also spiritual, imparting union with Christ as the true bread of the soul; as our Lord says (John vi. 63), 'the flesh profiteth nothing.'" They seem to have rejected or wildly

---

[1] See *ante*, p. 310.

[2] Both contemporary writers and most modern historians call these sectaries Manichæans, but their doctrines connect them with the Gnostics rather than with Manes. All our information regarding them comes through their enemies.

distorted the Old Testament revelation; and yet at the same time to have accepted the precepts of Christ in their faithful and literal sense, condemning war, the shedding of blood, and all asseveration beyond the simple Yea and Nay.

"There must," remarks Neander, "have been something peculiarly affecting and animating in the private assemblies of these heretics. Those who wished to be admitted into their society were to come to them by night; the doors were closed, and the walls hung with lights. The brethren in devout silence formed a circle, into which the president, holding a copy of the Gospels in his hand, introduced the novice; and after a short discourse, in which he exhorted him to ground his belief and hope of eternal salvation on God alone, he set the book on his head, prayed the Lord's prayer, and uttered over him the first words of the gospel of John. The new member then gave to the president, and to all in succession, the kiss of brotherhood; they united in prayer, and he was henceforward regarded as a brother."[1] For a while these sects increased without being regarded as heretical, for they waged no open war with the Church; they frequented the public worship in order to escape suspicion, and if questioned concerning their faith, they repeated the Apostles' Creed. It was only in secret that they sought to disseminate their tenets; and their unobtrusive piety and active benevolence had won for them the love and esteem of all men before the discovery of their heresy.

The new opinions first made their appearance in Italy.[2] In 945 Atto bishop of Vercelli wrote to his flock: "There are amongst you many persons who despise the divine service of the Church; these men, who utter only words of brute ignorance and simplicity, you, forsaking your holy mother the Church and the priests, call prophets." Besides agreeing with the Cathari in regard to the "sacraments," and the unlawfulness of oaths and of the taking of life, the "prophets" maintained that the law of Moses is no rule for Christians; that man cannot be saved by faith without works; and that the Church has no authority to persecute any, even the wicked. They also avowed the untenable dogma of the Novatians and Donatists[3] that the Church, even as an outward institution, can

---

[1] Admission into the community was followed in due time by adoption into the inner circle of the *Perfect*. This was called *Consolamentum*.

[2] Some writers refer the origin of this early dissent to a period antecedent to the arrival of the Paulicians—to Claude of Turin, or even to the primitive ages of the Church.

[3] See *ante*, p. 146.

consist of good men only. They are represented as being decent in their deportment, modest in their dress and discourse, and irreproachable in their morals: their bishops and deacons were mechanics who maintained themselves by their industry. By the year 1040 they had become very numerous at Milan, which was their chief centre.

In the time of Heribert archbishop of Milan,[1] there was a sect whose head-quarters were at the Castle of Montfort, near the town of Asti in Piedmont. Many of the clergy and laity were numbered amongst its adherents, and it was protected by the nobles. If the accounts which their enemies have transmitted are at all to be relied upon, the tenets of these enthusiasts were of a very mystical kind, resembling those of the Euchites and Bogomiles.[2] Moreover they rejected marriage, married persons being admitted amongst them only on the condition of living apart; they led a life of prayer and rigid abstinence, and renounced all earthly possessions. The archbishop despatched a military force against the castle, which was taken, and a number of prisoners were conveyed to Milan. They were led into the market-place, on one side of which stood a cross, on the other a pile of burning wood, and were told to take their choice, either to bow before the cross and confess the Catholic faith, or to plunge into the flames. A few chose the former; but the greater number, covering their faces with their hands, rushed into the fire and were consumed. Some years later (A.D. 1075) Pope Gregory VII. (Hildebrand), writing to the King of Denmark, tells him of a province not far from Rome occupied by heretics, and invites him to send one of his sons with a small force to conquer it. Why the pope did not borrow a sword nearer home for the extirpation of this new growth we are not told.

This side the Alps the Paulician doctrines first attracted attention in Champagne, where a Manichæan named Fortunatus is said to have converted the prince of the country, and where the archbishop of Rheims who had imbibed the heresy was compelled to abjure, A.D. 991. One of the converts, described as a Catharist, put away his wife, and destroyed the cross and the image of Christ. He had many followers. He was reduced to silence by the bishop of Châlons. In the province of Aquitaine (Guienne), in 1010, and again in 1017, certain heretical teachers are accused of " persuading the people to deny baptism, the sign of the Holy Cross, the Church, and the Redeemer of the world Himself, the veneration of the saints, lawful

---

[1] About the year 1028.
[2] See *ante*, p. 310.

marriage, and the eating of flesh, by which means they turned away many simple persons from the faith."[1]

The earliest instance of ecclesiastical action in France against the new heresy, of which we have any account, took place at Orleans A.D. 1022. An Italian lady sojourning in that city, communicated the doctrine she had learned in her own country to several of the clergy, especially to two canons of the "Holy Cross," Stephen, confessor to Queen Constantia, and Lisoius. Amongst the converts was Herebert, chaplain to Arefaste a knight of Rouen. The chaplain boasted to his patron that Orleans was blessed above all other cities with the light of true wisdom. Arefaste suspecting heresy, communicated what he had heard to Duke Richard, who reported it to the king, by whose command he went to Orleans to investigate the matter. The more completely to do this he feigned himself a disciple, and for the protection of his own soul from the poison of the heresy, by the advice of an aged priest of Chartres, he received the Communion daily. Supposing they had to do with an honest inquirer, Stephen and Lisoius unfolded to him their doctrine without reserve. They declared, so Arefaste reported, that Christ was not born of the Virgin Mary, did not suffer for mankind, was not really laid in the tomb, and did not rise from the dead; that water-baptism cannot wash away sins; and that the consecrating words of the priest cannot convert the bread and wine into the body and blood of Christ; that it is a vain thing to make prayers to the saints and martyrs; and that works of righteousness and charity cannot purchase eternal life.[2] "If," objected the pretended inquirer after truth, "I am not to look to good works for salvation, tell me I pray you what I may look to, lest I fall into despair." He was answered that in their further instructions they would show him how he might be cleansed from every stain of sin, and receive the Holy Spirit by the laying on of their hands; and that then he should eat heavenly food, and often see angels, with whom he should travel whither he pleased with ease and despatch. The

---

[1] There is no doubt that some of these sects trod in the footsteps of the monks and hermits both as to celibacy and fasting. In some instances, however, the charge that they rejected marriage probably meant no more than that they "denied it to be a 'sacrament,' and disputed the endless impediments of affinity created by the Romish Church." At the Diet of Worms Aleander absurdly accused Luther of "shamefully vilifying the unalterable law of holy marriage."

[2] Another account makes them reject the revelation of the Scriptures with regard to creation and the Trinity, and deny the necessity of a virtuous life and the future punishment of the wicked.

heavenly food they spoke of he interpreted to be nightly orgies, at which, as was reported of the Early Christians, they indulged in Thyestean banquets.

Whilst Arefaste was thus deceitfully collecting evidence, King Robert arrived with his queen at Orleans; and the next day, having caused the chief men of the party to be apprehended at one of their private meetings, he assembled a council of bishops, before whom they were brought in chains for trial. Called upon to confess their faith, they did this in so guarded a manner as to afford no ground for accusation. But when Arefaste stood forward and recounted the conversations he had had with them, and reminded them of their boast that neither torture nor death would ever move them, they admitted the charges and said they had long held such doctrines. Nay more, they asserted their expectation that both their judges and all the world would, sooner or later, embrace the same faith; and as to the fire with which they were threatened, they spoke as though they expected to be delivered from it unhurt. Their last words to the council were: "Speak to those who mind earthly things and who believe the figments of men written on parchment; to us who have the law written on the heart by the Holy Spirit, and relish nothing but what we have learned from God, the things you speak of are vain. Cease therefore to question us; do with us as you will; for now we see our King ready to receive us to heavenly joys at his right hand." After a nine hours' examination they were condemned to death; and, such of them as were priests being first stripped of their clerical vestments, they were led away, thirteen in number, to a great fire kindled outside the city walls. As they passed the church-door, Queen Constantia with a stick struck her confessor Stephen, and dashed out one of his eyes. When they were bound to the stake, a smile was seen on their faces which continued even in the midst of the flames.[1] Ten of those who were burnt were canons, the remaining three being laymen of distinction. Two, a priest and a nun, drew back. The corpse of another canon who had died in the heresy three years before was, at the command of the bishop, exhumed and cast out on the highway.

---

[1] This is the statement of the more copious narrator. The other principal authority, Glaber Rodulphus, says, "they leaped exulting into the flames, but no sooner felt the heat than they cried out that they had been deceived, and were about to perish for ever. The by-standers moved with pity made efforts to draw them out, but it was too late; they were reduced to ashes." He adds that others of the sect being afterwards discovered were put to death in the same manner.

What was the real creed of these confessors it is difficult to say; it must be borne in mind that all we know of them is derived from the evidence of a spy and the records of a prejudiced court. Such testimony is to be received with the utmost caution. The charge of abominable practices is in direct contradiction to their known character, since their enemies themselves bear witness to their intelligence and the purity of their lives.

Thus for the first time in Europe were men burnt at the stake by the Church which called herself Christian. This deed marks the beginning of the saddest era in the history of the Church. To France was offered the priceless boon of a revival in religious life. She knew not the day of her visitation, and quenched the upspringing light in blood. She did not foresee the long and dark reign of injustice and cruelty she was then inaugurating, and how when the bitter cup was full, it would be given back to her to drink to the very dregs. The *Auto-da-Fés* of the eleventh and twelfth centuries were the forerunners of the sanguinary crusades against the Albigenses, Waldenses and Huguenots, and more remotely, of the national infidelity and the French Revolution. Again and again, with a remorseless hand, the salt was cast out, until nothing remained to save the nation from corruption. If the attempts at reformation so often renewed in France had had free course, the unbelief of the eighteenth century had surely never so stifled the voice of truth as to leave the nation a prey to the curse of intellectual without spiritual life. The seeds of this bitter harvest were sown in the blazing faggots of Orleans.

Three years after the burning at Orleans we find similar opinions reappearing at Arras in French Flanders. In 1025 Gerhard, archbishop of Cambray and Arras, being in the latter city, was informed that a new kind of heresy had been introduced by certain Italians, "who disputed against the sacraments of the Church and overthrew the established religion." The accused were cast into prison, brought before the bishop and examined as to their faith and manner of life. They answered that they were the disciples of one Gundulph, an Italian, by whom they had been instructed in the gospels and epistles—the only Scriptures which they acknowledged —and that they adhered to these in word and life. They discarded the use of the bread and wine, and rejected water-baptism, especially the baptism of infants. They condemned images, denied the sanctity of churches, altars and crosses, and disapproved of incense, oil and bells. They condemned marriage, and asserted that funeral rites were invented by the priests to gratify their avarice, and that it mattered nothing where the dead were interred. They objected to penance as then practised, and denied that the sins of the dead can be expiated by masses or by gifts to the poor. They protested against the difference of rank amongst the clergy, and in their zeal for a spiritual Christianity, they denied the divine authority of Church offices. They summed up the doctrines of Christ and the Apostles in these few comprehensive articles: "To forsake the world, to overcome the flesh, to support one's self by labour, to injure no one, to love the brethren." The bishop was a prudent man. Desiring the reclamation, not the destruction, of these seceders, he ordered his clergy and the monks to fast and pray for them, whilst he himself reasoned with them in a laborious and temperate manner. To afford them time for reflection, he remanded them to prison for three days; at the end of which, whether influenced by the bishop's arguments, or by the thickness of the prison walls, or by the fear of a worse fate, they submitted and sued for pardon. A paper of retractation was drawn up which they signed, and they were then dismissed in peace with the episcopal benediction. But it is to be noted that the recantation was in Latin, a language they did not understand, and that it was explained to them by an interpreter.

Several councils for the suppression of heresy, one at Charroux near Poictiers in 1028, another at the royal city of Rheims in 1049, and a third at Toulouse in 1056, serve to show how wide-spread the religious fermentation had become.[1] By the last two all who kept company with the heretics were declared to be excommunicate. About the same time Berengar, head of the Public School at Tours, drew much attention by assailing the doctrine of transubstantiation. His writings were condemned, 1050—1055, by several councils, and lacking the fortitude of a martyr he recanted.[2] Besides maintaining that the Lord's Supper was to be a spiritual, not an outward communion, he is said to have rejected the baptism of infants, and marriage; and to have declared that the see of Rome is the seat of Satan.

In the midst of the emulation, shown by the bishops for the detection and extinction of heresy, it is refreshing to meet with the name of one who protested manfully, and so far as we know single-

---

[1] Other localities are mentioned. The infection extended even to Goslar, in the Harz Mountains, where in 1052 some "Manichæans" were put to death by order of the Emperor Henry III.

[2] When Lanfranc, archbishop of Canterbury, reproached him with changing his opinions on coming to Rome, Berengar replied: "Human wickedness by outward force can extort a recantation from human weakness; but it is God's Almighty power alone that can effect a change of conviction."

handed, against the intolerant spirit of the times. This was Waso, bishop of Liège, who died about 1047. During the spread of heretical tenets in the diocese of Châlons-sur-Marne, his opinion was asked on the right mode of dealing with heretics. In the spirit of Theodore Studites,[1] he answered: "Although such doctrines must be condemned as unchristian, yet after the example of our Saviour we are bound to bear with those who hold them. The parable of the wheat and the tares teaches us not at once to condemn sinners, but to wait with long-suffering for their repentance. By the servants who were for pulling up the tares as soon as they appeared, are to be understood over-hasty priests. Those who are of the tares to-day may to-morrow bring forth good fruit; and whilst we are thinking of exercising justice by punishing the wicked we may be counteracting the purposes of Him who wills not the death of the sinner, but seeks by patience and long-suffering to bring back all to repentance. Let these men be reserved then to the last harvest of the great Master of the house, for whose sentence we ourselves also must wait with fear and trembling. He can make those who now fight against us, occupy in that heavenly country a higher place than we. And we bishops ought certainly to remember that we did not, at our ordination, receive from God any vocation to slay, but only the vocation to make alive."

In this century the attempts at reformation were of a sporadic nature, often questionable as to Scriptural doctrine, and avoiding rather than courting publicity. In the next century we shall come upon a clearer faith, a wider and more general action, and a fearless assault on the stronghold of ecclesiastical abuses.

CHAPTER V.

The Reformers of the Twelfth Century.

The first noteworthy preacher of the reformed doctrines in this century is a priest named Peter of Brueys. Through the diligent study of the New Testament he had acquired a clear conception of the worship of God in spirit and in truth. Regarding faith as necessary to baptism, he rejected the baptism of infants; and when in consequence of re-immersing those who joined them his followers were called Anabaptists, they demurred to the name, alleging that

---

[1] See *ante*, p. 309.

the baptism performed in infancy was no baptism at all. He rejected the celebration of the Lord's Supper, holding that Christ once for all, before He suffered, having broken His body in the bread and distributed it to His disciples, the same thing could not be repeated. He vehemently opposed the sacrifice of the Mass, which he regarded as the pillar on which the dominion of the priesthood chiefly rested. "Trust not," he exclaimed to the people, "in your misleading clergy, when they pretend to produce for you the body of Christ and to deliver it to you for the salvation of your souls." He condemned prayers, offerings and alms for the dead. "The state of a man after death," he said, "depends on his conduct during life, nothing that is done afterwards can be of any avail." Burdened with the pomp of public worship, the multiplied ceremonies which had converted it into a mechanical service, and the artificial chanting which affected the senses rather than the heart, he says: "God is mocked by such services; He to whom pious feeling alone is acceptable is neither brought near by loud vociferation, nor propitiated by musical melodies." In like manner he despised *consecrated* buildings : " God is to be worshipped in the shop or in the market-place equally as in the church; He hearkens to the sincere suppliant whether praying before an altar or in a workshop."

But although Peter had a clear insight into the teaching of the New Testament, he was far from having imbibed its genuine spirit. Lamentably deficient in judgment and charity, he suffered his zeal to betray him into fanaticism. He not only condemned the superstitious reverence for the Cross, but insisted that as the memorial of Christ's sufferings, every representation of it ought, by way of avenging His death, to be cast away and destroyed.[1] This maxim was carried out by his followers only too literally. On a certain Good Friday they brought together all the crucifixes they could collect, and making of them a great fire, roasted meat thereat and invited every one to partake. They even proceeded to pull down altars, scourge priests, and compel monks to marry, "What other result," asks Neander, "could be anticipated from the spirit of unbridled liberty pervading so rude an age, when we see that at the more advanced era of the Reformation, all the caution of the reformers was insufficient to prevent men from confounding earthly licentiousness with Christian freedom, and to restrain the wild bursts of human passion ?"

Peter preached first in Dauphiné, his native country; being driven thence, he travelled up and down for twenty years in Gascony, Languedoc and Provence, waging war against superstition,

---

[1] In this respect he resembled Claude of Turin. See *ante*, p. 315.

and making many proselytes. " In Provence there was nothing to be seen but Christians re-baptized, churches profaned, altars pulled down, and crosses burnt." But about 1124, being at the city of St. Gilles in Languedoc, Peter, at the instigation of the clergy, was seized by an infuriated mob, hurried away and burnt at the stake, "thus passing," says even the large-hearted Peter of Cluny, " from temporal to eternal fire."

In 1119 a council at Toulouse issued the following canon in reference to Peter and other schismatics. " We condemn as heretics, and exclude from the Church of God, those who under the pretence of religion reject the Sacrament of the body and blood of Jesus Christ, Infant Baptism, Priesthood, Holy Orders, and lawful Marriage; and we enjoin that they should be suppressed by the secular power."

Not many years afterwards, Peter of Cluny, being on a tour in Gascony, set himself to repair the breaches which he everywhere found in the Church. He drew up a refutation of the errors, as he deemed them to be, of the Petrobrusians (the followers of Peter de Brueys), and sent it to the bishops of the province, telling them that it was their duty by preaching to drive the sectaries from their hiding-places, and if unable of themselves to do this they must invoke the secular power. " But since," he says, " it becomes Christian charity to labour rather for the conversion than for the extirpation of heretics, authority and reason are the great means to be employed, so that if they profess themselves to be Christians, they may bow to the one, or if they desire to be considered as men, they may acknowledge the other." [1]

Whilst the abbot of Cluny was thus unconsciously seeking to quench gospel light, a denizen of his own cloisters had been visited by heavenly illumination and prepared to be a Witness for the truth. This was Henry of Lausanne, a monk of Cluny and a deacon, who, like Peter, taking the New Testament for his guide, saw that the Gospel points to a life of practical activity, not to one of contemplative inaction, and felt himself called to minister to the wants of the people, who were either totally neglected or led astray by a hireling clergy. Accordingly he sallied forth in his monkish attire, and waiting for no invitation took up his abode, in one house after another, preaching the spiritual life, and contented with such fare as was set before him.

From Lausanne, where he appears to have first preached, he

---

[1] The abbot traces the new doctrines to the Cottian Alps, " whence," he says, " they had spread over all the south of France."

came into Central France. Men like-minded joined him as he went along, and an apostolical society was formed under his direction. Having no controversy, as Peter of Brueys had, with the symbol of the Saviour's passion, he caused to be carried before him a banner on which was worked a figure of the cross,[1] as an invitation to all men to take up the cross of Christ. At first he confined himself to preaching repentance, and denouncing that sham Christianity in which the fruits of a godly life are wanting. Soon however he proceeded to warn men against a worldly-minded clergy, those false guides whose teaching and example did more to promote wickedness than to restrain it. Especially he attacked their unchastity; and less enlightened than his compatriot on the subject of celibacy, he joined the monks in supporting the harsh decrees of Gregory VII. (Hildebrand) against the married clergy.[2]

Henry's appearance was such as of itself to command attention. The rapid changes in his countenance are likened by the contemporary chronicler to " a ruffled and tempestuous sea. He was as yet very young; he wore short hair, his beard shaved; was large in stature, but very sorrily clothed; walked apace, and barefooted even in the hardest time of winter. His ordinary retreats were the cottages of peasants; he lived all day under porticoes; ate and slept on some hill or other in the open air. The women cried him up for a great Servant of God,"—it is, as usual, a hostile pen which is describing him—" and gave out that no person could have a greater faculty than he of converting the most obdurate hearts; and that he was endued with the spirit of prophecy, to discern the most inward recesses of the conscience, and the most private sins. He had a natural eloquence, and a tone of voice resembling thunder." Contrited under the searching ministry of this Whitfield of the Middle Ages, the people hastened to confess their sins and to renounce their loose manner of life.

On Ash-Wednesday A.D. 1116, two of Henry's disciples in the garb of penitents appeared with their banner at Le Mans, the chief city of the province of Maine. They came to see if their master might visit the city as a preacher of repentance during the season of Lent. Henry's fame had preceded him, and the messengers " were received by the people as angels." The bishop Hildebert, a discreet and pious man, gave them a friendly reception, Henry not having as yet come under suspicion of heresy. Himself about starting for Rome, the bishop gave directions to his archdeacon

---

[1] Or it may have been an iron cross on a staff.
[2] Gregory was pope from 1073 to 1085.

that Henry should have liberty to preach. The effect of his preaching was wonderful. Not only were the common people drawn and bound to him by an invisible chain, but the younger clergy eagerly gathered round him, and prepared a stage in a public place from whence he could be heard by the whole city. Nevertheless the higher clergy set their faces against him, and when the citizens, in revenge, withdrew from the churches and insulted the priests, they applied for protection to the civil power. At the same time they addressed a letter to Henry upbraiding him with abusing the confidence reposed in him, and with instigating the people to schism, sedition and heresy. They forbade him under pain of excommunication to preach in any part of the diocese. Henry refused to recognize their authority, and when the prohibitory letter was read in public he shook his head at every sentence, and exclaimed, "Thou liest!" Not the working-classes only, but substantial citizens looked up to Henry as their spiritual guide; gold and silver were freely placed at his disposal, so that if he had been actuated by sordid motives he might easily have made himself rich. If he failed to restrain his own and the people's passions in the good cause he had at heart, he did not at least use his great influence for his own emolument, but only to raise the moral character of the people. Although he insisted on the celibacy of the clergy, Henry strenuously promoted marriage amongst the laity, striving to break down the arbitrary barriers of relationship which the Church had set up, as well as those of caste which had grown up between the free-born and the serfs. He also set himself against the prevalent custom of choosing a wife for the sake of her dowry.

When Hildebert returned from Rome he found the tone of feeling in Le Mans strangely altered. He himself was no longer received with the customary demonstrations of joy and reverence. His episcopal blessing was despised. "We have," said the people, "another father, priest and intercessor, more virtuous in life, more eminent in knowledge, more exalted in authority. The clergy hate him because they are afraid that by means of the Scriptures he will expose their vices, their incontinence and their false doctrine." Hildebert as we have said was a prudent man ; he saw the danger of attempting to put down Henry's influence by force. Accordingly he sought a private interview, in which he prevailed upon him, either by authority or argument, quietly to leave the diocese and betake himself to some other field.[1]

---

[1] "The bishop," says Milman, "bade him repeat the Morning Hymn, which finding he was unable to do, he concluded him to be a poor ignorant man."

Notwithstanding the allusion just made to the false doctrines of the priests, it does not appear that Henry, whilst he was at Le Mans, made any distinct attack either upon the dogmas or the ceremonial of the Church. It was otherwise when, directing his course southward, he came to the country in which Peter of Brueys had already laboured. The abbot of Cluny in his treatise speaks of Henry of Lausanne as the heir to Peter's wickedness.[1] Here Henry published a tract against the abuses of the Church, in which he gave a more systematic shape to the teaching of his predecessor. The clergy were greatly alarmed, and the archbishop of Arles, having succeeded in getting possession of Henry's person (A.D. 1134), carried him to the Council of Pisa, at which Pope Innocent II. presided. By this council he was pronounced a heretic, and placed under the custody of Bernard of Clairvaux. Recovering his liberty, he returned to the south of France, and recommenced preaching around Toulouse and Albi, where the anti-Romish tendencies were strong and were favoured by the feudal lords who were striving to render themselves independent of their sovereigns. Here he laboured for ten years with remarkable success.[2] Bernard of Clairvaux, whose watchful eye took in the whole Gallic Church with its wants and perils, roused himself, and called upon the count of St. Gilles and Toulouse to put down the heresy. "We have heard," he tells him, "what great things Henry the heretic is doing every day in the churches of God, wandering up and down, a ravenous wolf in sheep's clothing. The churches are without people; the people without priests; the priests without becoming reverence; and Christians without Christ. The invocation of saints, offerings for the dead, pilgrimages, festivals, are all neglected, and baptism is denied to infants, who are thus robbed of salvation."

Pope Eugenius III., who had been driven from Rome by a rival and was keeping his court at Avignon, saw the necessity of adopting energetic measures if the new heresy was to be prevented from overspreading the land. He sent into Languedoc the cardinal bishop Alberic of Ostia, who however refused to undertake the task unless Bernard would go with him. "Henry," he said, "is an antagonist, who can only be put down by the vanquisher of Abelard and of Arnold of Brescia." Bernard's strength was failing, and he hesitated; but his old zeal for the Church prevailed, and he set out for the heretical provinces, where he not only preached with extra-

---

[1] Milman says Henry joined Peter, and after the latter was burned retired into Gascony.

[2] His followers were called after him Henricians.

ordinary success, but is said to have performed many miracles. The legate had come in all the pomp of office with a train of attendant clergy. The intelligent weavers and the spiritually-minded priests who had left the Romish communion despised such show, and set his authority at nought. But Bernard's appearance, which refuted the common charge that the ecclesiastics had all become worldly, produced a totally different impression. At Albi, a focus of the defection, a vast multitude assembled to hear him. In his discourse he examined in succession the several articles of the heresy, and showed their deviation from the Roman Catholic faith, and then called upon the people to declare which of the two they would choose. Carried away by his eloquence and the mastery of his spirit, they exclaimed that they abhorred heresy, and were desirous only to return to the bosom of the Church. "Return, then," replied Bernard, "and that we may the better distinguish those who are sincere, let all true penitents lift up their hands." It is said that every hand was lifted up.

The bishops once more laid hands on Henry, and he was carried in chains before a council held at Rheims in 1148. Here he was condemned to death, but at the intercession of archbishop Samson, who presided, and who deprecated the shedding of blood, the sentence was commuted to "imprisonment for life, with meagre diet, that he might be brought to repentance."

At the same time there was a stirring in the provinces of Périgueux, Guienne and Dauphiné. In Périgueux, a monk named Pontius drew away from the Catholic Communion nobles, clerics, monks and nuns. He preached the same doctrine as Henry, treated the Host with the utmost contempt, and seems to have altogether rejected the bread and wine. It is said the most unlettered peasant who joined him acquired in a week sufficient knowledge of Scripture to put the priests to silence. The followers of Pontius were credited by the common people with being consummate sorcerers. Especially it was impossible to bind them. "Loaded with chains, stowed carefully in a wine butt turned bottom upwards, and well watched by a strong guard, they yet in the morning were found to have evaporated, as it were, and were not seen again till they chose to show themselves." A letter to Pope Lucius II. from Dauphiné in 1144, complains that the plague of heresy has broken out in that province. "Baptism, the Mass, and the imposition of hands by the priests, are counted for nothing. The sectaries have their neophytes, their priests and even their bishops, as we have. Every part of France," it is added, "is corrupted by the poison issuing from this province."

The Catholic world now began to awake to the magnitude of the danger with which it was threatened, and to devise comprehensive measures to avert it. In 1162 Pope Alexander III., who like Eugenius had fled from Rome to Avignon, declared that every secular prince who should not employ his authority for the suppression of heresy should be accursed; and the next year he called a council at Tours for the purpose of giving effect to this declaration. A large number of bishops, abbots, priests and laymen, chiefly French and English, assembled; and the decrees issued by them constitute the first solemn act of the Church of Rome, which can properly be called *inquisitional*. "There has," they say, "sprung up in the country about Toulouse a damnable heresy, which creeping on like a cancer, has spread into Gascony and infected many other provinces. Serpent-like it conceals itself in its own windings, and glides along, threatening danger to the simple and unwary." As an antidote to this poison, they prescribe the same remedy which, a few years ago, was made so much use of in Ireland for political purposes. "Wherefore we command all bishops and priests to keep a watchful eye upon the heretics, and to forbid all men under pain of excommunication to harbour or assist or *trade with them*, that so, through deprivation of the benefits of society, they may be forced to repent of their error. And whosoever shall attempt to oppose this decree shall be smitten with the same anathema."[1] To which these words were added: "Forasmuch as they frequently assemble in hiding-places, let such conventicles be closely searched, and if the attenders be found guilty, let them be restrained with canonical severity."

A few years afterwards (1176), a party of Henricians (called by themselves *Boni-Homines*, Good Men) were apprehended in Languedoc, and brought before a council at Lombers near Albi. They held that the sacrament of the body and blood of Christ may be consecrated by every good man, whether priest or layman. Respecting confession, they would go no further than the apostle James: "Confess your sins one to another, and pray one for another that ye may be healed." They regarded all oaths as unlawful. Of the Scriptures, they received only the New Testament and such parts of the Old as are referred to by Christ Himself or his apostles. They held that when men of unworthy lives are

---

[1] On Alexander's return to Rome he held a general council (the third Lateran, A.D. 1179), at which the decrees of the Council of Tours were re-enacted with additional severities. His successor Lucius III., at the Council of Verona, A.D. 1184, made a law of the same kind, and with a still nearer approach to the office of the Inquisition.

ordained to the priesthood they are not priests or bishops, but hypocrites. When the president of the council, after citing many Scripture passages, proceeded to pass sentence on them as heretics, they retorted that it was he who was a heretic and not they, and that they were not careful to answer him further, because the Lord had commanded to beware of false prophets. Then turning to the people they made a Catholic confession in accordance with the creed of the Church, and to which little or no exception could be taken; but when required to swear to it they refused, because Christ has forbidden all swearing. Their confession was in consequence held to be invalid, and they were condemned accordingly. Their symathisers however seem to have been too powerful to allow the punishment to follow.

The next place to be stained by the red hand of persecution is Vezelay in Burgundy. This little town was famous for a Benedictine monastery founded in the ninth century, and rendered especially sacred by the supposed relics of Mary Magdalene brought thither in the tenth. The town and the church (the latter being now the only remains of the monastery) crown the summit of a steep hill, and are conspicuous from all the country around. The pleasant river Cure flows far below, and the prospect looking up the winding valley to the south, and the granite ravines to the north, is one of the most picturesque in Central France. The abbey-church, a magnificent structure, was a great shrine of pilgrimage, and attracted commerce and wealth to the town.

Several notable events happened at Vezelay in the twelfth century. Here in 1146 Bernard of Clairvaux preached the second Crusade, Louis VII., with his Queen, the beautiful and haughty Eleanor, and a great train of nobles and retainers coming there to meet him. The castle being too small they assembled on an adjacent hill, where a platform was erected for the king and the preacher. Both wore the white cross. Bernard in his eloquence rivalled Peter the Hermit at Clermont in the previous century, and when he had spoken the whole multitude rent the air with shouts of "Crosses, crosses!"[1] They crowded to the stage to receive the holy badge which, in the words of an eye-witness, "he flung abroad rather than distributed." The great sheaf of crosses he had brought

---

[1] On another occasion Bernard "preached to the Knights Templars, then in the dawn of their valour and glory. The Koran," says Milman, "is tame to this fierce hymn of battle. 'The Christian who slays the unbeliever in the Holy War is sure of his reward, more sure if he is slain. The Christian glories in the death of the pagan, because Christ is glorified; by his own death both he himself and Christ are still more glorified.'"

being dispersed, he tore up his own garments to satisfy the eager claimants, and as long as he remained in the town he did nothing else than make crosses.[1] Another famous event is the excommunication of his adversaries pronounced in 1165 by Thomas à Becket in this church. Again a few years later, in 1180, Richard Cœur de Lion and the French King Philip Augustus, with a splendid host of mail-clad knights and men-at-arms, lodged at Vezelay on their way to the third Crusade. These events filled the trumpet of fame. What we are about to relate is an obscure transaction which has to be sought in the by-ways of history.

Two years after Becket had anathematized his enemies, a few ignorant men, to whom the names of Publicani and Telonarii are given, were apprehended at Vezelay on a charge of heresy. They were put to the torture, but nothing tangible being elicited they were remanded by the abbot to separate prisons. The clergy in alarm collected their whole strength to convert or crush this handful of poor Christian men. The archbishops of Lyons and Narbonne came to the monastery, with the bishops of Nevers, Laon and Nismes, and many abbots and learned theologians, and were occupied sixty days with the examination and judgment. The accused were pronounced guilty of denying everything but God; but this may mean no more than that they would not subscribe the errors which a faithless Church had engrafted on the truth. They were condemned for rejecting "the sacraments, infant-baptism, the Eucharist, the sign of the life-giving cross, holy water, consecrated churches," tithes and oblations, marriage, the monastic life and the priesthood. Two of them were disposed to recant, and were allowed the water ordeal. One passed through safe; the other case being more doubtful, the man was plunged again, and condemned, to the general satisfaction. But the abbot having still some doubt, he was put to a death less tormenting than the flames. Then the abbot appealed to the assembly: "What, my brethren, think ye we ought

---

[1] Regarding this crusade, Dean Waddington observes, "the history of religious war has not recorded any expedition at the same time more fatal or more fruitless. After two or three years of suffering and disaster almost uninterrupted, a miserable remnant of survivors returned to relate their misfortunes and marvel at their discomfiture. A general outcry was raised against St. Bernard; innumerable widows and orphans demanded of the prophet their husbands and their sires; or at least they claimed the sacred laurels which he had promised. . . . He asserted that his prophecies were only conditional; that in foretelling the success of the crusaders, he had *assumed* their righteousness and the purity of their lives; that their own enormous crimes had averted or suspended the designs of Providence!"

to do with those who persevere in their obstinacy?" The whole assembly shouted: "Let them be burned! let them be burned!" Accordingly they were carried down, seven in number, to the neighbouring valley of Ecouan and burned. We do not even know the names of these martyrs.

> "They lived unknown
> Till persecution dragged them into fame,
> And chased them up to heaven. Their ashes flew
> —No marble tells us whither. With their names
> No bard embalms and sanctifies his song:
> And history so warm on meaner themes
> Is cold on this."

Again, at Arras in Flanders in 1188, four heretics, called Paterini, after examination in the presence of the archbishop of Rheims and the count of Flanders, were committed to the flames. At a council held at Sens in 1198, the abbot of St. Martin in Nevers was deposed, and the dean of the cathedral suspended on an accusation of belonging to the sect of the Publicani. Some of the doctrinal views propounded in this age were highly spiritual. The abbot Joachim, who at first presided over the monastery of Corace in Calabria and afterwards founded that of Floris, says: "So long as we see only through a glass, darkly, it is necessary for us to cling to symbols, but when the Spirit of truth shall come and shall teach us all truth, what further need shall we have of symbols?"

Persecution, in the unsystematic way in which it was then carried out, seems to have done little towards effecting its object. We find the archbishop of Narbonne complaining to Louis VII. towards the end of his long reign: "We are pressed with many calamities, among which there is one which most of all affects us, namely, that the Catholic faith is extremely shaken in this our diocese; and St. Peter's boat is so violently tossed by the waves that it is in danger of sinking." In 1178 a delegation of papal visitors describes Toulouse as "the abomination of desolation, where the heretics exercise the chief power over the people and lord it among the clergy." About the same year an edict cited by Hoveden speaks of the "heretics whom some call Cathari, others Publicani, others Paterini, as being on the increase in Gascony, Albi and other places, and no longer exercising their impiety in private, but stalking abroad." In like manner Stephen of Tournay, writing to John de Bellesmains bishop of Poictiers, 1181, describes Languedoc, Gascony and Septimania (Roussillon) as countries where infidelity had taken root, and inconceivable treachery and trouble prevailed. "In my passage to Toulouse," he says, "whither the king sent me, I saw the walls of half-ruined churches and half-burnt monasteries, and where formerly stood the dwellings of men, now only the abode of wild beasts."[1]

Thus before fifty years had elapsed from the date of Bernard's progress in Languedoc, the whole south of France may be said to have swarmed with Protestants, who in the next century received the general name of Albigenses.[2]

A similar movement was at work in Italy. Unhappily we know little of the men by whom it was carried on. The name chiefly known to history is associated with a political revolution. Arnold, a priest of Brescia in Lombardy, conceived the idea of bringing back the priestly order to the apostolic pattern. Not the luxury and debauchery of the clergy only, but their possession of worldly property, and their interference with secular business, seemed to him at variance with the teaching of the New Testament. Like the French Reformers, he held that worldly ecclesiastics were not only unfit to discharge the priestly functions, but were in fact not bishops or priests at all, and that the secularised Church was no longer the House of God. His life corresponded with his doctrines; he assumed the monastic garb, and lived in poverty and ascetic severity. Brescia and the Lombard cities in general were ripe for such teaching; his invectives against the pope and the bishops fell on his hearers like a spark on tow. His eloquence is described by Bernard as " sweet yet powerful, sharp as a sword yet soft as oil." The agitation spread to Rome. Pope Innocent II. hastened to interfere, and by a decree of the second Lateran Council, 1139, Arnold was condemned and banished from Italy. He fled to France and thence to the Alps, where he may have rekindled the embers still remaining of the teaching of Claude of Turin three centuries

---

[1] To the same effect testifies a troubadour, who sang the destruction of the heretics: "This heresy, which the Lord cursed, had in its power the whole land from Béziers to Bordeaux."

[2] The names under which the reformers were known were numerous. Cathari is Greek for Puritans; it was often corrupted into Gazari. Publicani or Poplicani is taken to be a corruption of Paulicani (Du Cange); and as the name so corrupted (our Publicans) is in the Latin Vulgate the equivalent of telōnai, the tax-farmers of the New Testament, the heretics were also called Telonarii. Poplicani was sometimes corrupted into Piphles. Bulgari (French, Bougres) plainly connects them with Bulgaria, part of the Balkan country colonized by the Paulicians. In Italy the usual designation was Paterini (otherwise Patellini), derived, according to Mosheim, from the name of a place where they held their meetings; according to others it signifies smooth and flattering hypocrites. Tisserands (weavers) has already been referred to, as also Boni-Homines (in Provençal, Bos Homos).

before. The Church of the Waldenses has inscribed Arnold's name as well as Claude's in her spiritual genealogy. Bernard wrote to the pope to secure Arnold's person and to burn his books: but he remained unharmed in Switzerland five years, and then reappeared in Rome. The political agitation set going by his impassioned preaching had produced a revolution in that city. The people had thrown off both papal and imperial rule, and had reinstated the ancient government by consuls. The Republic lasted ten years, at the end of which time its inherent weakness, and the combined power of the Emperor Frederic I. and Pope Adrian IV. caused its destruction. Arnold was given up to the authorities, and hanged at Rome by order of the prefect. His body was burned and his ashes thrown into the Tiber, lest his bones should be preserved as relics by the Romans who were devoted to him.

Later in the twelfth century we find Protestant doctrines making alarming progress, especially in the north of Italy. The headquarters of the sectaries were at Milan. In 1199 a papal lieutenant was slain at Orvieto; and in 1207 Innocent III. went himself to Viterbo to "sponge out the filthiness of the Paterini with which the city was violently infected." Warned of his approach, the Paterini fled. Search was made for all their harbourers, abettors and defenders; their houses were razed to the ground, their property seized, and unlimited power given to the city authorities to extinguish the heresy.

If now we look towards the Rhine we shall find the same tokens of religious fermentation. In the year in which Henry of Lausanne was put to death, 1147, Evervinus, provost of Steinfeld, near Cologne, wrote thus to Bernard: "There have been lately some heretics discovered amongst us, two of whom stood forth before an assembly, the lord archbishop himself and many of the nobility being present, and maintained their tenets from the words of Christ and the Apostles. But when they could proceed no further, they desired that a day might be appointed when they might bring more skilful advocates, promising if these should fail to return to the Church. Whereupon, after they had been admonished for three days, and were still unwilling to repent, the people, incited by overmuch zeal, seized upon them, and hurried them to the stake, where they perished. What is most wonderful in all this is, that they bore the flames not only with patience, but with joyfulness, so that I should be glad, holy father, if thou couldst tell me how these members of the devil could exhibit a courage and constancy scarcely to be found in the most pious of the faithful. These people," he continues, "assert that the

Church is to be found with them only, because they alone tread in Christ's footsteps, and lead an apostolic life. 'We are Christ's poor,' they say; 'we have no certain abode, but flee from city to city, like the apostles and martyrs, enduring persecution; and this notwithstanding that we lead a holy life with fasting and abstinence, persevere day and night in prayers and labours, and from the world seek only what is necessary to preserve life. As for you, ye have peace with the world because ye are of the world.' That which we call the sacrament they stigmatize as a shadow and a mere tradition of men, but they themselves at their daily meals, according to the example of Christ and his Apostles, consecrate by the Lord's Prayer their meat and drink into the body and blood of Christ to nourish themselves therewith. Besides water-baptism, they baptize, so they pretend, with the Holy Ghost and fire, alleging the testimony of John the Baptist, and assert that every one of the elect has power to baptize and to consecrate at their meals the body and blood of Christ. In their diet they use neither meat nor milk; they also condemn marriage, the reason of which I could not discover." [1]

Evervinus then proceeds to speak of another kind of heretics, through whose dissensions with the former both sects had been discovered. "These," he says, "deny that the body of Christ is laid on the altar, because the priests have lost the power of consecration. They reject infant-baptism as not requiring faith. Second marriages they look upon as adultery. They put no confidence in the intercession of the saints, nor in fasting and penance, because at whatsoever time a sinner repents his sins are forgiven; nor in the fire of purgatory, because souls, as soon as they leave the body, enter either into rest or punishment, as saith Solomon: 'In the place where the tree falleth, there shall it be.' Those who were burned told us their heresy had been hidden from the time of the ancient martyrs, and had been preserved in Greece and some other countries. We, therefore, holy father," he concludes, "entreat thee to use thy vigilance against these manifold mischiefs, and direct thy pen against these wild beasts of the reeds; not deeming it sufficient to answer us that the tower of David to which we may flee is fortified with bulwarks, that a thousand bucklers hang on its walls, all shields of mighty men. For the sake of us who are simple and slow of understanding be pleased to gather all these arms into one place that they may be readily found, and mighty to resist these monsters. For those of them who have returned to the

---

[1] Marriage by a Romish priest should probably be understood, for in the same account the wives of the heretics are spoken of.

Church tell us that these people are everywhere to be found in great numbers, and amongst them are many of our clergy and monks."

Bernard was just then writing his discourses on the Canticles, and in two of these, under the text, "Take us the foxes, the little foxes that spoil the vineyards" (ii. 15), he disposes of the heretics. "Inquire of them the author of their sect, and they will assign none. All other pests of this stamp have had their founders, and been called by their name; as the Manichæans from Manes, the Arians from Arius, the Nestorians from Nestorius; but this heresy has no title, for it is not derived from man, nor received through man, but from demons. That they are not convinced by reasons is because they understand them not; nor corrected by authority, because they acknowledge it not; nor influenced by persuasion, because they prefer death to conversion. I approve the zeal of those who were so ready to inflict the punishment, but I do not applaud the deed, because faith should spring from persuasion, not from force. Yet it is unquestionably better that such should be restrained by the sword than be suffered to seduce others into their own error. . . . Those who wonder that the offenders went to execution, not with fortitude only, but as it appears even with joy, have not observed how great is the power of the devil over the hearts as well as the bodies of such as have given themselves up to him. The constancy of martyrs and the pertinacity of heretics have nothing in common; in the one it is the fruit of piety, in the other it is nothing but obduracy." The admissions, however, which Bernard elsewhere makes outweigh all the reproach which he casts upon this despised people: "If you interrogate them respecting their faith, nothing can be more Christian; if as to their conversation, nothing can be more blameless; and what they say they confirm by their deeds. They attack no one, they circumvent no one, they defraud no one. Their faces are pale with fasting. They eat not the bread of idleness, but labour with their own hands. Where is now the fox? By their fruits ye shall know them. Women forsake their husbands, and husbands their wives, to join them; clergy and priests, quitting their people and their churches, are found among them, unshorn and unshaven, herding with weavers and spinsters."

Tidings of the heresy and of the cruel death of its authors came to the ears of the pious Hildegarde, abbess of St. Rupert on the Rhine, one of the most enlightened women of the day.[1] Her

---

[1] Hildegarde was as bold as she was wise. The German clergy at that time had sunk into a depraved condition; she thus addressed the ecclesiastics of

judgment was that such offenders should be deprived of their goods and driven from the Church, but not put to death, for even they, she said, bear the image of God. Hildegarde's opinion represents the limit of toleration which the gentlest and most charitable spirits in that age were prepared to grant. Even Peter the Venerable would have found it hard to go further. The real temper of the time is seen in the reply which William of Paris made to the same reformers when they referred to our Lord's parable of the tares and the wheat. "Christ," so writes this dutiful son of papal Rome, "could not mean that the tares should be spared at the expense of the wheat. Whenever the ungodly increase to the injury of God's people they must be extirpated. It is true that those who belong to the tares may possibly be converted into wheat, but this is a matter of uncertainty; whereas that by their means the wheat is being changed into tares is a matter of perfect certainty. A few tares are sufficient to choke a large field of wheat. Very rare and difficult is it to convert a heretic, but very easy and common to subvert the faithful."

The Cathari of whom these Cologne reformers were a branch are said further to have rejected the authority of tradition, priestly assumption, pilgrimages and the worship of saints and images, to have practised a rigid asceticism, and laid great stress on good works. Some denied the lawfulness of war, objected to capital punishment, and would admit of no other asseveration than a simple yea and nay. They were zealous in disseminating their principles, travelling from village to village, and from house to house. Frequenting as merchants fairs and markets, they used the intercourse of trade as a means of introducing their tenets. They did not despise learning, but sent their sons to Paris for education. A beautiful feature of their life was the close fellowship which subsisted between the members. As was the case in the early days of Christianity, every stranger who brought from the brethren a letter of recommendation met with a hospitable reception; whilst a liberal collection was made for such as fell into indigence.

A few years later, A.D. 1160, the same people are described by Eckbert, abbot of Schönauge in Trèves: "They are increased to such multitudes that the Church of God is in much danger. They are well-armed with passages of holy Scripture. They boast that

---

Cologne: "By the teaching of the Holy Scriptures, which are the out-pouring of the sacred fire of the Holy Spirit, ye should be the fathers of the Church; but ye are debased and fallen, being devoted to the pursuit of riches and all vanity. Under the pretence that you cannot attend to everything, you have abandoned the teaching of your people."

the true faith and worship of Christ is nowhere to be found but in their meetings, which they hold in cellars and weaving-rooms. In such underground dwellings they lead as they pretend the life of the apostles. They scoff at the ringing of bells, piously used in our churches, by which men are warned to pray for the dead and reminded of their own end. As for the mass they utterly contemn it, and they pretend that the blessed pope Sylvester [in the fourth century] was the Antichrist of whom Paul speaks, and that since his time the Church is dead."

In 1163 some Cathari (from Flanders), four men and one young girl, again ventured to approach Cologne, and took up their abode secretly in a barn near the city. But as they did not attend public worship on the Lord's day they were seized by the neighbours and brought before the priests. After a long examination, in which they steadfastly persisted in their doctrines and in their resolution not to conform to the Romish worship, they were excommunicated, and delivered over to the secular arm. Being led out of the city, they were committed to the flames, but through the compassion of the by-standers the girl was held back, in the hope that terrified by the torment of the others she might recant. Her ardour however was equal to that of her companions; loosing herself by a sudden effort she sprang into the flames and was consumed.

In 1160 a little band of zealous reformers came from Germany to England to preach the truth which they had learned. They were known under the name of Publicani; and the history of their unsuccessful mission is related by one of our monkish chroniclers, William of Newbury, who, full as he is of detestation for the heresy, is little aware how moving an appeal to posterity he is making on their behalf. Nothing in the annals of the martyrs is more touching than the patience, the undeserved suffering and pitiful death of these witnesses, obscure on earth, but crowned (we may believe) with everlasting glory on high.

"There were of these vagrants," writes the chronicler, "men and women over thirty. Dissembling their error they entered the country quietly, their object being the propagation of that pestilential heresy. Their leader, one Gerard, was in some small measure literate, the rest were evidently uninstructed and rustic. During their sojourn in England they added to their company one only, a woman, who was circumvented by their poisonous whisperings, and fascinated, so it is reported, by magical arts. They could not long be concealed. Inquiries concerning them were made by some persons out of curiosity, and being foreigners, they were apprehended and kept in public custody.

"The king, Henry II., unwilling either to dismiss or punish them without investigation, ordered a council of bishops to be assembled at Oxford. Before this council the accused answered, through the mouth of one who was instructed amongst them, that they were Christians, and revered the doctrine of the Apostles. Being interrogated on the several articles of our sacred faith, they answered rightly indeed, concerning the nature of the heavenly Physician, but perversely concerning the remedies whereby he deigns to heal man's moral infirmity; for they spoke against the divine sacraments, expressing detestation of holy baptism, the Eucharist, and marriage; and wickedly derogating from the Catholic unity to which these divine aids belong. When they were pressed with arguments from holy Scripture, they answered that they believed as they had been taught, but were unwilling to dispute concerning their faith. Then being admonished to do penance, and to be re-united to the body of the Church, they spurned that salutary counsel. The threats too which were piously held up before them, in order that they might retract through fear—if through no other motive,—they treated with derision, absurdly applying to themselves those words of our Lord, 'Blessed are they that have been persecuted for righteousness' sake, for theirs is the kingdom of heaven.' Then the bishops in order that the heretical poison might not spread, having publicly pronounced them heretics, delivered them over to the Catholic prince for the infliction of corporal punishment.

"Henry's sentence was that the mark of heretical infamy should be branded on their foreheads, and that they should be publicly beaten with rods out of the city, strictly enjoining that no one should presume either to receive them under his roof, or minister to them any consolation. The sentence having been proclaimed, they were led forth to that most just punishment, and they went rejoicing with light steps; their teacher going before them and singing, 'Blessed are ye when men shall reproach you.' To such a pitch had the spirit of seduction deceived them! The woman whom they had led astray, induced by fear of suffering, left them, confessed her error and obtained reconciliation. But the hateful company of heretics underwent the just penalty of being cauterized on their foreheads; their leader suffering the disgrace of a double branding, one on the forehead, and one round the chin. Further, their garments being cut down to the girdle, they were publicly scourged, and with the sounding of the whip cast out of the city. After which, through the inclemency of the weather (for it was winter), and as no one showed them even the slightest act of compassion, they perished miserably."

CHAPTER VI.

THE WALDENSES.

THE ground over which we have hitherto travelled in tracing the spread of the reformed doctrines has been very various. In some instances the clearer insight of the reformers into the nature of the New Covenant has been darkened by strange delusions and by doubts respecting the authority of the Old Testament. In others an honest and well-founded testimony against the innumerable abuses of the Church has been weakened by an uncharitable and even anarchical spirit. We have indeed found many Protestants sound in doctrine and examplary in life; but it is not until we come to the WALDENSES that we meet with a united Church both holding a pure faith, and animated by a charitable spirit.

Peter Waldo was a citizen of Lyons, who had become rich by usurious practices. One day whilst he was attending a civic assembly, one of the company suddenly expired. The event powerfully impressed him; the fate of his fellow-citizen might at any time be his own. In this frame of mind his attention was arrested on a Sabbath (A.D. 1173) by hearing a troubadour in the streets of the city recite passages from a Romaunt called the Life of St. Alexis. Waldo took the minstrel home with him that he might hear the whole poem and converse with him on the momentous subject of the Christian life.

The next morning he went to a priest of high reputation, to ask how he should attain to holiness. "If thou wouldst be perfect," was the answer, "go sell all thou hast and give to the poor." Waldo, who was prepared to make any sacrifice to obtain what he sought, obeyed the injunction to the letter. He converted his property into money for the use of the poor, fed all who came to him three days in the week, placed his two daughters in a convent, and publicly announced his intention to abandon the service of mammon for that of God. At the same time he invited his fellow-citizens to follow his example. His wife, alarmed at his conduct, entreated the archbishop of Lyons to put a check to her husband's imprudent zeal. Not even episcopal authority however could damp his ardour; he persevered in his life of self-denial, and was joined by a number of companions, who formed themselves into a fraternity under the name of the Poor Men of Lyons. A season of famine gave them ample opportunity for the exercise of charity.

At first Waldo and his disciples were conspicuous only by the sanctity of their lives; soon however they began to attract notice by their censure of the rapacity and corrupt manners of the monks and clergy. To this grave cause of offence another was presently added. Longing to know more of the Scriptures than could be learnt from the Church lessons or from sermons, Waldo conceived the design of translating the Bible into the vernacular tongue, the Gallo-Provençal[1] idiom. With this object he obtained the assistance of three scholars—Bernard of Ydros, afterwards held in great estimation among the Dominican Friars; Stephen of Ansa, who was promoted to a benefice in Lyons; and John of Lugio, who became the head of a religious congregation in Lombardy. The last alone of the three remained faithful in after-time to the reformer. Stephen made the translation, which was revised by John, and transcribed by Bernard for the use of the copyists. The whole of the New Testament, the Psalms and many other books of the Old, were thus for the first time rendered accessible to the bulk of the people. At the same time Waldo made a collection of passages from the Fathers in illustration of Scripture, especially from Ambrose, Jerome, Augustine and Gregory the Great.

Taking with them the precious books which had thus been prepared, the master and his disciples went forth into the streets and houses of the city and into the neighbouring villages, everywhere declaring the Gospel message with ardour and success. In imitation of the seventy disciples they went two and two without staff or script, their feet being shod with wooden sandals.[2] In some few places the churches were opened to them by the clergy; more usually they preached and expounded in the streets and on the highways. The fears and jealousy of the priests could not suffer such a work to go on unhindered, and the archbishop of Lyons issued an order forbidding Waldo and his companions to expound the Scriptures or to preach. But the Spirit of truth by which they were inspired was not thus to be silenced. Conscious of integrity, and willing to believe that reason and justice were still to be found in the Catholic Church, two of Waldo's followers made a journey to Rome (1179) to see Pope Alexander III. and solicit his approbation

---

[1] Or Gallo-Roman.

[2] In French, *Sabots*, Latin *Sabates*, whence they were called *Sabatati* (or *Insabatati*). Coming afterwards into greater freedom of spirit, they discarded these outward tokens of poverty and asceticism.

of their work. They carried with them their translation of the Bible. The pope received them graciously and expressed his approbation of their profession of voluntary poverty.[1] The third Lateran Council was then in session, one of whose objects was the reformation of abuses in the Church. Waldo's petition was referred by the pope to the council, which after deliberating upon it appointed a commission to inquire into the tenets and objects of the fraternity.

One of the commissioners, an Englishman, Walter Mapes,[2] has left notes of the conference. "These people," he says, "have no settled place of abode, but go about the country barefoot, two and two, clad in woollen garments; they possess no private property, but like the Apostles have all things in common." He describes them as "uneducated laymen with whom it was not worth while for the council to trouble itself"; but this was a mere affectation of contempt, since he evidently regarded them as a formidable power. "They have begun in a humble manner, because they had not yet acquired any firm footing, but if we once suffer them to gain an entry, we ourselves shall be driven out." The pope however did not think it wise to put an extinguisher upon the work, but granted to Waldo and his friends a limited license to preach, subject to the control of the clergy.[3]

Up to this time the conduct of the "Poor Men of Lyons" had afforded no ground for ecclesiastical censure; "they had acted only as dutiful sons of the Catholic Church. It was a monkish legend which led Waldo to forsake the world; it was to a priest that he went for spiritual counsel; he had placed his daughters in a convent; the volume which the Church professed to take as her rule of faith was his constant study, and his translators were members of the priestly order." So far was he from any purpose of forsaking the Church, or resisting authority, that for a time he and his followers forbore to preach except within the limits imposed by the pope. At length their zeal, quickened by the opposition of the clergy, who could not endure a fervour which shamed their own lukewarmness, could no longer be restrained. They threw off the shackles of ecclesiastical control, and declared the truth in the

---

[1] Gilly says Waldo himself went to the pope, who "embraced him."

[2] He was canon of Salisbury, archdeacon of Oxford and some time chaplain to Henry II.

[3] Milman adds: "Their knowledge of Scripture seems to have perplexed John of Salisbury [another English divine, made bishop of Chartres], who writes of them with the bitterness of a discomfited theologian."

liberty of the Spirit; and when commanded to abstain altogether from preaching, they made the same answer as Peter and John before the council: "Whether it be right in the sight of God to hearken unto you rather than unto God, judge ye." Upon this they were reproached with presumptuously usurping the apostolic office, and threatened with the severest penalties. But they disregarded the menace, and in consequence by order of the archbishop of Lyons were deprived of the ordinances of religion and driven into exile. This sentence was followed at the Council of Verona in 1184, under the presidency of Pope Lucius III., by a formal act of excommunication. "To quench the malignity of divers heresies, which of late time have sprung up in most parts of the world, . . . we declare all Cathari, Paterini, those who call themselves the Poor Men of Lyons [and others], to lie under a perpetual anathema. . . . We direct that every bishop, once or twice in the year, shall visit the parishes in which it is reported that heretics dwell, and there cause two or three men of good credit, or if need be the whole neighbourhood, to declare on oath if they know of any heretics in that place, or any that frequent private meetings, or differ from the common conversation of mankind."

Before we follow the Lyons brotherhood in their exile, mention must be made of an attempt by a succeeding pope, Innocent III., to retain these ardent men within the pale of the Church. That sagacious pontiff endeavoured to transform the community into a monkish association of poor Catholics, to whom, subject to the control of the bishops, permission was to be granted to preach and expound the Scriptures. As Waldo and his followers looked upon oaths and the shedding of blood as unchristian, the pope made a show of conceding to them exemption both from judicial swearing and military service; but this exemption was rendered nugatory by the clause which was added: "So far as this may be done without prejudice or offence to any, and with the sanction of the secular rulers." It is not to be supposed however that any concession by the papal see would have brought Waldo's Gospel work within Romish lines. As it was there was little disposition on the part of the bishops to promote the pope's scheme.

Thus cast out of their native land, Waldo and his disciples spread themselves in all the countries around, Provence, Languedoc, France, Lombardy, Italy, Germany, and Spain.[1] Everywhere

---

[1] That they met with great success in the last-named country is shown by an edict of Ildefonso, King of Aragon, A.D. 1194. . . "We do command and charge the Waldenses, Insabatati, otherwise called the Poor Men of Lyons, and all other heretics, who cannot be numbered, being excommunicate from the holy

they found the soil prepared to receive the precious grain of truth. In some places doubtless the word which they preached came to the hearers like a new gospel; in others it was as a fertilizing shower falling upon seed sown by former generations, but long hid in the earth.

Peter for a while preached in Dauphiné, but the persecution was too hot to permit of his remaining so near Lyons; he fled northwards, and took refuge in Picardy. Here he gathered many followers, rich as well as poor; and his adherents became so numerous that the French king Philip Augustus, at the instigation of the clergy, sent an army against them. Three hundred country-houses of the gentry were demolished, several towns sacked, and the fugitives pursued into Flanders, where many of them were burned. From Picardy Waldo passed into Bohemia, where he was beyond the reach of the papal police. Here he founded a Church, sheltered and safe, which became so numerous that Reinerius Saccho, writing half a century after Waldo's death, speaks of forty-one societies in the diocese of Passau alone; and in 1315 the number of communicants was estimated at 80,000.[1] Of Waldo's last days and death no record has come down to us.

Reinerius, who was originally a Catharist, but who became a tool of the papal inquisition, in his endeavour to blacken the memory of the Waldenses, unwittingly discloses the causes of their success. He admits the ignorance, immorality and profanity of the Romish clergy, and owns that the craftsmen amongst the heretics, after toiling all day, gave up the night to learning and teaching, and that many of them knew the whole of the New Testament by heart. In Provence and the cities of Lombardy there were, he says, more schools of heretics than of theologians; forty-one were counted within the bishopric of Pavia. They blasphemously taught, he tells us, that the Romish Church is the harlot of the Apocalypse, and the pope the head of all error; that in the Eucharist transub-

---

Church, to depart out of our dominions; and that whosoever shall presume to receive the said Waldenses or other heretics into their houses, and supply them with meat or any other succour, shall thereby incur the indignation of Almighty God, as well as ours, and shall have his goods confiscated and be punished as if he were actually guilty of high treason. . . . Furthermore (though this may seem contrary to our duty and to reason), we grant to these wicked miscreants respite till the day after All Saints' day; but all who shall not be gone by that time, or at least preparing for their departure, shall be spoiled, beaten, cudgelled, and shamefully entreated."

[1] The French historian De Thou (A.D. circa 1600) tells us that the followers of Waldo were still extant in Bohemia in his day, and were called Picards.

stantiation does not take place in the hand of him who unworthily consecrates, but in the mouth of him who worthily receives; that the mass is a vain thing invented for the sake of gain; that there is no such state as purgatory, for as the tree falls there it shall be; and lastly, that whatsoever is taught that cannot be proved by Scripture is to be accounted false.[1]

Still more valuable is the testimony of Innocent III. himself, contained in a letter addressed to the Christians of Metz, A.D. 1199. The archbishop of that city had informed him that a large number of laymen and women presumed in their secret meetings to "belch out" to one another the gospels and other books of Scripture in the Gallic speech, and to preach by turns. The pope admits that the "desire to understand the divine Scriptures, and zeal in exhorting in accordance with the same, is not blameworthy but rather to be commended;" but censures the secrecy with which the heretics held their meetings, their assumption of the office of preaching, their mocking the "simplicity" of the priests, and their despising the fellowship of those who did not adopt their views. From another letter of the pope it appears that the archbishop had not accused them of any errors of faith or doctrine.

Except in Bohemia, persecution everywhere tracked the steps of the Waldenses. Stephen of Bourbon relates that he was present in a certain place when eighty persons of this sect were condemned to the flames; and Alberic, in his chronicle, speaks of the immolation of 182 at one time, which he calls "a sacrifice well-pleasing to the Lord." Thirty-five perished in one fire at Bingen, at Mayence eighteen, and eighty at Strasburg.

The branch of Waldo's followers which has attained the greatest historical celebrity is that which settled in the valleys of Piedmont. Here they became fused with an ancient Protestant community, of which we have several times in our survey caught a glimpse; and it is to the united Church thus formed that the name of Vaudois or Waldenses has been especially applied. Such seem to be the facts of the case, but it must be observed that the question of origin has been the subject of animated and protracted controversy, some writers contending that the Mountain Church of Piedmont had no existence prior to the immigration of the followers of

---

[1] Peter de Vaux-Cernay names as the four chief errors of the Waldenses, the wearing of sandals like the Apostles, the denial of the lawfulness of oaths, and of taking human life on any ground, and the assertion that any man without episcopal ordination "could make the body of Christ." Another opponent classes amongst their heresies the maxim that all lying is a mortal sin!

Waldo; others that it dates from the time of Constantine the Great.[1]

The Waldenses themselves do not appear to share in either of the above opinions; they refer their origin to Claude of Turin.[2] In the year 1805, Napoleon Bonaparte went to Milan to place the iron crown of Lombardy on his own head; on his way, a deputation of the Vaudois clergy waited upon him at Turin with an address from their Church. Their speaker was M. Peyran, a man of learning and of a fine Christian character, who thus relates the interview. Addressing himself to M. Peyran in a tone of unusual condescension, Napoleon began:

You are one of the Protestant clergy of this country?

Peyran. Yes, sire, and moderator of the Vaudois Church.

Napoleon. You are schismatics from the Church of Rome.

Peyran. Not schismatics I hope, but separatists for conscience' sake, on grounds which we hold to be Scriptural.

Napoleon. You have had brave men among you. But your mountains are your best defence. Cæsar found some trouble in making his way through your defiles with five legions. Is Arnaud's *Rentrée Glorieuse* accurate?[3]

Peyran. Yes, sire; but we believe that our people were aided by Divine Providence.

---

[1] "Confusion," remarks Gieseler, "has been introduced by both friend and foe into the history of the Waldenses. At first they were confounded with the Cathari or Albigenses by Catholics, in order to represent them as Manichæans, by Reformed writers, in order to clear the Albigenses also from the charge of Manichæism. Further, the origin of the Waldenses is often referred to an earlier period than that of Peter Waldensus, though it is so clearly proved by the witness of contemporaries that he is the founder of the sect."

[2] See *ante*, p. 317.

[3] This refers to an episode in the great persecution of the Vaudois under Louis XIV. of France and their own sovereign, Duke Victor Amadeus II. The cruelty of the French general Catinat marks this transaction as one of the foulest blots on the page of history. In 1689, 800 of the Piedmontese exiles who had taken refuge in Switzerland set out under one of their pastors, Henry Arnaud, to regain their native valleys, and in the course of their march heroically maintained their position against overwhelming numbers among the mountains of Angrogna, until the nefarious alliance between the king of France and the duke of Savoy was dissolved. The dissolution of this alliance was succeeded by hostilities between the two powers, and in the new turn which was thus given to affairs, the faithful Vaudois, forgetting their wrongs, freely shed their blood in the service of Victor Amadeus. It is deplorable to relate that on the return of peace and his reinstatement to power, the duke suffered himself to become the tool of the pope and the French king, interdicting all communication between the Vaudois and the French Protestants, and expelling from the valleys 3000 of the latter, who had found an asylum there.

Napoleon. How long have you formed an independent Church?

Peyran. From the days of Claude, bishop of Turin, about the year 820.

Napoleon. What stipend have your clergy?

Peyran. We have no fixed stipend at present.

Napoleon. You used to have a pension from England?

Peyran. Yes, sire; the kings of Great Britain have always been our protectors and benefactors till recently.

Napoleon. How is that?

Peyran. The Royal pension has been withheld ever since we became your Majesty's subjects.

Napoleon. Are you organized?[1]

Peyran. No, sire.

Napoleon. Draw out a memorial; send it to Paris; you shall be organized immediately.

Whatever may have been its precise origin, or the derivation of its name, it is certain that the Waldensian Church at the close of the twelfth century stands forth in the face of all Europe, as the foremost and clearest witness to the authority of the New Testament and the spiritual nature of the Gospel.

This Church possesses some early manuscripts, amongst which may be noticed a poem entitled *The Noble Lesson*.[2] It is, says Milman, "a remarkable work, from its calm almost unimpassioned simplicity. It is a brief, spirited statement of the Biblical history of man, with nothing of fanatic exaggeration, nothing even of rude vehemence; it is the perfect clear morality of the Gospel. The close which arraigns the clergy has nothing of angry violence; it calmly expostulates against their persecutions, and its strongest

---

[1] A law for the organization of the Protestant Churches in France had been promulgated in 1802, but some years elapsed before it was completely carried out.

[2] For the date of this manuscript see note at the end of this chapter. A valuable collection of Waldensian manuscripts, including *The Noble Lesson*, was brought to England by Sir Samuel Morland, Cromwell's ambassador to the duke of Savoy (1650). Some days before Morland left England, archbishop Ussher sent for him to his chamber, and charged him to use his utmost diligence in inquiring after, and to spare no cost in purchasing such manuscripts and authentic documents as might throw light on the ancient doctrine and discipline of the Waldensian Churches; declaring "there was nothing in the world he was more curious and impatient to know as being a point of exceeding great weight and moment for stopping the mouths of popish adversaries, and discovering the footsteps of our religion in those dark intervals of the eighth, ninth, and tenth centuries." The manuscripts collected by Morland were bound in six volumes and deposited in the library of Cambridge University.

sentence is an emphatic assertion that the power of absolving from mortal sin is in neither cardinal, bishop, abbot, pope, but in God alone." The reader will be interested in a few lines.

O brethren hear a noble lesson!
We ought often to watch and pray,
For we see the world is near its end.
  * * * * * *

A thousand and a hundred years have been already completed,
Since it was written that we are in the last time.
  * * * * * *

Whosoever will do good works
Ought to begin with paying honour to God the Father;
He ought likewise to call upon his glorious Son, the dear Son of holy Mary,
And on the Holy Ghost, who shows us the way.
These three are the holy Trinity, and the only God, who ought to be invoked,
Full of all power, all wisdom, and all goodness.[1]

The author then gives a summary of the Old and New Testament history; after which he contrasts the two dispensations.

The Ancient Law permits divorce;
But the New forbids to marry her who is put away,
[Saying] what God has joined let no man separate.
The Old Law forbids perjury only;
But the New says, Swear not at all,
And let thy speech be no more than yea and nay.
The Old Law commands to fight against enemies and render evil for evil;
But the New says, Avenge not thyself,
But leave vengeance to the heavenly king,
And let those live in peace who do thee harm;
And thou shall find pardon with the heavenly king.
The Old Law says, Thou shalt love thy friend, and hate thy enemy;
But the New says, Thou shalt no more do this,
But love your enemies, and do good to those who hate you,
And pray for them who persecute you, and seek occasion against you;
That ye may be the children of your Father who is in heaven.
The Old Law commands to punish malefactors;

---

[1] "O frayre entendé una nobla Leyçon.
Sovent deven velhar e istar en oreson,
C. nos veen aquest mont esser presdel chavon.
  * * * * * *
Ben ha mil e cent an compli entierament,
Que fo scripta lora, C. son al derier temp.
  * * * * * *
M. casçuna persona que vol ben obrar,
Lonor de Dio lo payre deo esser al commençar.
E apelar en aina lo sio glorios filli car filli de Santa Maria,
E lo Sanct Sprit que nos don bona via.
Aquisti 3. la Sancta Trenità enayma un Dio, devon esser aurà,
Plen de tota poysença e de tota sapiença e de tota brontà."

But the New says, Pardon all people,
And thou shalt find pardon with the Father Almighty;
For if thou dost not pardon thou shalt not be saved.

The author excuses the persecutors of the Apostles and early Christians, because they had not the faith of Jesus Christ, and contrasts with them those who in his day called themselves Christians, and yet were persecutors. The successors of the Apostles, he avers, had continued down to his time, but because of persecution were hardly able to show themselves.

The rekindling of the lamp of Gospel truth in the valleys of Piedmont, stirred up the envy and malevolence of the priesthood. In 1198 at the instance of the bishop of Turin, the German Emperor Otho IV. issued a decree for the expulsion from the diocese of " the heretical Waldenses and all who sow the tares of falsehood." In 1220 a certain count Thomas and the magistrate of Pignerol made a joint order, " that whosoever should show hospitality to any Waldensian man or woman should pay a fine of ten soldi." It does not fall within our limits to trace the subsequent history of this Church. Persecutions, conflicts and scenes of massacre were witnessed in one valley or another by nearly every age from the year 1300 to the Reformation, and again from the Reformation to the close of the seventeenth century.

We have seen what Reinerius Saccho has to say respecting the doctrines of the Waldenses. His testimony to their manner of life is equally valuable. He describes the heretics under the general name of Cathari, but especially distinguishes the Leonists (Poor Men of Lyons). The date is the middle of the thirteenth century. " The Waldenses are older, more universal, more orthodox and more sanctimonious than any other. They are sedate and modest; they have no pride in clothes, wearing such as are neither costly nor mean. To avoid fraud and oaths, they eschew commerce and live by manual labour; even their teachers are shoemakers and weavers. They do not amass wealth, are temperate in meat and drink, avoid taverns and dances, and are of chaste life. They resort to a crafty device to gain the ear of the noble and great. In the guise of pedlars they carry about jewels and ornaments of dress which they show to ladies and gentlemen. When one of them has disposed of his rings and kerchiefs, and is asked, ' Hast thou anything more to sell,' he answers, ' I have jewels more precious than these which I will show thee if thou wilt not betray me to the priests.' On receiving the required assurance, he says, ' I have a gem so brilliant, that by its light a man may see God; another which radiates such a flame as to kindle the love of God in the heart of its possessor';—and so on. By these jewels he means passages of Holy Scripture in their several applications, and he begins to recite some of them; such as the Annunciation, or our Lord's discourse after washing his disciples' feet. Then when he sees his hearers are interested, he repeats the woes pronounced by Christ on the Pharisees; and if asked of whom these imprecations are to be understood, he answers, of the clergy and the monks. After which the heretic draws a comparison between the Romish Church and his own sect. . . . In prayer they are very reverent, kneeling in silence when they leave their beds in the morning, before and after noon-day, and at night. Before they eat they give thanks, the eldest of the company saying in their vernacular tongue: ' God who blessed the five loaves and the two fishes in the desert, bless this table and that which is upon it (then they all make the sign of the Cross), in the name of the Father, the Son, and the Holy Ghost.' And when they rise from table the eldest amongst them repeats the doxology; 'Worthy is the Lamb that hath been slain, to receive the power, and riches, and wisdom, and might, and glory, and blessing'; adding, ' God plentifully reward all our benefactors; the God who hath given us food for the body, vouchsafe to us also the life of the Spirit, and be with us, and we with Him for ever!'; all the company meanwhile raising their clasped hands towards heaven."

The Waldensian Candlestick (*Convallium antiquissima Insignia*). See John i.5. From Léger, *Histoire des Eglises Evangeliques de Piemont*.

NOTE ON *The Noble Lesson*.

The line of this poem quoted above at page 40 —

A thousand and a hundred years have been already completed,

was thought until recently to determine its age, namely, the 12th century. Some difference of reading however in the Cambridge MSS. from those which have been followed by historians has within the last few years thrown doubts upon this date Mr. Bradshaw, the late librarian of the University, examining the MS. in its possession (a diminutive quarto on paper), discovered an erasure before the word cent, and with a magnifying-glass made out that the figure 4 had once occupied the space:

Ben ha mil e 4 cent an compli entierement.

He also found a single first leaf of another copy of the poem, in which are four c's between e and cent:

Ben ha mil e cccc cent anz compli entierament.

This discovery removes the poem to the 15th century. It is true that the reading hitherto received is supported by a manuscript of the poem in the University College, Dublin, and another in the Public Library, Geneva; the former reading

Ben ha mil e cêt an cpli entieramment;

the latter,

Ben ha mil ecêt ancz compli entieramt;

but Mr. Bradshaw has pronounced these copies to be later than the Cambridge; and whilst there would be an obvious motive for altering 1400 into 1100, there could be none for changing 1100 into 1400. Accordingly some deductions in the first edition of this work drawn from the supposed earlier date of the poem are now omitted. We tender our thanks to W. G. Searle, Vicar of Hockington, and to the librarians of the Cambridge, Geneva and Dublin libraries, for their kind assistance in this matter.

CHAPTER VII.

THE CRUSADE AGAINST THE ALBIGENSES.

The last of the Crusades, when the Shepherd handed his stray sheep over to the wolves, and bigotry, consecrating license, ran riot from Provence through Languedoc.—*Times*.

THE name Albigenses is not that of a sect, but is a generic term covering a wide group of Christian communities, spread over the whole south of France — Cathari, Paterini, Tisserands, Petrobrusians, Henricians, Boni-Homines, Waldenses; and it seems not to have been used prior to the Crusade of which we are about to speak. Some of these sects, as we have already seen, were the offspring of the Paulicians of Thrace, and clung to the Oriental theosophy and the practice of severe asceticism; others were indigenous, and were of two kinds, those which were chiefly distinguished by their opposition to the Romish priesthood and superstitions; and those which, especially after the preaching of Waldo, upheld the part of sound Biblical reformers. From one cause or other the land teemed with Christian people in revolt against the ruling Church. The heresy was not confined to the lower or even the middle ranks. If not the princes themselves, yet in many instances their wives and families were deeply implicated in the religious insurrection, the greater part of the daughters of the nobility being brought up in the educational establishments of the *Perfectæ*, who lived together in monastic style.

Side by side with this religious life there flourished another life of a very different kind. The nobles and knights of Languedoc and Provence, although not less warlike, were more cultivated and perhaps more luxurious than any in Europe. It was a land of castles and tournaments, the very focus of chivalry, where counts and barons "vied with each other in splendour and gallantry. The count of Toulouse and his vassals had been amongst the most distinguished of the Crusaders, and had brought home many usages of Oriental luxury." It was too the land of song. The troubadours of Provence opened to Europe a new world of romance and poetry; in their lays they touched many themes, sacred and profane, but especially love, which they sang in voluptuous strains. Moreover the soil was fertile, the people industrious, the cities wealthy; earth could boast no fairer region.

In 1198 there ascended the papal throne a learned ecclesiastic named Lothaire Conti, then aged thirty-seven years, who took the title of Innocent III. Rome has never seen an abler or more ambitious pontiff. "Pious and virtuous in private life," his sole aim as pope was to make the papal see supreme over all Christian states, princes and people, and to this object he sacrificed every Christian principle. He commenced his reign with an assumption for which it would be difficult to find an epithet strong enough: "Ye see what manner of servant the Lord hath set over his people, the vicegerent of Christ, the successor of Peter. He stands between God and man; below God, above man; less than God, more than man. He judges all, is judged by none, for it is written: 'I will judge.'" Innocent saw that so long as the south of France continued in a state of revolt the papacy itself was insecure. In the words of Sismondi, "both from character and policy he came at once to the conclusion that no measures must be kept with the sectaries. If they were not crushed, if the whole race was not exterminated, and Christendom struck with terror, the mischief would spread, and the intellectual fermentation which was everywhere going on would involve the whole world in universal conflagration."[1]

In the very first year of his pontificate Innocent addressed a letter to the archbishops, bishops, princes and counts in the south of France, declaring the Cathari, Paterini, Waldenses and all other heretics[2] to be outlaws, and calling upon the temporal lords to confiscate, banish and put to death all who should persist in their heresy. Spiritual indulgences, with the possession of the confiscated estates, were promised to all who should obey this mandate. At the same time he sent two Cistercian monks as his legates to see that these orders were carried into effect. But the lords of the great fiefs were not to be caught by either the spiritual or the temporal bait, and the pope's bull remained a dead letter.

Stronger measures were required. The pope chose two other Cistercians, Peter of Castelnau, and Raoul, whom he invested with extraordinary powers, the whole episcopal authority in the provinces being transferred to them. They went first to Toulouse, and extorted from the count and the civic authorities an oath to expel the Boni-Homines from the land. Still nothing was actually done; "Toulouse the deceitful[3] went on in its calm tolerance." A third legate was now added, Arnold d'Amauri, abbot of Citeaux, than whom no fitter tool could have been found for the work.

Thus reinforced the papal legates again set forth, and travelled through the land from city to city with great pomp, a retinue in rich attire, and a vast cavalcade of horses and sumpter mules. Wherever they came they admonished the heretics to return to the true Church, and exhorted the faithful to assist in compelling them. Their usual text was, "Who will rise up for me against the evil doers? Who will stand up for me against the workers of iniquity?" And the sermon generally ended with: "You see, most dear brethren, how great the wickedness of the heretics is, and by what pious methods the Church labours to reclaim them. But these all

---

[1] "Innocent was charitable to the poor who surrounded his palace, steeled against the wretch who deviated from his faith—generous in the profusion of his private expenditure, avaricious in the exactions which he levied for the apostolical treasury—humane in his mere social relations, merciless in the execution of his ecclesiastical projects—pious in the expressions of internal devotion, impious and blasphemous in his repeated profanation of the name of God and of the cross of Christ." To English readers he is best known as compelling King John to do penance and receive back his kingdom as a papal fief.

[2] The pope acknowledges that the heretics performed works of love, but ascribes these to dissimulation in order to obtain proselytes.

[3] *Tolosa, tota dolosa*, says the monk of Vaux-Cernay.

prove ineffectual; therefore, though with great reluctance and grief, our holy mother the Church calls together against them the Christian army. If then you have any zeal for the faith, if any concern for the honour of God, if you would enjoy the benefit of this great indulgence, come and receive the sign of the cross and join yourselves to the army of the crucified Saviour."

On their second circuit the legates fell in, near Montpellier, with the Spanish bishop of Osma in Castile, who was travelling northward. He was accompanied by Dominic, a Spaniard of noble family, who burned with hatred against the heretics. "The dejected legates bitterly mourned their want of success. 'How expect success with this secular pomp?' replied the severer Spaniards. 'Sow the good seed as the heretics sow the bad. Cast off those sumptuous robes, renounce those richly-caparisoned palfreys, go barefoot, without purse and scrip, like the Apostles; out-labour, out-fast, out-discipline these false teachers.' The Spaniards were not content with words only; the bishop of Osma and Dominic sent back their own horses, stripped themselves to the rudest monkish dress, and led the way on the spiritual campaign. The legates were constrained to follow."

But this new demonstration met with no better success than the former. The monks indeed, accustomed to the subtleties of the schools, often puzzled their opponents; but even this was far from being always the case. We have a note of one of these conferences, in which the legates were completely silenced. It took place at Montreal, near Carcassonne, in the year 1206. On this occasion the Albigenses challenged the Catholics to a public disputation on the errors of the Church of Rome. Many bishops and monks, including Peter of Castelnau, the bishop of Osma and Dominic, were present. Two noblemen and two commoners were chosen as arbitrators. It was agreed that the side which could not maintain its opinions by Scripture should be considered as vanquished. Arnold Hot, an Albigensian pastor, propounded six theses: I. That the mass was not instituted by Christ or his Apostles. II. That transubstantiation is an invention of man, and an erroneous doctrine; and that the worship of the Host is manifest idolatry. III. That the Church of Rome is not the Spouse of Christ, but the Church of confusion, the mother of abomination, drunk with the blood of the saints. IV. That the prayers of the living are not profitable for the dead. V. That purgatory is a human invention devised to gratify the avarice of the priests. VI. That prayer ought not to be made to the saints. These propositions, or some of them, Arnold sent in writing to one of the bishops who demanded a fortnight to prepare his answer. On the appointed day the bishop appeared with a voluminous paper which was read. Arnold undertook to reply to it extempore, if the judges and the audience would give him time; so long a treatise he said would require a long answer. This was granted, and Arnold discoursed for several hours each day on four days in succession, and this with so much skill that his opponents would gladly have been elsewhere; for he made it evident that though the bishop had written much he had proved nothing. In conclusion, Arnold challenged his opponents to prove from Scripture that the mass was instituted by Christ and sung by his Apostles in the same manner as it was accustomed to be sung in the churches. This the bishops could not do, and Arnold followed up his advantage by asserting that the Lord's Supper is not the mass. "If," said he, "the mass were the Lord's Supper, there would after the consecration be all there was before; but in your mass no bread is left, for by transubstantiation the bread has vanished; wherefore the mass cannot be the Lord's Supper, in which, as we all know, there is bread still. Jesus Christ brake bread, and Paul brake bread; but the priest breaks the body, not bread; wherefore the priest neither does what Jesus Christ did nor what St. Paul did." Upon this the monks, bishops, legates and priests rose up abruptly and left the assembly, fearful lest the faith of the audience in the mass should be altogether shaken.

For eight years did the papal emissaries preach, dispute, and threaten in vain. "Why," they demanded of the Catholic inhabitants, "why do you not drive the heretics out of the country?" "We cannot," was the answer; "we have been brought up with them, they are our kindred; besides, we see the goodness of their lives."

A more drastic remedy was needed. There yet remained the sword of the secular power; and Innocent was not troubled with scruples. He hastened to summon the princes to his side, and with malicious cunning, cast his eyes on the sovereign of the land as the fit executioner of the papal vengeance upon his own people.

Raymond, sixth count of Toulouse, was a "gay, voluptuous,[1] generous man, without strength of character enough to be either heretic or bigot." Some of his feudal lords, the king of Aragon, and himself were at war with one another. The legates peremptorily called on the belligerent parties to make peace and to combine their forces against the heretics. Raymond declined to obey the

---

[1] He had three wives living at the same time.

summons; upon which Peter of Castelnau issued sentence of excommunication against him, and placed his territory under an interdict; and Innocent from his lofty seat addressed to him a letter "perhaps unexampled in the furious vehemence of its language. It had no superscription, for it was to a man under sentence of excommunication. 'If with the prophet, I could break through the wall of thy heart, I would show thee all its abominations. . . . Who art thou, who, when the illustrious king of Aragon and the other nobles, at the exhortation of our legates, have consented to terms of peace, alone looking for advantage in war, like a carrion bird preying on carcases, refusest all entreaties? Impious, cruel and direful tyrant, thou art so far gone in heretical pravity that thou hast said thou wouldst find a bishop of the heretics who would prove his faith to be better than that of the Catholics.'"

The blow followed sharp upon the word. A papal letter was addressed to the king of France, his nobles and all his Christian subjects, and to sundry other princes, commanding them to take up arms for the suppression of the heretics, and placing their lands whilst so engaged under the special protection of St. Peter and the pope. The estates and goods of the heretics were to be divided amongst those who should take part in this holy enterprise; the interest of their debts was to cease; and the same spiritual indulgence was to be granted them as for a crusade in the Holy Land. At the same time Peter of Castelnau secretly stirred up the lords of Languedoc against Raymond. The latter in alarm hastened to make peace with his enemies, by which act he fondly supposed himself to be delivered from the excommunication. "But the inexorable Peter stood before him, reproached him to his face with cowardice, accused him of perjury and of abetting heresy, and renewed the excommunication in all its plenitude."

At this crisis (A.D. 1208) a deplorable event took place. The legates were crossing the Rhone when Peter of Castelnau was transfixed with a lance by a servant of Raymond and died almost instantly.[1] Suspicion naturally fell upon the count, but his innocence of the crime has been satisfactorily proved. The pope however at once assumed his guilt, and ordered his excommunication to be published throughout the provinces every Sunday and Holy-day; the only terms on which he could look for pardon being the expulsion of all heretics from his dominions. Innocent moreover seized the moment of public indignation at this crime to quicken the tardy

---

[1] He lived only long enough to breathe out, "God pardon them, as I pardon them."

zeal of the king of France and the princes. "Up, soldiers of Christ! Up, most Christian king! hear the cry of blood; aid us in wreaking vengeance on these malefactors."

The call was promptly responded to. Political ambition, the appetite for plunder, the chivalrous passion for war and enterprise, were all called into activity, whilst the conquest of a wealthy country close at hand offered an easier way to win heaven than the long and costly journey to Palestine and a perilous warfare amongst its stony hills. From all parts of France knights and armed men assembled at Lyons in countless numbers. Hopeless of resisting so mighty a force, Raymond submitted. The terms of his pardon were cruel. After surrendering seven of his chief castles, " he was led, naked to the girdle, to the porch of the abbey-church [it was at Valence], and in the presence of the legates and twenty bishops, before the Eucharist, with relics and the wood of the true cross, his hand laid on the Gospels, he acknowledged the justice of his excommunication, and swore full allegiance to the pope and to his legate." Then with a rope round his neck, and scourged on his naked shoulders as he went, he was led past the tomb of the murdered Castelnau, up to the high altar, where he received absolution.

But his relentless enemies were still unsatisfied; his humiliation was not yet complete. He himself must take up the cross against his own loyal subjects; "he must appear at the head, he must actually seem to direct the operations of the invading army;" for the war, so it was pretended, was not waged against the princes or people of Languedoc, but against the heretics. "Never in the history of man," such are Milman's words, "were the great eternal principles of justice, the faith of treaties, common humanity, so trampled under foot as in the Albigensian war. Never was war waged in which ambition, the consciousness of strength, rapacity, implacable hatred, and pitiless cruelty played a greater part. And throughout the war it cannot be disguised that it was not merely the army of the Church, but the Church itself in arms. Papal legates and the greatest prelates headed the host and mingled in all the horrors of the battle and the siege. In no instance did they interfere to arrest the massacre, in some cases urged it on." Arnold was the captain-general of the host. Fulk bishop of Toulouse, formerly a dissolute troubadour, and the deadly enemy of count Raymond, might be regarded as the second in command. The archbishops and bishops led the several armies in person. The head engineer was the archdeacon of Paris. Peter, monk of Vaux-Cernay, attendant on his uncle, the abbot of that monastery, was the historian of the crusade, and in his history he revels in all the deeds of blood. With him "the heretic was a beast of prey, to be slain wherever he might be found." The chief secular leaders were the duke of Burgundy, the count of Nevers, the count of St. Pol, and Simon de Montfort.[1]

It does not belong to our purpose to follow in all its harrowing detail the course of the war. The historians of the time depict, in vivid colours, the march of the armed host, the siege and sack of towns and castles, the heroic defence of despairing garrisons, the massacres, the burnings, the endless barbarities. They do not however take us into the sanctuary. Who shall describe the terror which seized the Churches at the approach of the pitiless host? Who can count the tears and prayers which were poured out in secret, day and night, in thousands of chambers; the trembling of the feeble-minded; the wrestling of the strong man that he might have faith to confess Christ in the presence of the sword, the gibbet, or the stake; the mortal shrinking of those who had a name to live and yet were dead? Or who shall tell how, when faith had fully laid hold of Christ, the peace of God flowed into the soul, lifting it above all the terrors of earth and hell? Some of the Churches, as we have seen, looking deeper into the Gospel than even Zwingle or Luther, held that Christ's disciple cannot use the sword. Were these faithful in the hour of trial? The perpetual din of arms, the shouts of triumph, the shrieks of woe, the cries of despair drown these gentler voices. History in this case, as in so many others, has filled her page with the coarser and the meaner traits, leaving the nobler and more spiritual to be revealed at the last day.

In the spring of 1209 the crusading army was put in motion. The first blow fell on the brave young viscount of Béziers, nephew to Raymond. Crowds of people from the surrounding country had taken refuge in the city. When the army arrived under its walls, the bishop, who had given to the legate the names of the suspected, exhorted the "faithful" to deliver these up, and so save themselves from ruin. "Tell the legate," was the noble reply of the Catholic citizens, "that rather than commit such baseness, we will devour our own children." The city was stormed, and the inhabitants massacred. When the crusaders asked the abbot of Citeaux, "Sir, how shall we do? we cannot distinguish between the good and the bad," he answered in the memorable words: "Kill all, God will know his own." At the same time he wrote to the pope: "We

---

[1] This man, created Earl of Leicester by King John, was father to the Simon de Montfort who led the English barons against King Henry III.

have spared neither rank, sex nor age; about 20,000 have perished by the sword; the whole city is spoiled and burnt, the divine vengeance wonderfully raging against it." In one church alone 7,000 were slain. The viscount escaped and threw himself into Carcassonne, to which the crusaders now laid siege. Water failed, a pestilence broke out, and the unhappy town surrendered; most of the inhabitants were permitted to leave, and wandered amongst the woods and mountains in an utterly destitute condition. Three hundred knights gave themselves up on promise of their lives and liberty. But Simon acted on Innocent's maxim, "To keep faith with those who have it not is an offence against the faith." They were burnt alive. The viscount was kept close prisoner and soon died, not without suspicion of being poisoned by order of Simon de Montfort.

Now arose the question, to which of the victorious leaders the viscount's lands should be given, as "the first-fruits of the conquest." The duke of Burgundy disdainfully refused them, saying "he had plenty of domains and lordships, without taking what would disinherit the viscount of Béziers, to whom he thought they had done evil enough without despoiling him of his inheritance." His example was followed by the counts of Nevers and St. Pol, but Simon de Montfort had no such scruples. He accepted the proferred spoil, and was invested on the pope's authority with all the lands conquered or to be conquered during the Crusade.

Raymond had submitted; he was with the crusading army; but it was necessary for the reduction of Languedoc that he should be completely separated from the other feudal lords, and reduced to a cipher. The legates demanded of him the instant surrender of all heretics in his dominions, with all their possessions. The count in dismay appealed to the pope, and went himself to Rome. Innocent received him with smooth words, and gave him absolution. Nevertheless he had to appear before a council in order to purge himself from the charge of abetting heresy. At the same time Innocent wrote to the legates: " We counsel you to use guile, as the Apostle Paul did. Leave for a time the count of Toulouse, employing towards him a wise dissimulation, that the other heretics may be the more easily defeated, and that afterwards we may crush him when he shall be left alone."

Meanwhile the Crusade went forward. Five hundred castles and towns either surrendered without resistance, or yielded after a short siege. The defenders were massacred, hanged, burned or mutilated. Minerve, a fortress of great strength, made a long and vigorous resistance; but provisions and water failed, and the garrison was forced to capitulate. One of the articles provided that such of the heretics as recanted should be spared. A fierce knight was indignant at such leniency! "Fear not," replied Arnold, who was himself vexed with the article, "they will be very few who will be spared." The crusaders marched into the castle singing the *Te Deum*. The Albigenses had assembled, the men in one house, the women in another, and on their knees in prayer, awaited the end. The abbot of Vaux-Cernay exhorted the men to return to the true Church. He was interrupted by a unanimous cry: "Your labour is in vain; we have renounced the Church of Rome; neither death nor life shall make us abandon our faith." He then proceeded to the women, whom he found equally resolute and more enthusiastic. Next came Simon de Montfort. He had raised a great pile of wood: pointing to it he said, "Return to the Catholic faith, or ascend that pile." No one moved. The pile was set on fire, until the square was filled with flame, and the heretics were marched out. One hundred and forty of the *Perfect*,[1] commending their souls to God, rushed of their own accord into the flames.

When the count of Toulouse offered to justify himself before the council (which met at St. Gilles), he found his enemies so utterly implacable that he burst into tears; upon which Theodisc, a canon sent by the pope to assist Arnold, mockingly cried out, "How great soever the flood of waters they will not reach to God." The terms proposed by the council were preposterous; compliance with them was impossible. The count heard them with bitter laughter; and seeing that his utter ruin was resolved upon, quitted the town, and rode off to Toulouse to put himself at the head of his people. He was received with enthusiasm. This event changed the aspect, although not the character of the war. It was still the Church employing the secular arm for the extirpation of heresy; but it was also a prince and his people defending their lands and liberties against a foreign enemy.[2]

The war was carried on with undiminished fury. Before Lavaur, five leagues from Toulouse, the bishops and legates amid the horrible tumult of the siege stood chanting, "Come Holy Ghost!" The capture of this fortress was followed by a frightful carnage. The commander, with eighty nobles and knights, were brought before De Montfort. He ordered them to be hanged; the over-

---

[1] See *ante*, pp. 372, 408.

[2] The French (in the annals of the period, *Franks*) were almost as much foreigners to the people of Provence and Languedoc as the English were to the Welsh before the reign of Edward I.

loaded gibbets broke down, and the survivors were hewn in pieces. Geralda, the Lady of Lavaur, "from whose door no poor man was ever turned away," was thrown into a well, and huge stones rolled down upon her. Men, women and children were indiscriminately massacred; "after which," says the monk of Vaux-Cernay, "our pilgrims, collecting the innumerable heretics the castle contained, burned them alive with the utmost joy." In 1211, although the cities of Toulouse and Montauban were still uncaptured, De Montfort assumed the title of Sovereign Prince of Languedoc. At the same time, the legate Arnold was made archbishop and even duke (!) of Narbonne; the abbot of Vaux-Cernay received the bishopric of Carcassonne; and other monks wealthy benefices.

But now complaints began to be made to the pope against De Montfort and Arnold: they had seized the lands of good Catholics, and amongst others some territory of the king of Aragon, who was related to Raymond, and supported his cause. At the same time Raymond offered to surrender his dominions in favour of his son, against whom there was no suspicion of heresy. The pope saw that the time had come to check the career of conquest; moreover he regarded the young Raymond with personal favour; nevertheless he found himself powerless to arrest or control the terrible engine he had set in motion. The churchmen of the Crusade would listen to no terms. In their reply to the pope's letter they exclaim: "Arm thyself with the zeal of Phinehas! annihilate Toulouse, that Sodom and Gomorrha, with all the wretches it contains; let not the tyrant, the heretic Raymond, nor even his young son, lift up his head; already more than half-crushed, crush them to the very uttermost." Innocent was forced to yield.

In 1213 at Muret, Simon de Montfort totally defeated the combined forces of Count Raymond and the king of Aragon, who was slain on the field. The city of Toulouse submitted, and was spared only because De Montfort was unwilling to destroy his newly-acquired capital. Its walls however, as well as those of Narbonne, were thrown down. At a council at Montpellier in 1215, De Montfort was formally invested with the "sovereignty of the whole land; all the native princes were deposed; and the ancient house of Toulouse, hitherto the greatest territorial principality in France, was stripped of everything."

The same year the pope assembled the fourth Lateran Council, one of the largest ever held.[1] Its avowed objects were the correc-

---

[1] It was attended by seventy-one archbishops, four hundred and twelve bishops, eight hundred and sixty abbots or priors, besides princes and other

tion of abuses and corrupt manners in the Church, the extinction of heresy, and a new crusade against the Turks. In reference to the first, Innocent spoke out boldly: "It is time, as the apostle saith, that judgment should begin at the House of God. The corruption that is in the world proceeds chiefly from the clergy!" Nevertheless this matter was soon suffered to drop. The third object was effected in the sixth crusade under Innocent's successor, Honorius III. The second, as we have seen, was in a fair way of being accomplished. But the council now made new and more stringent regulations, and decreed that "persons suspected of heresy, unless they can clear themselves, are to be smitten with the anathema and shunned by every one; and if they persist for a year in excommunication they are to be condemned as heretics. The temporal lord who shall neglect to purge his land from heretical defilement is to be excommunicated, and after one year his territories are to be taken possession of by Catholics, who may sweep off the heretics and purify the faith. All who resist the decisions of the council are pronounced infamous, incapable of holding any public office, exercising civic rights, bequeathing property, or having heirs to their estates. In distress none are to show them pity; after death none are to give them Christian burial." The council then proceeded to dispose of the conquered provinces. Count Raymond was for ever excluded from the sovereignty of the land; but Provence, and some other fiefs yet unconquered, were to be reserved for his son, if when he came of age he should show himself obedient to the Church.

The decree of the council regarding the sovereignty of Languedoc was not arrived at without strenuous resistance on the part of the princes who had lost their estates. The result was a renewal of the war. Raymond with his son again threw himself upon his people; many of the captured cities opened their gates to him, and De Montfort's party were driven out of Toulouse. But the Albigenses were not strong enough to hold the city; it was retaken by the crusaders, its fortress demolished, and the inhabitants plundered to the last piece of cloth and last measure of meal. Once more the patriots drove the foreigners out of the city, but this success availed them little. Innocent was dead, but Honorius carried on the work of extermination in a spirit even more relentless than his predecessor. A new crusade was preached, and De Montfort and the French lords again beleaguered the town (A.D. 1217).

---

laymen. So great was the concourse that the good bishop of Amalfi was suffocated in the throng.

The abbot of Citeaux harangued the army: "You are about to reconquer the city, to break into the houses, out of which no single soul, man nor woman, shall escape alive! not one shall be spared, in church, in sanctuary, in hospital! It is decided in the secret counsels of Rome that the deadly and consuming fire shall pass over it."

"But the counsels of Rome were not those of Divine Providence." Simon de Montfort had constructed a movable wooden tower called the Cat, which with its paw, an immense beam armed with iron hooks, laid hold of the walls. The besieged in a sortie got possession of the machine and were about to set fire to it. De Montfort was at mass when the news was brought to him. "Let me," he cried, "finish the service, and behold the sacrament of our redemption." Another messenger arrived: "Hasten to the rescue, our men can hold out no longer." "I will not stir," he answered, "until I have seen my Saviour." As soon as the priest lifted up the Host he exclaimed still kneeling, "Now let thy servant depart in peace, for mine eyes have seen thy salvation." He then called for his arms, and putting himself at the head of his old warriors he once more repulsed the Toulousians. He was standing beside the Cat which he had recaptured, when an enormous stone thrown from the wall by a catapult struck him on the head and stretched him lifeless on the ground. The crusaders maintained the siege a month longer, after which time they were forced to abandon it.[1]

A few years afterwards (1222) Raymond died, and being excommunicate, his body could not be buried in holy ground; it remained uninterred in the sacristy of the Knights Templars for 300 years. The war still lingered on, even after the heresy had to all appear-

---

[1] The Albigenses thus celebrated their deliverance:—

La mort du Loup,	The death of the wolf,
ou de Simon de Montfort.	Simon de Montfort.
Montfort	Montfort
Es mort!	Is dead!
Es mort!	Is dead!
Es mort!	Is dead!
Viva Tolosa,	Long live Toulouse,
Ciotat gloriosa,	City glorious,
Et poderosa!	And powerful!
Tornan lo paratge et l'onor!	Nobility and honour return!
Montfort	Montfort
Es mort!	Is dead!
Es mort!	Is dead!
Es mort!	Is dead!

ance been stamped out; it was not until 1229 that peace was finally made.[1] The younger count Raymond was permitted to receive absolution, but not before he had undergone the same cruel indignities as his father. "He rose from his knees, no longer sovereign of the south of France, but a vassal of limited dominions. His father on his penance renounced seven castles, the son, seven provinces."

Amongst the sources from which this dark history is derived is the contemporary lay of a Provençal poet, entitled *History of the Crusade against the Albigensian Heretics*.[2] Its merit as a history is great, and its statement of facts is considered of equal authority with the prose chroniclers of the time. The author was for the most part an eye-witness of what he relates. The effect at Rome of the news of Castelnau's murder is graphically described.

From Cantos V.—VIII.

When the pope heard the news
That his legate had been slain, it fell heavy upon him.
But he restrained his rising anger,
And began to pray to St. James of Compostella,
And to St. Peter who is buried in the chapel of Rome.
When he had made his prayer he put out the taper,
And there come to him brother Arnold, abbot of Cîteaux,
Master Milon speaking Latin,
And the twelve cardinals all in a circle.
The resolve was made by which this whirlwind was set in motion,
By which so many men were to perish, cleft asunder,
By which many a fair maiden and many a noble dame
Were to be left without robe or mantle.
The abbot of Cîteaux, who had been sitting with his head down,
Rose and stood against a marble pillar,

---

[1] "In this war," says Sismondi, "the slaughter had been prodigious, the massacres universal, the terror profound. . . . Hundreds of villages had seen all their inhabitants butchered with a blind fury, without the crusaders giving themselves the trouble to examine whether they contained a single heretic. The crusading armies, said to have amounted at one time to 500,000 men, were undisciplined, without pay, and without magazine, and all the harvests of the peasants, all the provisions and merchandise of the citizens, were rapaciously seized on every occasion. . . . There was scarcely a peasant in whose family some one had not been cut off by the sword of De Montfort's soldiers; not one but had repeatedly witnessed the ravaging of his property by them. More than three-fourths of the knights and landed proprietors had been spoiled of their castles and fiefs."

[2] The original manuscript, which is unique, is in the National Library at Paris. It is embellished with thirteen drawings, mostly war-scenes, and appears to be of the second half of the thirteenth century.

And said to the pope, "By St. Martin, my lord,
We speak too many words and make too much noise.
Cause letters to be written in Latin,
As it shall seem good to you, and I will straightway set forth
To carry them into France and through the Limousin,
To Poictou, Auvergne, and as far as Perigord.
Proclaim indulgences through all these countries
As far as Constantinople and in every land."
Whereupon the pope with a sad countenance
Answered, "Brother, go to Carcassonne,
And to Toulouse the great, which is on the Garonne,
You shall lead the host against the miscreant race.
Give to the faithful pardon for sins in the name of Jesus Christ,
And entreat them, exhort them from me
To drive the heretics from their midst."
Behold, the abbot prepares himself to set forth at the hour of nones.[1]
He rides forth from the city at full spur.
He betakes himself to Cîteaux, where, according to custom,
All the monks in white robes and tonsured
Were assembled in full chapter,
At the feast of the Holy Cross which is kept there in summer.
In the presence of the whole monastery he chants the mass.
The mass finished, he begins to preach.
He tells them he brings the words of the council,
And shows to each the bull with the seals.
By him and others it is displayed everywhere
As far as Holy Christendom extends,
In France and in all the other kingdoms.
As soon as they hear of the pardon of their sins the people put on the cross;
And never I think was so great a host gathered
As this against the heretics and the Sabbati.[2]
The duke of Burgundy donned the cross;
The count of Nevers and many other lords.
I will not speak of the cost of the gold embroidery and silk for the crosses,
Which they wore on the right side of the breast.[8]
I take no count of their coats of mail,
Of their charges and their ensigns;
Or of their horses cased in iron;
God never made Latinist or clerk so learned
Who could reckon up the half or the third;
Or even write the names of the priests and the abbots
Assembled in the host under Béziers,
Outside the walls in the open country.

The poet is nowhere more graphic than in his narration of the debates in the Lateran Council on the appropriation of the con-

---

[1] Three o'clock in the afternoon.
[2] See *ante*, p. 397.
In the Crusades against the Saracens the cross was worn on the shoulder.

quered provinces. It opens with the lines which our artist has copied from the frontispiece of M. C. Fauriel's edition.[1] They are appended in Roman type with a translation.

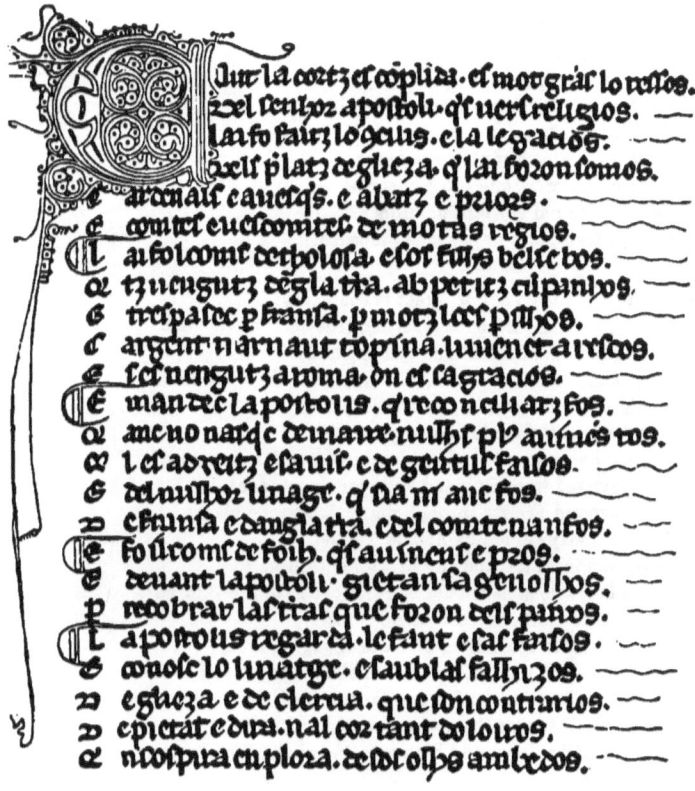

CANTO CXLIII.

Cant la cortz es complida es mot grans lo ressos
Del senhor Apostoli ques vers religios
Lai fo faitz lo concilis e la legacios
Dels prelatz de glieza que lai foron somos
Cardenals e avesques e abatz e priors
E comtes e ves comtes de motas regios
Lai fol coms de Tholosa e sos filhs bels e bos
Quez vengutz dEnglaterra ab petitz cumpanhos
E trespasec per Fransa per motz locs perilhos
Car gent nArnaut Topina li menet a rescos

---

[1] In the original these lines are surmounted by a drawing of the Troubadour in a castle, book in hand, reciting his lay to a group of noble ladies and knights.

E ces vengutz a Roma on es sagracios
E mandec lApostolis que reconciliatz fos
Quano no nasquec de maire nulhs plus avinens tos
Quel es adreitz e savis e de gentils faisos
E del milhor linage que sia ni anc fos
De Fransa e dEnglaterra e del comte nAnfos
E fo il coms de Foih ques avinens e pros
E denant lApostoli gietans agenholos
Per recobrar las terras que foron dels pairos
LApostolis regarda lefant e sas faisos
E conosc do linatge e saub las falhizos
De glieza e de clercia que son contrarios
De pietat e dira nal cor tant doloiros
Quen sospira en plora de sos olhs ambedos.

When the court is complete, great is the uproar,
[The court] of the lord pope (*apostle*), true chief of religion.
There was held the council and the assembly
Of the prelates of the Church, who had been all convoked ;
Cardinals and bishops and abbots and priors,
And counts and viscounts of many lands.
There was the count of Toulouse and his son, fair and good,
Who had arrived from England with young companions,
Having traversed France through many dangerous places
Well and secretly guided by Arnold Topina.
He is arrived in Rome, the city of sacred things.
The pope is desirous he should be reconciled [to the Church ;]
For never bore mother a child more comely,
More adroit, more sensible or of more engaging mien ;
To say nothing of lineage, the most noble which is or has been,
In France, in England, or [in the domains] of count Alphonso.
The count de Foix was there also, comely and brave.
[The count of Toulouse and his son], throwing themselves on their knees before the pope
Beg again the lands which belonged to their fathers.
The pope looks upon the child and his [princely] bearing.
He is acquainted with his lineage, he knows the wrongs [he has suffered]
From the Church and the clergy, his enemies;
With pity and care his heart is so troubled,
That he sighs over them and weeps with both his eyes.

The heretics had been exterminated or reduced to silence. Their public worship had ceased ; their teachers had perished or escaped to foreign countries ; the few faithful who survived preserved their lives only by burying the secret of their faith in their own bosoms, fearful even of communicating it to their children. But the root of the hated plant still remained in the earth, and whenever political occasion served, the proscribed came out of their hiding-places, to the dismay of the dominant Church. It was reserved for the

Inquisition, that new engine which for half a century had been maturing, to put the finishing stroke to the work.

During the war Dominic had founded at Toulouse an order of preachers for the defence of the Church against heretics. In 1216 the new order received the papal sanction, and taking the name of its founder became one of the great Mendicant orders.[1] Dominic was of a severe, enthusiastic and bigoted nature; he is said to have sanctioned all the barbarities of the war.[2] To his first band of preachers he added another corps, which he called Christ's Militia. These were all gentlemen, wearing a handsome court dress, and a sword which they were sworn to use against heretics. They were assisted by their wives, who were distinguished by a dress of mingled black and white.[3]

For a while the inquisition for heretics remained in the hands of the bishops. At a council held at Toulouse in 1229, statutes were framed for their direction in the duty of wiping out all lingering traces of heresy.[4] The bishops were to appoint a priest and two or three laymen of good repute in every parish, who should be sworn

---

[1] There were several other mendicant orders, the most famous of which was that of the Franciscans or Minor Friars. It was instituted about the same time as the Dominicans by Francis d'Assisi, an Italian, and had for its object the restoration of apostolic poverty and labour in strict obedience to the see Rome. Francis was remarkable for susceptibility to religious impressions, and love to God and man. In him grace and self-mortification strove long for the mastery. Once whilst painfully ruminating on some scenes of his earlier life, the assurance of the forgiveness of all his sins flowed into his heart and filled him with joy, so that he is said for a time to have laid aside his austerities. But the mistaken notions of the age seem again to have prevailed, so that when one night he thought he heard a voice say, "There is not a sinner in the world whom God would not forgive if he turned to Him, but he who destroys himself by severe exercises of penance will never find mercy," he was unable to accept the lesson, and concluded it was the voice of the deceiver. Still later however truth again became uppermost; and he ceased to regard self-mortification as in itself of any value, but solely as a means to promote purity: love appeared to him to be the soul of all.

[2] The gravest charges of cruelty have been brought against Dominic, and they are supported by Roman Catholic authorities. Milman however points out that these charges are not to be found in contemporary writers, but appear first in the Dominican authors of the following century, who to honour their leader, boast of his infuriate zeal in destroying the heretics.

[3] These military brethren and sisters, because they were attached to the first *family* or order, yet not subject to its rule, were styled *familiares*, familiars, a name which afterwards became notorious in the history of the Inquisition.

[4] The acts of this council were foreshadowed by those of Tours, Lombers, Verona and the third Lateran, already referred to, and also by that of Avignon, A.D. 1209.

to search out heretics in houses, caverns and other hiding-places, and report them to the bishop, or to the lord of the place. The lords were required to make a similar search in villages, houses and woods; and if any lord should suffer a heretic to take refuge on his domain, he was to be himself punished. Houses wherein the guilty had found shelter were to be pulled down. Converted heretics were not to live in a village suspected of heresy; "and to show their detestation of their former error they were to wear a yellow cross on each breast." Persons "converted against their will" were to be kept in perpetual imprisonment.[1] A list was to be made of the inhabitants in each parish. Every male over fourteen, and every female over twelve, was to swear that they utterly renounced heresy, and would persecute and inform against heretics. All who refused were to be written as suspected of heresy, as well as all who failed to confess and communicate three times in the year.[2]

The episcopal tribunal, being too tardy or too indulgent, was soon superseded by that of the Dominican Friars (afterwards appointed by Gregory IX.[3] to be the standing papal inquisitors). These active and zealous emissaries of the Church were untrammelled by custom, institutions, or public opinion, and subject to no authority but that of the pope. Finding the provisions of the Council of Toulouse insufficient for their hideous work, they invented new safeguards for the purity of the faith. The witnesses were now concealed from the accused, criminals were admitted to give evidence, confession was extorted by torture. In the examination of the accused the interrogatories were framed like a net, from which, if there was the least shadow of suspicion, it was impossible to escape. So flagrant was the injustice thus perpetrated that in 1234, the year following that in which the new court was opened, the inhabitants of Narbonne rose against it, whilst in the next year the inquisitors were driven out of Toulouse, and in 1242 four of them were murdered in that city. But all was of no avail; the iron grip of the oppressor closed tighter and tighter upon its victims, and for many generations there was none to deliver.

---

[1] The condemned under this statute appear not to have been consigned to ordinary prisons; it is provided "that they be enclosed in a wall" (*in muro includantur*) in such a manner that they may have no power of corrupting others; and when they were brought up for judgment they were said to be brought "out of the wall" (*educti de muro*).

[2] This Council of Toulouse is also noted as being the first at which, by a formal enactment, the laity were forbidden to read the Holy Scriptures. Aged persons might possess a Latin Psalter, a breviary, or the Hours of the Virgin, but were strictly forbidden to have even these books in a translation into a vulgar tongue.

[3] 1241—1243.

The mode of procedure in these detestable courts is to be learned from a book of instructions still extant, compiled for the use of the inquisitors in Carcassonne and Toulouse. "The accused is to be sworn on the Gospels that he will fully declare all he knows of the crime of heresy, or *Vaudoisie*, as well concerning the living as the dead. If he conceals or denies anything, he is to be put in prison and kept there until he confesses; but if he tells the truth his confession is written down. When a sufficient number have confessed to make a 'sermon,'[1] the inquisitors convoke some jurisconsults, preachers, and the bishops, to whom they submit a short extract from the confession of each accused person, but without the name. The counsellors having considered the same, give sentence: Let this man perform penance; let the other be immured; a third is to be delivered over to the secular arm. The following Sunday the inquisitors summon the prisoners before them, class by class, and pronounce the sentences, first in Latin, then in French. Those who are delivered to the secular arm are not to be burned the same day."

In order to reclaim as many as possible, other and secret instructions were at the same time given to the inquisitors. "He who is most deeply sunk in heresy may sometimes be brought back by the hope of life, if he confess his errors and denounce others. If he refuses to do this, let him be shut up in prison and be told there are witnesses against him, and that if once convicted there will be no mercy for him. At the same time let his food be diminished, for fear and suffering will help to bring him down.[2] Let none approach him but two adroit believers, who cautiously, and as if they had compassion upon him, may advise him to confess, with promise of his life. Let them say to him, 'Be not afraid to confess, if thou hast believed in these men when they said such and such things. If thou hast listened to them, assisted them, or confessed to them, it was because thou loved all whom thou believed to be good people, and because thou knew nothing evil respecting them. The same might happen to men much wiser than thyself.' If he should begin to soften, and to admit that he has heard the teachers speak concerning the gospels or epistles, he must then be asked, but cautiously, if they denied Purgatory, or

---

[1] What was afterwards called an *Auto-da-Fé* (Act of Faith) was at this time styled a General Sermon of Faith, because the proceedings of these gaol deliveries were opened by a sermon.

[2] The devil, when he sought to overcome our Lord, made use of his exhausted condition after the forty days' fast.

prayers for the dead, or what they had to say about the sacraments of the Church. He must be treated warily, for if questioned bluntly he will not answer, because he will suspect that you wish to take advantage of him. These are very subtle foxes, and you can only take them by subtlety. Note also that the inquisitor ought always to suppose a fact, and inquire only respecting the circumstances. For example, he should ask, 'How many times hast thou confessed thyself to the heretics'? or; 'In what chamber in thy house have heretics slept'? And when a heretic either does not make full confession, or does not accuse his accomplices, you must, in order to terrify him, say, 'We see how it is: think of thy soul, fully renounce thy heresy, for thou art about to die.' If then he says, 'Since I must die, I had rather die in my own faith,' then it is certain that his repentance is feigned, and he may be delivered up to justice."[1]

At length the tragedy was played out; the fruitful land had been turned into a desert; the heretical Church lay prostrate as one dead. It was as when the High Priests and the Roman governor joining hands, had crucified the Lord of life. It was laid in the tomb; a great stone was rolled to the mouth and sealed; and the watch was set. But Truth, like Him who bears her name, is immortal. Hardly had the note of Gospel freedom died away in Languedoc, than it was taken up by Wicliffe in England, and after him by Huss in Bohemia, whilst in every age down to the Reformation a clear and continuous testimony issued from the mountains of Piedmont. Rome, it is true, flattered herself that the witnesses were at length slain, to rise no more. "As the sixteenth century opened," says Mosheim, "no danger seemed to threaten the Roman pontiff. The agitations excited in former centuries by the Waldenses, Albigenses, Beghards, and Bohemians, had been suppressed and extinguished by craft and the sword. The surviving remnant of the Waldenses lived hardly, pent up in the narrow limits of the Piedmontese valleys; the Bohemians through their weakness and ignorance could attempt nothing. . . . The bishops of Rome reigned secure and free from all fear, and indulged their lusts and all their vicious propensities as freely as their innate de-

---

[1] Augustine, although, alas! he gave his sanction to persecution, set his face against falsehood and treachery. Being asked whether it was not lawful to make use of lies to discover the Priscillianists who lied to conceal their error, he declared that the Catholics who feigned themselves Priscillianists were worse than the Priscillianists who feigned themselves Catholics.

pravity demanded."[1] At the fifth Lateran Council, ninth session (1514), the preacher of the day exclaimed: "Now no one gainsayeth, there is none to oppose!"; and in the bull issued by Leo X. for its dissolution (March, 1517) he congratulates the council on having happily and successfully accomplished all the objects for which it had been called, amongst which was the *total extirpation of heresies*.

But the popes were like Belshazzar drinking at the feast when, lo, a strange handwriting appeared upon the wall. In the selfsame year, at mid-day on the 31st of October, the eve of the festival of All Saints, an Augustinian monk named Martin, the son of Hans Luther, and a professor in the university of Wittenberg, nailed with his own hand on the outer pillars of the great church of that city ninety-five theses, the effect of which was to shake the huge fabric of Popery to its foundation. The long dark night of apostacy was over. The day had dawned.

CONCLUSION. The office of the Church of Christ is to witness for Him, and this function was fulfilled in her early days when "with great power gave the apostles their witness," and when the servant followed his Lord in humility of life. But if we ask the question, how far has the outward Church maintained her witness, the answer furnished by these pages will be a mournful one.

In our former work we saw that departures from primitive simplicity took place at a very early period of the Church's life. The establishment of Christianity by Constantine as the religion of the Empire brought in new errors. The stormy blasts of persecution had tended to preserve a pure and living faith; but the sun of worldly prosperity favoured the growth of new corruptions, by which

---

[1] These popes were Alexander VI., Julius II. and Leo X. It is said that John Huss and his friend Jerome of Prague predicted the Reformation. Whilst in his dungeon at Constance, a few nights before his martyrdom, Huss "dreamed. It seemed as if some pictures of Christ, which he had been painting on the walls of his oratory, were effaced by the pope and the bishops. The dream afflicted him. But the next night he dreamed again, and seemed to see painters more in number, and with more of effect, restoring the pictures of Christ. He told the dream to his friends. 'I am no vain dreamer,' he said; 'but hold for certain that the image of Christ shall never be effaced. They wished to destroy it; but it shall be painted afresh in the hearts of gospel-preachers better than myself. And *awaking* as it were *from the dead*, and *rising from the grave*, I shall rejoice with exceeding great joy.'" His fellow-martyr Jerome even named the time, a hundred years to come. To his judges he said, "You are condemning me an innocent man, unjustly and wickedly; but I appeal to the most high and righteous judge—God Almighty, that within a hundred revolving years ye shall answer for it in his presence." Huss was burned in 1415, Jerome in 1416.

the witness of the Church to her Lord was continually obscured. The fourth century, rich as it is in churchmen of surpassing genius as well as piety, left the Church far more burdened by human inventions than before. In the dreary controversies of the two succeeding ages, it was as though the witness for Christ had fallen to a mere intellectual contention for his existence and attributes. It fell to a yet lower ebb during the long dark period which followed, a period in which monkery with all its accessories dominated the Church, and which saw also the rise and the palmy days of the papal power. The weight of tradition pressed ever more heavily upon the free spirit of the believer, whilst between the disciple and his Lord intervened a pretentious priesthood and an army of glorified saints and virgins. When the Church had thus become degenerate and lost to her pristine duty, the doctrine of infallibility came in as a crowning sin to crystallize her deformity, and to cut off all hope of reform.

But the Lord "left not Himself without witness"; and it has been the main purpose of these volumes to show how, from one age to another, men were visited and enlightened by the Spirit of Christ, and made ready to testify of Him. In some of these witnesses the truth was mixed with error: in many the professing Church saw only heretics, and invoked the powers of the world to put out the light they held up. Such were the early reformers of the fourth and ninth centuries, and such were those who from the eleventh century onward never suffered the torch of truth to be wholly quenched in Western Europe. An honourable place too must be given to the missionaries, who, although their eyes were not opened to the corruptions of the professing Church, bore witness in their Christ-like lives to the love of their Saviour.

It is not unprofitable for us, nay, it is necessary to a just discernment of the present times, to inquire what were the by-paths on which the Church went astray, and how it came to pass that the witness she was called to bear became almost wholly lost. No one cause of her declension has been probably so potent as the setting-up of a priesthood. The Lord Jesus designed his Church to be a brotherhood; and the only human priesthood mentioned in the New Testament is that of all believers. Jewish and pagan ideas, with the natural craving for distinction and rule, combined to establish an order of human mediators. From this grand mistake has flowed untold mischief and loss, both to the laity and to the clergy themselves. The life of the Church is the life of its individual members, and when these are resting, not upon the Saviour who bore their sins, but upon their fellow-men who "confess and absolve them,"[1] upon rites and ceremonies apart from the worship of the heart, upon angels and saints from the Virgin Mary downwards, then the life of the Church as the body of Christ is at an end.

Next to the priesthood, the ascetic element has had perhaps the largest share in destroying this spiritual life. It was early in the Church's history when the idea first took root, that man can lead a holier life by withdrawing from the world than by remaining in it. Fostered by the fourth-century Fathers, monachism became a great power, and during the dark ages it flourished like a fungus-growth upon the decaying Church. "The Son of Man came eating and drinking" and dwelling amongst his brethren, giving us in that holy and perfect life no ascetic example. It was a spirit alien to the Saviour's teaching which created the monastic system, in which the rule of the cloister took the place of personal holiness, and which thus struck a fatal blow at the responsibility of each disciple for a faithful life. It is true that Bernard and many other monks bore a true witness for Christ, but this must not blind us to the errors of the system under which they lived, and which caused superstition to be mixed with their faith, and spiritual arrogance with their humility.

Throughout the period under review, the Church was intolerant of any departure from her doctrine or practice. It was the spirit of the self-willed disciples: "We forbad him because he followeth not with us." When her own days of persecution were over and she acquired power, the Church became herself a persecutor. It was in vain that here and there some of her enlightened sons taught in a more Christ-like spirit; the course once entered upon must be followed to the bitter end, until the cup of iniquity should be full.

The crowning error of the Romish Church is the claim to infallibility, a claim not merely presumptuous but self-ruinous; for it effectually closes the path of return to first principles, and every avenue to a purer and higher state. Whatever has been decreed and done (such is the pretension) is right. Has a priesthood more exacting than that of Levi been set up? Have rites and ceremonies been multiplied? Has a mock-sacrifice been instituted? These are irrevocable parts of the Church's fabric. The worship of the

---

[1] Philip II. of Spain is said to have sent the following to his confessor a few days before he died: "Father confessor! as you occupy the place of God, I protest to you that I will do everything you shall say to be necessary for my being saved; so that what I omit doing will be placed to your account, as I am ready to acquit myself of all that shall be ordered to me."

saints and of Mary, and all the cumbrous system belonging to it, are fixed for ever. Was it right in past centuries to burn heretics and to employ against them the detestable engine of the Inquisition? Then it is right now; it will be so again. There may be hope for all men and for all institutions, excepting only the "infallible;" for such there is none.

But if the records of the Church seem too often to be an "inventory of human error," of good marred by abounding evil, we must still acknowledge with thankful hearts the faithfulness of God. Even in the darkest times and through all the Church's wanderings, He has not failed to raise up true witnesses, or to keep alive the lamp of truth; and now we look hopefully forward to yet brighter days. "Heaven's light for ever shines; earth's shadows flee."

AUTHORITIES.

In the First Edition the Authorities were cited with full particulars in footnotes. To save space the notes have been omitted in this edition, and a list of the principal authors is subjoined instead.

Socrates Scholasticus, Sozomen, Theodoret, Sulpicius Severus, Ammianus Marcellinus, Augustine, Bede; with occasional reference to others of the Fathers.
Smith and Cheetham, 'Dictionary of Christian Antiquities.'
Smith and Wace, 'Dictionary of Christian Biography.'
Neander, 'Church History,' 'Memorials of Christian Life,' 'St. Bernard.'
Mosheim, 'Institutes of Ecclesiastical History.'
Gieseler, 'Ecclesiastical History.'
Milman, 'History of Christianity.'
Robertson, 'History of the Church.'
Schaff, 'Nicene Christianity.'
Philip Smith, 'Students' Ecclesiastical History.'
Roberts, 'Church Memorials.'
Waddington, 'History of the Church.'
Newman, 'Church of the Fathers.'
Ruffner, 'Fathers of the Desert.'
Du Pin, 'History of Ecclesiastical Writers.'
Isaac Taylor, 'Ancient Christianity.'
R. T. Smith, 'St. Basil the Great.'
Ullmann, 'Gregory of Nazianzum.'
Scott, 'Ulfilas,' and an Article by Dr. Hodgkin in the 'Edinburgh Review.'
Stephens, 'Life of St. Chrysostom.'
Cutts, 'St. Jerome and St. Augustine.'
Elliott, 'Horæ Apocalypticæ.'
'The Church in the Middle Ages.'
Maitland, 'The Dark Ages.'
Morison, 'Life and Times of St. Bernard.'
Jones, 'Ecclesiastical History.'
Allix, 'Ancient Churches of Piedmont, Albigenses.'

Many other writers have been occasionally consulted.

The editor finds that the notice of Malachy in the preceding pages (pp. 359, 360) is derived too exclusively from his *Life* by Bernard of Clairvaux. For a more impartial estimate of Malachy's character and work the reader is referred to Dr. Healy's *Ancient Irish Church*.

INDEX.

A.

Abelard, 348, 361
Acacius, 78, 84, 89
Acta Sanctorum, 58 n., 169 n.
Adeodatus, 137
Adrian, abbot, 293 n
Adrianople, battle near, 37, 54
Adulatory titles, 123 n.
Aërius, 182
Africa, North, 154
Agilbert, 275
Agobard, 317
Aidan, 273
Aix-la-Chapelle, 313 n.
Alaric, 9, 124
Alban, St., 257
Aleric, 346, 383
Albi, 383
Albigenses, 352, 389
Alboin, 242
Alcuin, 312, &c.
Aldhelm, 346 n.
Aldred, 282
Aldwin, 294
Aleander, 374 n.
Alexander of Hierapolis, 211; III. pope, 385; VI. pope, 428 n.
Alexandrian School, 201
Alfred, king, 293 n.
Alfrid, prince, 274
Alith, 347
Almsgiving, 167
Altars, 159, 376
Alypius, 134, 255
Ambo, 81
Ambrose, 61, &c., 135, 162, 183
Ammianus Marcellinus, 5, 181
Ammonius, 11
Anacletus II. pope, 356
Anastasia, 40
Anastasius, 203
Anatolius, 218
Andreas, 210 n.
Annunciation, Feast of, 234
Anschar, 317, &c.
Anselm, 295 n., 360
Anthimus, 30
Anthony, 11 n, 15, 138
Anthusa, 71
Antioch, Council of, 92; see of, 42, 112

Antiochian School, 201, &c.
Antiochus of Ptolemais, 84, 89
Apocryphal Gospels, 231
Apollinaris, 44, 201, 210
Aquinas, Thomas, 235
Arcadius, Emperor, 69, 77, 193
Archimandrite, 207
Arefaste, 374
Arians, 5, 14, 36 n., 62, 84
Arianzus, 16
Ariminum, Creed of, 24, 52
Aristotle, 134
Arius, 4
Armorica, 258
Arnaud, Waldensian pastor, 402 n.
Arnold of Citeaux, 409; of Brescia, 389
Arras, 376, 388
Arsacius, 94
Art in Worship, 227
"Assumption" of the Virgin, 230
Astrologers, 133
Asylum, 80, 125 n
Athanasian Creed, 13 n., 361
Athanasius, 5, 6, 10, &c., 36, 149 n., 162, 163, 166
Athens, 16, 18 n.
Atticus of Constantinople, 95
Attila, 221 n.
Atto of Vercelli, 372
Audius, 52
Augustine, of Hippo, 37 n., 74 n., 105 n., 121, 128, 130, &c., 162, 171, 185; monk, 254, 263
Augustinian order, 141 n.
Aureole, 226
Auxentius of Dorostorus, 51, 55
Ave Maria, 234
Avignon, 383

B.

Babylon, 49
Bamborough Castle, 273
Bangor, 268, 294
Baptism, 72, 161, 371, 376, 377, 378, 384, 387
Baptismal vow, 302
Barbatianus, 185
Baronius, 370
Barsumas, 216
Basil, 15, 16, &c., 109, 128, 161, 169, 172

INDEX.

Basilius, 71, 73
Becket, Thomas à, 387
Bede, 258, 269, 274, 277, 290, &c.
Belisarius, 223
Bellarmine, 169 n., 250 n.
Bells, 187 n., 376
Benedict of Nursia, 235, &c.
Benignus, 261
Berengar, 360, 377
Bernard of Clairvaux, 335, &c., 352, &c., 383, 386; Morlaix, 367 n.; Ydros, 397
Berno, 334
Bertha, Queen, 264
Bethlehem, 117
Billfrith, 281
Biscop, 285
Bishops, 182
Blesilla, 113
Blood, shedding of, 384, 393, 399
Boa, 183 n.
Bobbio, 298
Bogomiles, 310
Bohemia, 400
Bollandists, 169 n.
Bonaven, 258
Bonaventura, 232
Boniface IV. pope, 297; VIII. pope, 255 n.
Boniface, missionary, 298
Boni Homines, 385
Bonosus, 231
Borri, 175
Bosham, 276
Bosnia, 311
Brahmanism, 166 n., 173
Braithwaite, 124
Bregenz, 297
Brethren, the Tall, 11, 85
Britain, 49 n., 106 n., 257, &c.
Bruno, 345 n.
Buddhism, 174
Bulgarians, 389 n.
Bull-fights, 10 n.
Burgundians, 9, 295
Burgundy, duke of, 364 n.

C.

Cædmon, 277, &c.
Cælestius, 150
Caerleon, 270
Cæsarea in Cappadocia, 96
Calagorris, 186
Calixtus II. pope, 334
Candidian, count, 205
Candlemas, 234
Canterbury, 264
Carcassonne, 415
Cardinal, 256 n.
Caroline Books, 314
Carthage, 131, 133, 145; Council of, 150; Conference at, 145
Carthusians, 345 n,

Cassiacum, 140
Cassianus, John, 176, 236
Cassiodorus, 239
Cathari, 371, 393
Catholic, 8 n.
Cedd, 275
Celcyth, Council of, 277 n.
Celestine, 204, 212
Celibacy, 194
Celsus of Armagh, 359
Ceolfrid, 288
Chalcedon, Council of, 218
Châlons, Council of, 316
Charlemagne (Charles the Great), 312
Charles Martel, 300
Charroux, Council of, 377
Chartreuse, La Grande, 345 n.
Chichester, 276
Chrysostom, 23 n., 70, &c., 161, 163, 166, 167, 170, 180
Church, the, 144, 146
Cicero, 110, 131
Circumcelliones, 148 n.
Circus, 180
Cistercians, 336, 342, 352
Cîteaux, 335, 344, &c.
Clairvaux, 335, 352, &c.
Classical studies, 131, 341
Claude of Turin, 315, &c.
Cleanliness, 189
Clement of Alexandria, 165; Irish missionary, 300
Clovis, 51 n.
Cluny, 333, &c.
Codex Argentius, 56
Cohen, Joseph, 285
Coifi, 271
Colman, 274
Cologne, heretics of, 390
Columba, 262
Columbanus, 294, &c.
Comana, 99
Comgall, abbot, 294
Commendam, In, 352
Compline, 239 n.
Constans, emperor, 4
Constantia, queen, 374
Constantine Chrysomalos, monk, 311; Copronymus, emperor, 310, 371; the Great, 3, 94; II., 4; founder of the Paulicians, 306
Constantinople, 8, 41
Constantius, emperor, 4, 24, 193
Corbie, abbey, 318
Corvey, 319
Cosmas, monk, 13 n.; patriarch, 311
Crediton, 298
Crescentius, 326
Cross, the, 316, 379
Crucifix, 377
Crusades, 386
Cucusus, 96
Cuthbert, 279, &c., 291

INDEX. 485

Cyprian, 365
Cyril of Alexandria, 201, &c., 232

D.

Dagan, 274 n.
Dalmatius, 207
Damasus, 27 n., 116, 126
Dames, 293, 294
Daniel of Winchester, 300; pillar saint, 179
Dauphiné 379, 400
Decretals, 183, 256
Deer in St. Paul's Church, 266 n.
Demophilus, 40
Demosthenes, Imperial cook, 33, 47
Denmark, 319
Desiderius, 192
De Thou, 400 n.
Dianius, 24
Diemudis, 343
Dijon, 347
Dinooth, 268
Diodorus of Tarsus, 202
Dionysius Exiguus, 267 n.
Dio-petes, 206 n.
Dioscorus, 214
Dokkum, 301
Dominic, 410, 424
Dominicans, 235, 241 n., 242
Domnus, 214
Donatists, 143, &c.
Donatus, 109
Dorotheus, 174 n.
Druids, 260
Duns Scotus, 235
Du Pin, 197 n.
Durham, 273, 281, 294; Book, 281

E.

Eadburga, 300
Eadfrith, 281
Eanfled, 274
Easter, 267, 297
Ebbesfleet, 264
Eckbert, 398
Edessa, 212
Edwin, king of Northumbria, 271
Egfrid, 285
Eginhardt, 313
Eleanor, queen of France, 386
Emmelia, 15
Emperors, semi-divine homage, 91
Ennodius, 225
Ephesus, Councils, 205, 215
Ephrem, 10 n.
Epiphanius, 85, 113, 230
Erasmus, 128
Essex, 266
Ethelbert of York, 312; king, 264
Ethelburga, 270
Ethelfrid, 269
Ethilwald, 281
Eucharist, 101, 161, 371, 376, 377, 379, 384, 387

Euchites, 310
Eudoxia, 82, &c.
Eugenius III. pope, 340, 365, 383
Eunapius, 167 n.
Eusebian canons, 56
Eusebius of Cæsarea in Cappadocia, 25, 27; of Dorylæum, 203; monk, 174 n.; of Nicomedia, 51; of Samosata, 28, 31
Eustathius, 20 n.
Eustochium, 113
Eutropius, 77, &c.
Eutyches, 202, 214
Eutychians, 214
Evagrius, 218
Evervinus, 390
Evetheus, 97
Exarch, 27
Exuperius, 194

F.

Fabiola, 115 n., 120
Facundus, 223
Fairbairn, 256
Familiars, 424
Farne Islands, 280
Fasting, 165
Faustus, 167 n.
Felix, 63, 187
Ferté, La, 351, 352
Flavian, 76, 214
Flowers, 160
Fontaines, 295, 347
Fortunius, 144
Forty martyrs, 29
Fountains Abbey, 361 n.
Francis d'Assisi, 424 n.
Franciscans, 235, 241 n., 242
Franks, 50
Freeman, 226
Friesland, 298, 301
Frithigern, 54
Fulda, 301
Fulk, 413
Fuller, 270, 345
Furness Abbey, 351 n.

G.

Gaeta, 327
Galileo, 361 n.
Galloway, 257
Gallus, 297
Gazari, 389 n.
Genseric, 153
Geoffrey, 358
George, St., 169 n.
Geralda, 417
Gerard, 348
Gerhard, 376
Germanus, 232, 257
Gervasius, 63
Gibbon, 13
Gieseler, 234 n.

Gildas, 262
Gilles, St., 380
Gladiators, 9, 134
Glass, 285
Glastonbury, 257 n.
Gnostics, 306
Godiva, 234 n.
Goodmanham, 272 n.
Gorm, 320
Goslar, 377 n.
Goths, 37, 50, 53, 79
Grace, 153
Gratian, 7
Gregorian chant, 247
Gregory Nazianzen, 9, 11 n., 16, &c., 77, 83, 112, 163, 170, 180 n., 231; of Nyssa, 6, 29, 161, 163, 170; I. pope, 172, 245, &c., 263, 297, 314 n.; II. pope, 255 n., 314 n.; V. pope, 326; VII. pope, 358 n., 373; IX. pope, 425; Thaumaturgus, 15; of Utrecht, 299
Green, Mrs., 351 n.
Guibert, 353
Guido, 348
Gundulph, 376

H.

Harald, 319, 320
Heathen, 4 n.
Hebrew, 126
Henricians, 383 n.
Henry IV., emperor, 358 n.
Henry I. of England, 356
Henry II. of England, 395; of Lausanne, 380, &c.
Heloise, 364
Helvidius, 114, 231
Heraclius, emperor, 232
Herefrid, 280
Heresy, 8 n.
Herebert, 373
Hilary, 5, 6
Hilda, 275
Hildebert, 381
Hildegarde, 392
Hippo, 141
Hodgkin, 5 n.
Holy Spirit, 36, 45, 142; water, 387
Home synod, 215
Homer, 118, 130
Homo-ousian and Homoi-ousian, 6
Honorius, emperor, 9, 69, 147, 150, 183; II. pope, 356; III. pope, 418
Hook, 269 n.
Hooker, 13, 36 n., 214
Hooper, 170
Hosius, 6
Host, 159 n.
Hottentot, Mohammedan, 305 n.
Hours, 128
Huguenots, 147
Huns, 50, 53, 119

Huss, 428 n.
Hypsistarians, 16

I.

I-colm-kill, 262
Iconoclasts, 309, 314
Idolatry, Christian, 250
Idols, 272, 297
Image-worship, 314, 376
Immaculate conception, 284
Incense, 376
Index expurgatorius, 317 n.
Infallibility, papal, 430
Ingelheim, 313 n., 319
Innocent I. pope, 255; II. pope, 356, 360, 383, 389; III. pope, 311, 390, 399; IV. pope, 342
Inquisition, 385, 424
Iona, 262
Ireland, 259, 262
Irenæus, on Mary, 230
Irish ornamentation, 286
Isaurians, 97, 124
Isidore, monk, 11; of Pelusium, 11 n., 248; of Seville, 256

J.

Jameson, Mrs., 227
Jarrow, 288, 294
Jellinge, 320
Jeremiah's prophecy, 369
Jerome, 6, 37 n., 73, 109, &c., 162, 176, 184, &c., 231; of Prague, 428 n.
Jerusalem, 7, 116
"Jerusalem the Golden," 367 n.
Jessopp, Dr., 37 n.
Jews, 305
Joachim, 388
Joannites, 95
John the Almsgiver, 224 n, 248; of Antioch, 205, 210; de Bellesmains, 388; of Constantinople, 249; the Deacon, 247 n.; king of England, 414 n.; of Jerusalem, 150; of Lugio, 397; of Placenza, 326; of Salisbury, 398 n.; Zimisces, 310, 371
Jonas, bishop of Orleans, 316
Joppa, 120
Jordanes, 52, 54
Joseph Studites, 328
Jovian, 7
Jovinian, 114, 182, &c.
Julian the Apostate, 6, 18, 25, 167
Julius Africanus, 73; Soranus, 53
Junius, F., 279
Justin Martyr, 149 n., 230
Justina, 64
Justinian I., 94 n., 226, 232
Justus, 249
Jutland, 319

K.

Kent, 264
Kilpatrick, 258

INDEX.

Koran, 305
Kornerup, 323 n.

L.
Lampon, 204
Lanfranc, 360, 377 n.
Languedoc, 385, 408
Lateran Council, 385
Latin, 127
Latria, 172
Laurentius, 274 n.
Lavaur, 416
Leo the Armenian, 309; the Isaurian, 315; I. pope, 217, 256; X. pope, 428 n.
Libanius, 16, 71
Liberius, 6
Library, 343
Lindisfarne, 273, 294
Lisoius, 374
Liturgy, 247
Lombards, 246
Lombers, Council of, 385
Louis the Pious, 315; VI. of France, 334; VII. of France, 364, 386, 388
Lucilla, 172
Lucius II. pope, 384; III. pope, 385, 399
Lupercalia, 234
Lupus, 257
Luthardt, 229
Luther, 70, 367, 374 n.
Luxeuil, 296
Lyons, 396

M.
Macrina, 15, 48
Madonna, 227
Magic, 74
Mai, 56 n.
Maitland, 113
Malachy, 359
Malchus, 111
Manicheism, 132, 371
Manning, Cardinal, 233 n.
Mans, Le, 381
Marcella, 112, 125
Marcellinus, 144
Marcian, 218
Marcionites, 306
Marriage, 267, 373
Martin of Tours, 51 n., 58, &c., 186; Abbé, 217
Martinmas, 60
Martyn, Henry, 99 n.
Mary, 165, 201, 225, 229
Mary-worship, 227, &c.
Mass, 159 n., 379, 384
Maurice, archbishop, 359; emperor, 250
Meletius, 42, 211
Mellitus, 266
Melrose, 279
Memnon, 205

Memory, the, 157
Merseburg, 302
Metropolitan, 27
Michael, patriarch, 311; I. emperor, 309
Middle ages, 245
Middleton, 168
Milan, 4, 6, 135, 357, 373, 390
Milman, 127, 177, 202, 217 n., 230, 245, 279, 345, 382 n., 386 n., 398 n.
Milton, 279
Minerve, 415
Ministry, the true, 251
Miracles, 253
Modestus, 33
Mohammed, 303, &c.
Molesme, 344
Monachism, 173, 238
Monastic life, 75, 333, &c.
Monkwearmouth, 285, 294
Monnica, 130
Monophysites, 222
Monothelite, 222 n.
Montalembert, 296, 304
Monte Casino, 237, 327
Montesquieu, 176
Montfort, Simon de, 414
Morison, 346, 354
Morland, 403 n.
Morris, 323 n.
Mosheim, 222 n., 304, 333
Mozley, 152

N.
Nabor, 63
Napoleon, 342
Narbonne, 425
Narses, 232
Natural goodness of man, 149 n.
Neander, 185, 299, 371
Nebridius, 136
Nectarius, 69 n., 77
Neo-Cæsarea, 15
Neo-Platonists, 137
Nestorians, 201, &c., 212
Nestorius, 151 n., 202, &c.
Netley, 351 n.
New Covenant, 369
Newman, Cardinal, 60, 194
Nicæa, 28, 96, 218
Nicene Creed, 8
Nicephorus, emperor, 308
Nicholas II. pope, 256 n.; secretary, 340
Nilus, 324, &c.
Nimbus, 226
Ninyas, 257
Niphon, 311
Nitria, 117
Nivard, 348
Noble Lesson, The, 403, 407
Nola, 187
Nones, 239 n.
Nonna, 16

Northmen, 282, 319
Northumbria, 270, &c.
Novatian, 146
Novella, 334
Nursia, 236

O.

Oak, Augustine's, 268; synod of the, 87
Oaths, 385
Odo, abbot, 334
Olympias, 83, 94
Ora pro nobis, 227
Origen, 23, 120, 163, 190, 361
Orleans, 374
Orosius, 150
Osma, 410
Ostrogoths, 53
Oswald, 274
Oswy, 274
Otho III. emperor, 326; IV. emperor, 405
Oxford, 360

P.

Pagan, 4 n.
Palatine school, 313
Palladius, 72, 87, 175 n.
Pallium, 359
Pammachius, 183
Pantheon, 167, 168
Papacy, 255
Paris, 355, 360
Parthenay, 358
Paschal I. pope, 315
Paschasius Radbert, 319
Paterini, 388
Patrick, 258, &c.
Paul, St., chains of, 251
Paul, the hermit, 129
Paula, 113, 123
Paulicians, 306, &c., 369, &c.
Paulina, 113
Paulinus, of Nola, 186; of York, 270
Paulus, 234 n.
Pelagius, 149
Penance, 377
Penitents, 159
Pepin, 301
Pera, 86
Perfect, the, 372
Persecution, 14
Peter, St., 250; of Brueys, 378, &c.; of Castelnau, 409, 412; de Vaux Cernay, 413, 417; the Venerable, 334, &c., 364, 380
Petilian, 145
Petrobrusians, 380
Petrus Gnapheus, 231
Peyran, 402
Pharetrius, 96
Philip Augustus, 387, 400; II. of Spain, 430
Philippopolis, 310

Philocalia, 23
Philostorgius, 51
Phocas, St., 169 n.
Picardy, 400
Picts, 258
Pictures in churches, 187
Pilgrimages, 49, 316
Pillar saints, 178
Piphles, 389 n.
Pisa, council of, 383
Pityus, 98
Plato, 118, 149 n.
Plautus, 110
Poictiers, 58
Pontigny, 351
Pontitianus, 138
Pontius, 336, 384
Pope, *papa*, 123 n., 255
Possidonius, 154
Posting system, 186
Postumian, 188
Prætextata, 114
Prayer, 107
Preaching, 142
Predestination, 153
Priesthood, 100
Prime, 239 n.
Principia, 125
Priscillian, 59
Proclus, 203, 211, 232
Protasius, 63
Provence, 380, 400
Prudentius, 171
Publicani, 387, 394
Pulcheria, 99
Pulpit eloquence, 76
Purification, festival of, 234
Pusey, 171 n.

Q.

Quarto-decimanians, 267
Quichelm, 271

R.

Raoul, 409
Ravenna, 225
Raymond of Toulouse, 411, &c.
Reinerius Saccho, 400
Relics, 172, 192
Repentance, 107
Rheginus, 205
Rheims, council, 377, 384
Ric, 265
Richard I., 387
Richelieu, 368
Rievaulx, 351 n.
Riparius, 191
Ripon, 280
Robber Synod, 217
Robert, king of France, 375; of Cîteaux, 336
Roberts, 27 n., 103 n., 128, 202, 266
Robertson, 8

Romanus, 236
Rome, 9, 124
Rosary, 234
Rosweyd, 169 n.
Ruffner, 149 n., 163
Rufinus, 67, 109, 120, 149 n., 190
Runic, 322

S.

Saba, 52
Sabatati, 397 n.
Sabbath, 327
Sacraments, 371
Saints, 167, 169 n., 172, 193
Salvian, 180
Samosata, 306
Samson, 384
Saracens, 306
Sarmateo, 185
Sasima, 30
Satyrus, 162
Saxons, 258
Schaff, 152, 155, 224
Scholastica, 241
Scot, 150 n.
Scott, 54
Scriptorium, 343
Scriptures, 105, 189, 252, 314, 397
Seleucia, 96
Selsey, 276
Sens, 363, 388
Serenus, 314 n.
Sergius, 307
Severian, 82, 89
Sexte, 239 n.
Shakspeare, 350
Sherborne, 346 n.
Simeon Stylites, 178
Simonians, 213
Simplician, 70, 137
Sin, 106, 151
Singing in churches, 311, 379
Siricius, 116, 183, 255
Sismondi, 420 n.
Sixtus III. pope, 262; IV. pope, 235
Slavery, 224 n., 247
Smith, Philip, 263
Soissons, council, 361
Sophia, St., 40, 94
Sozomen, 51
Spain, 399
Stanley, 257 n.
Stephen, of Ansa, 397; of Bosnia, 312; of Orleans, 374; Harding, 345, 346, 351; of Tournay, 388
Stigmata, 170
Stilicho, 70
Subiaco, 336
Suevi, 9, 297
Sulpicius Severus, 59, 118, 171, 186, 188 n.
Sunderland, 286
Supper, see Eucharist
Sussex, 276

Sweden, 319
Symbolism, 148 n.
Symmachus, 135, 255
Syrianus, 12

T.

Tapers, 192
Taylor, Isaac, 129, 155, 165, 173, 178, 304
Telemachus, 10
Telonarii, 387, 389 n.
Tessilin, 347
Teutons, 50
Thagaste, 130, 141
Theatre, 180
Theodemir, 315
Theodisc, 416
Theodora, 309
Theodore, of Canterbury, 298 n.; of Mopsuestia, 73, 149 n., 202; Studites, 309
Theodoret, 205, 210, 221
Theodoric, 225
Theodorus, 74 n.
Theodosius I., 7, 40, 58, 65, 69, 172; II., 99, 202, 205
Theophilus, 78, 85, 90
Theotimus, 85
Theotokos, 201
Thessalonica, 67
Thierry, 126; II. king of the Franks, 297; St., 336, 354
Three Chapters, the, 224
Thuringia, 300
Thyra, 320
Tierce, 239 n.
Timotheus, 223
Tintern Abbey, 351 n.
Tisserands, 389 n.
Toleration, 14, 45, 104
Tonsure, 267
Totila, 241
Toulouse, 377, 380, 385, 388
Tours, 385
Traditions, 128
Trent, council of, 127, 153
Trinity, 156
Troubadours, 408
Troyes, 368 n.
Truthfulness, 73
Tuam, 359 n.
Tuke, 227
Tusculum, 328
Tyana, 30

U.

Ulfilas, 50, &c.
Urban VIII. pope, 361 n.
Ursicinus, 27 n.
Ussher, 279, 403

V.

Valence, 413
Valens, 7, 13, 26, 33, 74 n.

Valentinian I., 7; II., 7, 64, 65; III., 255
Valerius, 141
Vandals, 9, 153
Veile, 320
Vespers, 239 n.
Vezelay, 386
Victor, 188
Victor Amadeus II., 402 n.
Victorinus, 137
Vigilantius, 186, &c.
Vigils, 239 n.
Virgil, 118, 130
Virgilius, 300
Virgin, see Mary
Virginity, 162
Visigoths, 9, 53
Votive-offerings, 160
Vow, monastic, 238
· Vulgate, 126, 313

W.

Waddington, 387 n.
Waldenses, 396, &c.
Walter Mapes, 398
Waso, 378

Waverley, 351 n.
Westcott, 127
Whitby, 275, 277
Whithorn, 282
Wicliffe, 268 n.
Wilfrid, 274, 275, &c.
Willehad, 302
William, of Aquitaine, 358; the Pious, 334; of Champeaux, 348, 354, 361; the Conqueror, 346; of Newbury, 394; of Paris, 393
Wimbert, 300
Wiseman, Cardinal, 233 n.
Wittenberg, 428
Wormwood, Valley of, 352
Worship, public, 103, 158

Y.

York, 275, 281, 293

Z.

Zacharias, pope, 301
Zosimus, 150, 255
Zug, 297